Victim Next Door," to its 1977 cover story on "Sexual Harassment on the Job and How to Stop It" that preceded by nine years the Supreme Court's sexual harassment decision, by nearly fifteen years Anita Hill's landmark testimony, and by more than forty-five years the #MeToo movement . . . here is the best reporting, the most resonant photography, the most provocative features and advertising that reveal and reflect the changes set in motion by *Ms.* magazine, along with its iconic covers that excited and galvanized readers.

Here are essays, profiles, conversations with, and features by Nancy Pelosi, Cynthia Enloe, Pauli Murray, bell hooks, Alice Walker, Billie Jean King, Eleanor Holmes Norton, Alison Bechdel, Brittney Cooper, and Joy Harjo, as well as fiction and poetry by Joyce Carol Oates, Audre Lorde, Adrienne Rich, Rita Dove, and Sharon Olds, among many others.

A rousing, inspiring celebration of the magazine's fifty years that helped to change the world and forge a path forward in the continuing fight of freedoms for us all.

50 YEARS of Ms.

50
YEARS *of*
Ms.

The BEST of the Pathfinding Magazine
That Ignited a Revolution

Edited and with commentary
by **KATHERINE SPILLAR** *and* **the editors of *Ms.***

Introduction by KATHERINE SPILLAR and ELEANOR SMEAL

Foreword by **GLORIA STEINEM**

ALFRED A. KNOPF | NEW YORK | 2023

THIS IS A BORZOI BOOK PUBLISHED BY ALFRED A. KNOPF

Copyright © 2023 by Liberty Media For Women, LLC
Foreword copyright © 2023 by Gloria Steinem

Published in the United States by Alfred A. Knopf,
a division of Penguin Random House LLC, New York,
and distributed in Canada by Penguin Random House Canada Limited, Toronto.

www.aaknopf.com

Knopf, Borzoi Books, and the colophon
are registered trademarks of Penguin Random House LLC.

Pages 517 and 519 constitute an extension of this copyright page.

Library of Congress Cataloging-in-Publication Data
Names: Spillar, Katherine, editor, writer of added commentary, writer of introduction, |
Smeal, Eleanor, writer of introduction. | Steinem, Gloria, writer of foreword.
Title: 50 years of *Ms.* : the best of the pathfinding magazine that ignited a revolution /
edited and with commentary by Katherine Spillar and the editors of *Ms.* ;
introduction by Katherine Spillar and Eleanor Smeal; foreword by Gloria Steinem.
Other titles: Fifty years of *Ms.* | *Ms.* (U.S. : 1971)
Description: New York: Alfred A. Knopf, 2023.
Identifiers: LCCN 2022017588 (print) | LCCN 2022017589 (ebook) |
ISBN 9780593321560 (hardcover) | ISBN 9780593321577 (ebook)
Subjects: LCSH: *Ms.* (U.S. : 1971)—History. | Feminism—United States—History—20th century. |
Women—United States—History—20th century.
Classification: LCC HQ1402 .A15 2023 (print) | LCC HQ1402 (ebook) |
DDC 305.42/097305—dc23/eng/20220414
LC record available at https://lccn.loc.gov/2022017588
LC ebook record available at https://lccn.loc.gov/2022017589

Jacket design by Emily Mahon

Manufactured in China

First Edition

This book is dedicated to *Ms.*'s loyal supporters and readers. And to the millions of women and men in the United States and around the world who have marched and mobilized, been arrested and imprisoned, and spoken out at great personal cost in support of the simple belief that women and girls have fundamental human rights to equality, self-determination, autonomy, and dignity.

Our work together has only just begun.
Here's to the next fifty years.

Contents

CHAPTER 1 1970s

CHAPTER 2 **1980s**

CHAPTER 3 1990s

CHAPTER 4 ## 2000s

CHAPTER 5   # 2010s

CHAPTER 6   **2020s**

Foreword

BY **GLORIA STEINEM**

IF YOU ASKED ME FIFTY YEARS AGO, when we started *Ms.* magazine, if this first woman-controlled magazine would still be alive half a century later, I would have said absolutely not.

Although there were no other magazines for women that weren't about food, fashion, and family—and women's magazines survived only through support from those same categories of ads—I believed that advertisers would soon realize that women's interests were just as wide and deep as men's interests are and there would be new magazines that were at least like, say, *Esquire* for women.

What I didn't understand then was how little advertising would change over the decades. Though women actually buy more books than men do—and also buy wine, cars, and insurance—the full range of women's interests is still not supported by advertisers of the products we actually buy.

Indeed, *Ms.* would not have been able to prove that women would buy even one issue of such a magazine if Clay Felker at *New York* magazine, where I was an editor, had not agreed to publish a sample of *Ms.* in its pages, and then an entire preview issue that was placed on newsstands nationwide. That gave women themselves a chance to show the breadth of their interests.

What was in that first issue? An article by Johnnie Tillmon, a brave organizer of women on welfare, called "Welfare Is a Women's Issue." We were told we absolutely could not include an article by or about lesbians in that preview issue, since, at the time, all feminists were characterized as lesbians. This only reinforced our conviction that we had to, and we did (with a piece titled "Can Women Love Women?").

And since abortion was then against the law, yet we knew that about one in three American women had needed one at some time in her life, we asked women if they would sign a petition, "We Have Had an Abortion," demanding its legality and safety. Hundreds of women, some well known and some not, many of whom had never even told their families, signed this historic and politically powerful petition.

The cover was a challenge because we wanted all women to feel included.

An early version showed a woman's face divided into various skin colors, but this didn't feel real. Since I had been living in India, I suggested a woman who was blue and had many arms, like the goddess Kali, with hands holding symbols—from the cooking spoon to the car wheel—of women's many tasks. Miriam Wosk, an artist then living in California, painted the perfect multitasking woman, and even put a tear running down her cheek and a baby in her body. It was titled "The Housewife's Moment of Truth." (*Ms.* recently published a modern-day reprise calling attention to the overburdening of women during the COVID-19 pandemic and this time putting the onus where it belongs: it's titled "The Nation's Moment of Truth.")

At the time that first issue was published, there were local feminist publications here and in some other countries, but there was no national voice for those of us who had the radical idea that women are people. I didn't know what the response would be, especially on newsstands, with no precedent or place for a women's magazine that wasn't about home, family, and children.

The response was shocking. Though that first issue was released in January 1972 and dated "spring 1972" so it could stay on the newsstand for months, it sold out in eight days. Soon, bags of mail began arriving in our offices, so many that there was room for little else.

The letters were irresistible to read, personal notes or small novels, as if *Ms.* were a friend who had entered readers' homes. One common theme was "At last, I know I'm not alone." A movement is a contagion of truth telling: at last, we know we are not alone.

The mail came from writers of all different ages. One was written in crayon and concluded, "We girls are angry as turnips." The very young writer explained that the boys got the best part of the playground and the girls had only a little corner to play jacks. I answered her letter. I bet she became a leader in expanding playgrounds to include us all.

Readers' letters were a source of encouragement and support and editorial ideas. They were our lifeline, from the little girl on the playground to women talking about raising children on welfare or running for political office or confronting the double discrimination of race and sex. Readers have always told *Ms.* what they think and what they need. They were and are the source of what appears in *Ms.*

This is why *Ms.* brought national attention to issues years before they were covered elsewhere: domestic abuse, sexual harassment, acquaintance rape, sweatshop work, the national need for child care, limits on military spending. And there was always this feeling of unity with feminists around the world, this understanding that we could learn from each other, and *Ms.,* because of its dedication to global reporting, could bring home those important facts, movements, issues, and ideas that might not otherwise get U.S. attention.

In 1973, our cover was "Chisholm/Farenthold: The Ticket That Might Have Been." Even though she was on the ballot in only fourteen states, Shirley Chisholm declared for the presidency and single-handedly took the "White Male Only" sign off the White House door. Half a century later, a woman of color finally walked through that door.

Of course, all change is ridiculed at the beginning. In 1972, the *60 Minutes* co-founder Harry Reasoner famously said that he would give us six months before the magazine ran out of things to say. (When *Ms.* celebrated its fifth anniversary, Reasoner apologized.)

The New York Times refused to use "Ms." as a form of address for a dozen years; thus I remained "Miss Steinem of *Ms.* magazine." For this and other reasons, women picketed. And when the *Times* finally relented in 1986, we took the editor Abe Rosenthal flowers. The most annoying thing he did was to say, "If I'd known it mattered that much to you, I would've done it much sooner."

The biggest challenges we faced, though, were financial. We were going against the women's magazine practice of editorial that praised advertisers, known as "complementary copy"; of newsstand distribution with covers that focused on beauty and celebrity; indeed, of pretty much everything in the magazine business.

In addition to dictating editorial content in women's magazines, there was a profound belief in the advertising industry that magazines had to be racially segregated, yet we were a diverse magazine. That was a big part of the reason we eventually became an ad-free foundation, supported by subscriptions and contributions. After all, we buy books without ads, why not magazines?

But in the mid-1980s, when *Ms.* was still struggling to survive, it was bought by a couple of commercial publishers who didn't understand its spirit. *Ms.* ultimately found a home with the Feminist Majority Foundation, as part of the movement and, thus, a nonprofit. This move was crucial to the survival of *Ms.* and its service to women and a movement.

There is now a big majority of the country that supports the radical idea that people are people, regardless of gender or race or sexuality or class or ethnicity. Yet there is still about a third of this country that is in backlash against this new consciousness. They feel robbed of privilege and have the power of resentment. We must be aware of the threat they pose, but make no mistake: they are not the majority anymore.

Patriarchy was the beginning of hierarchy, reinforced by racism and classism and nationalism, but since this began with controlling reproduction, free women can bring down the hierarchy. There is now a widespread understanding that democracy starts with the ability of women to make decisions over our own bodies, and that's exactly what we are doing. At the same time, men get to be whole human beings by being active in the home as well as outside. Both men and women have our whole humanity to gain.

I won't be around for the next fifty years, but you who are reading this may be. Imagining is the first step to creating. Let's do it together!

At my age, in this still hierarchical time, people often ask me if I'm "passing the torch." I explain that I'm keeping my torch, thank you very much, and I'm using it to light the torches of others.

Because only if each of us has a torch will there be enough light.

Introduction

BY **KATHERINE SPILLAR,** EXECUTIVE EDITOR,
AND **ELEANOR SMEAL,** PUBLISHER

THIRTY YEARS into *Ms.*'s first half century, we received a call from Gloria Steinem. She wanted to know whether the Feminist Majority Foundation would consider taking over publishing *Ms.* Having rescued the magazine from a series of commercial publishers (four in eleven years), Steinem and the then editor in chief, Marcia Ann Gillespie, were in search of a home for *Ms.,* this time within the feminist movement. Together with the editors and staff of *Ms.,* they thought the Feminist Majority Foundation might be a good fit, with our focus on research and advocacy and our national and global programs. Stunned, we said we would have to think about it and get back to her.

At the time, the magazine industry was undergoing rapid change, grappling with skyrocketing costs of production and the challenges created by the digital age. Brick-and-mortar bookstores and newsstands were disappearing as consumers increasingly purchased from online retailers. To compound matters, *Ms.* was laboring under significant debt, most of it in the form of short-term obligations, including tens of thousands of dollars in unpaid rent.

It would take several weeks before we finally arrived at a decision. We understood the outsized role *Ms.* had played in raising consciousness and building a feminist community. After all, advances in women's rights are driven not solely by mass demonstrations, precedent-setting litigation, and political activism but also through the spread of ideas and information. We couldn't allow *Ms.* to disappear. Having arrived at our decision not based on reason but with our hearts, we said yes.

We quickly set about making the changes that would be needed if *Ms.* was to survive. The group of investors who had provided the $2.5 million in funding to create Liberty Media for Women (the entity publishing *Ms.* when ownership was transferred from MacDonald Communications Corporation, the last commercial publisher) gave its shares to the Feminist Majority Foundation.

Through a legal restructuring, subscribers became "members of the *Ms.*

community," the magazine being one of the benefits of membership. We closed the New York City offices after arranging a sublease at a rate that would eventually pay off the back rent debt and moved the editorial side of the magazine to the new Feminist Majority Foundation offices in Beverly Hills and the publishing side to our metro Washington, D.C., office, placing the magazine at the center of U.S. feminist advocacy. The chair of the Feminist Majority Foundation's board, Peg Yorkin, pledged $5 million toward the magazine's operations, a critical investment that sustained operations during the transition and in the months after.

To expand the roster of writers for the magazine, we worked with the Ford Foundation program officer Irma McClaurin to secure a grant to develop and conduct a series of intensive writers' workshops to train feminist scholars to write for the popular press, thereby expanding the reach of new research beyond the ivory tower and into the mainstream. At the same time, we reconstituted the Ms. Committee of Scholars, which connects *Ms.* to the vast network of women's and gender studies programs at colleges and universities nationwide. Eventually, these connections became the base for our innovative Ms. Classroom program offering a first-of-its-kind digital textbook series used by professors and instructors for all levels of women's and gender studies, sociology, political science, history, English, and journalism courses in hundreds of colleges (and a growing number of high schools) in the United States and Canada.

Published four times a year in print, the magazine is sent to members and sold on newsstands and in bookstores; in addition, magazines are distributed at feminist events and conferences nationwide and to state and national policy makers, as well as sent free to domestic violence shelters and to women in prison in an effort to bring strategies and solutions to some of the places where they are needed most. As technology changed, *Ms.* launched MsMagazine.com, a vibrant website providing up-to-date reporting and opinion and reaching millions in the United States and around the globe. Its social media platforms are followed by hundreds of thousands, and its digital publications include daily and weekly newsletters featuring the most important feminist stories of the week from the United States and globally. To provide opportunities for the youngest generation of feminist writers, "The Future Is *Ms.*" (news reports by young feminists made possible by a grant from SayItForward.org) appears in print and on the website.

In 2020, we launched a biweekly podcast, *On the Issues: Reporting, Rebelling & Telling It Like It Is,* hosted by the renowned feminist legal scholar Michele Goodwin. The podcast attracts tens of thousands of listeners and has ranked in the top tier of podcasts since its launch; its occasional companion podcast, *Fifteen Minutes of Feminism,* provides a short dose of information and action ideas. And the recently launched *Ms.* Studios offers a range of audio and video programming that reports, engages, and entertains, bringing fresh takes on news, creating multiplatform programming, and organizing live and virtual Ms. Talks events.

This book is mostly focused on the award-winning print magazine. In the pages that follow, we include important pieces from the last fifty years: some will be immediately recognizable; others may be less familiar but are no less significant.

Brought together in this way, these pieces demonstrate the evolution of ideas—of problems and solutions—over the past five decades as told through groundbreaking articles, iconic covers, opinion essays, and letters. Thus, this book serves both to acknowledge *Ms.* magazine's tremendous institutional memory, its prescience and impact, and to herald its future necessity.

"We believed," the co-founding editor Joanne Edgar reminisced regarding *Ms.*'s launch, "that if we explained the problem clearly enough, people would understand the injustice of discrimination against women. Then it would just go away." While this underestimated how entrenched misogyny and racism were—and still are—in U.S. cultural and political institutions, the early days of *Ms.* proved that naming and explaining really were vital first steps toward gender equality.

Raising awareness, making visible the structures that severely constrained, and sometimes endangered, women's lives, served as a critical wake-up call. These revelations were named by Jane O'Reilly in *Ms.*'s first issue as "click!" moments, "that parenthesis of truth around a little thing that completes the puzzle of reality in women's minds—the moment that brings a gleam to our eyes and means the revolution has begun." Thousands of the early letters to *Ms.* that recounted readers' stories ended with "click!"

From its inception in 1972, *Ms.* has been at the forefront in tackling some of the biggest challenges in the fight for gender equality. In what *The Washington Post* says "changed the course of the abortion rights movement," *Ms.* published "We Have Had Abortions" in its first issue, featuring the signatures of fifty-three prominent American women. A year later, in its coverage of the landmark *Roe v. Wade* Supreme Court decision that legalized abortion nationwide, the magazine included a shocking photo of a woman covered in blood on a motel room floor, dead from a back-alley abortion, as a memorial to the countless numbers who died or suffered because of illegal and unsafe abortions ("Never Again").

In fact, *Ms.* was the first or one of only a few outlets to name and explore issues that ran the gamut: horrifying legacies of our past, strategies to change our present, and hopes for the future. *Ms.* offered readers strategies for dealing with the constraining effects of gender roles and stereotyping in their own lives while simultaneously providing a window on the world—an acknowledgment that sexism, racism, religious bigotry, and ethnic bias are universal problems even if they take on different forms in different places and at different times.

Ms. played a key role in recovering and substantiating the need for "women's history," what the feminist historian and frequent *Ms.* contributor Gerda Lerner defined as "women's right." As women's studies programs were created in colleges and universities across the country, many of the magazine's accounts of women's history were taught as part of these new curricula. The magazine also published poetry and fiction by up-and-coming as well as famous women writers, including Alice Walker, Ursula K. Le Guin, Joy Harjo, Ntozake Shange, Curtis Sittenfeld, Audre Lorde, and Margaret Atwood.

As the women's movement grew and the country changed, *Ms.* adapted. By the mid-1980s, a majority of women in the United States called themselves feminists. The problems no longer needed names; they needed solutions. The magazine's role shifted toward mobilizing a feminist majority and becoming a force to hold people accountable, change policy, and inform culture—a role that remains at the core of *Ms.*'s mission.

Ms. is more than a magazine. *Ms.* is a movement. As a cultural touchstone, it has achieved success beyond all standard benchmarks, reaching a readership of millions and providing community and connection for feminists across multiple generations in the United States and around the globe.

Where We Are Now

At a time when we are facing a significant patriarchal backlash to the fifty years of progress that *Ms.* has witnessed and helped to propel, the magazine's analysis continues to fill an ongoing stubborn hole in mainstream journalism. Newsrooms frequently overlook stories and issues that profoundly impact the lives of women and girls, here in this country and globally. *Ms.*'s reporting and analysis remain critical for understanding the role of gender in the expansion of right-wing extremism and violence, as well as the implications of the rise in authoritarianism in the United States and around the globe, and for helping construct a way forward.

If we have learned nothing else from the past fifty years, it should be that change can happen swiftly and singularly, both for better and for worse. We watched in horror in the summer of 2021 as the Taliban reseized power in Afghanistan. Despite twenty years of progress for women and girls under a constitutional democracy, the Taliban rapidly reimposed its gender apartheid edicts, severely constricting the rights of women and girls to education, employment, and freedom of movement. Almost overnight, women's voices were obliterated from the media. Women who protested the harsh restrictions were apprehended, beaten, tortured, their lives threatened, and some even murdered.

Here in the United States, our democratic institutions and women's rights are under intensifying attack. As under authoritarian regimes around the world, women are "canaries in the coal mine." State legislatures enacted more stringent laws on abortion in 2021 than ever before, including outright bans and adding to existing restrictions on abortions for poor women and young women. Domestic terrorists attack clinics that provide abortions and threaten, stalk, and murder doctors and staff. On June 24, 2022, the Supreme Court overturned *Roe v. Wade,* the 1972 decision that ensured a woman's constitutional right to abortion no matter in which state she lived. Immediately, feminists organized massive demonstrations at the Supreme Court and in every state to protest the Court's cruel decision—a decision that also threatens other fundamental rights, including the right to contraception, same-sex marriage, and interracial marriage. The fight for abortion rights is at its core the fight for self-determination and equality, and thus is critical to a truly representative democracy.

Meanwhile, gender and race disparity in representation in the Senate and the House, as well as state legislatures, persists, stymieing significant progress for women's equality. The same procedural roadblocks being used to thwart and undermine reproductive, civil, and voting rights are similarly used to derail critical gender equality advances, including the Equal Rights Amendment and the Violence Against Women Act. Despite these challenges, women possess tremendous political power. The gender gap—the measurable differences between women and men in public opinion and in voting—is growing and increasingly shapes election outcomes and the public debate on what the government should do to advance the common welfare.

Spanning Decades and Still at the Forefront

Despite more feminist news sources today from which to choose, accounting for a rich diversity of perspectives, the editorial impact of *Ms.* is unmatched. *Ms.* covers the news and makes it, reports on trends and helps create them. *Ms.* has generated new vocabulary, sparked laws and judicial changes, influenced policy, and advocated on issues too long ignored. Articles in *Ms.* have led to dozens of movies and books, have sparked new scholarship and action groups, and are widely reprinted and included in textbooks and collections.

The magazine's influence has threaded through all the significant social movements of the past fifty years and arrived here, in a moment when feminist ideas and innovations are more necessary than ever. The magazine remains a stalwart reminder of the power of feminist voices and is sharply focused on the ever-changing needs of the movement.

This book, then, serves not as an archive of the past but as a reflection of how far we have come and an assurance of the continued need for a feminist future. Over the years, the magazine has adapted to serve the needs of contemporary feminists, always sustaining a community. *Ms.* is as essential a voice of the movement as it has ever been—as the selections in this collection, carefully crafted and curated, bear out.

50
YEARS *of*
Ms.

CHAPTER 1

1970s

EVEN WITH THE MANY HURDLES we have left to clear in pursuit of gender equality, it is difficult to fathom how fundamentally different life was for the average woman or girl in the years prior to the founding of *Ms.* It is equally difficult to convey how quickly the social and cultural winds were shifting in the 1960s and 1970s. These shifts were owed in large part to the tremendous exertions of the women's, civil rights, gay and lesbian rights, and other political and social movements of the era.

Feminist organizations were gaining significant traction, including the National Organization for Women, the Women's Equity Action League, the National Association for the Repeal of Abortion Laws, and Redstockings, to name a few. Despite all this, the belief that the "natural" function of a woman was to be a wife and mother still ran rampant.

Ms. emerged to fill a gap between a determined, vibrant movement and the continued curtailment of women's rights in virtually every aspect of American life. In early 1971, the writer Gloria Steinem and the attorney Brenda Feigen brought together activists, writers, journalists, and artists to discuss creating a new print outlet for feminist voices. Steinem, already a familiar face of the movement, initially proposed a newsletter, but others—including Patricia "Pat" Carbine (then newly appointed editor of *McCall's* who would become *Ms.*'s publisher)—convinced her that a magazine would offer a truly women-centered alternative to the so-called women's magazines of the era, like *Ladies' Home Journal* and *Good Housekeeping,* that did not speak to the lives, needs, or ambitions of most women.

Driven by a combination of careful research, wisdom, conviction, tenacity, bravery, and luck, the magazine's first writers and editors saw a chance to launch a movement within a movement—a magazine women could call their own. The new magazine would be a place where women could fully express themselves, where their articles about politics, reproductive rights, sex and sexuality, and racial discrimination would not be turned away or paired with a negative article to "balance" a magazine's coverage of feminist ideas. The hope was to create a magazine that spoke to the real issues faced

by American women—married or unmarried, employed or at home, with or without children, lesbian or straight—especially those who had been marginalized or outright ignored in print media. The magazine's title, then, had to reflect that optimism of unity without limiting the diversity of its readership.

Titles such as *Everywoman, Sisters, The First Sex,* and *The Majority* were floated, but Steinem eventually landed on *Ms.* It was memorable, encouraged explanation and reflection, and became symbolic of feminism itself. In years to come, choosing to go by "Ms." rather than "Mrs." or "Miss" was a feminist gesture, signaling a woman's refusal to be circumscribed by her marital status.

ABOVE Meeting in the *Ms.* offices. *Left to right:* Patricia Carbine, Mary Peacock, Karin Lippert, Mary Scott, Pat Sweeting, Susanna Goldman, Ingeborg Day, and Gloria Steinem.

RIGHT The original *Ms.* staff in 1973. *Left to right, standing:* Lynn Thomas, Susan Thom Loubet, Patricia Carbine, Mary Thom, Dena Pender, Bernard Schick, Gloria Steinem, Letty Cottin Pogrebin, Susanna Goldman, Bea Feitler, Dinah Robinson, Ruth Sullivan, Donna Handly, Joanne Edgar, Susan Huberman, Mary Scott, Suzanne Levine. *Seated:* Margaret Sloan, Cathleen Black, Mary Peacock, Margaret Cleary, Margaret Hicks, Rita Waterman, Harriet Lyons, Catherine O'Haire, Joann Fairchild, Carl Barile, Pony Baptiste.

Editors Margaret Sloan *(right)* and Letty Cottin Pogrebin

Steinem and her compatriots, however, had little luck raising the necessary funds to start a magazine. Then Steinem was approached by Clay Felker, editor in chief of *New York* magazine, an outlet she had helped get off the ground only a few years prior and for which she was a regular contributor. Felker offered to print a forty-page issue of *Ms.* in the pages of *New York* in December 1971, with an expanded, stand-alone preview issue to follow in the spring of 1972.

"Until now, the Women's Movement has lacked an effective national publication to give voice to its ideas," Felker wrote in his foreword to the initial *Ms.* insert. "We have placed our own knowledge and experience at Gloria's disposal to help shape such a magazine."

Joining Steinem to work on the first issue were Joanne Edgar, Letty Cottin Pogrebin, Mary Peacock, and Nina Finkelstein. They were soon joined by Carbine and Suzanne Braun Levine, who took the reins as managing editor, and a tight-knit team of writers and editors including Margaret Sloan, Alice Walker, Susan Braudy, Harriet Lyons, Ruth Sullivan, Donna Handly, and Mary Thom.

The stand-alone preview issue of *Ms.* surpassed all expectations. The issue had been dated Spring 1972 even though it came out in January to give the fledgling magazine more time on newsstands, but its initial 300,000 print run, meant to last eight weeks, sold out within eight days. Twenty-six thousand readers mailed in subscriber cards, and *Ms.* editors received twenty thousand letters from girls and women around the country in response to their new venture.

Ms. had its share of growing pains—the push-pull between what to include and what to exclude, what aspects of the movement to highlight, and how to appeal to the average reader at the newsstand without diluting messages that to many were still considered controversial. Some feminists felt *Ms.* was not radical enough, while many advertisers balked at the magazine's frank portrayal of reproductive rights and abortion, its openness about sex, its willingness to include lesbian voices, and its inclusivity of Black and brown women.

But, at its heart, *Ms.* was—and still is—aspirational. Trying to balance the needs of its readers with the whims of an ever-changing media landscape, *Ms.* began as an effort to wrest control of the messaging about the feminist movement from mainstream media and put it back in the hands of women. Few could have imagined that *Ms.* would become the landmark institution in both women's rights and American journalism that it is today.

"If you asked us our philosophy for ourselves and for the magazine, each of us would give an individual answer," *Ms.* editors confessed in its first real issue, in July 1972. "But we agree on one thing. We want a world in which no one is born into a subordinate role because of visible difference, whether that difference is of race or of sex. That's an assumption we make personally and editorially, with all the social changes it implies. After that, we cherish our differences. We want *Ms.* to be a forum for many views. . . . So keep writing. *Ms.* belongs to us all."

.   .   .

The preview's cover, under the line, "Jane O'Reilly on the Housewife's Moment of Truth," was a painting of a many-armed, Shiva-like woman, her skin blue, her eight hands busy with typewriter, frying pan, phone, mirror, steering wheel, clock, iron, and feather duster. "It was the image that had come out of my Indian past," [Gloria] Steinem said, referring to the years she had spent in India as a young woman just out of college. Despite the tears falling from the blue woman's eyes, there is a peaceful, balanced feeling to the painting, and a serene cat sitting to the side.

—from *Inside* Ms.: *25 Years of the Magazine and the Feminist Movement*
by Mary Thom (1997)

OPPOSITE *Ms.* first appeared as an insert in *New York* magazine with this image as the insert's cover.

SPRING/72 PREVIEW ISSUE $1.50

Ms. ™

THE NEW MAGAZINE FOR WOMEN

Gloria Steinem
On Sisterhood

Letty Pogrebin
On Raising Kids
Without Sex Roles

Sylvia Plath's
Last Major Work

Women Tell
The Truth About
Their Abortions

Jane O'Reilly on The Housewife's Moment of Truth

Click! The Housewife's Moment of Truth

BY **JANE O'REILLY** • PREVIEW ISSUE/SPRING 1972

AMERICAN WOMEN ARE ANGRY. Not red-neck angry from screaming because we are so frustrated and unfulfilled angry, but clicking-things-into-place angry, because we have suddenly and shockingly perceived the basic disorder in what has been believed to be the natural order of things.

> "In the end, we are all housewives, the natural people to turn to when there is something unpleasant, inconvenient, or inconclusive to be done."

In Houston, Texas, a friend of mine stood and watched her husband step over a pile of toys on the stairs, put there to be carried up. "Why can't you get this stuff put away?" he mumbled. Click! "You have two hands," she said, turning away.

Last summer I got a letter from a man who wrote, "I do not agree with your last article, and I am cancelling my wife's subscription." The next day I got a letter from his wife saying, "*I* am not cancelling *my* subscription." Click!

On Fire Island my weekend hostess and I had just finished cooking breakfast, lunch, and washing dishes for both. A male guest came wandering into the kitchen just as the last dish was being put away and said, "How about something to eat?" He sat down, expectantly, and started to read the paper. Click!

A woman I know in St. Louis, who had begun to enjoy a little success writing a grain company's newsletter, came home to tell her husband about lunch in the executive dining room. She had planned a funny little anecdote about the deeply humorous pomposity of executives, when she noticed her husband rocking with laughter. "Ho ho, my little wife in an executive dining room." Click!

Attitudes are expressed in semantic equations that simply turn out to be two languages: one for men and another for women. One morning a friend of mine told her husband she would like to hire a babysitter so she could get back to her painting. "Maybe when you start to make money from your pictures, then we could think about it," said her husband. My friend didn't stop to argue the inherent fallacy in his point—how could she make money if no one was willing to free her for work? She suggested that instead of hiring someone, he could help with the housework a little more. "Well, I don't know, honey," he said. "I guess sharing the housework is all right if the wife is really contributing something, brings in a salary . . ." For a terrible minute my friend thought she would kill her husband, right there at breakfast, in front of the children. For ten years, she had been hanging wallpaper, making curtains, and refinishing floors so that they could afford the mortgage on their apartment. She had planned the money-saving menus so they could afford the little dinners for prospective clients. She had crossed town to save money on clothes so the family could have a new hi-fi. All the little advances in station—the vacations, the theater tickets, the new car—had been made possible by her crafty, endless, worried manipulation of the household expenses. "I was under the impression," she said, "that I *was* contributing something. Evidently my life's blood is simply a nondeductible expense."

In an office, a political columnist, male, was waiting to see the editor in chief. Leaning against a doorway, the columnist turned to the first woman he saw and said, "Listen, call Barry Brown and tell him I'll be late." Click! It wasn't because she happened to be an editor herself that she refused to make the call.

In the end, we are all housewives, the natural people to turn to when there is something unpleasant, inconvenient, or inconclusive to be done. It will not do for women who have jobs to pretend that society's ills will be cured if all women are gainfully employed. In Russia, 70 percent of the doctors and 20 percent of the construction workers are women, but women still do all the housework. Some revolution. As the Russian women's saying goes, it simply freed us to do twice the work.

It will not do for women who are mostly housewives to say that women's liberation is fine for women who work but has no relevance for them. Equal pay for equal work is only part of the argument—usually described as "the part I'll go along with." We are all housewives. We would prefer to be persons. That is the part they don't go along with. "That broad . . ." begins a male guest who Hasn't Thought. "Woman," corrects the hostess, smiling meaningfully over her coffeepot. "Oh, no," groans the guest. "Don't tell me you believe in this women's lib stuff!" "Yes," says the hostess.

"Well, I'll go along with some of it, equal pay for equal work, that seems fair enough," he concedes. Uneasy now, he waits for the male hoots of laughter, for the flutter of wives rushing to sit by their husbands at the merest breath of the subject of women's liberation. But that was three or four years ago. Too many moments have clicked in the minds of too many women since then. This year the women in the room have not moved to their husbands' sides; they have . . . solidified. A gelid quality settles over the room. The guest struggles on.

"You can't tell me women's lib means I have to wash the dishes, does it?"

"Yes."

They tell us we are being petty. The future improvement of civilization could not depend on who washes the dishes. Could it? Yes. The liberated society—with men, women, and children living as whole human beings, not halves divided by sex roles—depends on the steadfast search for new solutions to just such apparently trivial problems, on new answers to tired old questions. Such questions as: Denise works as a waitress from 6:00 a.m. to 3:00 p.m. Her husband is a cabdriver who moonlights on weekends as a doorman. They have four children. When her husband comes home at night, he asks, *"What's for dinner?"*

In moments of suburban strife, Fred often asks his wife, Alice, "Why haven't you mended my shirt and lubricated the car? *What else have you got to do but sit around the house all day?*"

How dare he ask such a question? What sort of bizarre social arrangement is post–Industrial Revolution marriage? What kind of relationship involves two people sharing their lives without knowing, or apparently caring, what the other does all day?

According to insurance companies, it would cost Fred $8,000 to $9,000 a year to replace Alice's services if she died. Alice, being an average ideal suburban housewife, works 99.6 hours a week—always feeling there is too much to be done and always guilty because it is never quite finished. Besides, her work doesn't seem important. After all, Fred is paid for doing whatever it is he does. Abstract statistics make no impact on Alice. "My situation is different," she says. Of course it is. All situations are different. But sooner or later she will experience—in a blinding click!—a moment of truth. She will remember that she once had other interests, vague hopes, great plans. She will decide that the work in the house is less important than reordering the work so she can consider her own life.

The problem is, what does she do then?

The first thing we all do is argue. We present our case: it is unfair that we should bear the whole responsibility for the constant schema of household management.

We may get agreement, but we will never get cooperation or permission. Rebuttals may begin at the lowest level: "It is a woman's job to wash dishes." Men at a higher stage of enlightenment may argue, "Why do we need a washing machine? I wash my socks and we send everything out." They simply cannot understand that we are the ones who must gather and list and plan even for the laundry we send out. It is, quite simply, *on our minds.* And *not* on theirs. Evenings of explanation and understanding will still end with "Honey, do I have any clean shorts for tomorrow?" Most women will decide that it is not worth making an issue out of shorts.

In fact, underwear is as good a place to begin as anywhere. Last summer I carried the underwear downstairs, put it in the hamper, sorted it, washed and dried it, folded it, carried it upstairs, and put it away. One day, I decided that as an act of extreme courage I would not carry the laundry upstairs. I put it on the couch in the room with the television set. The family moved it to one side of the couch so they could sit down. I left it there. I put more on the couch. They piled it up. They began to dress off the couch. I began to avoid the television room. At last, guilty and angry, my nerve failed and I carried the laundry upstairs. No one noticed. Out of that experience, I formulated a few rules that I intend to follow as soon as I finish the painful process of thinking about the assumptions that make them necessary.

1. Decide what housework needs to be done. Then cut the list in half. It is no longer necessary to prove ourselves by being in motion all day and all night. Beds must be made and food cooked, but it is unfair to demand that the family share the work if your standards include cooking like Julia Child and bouncing dimes on the bedspread. Beware of useless and self-defeating standards. It is preposterous and not unusual for a woman to feel her house must look as though no one lived there. Who's looking? Who cares?

2. Decide what you will and will not do. Keep firmly in mind the notion of personal maintenance as an individual responsibility. If children cannot put away their clothes and therefore cannot find them and have to go to school looking like ragpickers—well, presumably they will learn from experience. Their appearance does not make you a bad person. (If you can acknowledge and act on that fact, you are becoming liberated.) If you spend four or five hours a day driving your children places, ask yourself why. Are there no safe streets they can walk along? Why? Seizing responsibility from children has been women's way to compensate for their own lack of responsibility for themselves, and it has resulted in two generations of non-adults.

3. Make a plan and present it as final. There will, of course, be democratic argument, but it is only fair to state your purpose. Not that anyone will pay attention. They will laugh nervously and expect life to go on as usual. Do not be distracted by sophisticated arguments, such as "Well, let's take the relative value of our days." Yes. Let's. A wife who figures out that his important business meeting is no different from her PTA committee meeting may opt for equal hours and quit her own work at five o'clock.

Another diversionary remark is "But, honey, this isn't a business agreement. This is a home. It is a question of helping each other reach fulfillment." In my home, when I am working against a deadline, I sit in front of a typewriter and shout, "More tea!" The whole family hustles in with more tea. I call out, "Go to bed." "Get some lamb chops." It is an emergency situation and they all spring to, helping me fulfill myself. But *I* am still in charge of remembering to get the lamb chops. It is a problem that may not be solved in my lifetime.

4. Think revolutionary thoughts. The nineteenth century ended seventy-two years ago, but we are still trying to arrange our households according to that "ideal" image of family life. Think of something new. I know a man and woman who decided to stop eating dinner. She had been rushing around putting children to bed and then laying out a candlelit dinner with three kinds of food on the plate for her husband. They liked chatting at dinner. He helped clean up. They never finished before ten. But one night they discovered that both were dreaming of long cozy evenings reading by the fire. So they have skipped the ritual feast and replaced it with sandwiches. They get up earlier and have family talks at breakfast. Who knows what daring innovations may follow? He may demand an end to success based on overtime. Both may demand less homework so the children can assume some responsibilities.

5. Never give in. Empty one dishwasher, and it leads to a lifetime of emptying dishwashers. Remember that nothing will ever get done by anyone else if you do it. If you are the only person who worries about it, perhaps it isn't worth worrying about. If it is very important to you that you not live in a sty, then you must persuade everyone else that what is important to you counts.

6. Do not feel guilty. I have never met a woman who did not feel guilty. We can post signs in our hearts and on our walls saying, "It is not wrong to inconvenience my family; it is making us all responsible, ego-strong adults." But when a man we are attached to goes out with a button off his coat, we—nonetheless—feel feckless. The only near cure is to have something more interesting to think about. Even if "something to do" means going back to easy courses in school—back to the point where we abdicated for marriage—it is a beginning, and we are older now and will learn rapidly, because at least we know we want things some other way.

I cannot imagine anything more difficult than incurring the kind of domestic trauma I describe. It requires the conscious loss of the role we have been taught, and its replacement by a true identity. And what if we succeed? What if we become liberated women who recognize that our guilt is reinforced by the marketplace, which would have us attach our identity to furniture polish and confine our deepest anxieties to color coordinating our toilet paper and our washing machines. What if we don't allow ourselves to be treated as people with nothing better to do than wait for repairmen and gynecologists? What if we finally learn that we are defined not by our children and our husbands but by ourselves?

50 YEARS OF MS. is published on the heels of a global pandemic, which shined a light on the plight of modern caregiving in America and glaring gaps in its care infrastructure. One concrete result: a renewed demand for public investment in families (especially in mothers) and broad recognition of the need for long-sought feminist proposals like expanded access to affordable child care, paid federal family and medical leave, and financing for universal early education.

In 1971, when Congress passed nationally funded child care, it was vetoed by President Richard Nixon, who aligned it with communist ideas. Today's diverse cohort of advocates and progressive lawmakers are finally moving the needle in making the case that such reforms are essential not only to a strong, inclusive economy but to the fight for gender equality and justice. The U.S. congresswoman Jackie Speier wrote for *Ms.* in June 2021, "For too long, women—and particularly women of color—have been treated as second-class citizens as they've struggled to juggle it all. Women can't wait any longer for policy to catch up with reality. Otherwise this 'she-cession' will usher in nothing more than a 'he-covery.'"

Welfare Is a Women's Issue

BY **JOHNNIE TILLMON** • PREVIEW ISSUE/SPRING 1972

'M A WOMAN. I'm a Black woman. I'm a poor woman. I'm a fat woman. I'm a middle-aged woman. And I'm on welfare.

In this country, if you're any one of those things, you count less as a human being. If you're all those things, you don't count at all. Except as a statistic.

I am forty-five years old. I have raised six children. There are millions of statistics like me. Some on welfare. Some not. And some, really poor, who don't even know they're entitled to welfare. Not all of them are Black. Not at all. In fact, the majority—about two-thirds—of all the poor families in the country are white.

> **"Welfare is like a super-sexist marriage. You trade in a man for *the* man."**

Welfare's like a traffic accident. It can happen to anybody, but especially it happens to women.

And that's why welfare is a women's issue. For a lot of middle-class women in this country, women's liberation is a matter of concern. For women on welfare, it's a matter of survival.

Survival. That's why we had to go on welfare. And that's why we can't get off welfare now. Not us women. Not until we do something about liberating poor women in this country.

Because until now we've been raised to expect to work, all our lives, for nothing. Because we are the worst-educated, the least skilled, and the lowest-paid people there are. Because we have to be almost totally responsible for our children. Because we are regarded by everybody as dependents. That's why we are on welfare. And that's why we stay on it.

Welfare is the most prejudiced institution in this country, even more than marriage, which it tries to imitate. Let me explain that a little.

Ninety-nine percent of welfare families are headed by women. There is no man around. In half the states there can't be men around, because AFDC (Aid to Families with Dependent Children) says if there is an "able-bodied" man around, then you can't be on welfare. If the kids are going to eat, and the man can't get a job, then he's got to go.

Welfare is like a super-sexist marriage. You trade in a man for *the* man. But you can't divorce him if he treats you bad. He can divorce you, of course, cut you off anytime he wants. But in that case, he keeps the kids, not you.

An early *Ms.* reader responds to Johnnie Tillmon's article.

Los Angeles
February 6, 1972

Dear Ms.,

Congratulations to both yourselves and Johnnie Tillman! Her article on welfare, and especially her discussion of Nixon's F.A.P. program, is the most perceptive writing on this subject that I have come across yet.

I have been a caseworker on the AFDC program for the past two years and during that time I have seen how many new caseworkers are subtely conditioned to believe "that the only reason people are on welfare is because there's something wrong with their character." Such beliefs come about because caseloads are so high and the workload is so heavy that we rarely have enough time with our clients to see them as human beings caught in an impossible

2.

situation. Eventually you're sensitivity to other people becomes dulled and you begin to relate to them in increasingly more simplistic terms.

Then along comes an article by someone like Ms. Tillman and you're pulled back into reality. If there are ever going to be any meaningful changes in this welfare system we must reawaken our sensitivity and keep it operating at a high level. To that end I would appreciate information as to how to obtain reprints of her article -- I plan to distribute it among my fellow workers in the fervent hope that it will do some good.

Sincerely,
Boyd Grant
1477 S. Barrington #21
L.A., Cal. 90025

The man runs everything. In ordinary marriage, sex is supposed to be for your husband. On AFDC, you're not supposed to have any sex at all. You give up control of your own body. It's a condition of aid. You may even have to agree to get your tubes tied so you can never have more children just to avoid being cut off welfare.

The man, the welfare system, controls your money. He tells you what to buy, what not to buy, where to buy it, and how much things cost. If things—rent, for instance—really cost more than he says they do, it's just too bad for you. He's always right.

That's why Governor Ronald Reagan can get away with slandering welfare recipients, calling them "lazy parasites," "pigs at the trough," and such. We've been trained to believe that the only reason people are on welfare is that there's something wrong with their character. If people have "motivation," if people only want to work, they can, and they will be able to support themselves and their kids in decency.

The truth is a job doesn't necessarily mean an adequate income. There are some ten million jobs that now pay less than the minimum wage, and if you're a woman, you've got the best chance of getting one. Why would a forty-five-year-old woman work all day in a laundry ironing shirts at ninety-some cents an hour? Because she knows there's someplace lower she could be. She could be on welfare. Society needs women on welfare as "examples" to let every woman, factory workers and housewives alike, know what will happen if she lets up, if she's laid off, if she tries to go it alone without a man. So these ladies stay on their feet or on their knees all their lives instead of asking why they're only getting ninety-some cents an hour, instead of daring to fight and complain.

Maybe we poor welfare women will really liberate women in this country. We've already started on our own welfare plan. Along with other welfare recipients, we have organized so we can have some voice. Our group is called the National Welfare Rights Organization (NWRO). We put together our own welfare plan, called Guaranteed Adequate Income, which would eliminate sexism from welfare. There would be no "categories"—men, women, children, single, married, kids, no kids—just poor people who need aid. You'd get paid according to need and family size only, and that would be upped as the cost of living goes up.

As far as I'm concerned, the ladies of NWRO are the front-line troops of women's freedom. Both because we have so few illusions and because our issues are so important to all women: the right to a living wage for women's work, the right to life itself.

. . .

JOHNNIE TILLMON, born in Arkansas in 1926, was the daughter of a migrant sharecropper and an American welfare rights activist. She moved to California in 1959 and worked as a union shop steward in a Compton laundry. When Tillmon became ill in 1963 and was advised to seek welfare, she saw firsthand the prevalence of harassment by caseworkers. Tillmon organized in the housing projects and founded one of the first grassroots mothers' organizations, ANC (Aid to Needy Children) Mothers Anonymous, in 1963. ANC Mothers later became a part of the National Welfare Rights Organization, where Tillmon quickly emerged as a leader. Together with other mothers, she fought for adequate income, dignity, justice, and democratic participation. In 1979, she married the jazz musician Harvey Blackston and continued to live in Los Angeles and lead NWRO initiatives. Even after she achieved economic stability, Tillmon remained committed to welfare rights until her death in 1995 at age sixty-nine. Her name now graces daycare centers and housing developments—a reminder of her lasting influence on "welfare as a women's issue."

In the United States, women continue to live in poverty at higher rates than men—a figure that cuts across race. Even prior to the pandemic, women of color were disproportionately represented among those living in poverty: Latinas represented 18.1 percent of all women in the U.S. population and constituted 27.1 percent of women in poverty; Black women represented 12.8 percent of all women in the U.S. population and constituted 22.3 percent of women in poverty.

In 2020, those statistics were further exacerbated as women were forced by the pandemic to drop out of the labor force in alarming numbers. As safety nets faltered and schools shuttered, those numbers spiked. Worldwide, nearly fifty million women and girls had been pushed into extreme poverty by 2021—a figure that is not projected to revert to pre-pandemic levels until 2030.

The Mississippi-based Magnolia Mother's Trust is the longest-running guaranteed-income pilot in the country. Designed and run by and for women of color, this nonprofit initiative provides recipients with monthly, restriction-free cash awards. The results speak volumes: beneficiaries are 40 percent less likely to report debt from emergency loans, 20 percent more likely to have children performing at or above grade level, 27 percent more likely to seek medical care for sickness or chronic illness, and able to budget up to $150 more for groceries and household costs, resulting in lowered food insecurity and struggles with basic needs. It makes a strong statement about what we must demand from all our social safety nets.

IN THE PREVIEW ISSUE OF *MS.*, a historic declaration signed by fifty-three prominent women—including Billie Jean King, Judy Collins, Susan Sontag, Nora Ephron, Dorothy Pitman Hughes, Barbara Tuchman, Susan Brownmiller, Grace Paley, and Gloria Steinem—came with a simple headline: "We Have Had Abortions."

Not all who signed the *Ms.* petition had had abortions, and there was a ground rule not to ask nor to reply to that question, says Barbaralee Diamonstein-Spielvogel, the author of the original "We Have Had Abortions" article. "Signers responded in the evocative and then-current spirit of JFK's 'Ich bin ein Berliner.' Anything that impacts a woman—has resonance and touches on the rights of one woman—impacts each and all of us, with each of us understanding that there was and still is strength in a constituency, which we were hoping to ignite."

Today, social media has become a powerful tool for much of the same kind of truth telling. Among the modern viral moments: 2015's #ShoutYourAbortion campaign, followed by the 2019 hashtag #YouKnowMe, was the impetus for many thousands of people, from teens to older women, as well as celebrities and lawmakers—the likes of Busy Philipps and Amber Tamblyn, and Congresswomen Pramila Jayapal and Jackie Speier—to take to Twitter and Instagram to go public with their abortion stories.

This storytelling strategy is also having its day in court. When *Whole Woman's Health v. Hellerstedt* was argued in the U.S. Supreme Court in 2016, a friend-of-the-court brief was submitted by more than 110 lawyers; it is filled with their testimonies about how having had access to abortion enabled them to go on to become preeminent members of the legal profession. A similar lawyers' brief was filed in *June Medical Services v. Gee* in 2019, this time with more than 350 signatories. And in 2021, among the briefs filed in *Dobbs v. Jackson Women's Health Organization* was one from 500 all-star athletes—including 26 Olympians, 73 professional athletes, 276 college athletes, and top players like the U.S. soccer star Megan Rapinoe, the WNBA veteran Sue Bird, and the gold medalist in swimming Crissy Perham—as well as another signed by 6,600 everyday citizens, all of whom have had abortions.

In 2022, *Ms.* relaunched the petition in advance of the Supreme Court's decision overturning women's constitutional right to abortion, collecting thousands of names in just a few days. Women who have had abortions have spoken out many times during the past fifty years, and millions of women and men have marched in countless rallies and demonstrations for abortion rights. The result: by a margin of two to one, Americans oppose the repeal of *Roe*.

"We have had

These 53 American women invite you to join them in a campaign for honesty and freedom

Last year, 343 prominent and respected Frenchwomen were willing to sign a public manifesto declaring that they had undergone abortions. This *acte de révolte* dramatized their individual determination to take their lives and liberation into their own hands. It also showed their willingness to stand with and to speak for their less well-known sisters, who were forced to suffer unwanted pregnancies or illegal abortions in silence.

To many American women and men it seems absurd, in this allegedly enlightened age, that we should still be arguing for a simple principle: that a woman has the right to sovereignty over her own body. Still, there are tragically few places in the country where a woman can obtain an abortion without the expense and deception of conforming to inhuman laws, or the expense and physical danger of going outside the law. (Organizations offering information on the laws and on abortion availability are listed on page 126 of this issue.) The vast majority of abortion laws in this country are remnants of obscurantist attitudes and medieval prejudices.

In fact, at least one of every four women in the United States has had an abortion. Until the recent legal reform in two states, all of those had to be either therapeutic or illegal. Given the difficulty of securing a therapeutic abortion, the great majority of abortions endured by American women have been illegal—and therefore dangerous. This has caused untold suffering, especially on the part of poor women who must resort to self-induced or butchered abortions. Some idea of the lives to be saved by repealing abortion laws is suggested by the recent drastic reduction in deaths from childbirth, a statistic that includes deaths from bungled abortions, in New York City alone. During the first nine months of the new legal abortion program, "deaths from childbirth" dropped by at least 60 per cent.

To save lives and to spare other women the pain of socially-imposed guilt, 53 respected women residents in the United States have volunteered to begin the American Women's Petition by signing the statement below. Our purpose is not to alienate or to ask for sympathy, but to repeal archaic and inhuman laws. Because of the social stigma still wrongly attached to abortion, many women in public life, or with husbands in public life, have felt unable to join us. We are mostly women active in community work, or in the arts. But we invite all women, from every walk of life, to help eliminate this stigma by joining us in this petition, and signing the statement below. The complete list will be sent to the White House, to every State Legislature, and to our sisters in other countries who are signing similar petitions for their lawmakers.

Barbaralee D. Diamonstein

abortions"

Eve Auchincloss
Sunny Aurelio
Lorraine Beebe
Joan Bingham
Patricia Bosworth
Kay Boyle
Adelyn D. Breeskin
Susan Brownmiller
Hortense Calisher
Jaqueline Michot Ceballos
Lucinda Cisler
Shirley Clarke
Judy Collins
Mary Cunningham
Anselma Dell 'Olio
Karen De Crow
Barbaralee D. Diamonstein
Susan Edmiston

Nora Ephron
Lee Grant
Gael Greene
Nancy Grossman
Barbara Barrie Harnick
Lillian Hellman
Dorothy Pitman Hughes
Elizabeth Janeway
Lucy Jarvis
Jill Johnston
Billie Jean King
Maxine Kumin
Irma Lazarus
Viveca Lindfors
Marya Mannes
Dorothy Millstone
Marcia Colman Morton
Anaïs Nin

Grace Paley
Beverly Pepper
Eleanor Perry
Frances Fox Piven
Letty Cottin Pogrebin
Mary Rodgers
Naomi Ellen Rubin
Nora Sayre
Anita Siegel
Marcia B. Siegel
Anne Sexton
Ruth P. Smith
Susan Sontag
Gloria Steinem
Lena Tabori
Barbara W. Tuchman
Shirley Ann Wheeler

Barbaralee Diamonstein is a freelance writer who was Director of Cultural Affairs for New York City. Her book of interviews with 94 women, "Open Secrets," will be published in February.

The Shulmans' Marriage Agreement

BY **SUSAN EDMISTON** • SPRING 1972

I. PRINCIPLES

We reject the notion that the work which brings in more money is more valuable. The ability to earn more money is a privilege that must not be compounded by enabling the larger earner to buy out of his/her duties and put the burden on the partner who earns less or on another person hired from outside.

> **"We believe we must share all responsibility for taking care of our children and home—and not only the work but also the responsibility."**

We believe that each partner has an equal right to his/her own time, work, values, choices. As long as all duties are performed, each of us may use his/her extra time any way he/she chooses. If he/she wants to use it making money, fine. If he/she wants to spend it with spouse, fine.

As parents we believe we must share all responsibility for taking care of our children and home—and not only the work but also the responsibility. At least during the first year of this agreement, *sharing responsibility* shall mean dividing the jobs and dividing the *time*.

II. JOB BREAKDOWN AND SCHEDULE

A. CHILDREN

1. Mornings Waking children; getting their clothes out; making their lunches; seeing that they have notes, homework, money, bus passes, books; brushing their hair; giving them breakfast (making coffee for us). Every other week each parent does all.

2. Transportation Getting children to and from lessons, doctors, dentists (including making appointments), friends' houses, and so on. Parts occurring between 3:00 and 6:00 p.m. fall to wife. She must be compensated by extra work from husband.

3. Help Helping with homework, personal questions; explaining things. Parts occurring between 3:00 and 6:00 p.m. fall to wife. After 6:00 p.m. husband does Tuesday, Thursday, and Sunday; wife does Monday, Wednes-

How to Write Your Own Marriage Contract

Susan Edmiston

First we thought marriage was when Prince Charming came and took you away with him. Then we thought that marriage was orange blossoms and Alençon lace and silver patterns. Then we thought that marriage—at least—was when you couldn't face signing the lease on the new apartment in two different names.

But most of us never even suspected the truth. Nobody ever so much as mentioned that what marriage is, at its very heart and essence, is a contract. When you say "I do," what you are doing is not, as you thought, vowing your eternal love, but rather subscribing to a whole system of rights, obligations and responsibilities that may very well be anathema to your most cherished beliefs.

Worst of all, you never even get to read the contract—to say nothing of the fine print. If you did, you probably wouldn't agree to it. Marriage, as it exists today, is a peculiarly vague, and yet inflexible, arrangement of institutionalized inequality which goes only one step beyond the English common-law concept of husband and wife as one, and, as the saying goes, "that 'one' is the husband." We have progressed from the notion of wife as legal nonentity to the notion of wife as dependent and inferior.

In recent years, many people have taken to writing their own marriage ceremonies in a desperate attempt to make the institution more relevant to their own lives. But ceremonies, they are finding, do not reach the heart of the matter. So some couples are now taking the logical next step of drawing up their own contracts. These agreements may delineate any of the financial or personal aspects of the marriage relationship—from who pays which bills to who uses what birth control. Though many of their provisions may not be legally binding, at the very least they can help us to examine the often inchoate assumptions underlying our relationships, help us come to honest and equitable terms with one another, and provide guidelines for making our marriages what we truly want them to be.

Before their first child was born, Alix Cates Shulman and her husband had an egalitarian, partnership marriage. Alix worked full time as

Susan Edmiston is a writer, editor, columnist and contributor to many national magazines. She is now at work on a book, "A Literary Guide to New York."

BEFORE their first child was born, Alix Kates Shulman and her husband had an egalitarian partnership marriage. Alix worked full time as an editor in New York, and both shared the chores involved in maintaining their small household. After two children, however, the couple found that they had automatically fallen into the traditional sex roles: he went out and worked all day to support his family; she stayed home and worked from 6:00 a.m. to 9:00 p.m. taking care of children and housework. Unthinkingly, they had agreed not only to the legalities of marriage but to the social contract as well.

After six years at home—six years of chronic dissatisfaction—Alix became involved in the women's liberation movement and realized it might be possible to change the contract under which she and her husband lived. The arrangement they worked out, basically a division of household duties and child care, rejected "the notion that the work which brings in more money is more valuable. The ability to earn . . . money is a privilege which must not be compounded by enabling the larger earner to buy out of his/her duties."

—from "How to Write Your Own Marriage Contract"
by Susan Edmiston, Spring 1972

day, and Saturday. Friday is free for whoever has done extra work during the week.

4. Nighttime (after 6:00 p.m.) Getting children to take baths, brush their teeth, put away their toys and clothes, go to bed; reading with them; tucking them in and having nighttime talks; handling if they wake in the night. Husband does Tuesday, Thursday, and Sunday. Wife does Monday, Wednesday, and Saturday. Friday is split according to who has done extra work.

5. Babysitters Babysitters must be called by the parent the sitter is to replace. If no sitter turns up, that parent must stay home.

6. Sick care Calling doctors; checking symptoms; getting prescriptions filled; remembering to give medicine; taking days off to stay home with sick child, providing special activities. This must still be worked out equally, since now wife seems to do it all. In any case, wife must be compensated.

7. Weekends All usual child care, plus special activities (beach, park, zoo). Split equally. Husband is free all Saturday; wife is free all Sunday.

B. HOUSEWORK

1. Cooking Breakfasts during the week are divided equally; husband does all weekend breakfasts (including shopping for them and dishes). Wife does all dinners except Sunday nights. Husband does Sunday dinner and any other dinners on his nights of responsibility if wife isn't home. Whoever invites guests does shopping, cooking, and dishes; if both invite them, split work.

2. Shopping Food for all meals, housewares, clothing and supplies for children. Divided by convenience. Generally, wife does daily food shopping; husband does special shopping.

3. Cleaning Husband does dishes Tuesday, Thursday, and Sunday. Wife does Monday, Wednesday, and Saturday. Friday is split according to who has done extra work during week. Husband does all the housecleaning in exchange for wife's extra child care (3:00 to 6:00 daily) and sick care.

4. Laundry Home laundry, making beds, dry cleaning (take and pick up). Wife does home laundry. Husband does dry-cleaning delivery and pickup. Wife strips beds; husband remakes them.

Wonder Woman: Revisited

BY JOANNE EDGAR • JULY 1972

"ONE *SUPERMAN* is worth three *Wonder Woman*s," I conceded, stacking, counting, and restacking comics on the sidewalk. I was an avid comic book reader, but I pretended not to like *Wonder Woman.* After all, it wasn't a real advantage in our daily comic trades. The boys on my block always bid for *Superman, Green Lantern,* or *Batman;* even *Donald Duck.* But never *Wonder Woman.* "She's just a girl," they said. And so, being "just a girl" myself, I hid my admiration for Wonder Woman and put my stakes on Superman.

But up in my apple tree, I read *Wonder Woman* anyway. "Breaking the fetters of evil with her strength; parrying bullets with her steel bracelets; sweeping through dimensions of time and space in her invisible plane,

> "In the mid-1940s she even jumped into politics with a campaign for president—a woman to save the country from war and destruction."

Wonder Woman, the Amazonian princess from Paradise Isle, brought enemies to their knees and to her command with her golden magic lasso." Who could resist a role model like that? In America she lived as Diana Prince—secretary, nurse, army intelligence officer—but she could change into her Wonder Woman costume and appear from nowhere to do battle with the forces of evil. In the mid-1940s she even jumped into politics with a campaign for president—a woman to save the country from war and destruction.

I loved her comic cohorts, too.

Etta Candy: fat and frustrated, who stuffed her problems with chocolate and her comments with "Woo Woo!"

Mer-Boy: her underwater boyfriend—all boy above and all fish below.

Hippolyta: her mother and queen of the Amazons (like the mythical Hippolyta), who taught goodness and justice and kept close tabs on her daughter through a mental radio-TV.

As a kid trading comics on the sidewalk, I wish I'd known that, even though Superman never existed outside the comic book world, Amazonian princesses did. In sixteenth-century Brazil, for instance. Picture a civilization of jungle women living in caves deep in the rain forests of the Amazon River. These fierce female warriors and powerful victors kidnapped males from neighboring tribes and brought them to a copulatorium for a mating ritual complete with dancing and flute music. (In memory of this fearful time of women's superiority, some modern-day tribes of Indians in Brazil

GLORIA STEINEM ON HOW WOMEN VOTE
MONEY FOR HOUSEWORK
Ms.
NEW FEMINIST: SIMONE DE BEAUVOIR
BODY HAIR: THE LAST FRONTIER
WONDER WOMAN FOR PRESIDENT
JULY/1972
$1.00
PEACE AND JUSTICE IN '72
MURPHY ANDERSON

Wonder Woman was featured on *Ms.*'s cover for the first time in July 1972 (*opposite*); she's appeared on the cover four more times since then.

will not allow their women to play flutes.) Mothers slaughtered their male infants or maimed them so that they could be used as servants. Daughters were raised in the strong, self-sufficient, and ruling-class images of their mothers.

Many historians have rejected this Amazon society as pure myth, an expression of men's fear of women. But recent archaeological discoveries support the stories of such tribes. Caves painted with triangular female symbols, a copulatorium where a male symbol appears for the first and only time, and a slaughtering basin for male infants or animal sacrifices; all this evidence has been found deep in the jungles of Brazil by German and Brazilian scientists.

Hundreds of similar societies might have existed in other cultures over a period of several thousand years. They were probably backlash societies—a reaction to the cruel, patriarchal takeover of a previously gynocratic world.

Greek myths and legends abound with stories of Amazons. Herodotus and other ancient historians and geographers wrote of such societies in the Black Sea area, Greece, and northeast Africa.

Wonder Woman captured the Amazonian spirit of strength and self-sufficiency, but added the peacefulness and revulsion toward killing that have culturally distinguished women from men.

Wonder Woman herself first appeared in 1941, the invention of a psychologist named William Moulton Marston. Attorney, inventor of the lie detector, prison reformer, and businessman, Marston (who wrote comics under the thinly disguised pen name of Charles Moulton) conceived of *Wonder Woman* as a counter to the "bloodcurdling masculinity" of most comic books. Both plot and character were based on Marston's self-styled vision of feminist philosophy. "Women represent love; men represent force," he wrote. "Man's use of force without love brings evil and unhappiness. But Wonder Woman has force bound by love and, with her strength, represents what every woman should be and really is. She corrects evil and brings happiness. Wonder Woman proves that women are superior to men because they have love in addition to force."

Not all of Marston's characters were heroines. "Women have been submissive to men and taken men's psychology [force without love] as their own," explained Marston, so women villains still existed and appeared regularly in *Wonder Woman* comics. Cheetah, for example, was a feline fury who represented "uncontrolled power."

So much for Marston's theories. Though Wonder Woman in battles reigned supreme, Wonder Woman in love, as if lassoed back into conventionality, became the simpering romantic maiden, willing to relinquish her Amazonian birthright to follow a man. In fact, what brought her to America in the first place was her love (illicit for an Amazon) for Captain Steve Trevor, U.S. Army.

Wonder Woman's adventures were and are full of violence, but Marston insisted that Wonder Woman herself never sought revenge, nor hurt any villain. "Evil destroys itself, unless Wonder Woman can bind it for constructive use," Marston explained. (After six pages of fierce battle in which Wonder Woman defeats a Nazi spy, for instance, he accidentally slips off a pier and drowns.) Usually Wonder Woman saved her worst enemies and reformed their characters. Exceptions included the distorted and villainized Nazis and Japanese who invaded all good American comics during World War II.

Marston died in 1947, but Wonder Woman lived on. The new writers didn't understand her spirit, however, and she lost some of her original feminist orientation. Her superhuman strength remained, but her violence increased. Rather than proving her superiority over men, she became more and more submissive. In 1968, she relinquished her superhuman Amazon powers along with her bracelets, her golden magic lasso, and her invisible plane. She became a human being. Diana Prince, clad now in boutique pantsuits and tunics, acquired conventional emotions, vulnerability to men, the wisdom of an adviser (a man, of course, named I Ching), and the skills of karate, kung fu, and jujitsu. In other words, she became a female James Bond, but without his sexual exploits. The double standard applied even to her.

Next year, Wonder Woman will be reborn. With the help of her first woman editor, Dorothy Woolfolk, she will rise again as an Amazon, complete with superhuman powers. Ms. Woolfolk also plans to decrease violence in the plots and return our heroine to the feminism of her birth. And maybe to politics, too?

"Great Hera!" says one of the new 1973 comic book covers. "Wonder Woman, the beautiful Amazon princess, is alive and well and living on Paradise Isle." And why not? After all, even Wonder Woman needs a Key Biscayne.

But will she still have to trade three for one against Superman?

Women Voters Can't Be Trusted

BY **GLORIA STEINEM** • JULY 1972

MEN IN POLITICS have made a lot of assumptions about the way women vote:

- that we vote like our husbands if we're married or like our fathers if we're not;
- that, given our choice of male candidates, we'll choose the sexually attractive one;
- that we're much less likely to vote for a woman candidate than men are;
- that we consider politics a male province, and so are less likely to get into the process, to form political opinions, or to vote at all;
- that Black women are less concerned than white women with issues of sex discrimination and more turned off by the women's liberation movement as a whole;
- that women are more conservative than men, and possibly even more violent and vengeful ("the real haters," as Richard Nixon once put it);
- finally, and somewhat paradoxically, that the Nineteenth Amendment didn't amount to much, because the women's vote is never going to make a fundamental difference anyway.

Women have tended to go along with these assumptions. After all, they fit our popular image as nonpolitical, limited people, an image we have internalized so well that we may accept it as true of women as a group, even though we have disproved it in our individual lives. The truth is that these ideas have been acted upon with little proof of their accuracy, and often with no serious study at all.

In the early days of opinion taking, pollsters went to offices and factories where few women were present, or went door-to-door asking for "the man of the house." Modern pollsters talk to women, but often fail to analyze sex—as they would, say, age or economic level—for its possible influence on opinion.

Religion, marital status, ethnic origin, geographic region, education, parents' voting habits, property ownership, urban versus rural or suburban lifestyle, blue collar versus white collar: all are more likely to be studied for their effect on voting habits, both by politicians and by scholars, than are political differences based on sex.

Some prominent women have taken positive pride in ignoring the women's vote or insisting there was no such thing. After all, if men were the acknowledged political grown-ups, then any difference from them was the measure of our immaturity. Why prove male-female opinion differences when they were bound to be used against us? Better to get "educated on the issues" so we could prove ourselves by voting exactly like men. True, brave women fought for and earned the right to vote fifty-two years ago, but too few of their sisters had the ego strength to believe their cultural differences from men might have a positive value—ever.

> "Brave women fought for and earned the right to vote . . . but too few of their sisters had the ego strength to believe their cultural differences from men might have a positive value."

We are just beginning to look unashamedly at how we think, whether it is like, or different from, men. We are just beginning to flex our muscles, and figure out what kind of political force we might be.

Apparently, we are becoming less "conservative." Even about ourselves.

ARE BLACK WOMEN AGAINST THE WOMEN'S LIBERATION MOVEMENT?

One unmissable trend in all available polls is that Black women are even more interested in changing their status as women than white women are. White women say yes to change by 45 to 39 percent in the Harris-Setlow poll, but among Black women the positive balance is 62 to 22 percent.

Furthermore, Black women come out stronger on just about every feminist issue, whether it's voting for a woman candidate, ending violence and militarism, or believing that women are just as rational as men and have more human values.

Black women are also more favorably disposed to the phrase "women's liberation" than white women are, in spite of the white or middle-class connotations often given it by the press: 67 percent of Black women reacted favorably to it, as opposed to 35 percent of white women. Perhaps most surprising, Black women more often put white feminist leaders on their list of "greatly respected" women than white women did.

THERE'S NO SUCH THING AS A WOMEN'S BLOC VOTE. OR IS THERE?

All the available polls show one thing very clearly: women are changing more rapidly than any other group. We are just beginning to act forcefully and to express the ways in which we are culturally different from men: the more humane, less violent values of the women's culture.

Even a small difference can be crucial when it involves 51 percent of the population. It may only take a few thousand people in each state to change an election. In most countries, 5 percent of the population is the activist group that makes social change.

We've been voting differently for quite a long time, but we've been delivering our votes for nothing. Now women want something in return. Nineteen seventy-two is just the beginning.

·   ·   ·

STARTING IN 1980, Election Day exit polls began being reported out by gender, thus revealing the "gender gap"—the difference between the way women and men vote. This provided the first concrete polling data to prove that "women voters can't be trusted."

In 2008, *Ms.* commissioned Election Day polling to track which voters identified as feminist, with 48 percent of the female electorate claiming the title. In 2012, *Ms.* coined the term "feminist factor" to reflect the proportion of feminist-identifying voters and their subsequent voting behavior. By 2020, it was stronger than at any time in the past—driving the gender gap to become a "gender gulf," as 61 percent of all women polled said the term "feminist" described them "very well" or "somewhat well" (19 percent and 42 percent, respectively).

The finding cut across all racial and ethnic lines, with 64 percent of Black women, 63 percent of Latinas, and 59 percent of white women responding "very" or "somewhat well." Others proudly claiming the title were young women (68 percent), Democrats (75 percent), and those with a college degree (72 percent). And among men, four in ten called themselves a feminist.

Notes from **Abroad**

SINCE THE JULY 1972 ISSUE, when Germaine Greer wrote "Down with Panties," the first of many "Notes from Abroad," *Ms.* has chronicled the struggles and successes of women's rights movements around the globe.

On November 29, 1974, at 3:45 a.m., an exhausted woman stepped out from the French National Assembly into a cold, fine Paris rain. After a dramatic thirty-hour debate, Simone Veil (pronounced "Vay") had just won the right to abortion for all Frenchwomen by a vote of 284 to 189. The Senate ratified the law on December 14, making France the first nation of Latin and Catholic background to legalize abortion.

Suddenly journalists of every political persuasion were scrambling for interviews with this young, green-eyed grandmother who is the only woman to occupy a full-rank cabinet post in the government. Although French feminists had been fighting for this legislation for five years, there is no doubt that in the crucial weeks of November 1974, Simone Veil was in the right place at the right time. For it was her skill and determination in the position of minister of health that made the difference; she exemplifies what a woman in a position of power can accomplish to improve the lives of all women.

—from "Simone Veil: 20 Million Frenchwomen Won't Be Wronged"
by Claude Servan-Schreiber, February 1976

The ferry chugs for nearly an hour to reach the tiny Danish island of Femø. As the only link to the mainland, the boat is always loaded with cars, boxes, milk cans, and people. In the summer, the ferry is weighted even more; it underlines the separation between a male-dominated, traditional society and a female society where values and ideas supersede things and position. The Women's Camp gathered for the second time last summer on Femø.

—"Denmark: The Women's Island Camp"
by Barbara Robin, November 1972

Economic survival for a woman in Italy means marriage, and the mystique of romantic love helps to blind her to its probable consequences. Most women are not even aware of the legal servitude they will be subjected to. The Italian juridical structures, even more than those in other industrialized societies, blatantly support the accepted inferiority of women.

—"Italy: Violent Reactions"
by Julienne Travers, April 1973

Because of modesty and tradition, Muslim women will see only female physicians, and the only female physicians available were Hindus from India. . . . Although I am Kashmiri, I was not accepted by the people—I was a curiosity, a Muslim woman who was a physician. No one could fathom it. The British came to investigate my degree, and in the street the men threw earth at me, which means "you will die soon."

—"Kashmir: Some Call It Paradise"
by Gulshan Nallazarilli (as told to Carol Muske), July 1974

Nothing better symbolizes the paradox that is India than the enigma of its women. How does one understand a nation that has distinguished women politicians, administrators, entrepreneurs, and attorneys, and yet remains to a great extent a stagnant, dormant giant in regard to the everyday lives of its women? How can one explain the paradox within the individual woman who holds a position of authority in her professional life but retreats to a secondary or passive role in her private life?

—"Six Faces of India"
by Rami Chhabra, December 1974

Mae-fun and three other women work in a hot loft without air-conditioning. Her job is pushing a fifty-pound roll of plastic to her machine, unwinding it by hand, and pulling one end under the arm of a machine that resembles an electrified paper cutter. She then presses a foot pedal, which drops the electrified arm down on the plastic, seaming the bag—motions that take a few seconds and could be completely mechanized except for the variety of sizes and shapes of bags produced. "We women are cheaper than machines," she claims, "because a machine costs more than $2,000 [U.S. currency] and would only replace two of us, and then a mechanic would have to be hired to service the machine, and a mechanic's wages are $120 a month." Mae-fun earns a dollar for every thousand bags she seams—about two hours' work.

—"Hong Kong: Inside the Factory"
by Janet Salaff, February 1975

Its tourist brochures may feature come-on close-ups of itty-bitty string bikinis, but the government of Brazil takes a somewhat different view of female sexuality when the subject is treated seriously. This past fall, after several weeks at the top of the best-seller list, *The Hite Report* was hurriedly yanked off the nation's bookstore shelves because—according to the official government censor—the book is "against the morals and good customs of Brazil." (The author Shere Hite noted that "it must also be a break with Brazilian customs for a woman to have an orgasm.") The government's 1968 censorship decree has banned various explicitly feminist publications (including *Ms.*).

—"A Brazilian Censor Tells All"
by Marlise Simons, January 1979

Populist Mechanics

THE JULY 1972 ISSUE also launched the series "Populist Mechanics." These practical, how-to guides empowered women to gain self-reliance, with topics ranging from "Tires—One More Thing Women Can Change" to "The Fine Art of Used Car Buying" and "Cameras Less Obscura."

There's a reason why men have kept cars an arcane secret all these years, and why women on campus are now demanding courses in auto mechanics as part of women's liberation. It's all very simple. To understand is to be free.

Here's a simple explanation of how a car works. Clip it, put it in your glove compartment, and never again be intimidated by a rattle or a hiss under the hood.

—from "Demystifying Your Car"
by Elizabeth Hemmerdinger, July 1972

Anyone who has stood in the midst of a project muttering, "There must be a better way!" is a potential inventor. You don't have to be a tinkering genius; most inventors have simply recognized the significance of change.

—"How to Patent Your Invention"
by Victoria Frigo, February 1976

Once, when I was wondering (in a rather despondent tone) how I could escape spending the rest of my life as a secretary, a friend suggested that my trouble might be that I never thought of trying anything really different. For instance, he said, he had been talking to an exterminator, and it seems that they had a good thing going. I didn't want my friend to know how truly bereft of ideas I was at that point, so I just said "hmm," but I secretly resolved in that moment to become an exterminator, and I did.

—"How to Be Your Own Exterminator"
by Sally George, February 1977

Imagine this potential: if the thirty-three million women who constitute the memberships of organizations associated with creating the

National Women's Agenda contributed a *dime* each, we could afford a computer system large enough to connect and serve us all—to maintain our network, exchange information, alert each other to crises, and build data banks of crucial lists, statistics, projections. Computer techniques and computers themselves are becoming an increasingly pervasive part of the world we live in. Not understanding our world is oppressive, and there is danger in ignorance.

—"Overcoming Computer Anxiety" or "Can a Computer Be Your Sister?"
by Dana Densmore, May 1979

Manners for Humans

THE ETIQUETTE COLUMN "Manners for Humans" was a feminist alternative to the prevailing "myth that manners differ for each sex and therefore have little to do with relationships between human beings," as Jane Trahey described the work of Emily Post and Amy Vanderbilt in the first piece in the series, "Good-Bye to Emily and Amy" (July 1972).

Doorways: If the truth were known, the only reason a woman went through a door ahead of a man was simply that her life was infinitely more expendable than his. If someone jumped on someone, you know who got it. Anyone can hold doors for anyone else. It is also only decent to see that it doesn't slam behind you.

—"Good-Bye to Emily and Amy"
by Jane Trahey, July 1972

Women are throwing their bras and girdles away not because they want it all to hang out but because most underclothes *hurt.* Our children sit on curbs and read on the floor because they are more interested in comfort than in keeping themselves presentable. They don't care if their blue jeans get dirty. In the same sense, the millions of women who now wear pants in public are not captives of changing fashion; they simply want to feel at ease in their bodies and unhampered in their activities.   —"T-Shirts for Tea"
by Maria Josephy Schoolman, February 1973

I know he is still my husband because of a letter I got asking for a divorce. The letter came from Israel and it said, "Our divorce has got to have a little pizzazz in it. Rabbi Kahane recommends the Rabbinical Council of America." I wrote back indicating that the only pizzazz I was looking for in "our divorce" was a clause requiring him to give me some financial support for the baby (now four and a half).

—"Wednesday the Rabbi Called About My Divorce"
by Marcia Karmen, January 1974

Body Hair: **The Last Frontier**

BY **HARRIET LYONS** AND
REBECCA ROSENBLATT • JULY 1972

THE ACTRESS Faye Dunaway boldly reveals her unshaven armpits for a photograph in a national magazine and says that that's the way she will appear in all future film roles.

Eunice Lipton, an art historian in her thirties, strokes the growth on her legs and says, "It may seem ugly, but it's me."

The graduate student Grace Boynton, twenty-three, explains that she has thrown away her razor because "I got insulted that my natural body processes were considered disgusting by society."

And the social worker Peg Brennan, forty-seven, has decided "not to add anything that isn't me—and not to remove anything that is me."

> **"Given the . . . stares directed at the unshaven woman, we are not surprised to discover that even the most liberated woman backslides when beach weather arrives."**

While cosmetics imply the real woman is not enough, shaving says the real woman is too much. There is probably nothing more tedious, messy, or hazardous in the feminine beauty regimen than the removal of hair from underarms, legs, eyebrows, lips, chin, and breasts.

Ah, the pain . . . a splash of cologne or, heaven forbid, a dip in the ocean after shaving could produce a strong desire for Darvon. Several moments of teeth gnashing usually follow a dab of deodorant to a newly depilated armpit. And who among us has not hacked ankles, shins, and knees in hurried preparation for a date, and then tried desperately to stop the bleeding with dainty dots of toilet paper when a tourniquet would have been more appropriate?

Because anything that destroys hair is likely to have a similar effect on skin, depilation can also be dangerous—particularly if it's electrical or chemical.

Electrolysis, the use of shortwave electric current to remove hair permanently, must be done expertly if permanent scarring is to be avoided. If the follicle is not thoroughly destroyed, those cursed hairs, for whose eternal removal you suffered and paid dearly, will resurface. Home electrolysis devices are downright unsafe and rarely successful.

Cream depilatories smell awful and, if the explicit label instructions are not carefully followed, can cause irritation, allergic reactions, and eye injuries. Waxing, one of the oldest methods of hair removal, can be a masochistic trip. After the wax preparation is applied and allowed to harden, it is pulled off, taking both your hair and your breath away.

An emerging feminist consciousness tells us that all this punishing depilation reflects the depth of our socialized distaste for our bodies. We slavishly remove body hair and substitute artificial scents for natural body odors because we dare not expect approval if we look or smell as we really are.

Despite the all too familiar bother and pain—as well as the new feminist mandate to let it all hang out—the custom of depilating is still alive and well. Those who do vastly outnumber those who don't, but discussions of female body hair reveal disquieting associations.

In psychoanalytic parlance, hair is the accepted symbol of the genitals, so sexual behavior and hair-removal rituals are closely associated. Hairiness, in this lexicon, is translated as unrestrained animal sexuality. Conversely, extremes of haircutting and shaving are symbolic of castration or the repudiation of the very existence of sex. Anthropological evidence linking shaving customs to celibacy and ceremonial mutilation rites (such as the cutting off of finger joints) supports this symbology.

The year *Ms.* first hit newsstands also happened to mark the tenth anniversary of the death of Marilyn Monroe. Harriet Lyons, the co-author of "Body Hair" and an early editor at *Ms.*, was the catalyst behind the 1972 cover and its caption, "The Woman Who Died Too Soon." Gloria Steinem remarked of it in 1986, "As the writer of this brief essay about women's new hope of reclaiming Marilyn, I was astounded by the response to the article. It was like tapping an underground river of interest."

With hairiness equated to animal sexuality, the unchecked or uncovered appearance of hair in the armpits and on the legs of women collides with the culture's premise of female sexuality as passive. The implication that a woman's underarm and leg hair is superfluous, and therefore unwanted, is but one embodiment of our culture's preoccupation with keeping women in a kind of state of innocence and denying their visceral selves. Some women will even shave pubic hair, thereby emulating the infantile sexlessness of a little girl. And only within the last year has the men's magazine *Playboy* conceded that adult women have pubic hair at all.

The acceptance of hairiness in men, like its suppression in women, is connected to animality, but, ironically, the association is misguided. Man/woman is the only animal sexually active beyond the need to reproduce; the only animal that can experience orgasm at times when conception is impossible. We are both the most sex-driven and the least hairy of the animal kingdom, yet we persist in equating sexuality with furriness. The bald or non-hairy-chested man suffers a minor discrimination all his own.

While our puritanical attitude makes the hairless female body the quintessence of femininity, our obsession with cleanliness works to modify the acceptance of hairiness even in men. Long hair and beards are for dirty hippies. The clean-shaven and the crew cuts satisfy the American ideal.

Hair shares with feces, urine, semen, menstrual blood, spittle, and sweat a centuries-old association with impurity. As a result, fastidious women throughout history have felt obliged to remove hair that appeared anywhere but on the head or pubis. In the 1850s, women were so devoted to their hygienic images that they inflicted skin ulcers upon themselves by reckless use of depilatories made from lime, arsenic, and potash.

Biologists have given shaving yet another crude rationale. In their belief, hair is a surplus human product; its original function—to provide protection from the elements, extremes in temperature, insect bites, and the sun's rays—technology. Hair growth is becoming a vestigial process, which will eventually disappear. Therefore its removal by shaving is, in the biologists' view, as natural a way for human beings to get rid of it as shedding is for animals.

Race and class, with their attendant prejudices, determine special cultural attitudes toward body hair. The connotation of dirty foreigner versus clean American has always been evident in our national thoughts on hair. A young woman involved in a bicycle accident was asked by a New York policeman examining her injured, unshaven leg, "You're not Puerto Rican, are you?"

It's true that in Puerto Rico women do not remove body hair unless they are upwardly mobile or mainland oriented. In France, only lower-class or provincial women remain hairy. Even the supposedly earthy Italian women have begun shaving underarms to conform with standards of chicness. In Spain, a mustache on a woman is considered sexy, but not necessarily bred.

Hair underscores the various myths and mysteries that have arisen from our different skin colors. Intimidated racial groups try to lose their identity by adapting the hair texture and styles of the majority or ruling class. The kinky hair of American-born Black people has been obscured for generations by straighteners, pomades, and pageboy wigs. In Sweden, where most women are fair enough to make shaving a nonissue, dark-complexioned women shave to be less conspicuous in the homogeneous population.

The Afro-coifed Black and the unshaven woman, regardless of hair color, nationality, and class, make of their personal grooming a political statement. They reject an image of beauty and acceptability imposed by society, and risk the censure reserved for the rebel. In America in the 1970s, the hirsute woman is not yet an idea whose time has come. The shaving of body hair by women stubbornly defies extinction. Given the convoluted symbolism of the ritual and the repellent stares directed at the unshaven woman, we are not surprised to discover that even the most liberated women backslide when beach weather arrives.

But more and more individual women are risking those stares to affirm their natural femaleness. Eventually, this small but intimate tyranny will be resisted so that one more oppressive hang-up can be retired forever and the hirsute will live happily with the hairless.

MEN

Clubbishness

BY **MARC FASTEAU** • AUGUST 1972

It used to surprise me that men's attitudes toward the women's movement did not follow familiar political lines. I expected men who thought of themselves as liberal to be much less traditional and paternalistic toward women and much more favorably disposed toward the women's movement. In fact, the difference is more in style than substance.

Nearly all liberals will say they agree with the basic demands of the women's movement. On the other hand, they still believe that it isn't a "high-priority problem," that it somehow isn't "serious." Furthermore, there's a big difference between rhetoric and practice. Many will agree that women deserve equal employment opportunity, for instance, but very few are willing to share housework and child care so that their wives can make use of this opportunity. This can be explained at least in part by a universal, if selfish, desire to avoid drudgery (or work, such as child care, that is often rewarding but has been downgraded by the label "woman's work"). But men of all political persuasions also seem to want to exclude women from their worlds for reasons that have nothing to do with convenience.

Liberal senators give speeches urging U.S. withdrawal from Vietnam and a reordering of our priorities toward more humane concerns and then ride across Washington to meet their friends at the

(continued on next page)

MEN Clubbishness

(continued from previous page)

all-male Cosmos Club. In New York, foundation executives, whose professional careers are dedicated to the fight against poverty and discrimination, lunch at the Harvard Club, where only male graduates of the university may apply for membership. Senior partners of prestigious law firms and investment banking firms who have served in high positions in liberal Democratic administrations meet to cultivate business friendships and to close deals in men-only luncheon clubs.

The exclusion of women from social groups is not limited to the upper levels of society. Less prestigious and powerful clubs and groups—the Elks and the Moose, for example—do the same thing. Nor is the exclusion of women simply an unthinking hangover from an earlier era.

The younger establishmentarians aren't much better. When I tried to get women admitted to an eating club at law school several years ago, the responses from many liberal, antiwar classmates were "We'll have to get up every time they come into the room," or "We won't be able to talk about sports," or "We'll have to invite them to Christmas dinner."

Why, I'm not sure, but I've taken part in enough of these gatherings to guess. First of all, "acting like a man" in our society means being tough all the time, being emotionally invulnerable, and always being in control of yourself, your friends, and "your woman." Since living up to this ideal isn't easy, men have developed a few crutches. One is to label certain activities as distinctively masculine: foreign policy and high finance, for example. Participating in these activities then takes on the added dimension of a masculinity-affirming ritual. When women participate, this dimension is lost. The activity and the men participating in it can no longer be so clearly labeled as masculine.

Another masculinity-affirming ritual is simply for men to separate themselves from women. Part of being a man in our culture is not acting "like a woman." By getting together as a group and explicitly excluding women, men affirm that they are different from and better than women. I am reminded of nothing so much as my old tree-house gang trying to place the foot- and handholds leading up to the tree house so that "no girls would get up there." There were no secret male ceremonies we wanted to be free to indulge in. It just made us feel manly and powerful to keep the girls out.

> **"Part of being a man in our culture is not acting 'like a woman.'"**

Men complain that the atmosphere of their clubs will change if women are admitted. If the women who join have enough self-confidence to be themselves instead of trying to be one of the boys, those men are probably right. Women, whatever other problems they may have, are not preoccupied with a need to demonstrate their masculinity, and they do not feel the constraints that grow out of this concern. In fact, women may inject into the formal and informal "clubs" which make up our decision-making establishment the irreverence and flexibility that are so badly needed.

MARC FASTEAU wrote about men for *Ms.* In 1968 while in law school, he met and married his classmate Brenda Feigen, who hosted one of the first meetings to brainstorm the birth of *Ms.* During their twenty-year marriage they partnered to practice law and tackle gender discrimination.

Stories for Free Children

X: A FABULOUS CHILD'S STORY

BY **LOIS GOULD** • DECEMBER 1972

ONCE UPON A TIME, a baby named X was born. This baby was named X so that nobody could tell whether it was a boy or a girl. Its parents could tell, of course, but they couldn't tell Baby X, at first.

You see, it was all part of a very important Secret Scientific Xperiment, known officially as Project Baby X. The smartest scientists had set up this Xperiment at a cost of Xactly $23,000,000,000.72, which might seem like a lot for just one baby, even a very important Xperimental baby. But when you remember the prices of things like strained carrots and stuffed bunnies, and popcorn for the movies and booster shots for camp, let alone twenty-eight shiny quarters from the tooth fairy, you begin to see how it adds up.

Also, long before Baby X was born, all those scientists had to be paid to work out the details of the Xperiment, and to write the *Official Instruction Manual* for Baby X's parents, and, most important of all, to find the right set of parents to bring up Baby X. These parents had to be selected very carefully. Thousands of volunteers had to take thousands of tests and answer thousands of tricky questions. Almost everybody failed because, it turned out, almost everybody really wanted either a baby boy or a baby girl, and not Baby X at all. Also, almost everybody was afraid that a Baby X would be a lot more trouble than a boy or a girl. (They were probably right, the scientists admitted, but Baby X needed parents who wouldn't *mind* the Xtra trouble.)

> "How *could* X have passed the whole Xamination? Didn't X have an *identity* problem? Wasn't X mixed up at *all*?"

There were families with grandparents named Milton and Agatha who didn't see why the baby couldn't be named Milton or Agatha instead of X, even if it *was* an X. There were families with aunts who insisted on knitting tiny dresses and uncles who insisted on sending tiny baseball mitts. Worst of all, there were families that already had other children who couldn't be trusted to keep the secret. Certainly not if they knew the secret was worth $23,000,000,000.72 and all you had to do was take one little peek at Baby X in the bathtub to know it was a boy or a girl.

But, finally, the scientists found the Joneses, who really wanted to raise an X more than any other kind of baby—no matter how much trouble it would be. Ms. and Mr. Jones had to promise they would take equal turns caring for X, and feeding it, and singing it lullabies. And they had to promise never to hire any babysitters. The government scientists knew perfectly well that a babysitter would probably peek at X in the bathtub, too.

The day the Joneses brought their baby home, lots of friends and relatives came over to see it. None of them knew about the secret Xperiment, though. So the first thing they asked was what kind of a baby X was. When the Joneses smiled and said, "It's an X!" nobody knew what to say. In fact, they all thought the Joneses were playing some kind of rude joke.

But, of course, the Joneses were not joking. "It's an X" was absolutely all they would say.

The *Official Instruction Manual* had warned the new parents that this would happen, so they didn't fret about it. Besides, they were too busy with Baby X and the hundreds of different Xercises for treating it properly.

Ms. and Mr. Jones had to be Xtra careful about how they played with little X. They knew that if they kept bouncing it up in the air and saying how *strong* and *active* it was, they'd be treating it more like a boy than an X. But if all they did was cuddle it and kiss it and tell it how *sweet* and *dainty* it was, they'd be treating it more like a girl than an X.

On page 1,654 of the *Official Instruction Manual,* the scientists prescribed "plenty of bouncing and plenty of cuddling, *both.* X ought to be strong and sweet and active. Forget about *dainty* altogether."

Meanwhile, the Joneses were worrying about other problems. Toys, for instance. And clothes. On his first shopping trip, Mr. Jones told the store clerk, "I need some toys and clothes for my new baby." The clerk smiled and said, "Well, now, is it a boy or a girl?" "It's an X," Mr. Jones said, smiling back. But the clerk got all red in the face and said huffily, "In that case, I'm afraid I can't help you, sir." So Mr. Jones wandered helplessly up and down the aisles trying to find what X needed. But everything in the store was piled up in sections marked "Boys" or "Girls." There were "Boys' Pajamas" and "Girls' Underwear" and "Boys' Fire Engines" and "Girls' Housekeeping Sets." Mr. Jones went home without buying anything for X. That night he and Ms. Jones consulted page 2,326 of the *Official Instruction Manual.* "Buy plenty of everything!" it said firmly.

So they bought plenty of sturdy blue pajamas in the Boys' Department

LOIS GOULD was a much-admired fiction writer who became a center-piece of the women's movement. Born in Manhattan, she graduated from Wellesley and began a career in journalism. Upon the untimely death of her first husband, she discovered a diary, written in code, that detailed his extramarital affairs, including with her close friends. This animated her writing—her 1970 best-selling debut novel, *Such Good Friends,* as well as memoirs and essays about feminism, families, marriage, sexual politics, and the intricacies of women's lives. Over the course of her storied career, Gould also served in columnist and editorial roles at major newspapers and maga-zines, including as executive editor of *Ladies' Home Journal.*

and cheerful flowered underwear in the Girls' Depart-ment. And they bought all kinds of toys.

The head scientists of Project Baby X checked all their purchases and told them to keep up the good work. They also reminded the Joneses to see page 4,629 of the *Manual,* where it said, "Never make Baby X feel *embarrassed* or *ashamed* about what it wants to play with. And if X gets dirty climbing rocks, never say, 'Nice little Xes don't get dirty climbing rocks.' "

Likewise, it said, "If X falls down and cries, never say, 'Brave little Xes don't cry.' Because, of course, nice little Xes *do* get dirty, and brave little Xes *do* cry. No matter how dirty X gets or how hard it cries, don't worry. It's all part of the Xperiment."

By the time X grew big enough to play with other children, the Joneses' troubles had grown bigger, too. Once a little girl grabbed X's shovel in the sandbox and zonked X on the head with it. "Now, now, Tracy," the little girl's mother began to scold, "little girls mustn't hit little—" and she turned to ask X, "Are you a little boy or a little girl, dear?"

Mr. Jones, who was sitting near the sandbox, held his breath and crossed his fingers.

X smiled politely at the lady, even though X's head had never been zonked so hard in its life. "I'm a little X," X replied.

"You're a *what?*" the lady exclaimed angrily. "You're a little b-r-a-t, you mean!"

"But little girls mustn't hit little Xes, either!" said X, retrieving the shovel with another polite smile. "What good does hitting do, anyway?"

X's father, who was still holding his breath, finally let it out, uncrossed his fingers, and grinned back at X.

And at their next secret Project Baby X meeting, the scientists grinned, too. Baby X was doing fine.

But then it was time for X to start school. The Joneses were really worried about this, because school was even more full of rules for boys and girls, and there were no rules for Xes. The teacher would tell boys to form one line and girls to form another line. There would be boys' games and girls' games, and boys' secrets and girls' secrets. There would even be a bathroom marked "Boys" and another one marked "Girls." Pretty soon boys and girls would hardly talk to each other. What would happen to poor little X?

The Joneses spent weeks consulting their *Instruction Manual* (there were 249½ pages of advice under "First Day of School") and attending urgent special conferences with the smart scientists of Project Baby X.

The scientists had to make sure that X's mother had taught X how to throw and catch a ball properly, and that X's father had been sure to teach X what to serve at a doll's tea party. X had to know how to shoot marbles and how to jump rope and, most of all, what to say when the Other Children asked whether X was a boy or a girl.

Finally, X was ready. The Joneses helped X button on a nice new pair of red-and-white-checked overalls, and sharpened six pencils for X's nice new pencil box, and marked X's name clearly on all the books in its nice new book bag. X brushed its teeth and combed its hair, which just about covered its ears, and remembered to put a napkin in its lunch box.

The Joneses had asked X's teacher if the class could line up alphabetically, instead of forming separate lines for boys and girls. And they had asked if X could use the principal's bathroom, because it wasn't marked anything except "Bathroom." X's teacher promised to take care of all those problems. But nobody could help X with the biggest problem of all— Other Children.

Nobody in X's class had ever known an X before. What would they think? How would X make friends?

After school, X wanted to play with the other children. "How about shooting some baskets in the gym?" X asked the girls. But all they did was make faces and giggle behind X's back.

"How about weaving some baskets in the arts and crafts room?" X asked the boys. But they all made faces and giggled behind X's back, too.

That night, Ms. and Mr. Jones asked X how things had gone at school. X told them sadly that the lessons were okay, but otherwise school was a terrible place for an X. It seemed as if Other Children would never want an X for a friend.

Once more, the Joneses reached for their *Instruction Manual*. Under "Other Children," they found the following message: "What did you Xpect? *Other Children* have to obey all the silly boy-girl rules, because their parents taught them to. Lucky X—you don't have to stick to the rules at all! All you have to do is be yourself. P.S. We're not saying it'll be easy."

X liked being itself. But X cried a lot that night, partly because it felt afraid. So X's father held X tight, and cuddled it, and couldn't help crying a little, too. And X's mother cheered them both up by reading an Xciting story about an enchanted prince called Sleeping Handsome, who woke up when Princess Charming kissed him.

The next morning, they all felt much better, and little X went back to school with a brave smile and a clean pair of red-and-white-checked overalls.

There was a seven-letter-word spelling bee in class that day. And a seven-lap boys' relay race in the gym. And a seven-layer-cake baking contest in the girls' kitchen corner. X won the spelling bee. X also won the relay race.

More "Stories for Free Children"

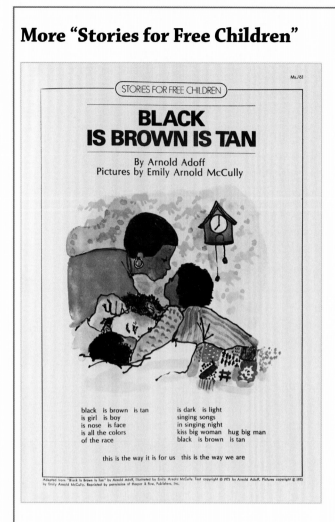

STORIES FOR FREE CHILDREN

Ms./61

BLACK IS BROWN IS TAN

By Arnold Adoff
Pictures by Emily Arnold McCully

black   is brown   is tan
is girl   is boy
is nose   is face
is all the colors
of the race

is dark   is light
singing songs
in singing night
kiss big woman   hug big man
black   is brown   is tan

this is the way it is for us   this is the way we are

Adapted from "Black Is Brown Is Tan" by Arnold Adoff, illustrated by Emily Arnold McCully. Text copyright © 1973 by Arnold Adoff. Pictures copyright © 1973 by Emily Arnold McCully. Reprinted by permission of Harper & Row, Publishers, Inc.

CONTRARY TO STEREOTYPES that painted feminists as antifamily, the early editors of *Ms.* made a concerted effort to include a special section for children in each issue of the magazine. These "Stories for Free Children" broke the mold of early 1970s children's book publishing with characters who weren't exclusively straight, white, able-bodied, and gender conforming.

• "black   is brown   is tan
is girl   is boy
is nose   is face
is all the colors
of the race"

—"Black Is Brown Is Tan"
by Arnold Adoff, February 1974

• "There are many kinds of guns. One kind is called a pistol. Or a rod. Police officers carry it. So do crooks. It kills people. Last year, in accidents and in crimes, all types of guns killed thirty thousand children, women, and men in the United States."

—"A Gun Is No Fun"
by Shirley Camper Soman, June 1975

• "Every morning, Jon, David, and Adam go to school. While they are at school, when they are playing . . . or having a snack, they sometimes think, I wonder what Mommy is doing?"

—"Mommy Is a Doctor"
by Sally E. Shaywitz, MD, September 1976

• "My mother is tall. This is my mother, Mariana, in her mail-carrier uniform. Isn't she tall and wonderful?

Mi mamá es alta. Ésta es mi mamá, Mariana, llevando su uniforme de cartera. ¿No se ve alta y maravillosa?"

—"My Mother the Mail Carrier"
by Inez Maury, March 1977

- "There was me, Judy. That's one. And my mother and father. They made two. And together we made three.

"Then my mother took me out for ice cream and told me that she and my father were getting a divorce, and she was marrying a wonderful man named Frank. . . . One father, two fathers. That made four."

—"One Father, Two Fathers"
by Joan Lowery Nixon, June 1977

- "When she was born, three fairies had come to her cradle to give her gifts as was usual in that country. The first fairy had given her beauty. The second had given her grace. But the third, who was a wise old creature, had said, 'I'll give her common sense.'

" 'I don't think much of that gift,' said King Ludwig, raising his eyebrows. . . .

"Nonetheless, when Bedelia was eighteen years old, something happened which made the king change his mind."

—"The Practical Princess"
by Jay Williams, August 1972

- "My daddy don't go to work. He would, if he could. He goes out looking for a job every day. But he can't find a place that needs him. He says, Things are tough.

"My mama says, Don't you worry. You'll find something. And I still got my job. We're okay."

—"My Daddy Don't Go to Work"
by Madeena Spray Nolan, August 1979

The stories in *Ms.* focused on themes considered taboo in children's literature of the time—from gender roles to interracial families to divorce.

And X almost won the baking contest, except it forgot to light the oven. Which only proves that nobody's perfect.

One of the Other Children noticed something else, too. He said, "Winning or losing doesn't seem to count to X. X seems to have fun being good at boys' skills *and* girls' skills."

"Come to think of it," said another of the Other Children, "maybe X is having twice as much fun as we are!"

From then on, some really funny things began to happen. Susie, who sat next to X in class, suddenly refused to wear pink dresses to school anymore. She insisted on wearing red-and-white-checked overalls—just like X's.

Then Jim, the class football nut, started wheeling his little sister's doll carriage around the football field. He told his family that X did the same thing, so it must be okay. After all, X was now the team's star quarterback.

Susie's parents were horrified by her behavior, and Jim's parents were worried sick about his. But the worst came when the twins Joe and Peggy decided to share everything with each other. Peggy used Joe's hockey skates and his microscope, and took half his newspaper route. Joe used Peggy's needlepoint kit and her cookbooks, and took two of her three babysitting jobs. Peggy started running the lawn mower, and Joe started running the vacuum cleaner.

Their parents weren't one bit pleased.

Peggy and Joe were forbidden to play with X anymore. So was Susie, and then Jim, and then *all* the Other Children. But it was too late; the Other Children stayed mixed up and happy and free, and refused to go back to the way they'd been before X.

Finally, Joe and Peggy's parents decided to call an emergency meeting of the school's Parents' Association to discuss the "X Problem." They sent a report to the principal stating that X was a "disruptive influence." They demanded immediate action. The school psychiatrist must Xamine it physically and mentally, and issue a full report. If X's test showed it was a boy, it would have to obey all the boys' rules. If it proved to be a girl, X would have to obey all the girls' rules.

And if X turned out to be some kind of mixed-up misfit, then X should be Xpelled from the school. Immediately!

The principal was very upset. Disruptive influence? Mixed-up misfit? But X was an Xcellent student. All the teachers said it was a delight to have X in their classes.

Nevertheless, insisted the Parents' Association, X is a Problem Child.

So the principal reluctantly notified X's parents that numerous complaints about X's behavior had come to the school's attention. And that after the psychiatrist's Xamination, the school would decide what to do about X.

The Joneses reported this at once to the scientists, who referred them to page 85,759 of the *Instruction Manual*. "Sooner or later," it said, "X will have to be Xamined by a psychiatrist. This may be the only way any of us will know for sure whether X is mixed up—or whether everyone else is."

At Xactly nine o'clock the next day, X reported to the school's psychiatrist's office. The principal, along with a committee from the Parents' Association, X's teacher, X's classmates, and Ms. and Mr. Jones, waited in the hall outside. Nobody knew the details of the tests X was to be given, but everybody knew they'd be *very* hard, and that they'd reveal Xactly what everyone wanted to know about X but was afraid to ask.

It was terribly quiet in the hall. Almost spooky. Once in a while, they would hear a strange noise inside the room. There were buzzes. And a beep or two. And several bells. An occasional light would flash under the door. The Joneses thought it was a white light, but the principal thought it was blue. Two or three children swore it was either yellow or green. And the Parents' Association missed it completely.

Through it all, you could hear the psychiatrist's low voice, asking hundreds of questions, and X's higher voice, providing hundreds of answers.

The whole thing took so long that everyone knew it must be the most complete Xamination anyone had ever had to take. Poor X, the Joneses thought. Serves X right, the Parents' Association thought. I wouldn't like to be in X's overalls right now, the children thought.

At last, the door opened. Everyone crowded around to hear the results. X didn't look any different; in fact, X was smiling. But the psychiatrist looked terrible. He looked as if he was crying! "What happened?" everyone began shouting. Had X done something disgraceful? "I wouldn't be a bit surprised!" muttered Peggy and Joe's parents. "Did X flunk the *whole* test?" cried Susie's parents. "Or just the most important part?" yelled Jim's parents.

"Oh, dear," said Mr. Jones, with a sigh.

"Oh, dear," said Ms. Jones, with a sigh.

"Sssh," ssshed the principal. "The psychiatrist is trying to speak."

Wiping his eyes and clearing his throat, the psychiatrist began, in a hoarse whisper. "In my opinion," he whispered—you could tell he must be very upset—"in my opinion, young X here—"

"Yes? Yes?" shouted a parent impatiently.

"*Sssh!*" ssshed the principal.

"Young *Sssh* here, I mean young X," said the doctor, frowning, "is just about—"

"Just about *what*? Let's have it!" shouted another parent.

"—just about the *least* mixed-up child I've ever Xamined!" said the psychiatrist.

"Yay for X!" yelled one of the children. And then the others began yelling, too. Clapping and cheering and jumping up and down.

"SSSH!" ssshed the principal, but nobody did.

The Parents' Association was angry and bewildered. How *could* X have passed the whole Xamination? Didn't X have an *identity* problem? Wasn't X mixed up at *all*? And why was the psychiatrist crying?

Actually, he had stopped crying and was smiling politely through his tears. "Don't you see?" he said. "I'm crying because it's wonderful! X has absolutely no identity problem! X isn't one bit mixed up! As for being a misfit—ridiculous! X knows perfectly well what it is! Don't you, X?" The doctor winked. X winked back.

"But what *is* X?" shrieked Peggy and Joe's parents. "*We* still want to know what it is!"

"Ah, yes," said the doctor, winking again. "Well, don't worry. You'll all know one of these days. And you won't need me to tell you."

"What? What does he mean?" some of the parents grumbled suspiciously.

Susie and Peggy and Joe all answered at once. "He means that by the time X's sex matters, it won't be a secret anymore!"

With that, the doctor began to push through the crowd toward X's parents. "How do you do?" he said, somewhat stiffly. And then he reached out to hug them both. "If I ever have an X of my own," he whispered, "I sure hope you'll lend me your instruction manual."

Needless to say, the Joneses were very happy. The Project Baby X scientists were rather pleased, too. So were Susie, Jim, Peggy, Joe, and all the Other Children. The Parents' Association wasn't, but they had promised to accept the psychiatrist's report and not make any more trouble. They even invited Ms. and Mr. Jones to become honorary members, which they did.

Later that day, all X's friends put on their red-and-white-checked overalls and went over to see X. They found X in the backyard, playing with a very tiny baby that none of them had ever seen before. The baby was wearing very tiny red-and-white-checked overalls.

"How do you like our new baby?" X asked the Other Children proudly.

"It's got cute dimples," said Jim.

"It's got husky biceps, too," said Susie.

"What kind of baby is it?" asked Joe and Peggy.

X frowned at them. "Can't you tell?"

Then X broke into a big, mischievous grin. "It's a Y!"

.   .   .

56/Ms.   Ms./57

GIFTS 'R FREE CHILDREN
by Letty Cottin Pogrebin

A toy must be:
- Safe
- Made to last
- Respectful of a child's intellect, self-esteem, and creativity
- Nonracist and nonsexist in the way it is packaged, conceived, and planned for play
- Moral in terms of the values it represents

This is the Ms. standard, developed over four years of reviewing and testing thousands of toys, games, and crafts. It has guided parents and other buyers of children's gifts, and has been adopted as a checklist for schools and child-care centers all over the country.

What it has *not* done is made a really measurable dent in the overall practices of the $3 billion toy industry in the United States.

This year, as in the past, I have tried to find the exceptions to the rule of toy mediocrity—and there *are* joyful, inventive, even audacious exceptions in the wasteland of kiddie hype.

But a few hundred acceptable toys, out of some 150,000 novelties and playthings, can't be enough to satisfy the diverse needs, interests, and economic limitations of American households. Moreover, many of the best toys are produced by country craft shops or cottage industries that cannot underwrite or fulfill national distribution.

While children's parents and friends stalk the toy counters in their search for life-enhancing play materials, most toy industry people pursue a less elusive ideal: profit. And while we celebrate quality in toys and its child development, they are busy counting children and anticipating sales revenues.

The United States is starting to experience a boom in first births, which should be very favorable to the toy industry," states a news item in *Toy & Hobby World* (a trade publication), now that millions of women and men born during the postwar baby boom are having babies of their own. In 1975, there were 15.2 childbirths per thousand people; by 1980, this will rise to 16.2 births.

Commenting on the new boom, *Playthings* magazine rejoices: "Preschool manufacturers and retailers alike should be passing out cigars!"

Not so fast. No matter how many children there are, it is adults who make spending decisions, and we're not pleased with the selection in the toy chest. A Ralph Nader poll of 2,500 urban households found that among four different product categories, toy products received the greatest number of "unsatisfactory" ratings. The study also noted that only one in three unhappy consumers register their complaints to manufacturers. So there's more dissatisfaction than meets the toymakers' eye. It's vital that we tell them not only what we deplore but what we want—and we must communicate both by complaining about poor toys and by spending our dollars only for worthwhile products.

At present, according to the Toy Manufacturers of America, the average family (whatever that is) spends on toys $85 per child per year. And the industry hopes to increase that figure by putting about $100 million a year into toy advertising.

It may take more time and effort to seek out the superior plaything, especially during the holidays when we do 60 percent of our toy-buying. But the way you spend each child's $85 (or less or more) is not only an investment in the child's pleasure but a vote of confidence in the best that toyland has to offer.

If you're shopping for your own children, you have the advantage of knowing exactly what they have, want, and "need." What they "need" is what has least occurred to them, unadvertised toys that take them in a new direction. Before setting out with a shopping list, why not comb through the kids toy closet yourself? Look for one-dimensional toy collections, or noticeable gaps in various categories—games, active toys, books, nurturant toys, for example.

A study of the toy inventory in upper-income homes of North Carolina children, aged one to six, found that girls' rooms had more dolls, dollhouses, homemaker toys, and floral-craft decorations. Boys' rooms had more vehicles, educational/art materials, sports equipment, toy animals, military toys, and animal decorations. The numbers of musical instruments, books, juvenile furniture, and stuffed animals were about equal for girls and boys.

These differences cannot simply be dismissed as a matter of personal taste. A 1968 study by psychologist Brian Sutton-Smith found that "both boys and girls can derive more creative ideas from traditional boys' toys than they can from traditional girls' toys." This finding was reinforced by E. F. Rosenfeld's 1974 study on the relationship of toys to the development of competence. Here it became clear that both girls and boys discovered many more things to do with "boys' toys" than with "girls' toys."

The long-term effect of children's play experiences on their sex-role behavior and on eventual career interests is a new area of inquiry. But we don't need experts to tell us that our children deserve the best. We need only our own good sense and a larger selection of wonderful toys to choose from.

Vaginalis, Masks, Ethnic Dolls, and Garden Set (see pages 66 and 90)

BABY HUMANS/TODDLERS

For this age toymakers exercise their best social conscience, show the most concern for safety and the least concern for sex-role rigidity.

WIND-ME-NOT 3-IN-1 ELECTRIC MOBILE is a soft night-light, music box, and dangling community of animal figures, all under a checked umbrella (Dolly Toy, $23). Birth-6 years.
BABY BUNNY BALL is a beige plush "thing" with floppy ears (Playskool, $5). 3-24 months.
KATIE KANGAROO. Squeeze the bulb, and Katie hops along with a boing-boing noise (Fisher-Price, $6.25). 2-4 years.
PUZZLE PUPPY is a put-together mutt in six parts. Package shows black boy and white girl (Fisher-Price, $3.75). 6 months-3 years.
LOLLY, a charming gingham crib-and-play-pen doll, is machine-washable (Fisher-Price, $5). 3 months-2 years.
TUBBY is a cushiony inflatable baby bath versatile enough to be a bath or bed for infants and later a wading pool or float for toddlers (Newman-Fine, Inc., P.O. Box 2004, New York, N.Y. 10017, $12).
PEAS 'n CARROTS BABY FOOD-GRINDER mashes cooked

ABOVE Each December, editor Letty Cottin Pogrebin created a holiday gift guide filled with toys that are "nonracist and nonsexist in the way [they are] packaged, conceived, and planned for play" and are "respectful of a child's intellect, self-esteem, and creativity"—this is the list from 1976.

Never Again

BY **ROBERTA BRANDES GRATZ** • APRIL 1973

THIS WOMAN was the victim of a criminal abortion. Her body was photographed exactly as it was found by police in a bloody and barren motel room; exactly as it had been abandoned there by an unskilled abortionist. Becoming frightened when "something went wrong," he left her to die alone.

The photograph is just one bit of evidence in the files of the Connecticut medical examiner who determined the technical cause of her death:

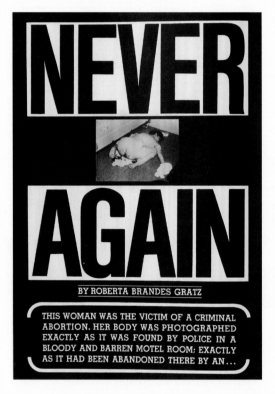

an air embolism resulting from the unskilled surgical procedure. But this visible evidence of butchery has come to symbolize far more than an individual case with an individual cause.

Because various abortion-law repeal and reform groups have used this photograph as one answer to the magnified fetus photographs so often displayed by antiabortion forces, this individual woman has come to represent the thousands of women who have been maimed or murdered by a society that denied them safe and legal abortions.

In January, the Supreme Court partially rewarded the long and courageous fight for women's right to choose by ruling that the state laws restricting early abortion were unconstitutional. But the woman in this photograph cannot be brought back to life, nor can the many, many women whose lives have been lost or tragically damaged in the past.

We must not forget. Now that a part of the battle is over, it is important to honor its victims and heroines.

•   •   •

The Ticket That Might Have Been . . . President Chisholm

BY **GLORIA STEINEM** • MAY 1973

I am a candidate for the Presidency of the United States. I make that statement proudly, in the full knowledge that, as a Black person and as a female person, I do not have a chance of actually gaining that office in this election year. I make that statement seriously, knowing that my candidacy itself can change the face and future of American politics—that it will be important to the needs and hopes of every one of you—even though, in the conventional sense, I will not win.

—June 4, 1972

The election is over, and there will be a familiar face, a familiar white and male face, in the White House for four more years. The months of feverish work and hard-earned dollars that went into the presidential candidacy of Shirley Chisholm are only memories now. Sometimes it seems they are discussed seriously only when veterans of her campaign happen to get together and reminisce.

In fact, there is some uncertainty and even disappointment in those discussions, too. What effect did the Chisholm campaign have on the country? On the excluded groups it was meant to help and encourage? What ideas did it launch or lives did it change? And finally, the heart of all the questions, was it all worth it?

From reading the postconvention and postelection reporting, it's impossible to tell. The Chisholm candidacy was rarely analyzed while it was going on, and even less so in traditional postmortems. Before and after the primaries, there were occasional tantalizing hints of Chisholm's significance. The Harris poll of last February, for instance, found the congresswoman getting 35 percent of the vote among Black independents and Black Democrats and support among women of all races that was three times greater than her support among men. (From this, the Harris summary concluded, "Ms. Chisholm must now be considered a distinct threat to Mayor Lindsay, Senator McGovern, and former Senator Eugene McCarthy in vying for the liberal and left-of-center vote.")

Of course, Chisholm herself had stated her intention of "keeping other candidates honest," of being one of the few forces pushing them to the left, not becoming a divisive force or a threat. But traditional analyses deal

> **"Perhaps the best indicator of her campaign's impact is the effect it had on individual lives."**

only with winning or losing in the traditional sense. Even Senator Hubert Humphrey was amazed by the showing Chisholm made in the Florida primary, and said often that with a little money and organization "she might have defeated us all." But neither of those clues to the significance or strength of the Chisholm campaign was pursued in deeper reports or taken very seriously in the press. (In fact, airtime for the major preprimary speech quoted above was made available by court order under equal time provisions of the Federal Communications Commission because of clear network failure to fairly cover the Chisholm candidacy.)

Perhaps the best indicator of her campaign's impact is the effect it had on individual lives. All over the country, there are people who will never be quite the same: farm women in Michigan who were inspired to work in a political campaign for the first time; Black Panthers in California who registered to vote, and encouraged others members of the Black community to vote, too; children changed by the sight of a Black woman saying, "I want to be president"; radical feminists who found this campaign, like that of Linda Jenness in the Socialist Workers Party, a possible way of changing the patriarchal system; and student or professional or "blue-collar" men who were simply impressed with a political figure who told the truth as she saw it, no matter what the cost.

The Chisholm candidacy didn't forge a solid coalition of those people working for social change; that will take a long time. But it began one. If you listen to personal testimony from very diverse sources, it seems that the Chisholm candidacy was not in vain. In fact, the truth is that the American political scene may never be quite the same again.

SHIRLEY CHISHOLM became the first Black woman elected to Congress, where she served for seven terms, from 1968 to 1983, and was known to all as Fighting Shirley. She was the first woman and Black person to seek the nomination for the presidency, in 1972. She faced discrimination from within—from fundraising to participation in primary debates—yet built a dedicated following and lasting legacy. Said Chisholm, "I want to be remembered as a woman . . . who dared to be a catalyst of change." No doubt, her impact was most profoundly felt in 2020 as America elected its first woman and woman of color as vice president. And yet executive branch representation remains far from equal: 100 percent of American presidents have been men, 97.8 percent have been white.

THE TICKET THAT MIGHT HAVE BEEN...

PRESIDENT CHISHOLM

I am a candidate for the Presidency of the United States. I make that statement proudly, in the full knowledge that, as a black person and as a female person, I do not have a chance of actually gaining that office in this election year. I make that statement seriously, knowing that my candidacy itself can change the face and future of American politics — that it will be important to the needs and hopes of every one of you — even though, in the conventional sense, I will not win."
—June 4, 1972

The election is over, and there will be a familiar face, a familiar white and male face, in the White House for four more years. The months of feverish work and hard-earned dollars that went into the Presidential candidacy of Shirley Chisholm are only memories now. Sometimes it seems they are discussed seriously only when veterans of her campaign happen to get together and reminisce.

In fact, there is some uncertainty and even disappointment in those discussions, too. What effect did the Chisholm campaign have on the country? On the excluded groups it was meant to help and encourage? What ideas did it launch or lives did it change? And finally, the heart of all the questions: was it all worth it?

From reading the post-Convention and postelection reporting, it's impossible to tell. The Chisholm candidacy was rarely analyzed while it was going on, and even less so in traditional postmortems. Before and after the primaries, there were occasional tantalizing hints of Chisholm's significance. The Harris poll of last February, for instance, found the Congresswoman getting 35 percent of the vote among black Independents and black Democrats, and a support among women of all races that was three times greater than her support among men. (From this, the Harris summary concluded, "Ms. Chisholm must now be considered a distinct threat to Mayor Lindsay, Senator McGovern, and former Senator Eugene McCarthy in vying for the liberal and left-of-center vote.")

Of course, Chisholm herself had stated her intention of "keeping the other candidates honest," of being one of the few forces pushing them to the left, not becoming a devisive force or a threat. But traditional analyses deal only with winning or losing in the traditional sense. Even Senator Hubert Humphrey was amazed by the showing Chisholm made in the Florida primary, and said often that, with a little money and organization, "she might have defeated us all." But neither of these clues to the significance or strength of the Chisholm campaign was pursued in deeper reports, or taken very seriously in the press. (In fact, air time for the major pre-primary speech quoted above was made available by court order under equal time provisions of the Federal Communications Commission, because of clear network failure to fairly cover the Chisholm candidacy.)

Perhaps the best indicator of her campaign's impact is the effect it had on individual lives. All over the country, there are people who will never be quite the same: farm women in Michigan who were inspired to work in a political campaign for the first time; Black Panthers in California who registered to vote, and encouraged other members of the black community to vote, too; children changed by the sight of a black woman saying, "I want to be President"; radical feminists who found this campaign, like that of Linda Jenness in the Socialist Workers' Party, a possible way of changing the patriarchal system; and student or professional or "blue-collar" men who were simply impressed with a political figure who told the truth as she saw it, no matter what the cost.

The Chisholm candidacy didn't forge a solid coalition of those people working for social change; that will take a long time. But it began one. If you listen to personal testimony from very diverse sources, it seems that the Chisholm candidacy was not in vain. In fact, the truth is that the American *(continued on page 120)*

THE TICKET THAT MIGHT HAVE BEEN...

VICE-PRESIDENT FARENTHOLD

On the last night of the 1972 Democratic Convention in Miami, there was officially put in nomination for the Vice-Presidency of the United States the name of Frances Tarlton Farenthold, commonly known as Sissy; a 46-year-old Texas state legislator, a reformer, and a woman.

By Elizabeth Frappollo

Many of the Convention delegates, 40 percent of them women, had never heard of her. Neither had television anchorman Walter Cronkite, who commented disdainfully, "A lady named Farenthold wants to be Vice-President." The CBS network then blacked out Sissy's nominating and seconding speeches with commercials, reinstating part of the nominating speech only after phone calls from women viewers and Congresswoman Bella Abzug's vociferous complaint on camera. By the end of that session, however, after tedious hours of speeches and floor maneuverings, Sissy Farenthold had emerged as the surprise victor. She received over 420 delegate votes, a total second only to that of Senator Thomas Eagleton and far surpassing former Governor Endicott Peabody of Massachusetts and Senator Mike Gravel of Alaska, both of whom had campaigned openly for the Vice-Presidential spot for months. Eagleton, McGovern's ill-fated choice, pulled ahead because of duty votes, committed-to-McGovern votes. Sissy's main support came from women delegates, who finally had a positive way of demonstrating their solidarity, and from black, Spanish-speaking, and youth delegates—many of whom saw her candidacy as a rallying point for excluded groups.

Before the Convention, Sissy had run in the Democratic gubernatorial primary in Texas, and that's when I first heard of her. Had I been a student of the baroque intrigue of Texas politics, I would have known all about her long ago. Elected to the State House of Representatives in 1968, Sissy had become a member of, and indeed a leader of, a group of liberal legislators who eventually earned the tag of Dirty Thirty, referring to their number and, ironically, to their tactics. They did not play the game the way it has always been played in Texas state politics. Following the Federal Securities Exchange Commission's unmasking of a cozy financial swindle known as the Sharpstown Bank scandal, the Dirty Thirty were so unaccommodating as to vote for an unsuccessful resolution introduced by Sissy calling for an independent investigation. The Sharpstown scandal grew out of a scheme in which laws were introduced for the hidden financial benefit of various state officials and their friends, but not for the benefit of the public. Everyone from Governor Preston Smith down was tainted, at least by association. The Dirty Thirty's relentless clamor resulted in public distrust of almost anyone connected with that legislature except the Dirty Thirty themselves, and led to the defeat in the '72 primaries of Lieutenant Governor Ben Barnes, the favorite of Lyndon Johnson and John Connally.

In 1971, Representative Farenthold got so tired of Texas politics-as-usual, that she made a very controversial decision: to run in the gubernatorial primary. To everyone's surprise, that primary, held in early May, 1972, was so close that it resulted in a second runoff election between Farenthold and Dolph Briscoe, a former legislator and millionaire rancher of mature years whose chief distinction lay in having remained back on the ranch long enough to avoid any suggestion of involvement in the Sharpstown Bank shenanigans. Briscoe was so bland that his oppo-

Letters

IN TODAY'S ERA of email, text, and an app for nearly any communication, the very act of writing a letter—written or typed, on notecard or scrap of paper, signed, sealed, and sent by post—seems delightfully quaint. For *Ms.,* letters were revolutionary. After a stunning twenty thousand responses arrived by mail following the inaugural issue in 1972, the "Letters to the Editor" feature fast became a beloved fixture. In the years that followed, readers' reflections continued to pour in, forming a rich tapestry of "Click!" moments: stories, questions, complaints, observations, declarations. Letters reprinted throughout this volume are just a fraction of the real-time thoughts and testimonies shared by women—girls and boys too, as well as men—whether they were grappling with burgeoning activism, simmering in anger, or brewing with purpose. Perhaps most important, letters to *Ms.* afforded radical connectivity, feminist engagement and interaction, and inspiration among strangers hailing from all corners of the country.

My husband says I used to be a bitch once a month but, since I subscribed to *Ms.,* now I'm a bitch twice a month.

CLAUDIA HELLER
Los Angeles
June 1973 issue

I am in the ninth grade and on the girls' varsity basketball team at our school. I'm captain of the team and lead it in scoring, steals, and assists. I love basketball.

During our whole season this year, we had only five games: we had to furnish rides to the games ourselves; we had to play in our gym suits, because we had no uniforms in which to play; we were able to use the gym only when the boys were through with it; and we had a grand total of about thirty spectators at all our games combined. Our principal did not announce any of our games and did not provide a late bus so that kids could stay and watch. One time I asked if it would be possible to get uniforms for our team. I was told to earn the money through car washes, dances, and bake sales. Yet each of the boys received $30 brand-new uniforms this year.

Everyone seems to think that girls playing basketball is a big joke, but I am dead serious. If we are good enough to be called varsity, aren't we good enough to be respected?

JANE LUNDQUIST
Bangor, Maine
June 1973 issue

I had just put the kids to bed, the house was a wreck, and I still had the dinner dishes to do. But this month's *Ms.* had just arrived, and I couldn't resist sitting down with it for a minute.

Well, one article led to another before I realized that any minute the door would open on the shambles around me. What would I say?

The door opened. It was time to practice what I'd been reading. "I left the dishes for you for a change," I said, cool as a revolutionary. Click!

My wife, home from her graduate-school class, was flabbergasted! I hope she doesn't cancel our subscription.

MIKE TIGHE
Davis, Calif.
July 1973 issue

Yeah, I watched that tennis match. Like a whole lot of people, I was anxious as hell, looking forward to it. Every time Bobby Riggs opened his mouth, I got madder. Sure, I know, most of his sounding was strictly promotion. But he was coming on too strong and uncool. Then I see this jive article about how the man really, in private, does not put women down and he didn't know there ever was such a thing as a women's movement. So, after all this nonsense, when it comes time for the match, I'm on the edge of my seat . . . digging Billie Jean's cool and ready for her to cream this cat. Now I got to admit that, deep down, there's that little doubt—can she really do it? After the first set—man, no more doubt. I'm yelling at the television. Real kicks! Billie Jean wins the second set, and I'm wild—shouting for a love set to really finish Mr. Riggs.

Then it hits me—something's happened to me. The fast heartbeat and the high emotion and the gulping beer without tasting it— damn! This scene I'm watching ain't just Billie Jean King versus Bobby Riggs. I am busting with a too-familiar excitement. This is Joe Louis fighting Max Schmeling . . . Jackie Robinson against the baseball world . . . Sugar Ray fighting Jake LaMotta . . . Althea Gibson playing Darlene Hard, and Jim Brown trying to run over Sam Huff, and, well, damn—for two hours Billie Jean King is Black!

Do you understand?

MEL WILLIAMSON
New York
December 1973 issue

In 1973, the world was captivated when Billie Jean King, just twenty-nine years old, defeated Bobby Riggs in an epic "Battle of the Sexes" tennis match—one of the greatest moments in sports history. An audience of fifty million tuned in, making it the most viewed U.S. match of all time. Her victory changed the game for women's tennis and female athletes and in many ways was a defining moment in modern feminism. In addition to *Ms.*'s cover story, King has remained a regular at the magazine—a proud signatory of our "We Have Had Abortions" petition and author of articles about the profound impact Title IX has had on sports and society.

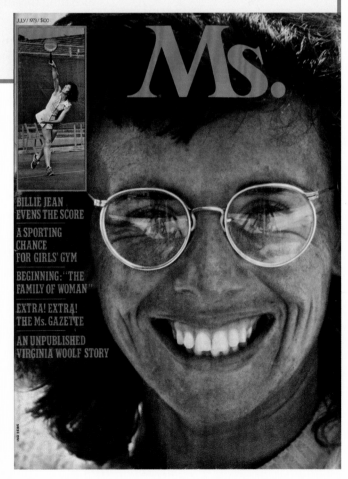

JULY / 1973 / $1.00

Ms.

BILLIE JEAN EVENS THE SCORE

A SPORTING CHANCE FOR GIRLS' GYM

BEGINNING: "THE FAMILY OF WOMAN"

EXTRA! EXTRA! THE Ms. GAZETTE

AN UNPUBLISHED VIRGINIA WOOLF STORY

Getting to Know Me: A Primer on Masturbation

BY **BETTY DODSON** • AUGUST 1974

MASTURBATION has been a continual part of my sex life since the age of five. It got me through childhood, puberty, romantic love, marriage, and it will, happily, see me through old age. I am not typical in this respect. As I have learned, very few women masturbate regularly once they're past childhood exploration, and a lot of women have no memory of even childhood masturbation.

But I am typical in most other respects: I was subjected to the same barrage of negative sexual conditioning all women get. I was made to feel ashamed and guilty about masturbation. Even as an adult, I felt that masturbating meant there was something wrong with my sex life.

> **"I discovered that . . . a vibrator pictured in one of the drawings made several men very hostile and defensive."**

Coming from the Bible Belt in Kansas, I knew very well where the church and moralists stood on the subject of masturbation. But even my liberal, intelligent friends put down masturbation, making clear that it was a second-rate sexual activity.

Even if masturbation was "wrong," I kept doing it. At twenty-nine, after much conflict over marriage versus art career and after several affairs that were superromantic and monogamous, I got married—just in time to escape the horrible fate of going over the hill alone. Quite typically, my marital sex soon got down to twice a month, but even then my husband would come too fast, and I wouldn't come at all. We would both be embarrassed, depressed, and silent. After he went to sleep, I would quickly and quietly masturbate under the covers. I did it without moving or breathing, feeling sick with frustration and guilt the whole time.

My marriage ended after five years of struggling to "adjust" and "work through our problems." Any possibility of substituting bridge, golf, or work for a diminished sexuality had been ruined by my moderately healthy sexual beginnings. I had a continuous reminder from my masturbation that pleasure through sexual expression could be available to me. When I got divorced, I was a thirty-five-year-old emotional virgin facing the terrors of "dating" again.

My first postmarital affair was a turning point. Both of us sexually starved, we plunged headlong into an intense, joyful, experimental physical exchange. My lover, just out of a seventeen-year marriage, was overjoyed to be completely open sexually, and so was I. Our exploratory conversations quickly got on to the subject of marriage, monogamy, and sexual repression, and I was able to tell him openly and honestly about my guilt-ridden marital masturbation. And he told me about his. He had longed for a more experimental relationship, but his only variety came from masturbation, which would have been okay if he could have done it positively and joyfully. But, like me, he had felt sick with frustration and guilt. He had begun to regard himself as a "dirty old man," and his self-esteem steadily sank.

As we shared information, I began to understand how our whole anti-sexual social system represses and controls us, and I was able to let go of my remaining sexual guilt. We both realized that masturbation had saved our sexual sanity, and we would never again consider it a second-rate sexual activity.

My art began to reflect my growing sexual affirmation. I felt so good about myself and my new sexuality that I started to transfer my discoveries in bed to the canvas.

My second show was devoted to the celebration of masturbation. Getting models to pose for me was difficult, but finally, with a little help from my friends, I drew four magnificent, life-sized classical nudes masturbating. Everyone said I was nuts, that the drawings would never sell (absolutely true), but what I learned was invaluable.

The response to the drawings was fascinating and informative. I discovered that a lot of people did not masturbate, that some people did not know women ever masturbated ("Why should they?"), and that a vibrator pictured in one of the drawings made several men very hostile and defensive. One man remarked, "If that was my woman, she wouldn't have to use that thing." I found myself fielding hundreds of questions. Yes, I did it myself and loved it. No, you don't get warts. Yes, I use live models. Yes, the woman with the vibrator in the picture has a boyfriend; he's standing right over there. No, despite what society tells us, intercourse isn't necessarily better; it's just different. I like to do both.

I explained many times that seeking sexual gratification should be a basic drive, and that masturbation is our first explicitly sexual activity. It's the way we discover our eroticism, the way we learn to respond sexually. Sexual skill and the ability to respond are not "natural"—at least not in our society. Doing what "comes naturally" for us is to be sexually inhibited. Sex is like any other skill or art form: it has to be learned and practiced.

It is my feeling that when a woman masturbates, she learns to like her own body, to enjoy sex and orgasm, and to become proficient and independent about sex. Our society does not really approve of sexually proficient and independent women. Which gets us to the double standard—the concept that men have the social approval to be aggressive (independent) and sexually polygamous, but that women should be nonaggressive (dependent) and sexually monogamous.

I think that one of the best ways to make women accept and conform to this double standard is to deprive us of direct sexual self-knowledge—especially masturbation. In other words, deprive us of our own bodies and of a way of discovering and developing orgasmic response patterns. Start early. Instill the notion that female genitals are deficient and inferior and that women's main social value lies in producing babies. Avoid any information about the clitoris and life-affirming orgasm. Prohibit touching of your genitals through the suggestion of supernatural punishment. Socially ostracize nonconforming women.

BETTY DODSON came to New York City from Wichita, Kansas, to be an artist. But it was her commitment to female masturbation that skyrocketed her to fame. During the course of her long life—she died in 2020 at the age of ninety-one, a *New York Times* obituary decreeing her "an evangelist of self-pleasure"—she led generations of women to know and rely upon their own bodies. She saw her work as a calling, inextricably linked to feminism—a way to end sexual dependence or the notion that sexual pleasure required men. This article in *Ms.* evolved into her 1987 book, *Sex for One: The Joy of Selfloving*.

An important part of our sexual development is learning to like and accept all of ourselves, including our genitals—to become what I call "cunt positive." Most women feel that their genitals are ugly, funny looking, disgusting, smelly, and not at all desirable—certainly not a beautiful part of their bodies. A woman who feels this way is obviously going to have a lot of reservations about intimate sharing with another person. We therefore need to become very aware of our genitals. We want to know how we look, smell, and taste—and how we vary.

Last year I produced a set of color slides of the genitals of twenty different women. The slides reveal a vast range of differences and similarities in the color, texture, size, and shape of women's genitals. Women with extended inner lips who thought themselves deformed saw many other women with the same genital configuration; the brownish color of some genitals turns out to be natural and not the result of aging or childbirth.

The range of differences in the distance between the clitoris and vaginal opening may explain why some women never achieve orgasm through penetration only: if the clitoris is close to the vaginal entrance, it is more likely to receive indirect stimulation with penetration. How many women are suffering or confused from this lack of fundamental information?

Some women I know have put such tremendous pressure on themselves to have orgasms that they have not developed the capacity for pleasure in the buildup of sexual tension. I encourage them to spend several self-lovemaking sessions without performance demands, just bringing themselves up slowly . . . experiencing the pleasurable sensations and the fantasies.

Joyful masturbation and self-love naturally flow over into a sexual exchange with another person. We can give and receive love best when we feel good about ourselves. Because I am secure about my sexual response and orgasm, I feel free to stimulate my clitoris along with penetration or to show my partner what turns me on. During oral sex, I can state my preference—giving my partner necessary feedback on what pleases me. There are many positions where I can use the vibrator while being penetrated, enhancing my partner's sensation as well. I have never met a person whom I would consider a good lover who wasn't totally turned on by any information I could give about what turned me on.

Exploring my sexual potential has taken me on many paths of learning and change. Reclaiming my body as a source of strength and pleasure has given me power over my own life and the freedom to design my sex life creatively, just like painting a picture. Self-sexuality, along with heterosexuality, homosexuality, bisexuality, and group sexuality, is simply part of human sexual behavior.

Ms./109

require more direct stimulation. I have also had orgasms by letting water run on my genitals in the bathtub. The pressure can be easily controlled and water is symbolically pleasing.

For the past two years I have been experimenting with different vibrators. I have found that the vibrator gives me the strongest and most consistent form of stimulation and is especially good for women who have never experienced orgasm. It also overcomes the problem of your hand or arm getting tired while masturbating manually. Some women complain that the vibrator simply makes them go numb. Of course, if you put the vibrator directly on your clitoris and don't move either the vibrator or your body, you will numb out. I always use a bit of material between me and my vibrator—a piece of velvet, satin, fur, a towel. I move the vibrator back and forth besides rocking my pelvis forward and back and around. It's very much like dancing, and I love to masturbate with music and follow the musical buildup to orgasm.

Some women I know have put such tremendous pressure on themselves to have orgasms, that they have not developed the capacity for pleasure in the buildup of sexual tension. I encourage them to spend several self-lovemaking sessions without performance demands, just bringing themselves up slowly . . . experiencing the pleasurable sensations and the fantasies. Sometimes when I feel I'm getting close to coming, I drop back—tease and please myself. When I have an orgasm, I don't stop stimulation. I just soften up, and stay with the good feelings. I'll let the pleasure come with movement, breathing, sounds, or words. If I feel like it, I'll go on to another buildup and a second orgasm, spending at least 30 minutes to an hour. We have been conditioned to make love as though we are rushing to an appointment.

Joyful masturbation and self-love naturally flows over into a sexual exchange with another person. We can give and receive love best when we feel good about ourselves. Because I am secure about my sexual response and orgasm, I feel free to stimulate my clitoris along with penetration—or to show my partner what turns me on. During oral sex, I can state my preference—giving my partner necessary feedback on what pleases me.

There are many positions where I can use the vibrator while being penetrated, enhancing my partner's sensation as well. I have never met a person whom I would consider a good lover who wasn't totally turned on by any information I could give about what turned me on.

Exploring my sexual potential has taken me on many paths of learning and change. Reclaiming my body as a source of strength and pleasure has given me power over my own life and the freedom to design my sex life creatively, just like painting a picture. Self-sexuality, along with heterosexuality, homosexuality, bisexuality, and group sexuality, is simply all part of human sexual behavior.

Betty Dodson is an artist turned writer-lecturer-teacher on the subject of human sexuality. She conducts bodysex workshops for women across the country. This article was adapted from her illustrated booklet, "Liberating Masturbation," which can be obtained by sending $3 to Betty Dodson, c/o "Ms." Magazine, 370 Lexington Avenue, New York, New York 10017.

A daily yoga-style workout helps Betty Dodson keep in touch with her body.

Baseball Diamonds Are a Girl's Best Friend

BY **LETTY COTTIN POGREBIN** • SEPTEMBER 1974

Whenever I play baseball with my brother and I get a hit, he says it was luck. But if I strike out it's because of my sex. Click!

—Moira Brennan, Providence, R.I.

ALL OVER THE COUNTRY, girls like Moira Brennan are hearing the click that tells them something unfair is going on. Boys have to worry about being good enough to play. But girls have to worry about being allowed to prove that they're good enough to play.

Thousands of girls are beginning to fight back. They are challenging old-fashioned ideas—like the belief that girls are too fragile, or the myth that girls are never as good as boys in athletics. Many of these young women have written to *Ms.* to share their anger and their plans for action.

Kelly Kirk of Winona, Minnesota, writes, "In junior high there are no sports (basketball, volleyball, softball, track) for girls. It's time for those of us who enjoy sports to start hollering."

Pat Viera of Pasadena, California, eighteen, writes, "I would like some-day to coach a National Basketball Association team, but I can't. I'd love to go to some big college on an athletic scholarship and eventually play on a professional team, but I can't. I'm not mentally or physically handicapped, but I'm a girl."

While these girls and young women are fighting their private battles, one battle has been fought in public, and the whole country has watched its outcome. The Little League—which puts more than two million eight- to twelve-year-old boys on baseball fields in thirty-one countries—has finally agreed to accept girls.

It all began in New Jersey in 1972, when a young ballplayer named Maria Pepe was accepted by the Hoboken Little League team. Maria's teammates had no objections to her, but the men in charge at the national headquarters of Little League refused to let the Hoboken team stay in the league if they kept a girl in their ranks.

The case eventually went to court, and the judges decided that it was against the law for Little League to stop any child from joining a team just because she happens to be a girl. Some Little Leagues voluntarily "desexegrated," while others insisted on keeping girls behind the fences.

In New Jersey, throughout last spring, two thousand teams refused to play rather than accept girls. There were angry demonstrations and arguments among parents. Some communities were fiercely split down the middle, and through it all, individual girls experienced the joys and embarrassment of being "female firsts" in a formerly male preserve.

Then, last June, officials of Little League Baseball Inc. announced that they would "defer to the changing social climate" and let girls play on their teams.

Little League tryouts in New Jersey on April 3, 1974.

TITLE IX, passed in 1972, prohibits discrimination on the basis of sex. One of the law's biggest impacts has been in sports—by way of increasing participation, opportunities, funding, and college scholarships for women and girls in schools receiving federal funds. According to the Women's Sports Foundation (WSF), by 2016 there was a 545 percent increase in the percentage of women playing college sports and a 990 percent increase in those playing in high school; by 2021, those numbers jumped to 614 percent and 1,057 percent, respectively.

In professional sports, demand for equal pay has been a major catalyst for activism, from the soccer field to the basketball court. The WSF founder Billie Jean King was an early trailblazer for equal pay, catalyzing the creation of the Women's Tennis Association and demanding pay equity or a boycott of the 1973 U.S. Open. And in 2022, after years of advocacy, walkouts, and lawsuits, the U.S. women's national soccer team finally won a collective bargaining agreement that guaranteed they will be paid the same as the men.

Letters

We have no words that can begin to express our joy, our gratitude, and our love for the Petition for Sanity you ran in your February issue. For those of us who are only now developing the courage to "come out" in public in order to inform others about our lifestyle, this petition is a rare gift from our sisters.

Some of us have suffered loss of jobs, loss of family love and support, and loss of legal rights. We have fought the heavy personal assaults as well as the legal ones, with little progress. But now, with the help of all of our sisters, there seems to be a light at the end of the tunnel.

> THE LESBIAN FEMINIST ALLIANCE
> Santa Clara County, Calif.
> January 21, 1975

I certainly want to sign the Petition for Sanity. I am just the mother of a gay son in California. After he and his lover had "come out," his lover lost his job, and my son's job was threatened. They were forty-six and forty-eight and could take no more, so they went into their garage, sealed it, and turned on the motor. I lost both of them. Two more tragic casualties to bigotry and injustice.

> SARAH V. MONTGOMERY
> New York
> June 1975 issue

The census taker came to our door today, counting noses as he went. Having established that we were a married couple, he was required to ascertain who was the "head of the household." First, he asked if I, the husband, were the head of the household. My wife politely explained to him that we do not believe that a household needs a "head," or that the husband, by virtue of male genes, is somehow naturally endowed as head of any household, or that his wife is naturally subordinate to him.

Our determined census taker scratched his head awhile, considered our answer, and then asked my wife if she were the head of the household. My wife answered no, for the same reasons. Undaunted, he tried again: Was it that she was the head of the household but let me *think* that I was?

An immediate protest call to the local Census Bureau office produced the explanation that someone must be designated as "head of the household" or else the computer won't know how to relate the various members of a household to one another.

The net result of the whole matter was that, somehow, my wife was listed as "head of household," and I as "other relative."

> JOHN MICHAEL BROUNOFF
> (OTHER RELATIVE)
> PATRICIA SEED
> (HEAD OF HOUSEHOLD)
> Madison, Wis.
> March 1975 issue

Joan Little:
The Dialectics of Rape

BY **ANGELA DAVIS** • JUNE 1975

RAPE, LYNCH NEGRO MOTHER

Columbus, Miss., Dec. 17—Thursday a week ago Cordella Stevenson was found early in the morning hanging to the limb of a tree, without any clothing, dead. . . . The body was found about fifty yards north of the Mobile & Ohio R.R., and the thousands and thousands of passengers that came in and out of this city last Thursday morning were horrified at the sight. She was hung there from the night before by a bloodthirsty mob who had gone to her home, snatched her from slumber, and dragged her through the streets without any resistance. They carried her to a far-off spot, did their dirt, and then strung her up. —*Chicago Defender,* December 18, 1915

NO ONE—not even the men in the mob—had bothered to accuse Cordella Stevenson of committing a crime. She was Black and that was reason enough. She was Black and a woman, trapped in a society pervaded with myths of white superiority and male supremacy. She could be raped and murdered with absolute impunity. The white mob simply claimed that a few months earlier Cordella Stevenson's son had burned down a white man's barn.

It was sixty years ago when this Black woman was raped and strung up on a tree. There are many who believe that incidents such as these belong to an era of racist terror now forever buried under the historical progress of the intervening years. But history itself allows only the naive to honestly claim these last sixty years as a time of unequivocal progress—especially when the elimination of racism and male supremacy is used as the yardstick.

> **"Rape is not one-dimensional and homogeneous, but one feature that does remain constant is the overt and flagrant treatment of women, through rape, as property."**

Twenty-year-old Joan Little, one of the most recent victims in this racist and sexist tradition, is the cultural grandchild of Cordella Stevenson. She says that she resisted when she was sexually assaulted, but as a result she is currently being tried on charges of first-degree murder. In the event of a conviction, she will automatically get a death sentence and will be placed on North Carolina's death row—the result of a "legal" process, but still too close to the lynch law of the past.

The story begins last August 27, when a guard at the jail in Beaufort County, North Carolina, was found dead in the cell of a missing prisoner. He had been stabbed eleven times with an ice pick, the same ice pick that he had kept in his own desk drawer. The jailer, Clarence Alligood, was white. The missing prisoner was Black, and the only woman in the entire jail. Because of a conviction on charges of breaking and entering, larceny, and receiving stolen property, Joan Little was serving a sentence of seven to ten years and had already been kept in the Beaufort County jail for three months at the time of her disappearance.

When the autopsy report was released, it contained this evidence of recent sexual activity on the part of Alligood: "His shoes were in the corridor, his socks on his feet. He was otherwise naked from the waist down. . . . The left arm was under the body and clutching his pants. . . . His right hand contained an icepick. There was blood on the sheet, cell floor, corridor. . . . Beneath his buttocks was a decorated, partially torn woman's kerchief. On the floor was a night gown and on the cell door was a brassiere and night jacket. . . . Extending from his penis to his thigh skin was a stream of what appeared to be seminal fluid. . . . The urethral fluid was loaded with spermatozoa."

After a week of evading police—who conducted their search with riot weapons and helicopters—Joan Little turned herself in, stating nothing publicly about the case except that she did what she had to do in self-defense. At her own insistence, Jerry Paul, the lawyer she contacted, received assurances that she would be incarcerated in the women's prison in Raleigh—not in the jail where the incident took place and where she feared that she would be subjected to further sexual assault and perhaps even that her life would be in danger. Shortly thereafter, Joan Little was charged with murder in the first degree.

The circumstances surrounding this case deserve careful attention, for they raise fundamental questions about the bringing of murder charges against her. Moreover, they expose conditions and situations many women prisoners must confront, especially in the small-town jails of this country.

1. Joan Little was being detained in a jail in which she was the only woman—among prisoners and guards alike.

2. Like any other prisoner, Sister Joan was being held under lock and key. Only her jailer, Clarence Alligood, had access to the key to her cell that night. Therefore, how could he have been present there against his will? A part of an escape attempt on the part of Joan Little, as the authorities then charged?

3. Alligood was apparently killed by stab wounds inflicted by the same ice pick that he was known to keep in his desk. What was a jail guard doing with an ice pick in the first place? And for what legitimate purpose could he have taken it into a prisoner's cell?

4. Alligood was discovered naked from the waist down. According to Karen Galloway and Jerry Paul, Joan Little's attorneys, the authorities maintained for a full three weeks that Alligood's pants were nowhere to be found. Were they afraid that the public would discover that, although he had been stabbed in the legs, there were no such holes in his pants? Were they afraid people would therefore realize that Alligood had removed his pants before the struggle began? In any case, how could such crucial evidence be allowed to disappear?

In fact, the reality of Joan Little's life as a prisoner, even before the rape, might have been one of sexual exploitation—a fate she consistently resisted. Jerry Paul has said, "One possibility is that she was being kept in Beaufort County Jail for openly sexual purposes."

She should have been moved to the women's prison in Raleigh shortly after her original conviction, but she was never transferred. According to Paul, a TV camera was focused on her cell at all times, leaving her no privacy whatever even when she changed clothes or took a shower. When she used her sheets to block the view, they were taken from her. Joan Little's lawyers have said that on one occasion a highway patrolman visiting the jail on business unrelated to Joan came into her cell and urinated on the floor.

Essential to a clear perspective on the Joan Little case is an analysis of what might have happened if the situation had been reversed. What if Alligood had overpowered her? What if he had stabbed her with the ice pick—as he might have intended to do if she could not otherwise be raped? What if the sexually violated body of Joan Little had been discovered in that cell on the night of August 27?

There can be little speculation about the turn events would have taken had Joan Little been killed by Alligood. A verdict of "justifiable homicide" would have probably closed the books on such a case.

But she had the courage to fend off her assailant. The price of her resistance was a new threat of death, this time issuing from the government of North Carolina. And so she is being tried—by the same state whose supreme court decided, in the nineteenth century, that no white man could be convicted of fornication with a slave woman.

Joan Little stands accused by a court system that, proportionate to its population, has sentenced more political activists to prison than any other state in the country. The number of state prison units in North Carolina is staggering—more than five times greater than in California, the most populous state in the country. In fact, North Carolina, along with Georgia, can claim more prisoners per capita than any other state, and they include, of course, an enormously disproportionate number of Black men and women.

As this article is being written, there are seventy-one prisoners on death row in North Carolina, making that state number one in the nation in condemning people to legal death. In the event of a conviction, the state's present sentencing policy could make Sister Joan Little the third woman in the country to be sentenced to death since the Supreme Court ruled in 1972 that the death penalty imposed at the discretion of judges and juries was cruel and unusual punishment. North Carolina subsequently mandated that a conviction on a first-degree murder charge automatically carried the death penalty. This procedure was appealed to the Supreme Court in late April. The other two women presently on death row are also in North Carolina—a Black and a Native American.

Joan Little's attorneys relate numerous possibilities of judicial bias against her. In Beaufort County, for instance, where families are generations old, virtually everyone knows everyone else. Living in the area are numerous Alligoods. One of these Alligoods sat on the grand jury that returned the indictment against Joan Little.

Without exception, every pretrial motion filed, as of this writing, has been flatly denied. Despite inflammatory publicity about Joan Little— including unfounded and malicious charges that she was a prostitute—and in spite of the unconcealed public sympathy for Alligood, the courts have refused to grant a change of venue for the trial.

Although Joan Little is indigent, her motion to have the court assume the costs of expert witnesses has been denied. It was denied even though the court does not have to pay her attorneys' fees, since the lawyers are donating their services.

Efforts to gain access to the evidence, in the form of discovery motions, have also been thwarted. The sheriff at first refused to release a list of female prisoners previously incarcerated in the jail, leading to a belief that the authorities feared the exposure of other sexual assaults by Alligood and his colleagues. Later, after the State Bureau of Investigation (SBI) had questioned sixty-five former prisoners, their names were released to Joan Little's lawyers, but even this SBI report stated that some of these inmates claimed Alligood and other jailers made sexual advances toward them.

After the difficulty in locating Alligood's pants, the defense attempted to have all the evidence assembled and placed in protective custody. This was denied.

Although Sister Joan seemed clearly eligible to be released on bail, District Attorney William Griffin employed every trick of his trade to prevent her release. When the defense attorneys attempted to post bail, for instance, Griffin, relying on a technicality, ordered the clerk not to accept the bond.

Finally, as a result of a nationwide outcry, she was released in February on bail of $115,000: an amount that is itself clearly exorbitant.

Over the last few years, widespread concern about the increasing incidence of sexual assaults on women has crystallized into a militant campaign against rape. In the Joan Little case, as well as in all other instances of sexual assault, it is essential to place the specific incident in its sociohistorical context. For rape is not one-dimensional and homogeneous, but one feature that does remain constant is the overt and flagrant treatment of women, through rape, as property. Particular rape cases will then express different modes in which women are handled as property.

Thus when a white man rapes a Black woman, the underlying meaning of this crime remains inaccessible if one is blind to the historical dimensions of the act. One must consider, for example, that a little more than a hundred years ago, there were few Black women who did not have to endure humiliating and violent sexual attacks as an integral feature of their daily lives. Rape was the rule; immunity from rape the exception. On the one hand, the slave master made use of his tyrannical possession of slave women as chattel in order to violate their bodies with impunity. On the

This clipping from the *Washington Star-News* was found in a file in the *Ms.* archives containing the magazine's correspondence with writer Angela Davis.

SLIGS

The Case of Joann Little

Washington Star-News Sunday, February 16, 197

Carl T. Rowan:
Ignore Rape, Cry Murder!

"This is the sort of case which puts the test to the women's liberation movement."

● In the wee hours of Aug. 27, 1974, Joanne Little was sleeping in a cell of the Beaufort County Jail where she had been for three months, awaiting appeal of a conviction for breaking and entering. She was the only woman in the cellblock, which was guarded solely by white males.

● The guard that morning was Clarence Alligood, a 62-year-old farmer and ex-truck driver who was known to keep an ice pick in his drawer.

● Alligood went into Miss Little's cell in the wee hours for some reason, carrying his own ice pick. He had left his shoes out by his desk. He wound up stabbed to death with his own ice pick, and when found was nude from the waist down.

● Joanne Little fled the jail, but later turned herself in when a friendly lawyer established precautions against her being shot on sight

● Some newspapers in the areas suppressed the fact that Alligood was naked from the waist down, and that Dr. Harry M. Carpenter, the county medical examiner, had found clear evidence of recent sexual activity by Alligood. On the contrary, they carried editorials portraying Alligood as a martyr who died a courageous law enforcer

● The Southern Poverty Law Center reports that "the state medical examiner was prepared to support Joanne's story from his observation of the evidence, but he was not allowed to testify before the grand jury which indicted her" for first-degree murder.

SOME READERS may complain that I not only presume Miss Little innocent prior to the trial, but I declare it in print. I assure you that I

would not do so if I could thi. of any explanation for a male jailer going barefoot and bare-bottomed into the cell of a single black woman inmate in the wee hours, wielding his ice pick. There are some rules of simple deduction here that ought not mystify even Beaufort County's excuse for Sherlock Holmes.

Still, I would not prejudge this case were it not for the fact that every bit of evidence I can find indicates that this is a classic move to railroad to prison or death a young, indigent, not-well-educated black woman who herself ought to be the complainant.

Even beyond that, I would not write this column if I felt there was a ghost of a chance of Joanne Little getting a fair trial in this area where a black juror is a rarity.

THIS IS THE sort of case which puts the test to the women's liberation movement. Will its members help, or is it just a pseudo-intellectual exercise in letting off personal steam or airing personal hang-ups and frustrations. Do the leaders of the movement truly care about the dehumanizing and brutalizing of a woman prisoner by a male guard?

Editorial from the local newspaper in Washington, N.C. (Beaufort County) on August 28, 1974.

Brutal Murder

The murder of Clarence G. Alligood, age 62, Beaufort County night jailer, is one of the most brutal ever to happen in this county.

At this very moment we look at what has happened, we look at his family and loved ones, and what is there to say? Here is a man who gave his life in the line of duty. Here is a good man who never made the headlines in life, but in death there must be an appreciation for him and what he did that he never lived to realize.

We look so often at the death of a law enforcement officer, and within a day the story belongs to history. We express great sympathy at the time, but all too soon the story fades away.

Clarence Alligood gave his best to his job. He gave his life in the performance of his duties. What more can any man give?

It is with deeper sympathy than words can express that we feel a part of this story. There will be other Clarence Alligoods . who give their lives, and there will be other stories of a similar nature. But this one is here at home, and it represents a brutal chapter of a continuing story.

He was a good man.

The autopsy report showed that:

"His [Alligood's] shoes were in the corridor, socks on feet, but otherwise naked from waist down with open yellow plaid shirt and undershirt on. The left arm was under the body and clutching his pants . . . extending from his penis to his thigh skin was a stream of what appeared to be seminal fluid . . . the urethral fluid was loaded with spermatozoa."

Join Women's International League For Peace And Freedom
NEW YORK METROPOLITAN BRANCH
201 WEST 13th STREET • NEW YORK, NEW YORK 10011 • (212) 242-4610

Ms. Little is now "free" on $115,000 bail. Trial date is April 15. At issue is her exoneration and exposure of the brutalization of women in prison. Buttons, posters, rally dates, etc., are available at the Joann Little Information Center, 4850 Blagden Ave. NW, Washington DC.

other hand, rape itself was an essential weapon utilized by the white master to reinforce the authority of his ownership of Black women.

Although the immediate victim of rape was the Black woman—and it was she who endured its pain and anguish—rape served not only to further her oppression but also as a means of terrorizing the entire Black community. It placed brutal emphasis on the fact that Black slaves were indeed the property of the white master.

In conjunction with the sexual exploitation of Black women, the stereotypical image of the Black woman branded her as a creature motivated by base, animal-like sexual instincts. It was therefore no sin to rape her. This bestial notion of the Black woman, incidentally, played and continues to play a significant role in justifying the overexploitation of her labor. For such a woman would hardly be distinguishable from a beast of burden. Again, she is openly defined as property.

If rape was, in effect, institutionalized during slavery, essentially the same institutionalized form of rape is present today in such vestiges of slavery as domestic work. How many Black women working in the homes of white people have not had to confront the "man of the house" as an actual or potential rapist?

The rape of the Black woman and its ideological justification are integrally linked to the portrayal of the Black man as a bestial rapist of white women—and, of course, the castration and lynching of Black men on the basis of such accusations. Struggle against the sexual abuse of Black women has demanded at the same time struggle against the cruel manipulation of sexual accusations against Black men. Black women, therefore, have played a vanguard role, not only in the fight against rape, but also in the movement to end lynching.

For Black women, rape perpetrated by white men, like the social stereotype of Black men as rapists, must be classed among the brutal paraphernalia of racism.

Whenever a campaign is erected around a Black woman who has been raped by a white man, therefore, the content of the campaign must be explicitly antiracist. And, as incorrect as it would be to fail to attack racism, it would be equally incorrect to make light of the antisexist content of the movement. Racism and male supremacy have to be projected in their dialectical unity. In the case of the raped Black woman, they are mutually reinforcing.

Joan Little's assailant had probably been exposed to all the racist myths about Black women and was aware of the lack of redress available to victims of white rapists. In the aftermath of the incident, in fact, vicious accusations were hurled at Joan Little: she was called a prostitute, and it was claimed that she engaged in sexual activities with jailers.

Of course, the conviction rate for rape is the lowest of all violent crimes—regardless of the victim's ethnic group. Only in those instances where the accused rapist is Black and the alleged victim is white can a long prison term or death penalty be anticipated. From 1930 to 1967, 455 men were executed as a result of rape convictions: 405 of them were Black, 48 of them were white, and 2 were of other ethnic groups. This means that almost 90 percent of all rape executions during this period involved Black men.

Courts have established the pattern of either acquitting or not trying the majority of white men who are charged with rape. In New York, for instance, in 1967, 30 percent of all felony indictments ended in convictions, but in only 13 percent of all rape indictments were there convictions.

There must be a reason behind this social and judicial encouragement given to rape. This reason, in turn, must be related to the social and political function of male supremacy in general.

The oppression of women is a vital and integral component of a larger network of oppression that claims as its foremost victims Black people, Chicanos, Puerto Ricans, Asians, Indians, and all poor and working-class people. Just as class exploitation, racism, and imperialist subjugation of peoples abroad serve to nourish this larger system and keep it functioning, so male supremacy is likewise essential to its smooth operation. The larger system, of course, is monopoly capitalism, and its overall driving motive is profit.

It is in the interests of the ruling class to cultivate the archaic patriarchal domination of women—based on male ownership of females as property—that flourished during the feudal era. As long as women are oppressed, enormous benefits accrue to the ruling class. Female labor can be even more flagrantly exploited than male labor. (White women's median wages are even lower than Black men's, and, of course, women of color receive the lowest wages of all workers.) The social definition of women as housewives provides, as Alva Buxenbaum states, the most effective "rationale for failing to make housework and child care a social responsibility." A list of examples could go on and on.

The social incentive given to rape is woven into the logic of the institutions of this society. It is an extremely efficient means of keeping women in a state of fear of rape or of the possibility of it. It is, as Susan Griffin wrote, "a form of mass terrorism." This, in turn, buttresses the general sense of powerlessness and passivity socially inflicted upon women, thus rendering them more easily exploitable. Yet, just as working-class and poor white people who exhibit racist attitudes toward people of color are unconscious agents of a higher power, so rapists (though they may be individually unaware of this) are performing deeds that give sustenance not to them but to the existing system.

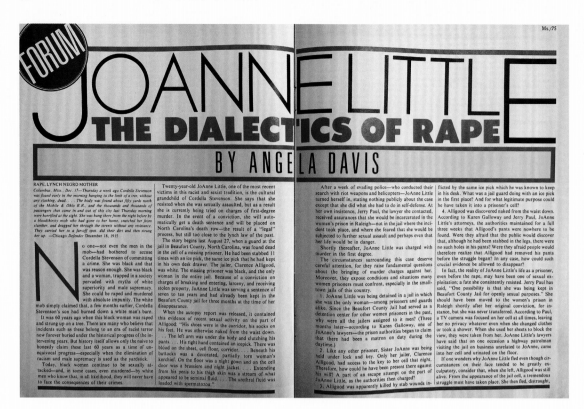

Ms./75

FORUM

JOANNE LITTLE
THE DIALECTICS OF RAPE
BY ANGELA DAVIS

RAPE, LYNCH NEGRO MOTHER

Columbia, Miss., Dec. 17—Thursday a week ago Cordella Stevenson was found early in the morning hanging to the limb of a tree, without any clothing, dead. . . . The body was found about fifty yards north of the Mobile & Ohio R.R., and the thousands and thousands of passengers that came in and out of this city last Thursday morning were horrified at the sight. She was hung there from the night before by a bloodthirsty mob who had gone to her home, snatched her from slumber, and dragged her through the streets without any resistance. They carried her to a far-off spot, did their dirt and then strung her up. —Chicago Defender December 18, 1915

No one—not even the men in the mob—had bothered to accuse Cordella Stevenson of committing a crime. She was black and that was reason enough. She was black and a woman, trapped in a society pervaded with myths of white superiority and male supremacy. She could be raped and murdered with absolute impunity. The white mob simply claimed that, a few months earlier, Cordella Stevenson's son had burned down a white man's barn.

It was 60 years ago when this black woman was raped and strung up on a tree. There are many who believe that incidents such as these belong to an era of racist terror now forever buried under the historical progress of the intervening years. But history itself allows only the naive to honestly claim that these last 60 years as a time of unequivocal progress—especially when the elimination of racism and male supremacy is used as the yardstick.

Today, black women continue to be sexually attacked—and, in some cases, even murdered—by white men who know that, in all likelihood, they will never have to face the consequences of their crimes.

Twenty-year-old JoAnne Little, one of the most recent victims in this racist and sexist tradition, is the cultural grandchild of Cordella Stevenson. She says that she resisted when she was sexually assaulted, but as a result she is currently being tried on charges of first-degree murder. In the event of a conviction, she will automatically get a death sentence and will be placed on North Carolina's death row—the result of a "legal" process, but still too close to the lynch law of the past.

The story begins last August 27, when a guard at the jail in Beaufort County, North Carolina, was found dead in the cell of a missing prisoner. He had been stabbed 11 times with an ice pick, the same ice pick that he had kept in his own desk drawer. The jailer, Clarence Alligood, was white. The missing prisoner was black, and the only woman in the entire jail. Because of a conviction on charges of breaking and entering, larceny, and receiving stolen property, JoAnne Little was serving a sentence of seven to ten years and had already been kept in the Beaufort County jail for three months at the time of her disappearance.

When the autopsy report was released, it contained this evidence of recent sexual activity on the part of Alligood: "His shoes were in the corridor, his socks on his feet. He was otherwise naked from the waist down. . . . The left arm was under the body and clutching his pants. . . . His right hand contained an icepick. From the blood on the sheet, cell floor, corridor. . . . Beneath his buttocks was a decorated, partially torn woman's kerchief. On the floor was a night gown and on the cell door was a brassiere and night jacket. . . . Extending from his penis to his thigh skin was a stream of what appeared to be seminal fluid. . . . The urethral fluid was loaded with spermatozoa."

After a week of evading police—who conducted their search with riot weapons and helicopters—JoAnne Little turned herself in, stating nothing publicly about the case except that she did what she had to do in self-defense. At her own insistence, Jerry Paul, the lawyer she contacted, received assurances that she would be incarcerated in the women's prison in Raleigh—not in the jail where the incident took place, and where she feared that she would be subjected to further sexual assault and perhaps even that her life would be in danger.

Shortly thereafter, JoAnne Little was charged with murder in the first degree.

The circumstances surrounding this case deserve careful attention, for they raise fundamental questions about the bringing of murder charges against her. Moreover, they expose conditions and situations many women prisoners must confront, especially in the small-town jails of this country.

1. JoAnne Little was being detained in a jail in which she was the only woman—among prisoners and guards alike. Since the Beaufort County Jail had served as a detention center for other women prisoners in the past, why were all the jailers assigned to it men? (Three months later—according to Karen Galloway, one of JoAnne's lawyers—the prison authorities began to claim that there had been a matron on duty during the daytime.)

2. Like any other prisoner, Sister JoAnne was being held under lock and key. Only her jailer, Clarence Alligood, had access to the key to her cell that night. Therefore, how could he have been present there against his will? A part of an escape attempt on the part of JoAnne Little, as the authorities then charged?

3. Alligood was apparently killed by stab wounds inflicted by the same ice pick which he was known to keep in his desk. What was a jail guard doing with an ice pick in the first place? And for what legitimate purpose could he have taken it into a prisoner's cell?

4. Alligood was discovered naked from the waist down. According to Karen Galloway and Jerry Paul, JoAnne Little's attorneys, the authorities maintained for a full three weeks that Alligood's pants were nowhere to be found. Were they afraid that the public would discover that, although he had been stabbed in the legs, there were no such holes in his pants? Were they afraid people would therefore realize that Alligood had removed his pants before the struggle began? In any case, how could such crucial evidence be allowed to disappear?

In fact, the reality of JoAnne Little's life as a prisoner, even before the rape, may have been one of sexual exploitation; a fate she consistently resisted. Jerry Paul has said, "One possibility is that she was being kept in Beaufort County Jail for openly sexual purposes." She should have been moved to the women's prison in Raleigh shortly after her original conviction, for instance, but she was never transferred. According to Paul, a TV camera was focused on her cell at all times, leaving her no privacy whatever even when she changed clothes or took a shower. When she used her sheets to block the view, they were taken from her. JoAnne Little's lawyers have said that on one occasion a highway patrolman visiting the jail on business unrelated to JoAnne, came into her cell and urinated on the floor.

If one wonders why JoAnne Little fled even though circumstances on their face tended to be greatly exculpatory, consider that, when she left, Alligood was still alive. From the appearance of the jail cell, a tremendous struggle must have taken place. She then fled, distraught,

---

Because her first name was pronounced Jo-Ann, early reports about Little, including by *Ms.*, often misspelled her name as "JoAnne" or "Joann."

Joan Little might not only have been the victim of a rape attempt by a white racist jailer; she has truly been raped and wronged many times over by the exploitative and discriminatory institutions of this society. All people who see themselves as members of the existing community of struggle for justice, equality, and progress have a responsibility to fulfill toward Joan Little. Those of us—women and men—who are Black or people of color must understand the connection between racism and sexism that is so strikingly manifested in her case. Those of us who are white and women must grasp the issue of male supremacy in relationship to the racism and class bias that complicate and exacerbate it.

Let us be sure that the leitmotif running through every aspect of the campaign is unity. Our ability to achieve unity may mean the difference between life and death for Sister Joan. Let us then forge among ourselves and our movements an indivisible strength, and with it let us halt and then crush the conspiracy against Joan Little's life.

·   ·   ·

Letters

Well, those Honda folks put an ad in *Ms.* that talked about rack-and-pinion steering, and it sold me their car. The car is terrific, and the steering is even better, and I think you should know that I wrote them and told them to keep advertising in *Ms.*

When I went down to look the Honda Civic over, I took the issue of *Ms.* in which the ad appeared with me, and the salesperson took me on a tour of the engine before he started going over the advantages of color schemes. I don't know whether he took me seriously because his consciousness had been raised or because Honda tells their salespeople to watch out for grim women clutching *Ms.* magazine and marching stoically along mumbling things about disc brakes. But he did take me seriously. It was a great change for the better, and they should all be told it works.

> MALLORY KIRK-MARSHALL
> Yarmouth, Maine
> June 1975 issue

I thought you might enjoy hearing a discussion I heard between my son and his neighbor friend. They were playing together and the little boy got the giggles. "Hee-hee-hee-hee," he giggled, whereupon my son replied in a very condescending tone, "What are you, Danny, some kind of chauvinist? In this house we say, 'Her-her-her-her!'"

> Her who laughs last,
>
> NAME WITHHELD
> August 7, 1975

When I saw that in my spelling book they had "the Queen is the wife of a King," I got really mad. Even though I'm only nine years old, and only in the fourth grade, I've written five poems. One from the five I thought you might want to put in *Ms.* Here it is:

> If you think I'm going to slave
> in the kitchen for a man who is
> supposed to be brave,
> Then I'm sorry to say,
> but you're wrong all the way,
> Because I'm going to be an
> astronaut.

> ANITA BUZICK II
> Killeen, Tex.
> June 1975 issue

The March 1975 article reminded me of the time I brought my son, Karl, to work with me three or so years ago. I was teaching at a small college in Minnesota, and the babysitter canceled out twenty minutes before one of my classes. I put Karl in the front pouch of the baby carrier and wore him on my chest for the two-hour class. He slept, and I lectured, and everything was fine—or so I thought. The department head heard about the "incident" and wrote me a letter of reprimand for unprofessional conduct.

The course I was teaching? Sociology of the Family. Click!

> JACK SATTEL
> Eugene, Ore.
> July 1975 issue

Testosterone Poisoning

BY **ALAN ALDA** • OCTOBER 1975

EVERYONE KNOWS that testosterone, the so-called male hormone, is found in both men and women. What is not so well known is that men have an overdose. Until now it has been thought that the level of testosterone in men is normal simply because they have it. But if you consider how abnormal their behavior is, then you are led to the hypothesis that almost all men are suffering from testosterone poisoning. It is well known that men don't look like other people. They have chicken legs. This is symptomatic of the disease, as is the fact that those men with the most aviary underpinnings will rank women according to the shapeliness of their legs.

> **"Your first reaction may be that you are sicker than anyone else, or that you are the one man in the world able to fight it off. . . . These are all symptoms of the disease."**

Testosterone poisoning is particularly cruel because its sufferers usually don't know they have it. In fact, when they are most under its sway, they believe that they are at their healthiest and most attractive. They even give each other medals for exhibiting the most advanced symptoms of the illness.

But there is hope. Sufferers can change. They must first realize, however, that they are sick. The fact that this condition is inherited in the same way that dimples are does not make it cute.

Eventually, of course, telethons and articles in *Reader's Digest* will dramatize the tragedy of testosterone poisoning. In the meantime, it is imperative for your friends and loved ones to become familiar with the danger signs. Have the men you know take this simple test:

1. **Do you have an intense need to win?** When having sex, do you take pride in always finishing before your partner?

2. **Does violence play a big part in your life?** Before you answer, count up how many hours you watched football, ice hockey, and children's cartoons this year on television. When someone crosses you, do you wish you could stuff his face full of your fist? If so, you're in big trouble, fella, and this is only question number two.

3. **Are you "thing" oriented?** Do you value the parts of a woman's body more than the woman herself? Are you turned on by things that even remind you of those parts? Have you ever fallen in love with a really great doorknob?

4. Do you have an intense need to reduce every difficult situation to charts and figures? If you were present at a riot, would you tend to count the crowd? If your wife is despondent over a deeply felt setback that has left her feeling helpless, do you take her temperature?

5. Do you tend to measure things that are really qualitative? Are you more impressed with how high a male ballet dancer can leap than with what he does while he's up there?

6. Are you a little too mechanically minded? Would you like to watch a sunset with a friend and feel at one with nature and each other, or would you rather take apart a clock?

7. Are you easily triggered into competition? When someone tries to pass you on the highway, do you speed up?

A man answering yes to more than three of the above questions is considered sick and not someone you'd want to have around in a crisis—such as raising children or growing old together. But there's hope:

1. Don't panic. Your first reaction may be that you are sicker than anyone else, or that you are the one man in the world able to fight it off, or that you are the one man ordained to lead others to health (such as writing articles about it). These are all symptoms of the disease. Relax. Sit back and enjoy yourself. Then find out how to enjoy somebody else.

2. Try to feel something. (Not with your hands, you oaf.) Look at a baby and see if you can appreciate it. (Not how big it's getting, just how nice she or he is.) See if you can get yourself to cry by some means other than getting hit in the eye or losing a lot of money.

3. See if you can listen while someone is talking. Were you the one talking? Perhaps you haven't got the idea yet.

4. Practice this sentence: "You know, I think you're right and I'm wrong." (Hint: It is useful to know what the other person thinks before you say this.)

FOR WOMEN ONLY: Only after he begins to get his condition under control and has actually begun to enjoy life should you let him know that there is no such thing as testosterone poisoning.

Letters

I am fifteen years old, and last summer I was raped by the closest friend of my boyfriend. I did not consider it rape at the time, because I knew the guy relatively well, and I didn't think you were raped by your "friends." I felt like a whore and a piece of trash, but worse than that I felt used. I felt that I had done something to make him want to have sex with me.

After school started, a woman from WOAR [Women Organized Against Rape] came and spoke to my class about rape. I realized that women can be raped by anybody, friends, neighbors, strangers, whatever, and if the woman is unwilling to commit the act, then it is rape, even if it's her husband. Although I still felt I had no one to turn to, at least I had a name for my hurt, and someplace to direct it and my anger.

NAME WITHHELD
February 24, 1976

Lost Women

RECLAIMING THE FORGOTTEN HISTORIES of women was the driving force behind *Ms.*'s monthly column "Lost Women." One of the column's early writers, Gerda Lerner, declared, "Women's history is women's right." She went on to be a key organizer of the first Women's History Week in 1979, which became a national celebration in 1982 and was expanded into Women's History Month in 1987.

Looking at Dickey Chapelle's photographs, from two wars and four revolutions, and reading her own story of how she got them, one wonders how she managed to live as long as she did. She was forty-seven years old and covering the Vietnam War in 1965 for *The National Observer* when she was killed.

During her unique career as a combat photojournalist, which began off Iwo Jima in 1945, she probably logged more front-line experience than any of her counterparts. War photographers, male and female, grow gun-shy after a time and usually switch to less hazardous subjects. Though shot at for twenty years, Chapelle kept going— never outwardly betraying fear or hesitation. "It's not that I'm not afraid," she admitted. "Courage is not the absence of fear, it's the control of fear." . . .

The photographs and first-person journalism Dickey Chapelle produced ranged from the bald, straightforward stuff of World War II to a more sophisticated blend of the ironies of less clear-cut revolutions and skirmishes. During the small-patrol era in Vietnam (before the giant pitched battles started), she protested in her dispatches and in complaints to the Overseas Press Club that correspondents and photographers were being misled about the war. She recognized early what we did not grasp until much later—that the Vietnam War was not being won.

—from "Lost Women: Dickey Chapelle: Two Wars and Four Revolutions"
by Stanley P. Friedman, April 1976

Name ten women who have made important contributions to American history and development. (Please: no presidents' wives, writers, or opera singers—and no one living today.) If this was difficult, try naming ten men. Easy? Does that suggest something to you? There is a good deal wrong with the history you were taught, the textbooks you read in high school and college, and the culture that has largely ignored what women have experienced and contributed to human development. It is time to change the narrow, male-centered view of the past, to redefine history as the history of men and women. . . . Women have a right to their history too.

—"So You Think You Know Women's History"
by Gerda Lerner, September 1972

Juana Inés de la Cruz hated the portrait that was painted of her in the 1670s, when, though not yet thirty, she had been Mexico's greatest literary figure for well over ten years. It shows a nun in white, posed in a dark study. The face is solemnly lovely; the body is half turned toward the beholder, a hand marking a place in an open book. The luster of the glance and smile are both turned low. One might suppose the artist had caught her inner calm. More likely, he had been conned by her patience. It is clearly the portrait of an intrusion.

—"Sister Juana: The Price of Genius"
by Judith Thurman, April 1973

Harriet Tubman's name has not been lost to us—it appears in history texts defined by such epithets as "Liberator," "Underground Railroad Conductor," and "Famous Negro"—but the credit Tubman received in her time and in our own has never been commensurate with her work, her vision, or her zeal. . . . In a time when being both Black and female meant extreme oppression, Tubman was an activist obsessed with liberation, and she expressed her driving concern

LOST WOMEN

HARRIET TUBMAN: THE MOSES OF HER PEOPLE

MARCY GALEN

Harriet Tubman's name has not been lost to us—it appears in history texts defined by such epithets as "Liberator," "Underground Railroad Conductor," and "Famous Negro"—but the credit Tubman received in her time and in our own has never been commensurate with her work, her vision, or her zeal.

Slave owners on the Eastern Shore of Maryland were not certain who "Moses" was, and for a time they did not know if the "black wretch" was male or female. During the 1850s a raider with this Biblical code name struck their plantations by night and carried off large groups of slaves worth thousands of dollars. Record-breaking rewards were offered, but Harriet Tubman, "the Moses of her people," was never captured.

Tubman was an escaped slave, a hunted fugitive, and one of the most effective conductors on that secret route North called the Underground Railroad. Her life contains so many elements of high adventure that it might appear melodramatic to modern, cynical eyes. Her combination of religious mysticism and militancy might call to mind a black Joan of Arc, but she was neither an adventurer nor a saint.

In a time when being both black and female meant extreme oppression, Tubman was an activist obsessed with liberation, and she expressed her driving concern pragmatically. In the space of one decade, she made 19 forays into the South to rescue more than 300 people from slavery. She joined the Anti-Slavery and Women's Suffrage movements, and joined the Union Army during the Civil War, becoming the only woman in American military history to plan and personally conduct an armed expedition against enemy forces. She was unpaid for her work and spent the last part of her life in poverty.

Harriet Ross Tubman was born into slavery on Edward Brodas's plantation in Dorchester County, Maryland, about 1821. She was of pure African lineage,

said to be descended from the warlike and rebellious Ashanti tribe. A homely, willful child, she was continually whipped for "insolence" as a nursemaid and domestic, and was later sent to work in the fields. Unusually short but stronger than most men, she split rails, carted heavy loads, and plowed. The hard labor prepared her for the physical endurance that would be essential to her later vocation.

Before she reached adulthood, Harriet saw her own sisters sold South and heard of Nat Turner's slave revolt in nearby Virginia. Her rebelliousness increased, and when she was a young woman, she deliberately stood between an overseer and an escaping slave. The enraged overseer hurled a heavy iron weight which struck Harriet in the head and nearly killed her. After months in a delirium she recovered, but her injury resulted in chronic narcolepsy, and for the rest of her life she was subject to sudden attacks of deep sleep from which no one could rouse her.

Always rebellious, she was further radicalized by this incident. She began to believe that God had called her to help her people, and she experienced

visions which increased her growing sense of mission. Her activism was probably postponed some years by her marriage to John Tubman, a freed slave whom she deeply loved, and by an abortive attempt to buy her freedom. As a hired-out hand, she attempted to save a portion of her meager wages, but when it became evident that she could never save enough to purchase freedom, her thoughts turned seriously to escape. In 1849, she learned that she and her brothers were to be sold South on a chain gang, and she finally resolved to escape with her brothers and John.

She reported that she had a dream before her escape: "I dreamed I was flying over cotton fields and cornfields and the corn was ripe, the tassels waving golden brown in the sun. I fly over Cambridge and the Choptank River, and I can see the gleam of the water under me like a mirror. I come to a mountain and I fly over that. But I always come to a barrier, sometimes it's a fence, sometimes a river, and I can't fly over it. It appears like I won't have the strength and just as I'm sinking down, there are ladies in white over there, and they put out their hands and pull me across."

Later she described how she came to the decision to escape: "I had reasoned this out in my mind, there was two things I had a right to, liberty and death. If I could not have one, I would have the other, for no man should take me alive."

John, however, was content in Maryland and forbade his wife to leave him. Her frightened brothers deserted her at the last moment. Harriet Tubman, placing personal freedom above her marriage, disappeared from the plantation alone one night.

She reached a woman in a nearby town who put her in touch with the Underground Railroad. The Railroad, a chain of hiding places, sustenance, and sometimes transportation for runaway slaves, was run by Quakers, freed slaves, and other sympathizers who were called

"I had reasoned this out . . . there was two things I had a right to, liberty and death."

pragmatically. In the space of one decade, she made nineteen forays into the South to rescue more than three hundred people from slavery.

—"Harriet Tubman:
The Moses of Her People"
by Marcy Galen, August 1973

In the ghettos of Nazi-occupied Europe, women did more than just survive and make soup out of stones. Their major role in the Resistance has been noted not only by ghetto historians but by the Germans as well. General Jürgen Stroop, sent especially to quell the Warsaw ghetto's revolt, was amazed by the presence among the Jewish fighters of females, "wearing knee-length trousers and flat caps," who put up "fanatical resistance." One of these fighters was Zivia Lubetkin, a legendary figure in the annals of the ghetto.

—"Zivia Lubetkin: A Last Stand
at the Warsaw Ghetto"
by Marie Syrkin, September 1973

Seventy-five years ago, in London, a woman escaped from prison with the help of a rabbit. It was not a modern prison, with facilities for education and recreation and a chance of parole, but a tall, dark, stuffy Victorian house; and the prisoner, who had been confined for most of her thirty-six years, was under sentence for life. The rabbit's name, of course, was Peter. It was Beatrix Potter's misfortune to be the only daughter of rich, pretentious, ultraconservative parents. They never allowed her to go to school, where she might have picked up unsuitable ideas and rude habits; and she never had any friends of her own age—her only companion was her brother, Bertram.

—"Beatrix Potter: More Than
Just Peter Rabbit"
by Alison Lurie, September 1977

.   .   .

Letters

IT WOULD BE IMPOSSIBLE to tell the story of *Ms.* in the 1970s without a special dedication to Gerald Robert Wildermuth, a man who took a "few minutes" out of his "busy schedule" in 1976 to tell *Ms.* what he really thought of feminism. An avalanche of reader responses followed—from across the country, women and men, teen girls and boys—and was published in subsequent issues. And gloriously clever and thoughtful these letters were! Among those shared here are ones that made it into the magazine, though many others were never made public, mostly on account of volume, according to Mary Thom in *Letters to "Ms.," 1972–1987.*

I thought I would take a few minutes out of my busy schedule to write this letter. Then perhaps you can get a better picture of what you're really up against and what other people really think about your opinions.

First, I would like to state I am a father of three girls, ages six, four, and two. Also, my wife shares my thoughts and ideals. You feminists all seem to think that you are hurting men's feelings or insulting them by calling them male chauvinist pigs. I would like to state that the greatest honor anyone can give me is to call me a male chauvinist pig. I'd consider it a great honor. I teach all my girls that all feminist women are "lesbians." I drill this into their heads so that the schools, churches, and their friends cannot set their futures on the wrong path. You always talk of what women can do to help women's lib. I would like to tell you what I and my family do to stop women's lib. Now, I know that one family cannot change women's lib, but we feel better for doing our part.

When we pull into a gas station and a broad is working there, we tell her that we don't believe in women working in service stations and that she can't put gas in our car. Then we drive off, and the woman stands there looking stupid.

My girl is taken to school by myself because we have a woman bus driver. I have told the school my reasons!

We screen all television shows. If any woman is playing a man's role, we don't watch those programs (*Police Woman* or *Get Christie Love!* or any of the news programs with women as reporters). If you're on television, we simply turn you off. If you're in a magazine, we simply throw it away.

We also screen all our friends. My wife doesn't hang around with any feminists.

I also wish to say that I support my own family. I am an over-the-road driver. My wife does not work. When my girls look for their mother, they know where they can find her.

I could sit here and write you all night long, but my time is valuable to me, and you are nothing to me but another bunch of feminists.

You can print any or all of this letter if you wish. My only desire is to show you that your time is wasted. You can't change me or my friends, no matter what you or television do.

GERALD ROBERT WILDERMUTH
Location withheld
May 1976 issue

Regarding Gerald Robert Wildermuth—is he for real?

SHARON K. CHAPMAN
Detroit
September 1976 issue

I think Gerald Robert Wildermuth is suffering from acute testosterone poisoning, complicated by severe closed-mindedness and bigotry.

> MARTHA ROOT
> Buffalo, N.Y.
> September 1976 issue

I'm fourteen years old, and I'm trying (successfully) to steer every child I know in the right direction. They're learning that everyone is to be treated as a person and everyone has a chance to make it. My little brother heard me read the Wildermuth letter, and he thought it was very stupid. I know more and more boys like my brother, and it makes me happy.

Also, Mr. Wildermuth says his wife doesn't work. What does he call cooking, cleaning, and taking care of the kids? A vacation?

> GRACE N. LUPPINO
> South Norwalk, Conn.
> September 1976 issue

I honestly believe *Ms.* ought to inform anthropologists Mary and Richard Leakey about Wildermuth; it seems we've very probably uncovered the missing link between humans and apes!

> M. CONSTANCE JENKINS
> Ogdensburg, N.Y.
> September 1976 issue

The Traiger family would like to express their deepest sympathy for the tragic loss of G. R. Wildermuth's mind.

> ROBIN, TERRIE, SY, AND
> MARILYN TRAIGER
> Bellmore, N.Y.
> September 1976 issue

It is probably best to ignore people like Gerald Robert Wildermuth (which is German for "wild mouth"). But I can't resist responding, because if there's anything I dislike more than chauvinism, it's illiterate chauvinism.

Fortunately, his species of mammal is fast becoming extinct.

> DIANE K. MITCHELL
> Los Angeles
> September 1976 issue

Thanks for writing, Mr. Wildermuth—even you know that you can't ignore us now.

> JERI S. DARLING
> Ann Arbor, Mich.
> September 1976 issue

Thank God for my daddy!

> BARBARA JOYCE SMITH
> Oklahoma City
> September 1976 issue

SUMMER SPECIAL:
30 PAGES
OF FICTION AND
PHOTOGRAPHY

WHEN MEN
COACH WOMEN—
DO THEY HAVE
TO SCORE?

Ms.

AUGUST/1976 $1.00

TRAVEL: GEORGE
WASHINGTON
NEVER SLEPT HERE

UNDERGROUND:
JEAN BOUDIN
TALKS ABOUT HER
FUGITIVE
DAUGHTER

Battered Wives
HELP FOR THE SECRET VICTIM NEXT DOOR

In a watershed moment, *Ms.* was the first-ever national magazine to address domestic violence—let alone issue a feature story complete with a haunting cover photo, a close-up of a woman's bruised face. Seen on newsstands and in homes nationwide, the August 1976 cover sparked controversy, conversation, and a movement. As Gloria Steinem shared in 2011, at the time *Ms.* published "Battered Wives: Help for the Secret Victim Next Door," phrases like "sexual harassment" and "domestic violence" weren't yet part of our public or political vernacular. Nor were interventions—from support services like rape crisis centers and women's shelters, to laws naming and criminalizing domestic abuse. It took until 1994 for Congress to pass meaningful federal reform: the Violence Against Women Act, which has been reauthorized over the years, even expanded to broaden protections, invest in prevention, and address emerging threats and issues, from firearms access to dating violence.

The laws that can be invoked to protect women from assaultive husbands vary from state to state. In every state it is against the law to physically attack another person, but if the assailant is married to his victim, the law is unlikely to be enforced. Though "domestic trouble" complaints constitute the majority of all calls for police assistance, police policy dictates that these calls result in few arrests. The International Association of Chiefs of Police training bulletin states, for example, that most family disputes are "personal matters requiring no direct action." The bulletin goes on to recommend that "once inside the home, the officer's sole purpose is to preserve the peace . . . attempt to soothe feelings, pacify parties . . . the power of arrest should be exercised as a last resort." In a number of cities, including New York, Oakland, and New Orleans, police have been specifically trained in mediation and conciliation techniques for use in family cases. While these tactics seem to reduce the number of injuries *police* incur while responding to domestic dispute calls, their protective value to the abused wife is debatable. "In one case that I know of, the cops asked the husband to walk around the block and cool off," says the Philadelphia social worker Jennifer Fleming. "The husband walked around the block. When he came back, he murdered his wife."

—from "One of These Days—Pow! Right in the Kisser:
The Truth About Battered Wives"
by Judith Gingold, August 1976

B.C. (Before Consciousness): there we were, pre-feminism, denying there was any problem, solitarily certain that each of us was herself the problem: "I self-loathe, therefore I am." There was no question about this, yet we all knew the answer—appearances mattered, after all. Therefore, we curled, plucked, dieted, bleached, straightened, shaved, uplifted, and otherwise adorned. One day we compared notes, went into a painful but hilarious labor, and gave birth—to ourselves, we thought.

—from "The Politics of Body Image"
by Robin Morgan, September 1977

The issue that beat out the sexual harassment cover as the bestseller of 1977 had another provocative cover image, but this time the controversy began in the *Ms.* offices. It was the September issue, and the cover line read, "Why Women Don't Like Their Bodies." The line itself was not subject to debate, but rather the way it appeared as an illustrated tattoo running the length of a shapely woman's bare back. Robin Morgan, who wrote the introduction for the coverage inside on body image, hated it. Having just published *Going Too Far: The Personal Chronicle of a Feminist* and about to join *Ms.* as a contributing editor, Morgan argued vehemently that the cover was exploitative, not necessarily because the back was naked but because it was only the torso of a woman, from neck to mid-buttocks, and that turned her into an object, a commodity, which was exactly what the patriarchy was always doing to her. Others complained that the woman was too perfectly proportioned; she looked like a model, not a real woman. The counterpoint was that a woman can never look perfect enough in a sexist world. . . .

Robin Morgan and others who disliked the cover could take some solace from readers who wrote in to complain. One letter that was published said it was outrageous to feature the bare back of "a skinny white woman" and that it was "appalling that *Ms.* would stoop to a cheap method of selling magazines."

—Mary Thom, *Inside "Ms."*

·   ·   ·

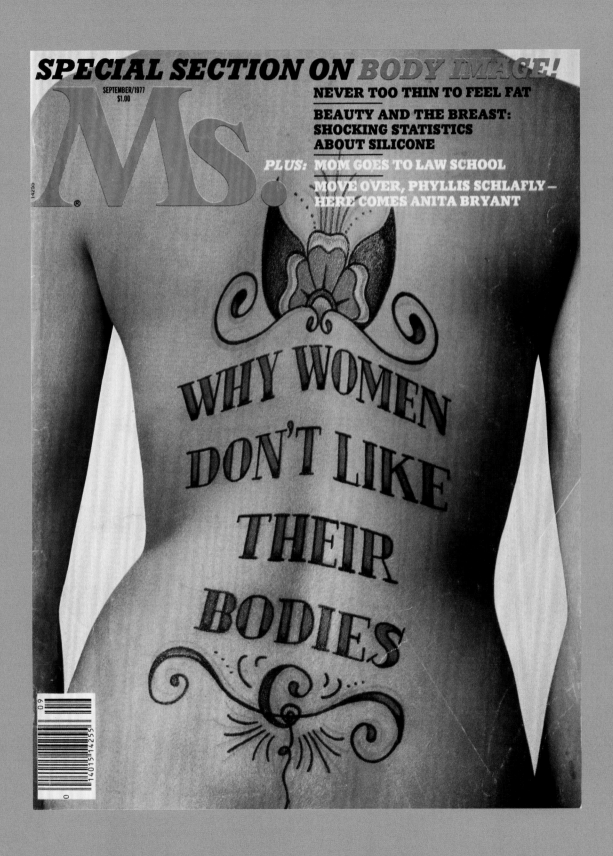

SEPTEMBER/1977
$1.00

SPECIAL SECTION ON BODY IMAGE!

Ms.

NEVER TOO THIN TO FEEL FAT

BEAUTY AND THE BREAST: SHOCKING STATISTICS ABOUT SILICONE

PLUS: **MOM GOES TO LAW SCHOOL**

MOVE OVER, PHYLLIS SCHLAFLY — HERE COMES ANITA BRYANT

WHY WOMEN DON'T LIKE THEIR BODIES

Lesbian Custody:
A Tragic Day in Court

BY **LINDSY VAN GELDER** • SEPTEMBER 1976

CENTRAL CASTING couldn't have picked a better test lesbian mother than Mary Jo Risher. Warm, articulate, and downright *straight* in every nonsexual sense of the word, the thirty-nine-year-old Texan is a college graduate and former Baptist Sunday school teacher, PTA president, and chaplain of the Order of the Eastern Star. After her divorce five years ago from Douglas L. Risher Jr., an aircraft mechanic, she was awarded custody of Jimmy, now eighteen, and Richard, now nine. For the past three years she has made her home with her lover, Ann Foreman, who is the mother of an eleven-year-old girl. The two women have recently started a small contracting business that specializes in interior decorating.

> **"Lesbian mothers . . . are routinely forced to answer two charges: that their sexuality is contagious . . . and that the 'stigma' of their lifestyle will hurt their offspring."**

They consider themselves "just like a heterosexual family," with the differences that "neither one of us depends on the other to fulfill any type of role." Theirs is a permanent commitment. They are each other's insurance beneficiaries, they have a joint checking account, and they co-own property. According to several psychologists, the children have an exceptionally loving stable family life.

Jimmy—who now maintains he's "ashamed" of his mother's lesbianism—lived with his father and stepmother for nine months. He is now married and had a child. His custody has not been an issue. But Richard wanted to stay with Mary Jo and Ann, and they chose to fight for him. That fight was lost last December, at least temporarily, when a Dallas jury ruled 10–2 that Richard should not, in the words of his father's attorney, be made "a guinea pig of someone else's social experiment." He was taken from Mary Jo and Ann's home the day after Christmas.

Mary Jo faced a particular legal handicap not shared by most lesbian mothers because of one child's desire to live with his father. (The courts traditionally feel that siblings should stay together.) The case was also atypical for another reason: although custody disputes are generally decided by lower court judges, the Risher case was tried by a jury. And as a comment on society's attitudes toward lesbianism and homosexuality—and on the broader feminist issue of sex roles—the Risher case threatens to set an ominous precedent.

Lesbian mothers (and gay fathers who want visitation rights or custody) are routinely forced to answer two charges: that their sexuality is contagious—that they will consciously or unconsciously teach their children to *be like them*—and that the "stigma" of their lifestyle will hurt their offspring. Mary Jo Risher's case was no different. Whereas the burden of proof should have fallen on her ex-husband to show that she wasn't a fit parent, it was she who had to prove that her lesbianism didn't "interfere" with her mothering.

In fact, Mary Jo's lawyers argued in a pretrial hearing that her sexuality shouldn't be an issue, but the judge ruled against them (a surprising variety of testimony is admissible in custody cases, even confidential doctor-patient information). As a result, lesbianism was on trial. Even jurors and witnesses were asked about their sexual preferences.

Much was made of the apparent heterosexual orientation of the children. According to a psychologist defense witness, Ann's daughter, Judie Ann, "is an especially pretty child, very charming, [who] espouses a traditional female role." Richard's sexual identity is "actually somewhat of a male stereotype. He wants to be a policeman." (One shudders to think of what would have been said if Richard wanted to be a nursery school teacher.) If the boy *did* decide to be gay, his mother said she would have him counseled "to see if that is truly what he wanted."

Despite all of this backward bending and egg walking, even the slightest deviations from traditional macho child-rearing practices were pounced on. A court-appointed psychologist conceded that Mary Jo was "a warm and loving parent," but urged the jury to take her son away anyway because she "exhibited poor judgment." He specifically cited two occasions when Richard showed up at the psychologist's office wearing "unsuitable clothing"—a suit belonging to Judie Ann and a YWCA T-shirt. Under cross-examination the psychologist acknowledged that the suit—actually jeans and a jacket—was a unisex outfit, and that since Richard was taking a gym course at the Y, the shirt was hardly high drag. He also admitted that he'd never mentioned the issue to Richard's mother. No matter. "It is not the actual fact of Richard wearing the clothing," he testified, "but Mary Jo was a lesbian and therefore should be more sensitive to Richard's appearance."

Mary Jo's witnesses included co-workers, friends, and Richard's pediatrician, as well as three prominent psychologists. In the words of one of them, "When a child is comfortable, happy, loved, I see no reason to remove the child . . . it would have detrimental effects. To remove this child would say we see something wrong with his mother and *this* would reflect on what he thinks of himself." Another witness was Ann's ex-husband, who also has remarried and who also considered instigating a custody fight until he had his daughter evaluated by a psychologist: "The psychologist said she and her mother had a good relationship and it would be much more harmful for us to try and remove her. It was more important to accept Ann for what she was."

Doug Risher's star witness was Jimmy, who recounted the joys of hunting and fishing with his father and asked the jury to "get my brother out of this particular home." Other witnesses included a Baptist minister, who noted that the Bible forbids homosexuality and also teaches women to "be submissive," and a social worker, who felt that Richard would be better off in a home where the mother didn't work. (At that time, Mary Jo was working extra shifts to help pay her legal defense costs.)

Doug Risher himself told the jurors, "I have a wife who could be there to attend to [Richard's] needs twenty-four hours a day. There would be a father and a mother image portrayed that he could model himself after. There would be outdoors and sports, vital to a young boy." Cross-examination revealed some interesting facts about this model dad. He once broke Mary Jo's nose during a fight. He has a drunken driving record. Between his marriages he hung out at singles' bars, had sex with several women, and was accused of impregnating an eighteen-year-old. Although he "had his doubts that he was the one responsible," he did cough up $150 toward an abortion when confronted by the young woman's father. None of this behavior apparently influenced the jury adversely. In fact, it might have come off as a machismo plus.

According to the jury foreman, the members of the panel believed that Mary Jo was a good mother, and "we tried to leave the homosexual issue out as best we could. [But] I felt the heterosexual family would be better for the child. . . . I felt we were taking him out of a good home just to put him in a better one." He added, "Not having a man there all the time had an effect on the decision." Lesbians, it would appear, are simply further along a continuum of second-rate parents that presumably includes single mothers and other people who don't adhere to the collie-dog-in-the-backyard nuclear-family model.

Not all lesbian mothers are as unfortunate as Mary Jo Risher. A major victory was won in Seattle in late 1974, when a superior court judge ruled that Madeleine C. Isaacson and Sandra L. Schuster no longer had to live "separate and apart" to keep their six children. Isaacson and Schuster had pushed their custody requirements to the limit by moving across the hall from each other. Nonetheless, their ex-husbands weren't able to meet the twofold test set down in Washington's 1973 Divorce Reform Act: proof that the current situation is "detrimental" to the children, and further proof that the harm caused by a custody change would be "outweighed" by new advantages. In general, the lesbian custody picture is still a bleak one, and to women like Mary Jo, other women's victories can't compensate for the loss of a child. The Risher case is in the process of being appealed.

"I'm one of those perceptive, aware forecasters who, five years ago, said, 'I give *Ms.* Magazine five months.'"

—*Harry Reasoner*

"That's what I said when I commented on the Preview Issue of *Ms.* 'They have said it all in this first little issue,' I remarked. 'After you've done marriage contracts, role-changing, female identity crisis, what do you do next? Organize foods for Christmas dinner, I expect.'

"But *Ms.* Magazine has shown us all—through personal writing, humor, political theory and first-class exposé journalism—that there is literally no subject feminism does not affect or transform.

"So happy 5th birthday and a big future to *Ms.*—from all of us who are glad we were wrong."—*Harry Reasoner*

Who reads *Ms.*? A higher percentage of women who worked for a political party than readers of *Psychology Today*; own life insurance than readers of *The New Yorker*; consume brandy or cognac than readers of *House Beautiful*.

Ms. is read by more than two million people who change minds and who aren't afraid of change themselves. Like our friend, Harry Reasoner.

And to all our friends, readers and advertisers, thank you for five history-making years.

Ms. Magazine. A good place to find yourself.

Ms. celebrated its fifth anniversary with a full-page ad in *The New York Times* in defiance of the skeptics who predicted the magazine would quickly run out of things to say.

Have You Ever Supported Equal Pay, Child Care, or Women's Groups? The FBI Was Watching You

BY **LETTY COTTIN POGREBIN** • JUNE 1977

ARE YOU NOW or have you ever been a member of the women's movement?

If so, you may find yourself in the 1,377 pages of memos, reports, teletypes, tape transcripts, press clippings, and leaflets released thus far from the material, gathered between 1969 and 1973, in the files of the Federal Bureau of Investigation under the subject heading "Women's Liberation Movement (WLM)."

Within its pages you may find your name (misspelled perhaps), your address, and in a few instances a physical description of yourself, your clothing, and your behavior; the names and addresses of groups you belonged to; the dates, times, and locations of meetings or rallies you might have attended; the slogans on your picket signs; and even the serial numbers on the bus that took you home.

> **"Wherever we were, they were—or tried to be: at street actions where we marched forty thousand strong, and at CR groups of as few as six women."**

"They" kept tabs on "us" with the aid of special agents, informers, observers, infiltrators, other law enforcement agencies, and red alert signals from conscientious citizens. They filed women's movement flyers, position papers, membership lists, newsletters, agendas, meeting notices, and conference reports. They listened to our radio interviews and clipped articles on us and by us, whether published in the straight press or the most obscure underground paper.

Wherever we were, they were—or tried to be: at street actions where we marched forty thousand strong, and at CR groups of as few as six women; at a building takeover at Harvard, and at a rally for Black Panther women at a New Haven, Connecticut, prison. They followed us to the Statue of Liberty, to women's studies courses, to a farm retreat in Pennsylvania, to protests against the Miss America pageant in Atlantic City, and to campuses from Oregon to Vermont.

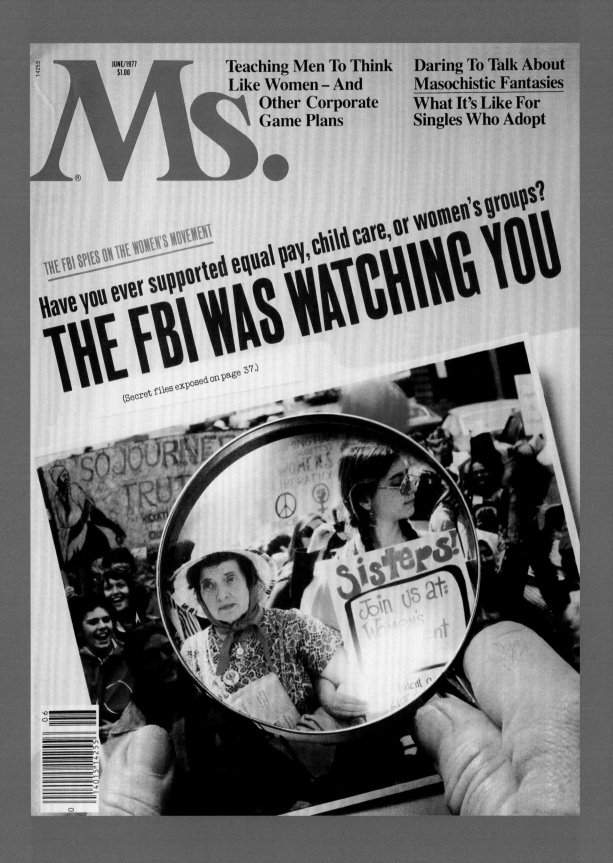

JUNE/1977
$1.00

Ms.

Teaching Men To Think Like Women – And Other Corporate Game Plans

Daring To Talk About Masochistic Fantasies

What It's Like For Singles Who Adopt

THE FBI SPIES ON THE WOMEN'S MOVEMENT

Have you ever supported equal pay, child care, or women's groups?

THE FBI WAS WATCHING YOU

(Secret files exposed on page 37.)

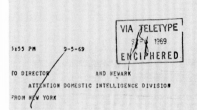

VIA TELETYPE
SEP 4 1969
ENCIPHERED

210PM   9-4-69
TO DIRECTOR AND NEWARK
    ATT DOMESTIC INTELLIGENCE DIVISION
FROM NEW YORK

WOMENS LIBERATION MOVEMENT

                    ADVISED   THE
WOMENS LIBERATION MOVEMENT FROM NEW YORK CITY IS PLANNING
TO GO TO ATLANTIC CITY SATURDAY SEPTEMBER SIXTH NEXT TO
DEMONSTRATE AT THE MISS AMERICA PAGEANT.
DESCRIBED THE GROUP AS A REACTIONARY GROUP OF WOMEN
FIGHTING FOR WOMAN'S EQUAL RIGHTS.
            IS ATTEMPTING TO DETERMINE HOW MANY WOMEN ARE
TRAVELLING TO ATLANTIC CITY AND TIME OF DEPARTURE.
NEW YORK WILL KEEP THE BUREAU AND NEWARK ADVISED.

VIA TELETYPE
SEP 5 1969
ENCIPHERED

5:55 PM   9-5-69
TO DIRECTOR   AND NEWARK
    ATTENTION DOMESTIC INTELLIGENCE DIVISION
FROM NEW YORK

WOMEN'S LIBERATION MOVEMENT

            FURNISHED INFORMATION CONCERNING WOMEN'S
LIBERATION MOVEMENT (WLM) ACTIVITY PLANNED IN CONNECTION WITH THE
MISS AMERICAN BEAUTY PAGEANT AT ATLANTIC CITY SEPTEMBER SIX
NEXT AS FOLLOWS:
    AN ANNOUNCEMENT WAS MADE AT A CITY-WIDE MEETING OF WLM,
ONE THREE THREE WEST FOURTH STREET, NEW YORK CITY ON SEPTEMBER
FOURTH LAST THAT BUSES WOULD DEPART FROM SEVENTEENTH STREET AND
UNION SQUARE, NEW YORK CITY AT NINE AM, SEPTEMBER SIXTH NEXT FOR
ATLANTIC CITY. THE NUMBER OF BUSES AND NUMBER OF PARTICIPANTS
WAS NOT KNOWN. AT ONE PM, SEPTEMBER FIVE INSTANT THE WLM GROUP WILL
PICKET, PERFORM GUERILLA THEATRE, SHOW MOVIES AND CONDUCT WORKSHOPS
ON THE BOARDWALD IN FRONT OF CONVENTION HALL. NO PLANS WERE
MADE TO DISRUPT THE PROCEEDINGS EITHER INSIDE OR OUTSIDE THE HALL.
THE WLM GROUP IS SCHEDULED TO RETURN TO NEW YORK AT ONE AM,
SEPTEMBER SEVEN NEXT.

An FBI file on the bureau's surveillance of the Miss America protest in Atlantic City in 1969, obtained by Letty Cottin Pogrebin, described the demonstrators as "a reactionary group of women fighting for woman's [*sic*] equal rights" (*top left*) and warned that the group was planning to "picket, perform guerilla theatre, show movies and conduct workshops on the boardwald [*sic*]" (*top right*). Furthermore, "they are protesting Miss America pageant to be racist and degrading to women" (*opposite*).

Early on, several field offices advised J. Edgar Hoover (FBI director from 1924 to 1972) that "active investigation" of the women's movement was unwarranted and that they wished to put the matter into "a closed status." The director flatly overruled them: "The Bureau does not concur with your recommendation that a report on WLM activity within your division is not warranted at this time. . . . [I]t is absolutely essential that we conduct sufficient investigation to clearly establish subversive ramifications of the WLM and to determine the potential for violence presented by the various groups connected with this movement as well as any possible threat they may represent to the internal security of the United States."

The FBI's mission was to discover violence in the women's movement. But the pickings were so pitifully slim that the agents resorted to describing what we didn't do wrong: "Demonstrations orderly and no violence occurred. No injuries to demonstrators or police. No incidents, no snipings, no looting, no arson, no damage to property, no arrests."

Among the most incriminating "facts" amassed against movement women were reports that we were not all heterosexual, nor were we all ladylike and attractive.

WLM attacks on "femininity" (as defined by the FBI) seem to have justified surveillance of the peaceful demonstrations at the Miss America

```
WASHINGTON
NEW YORK
1:20 AM /090/07/69/
TO DIRECTOR AND NEW YORK
     ( ATTN DOMESTIC INTELLIGENCE DIVISION )
FROM NEWARK

WOMEN'S LIBERATION MOVEMENT.


                                  ADVISED TODAY THAT
APPROXIMATELY SIXTY WOMEN MOSTLY IN LATE TWENTY'S AND EARLY THIRTY'S
DEMONSTRATED UNDER BANNER OF WOMEN'S LIBERATION AT KENNEDY PLAZA
OPPOSITE THE ENTRANCE TO CONVENTION HALL ATLANTIC CITYFROM ABOUT
THREE PM TO MIDNIGHT NINE SIX SIXTYNINE.
        THEY ARE PROTESTING MISS AMERICA PAGEANT TO BE RACIST AND DEGRADING
TO WOMEN.  DEMONSTRATION ORDERLY AND PEACEFUL.  NO INCIDENTS
TOOK PLACE.  NO FURTHER ACTION BEING TAKEN BY NEWARK.
```

pageant and the protest against the Bridal Show at the Felt Forum in New York City.

The FBI tabulated us by marital status, looks, age, class, race, and sexual preference. Perhaps they thought this bewildering, burgeoning movement could be reduced to some neat demographic profile. But they could never make sense of us. The Panther women showed up with the housewives. Revolutionary firebrands appeared to be comfortably middle class. High school hippies marched beside established professional women.

·   ·   ·

Ms.'s groundbreaking cover story preceded the Supreme Court's sexual harassment decision by nine years and Anita Hill's famous testimony by nearly fifteen years.

Some of the nonfeminist writing on sexual harassment still seems to assume that it has mostly to do with real sexual attraction; that women who are adept at "handling a pass" or at dressing and speaking in ways that aren't "provocative" will somehow be able to avoid it.

On the contrary, the range of ages and situations in which sexual harassment takes place makes clear that it is more often related to power than to sex. . . . The documentation that now exists also makes clear that what we have so far seen is only the tip of a very large and very destructive iceberg. . . .

Other preliminary evidence of this problem's seriousness are the first few lawsuits charging discrimination under Title VII of the Civil Rights Act. In one landmark case, Diane Williams, an employee of the Justice Department, was awarded $16,000 in back pay after being fired for refusing her boss's sexual advances. . . . The major question is what all the courts will conclude. The few lower courts that have reached decisions in these cases so far have not agreed on what forms of sexual harassment, if any, constitute sex discrimination. . . .

Whatever the possible remedy, there are some other conclusions to be drawn from the evidence now in. Logically enough, for instance, the women who are hardest hit by sexual harassment on the job are waitresses, clerical workers, and factory workers—women who are poorly paid to begin with and who cannot afford to quit their jobs (and are often heads of families, supporting themselves and their children on small salaries), or do not have the resources to pursue costly court cases. And, of course, their economic vulnerability is played on by their male bosses.

—from "Sexual Harassment on the Job and How to Stop It"
by Karen Lindsey, November 1977

Partly because of skittish newsstand policies, it was not the biggest seller of 1977. The device of using puppets for the cover was ingenious, and the image was powerful. The primary cover line, straightforward and inflammatory, read simply, "Special Report: Sexual Harassment on the Job and How to Stop It." Still, the magazine was pulled off the newsstands by one large distributor in the Midwest. Reports came back from a drugstore chain that the November issue would be too upsetting for its customers—they operated family stores, after all. The *Ms.* women suspected that the people upset were not customers at all but those who ran the businesses, men who like the members of the 1991 Senate Judiciary Committee [when Anita Hill testified] were immensely threatened by women who challenged the rules of the game by speaking out about sexual harassment. The cover won awards from both the Society of Illustrators and the Society of Publication Designers for that year. —Mary Thom, *Inside "Ms."*

.   .   .

If Men Could Menstruate

BY **GLORIA STEINEM** • OCTOBER 1978

A WHITE MINORITY of the world has spent centuries conning us into thinking that white skin makes people superior—even though the only thing it really does is make them more subject to ultraviolet rays and wrinkles. Male human beings have built whole cultures around the idea that penis envy is "natural" to women—though having such an unprotected organ might be said to make men vulnerable, and the power to give birth makes womb envy at least as logical.

> **"Men would brag about how long and how much."**

In short, the characteristics of the powerful, whatever they may be, are thought to be better than the characteristics of the powerless, and logic has nothing to do with it.

What would happen, for instance, if suddenly, magically, men could menstruate and women could not?

The answer is clear: menstruation would become an enviable, boastworthy, masculine event.

Men would brag about how long and how much.

Boys would mark the onset of menses, that longed-for proof of manhood, with religious ritual and stag parties.

Congress would fund a National Institute of Dysmenorrhea to help stamp out monthly discomforts.

Sanitary supplies would be federally funded and free.

Military men, right-wing politicians, and religious fundamentalists would cite menstruation ("*men*-struation") as proof that only men could serve in the army ("you have to give blood to take blood"), occupy political office ("can women be aggressive without that steadfast cycle governed by the planet Mars?"), be priests and ministers ("how could a woman give her blood for our sins?") or rabbis ("without the monthly loss of impurities, women remain unclean").

Male radicals, left-wing politicians, and mystics, however, would insist that women are equal, just different, and that any woman could enter their ranks if only she were willing to self-inflict a major wound every month ("you must give blood for the revolution"), recognize the preeminence of menstrual issues, or subordinate her selfness to all men in their Cycle of Enlightenment.

Street guys would brag ("I'm a three-pad man") or answer praise from a buddy ("Man, you lookin' good!") by giving five and saying, "Yeah, man, I'm on the rag!"

Men would convince women that intercourse was more pleasurable at "that time of the month." Lesbians would be said to fear blood and therefore life itself, though probably only because they needed a good menstruating man.

Of course, male intellectuals would offer the most moral and logical arguments. How could a woman master any discipline that demanded a sense of time, space, mathematics, or measurement, for instance, without that in-built gift for measuring the cycles of the moon and planets—and thus for measuring anything at all? In the rarefied fields of philosophy and religion, could women compensate for missing the rhythm of the universe? Or for their lack of symbolic death-and-resurrection every month?

Liberal males in every field would try to be kind: the fact that "these people" have no gift for measuring life or connecting to the universe, the liberals would explain, should be punishment enough.

And how would women be trained to react? One can imagine traditional women agreeing to all these arguments with a staunch and smiling masochism. ("The ERA would force housewives to wound themselves every month": Phyllis Schlafly.) Reformers and queen bees would try to imitate men and pretend to have a monthly cycle.

All feminists would explain endlessly that men, too, needed to be liberated from the false idea of Martian aggressiveness, just as women needed to escape the bonds of menses envy. Radical feminists would add that the oppression of the nonmenstrual was the pattern for all other forms of oppression. ("Vampires were our first freedom fighters!") Cultural feminists would develop a bloodless imagery in art and literature. Socialist feminists would insist that only under capitalism would men be able to monopolize menstrual blood.

In fact, if men could menstruate, the power justifications could probably go on forever.

If we let them.

> **STEINEM'S ESSAY** imagines a host of policies that seemed far-fetched at the time—among these, that menstrual products would be covered by federal funds and freely available. Today, these reforms are the heart of a global movement and legislative campaign.
>
> *Ms.* has been at the fore of reporting on advances for "menstrual equity," which include dozens of municipal and state laws that now mandate free pads and tampons in public schools, shelters, local jails and state prisons, and other public buildings. Scotland made headlines in 2020 when it became the first nation to ensure free menstrual products for all. Even the U.S. Congress addressed the issue: in 2018, it passed a law requiring menstrual products be freely provided in federal prisons; in 2020, as part of a pandemic relief package, it qualified menstrual products for inclusion in federal pretax allowance programs like Health Savings Accounts and Flexible Spending Accounts.

Letters

On Sunday, July 9, 1978, at 7:00 a.m., my daughter and I boarded a school bus at Philadelphia's Thirtieth Street Station bound for Washington, D.C., to demonstrate for the ERA. The waiting, the heat, the lack of sanitary facilities, the expense of money and energy, was shared by 100,000 other people.

When we returned home, nearly midnight, my husband told us how NBC Radio had covered the historic event: not with Gloria Steinem, Bella Abzug, Betty Friedan, or Ellie Smeal, but with Phyllis Schlafly, who claims to represent a nonexistent majority in opposition to the ERA.

It is true, violence was not anticipated. It is true, no one threatened to burn any bras. True, also, that efforts to pass the ERA have been going on since 1923. However, 100,000 demonstrators, albeit peaceful, are newsworthy.

NAME WITHHELD
July 10, 1978

While trying to complete the endless errands necessary to get married, my fiancé and I dutifully arrived at the county clerk's office with the items needed to obtain a marriage license. The woman behind the desk filled out several forms and then handed a large legal sheet to us for our signatures. My fiancé got to sign on the line marked "Principal," and I got to sign on the blank line underneath.

Next the woman handed me a suspicious-looking plastic bag marked "New Homemaker's Kit." It contained the following items: (1) a can of Spray 'n Wash; (2) some Bon Ami polishing cleaner; (3) a bottle of Fantastik; (4) a bottle of Bufferin; (5) coupons for *TV Guide* (so I know when the soap operas are on?), (6) panty hose, and (7) a long list of recommended magazines (*Ms.* was not on the list).

Saving the best for last, the kit included a paperback Harlequin romance! Inside the front cover were comments from satisfied readers. One summed up the attitude of the New Homemaker's Kit beautifully: "Harlequins help me to escape from housework into a world of romance, adventure, and travel."

PHEBE DUFF KELLY
Little Rock, Ark.
September 1978 issue

Final

BY **LINDA PASTAN** • FEBRUARY 1979

I studied
so long
for my life
that this morning when I waken
to it as if for the first time
someone is already walking
down the aisle
collecting the papers.

And indeed
all of the relevant blanks
have been filled in
with children lost
and found and lost again,
with meals served
and eaten
and cleared away.

Only one page
remains empty:
it is the hardest of all.
Its blanks are as white
as hospital corridors,
each of its question marks
is the shape
of a noose.

For I have been accused
of cheating, of writing
the same line
over and over again,
and once when I brushed my hair
sparks flew out
igniting
more than I intended.

Now is the time
for the shuffling of chairs,
the scribbling of excuses
on the margins. I did my best
but there were handicaps:
a low pain threshold,
so many words I couldn't choose
between them.

I studied
so long
for my life,
and all the time
morning had been parked
outside my window,
one wheel of the sun
resting against the curb.

Can so much light
be simply
to read by?
I open the curtain
to see,
just as the test
is over.

Letters

I started my *Ms.* subscription during my senior year in high school, some five years ago. The magazine fitted my radical image. I usually kept it hidden in my room, afraid of the reaction of Mom and Dad.

When I left for college, *Ms.* still came to my parents' home, and I picked it up during visits. A delightful thing happened because I wasn't there to intercept the magazine directly: Mom paged through it and began reading the articles. She'd ask me questions; we'd discuss a specific story or disagree over the tone of a letter.

Last year, Mom went back to school to pick up the required credits as a nurse's aide. Now, after raising eight children—ranging in age from nine to twenty-three—Mom has a new job: a career that is making her happy.

One day my father and I were talking, and he told me that he believed that I was the cause of Mom wanting to work. All my extreme ideas, all those "liberated magazines" I had sent to the house, he said, had influenced Mom to the point of rebellion. I was glad to be held responsible.

DIANE M. WILKE
St. Francis, Wis.
February 1979 issue

I don't believe what I did after reading the article by Maureen R. Michelson. Let me explain.

I work in the admitting office of a hospital, and women are admitted all the time suffering from tumors in the breast. If the tumors are diagnosed as malignant, a radical or partial radical mastectomy is performed. These women have decided upon surgery because of their doctor's advice, and he has not told them of other methods of treatment and recovery percentages. Patients have the right to be informed, and so also does the doctor.

What I did after reading the article was to take copies and covertly place one in each of the surgeons' mailboxes. If they were not aware of alternate treatments, they are now!

NAME WITHHELD
May 1979 issue

My husband ordered "you" last fall from a high school senior who was raising funds. It took me six months to get used to having a magazine of my own to read. I am writing this during my only "quiet, alone" time—five minutes before I dash off to teach fourth grade.

I have raised three daughters, aged twenty-two, twenty-one, and seventeen. My twenty-four-and-a-half-year marriage is as typical as a 1950s romance can be! As we try to change the roles of a male-dominated household, you can hear the creaks and cracks (or is it screams?).

LOUISE BEMENT
Lansing, N.Y.
October 5, 1979

Ms.

December 21, 1979

Dear Ms. Family:

The New Ms. isn't exactly in new clover, but nothing
should begin without a gesture of faith in each other
and in the future. If it weren't for the unmatchable
concentration of dedication, energy and talent in
these few rooms, there wouldn't be a New Ms. - and
the world might be a measurably different place for
many women who are far outside these rooms.

Therefore, the Salary Committee (Pat, Gloria and Suzanne) has voted to count up the years that each person has served and multiply by $100. The result is a
holiday bonus.

And the bigger result will be bread-cast-upon-the-
waters that comes back buttered in the future.

Happy New Ms.

Happy New Decade.

Happy holidays!

Pat
Gloria
Suzanne

370 Lexi
New York
21

Office memos to the *Ms.* staff—
the good and the bad.

Ms.

To: Rhoda, JE, PC

If our friend reappears again, call 911
and ask them to send someone over,
that a complaint has been previously
filed. Try to keep him here and quiet
and when cops arrive give them the
complaint number   31586.
It is in Joanne Edgar's name and
charges trespassing and harrassment -
we'd prefer to stay with trespassing
alone.

the complaint is filed with Midtown
South Precinct (239-9811) by officer
Jurgielski.

other info: Gary Skelton Sonerk
               47 morewood Oaks
               Port Washington NY 11050
     car: blue capri (NY) 737 YIJ

SL

CHAPTER 2

1980s

BY THE 1980s, with the rise of the religious right and its determination to reverse the gains of the women's, civil, and gay rights movements, *Ms.* covered the urgent fights of the moment—from rollbacks on abortion rights to the stalling of the drive for the Equal Rights Amendment. The editor in chief Suzanne Braun Levine led the magazine through much of this turbulent decade.

Ms. was published as a nonprofit magazine through the Ms. Foundation for Education and Communication. Unable to secure significant revenues from paid advertising, a persistent problem that would eventually lead to the decision to publish ad-free, *Ms.* began encountering financial troubles; Gloria Steinem and Pat Carbine fundraised to keep it afloat. In 1988, *Ms.* was sold to John Fairfax Ltd., in a deal brokered by Sandra Yates and Anne Summers, Australian women who'd started the teen magazine *Sassy* and were acquainted with the leadership at *Ms.* Right before the sale, in the December 1987 issue of *Ms.*, Steinem assured readers Yates and Summers were "real feminists with access to real financial support." Almost immediately, though, Fairfax underwent a reorganization and made moves to sell off *Ms.*; Yates and Summers quickly acquired it under a new company they formed called Matilda Publications. When *Sassy*'s advertisers became the target of a boycott organized by Jerry Falwell's Moral Majority, more financial instability ensued. *Ms.* changed hands again, through a sale to Lang Communications in 1989.

During the tumultuous two years, anxious staff stayed on and kept writing, even though, for a short period at the very end of the decade, publication of *Ms.* was temporarily suspended.

In the *Ms.* offices in 1980 (*left to right*): staffers Mary Thom, Susan McHenry, Gloria Steinem, Joan Philpott, and Cathy O'Haire.

The Question No One Would Answer

BY **NAWAL EL SAADAWI** • MARCH 1980

I WAS SIX YEARS OLD that night when I lay in my bed, warm and peaceful in that pleasurable state which lies halfway between wakefulness and sleep. I felt something move under the blankets, something like a huge hand, cold and rough, fumbling over my body, as though looking for something. Almost simultaneously another hand, as cold and as rough and as big as the first one, was clapped over my mouth to prevent me from screaming.

They carried me to the bathroom. I do not know how many of them there were, nor do I remember their faces, or whether they were women or men. The world seems enveloped in a dark fog; perhaps they put some kind of cover over my eyes. All I remember is that I was frightened and that there were many of them, and that something like an iron grasp caught hold of my hand, and my arms, and my thighs, so that I became unable to resist or even to move. I also remember the icy touch of the bathroom tiles under my naked body and unknown voices and humming sounds interrupted now and again by a rasping metallic sound, which reminded me of the butcher when he used to sharpen his knife before slaughtering a sheep for the Eid (festival).

> **"I did not know what they had cut off, and I did not try to find out."**

My blood was frozen in my veins. I thought thieves had broken into my room and kidnapped me from my bed. I was afraid they were getting ready to cut my throat, which was what always happened with disobedient girls in the stories my old rural grandmother told.

I strained my ears trying to catch the metallic, rasping sound. The moment it ceased, I felt as though my heart had stopped beating, too. I was unable to see, and somehow my breathing seemed to stop. Yet I imagined the rasping sound coming closer and closer to me. Somehow it was not approaching my neck as I had expected, but another part of my body, somewhere below my belly, as though seeking something buried between my thighs. At that very moment, I realized that my thighs had been pulled wide apart, and that each of my legs was being held as far away from the other as possible, as though gripped by steel fingers that never relinquished their pressure. Then suddenly the sharp metallic edge dropped between my thighs and cut off a piece of flesh from my body. I screamed with pain despite the tight hand over my mouth. The pain was like a searing flare that went through my whole body. After a few moments, I saw a red pool of blood around my hips.

I did not know what they had cut off, and I did not try to find out. I just wept and called out to my mother for help. But the worst shock of all was when I looked around and found her standing by my side. Yes, it was she. In flesh and blood, right in the midst of these strangers, she was talking to them and smiling at them, as though they had not just participated in slaughtering her daughter.

They carried me to my bed. Then I saw them catch my four-year-old sister in exactly the same way they had caught me. I cried out with all my might. No! No! I could see my sister's face held between the big rough hands. It had a deathly pallor. Her wide black eyes met mine for a split second, a glance of terror that I can never forget. A moment later, she was gone, behind the door of the bathroom where I had just been. The look we exchanged seemed to say, "Now we know what it is. Now we know where our tragedy lies. We were born of a special sex, the female sex. We are destined in advance to taste misery, and to have a part of our body torn away by cold, unfeeling hands."

My family was not an uneducated Egyptian family. On the contrary, both my parents had been fortunate enough to have a very good education, by the standards of those days. My father was a university graduate and that year had been appointed general controller of education for Menoufia, then a province of the delta region north of Cairo. My mother had been sent to French schools by her father, who was director general of army recruitment. Nevertheless, this custom of clitoridectomy for girls was very prevalent then, and no girl could escape having her clitoris excised, regardless of her social class or whether her family lived in a rural or an urban area. When I recovered from the operation and returned to school, I asked my friends about what happened to me, only to discover that all of them, without exception, had been through the same experience.

For years, the memory of my clitoridectomy continued to track me down like a nightmare. I had a feeling of insecurity, fear of the unknown, waiting for me at every step I took into the future. I did not know if there were other such surprises being stored up for me by my mother and father, or my grandmother, or the people around me. Since that day, society had made me feel that I was a girl, and I saw that the word *bint* (girl) when pronounced by anyone was almost always accompanied by a frown.

Time and again I asked myself why girls were made to undergo this barbaric procedure. But I could never get an answer to this question, just as I was never able to get an answer to the questions that had raced around in my mind the day that both my sister and I were clitoridectomized.

Somehow this question seemed to be linked to other things that puzzled me. Why did they favor my brother when it came to food? Why did he have freedom to go out of the house? Why could he laugh at the top of his voice, run and play as much as he wished, when I was not even supposed to look into people's eyes directly? My duties were primarily to help in cleaning house and cooking, in addition to studying. My brother, however, was not expected to do anything but study.

My father was a broad-minded man who tried as best he could to treat his children equally. I used to feel sorry for my young girl relatives when they were forced out of school in order to get married to an old man just because he owned some land, or when their younger brothers could humiliate and beat them because boys could act superior to their sisters. My own brother tried to dominate me, though my mother used to say that a girl is equal to a boy. I used to rebel, sometimes violently, and ask why my brother was accorded privileges not given to me, despite the fact that I was doing better than he was at school. Neither my mother nor my father ever had any answer except "It is so." I would retort, "Why should it be so?" and back would come the answer, unchanged: "Because it is so."

Even after I grew up and graduated as a doctor in 1955, I could not forget the painful incident that made me lose my childhood, that deprived me during my youth and for years of married life from enjoying the fullness of my sexuality and completeness of life that can only come from psychological equilibrium. Nightmares followed me throughout the years, especially during the period when I was working as a medical doctor in rural areas where I often had to treat young girls who had come to the outpatients' clinic bleeding profusely after this mutilation. Many died as a result of the primitive way in which clitoridectomies were performed. Others were afflicted with acute or chronic infections from which they sometimes suffered for the rest of their lives. And most, if not all, became the victims of sexual or mental distortions later as a result of this savage experience.

Since the day of my terror, I have realized that I had to find my own answer to the question that no one would answer.

SINCE 2008, thirteen countries have passed laws banning female genital mutilation (FGM). And in 2012, the UN General Assembly created the International Day of Zero Tolerance for Female Genital Mutilation, adopting a resolution to commit to ending the practice worldwide. These efforts are vital: today there are as many as 200 million girls and women around the globe who have been subjected to FGM—a number that could potentially increase by nearly seventy million by 2030.

·   ·   ·

The Life Story That Asks the Question: "Can a Girl from a Little Town in North Carolina Find Happiness

AS A PRIEST / POET/ LAWYER / TEACHER / REVOLUTIONARY / FEMINIST/ CIVIL RIGHTS ACTIVIST?"

BY **CASEY MILLER** AND **KATE SWIFT** • MARCH 1980

I WILL RESIST every attempt to categorize me, to place me in some caste, or to assign me to some segregated pigeonhole," Pauli Murray wrote soon after earning her law degree from Howard University. "No law which imprisons my body or custom which wounds my spirit can stop me."

That was in 1944. She had already been denied admission to the University of North Carolina because of her race and to Harvard Law School because of her sex. She had been jailed in Virginia for refusing to move to the back of an interstate bus. For the next three decades, as a constitutional lawyer, she played a significant, though rarely visible, role in advancing the cause of civil rights. Now an ordained priest of the Episcopal Church, she continues, at sixty-nine, to fight laws and customs that discriminate on the basis of race or sex.

> **"Murray confronted him. 'You and I have been told to use the back doors all our lives,' she said, 'I think you'll understand why I have no intention of doing so any longer.'"**

Murray sees her lifework—and her life—as the reconciliation of the most divisive conflicts in our society. Whenever biographical references describe her as "the granddaughter of a slave," she adds, "And great-granddaughter of a slave owner."

"True emancipation," she explains, "lies in the acceptance of the whole past, in deriving strength from all my roots."

It was Murray who, while a law student at Howard, developed the strategy for employing nonviolent civil action that was widely used in the South in the 1960s. She taught techniques of confidence and self-restraint to students who then applied them in sit-ins that successfully desegregated two Washington, D.C., restaurants in 1943–44. When Murray found a still

Gloria Steinem (*left*) with publisher Patricia Carbine in 1980.

extant nineteenth-century city ordinance prohibiting discrimination in public accommodations, she asked a number of lawyers to test it. "Nobody [was] interested," she recalls. "But eight years later the veteran suffragist Mary Church Terrell, at age ninety, picked up where we left off. Her case went to the Supreme Court and in 1953 ended segregation in public accommodations in the nation's capital. I've been both a winner and a loser, but after I lose, someone else wins, because this is a relay race."

Another lap in that race involved Murray's 1944 senior law thesis at Howard in which she examined the Supreme Court's civil rights decisions in the late nineteenth century. She stressed the futility of the "separate but equal" doctrine invented by the court in the *Plessy v. Ferguson* decision of 1896. "Not only is the doctrine a legal delusion," she wrote, "but its effect is to do violence to the personality of the individual affected." Her words were echoed ten years later in *Brown v. Board of Education,* when the Supreme Court held that separate schools generate "a feeling of inferiority" in Negro children and are therefore "inherently unequal."

Sometime after that decision, Murray called on one of her Howard professors and asked how she could get her senior thesis back, since she had turned in her only copy. "Oh, I have your paper," said the professor, who had helped prepare the *Brown* case. "When I first read it, I didn't think much of it. Then when we were right up against *Plessy v. Ferguson* in 1953, I read it again and it sounded better, and we were able to use it in *Brown.*" Although she never received credit for contributing to the pivotal argument in that landmark decision, Murray feels no bitterness. "Sexism isn't always deliberate," she says. "It's just that you don't count."

As the only woman in her law class at Howard, she had come to realize that male attitudes toward women were similar to whites' attitudes toward Blacks. First in her class, she won a Julius Rosenwald scholarship, specifically designated for graduate study in law at Harvard. But Harvard refused to admit her ("Your picture and the salutation on your transcript indicate you are not of the sex entitled to be admitted to Harvard"), and she earned her master's degree in law at the University of California at Berkeley. After several years practicing on her own, she joined the New York firm of Paul, Weiss, Rifkind, Wharton & Garrison.

In the late 1940s, Murray researched and compiled *States' Laws on Race and Color,* which the Supreme Court justice Thurgood Marshall once described as the "bible" of the NAACP legal staff during the breakthrough years in civil rights. But as the civil rights movement coalesced, opposition stiffened, foreshadowing the violence and racial polarization to come. In April 1959, a Black man named Mack Parker was lynched in Mississippi. Although his murderers were known, they were never indicted. "Each of us reaches a point where we can't take it anymore," Murray says. "I reached it with Poplarville. My depression was so deep I had to get away." She contracted to teach law at the University of Ghana, believing she would never return to this country.

But Africa proved to her that she was and wished to remain an American. "I could not evade the impelling conviction," she wrote, "that my own task was not to expound democratic values to Africans, but to realize those values in American Life." So, she came home and, as a Ford Foundation Fellow, earned a doctor of juridical science degree from Yale Law School in 1965. (In 1979, she received an honorary doctorate from Yale.)

A New Haven friend remembers an incident from those years that typifies this slight, wiry woman whose energy seems boundless. The two women were meeting for lunch at the Graduate Club. As they approached the front door, the doorman, who was Black, stopped them and said they would have to use the "Ladies' Entrance" at the back of the building. Murray confronted him. "You and I have been told to use the back doors all our lives," she said, "I think you'll understand why I have no intention of doing so any longer."

In the 1960s, Murray's activities began to reflect more explicitly this double burden of discrimination. She served on the Civil and Political Rights Committee of President Kennedy's Commission on the Status of Women, for example, and was an early consultant to the Equal Employment Opportunity Commission and a founder of the National Organization for Women.

In 1968, she began teaching at Brandeis University. Some of her students were active in the radical feminist movement, and their questions stirred many of her own, especially about the role her church was playing, had played for centuries, in the subordination of women. She had always been active in the Episcopal Church. "But one day," she says, "I simply couldn't take Communion. I sat there and said, 'Why can't women be crucifers? Why can't they be servers?'"

It was the beginning of her fight to open the eyes of the church's male

---

PAULI MURRAY, born in 1910, had emerged as a civil rights pioneer by the 1930s. The friendships Murray forged at that time included the then First Lady, Eleanor Roosevelt (see Patricia Bell-Scott's *The Firebrand and the First Lady*), after writing to her and President Franklin Roosevelt protesting segregation in the South. They would remain friends for twenty-five years. Murray went on to earn a JD and advanced law degrees—ever a brilliant strategist and seeker of justice whose constitutional interpretations and writing fueled watershed victories for public school desegregation, women's rights in the workplace, and an extension of rights to LGBTQ+ people under Title VII of the 1964 Civil Rights Act. When the National Organization for Women was founded in 1966, Murray helped write its statement of purpose. She served in key public leadership roles, ranging from President Kennedy's Commission on the Status of Women to academic appointments. Murray's vision influenced the jurisprudence of Thurgood Marshall and Ruth Bader Ginsburg.

A 2021 documentary about the life and contributions of Pauli Murray received critical acclaim, including the Alfred I. duPont–Columbia University Award for broadcast and documentary journalism. The feature-length film, *My Name Is Pauli Murray,* was created decades after Murray died in 1985 and is told through a combination of archival footage and interviews, including with family members, a generation of students, and classmates such as Congresswoman Eleanor Holmes Norton and Justice Ginsburg (before her own death in 2020). Murray's written words also animate the film, including published nonfiction and poetry, as well as personal letters. The film brings to life Murray's foresight and care in forging groundbreaking legal frameworks on racial, gender, and economic inequality.

hierarchy to a growing sense of alienation among women. Using her skills as a lawyer and teacher, she joined others in bombarding bishops, priests, and the laity with carefully reasoned, historically sound memorandums. Progress was slow, however, and for a year Pauli Murray left the church. "I literally wandered in the wilderness," she says, "walking my dog by the Charles River, searching for God." In 1973, a dear friend of many years died of cancer. Watching her die, Murray wrote later, was "a special gift of unremitting heartache which changed my life," for the experience led her not only back to the church but to her bishop to seek ordination. When she resigned her tenured post at Brandeis to enter the seminary and a new career, she was sixty-two years old.

In 1977, one week after the Episcopal Church officially accepted women into the priesthood, Murray was ordained.

Even as the nation's first Black woman priest, she still resists being pigeonholed or made a token. When asked, for example, to give the benediction at a U.S. Postal Service ceremony marking the issuance of the Harriet Tubman commemorative stamp, she was incensed to find herself the only woman among eight dignitaries chosen to honor another woman.

"So, before I give the benediction, will all the women and girls in the auditorium stand in silent tribute to Harriet Tubman?" The storm of applause that followed was a tribute to Pauli Murray as well.

Life on the Global Assembly Line

BY **BARBARA EHRENREICH**
AND **ANNETTE FUENTES** • JANUARY 1981

EVERY MORNING, between four and seven, thousands of women head out for the day shift. In Ciudad Juárez, they crowd into *ruteras* (rundown vans) for the trip from the slum neighborhoods to the industrial parks on the outskirts of the city. In Penang they squeeze, sixty or more at a time, into buses for the trip to the low, modern factory buildings of the Bayan Lepas free trade zone. In Taiwan, they walk from the dormitories—where the night shift is already asleep in the still-warm beds—through the checkpoints in the high fence surrounding the factory zone.

This is the world's new industrial proletariat: young, female, Third World. Viewed from the "First World," they are still faceless, genderless "cheap labor," signaling their existence only through a label or tiny imprint reading, "Made in Hong Kong SAR," or Taiwan region, Korea, the Dominican Republic, Mexico, the Philippines. But they may be one of the most strategic blocs of womanpower in the world. Conservatively, there are two million Third World female industrial workers employed now, millions more looking for work, and their numbers are rising every year.

> **"'Young male workers are too restless and impatient to do monotonous work with no career value . . . But girls? At most, they cry a little.'"**

It doesn't take more than second-grade arithmetic to understand what's happening. In the United States, an assembly-line worker is likely to earn, depending on her length of employment, between $3.10 and $5.00 an hour. In many Third World countries, a woman doing the same work will earn $3.00 to $5.00 a day.

And so, almost everything that can be packed up is being moved out to the Third World: garment manufacture, textiles, toys, footwear, pharmaceuticals, wigs, appliance parts, tape decks, computer components, plastic goods. In some industries, like garment and textile, American jobs are lost in the process, and the biggest losers are women, often those who are Black or Hispanic. But what's going on is much more than a matter of runaway shops. Economists are talking about a "new international division of labor," in which the process of production is broken down and the fragments are dispersed to different parts of the world, while control of the overall process and technology remains safely at company headquarters in "First World" countries.

The American electronics industry provides a classic example: circuits are printed on silicon wafers and tested in California; then the wafers are shipped to Asia for the labor-intensive process by which they are cut into tiny chips and bonded to circuit boards; final assembly into products such as calculators or military equipment usually takes place in the United States. Garment manufacture too is often broken into geographically separated steps, with the most repetitive, labor-intensive jobs going to the poor countries of the Southern Hemisphere.

So much any economist could tell you. What is less often noted is the gender breakdown of the emerging international division of labor. Eighty to 90 percent of the low-skilled assembly jobs that go to the Third World are performed by women in a remarkable switch from earlier patterns of foreign-dominated industrialization. Until now, "development" under the aegis of foreign corporations has usually meant more jobs for men and—compared with traditional agricultural society—a diminished economic status for women. But multinational corporations and Third World governments alike consider assembly-line work—whether the product is Barbie dolls or missile parts—"women's" work.

It's an article of faith with management that only women can do, or will do, the monotonous, painstaking work that American business is exporting to the Third World. The personnel manager of a light assembly plant in Taiwan told the anthropologist Linda Gail Arrigo, "Young male workers are too restless and impatient to do monotonous work with no career value. If displeased, they sabotage the machines and even threaten the foreman. But girls? At most, they cry a little."

A top-level management consultant who specializes in advising American companies on where to relocate gave us this global generalization: "The [factory] girls genuinely enjoy themselves. They're away from their families. They have spending money. Of course it's a regulated experience too—with dormitories to live in—so it's a healthful experience."

What is the real experience of the women in the emerging Third World industrial workforce? Rachael Grossman, a researcher with the Southeast Asia Resource Center, found women employees of U.S. multinational firms in Malaysia and the Philippines living four to eight in a room in boarding-houses, or squeezing into tiny extensions built onto squatter huts near the factory. Where companies do provide dormitories, they are not of the "healthful," collegiate variety. The American Friends Service Committee (AFSC) reports that dormitory space is "likely to be crowded—while one shift works, another sleeps, as many as twenty to a room."

Living conditions are only part of the story. The work that multinational corporations export to the Third World is not only the most tedious but often the most hazardous part of the production process. The countries these corporations go to are, for the most part, those that will guarantee no interference from health and safety inspectors, trade unions, or even freelance reformers.

Consider the electronics industry, which is generally thought to be the safest and cleanest of the exported industries. The factory buildings are low and modern, like those one might find in a suburban American industrial park. Inside, rows of young women, neatly dressed in the company uniform or T-shirt, work quietly at their stations. There is air-conditioning (not for the women's comfort, but to protect the delicate semiconductor parts they work with) and high-volume piped-in Bee Gees hits (not so much for entertainment as to prevent talking).

For many Third World women, electronics is a prestige occupation, at least compared with other kinds of factory work. They are unlikely to know that in the United States the National Institute for Occupational Safety and

In Ciudad Juárez, Mexico, Anna M. rises at 5 A.M. to feed her son before starting on the two-hour bus trip to the maquiladora (factory). He will spend the day along with four other children in a neighbor's one-room home. Anna's husband, frustrated by being unable to find work for himself, left for the United States six months ago. She wonders, as she carefully applies her new lip gloss, whether she ought to consider herself still married. It might be good to take a night course, become a secretary. But she seldom gets home before eight at night, and the factory, where she stitches brassieres that will be sold in the United States through J.C. Penney, pays only $48 a week.

In Penang, Malaysia, Julie K. is up before the three other young women with whom she shares a room, and starts heating the leftover rice from last night's supper. She looks good in the company's green-trimmed uniform, and she's proud to work in a modern, American-owned factory. Only not quite so proud as when she started working three years ago—she thinks as she squints out the door at a passing group of women. Her job involves peering all day through a microscope, bonding hair-thin gold wires to a silicon chip destined to end up inside a pocket calculator, and at 21, she is afraid she can no longer see very clearly.

Every morning, between four and seven, thousands of women like Anna and Julie head out for the day shift. In Ciudad Juárez, they crowd into ruteras (run-down vans) for the trip from the slum neighborhoods to the industrial parks on the outskirts of the city. In Penang they squeeze, 60 or more at a time, into buses for the trip from the village to the low, modern factory buildings of the Bayan Lepas free trade zone. In Taiwan, they walk from the dormitories—where the night shift is already asleep in the still-warm beds—through the checkpoints in the high fence surrounding the factory zone.

This is the world's new industrial proletariat: young, female, Third World. Viewed from the "first world," they are still faceless, genderless "cheap labor," signaling their existence only through a label or tiny imprint—"made in Hong Kong," or Taiwan, Korea, the Dominican Republic, Mexico, the Philippines. But they may be one of the most strategic blocs of womanpower in the world of the 1980s. Conservatively, there are 2 million Third World female industrial workers employed now, millions more looking for work, and their numbers are rising every year. Anyone whose image of Third World women features picturesque peasants with babies slung on their backs should be prepared to update it. Just in the last decade, Third World women have become a critical element in the global econ-

SPECIAL REPORT:

LIFE ON THE GLOBAL ASSEMBLY LINE

By Barbara Ehrenreich and Annette Fuentes

The "manual dexterity of the Oriental female is famous the world over," boasts a Malaysian brochure. (Left) Young women in a Taejon, Korea, leather factory.

It's cheaper to train teenagers than to pay for experience. Age 30 is over the hill in most industries. (Above) A garment sewer in Kaosiung, Taiwan.

Health (NIOSH) has placed electronics on its select list of "high health-risk industries using the greatest number of toxic substances." If electronics assembly work is risky here, it is doubly so in countries where there is no equivalent of NIOSH to even issue warnings. In many plants toxic chemicals and solvents sit in open containers, filling the work area with fumes that can literally knock you out. "We have been told of cases where ten to twelve women passed out at once," an AFSC field worker in northern Mexico told us, "and the newspapers report this as 'mass hysteria.'"

Some of the worst conditions have been documented in South Korea, where the garment and textile industries have helped spark that country's "economic miracle." Workers are packed into poorly lit rooms where summer temperatures rise above a hundred degrees. Textile dust, which can cause permanent lung damage, fills the air. Management may require forced overtime of as much as forty-eight hours at a stretch, and if that seems to go beyond the limits of human endurance, pep pills and amphetamine injections are thoughtfully provided.

In all the exported industries, the most invidious, inescapable health hazard is stress. Lunch breaks may be barely long enough for a woman to stand in line at the canteen or hawkers' stalls. Visits to the bathroom are treated as privileges. Rotating shifts—the day shift one week, the night shift the next—wreak havoc with sleep patterns. Because inaccuracies or failure to meet production quotas can mean substantial pay losses, the pressures are quickly internalized; stomach ailments and nervous problems are not unusual.

As if poor health and the stress of factory life weren't enough to drive women into early retirement, management actually encourages a high turn-over in many industries. "As you know, when seniority rises, wages rise," the management consultant to U.S. multinationals told us. He explained that it's cheaper to train a fresh supply of teenagers than to pay experienced women higher wages. "Older" women, aged twenty-three or twenty-four, are likely to be laid off and not rehired.

The lucky ones find husbands. The unlucky ones find themselves at the margins of society—as bar girls, "hostesses," or prostitutes.

There has been no international protest about the exploitation of Third World women by multinational corporations—no thundering denuncia-tions from the floor of the UN General Assembly, no angry resolutions from the Conference of the Non-aligned Countries. The sociologist Robert Snow, who has been tracing the multinationals on their way south and eastward for years, explained why. "The Third World governments want the multinationals to move in. There's cutthroat competition to attract the corporations."

The governments themselves gain little revenue from this kind of investment—especially since most offer tax holidays and freedom from export duties in order to attract the multinationals in the first place. Nor do the people as a whole benefit, according to a highly placed Third World woman within the UN. "The multinationals like to say they're contributing to development," she told us, "but they come into our countries for one thing—cheap labor. If the labor stops being so cheap, they can move on. So how can you call that development? It depends on the people being poor and staying poor." But there are important groups that do stand to gain when the multinationals set up shop in their countries: local entrepreneurs who subcontract to the multinationals, "technocrats" who become local management, and government officials who specialize in cutting red tape for an "agent's fee" or an outright bribe.

In the competition for multinational investment, local governments advertise their women shamelessly. An investment brochure issued by the Malaysian government informs multinational executives that "the manual dexterity of the Oriental female is famous the world over. Her hands are small, and she works fast with extreme care. . . . Who, therefore, could be better qualified by nature and inheritance, to contribute to the efficiency of a bench-assembly production line than the Oriental girl?" Many "host" governments are willing to back up their advertising with whatever brutal-ity it takes to keep "their girls" just as docile as they look in the brochures.

Even the most polite and orderly attempts to organize are likely to bring down overkill doses of police repression.

Then there is the World Bank, which over the past decade has lent several billion dollars to finance the roads, the airports, the power plants, and even the first-class hotels that multinational corporations need in order to set up business in Third World countries.

But the most powerful promoter of exploitative conditions for Third World women workers is the U.S. government itself. For example, the notoriously repressive Korean textile industry was developed with the help of $400 million in aid from the U.S. State Department. Malaysia became a low-wage haven for the electronics industry thanks to technical assistance financed by USAID and to U.S. money (funneled through the Asian Development Bank) to set up free trade zones.

But the most obvious form of U.S. involvement, according to Lenny Siegel, the director of the Pacific Studies Center, is through "our consistent record of military aid to Third World governments that are capitalist, [are] politically repressive, and are not striving for economic independence."

So far, feminism, First World style, has barely begun to acknowledge the Third World's new industrial womanpower. Jeb Mays and Kathleen Connell, co-founders of the San Francisco–based Women's Network on Global Corporations, are two women who would like to change that. "There's still this idea of the Third World woman as 'the other'—someone exotic and totally unlike us," Mays and Connell told us. "But now we're talking about women who wear the same styles in clothes, listen to the same music, and may even work for the same corporation. That's an irony the multinationals have created. In a way, they're drawing us together as women."

Saralee Hamilton, an AFSC staff organizer, says, "The multinational corporations have deliberately targeted women for exploitation. If feminism is going to mean anything to women all over the world, it's going to have to find new ways to resist corporate power internationally." She envisions a global network of grassroots women capable of sharing experiences, transmitting information, and—eventually—providing direct support for each other's struggles. It's a long way off; few women anywhere have the money for intercontinental plane flights or even long-distance calls, but at least we are beginning to see the way. "We all have the same hard life," wrote the Korean garment worker Min Chong Suk. "We are bound together with one string."

OPPOSITE The February 1981 cover featured an edgy biblical backdrop to convey the federal government's heavy-handed regulation of women's reproductive rights and warn of the danger posed by a so-called human life amendment, which would have given personhood to fertilized eggs and embryos. In the cover story, Gloria Steinem noted that "if the patriarchal state, church, and family lose their control over women's bodies as the most basic means of production—the means of *re*production—those structures eventually become more democratic, and not patriarchal at all."

•   •   •

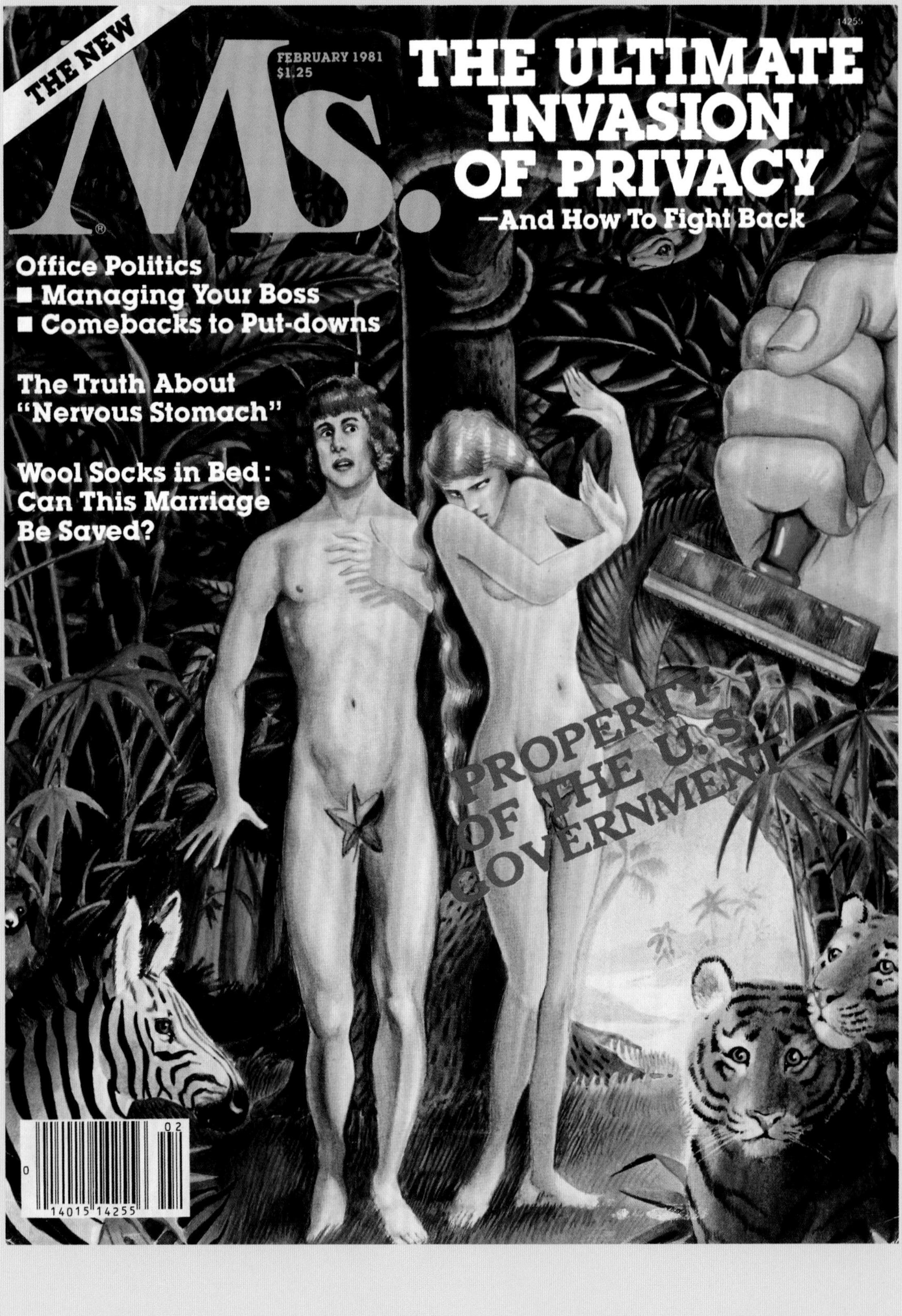
THE NEW
Ms.
FEBRUARY 1981
$1.25
THE ULTIMATE INVASION OF PRIVACY
—And How To Fight Back
Office Politics
■ Managing Your Boss
■ Comebacks to Put-downs
The Truth About "Nervous Stomach"
Wool Socks in Bed: Can This Marriage Be Saved?
PROPERTY OF THE U.S. GOVERNMENT
0 14015 14255 02

Letters

Letty Cottin Pogrebin's article really spoke to me and to issues I have been struggling with for years.

My twelve-year-old son is interested in cooking, building toy houses with very elaborate kitchens, and playing the female part in puppet shows. Most recently, he has built a dollhouse and furniture to go with it. Although he has studiously avoided team sports, he has exhibited lots of other interests, many considered traditionally masculine. But because I worried about what Pogrebin dubbed the "secret fear," I only paid attention to his feminine interests.

I blamed myself of course and tried to seek help. When I expressed my worries to the pediatrician, he said, "Don't worry, but if it continues . . ." The nursery-school teacher and later my therapist, both women, said, "Explore your feelings about it." I already knew my feelings. I was scared to death I had ruined my son somehow.

What Pogrebin gave me was information, a new perspective that fits my reality, and a sensible rationale to drop my attempts to make my son fit into a mold. The article laid to rest many of the ancient fears rattling inside me. I feel I can finally "stop worrying about gender and love my child."

NAME WITHHELD
February 1981 issue

I read your article "Hug a Tree Today" by Cynthia Cooke, MD, and Susan Dworkin [June 1981], while sitting under my favorite tree and smoking my favorite brand of cigarettes. I looked up at the leaves of the towering oak above me and took a puff on my cigarette. I breathed deeply of the oxygen emanating from the tree and took another drag on my cigarette. My anger rose. How dare they cut down trees? How dare they assault my health by depriving me of oxygen? I took two more puffs on my cigarette. Trees are a natural phenomenon, essential for life on earth. I lit up another cigarette. Thank God for *Ms.* At least you have my health in mind. Thank you for such an enlightening article, and most important of all, thank you for your cigarette ads. It's just me and my tree and my cigarette and my (pardon while I cough) health(?).

NAME WITHHELD
May 26, 1981

The Politics of Talking in Couples:
Conversus Interruptus and Other Disorders

BY **BARBARA EHRENREICH** • MAY 1981

N OT TOO LONG AGO, this magazine carried an article on how to talk to a man in bed. My only disappointment was that it was not followed up by a series of articles on how to talk to a man in other settings and on other items of furniture: "Talking in Living Rooms," "Talking on Straight-Backed Chairs." For it is my conviction, based on years of what sociologists call "participant observation," that far more male-female relationships die in the dining room than in the bedroom. And the problem is not the cuisine; it's the conversation.

The fact is that we are going through a profound Crisis in Intersex Conversation, and that this crisis has been the subject of a vast, systematic cover-up. I am not referring to the well-known difficulty of maintaining equity in public discourse—meetings, cocktail parties, seminars, and the like—a problem amply documented by our feminist foresisters in the late 1960s. I am referring to the much more insidious problem of intimate conversation between consenting adults of different sexes.

I can understand that there are solid artistic and commercial reasons for the cover-up. If art were forced to conform to conversational reality, *A Man and a Woman* would have been done as a silent film, and the Broadway hit *Lunch Hour* would have been condensed, quite adequately, into *Coffee Break*.

Nevertheless, the truth about male-female conversations has been leaking out. In her book *On Loving Men,* Jane Lazarre recounts a particularly disastrous conversational attempt with one of the objects of her love. Jane has just spent a long phone call consoling her recently widowed mother-in-law, who is hysterical with grief. She tells her husband about the call (after all, it was *his* mother), "after which we both lie there quietly." But she is still—understandably—shaken, and begins to fantasize about losing her own husband:

> "We are dealing not with individual problems— unfortunate conversational mismatches—but with a crisis of gender-wide proportions."

THE NEW

Ms.

MAY 1981
$1.25

14255

THE POLITICS OF TALKING

CAN WE TALK TO MEN THE WAY WE TALK TO EACH OTHER?

"Phyllis Schlafly: the Movie"
By Jane O'Reilly

The (Part-Time) Work Ethic

Too Fat, Too Chic,
Too Shrill, Too Weak:
The Plight of the
Woman Candidate

Street Harassment:
Men Tell
Why They Do It

Photo Story—
Triumph of a
Small-Town
Basketball Team

but..

Crying by now, due to the reality of my fantasy as well as the full compre-
hension of my mother-in-law's pain, I turn to James, then intrude upon
his perpetual silence and ask, "What are you thinking?" hoping for once to
be answered from some vulnerable depth. . . . And he admitted (it was an
admission because he was incredulous himself at the fact): "I was thinking
about the Knicks. Wondering if they were going to trade Frazier."

Jane Lazarre attributes her husband's talent for aborting conversations
to some "quality of character" peculiar to him and in the book goes off in
search of more verbose companionship. Thousands of other women have
also concluded that theirs was an individual problem: "I just can't talk to
him," and so forth. This, however, is a mistake. We are dealing not with
individual problems—unfortunate conversational mismatches—but with
a crisis of gender-wide proportions.

Much of the crisis must go to a few stealthy sociologists who have
devoted themselves to listening in on male-female conversations. Pamela
Fishman planted tape recorders in the homes of three couples and recorded
(with their permission) more than fifty hours of real-life chitchat. The picture that emerges from Fishman's work is that of women engaged in a more
or less solitary battle to keep the conversational ball rolling. Women nur-
ture infant conversations—throwing out little hookers like "you know?" in
order to enlist some help from their companions. Meanwhile, the men are
often working at cross-purposes, dousing conversations with "ummms,"
non sequiturs, and unaccountable pauses. And, in case you're wondering,
the subjects that Fishman's women nourished and men killed were neither
boringly trivial nor threateningly intimate: they were frequently about current events, articles read, work in progress. Furthermore, the subjects of
Fishman's research were couples who described themselves as "liberated"
from sex roles. One can only wonder what she might have found by leaving
her tape recorder in the average Levittown breakfast nook.

The problem is not that men are so taken with the strong, silent look
that they can't talk. The sociologists Candace West and Donald Zimmer-
man did some extensive eavesdropping at various sites around the University of California campus at Santa Barbara and found that men interrupt
women much more often than they interrupt other men and that they
do so more often than women interrupt either men or other women. In
analyzing her tapes of men and women who live together, Pamela Fishman found that topics introduced by men "succeeded" conversationally
96 percent of the time, while those introduced by women succeeded only
36 percent of the time and fell flat the rest of the time. Men can and will
talk—if they can set the terms.

There are all kinds of explanations for the conversational mismatch between the sexes, none of which requires more than a rudimentary feminist analysis. First, there's the fact that men are more powerful as a class of people and expect to dominate in day-to-day interactions, verbal or otherwise. Take any intersex gathering and—unless a determined counter-effort is undertaken—the basses and tenors quickly overpower the altos and sopranos.

For most men, public discourse is a competitive sport in which points are scored with decisive finger jabs and conclusive table poundings, while adversaries are blocked with shoulder thrusts or tackled with sudden interruptions. This style does not, of course, carry over well to the conversational private sector. As one male informant admitted to me, albeit under mild duress, "If you're just with a woman, there's no real competition. What's the point of talking?"

Male dominance is not the only problem. There's also male insecurity. When men have talked honestly about talking (or about not talking), under either psychiatric pressure or the lure of royalties, they tell us they are *afraid* to talk to women. Marc Feigen Fasteau confessed in *The Male Machine* that a "familiar blankness" overcame him in conversations with his wife, resulting from an "imagined fear that spontaneous talk will reveal unacceptable feelings—almost anything that would show vulnerability or indicate that the speaker doesn't 'measure up' to the masculine ideal."

Given the cultural barriers to intersex conversation, the amazing thing is that we would even expect women and men to have anything to say to each other for more than ten minutes at a stretch. The barriers are ancient—perhaps rooted, as some up-and-coming paleontologist may soon discover, in contrast between the occasional guttural utterances exchanged in male hunting bands and the extended discussions characteristic of female food-gathering groups. History does offer a scattering of successful mixed-sex conversational duos—Voltaire and Madame de Châtelet, Marie and Pierre Curie—but the mass expectation that ordinary men and women should engage in conversation as a routine activity probably dates back no further than the 1950s and the era of "togetherness." Until then, male-female conversation had served principally as an element of courtship, sustained by sexual tension and easily abandoned after the nuptials. After suburbanization threw millions of couples alone together in tiny tract houses for whole weekends at a stretch, however, media pundits decided that conversation was not only a healthy but a necessary marital activity, even if the topic never rose above the level of septic tanks and aluminum siding. While I have no direct evidence, the success of these early mixed-sex conversational endeavors may perhaps be gauged by the mass influx of women into the workforce and the explosive spread of feminism in the 1960s and 1970s.

It was feminism, of course, that raised women's conversation expectations. In consciousness-raising groups and National Organization for Women chapters, women's centers and caucuses, women discovered (or rediscovered) the possibilities of conversation as an act of collective creativity: the intimate sharing of personal experience, the weaving of the personal into the general and political, the adventure of freewheeling speculation unrestrained by academic rules or boundaries.

As men became aware of the heightened demands being placed upon them, their intellectual spokesmen quickly displaced the problem into the realm of sexuality. Thus Christopher Lasch, in discussing men's response to feminism, never even touches upon the conversational crisis, but tells us that "women's sexual demands terrify men," evoking images of "the vagina which threatens to eat them alive." But we could just as well invert this florid Freudiana and conclude it is women's verbal demands that terrify men and that the dread *vagina dentata* (devouring, toothed vagina) of male fantasy is in fact a mouth symbol, all set to voice some conversational overture such as "don't you think it's interesting that . . . ?"

Now that the crisis is out in the open, what do we do about it? Is there any way to teach a grown man, or short of that, a little one, how to converse in a manner that is stimulating, interesting, and satisfying to women? One approach might be to work through the educational system, introducing required mixed-gender courses in English Conversation. Or we might take a clinical approach, setting up therapeutic centers to treat Male Conversational Dysfunction. Various diagnostic categories leap to mind: "Conversational Impotence" (total inability to get a subject off the ground), "Premature Ejaculation" (having the answer to everything before anyone else gets a chance to utter a sentence), "Conversus Interruptus," and so forth. It may even be necessary, in extreme cases, to provide specially trained female Conversational Surrogates.

My own intuition is that the conversational crisis will be solved only when women and men—not just women—together realize their common need for both social and personal change. After all, women have discovered each other and the joy of cooperative discourse through a common political project—the feminist movement. So struck was I with this possibility that I tried it out loud on a male companion: "Can you imagine women and men together in a movement that demands both social and personal transformation?" There was a long, and I hoped pregnant, pause. Then he said, "Hmmmmm."

.   .   .

Letters

I would like to voice my agreement with your pro-choice position and suggest that there is an untapped resource for more support within the ranks of American womanhood that has traditionally been a very silent minority. We are those women who carry a secret just as painful as those who cannot admit to having had an abortion. We are the birth mothers of adopted children. We rarely speak out because we have been personally and publicly embarrassed, ridiculed, and patronized for having made the ultimate mistake. In the eleven years since I relinquished my child, I have not met one woman who has admitted to having a similar experience, yet there are many thousands of us out there.

I was one of the unwed teenage mothers "epidemic" in 1969, when abortions were all but impossible to obtain. In order to be referred to a doctor who would even consider examining me for the feared operation, I had to visit a pastor who required from me a release form stating that I had seriously considered suicide (which I had not), had ingested quantities of LSD and other dangerous drugs (which I had not), and was mentally, emotionally, physically, and financially incapable of caring for any child (which I was not). I was, in fact, a desperate first-year college student on the dean's list who wanted very much to continue in school.

As abortion negotiations wore on, it became clear that the safest method of terminating the pregnancy (and the most lucrative for the doctor) was similar to that of a cesarean procedure, although a saline injection method was offered with the dour comment that it was cheaper but more dangerous. The only viable solution in my opinion was to drop out of school and deliver the child, wrestling with relinquishment and adoption along the way.

Don't ever let anyone fool you into thinking that the answer to an unplanned pregnancy is to carry a child you cannot love. There is nothing holy about the experience, nothing satisfying. Antiabortion supporters use this argument frequently in response to the pregnancy problem, but as one who has been through it, it is not an option preferable to termination.

I deeply resent the treatment I received in a self-righteous society that turned a potentially beautiful experience into a horrid memory. It will not happen again.

NAME WITHHELD
June 1981 issue

At twelve years old, I had my first period. On discovery of this, I ran to where my parents were relaxing in the yard, yelling triumphantly, "I got my period!"

That night we toasted my womanhood with champagne. I still have the empty bottle.

NAME WITHHELD
June 16, 1981

Gerda Lerner
on the Future of Our Past

INTERVIEW BY **CATHARINE R. STIMPSON** • SEPTEMBER 1981

AFOUNDER of the study of women's history, Gerda Lerner was the president of the Organization of American Historians, the first woman in fifty years to hold that office, and the Robinson-Edwards Professor of History at the University of Wisconsin–Madison.

CATHARINE R. STIMPSON: You often speak of the need to connect the female experience and academic theory.

GERDA LERNER: That's right. A feminist style of learning implies the fusion of theory and practice. But I also happen to believe strongly that history is essential, not just as a specialty, but as an absolute lifeline to self-recognition and to giving our life meaning.

STIMPSON: Another of your fundamental contributions to women's history is the belief that women have been an active force. You had to counter the pervasive influence of Simone de Beauvoir's notion of women as the second sex, as passive.

LERNER: Mary Beard did that in her book, *Woman as Force in History.* I read it as an undergraduate. That really changed my intellectual life.

STIMPSON: Why was Simone de Beauvoir so popular, despite her ahistorical approach?

LERNER: Because of the brilliant concept and form of *The Second Sex* and because of the overwhelming evidence she amassed. The book provided an intellectual explanation for the status quo without really touching it. Mary Beard's insight absolutely challenges the status quo. The funny part is that Mary Beard seemed to be conservative and de Beauvoir radical, but Beard is much more radical. If you follow the insight that women have been a central agency in the shaping of civilization, you have

> **"Today we can be defeated in regard to laws, to appropriations, to representation, but if we are truly transforming consciousness, we cannot be defeated."**

to review the entire package of what we call culture, civilized knowledge. It leaves nothing untouched. De Beauvoir's description of patriarchal society and women in it was a tremendous contribution, but not a prescription for understanding the reality of women's role in the past.

STIMPSON: Do you think feminist scholars have come closer to a correct analysis of women's situation?

LERNER: Yes. The progress we have made is due to the collective nature of the enterprise and to the fact that we have found a way to break out of the isolation that our training imposes on us. This is exciting and new, just as the forms that the women's movement has found for solving social problems have been innovative. For instance, the women's group, the support group, women's health services, interage housing, and other living schemes. . . .

Then came another question, "What are women as a group, and how are they a group?" The hypothesis I have worked on all along is that the single thing, the major commonality women share, is the peculiar way in which men have controlled women's sexuality. Through historical time, women have been defined in their sexuality by men or male-dominated institutions, and they have been confined within the family as their assigned area of functioning.

Of course, there are also differences among women—of class, race, ethnicity—that are extremely important and must constantly be taken into consideration. . . . The family happens to be the common historical terrain of the vast majority of women. Ordinary housewives continue to work after they are married, but their main emphasis is family and children, and they fit their working lives within that matrix. Contrary to what the media make you believe, these women are the base out of which feminism is rising, and with whom we must have a constant connection. I've always had that connection because I am such a woman myself. I know what it is to live like that, the struggles involved, and the strength of it. There is some basis for collectivity and for common language. Many such women don't understand the advanced jargon of feminism, and even less the media distortion that wants to make feminism appear a threat to ordinary women.

STIMPSON: Do you still accept your theory that when we talk about the full emancipation of women, we must distinguish between women's rights and feminism?

LERNER: As the women's movement began to move into theoretical areas, there was often a great fuzziness of language, partially due to the fact that

we were speaking in a language we did not create and which is inappropri-
ate to that which we have to describe. Sharpness of definition becomes a
good. I found it useful to distinguish between women's rights, which are
akin to civil rights—that is, the right to participate fully in society, which-
ever it may be—and women's emancipation. This means not only rights
but autonomy and self-determination. This feminist struggle for emancipation is much older than the struggle for women's rights and goes on after
women's rights have been won. Knowing this, you understand the prob-
lematic of societies that have made revolutionary change and given women
rights, but in which women are still not emancipated.

STIMPSON: Where do you place men in the emancipation of women?

LERNER: We need to understand that men are structured into gender as well
as women and that it is as oppressive in some ways to men as to women.
But men do have an advantage out of it that women don't—lifelong personal service in the family. Men will have to lose that advantage, once
women make up their minds that men are not going to have it anymore
and educate their children so that they're not going to have it anymore. It's
always been within the power of women to withhold that, and we haven't
done it because we haven't seen it correctly.

If we wish to build, as we must, a mass social movement appropriate to
the twenty-first century, feminism is that movement. Then we must come
to terms with two basic realities: the ordinary woman has an experience
that we must respect, and we must deal with the gender oppression of men
to enlist some as allies.

STIMPSON: We have talked about history and about politics. What else do
you think connects women's history and feminism?

Gerda Lerner, who died in
2013, wrote eight books,
including *The Creation of
Patriarchy.*

LERNER: I now think that women's history is the primary tool for women's emancipation. I know that's a big, controversial statement, but I will make it. The subordination of women is built into the intellectual framework by which the whole Western world is ordered. Because of that, women and men have been raised without a concept of their relative significance, which assumed it was natural that women are persons who have no history. In this sense, Simone de Beauvoir was quite right, but she thought that was the reality. Now, because women have thought of themselves that way, even while being active in history, they have never connected with their own experience as the basis for thought. Men have drawn their thought from the experience of men. What has been missing is women's knowledge of the *actual* role they have played in making civilization, and that's called women's history. It is this that can change women's consciousness. No other analysis can do it as well, in my opinion. Not poetry, not myth, not psychology, not religion. The actuality of women's experience of the world for six thousand years and the way in which it has been structured into what we call knowledge—once we understand that, women's consciousness is irrevocably changed. That can provide the basis on which lasting coalitions and social change itself can be built.

In the process, we may have to find new forms of struggle. After 1920, women had to give up some of the forms of struggle they were used to, and they found new ones. But they did not give up striving for autonomy, independence, and self-determination. In this sense, there was no defeat of feminism in the 1930s. Today we can be defeated in regard to laws, to appropriations, to representation, but if we are truly transforming consciousness, we cannot be defeated. The situation of women in history and in society is knowledge of an order of significance akin to that of humans when we first began to understand how the universe is really put together. What we have to offer, for consciousness, is a correct analysis of what the world is like. Up to now, we have had a partial analysis. Everything that explains the world has in fact explained a world that does not exist, a world in which men are at the center of the human enterprise and women are at the margin "helping" them. Such a world does not exist—never has.

Men and women have built society and have built the world. Women have been central to it. This revolutionary insight is itself a force, a force that liberates and transforms.

.   .   .

Back Page

GIVE YOURSELF THE LAST WORD

DECEMBER 1981

THIS COLLECTION of perfect put-downs has been gathered by *Ms.* editors from our informal memory bank.

FLO KENNEDY: "For a man, the only sex-linked job is sperm donor; for a woman, wet nurse."

When people used to accuse feminists of being too "militant," Flo would say: "What about the Pentagon, General Westmoreland, General Mills, General Motors—they're the real militants. We don't even have a helicopter."

"If men could get pregnant, abortion would be sacrament."

"Men's jobs and women's jobs are only those that actually require a penis or a vagina."

GLORIA STEINEM: When a male student "streaked" nude during her speech at Wesleyan University in Connecticut, Gloria said, "For men, liberation may be taking their clothes off; for women, it's not having to take our clothes off."

Hans Conried violently disagreed with something Gloria said while both were guests on *The Dick Cavett Show.* "If you were a man, I'd punch you in the nose," he said. "Why don't you?" she answered. "At least then you'd be taking me seriously."

ROBIN MORGAN: At a college lecture, a jock in football clothes asked (in a tone of contempt), "Do you 'insist' on being called 'Mrs.' or 'Miss' or that stupid 'Ms.'? Just how do you want to be addressed?" Robin answered, "If you find 'Ms.' so distasteful, then a simple 'Your Majesty' will do."

"What is the single most earth-shattering, truly revolutionary phrase or slogan of the feminist movement? 'Herman, pick up your sock.'"

When faced with the "look at other species" argument and told about the inherent docility of female monkeys,

> THROUGH MUCH OF THE 1980S, *Ms.*'s "Back Page" offered famous feminist writers, actors, academics, and activists an opportunity to vent, advocate, and pontificate. The longtime *Cosmopolitan* editor in chief Helen Gurley Brown wrote about "what the women's movement meant to me—from the women's magazine editor who first admitted that women were sexual, too." Margaret Atwood asked, "What's a woman's novel? For that matter, what's a man's?" while Grace Paley reflected on memories of her late mother standing in the doorway.

ducks, and bears, Robin reminds her opponent, "The sex life of spiders is very interesting. He fucks her. She bites off his head."

SIMONE DE BEAUVOIR: When "pro-life" comes up, you might point out that many "pro-lifers" are also pro–capital punishment—and quote de Beauvoir on the Catholic Church:

"They have always reserved their uncompromising reverence for life to life in the fetal form."

CYNTHIA OZICK: Having heard Norman Mailer say that all a writer needs is his pen and his balls, Cynthia asked, "I've been wondering all evening. Mr. Mailer, in what color ink do you dip your balls?"

MARLO THOMAS: "To be ruthless, a man must be Attila the Hun; a woman just has to put you on hold."

SUZANNE LEVINE: If someone rejoices over the fact that the polls show that a majority of men now help out by doing grocery shopping, Suzanne reminds them that the same poll shows that 100 percent of the men go with shopping lists prepared by their wives.

UNATTRIBUTED: "Women will have achieved equality when a female schlemiel has just as much chance as a male schlemiel."

Commenting on the fact that she uses a different last name from her husband, a woman quipped, "I let him keep his own name."

If they say, "Feminism is the cause of divorce," answer, "No, marriage is the cause of divorce."

"A pedestal, like a prison, is a very small space."

MORE "BACK PAGES"

I wasn't looking for trouble. What I was looking for, actually, was a little tourist information to help me plan a camping trip to New England. But there it was, on the first page of the 1979 edition of the State of Vermont's *Digest of Fish and Game Laws and Regulations:* a special message of welcome from one Edward F. Kehoe, commissioner of the Vermont Fish and Game Department, to the reader and would-be camper, that is, me. This person (that is, me) is called "the sportsman."

—"The Great Person-hole Cover Debate"
by Lindsy Van Gelder, April 1980

BACK PAGE

The Great Person-hole Cover Debate
A modest proposal for anyone who thinks the word "he" is just plain easier...

A Giant Step for Womankind

BY LINDSY VAN GELDER

I wasn't looking for trouble. What I was looking for, actually, was a little tourist information to help me plan a camping trip to New England.

But there it was, on the first page of the 1979 edition of the State of Vermont *Digest of Fish and Game Laws and Regulations:* a special message of welcome from one Edward F. Kehoe, commissioner of the Vermont Fish and Game Department, to the reader and would-be camper, *i.e.,* me. This person (*i.e.,* me) is called "the sportsman."

"We have no 'sportswomen, sportspersons, sportsboys, or sportsgirls,' " Commissioner Kehoe has-tened to explain, obviously anticipating that some of us sportsfeminists might feel a bit overlooked. "But," he added, "we are pleased to report that we do have many great sportsmen who are women, as well as young people of both sexes."

It's just that the Fish and Game Department is trying to keep things "simple and forthright" and to respect "long-standing tradition." And anyway, we really ought to be flattered, "sportsman" being "a meaningful title being earned by a special kind of dedicated man, woman, or young person, as opposed to just any hunter, fisherman, or trapper."

I have heard this particular line of reasoning before. In fact, I've heard it so often that I've come to think of it as The Great Person-Hole Cover Debate, since gender-neutral manholes are in-variably brought into the argument as evidence of the lengths to which hu-morless, Newspeak-spouting femin-ists will go to destroy their mother tongue.

Consternation about woman-handling the language comes from all sides. Sexual conservatives who see the feminist movement as a unisex plot and who long for the good olde days of *vive la différence,* when men were men and women were women, none-theless do not rally behind the notion that the term "mankind" excludes women.

But most of the people who choke on expressions like "spokesperson" aren't right-wing misogynists, and this is what troubles me. Like the undoubt-edly well-meaning folks at the Vermont Fish and Game Department, they tend to reassure you right up front that they're only trying to keep things "sim-ple" and to follow "tradition," and that some of their best men are women, anyway.

Usually they wind up warning you, with great sincerity, that you're jeopar-dizing the worthy cause of women's rights by focusing on "trivial" side is-sues. I would like to know how anything that gets people so defensive and resis-tant can possibly be called "trivial,"

whatever else it might be.

The English language is alive and constantly changing. Progress—both scientific and social—is reflected in our language, or should be.

Not too long ago, there was a product called "flesh-colored" Band-Aids. The flesh in question was colored Caucasian. Once the civil rights move-ment pointed out the racism inherent in the name, it was dropped. I cannot imagine reading a thoughtful, well-in-tentioned company policy statement explaining that while the Band-Aids would continue to be called "flesh-colored" for old time's sake, black and brown people would now be consid-ered honorary whites and were perfect-ly welcome to use them.

Most sensitive people manage to describe our national religious tradi-tions as "Judeo-Christian," even though it takes a few seconds longer to say than "Christian." So why is it such a hardship to say "he or she" instead of "he"?

I have a modest proposal for any-one who maintains that "he" is just plain easier: since "he" has been the style for several centuries now—and since it really includes everybody any-way, right?—it seems only fair to give "she" a turn. Instead of having to pon-der over the intricacies of, say, "Con-gressman" versus "Congressperson" versus "Representative," we can sim-plify things by calling them all "Con-gresswoman."

Other clarifications will follow: "a woman's home is her castle . . ." "a giant step for all womankind" . . . "all women are created equal" . . . "Fisher-woman's Wharf." . . .

And don't be upset by the busi-ness letter that begins "Dear Madam," fellas. It means you, too.

Lindsy Van Gelder is a staff writer for "Ms.," and a United Feature Syndi-cate columnist. She was previously a reporter for United Press Interna-tional and the New York "Post," and has written for many national magazines.

120/Ms./April 1980

The latest argument of the right wing cites pseudoscientific "evidence" that women (and men of conscience) had better be prepared and equipped to refute. Two recent letters to the editor of *The Providence Journal/Evening Bulletin* claim that there exists well-known evidence that the increase in availability of elective abortion in the 1970s pro-duced an increase in child abuse. The apparent logic that links elective abortion with child abuse is that if parents feel they may "kill" a fetus, they are less likely to feel constrained from battering children. Both letters took us, as sociologists specializing in family violence studies, by surprise.   —"Watch on the Right: Beware the 'Research Shows . . .' Ploy" by Richard J. Gelles and Claire Pedrick Cornell, June 1981

At the Feminist Press, we used to be asked, "Where are the 'good' women's studies programs?" Recently, the questions from college-bound women or their parents have grown more complex: "Where can my daughter study marine biology *and* find good role models, women's studies courses, and team sports? She plays soccer." Or "I am planning to be an engineer, but I want to take some women's studies as well, and I'd like to be in or near a Chicano community."

"You want everything," was one of our early, surprised responses. But why should women *not* want everything? Shouldn't colleges serve the whole woman?

—"Is Your Campus Good for Your Health?"
by Florence Howe, September 1981

Why should the insurance industry be willing to spend more than $4 million (so far) on an advertising campaign in an attempt to defeat legislation that would save women money? Because discrimination pays—and pays well—for the practitioner. The bill, which would ban separate treatment of women in insurance policies, is backed by virtually all the national women's groups.

—"The Unisex Debate: What Are Insurance Companies Afraid Of?"
by Mary W. Gray, April 1984

What do Vanessa Williams, Janet Cooke, and Leanita McClain have in common with every other Black woman in this country? The answer, depending on whom you listen to these days, is everything and nothing. Both answers are wrong. Reality lies, naturally enough, somewhere in between. But as a Black woman, I'm more upset about the "everything" answer . . . an answer that the wider society seems determined to give, an answer that fundamentally strips Black women of our individuality. Somehow when one Black steps in a puddle, we all end up getting splashed. Vanessa Williams was, of course, the first Black to be Miss America; Janet Cooke, a *Washington Post* reporter, the first Black woman to win a Pulitzer Prize in journalism; and Leanita McClain, the first Black member of the powerful *Chicago Tribune* editorial board.

—"What Happens When a Black 'First' Fails?"
by Renee Poussaint, February 1985

Letters

While reading the article "Vintage Sex— Does It Get Better?" [by Sara Mandelbaum, January 1982], I was reminded of a story about my great-great-aunt Annie (now ninety-four years old).

At one of the many family gatherings we've had, a woman asked Aunt Annie (then in her late seventies) how old a woman is when she starts losing interest in sex. That spry little parakeet of a woman deadpanned, "Well, honey, you'll have to ask somebody older than me."

Priceless . . .

CECILIA M. BARFIELD
Ocala, Fla.
May 1982 issue

A Bloodsmoor Romance

BY **JOYCE CAROL OATES** • JUNE 1982

MISS CONSTANCE PHILIPPA ZINN and the Baron Adolf von Mainz were joined in holy matrimony on November 15, 1880, at Trinity Church of Bloodsmoor, the Reverend Silas Hewett presiding. The bride wore a gown of surpassing beauty, of the finest China silk, with a many-layered skirt and train, and a long veil of Brussels lace; and the groom was impeccably attired in a morning coat and tails, with a sprig of orange blossom in his lapel. There was only a moment's awkwardness, when, it appeared, the wedding band was too small for the bride's finger, and the groom, perhaps embarrassed by his role, seemed to grow impatient, and jammed it on: but an instant later all was well, and though slightly red-faced, the bridal couple continued with the ceremony, and Reverend Hewett pronounced them man and wife; and the organ sounded.

Wedding guests were driven to Kiddemaster Hall in special carriages, and received in the reception room at the east end of the house, which was sumptuously decorated with floral displays of all kinds, and had never looked more elegant. On a raised platform was a six-piece chamber orchestra, which played throughout the evening; in one corner, a display of wedding gifts (a great number of the most beautiful specimens of cut glass, china, silverware, side pieces, watercolors and oil paintings, linens, etc.), which all the guests inspected with delight, and congratulations to the bride and groom.

The wedding repast was served in the larger of the two dining rooms, which room had been given a marvelous pink cast, by the judicious selection and arrangements of roses, candles, napkins, and glassware of that hue, to the exclaimed admiration of the guests. The bride's table was circular in form, with a generous mound of tulle upon which were strewn a countless number of pink tea roses interspersed with little bows of pink-and-white-striped ribbon, the appearance of all being most beautiful. Before the bride was placed the bride's loaf, magnificently frosted, and at each of the twelve places about this table, occupied by the bridal party, were bouquets of pink and cream roses, large ones for the ladies, and smaller ones for the gentlemen. (Vivacious Malvinia created something of a scene, by presenting to her older sister Constance Philippa a prankish mock-bouquet of tea roses some hours past their prime, interspersed with weed flowers of a common ghastly whitish hue: turkey beard, fly poison, miterwort, and death camas!—a bouquet the bride accepted without comment, and laid beside her place at the table.)

The long dining table was adorned with pink and cream roses as well, and drew forth unstinting exclamations of delight, as did the delicious ten-course meal, which, as was the tradition at Kiddemaster Hall, disappointed neither in quality nor in quantity. Guests were overheard commenting to one another upon the festivities, in tones of fulsome praise. "The most brilliant social event of the Bloodsmoor season," was the general verdict; and I cannot but concur in their judgment.

A fair amount of champagne was consumed, inspiring Cousin Basil Miller to an impudent but high-spirited toast, delivered in rollicking song:

"It's we two, it's we two for aye, All the world and we two, and Heaven be our stay! Like a laverock in the lift, sing O bonny bride!

"All the world was Adam once, with Eve by his side! *All the world was Adam once—with Eve by his side!*"

In the busy months of her engagement Constance Philippa Zinn, the eldest of the five Zinn daughters, and in the eyes of most observers the most "difficult" of these attractive young women, had ample opportunity to acquaint herself, through her reading, with the sacred duties of Wifehood soon to be hers (she perused such helpful books as Eliza North's *Maiden, Wife, and Mother;* Mary Maderly Ogden's *Christian Mother;* Dr. Elias Riddle's *Counsels on the Nature and Hygiene of Womanhood;* and, of course, Dr. Naphey's excellent *The Physical Life of Women*). Her trepidatious maiden's heart was appeased somewhat by the good counsel of Dr. Riddle, who spoke with a refreshing forthrightness of matters Constance Philippa scarce dared to think:

In our most unitary of acts, which is the epitome and pleroma of life, we have the most intense of all affirmations of God's love for us creatures, and His will that the husband and wife participate in a true pangenesis. The supreme holiness of the wedding bond, symbolized in the solemn exchange of rings, is a measure of the holiness of God's bond with His creation.

In addition, Constance Philippa spent a great deal of time, as one might imagine, being fitted for her wedding trousseau and for her resplendent wedding gown. And during these sessions she acquired a curious—and, one might venture, somewhat morbid—interest in the dressmaker's dummy that was molded to her form. Oft she brooded over the shapely figure (for it was "her" form in its ideal, corseted state), observing it from all sides; upon one occasion, no one being near, she even removed the dummy's clothing—as if, with very little natural hesitation, she meant to examine the torso *naked*!

The mannequin was hers; yet, with its agreeably slender waist (some twenty inches), and its ample bosom (a consequence of some strategic padding), it struck the o'erly-censorious young lady as not hers at all, but a *lie.* "This is Constance Philippa," she inwardly murmured, "and yet quite clearly, it is not Constance Philippa. Nay, the riddle is most worrisome—it has made my head spin—I shall think of it no longer!"

(And so she resolved; yet, as we shall unhappily see, with no conspicuous degree of success.)

The honeymoon journey was to be an ambitious one, involving visits to Washington, D.C., Richmond, Atlanta, and New Orleans; and possibly the West Indies as well—where the Baron's sugarcane plantation was said to be threatened of late by labor difficulties. So the couple betook themselves to their carriage, and departed for Philadelphia, where they were scheduled to spend the night in the Baron's handsome suite in the Hotel de la Paix, overlooking Logan Square.

They were, it hardly needs to be said, a *subdued* couple, for Constance Philippa in particular was extremely shy, and not even the champagne poured for them by the Baron's silent manservant could loosen her tongue, though she drank, it may have been unthinkingly, several glasses in rapid succession. From time to time both the bride and the groom glanced around, as if expecting to see, in the room's corners, an unheralded visitor or witness. But of course they were alone—quite alone.

"Are you warm enough, my dear?" the Baron asked solicitously, having noticed his bride shivering; and before she had even time to reply, he had arisen, and fetched a lovely white cashmere shawl, and draped it about her shoulders. "Perhaps, my dear Constance Philippa," he murmured, "we can aspire to warmth together."

Constance Philippa murmured an inaudible reply, no doubt an assent.

He regained his seat, and in silence they finished their light repast of ham, scallops, and caviar toast, and drank the rest of the champagne, the Baron now eyeing his bride steadily, with a look of grimness leavened by some humor (for one must remember that, despite the romance of their courtship, the young man had been married before), and, from time to time, a slight quiver of his mustache; and the bride's cheeks appeared to have acquired a permanent blush, which gave to her ordinarily undistinguished complexion a look, almost, of maidenly delicacy. That the bride was nervous was evident in the trembling of her hand, as she lifted the glass to her mouth, and in a certain quickening of her breath; that the groom was similarly affected was evident in his breath, which soon became audible. "My dear," the Baron said, in a dry, gentle voice, "perhaps it is time to retire for the night—?"

At once the bride rose from her chair, so quickly her husband had not time to help her, and in a soft rushed tone she excused herself, and went into the bedchamber with no evident air of hesitation, and closed the door quietly behind her. The Baron, being a considerate, and as it were, a practiced husband, lingered behind, idly eating what remained of the ham, and, after some minutes, pouring an inch or two of brandy in a glass, the fumes of which he inhaled with evident pleasure. Time passed: he checked his pocket watch and decided to give the new Baroness another minute or two, to prepare herself. She had brought along for the honeymoon trip such a quantity of suitcases, trunks, and boxes, it would not have surprised him had she searched in vain for her nighttime apparel; and he smiled tightly to think of her growing desperation, should she *not* find it.

After a discreet space of time, the Baron went to the door, rapped lightly upon it, and, turning the knob (which he halfway feared might be locked against him—for that had happened once before), called out to his bride in as controlled a voice as he could manage, "You have no objection, my dear Constance Philippa, if I now join you?" and, receiving no reply, he added in jest, "Maidenly delicacy, even yours, my dear wife, exerts but a limited charm—and the hour is late."

He believed he heard her voice, and as it did not seem she was asking him to wait, he slipped quietly into the candlelit room, closing the door behind him, and locking it; now beginning to tremble with a necessary and altogether natural masculine desire, lustful only if one subscribes to the scruples of our Puritan ancestors, but entirely normal, if one recalls the admonition that male and female reproduce their kind, and populate the earth, under God's command. That the desire to reproduce the human species is native to the masculine sex, and by no means an aberrant tendency, still less an inclination of disgusting perversity, must be kept in mind by the reader, else the behavior of our Constance Philippa will not seem so blasphemous as in truth it was.

The bride had already retired, and lay motionless in the recesses of the handsome canopied bed, near lost in shadow, and the flickering phantasmagoric light cast by the candelabrum, upon which twelve candles burned to great effect. The Baron loosened his cravat, and, taking care to walk lightly around the various items of luggage, so as not to disturb his bride, locked both remaining doors of the bridal chamber—for, upon the occasion of his first marriage, now many years back, an unfortunate incident had transpired, owing to the infelicity of an unlocked door. He then retired to his dressing room, where, quickly stripping himself of his numerous garments, he felt his manly lust grow, and could not resist glancing at himself in the mirror, which, though dim, presented a countenance of small but regular features, and a mustache of striking fullness, wonderfully black.

Past experience had taught him that it was far more pragmatic to act boldly than to continue with a pretense of drawing-room manners, and so the Baron strode to the bed, and threw off the heavier of the covers, and, now nearly overcome by his natural masculine inclination, and by the labored dryness of his breath, he slid as adroitly as possible beneath the sheet, embraced his unresisting bride, mounted her, and in a single gesture of great force and authority, made her his wife in the *Flesh,* as Reverend Hewett had made her his wife in *Spirit.*

Grunting, he then flung himself from her, and lay, panting, on the pillow beside hers, one forearm across his face, his eyes half-shut, in an effort to recover himself; and, it may have been, the Baron murmured words of comfort or even of love to his spouse, in the throbbing tumult of those minutes; but none has been recorded. After a brief space of time the gentleman's breathing grew more regular, and he bethought himself to glance at his bride, who had, all this while, continued to lie motionless, with infinite tact, not disturbing the sanctity of the rite by moaning or sobbing, as others had done in the past—and I am scarcely able to force myself to reveal what the Baron Adolf von Mainz saw: not the face of his beloved bride, and not even her head, *but only the naked pillow.*

With a muttered exclamation he pulled the sheet away, and discovered, to his utter astonishment—alas, was ever a Christian husband so ill-treated?—that no woman lay beside him, no trembling Constance Philippa, nay, not even a human being, but a *dressmaker's dummy*—headless, armless, and possessing no nether limbs!

Letters

My father has been a very conservative man for most of his life. He used to believe that a woman's place was strictly in the home and that the man was to be in control.

A few years ago I started to notice a change slowly coming over him. My older sister wanted to go to law school. My mother gradually prepared him for the idea that woman lawyers were as good as men and that a bad woman lawyer was bad not because she was a woman but because she was a bad lawyer.

By the time my sister was ready to tell him of her decision to go to law school, he was ready to hear it. And, most important, he could accept it and be proud of it.

Probably the most significant change I've noticed in my father is his views on homosexuals.

When homosexuals were beginning to come out in the early 1970s, my dad's only response was "Disgusting." I never knew his attitude had changed on the subject until the palimony suit was brought against Billie Jean King. I thought Billie Jean would have one less fan. But to my surprise my very conservative father said, "I respect Billie Jean King more now than I did before." This personally was a great relief, since one day I will be telling him that I am a lesbian.

NAME WITHHELD
July/August 1982 issue

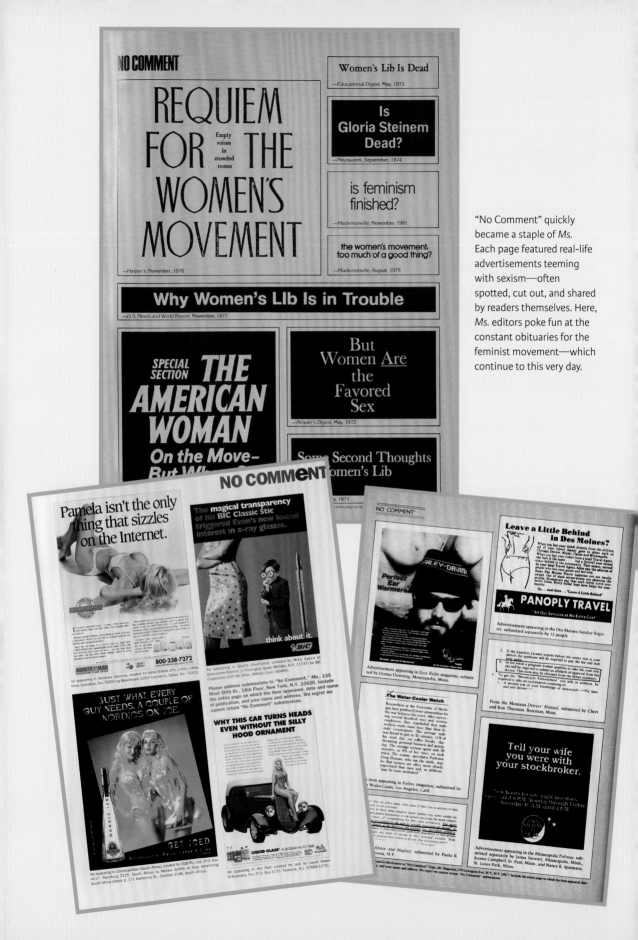

"No Comment" quickly became a staple of *Ms.* Each page featured real-life advertisements teeming with sexism—often spotted, cut out, and shared by readers themselves. Here, *Ms.* editors poke fun at the constant obituaries for the feminist movement—which continue to this very day.

Letters

On June 6, two days after the North Carolina legislature failed to ratify the ERA, I attended the ERA rally in Raleigh. Later that day I went to a restaurant with my family. There I met a nine-year-old girl, her hair in pigtails. She looked at my green ERA Yes buttons and white dress, and said, "You must be for the Equal Rights Amendment. Did you go to the rally?"

"Yes," I answered. "Did you?"

"No," she said. "I couldn't go because I had a softball game. We got creamed, as usual. I probably couldn't have gotten anyone to take me anyway. I have real dumb relatives who don't believe in equal rights."

Then, very tentatively, she asked, "Have we ever had equal rights?"

I answered, "No."

"Will we ever have them?" she wanted to know.

Who will answer this child?

NAME WITHHELD
August 25, 1982

The Nouveau Poor" [by Barbara Ehrenreich and Karen Stallard, July 1982] hit me at a precipitous moment. I read it the day before my mother went to court to involuntarily end a thirty-year marriage. My mother spent twenty years of that marriage at home raising three children; then, just when the college tuition and the other debts were finally paid off, my father decided to share his income (and himself) not with her but with a woman fifteen years his junior.

Because my parents reside in a "no-fault divorce" state, my mother was entitled to virtually nothing. Every attorney she consulted told her she had no right to my father's considerable assets. He has these assets because for thirty years he had a wife to raise his children, make his meals, clean his house, and provide support so that he could go out and earn a living. In the eyes of the law, however, this "women's work" is worth nothing. My mother, along with many other women, has become of the nouveau poor.

If we do anything in the next ten years, it must be to fight for the legal guarantee that our work and our daughters' work (whether in or out of the home) will be valued.

NAME WITHHELD
November 1982 issue

I thought you might be interested in this classified ad, which I ran across this week. It is not the usual promotion of T. and A. [tits and ass], but it is every bit as stereotypical:

Envelope stuffing. Persons with finger dexterity needed to work for a temporary help service. Must have phone & reliable transportation. Tedious work/minimum wage. Ideal for homemakers.

You'll excuse me if I cut this letter short. I must rush to line up that job. It's not every day that a good position, suited to my skills, comes along.

NAME WITHHELD
February 15, 1983

The Contrived Postures of Femininity

BY **SUSAN BROWNMILLER** • MARCH 1984

I WAS TAUGHT to sit with my knees close together, but I don't remember if I was given a reason. Somewhere along the way I heard that boys like to look up girls' skirts and that it was our job to keep them from seeing our panties, but I didn't put much stock in this vicious slur. "Put your knees together" seemed to be a rule of good posture like "Sit up straight," and nothing more. As with other things that became entrenched in my mind as unquestionably right and feminine, when I thought about it later, I could see an aesthetic reason. The line of a skirt did seem more graceful when the knees weren't poking out in different directions. Slanting them together was the way to avoid looking slovenly in a chair. (Sitting with legs crossed became an acceptably feminine posture only after skirts were shortened in the 1920s.)

Bending over to pick up a piece of paper was fraught with the danger of indecent exposure during the 1960s miniskirt era, and like other women who believed minis looked terrifically dashing when we stepped along the street, I had to think twice, compose myself, and slither down with closed knees if I dropped something. A breed of voyeurs known as staircase watchers made their appearance during this interesting time. Slowly it dawned on me that much of feminine movement, the inhibited gestures, the locked knees, the nervous adjustments of the skirt, was a defensive maneuver against an immodest, vulgar display that feminine clothing flirted with in deliberate provocation. My feminine responsibility was to keep both aspects, the provocative and the chaste, in careful balance, even if it meant avoiding the beautifully designed open stairway in a certain Fifth Avenue bookshop.

> **"The charge that feminists have no manners is true."**

But why did I think of vulgarity when the focal point at issue—I could no longer deny the obvious—was my very own crotch? And why did I believe that if I switched to trousers, the problem would magically be solved?

Spreading the legs is a biologically crucial, characteristically female act. Not only does the female have the anatomical capacity to stretch her legs farther apart than the average male because of the shape of her pelvis, but a generous amount of leg spread is necessary to the act of sexual intercourse, to the assertive demand for pleasure, and to the act of giving birth. There might have been a time in history when this female posture was celebrated with pride and joy, but in civilization as we know it, female leg spread is identified with loose, wanton behavior, pornographic imagery, promiscuity, moral laxity, immodest demeanor, and a lack of refinement. In other words, with qualities that the feminine woman must try to avoid, even as she must try to hint that somewhere within her repertoire such possibilities exist.

Students of Japanese history know that samurai warriors trained their daughters in the use of weapons to give them the requisite skill to commit hara-kiri when faced with disgrace. As part of the training, girls were taught how to tie their lower limbs securely so they would not embarrass themselves and their families by inadvertently assuming an immodest position in the agony of death. Traditional Japanese etiquette pays close attention to the rules of modest posture for women. In the classic squat position for eating, men are permitted to open their knees a few inches for comfort but women are not. Men may also sit cross-legged on the floor, but women must kneel with their legs together.

Studies by the psychologist Albert Mehrabian show that despite evidence of superior anatomical flexibility and grace, women are generally less relaxed than men. Mehrabian proposes that attitudes of submissiveness are conveyed through postures of tension. In his analysis of body language

Locked Knees, the Debutante Slouch, Hair Twisting:

The Contrived Postures of Femininity

I was taught to sit with my knees close together, but I don't remember if I was given a reason. Somewhere along the way I heard that boys like to look up girls' skirts and that it was our job to keep them from seeing our panties, but I didn't put much stock in this vicious slur. "Put your knees together" seemed to be a rule of good posture like "Sit up straight," and nothing more. As with other things that became entrenched in my mind as unquestionably right and feminine, when I thought about it later on I could see an aesthetic reason. The line of a skirt did seem more graceful when the knees weren't poking out in different directions. Slanting them together was the way to avoid looking slovenly in a chair. (Sitting with legs crossed became an acceptably feminine posture only after skirts were shortened in the 1920s.)

Copyright © 1984 Susan Brownmiller. Excerpted with permission from *Femininity*, by Susan Brownmiller, published by Linden Press/Simon & Schuster.

▶ BY SUSAN BROWNMILLER

among high- and low-status males, high-ranking men are more relaxed in their gestures in the presence of subordinates. Not surprisingly, men of all ranks generally assume more relaxed postures and gestures when communicating with women.

Small, fluttery gestures that betray nervousness or a practiced over-animation are considered girlishly feminine and cute. Toying with a strand of hair, bobbing the head, giggling when introduced, pulling the elbows in close to the body, and crossing the legs in a knee and ankle double twist are mannerisms that men studiously avoid.

Quaint postures that throw the body off balance, such as standing on one leg as if poised for flight, or leading from the hips in a debutante slouch, or that suggest a child's behavior (the stereotypical sexy secretary taking dictation while perched on the boss's knee), fall within the repertoire of femininity that is alien, awkward, and generally unthinkable as a mode of behavior for men. Reclining odalisque-style, such a shocker thirty years ago when Truman Capote posed in this manner for a book jacket, is a classic feminine tableau of eroticized passivity with an established tradition in art.

Of course, feminine movement was never intended for solo performance. It is in order to appeal to men that the yielded autonomy and contrived manifestations of helplessness become second nature as expressions of good manners and sexual goodwill. For smooth interaction between the sexes, the prevailing code of masculine action demands a yielding partner to gracefully complete the dance.

Nancy Henley, psychologist and author of *Body Politics,* has written, "In a way so accepted and so subtle as to be unnoticed even by its practitioners and recipients, males in couples will often literally push a woman everywhere she is to go—the arm from behind, steering around corners . . . crossing the street."

To be helped with one's coat, to let the man do the driving, to sit mute and unmoving while the man does the ordering and picks up the check—such trained behavioral inactivity may be ladylike, gracious, romantic and flirty, and soothing to easily ruffled masculine feathers, but it is ultimately destructive to the sense of the functioning, productive self. The charge that feminists have no manners is true, for the history of manners, unfortunately for those who wish to change the world, is an index of courtly graces addressed toward those of the middle classes who aspire to the refinements of their betters, embodied in the static vision of the cared-for, catered-to lady of privilege who existed on a rarefied plane above the mundane reality of strenuous labor. When a feminist insists on opening the door for herself, a simple act of physical autonomy that was never an issue for servants, field and factory workers, and women not under the protection of men, her gesture rudely collides with chivalrous expectations, for manly action requires manifest evidence of a helpless lady in order to demonstrate courtly respect.

The psychology of feminine movement, as we know and practice its provocative airs and graces, is based on the premise that direct acts of initiative and self-assertion are a violation of the governance of male-female relations, if not of nature itself. In place of forthright action we are offered a vision so exquisitely romantic and sexually beguiling that few care to question its curious imagery of limitations: a *Venus de Milo* without arms, a mermaid without legs, a Sleeping Beauty in a state of suspended animation with her face upturned, awaiting a kiss.

Letters

I just dashed out onto the busy streets of Boston to run an errand and was struck by an observation. Well-dressed businessmen traveling in twos and threes crowding the sidewalk expect "lessers" (read *women, racial or ethnic* minorities, less professionally dressed) to step aside and defer to them in using the crowded sidewalk space. I decided to practice being more aggressive (hard for me) and did not defer. These groups were irritated, surprised, and probably a few other things in realizing it was they who had to step aside. After all, who runs the world controls the sidewalks, and isn't their ongoing conversation of great importance, et cetera? Of course, common courtesy is that we all defer at times and share the space, but my tiny experiment was a real click.

> GAIL D. HINAND
> Boston
> April 13, 1984

Lindsy Van Gelder's "Marriage as a Restricted Club" [February 1984] took the words out of my mouth. It is so important to let our heterosexual friends, married or unmarried, know how this institution oppresses gay people. What hurts most is the fear my lover and I "can't take care of each other," not only because of homophobic attitudes, but also health-benefit laws and hospital regulations. Income tax and insurance laws are added expenses. We recently found that renter's insurance on the contents of our apartment recognizes only one owner, a law that, like many of the ones mentioned, also discriminates against heterosexual couples.

I recently participated in my brother's wedding, as a bridesmaid. My lover of ten years was not welcome at the event, but my sister-in-law asks when we are getting married. I will always be considered "single" by my parents and my parents' friends. Even if my heterosexual friends don't have a wedding ceremony, the law recognizes them as a legal couple if they live together long enough. The choice we've made to live together forces us to expose ourselves in ways that jeopardize our career choices and sometimes our friendships.

> NAME WITHHELD
> June 1984 issue

Letters

I am writing just moments after watching history being made: Geraldine Ferraro has been nominated for vice president of the United States! I happily admit I cried throughout the announcement and speeches. I cry because I was filled with gratitude, hope, and pride.

To me, the outcome of the election is almost irrelevant, for now I know that more great, pride-filled moments such as this one lie ahead for all Americans and that, as Gerry Ferraro suggested, more and more of those heavy old doors will be opening.

LUCY ALLEN
St. Louis, Mo.
October 1984 issue

I am married to a wonderful man who lives his life based on feminist principles. We share equally the mundane duties of everyday life; he supports my work as a counselor at a battered women's shelter, and I support his as a physician. Yet he has never been outspoken about his feminist philosophy. I have always found that particularly frustrating.

Not long after our first child, a daughter, was born, we found ourselves in the middle of a discussion of the New Bedford rape trial with my family. Someone made a disparaging remark about the woman involved. My usually soft-spoken husband rose to his feet and began an angry discourse on the cruelty of the remark, on rape and the fear most women are forced to carry with them, and on the general "injustice of the system" and our society where women are concerned. As my family sat stunned, he said finally, "What if it had been Rebekah (our daughter)? Would you still be so callous and unfeeling?" I felt like applauding.

When we watched Walter Mondale pick Geraldine Ferraro for his vice presidential running mate, the excitement was overwhelming. My husband told four-month-old Rebekah what the nation had been told: "If you want to, you can grow up to be a president."

Thank you, Rebekah, for helping your dad find his voice and for setting him free.

DARLENE FUREY
Abington, Pa.
November 1984 issue

Ms. featured Geraldine Ferraro as the October cover story just weeks before the 1984 presidential election, when she was the first-ever woman to run on a major-party ticket. The article concluded that, of course, a woman would make a difference, but the country would wait nearly four decades for its first woman vice president.

The Training
of a Gynecologist

BY **DAVID HELLERSTEIN, MD** • NOVEMBER 1984

"SCOOT DOWN to the edge of the table, hon," says Dr. Snarr. The small room is hot, the air stuffy. Our patient winces at the word "hon." She is a young woman with chronic pelvic pain, the bane of gynecologists, and I can tell she doesn't like Snarr's tone. She does scoot along the table, though, and Snarr kicks a wheeled stool toward me. I sit on it, slide between her legs, ready for my lesson of the day. Feet and calves and thighs surround me, suddenly very close. Snarr positions the lamp before my chest, so light pours on her. I warm the speculum in my gloved hand and with a twist insert it.

"Open it up," he says. "Tighten it all the way open. Pull down to keep away from the urethra. You hit the urethra and no patient will ever come back to you."

Snarr is my teacher, a gaunt and narrow-shouldered man, with a small potbelly below the best of his plaid pants. Before coming in here, he went over the information I had gathered and insisted it was nonsense. She couldn't possibly feel that kind of pain. I must not be asking the right questions. Hadn't I learned anything? Gynecologists have the reputation of being the dummies of medicine: surgeons laugh at their clumsiness in the operating room, internists at their ignorance of medical fact, psychiatrists at their insensitivity. And so far Snarr had done nothing to dispel that prejudice—which was too bad, considering that I was an impressionable third-year medical student, still trying to decide what field to go into.

> " 'I don't know why the heck she hurts,'
> he says when we are outside. 'Give her some estrogen cream.' "

"Okay," says Snarr. "Now swab it out real well. Get some cells on that."

I swab.

"Pull that speculum out now. Get a good look at those walls."

I see pink folds as I pull, pink moist walls bulging in against the metal of the speculum—aquatic territory, the scalloped forms of submarine life. It's out. Snarr is quick next with lubricating jelly on the first two fingers of my glove. I stand up, push the stool away. I begin.

"AIIEE!" the woman screams and slides up on the table. "God! Oh, God!"

"So that's . . . that's where it hurts," I say. I'm sweating. "Just . . . just a second, I'll try more gently."

I feel around again. This time she doesn't scream. She breathes deeply. I can't feel a thing, but with Snarr watching, I can't pull out right away. For a month I've been spending afternoons in gynecology clinic with Dr. Snarr—a month of women's bottoms on the edge of tables, of the hot lamp in front of my chest, the powdery-inside examining glove on my hand, the smells of femaleness. And the confidences of women, fascinating and at times overpowering, about their pains, their periods, their fertility, their husbands, their lovers. What gets to me, though, are the exams. The touching. Deep internal touching, feeling for the bulge of the uterus, for those small elusive olives, the ovaries, exploring for tenderness, creating sudden moments of pain. Technically I'm reasonably good—as good as can be expected for a third-year medical student rotating through ob-gyn. But I still find it strange to be touching intimately but without passion—as a doctor.

I'm not alone in this either; the other med students on ob-gyn seem just as awkward as I am. We hang around in the lounge when the pharmaceutical rep leaves free coffee and doughnuts, cracking jokes, laughing too much.

"All right," Dr. Snarr says, "let me try my hand." He steps in. I strip off my glove and wash my hands, ready to observe a deft exam, pinpointing the source of pain, exploring yet reassuring.

But in a second the woman is screaming, writhing on the table. Snarr is reaching way far in, clumsily it seems, pushing so hard her hips rise from the table, and she is crying, grabbing the table with her hands. I feel sick just watching. Is this necessary? I have no way of knowing what Snarr is finding, if anything, since he does not explain.

"All right, hon," he tells her. He pulls off his glove. "Wipe yourself off. We'll come back and see you in a minute."

"I don't know why the heck she hurts," he says when we are outside. "Give her some estrogen cream."

She's dressed when I come back in, pale and woozy; there's still pain in her eyes. I hand her the prescription.

"Come back if it gets worse," I say.

"Then what?" the woman says.

I am embarrassed. I murmur something, that I'm sorry we didn't come up with anything. Then I hurry out after my teacher.

I find him in the side room, having coffee and doughnuts, courtesy of the pharmaceutical rep. The next patient isn't ready yet.

"Have some," he says.

I decline. I'm too jittery to eat.

"That girl," says Dr. Snarr. "What do you think her problem is?"

I consider the possibilities: PID, endometriosis, cysts. I talk, but I don't say what I really think: That he has no sense of what he put her through. That he's insensitive. Clumsy. A jerk. I'm disappointed too, but I'm not sure why.

Thinking back on it now, five years later, perhaps it's that I wished he were a better doctor, a better role model. Certainly not all gynecologists are like Dr. Snarr, but at that moment it seemed as if they were—and what I needed so much was to know how to *be* with patients, how to deal with the feelings they evoked, how to make them feel at ease. If Dr. Snarr had been a better teacher, I conceivably might have gone into his field.

Dr. Snarr washes down the rest of his doughnut.

"So what else have we got out there?" he says.

A young Black woman in a white gown; she looks around nervously as we enter.

"Scoot down to the edge of the table, hon," says Snarr. Wincing at the word "hon," the woman nevertheless does scoot down.

Snarr kicks the wheeled stool over toward me.

And I begin.

·   ·   ·

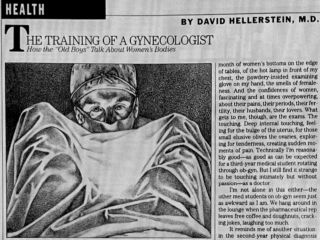

HEALTH

BY DAVID HELLERSTEIN, M.D.

THE TRAINING OF A GYNECOLOGIST
How the "Old Boys" Talk About Women's Bodies

month of women's bottoms on the edge of tables, of the hot lamp in front of my chest, the powdery-insided examining glove on my hand, the smells of female-ness. And the confidences of women, fascinating and at times overpowering, about their pains, their periods, their fertility, their husbands, their lovers. What gets to me, though, are the exams. The touching. Deep internal touching, feeling for the bulge of the uterus, for those small elusive olives the ovaries, exploring for tenderness, creating sudden moments of pain. Technically I'm reasonably good—as good as can be expected for a third-year medical student rotating through ob-gyn. But I still find it strange to be touching intimately but without passion—as a doctor.

I'm not alone in this either—the other med students on ob-gyn seem just as awkward as I am. We hang around in the lounge when the pharmaceutical rep leaves free coffee and doughnuts, cracking jokes, laughing too much.

It reminds me of another situation: in the second-year physical diagnosis course, when we had to examine each other. The idea was that we'd learn how to be more compassionate doctors if we practiced physical exams on one another first, before going on to patients. We were divided into small groups, men and women together, and sent to various examining rooms. Our exams began at the head and worked down. You couldn't get too upset about looking into your medical student buddy's eyes, but by the second session, when we got down to the chest, the protests began. First it was the women complaining and refusing to be examined, but as it became clear that genital and rectal exams were also part of the required curriculum, men started to protest as well. And finally there was a full-scale revolt. A petition was circulated, meetings were hurriedly arranged with various administrators, protests were loud and vocal. The class was boycotted. We ended up learning the pelvic exam on professional models, and doing rectal exams on plastic dummies. No one felt the course should be repeated.

I've always been sort of puzzled about why my fellow medical students got so upset. After all, we had done just about everything else together—cut open cadavers, crammed for exams,

"SCOOT DOWN TO THE EDGE OF the table, hon," says Dr. Snarr. The small room is hot, the air stuffy. Our patient winces at the the word "hon." She is a young woman with chronic pelvic pain, the bane of gynecologists, and I can tell she doesn't like Snarr's tone. She does scoot along the table, though, and Snarr kicks a wheeled stool toward me. I sit on it, slide between her legs, ready for my lesson of the day. Feet and calves and thighs surround me, suddenly very close. Snarr positions the lamp before my chest, so light pours on her. I warm the speculum in my gloved hand, and with a twist insert it.

"Open it up," he says. "Tighten it all the way open. Pull down to keep away from the urethra. You hit the urethra and no patient will ever come back to you."

Snarr is my teacher, a gaunt and narrow-shouldered man, with a small potbelly below the belt of his plaid pants. Before coming in here, he went over the information I had gathered and insisted it was nonsense. She couldn't possibly feel that kind of pain. I must not be asking the right questions. Hadn't I learned anything? Gynecologists have the reputation of being the dummies of medicine: surgeons laugh at their clumsiness in the operating room, internists at their ignorance of medical fact, psychiatrists at their insensitivity. And so far Snarr had done nothing to dispel that prejudice—which was too bad, considering that I was an impressionable third-year medical student, still trying to decide what field to go into.

"Okay," says Snarr. "Now swab it out real well. Get some cells on that."

I swab.

"Pull that speculum out now. Get a good look at those walls."

I see pink folds as I pull, pink moist walls bulging in against the metal of the speculum—aquatic territory, the scalloped forms of submarine life. It's out. Snarr is quick next with lubricating jelly on the first two fingers of my glove. I stand up, push the stool away. I begin.

"AIIEE!" The woman screams and slides up on the table. "God! Oh, God!"

"So that's . . . that's where it hurts," I say. I'm sweating. "Just . . . just a second, I'll try more gently."

I feel around again. This time she doesn't scream. She breathes deeply. I can't feel a thing, but with Snarr watching I can't pull out right away. For a month I've been spending afternoons in gynecology clinic with Dr. Snarr—a

MEL WILLGES

136 *Ms.* NOVEMBER 1984

Poem in Answer to the Question "Why Don't You Have Children?"

BY **JANA HARRIS** • FEBRUARY 1985

i

at noon you leave to teach
finding your way
through the many stray cats
who have come to your door,
one so hungry it eats horse chow,
in the field
the neighbor's cow has calved,
Kinderman's black-and-white dairy
watch at the fence,
so many of them
they look like Xeroxes

the newborn's
many jointed legs askew
injured insect
it cannot rise,
the mother does not
lick it clean with love,
but kneads the calf like bread,
beats it with her muzzle
runs away, grazing
out of sight while
Kinderman's dairy strains
against the fence
for a better view

ii

at school you teach
tireless teenagers poetry,
they want to compose
in-depth poems

about the symbolism
of the nomenclature
of the Junior Prom and Senior Ball
while listening to Michael Jackson,
you say: get serious,
and forbid the music,
tell them about the calf
born that morning

Lindsay hands you a poem
"The Lady Next Door,"
killed her twins,
banged their heads against
the bathtub rim,
at the funeral bruises
covered their tiny faces,
the poem titled "Lindsay"
tells you her father
poured gasoline
over his clothes, said
save me, and
struck a match

you ask her if she made that up,
she says, he's always
trying to get me,
he started picking on me
when I was twelve
and hasn't quit,
my theory is
I turn him on,
you tell the class

they can write poetry
about the Junior Prom
and listen to Michael Jackson

iii
driving home
you run three red lights,
at your door cats
are screaming for food,
there are more of them,
the tiny black-and-white calf
stands alone in the field

Kinderman's dairy has become
bored and gone home,
the newborn's bleatings
keep you from sleep,
over the phone
the farmer's wife tells you:
the cow's not
a bad mother, just
trying to make the calf walk,
what's the matter, lady?
aren't you used to
things being born?

If Women Had a Foreign Policy

MARCH 1985

THIS ROUNDTABLE—another in the *Ms.* series of roundtable discussions on major issues of our time—took place at the end of 1984 and included Gloria Steinem, writer, activist, and co-founder of *Ms.;* Perdita Huston, feminist author and expert on world development issues; Bella Abzug, former U.S. congresswoman and current president of Women USA; Patricia Derian, Washington writer and former assistant secretary of state for human rights and humanitarian affairs in the Carter administration; Robin Morgan, author and activist in the international feminist movement; and Marcia Ann Gillespie, activist, freelance writer, and former editor of *Essence* magazine.

> **"Why should national interest always be equated with male interest?"**

GLORIA STEINEM: This discussion started from the premise "What would happen if women had a foreign policy?" What if American women considered the situation of women in other countries a primary concern and influenced our *own* national policy to that end? What if we had the self-confidence to consider *ourselves* a primary concern, as well as the women in some other country? It's considered controversial to even talk about this because it is putting women's interests ahead of, or together with, national interests.

But after all, we've all said that women often have more in common with each other than we do with our own government. Why should national interest always be equated with male interest?

BELLA ABZUG: You know, the idea of women influencing foreign policy is not a new one. The women's suffrage movement regarded a foreign policy on the part of women to be crucial. In 1915, the International Suffrage Alliance arranged an international women's congress at The Hague. They established the International Committee of Women for Permanent Peace, which sent delegates to the heads of state of the nations fighting in World War I. There was a whole series of things in the 1920s—women involved in developing petitions, and there were twelve thousand public meetings in support of the Kellogg-Briand Pact to outlaw war; women were considered influential in getting the Senate to pass such a treaty. And then they formed another organization called the National Committee on the Cause and Cure of War in which many of our famous old organizations like the YWCA and the Business and Professional Women's Club were included. They were very instrumental in the general disarmament conference in 1932 where women from fifty-three nations brought, I think, ten million petition signatures into the League of Nations Hall in Geneva. The Women's International League for Peace and Freedom came right out of the suffrage movement and is still active; they were part of many of these events. Later, of course, in the 1960s, we had Women Strike for Peace, which was instrumental in helping secure the partial Nuclear Test Ban Treaty. So women having a foreign policy is not historically new.

I've been pressing lately for a sort of shadow State Department and National Security Council as starters.

As long as we're outside power, we've got to work a little differently. This is not to say that we won't continue to push to secure the power to bring us *inside* government itself. But in the meanwhile, we have to demand that women be a presence at any national and international conferences where the big decisions are made. At this point, we're not even present in the foreign policy debates on radio and television, except in very limited degrees. We should demand to be there.

ROBIN MORGAN: I want women in power as well. We do have a few women heads of state—pathetically few—and now quite a number of women at cabinet level around the world, but usually in "soft" areas: minister of education, or health, or sports, or welfare—"women's concerns." I want a woman as the minister of *trade* or *economics* or *foreign affairs* or *state* in every country in the world. Those are the real policy-making positions.

NATIONAL SECURITY

PERDITA HUSTON: Why don't we start by redefining national security? My premise is that there is no such thing as *national* security in today's world if there is no *global* security. The global resource base is being destroyed day by day. This enormous environmental degradation gives rise to hunger, chaos, political upheaval, and so on. And how on earth, if you don't take global security issues into consideration, can you expect to live in peace and security in a world where two-thirds of the population is in dire straits?

There is no weapon on earth that squelches people's need for freedom. And our country has based our entire concept of national security on weapons rather than on surviving as a species.

MARCIA ANN GILLESPIE: Another point to think of in redefining national security is "strength." Especially in light of Reagan's election where people kept saying "I'm going to vote for Ronald Reagan because he's going to make us strong," we have to help people ask, "What are you calling strong?" Because as long as that concept exists the way it does, it really comes down to more missiles and to knocking ideological heads. It does not create the kind of security I think we're talking about.

MORGAN: You also can't redefine national security in an ignorance vacuum. For example, we are fed a statistic that says the world literacy rate is rising. The world literacy rate, in fact, is rising for men; it is *falling* for women, and women are already two out of three of the world's illiterates. Hunger impacts most on women and children around the world. The majority of the world's refugees are women and children—which is the one major "grown-up" issue that the United Nations finally now will define as a women's issue. Population policy, however, is still generally and astonishingly regarded as separate from women. The problem of the elderly is not perceived as a problem of women. Yet women *are* the elderly in virtually every culture; plus we're the primary caretakers of the elderly. The problem of children's health is still seen as separate from women in most countries. Whether it's deforestation, refugees, hunger, war, education, health—it always is impacting most severely on women, who are the last consulted about any solution. So that when we redefine national security, this basic consciousness has to be there. I don't think it has to *wait* for that, because the kind of effort we're talking about would help create it.

DEVELOPMENT

HUSTON: I spent six weeks in Africa this summer looking at rural water supply projects and how they are helping women, and I came back with an incredible sense of impending disaster. Women may not have to walk six miles a day to find water anymore, but they sure have to go out and scratch, scratch, scratch to pay the pump fees. And are the women involved in the decision making as to where the fees go? No. This is a major policy issue.

And the population growth rate is putting enormous pressures on the environment, not only with water, but also with fuel. I came back with the feeling that in twenty years the whole continent of Africa would be a desert. Now that is a U.S. national security problem. We must start thinking in these long-term global security modes.

PATRICIA DERIAN: Women do tend to be the marketers and the base of the economy in an enormous part of the world. And the consequences of what you describe come just at the moment when development theory in the United States is being stood on its head. According to this new way of thinking, the only places where development has worked are West Germany, with the Marshall Plan after World War II; Japan, with postwar reparations; South Korea; and so on. So this new theory favors making capital investment in private economies. And it comes *just* at the time that the women—who *are* those basic producers in the Third World, and who are small-time entrepreneurs ineligible for large capital investment—are being wiped out of the picture.

WAR AND PEACE

ABZUG: Historically, for example, we know that women have always been much more amenable to a peaceful way of solving problems. All the polls show it. Women don't like a military approach in Central America; we're against an arms buildup; we're for a nuclear freeze.

And the Brandt Commission had a good idea. It proposed a tax on all arms sales to fund development. Even if it were a minimal percentage, even 1 percent, it would fund all the development projects in the entire world—primary health care, literacy, everything. Now there's one to go for.

HUMAN RIGHTS

DERIAN: I feel strongly that there is no way to plan a meaningful foreign policy for this country if it does not include fundamental human rights.

STEINEM: As it is, the list of human rights doesn't even include those that especially affect women—like reproductive freedom.

GILLESPIE: The women I've talked to from all over the world always seem to come back to the simple basics: peace, a safe environment for ourselves and our children, a safe place to grow. And the real basic is, can we feed ourselves?

DERIAN: Add this to your list: the fundamental human right of having a voice in your government. After all, that's why we're having this conversation. We women don't really have a voice—yet.

Solving the Great Pronoun Debate

BY **MARIE SHEAR** • OCTOBER 1985

MALE PRONOUNS are supposedly the hardest form of sexist language to overcome. Purists insist that "he," "his," and "him" are indispensable when the person in question is unidentified or archetypical. In apocalyptic terms, they warn that nonsexist alternatives are ostentatious and politicized. The purists sound like fifteenth-century cartographers warning Columbus about the sea monsters.

Despite the humbug, we *can* solve the Great Pronoun Problem. Nonsexist usage, like all first-rate writing and speech, requires skill placed in the service of an educated eye and ear. But we needn't exaggerate the difficulty. Practice is necessary. Genius is not.

THE SIMPLEST SOLUTION OF THEM ALL

Millions of people have been using "they," "their," and "them" as third-person singulars all along. They are eminently sensible. As a reformed pedant, I don't say that casually. Until a few years ago, I agreed with the columnist who called the singular "they" "grammatically repulsive." I scorned people who used it, considering them fundamentally uncouth—like public smokers. But I've seen the light.

Many word watchers endorse "they." During the last ten or fifteen years, they have alerted us to its surprisingly long and respectable history. Valuable scholarly discussions by Ann Bodine and Rosa Shand Turner teach us that "they" was widely accepted in written English until the end of the eighteenth century, when grammarians began attacking it. So "they" isn't some new, sloppy corruption of "correct" English, but rather a return to venerable usage. George Jochnowitz concludes that it is wrong, even astounding, to consider "they" incorrect for formal writing when it predates "he" and is nearly universal in colloquial and spoken English.

> " 'They' was widely accepted in written English until the end of the eighteenth century, when grammarians began attacking it."

Do pronouns matter? President Ronald Reagan thinks so. He calls Christians "we" and calls everyone else "they." In contrast, Jimmy Carter talks about the typical presidential candidate "himself or herself."

Way to go, Jimmy.

Date Rape:
The Story of an Epidemic and Those Who Deny It

BY **ELLEN SWEET** • OCTOBER 1985

It was the beginning of spring break when I was a junior. I was in good spirits and had been out to dinner with an old friend. We returned to his college (dorm). There were some seniors on the ground floor drinking beer, playing bridge. I'm an avid player, so we joined them, joked around a lot. One of them, John, wasn't playing, but he was interested in the game. I found him attractive. We talked, and it turned out we had a mutual friend, shared experiences. It was getting late, and my friend had gone up to bed, so John offered to see me safely home. We took our time, sat outside talking for a while. Then he said we could get inside one of the most beautiful campus buildings, which was usually locked

> "Date rape is among the least reported, least believed, and most difficult to prosecute [crimes], second only to spouse rape."

at night. I went with him. Once we were inside, he kissed me. I didn't resist, I was excited. He kissed me again. But when he tried for more, I said no. He just grew completely silent. I couldn't get him to talk to me anymore. He pinned me down and ripped off my pants. I couldn't believe it was happening to me.

Such denial, the inability to believe that someone they know could have raped them, is a common reaction of victims of date rape, say psychologists and counselors who have researched the topic and treated these women. In fact, so much silence surrounds this kind of crime that many women are not even aware that they have been raped. In one study, Mary P. Koss, a psychology professor at Kent State University, asked female students if they had had sexual intercourse against their will through use of or threat of force (the minimal legal definition of rape). Of those who answered yes, only 57 percent went on to identify their experience as rape. Koss also identified the other group (43 percent) as those who hadn't even acknowledged the rape to themselves.

"I can't believe it's happening on our campus" is usually the initial response to reports such as Koss's. She also found that one in eight women students had been raped, and one in four were victims of attempted rape. Since only 4 percent of all those reported the attack, Koss concluded that "at least ten times more rapes occur among college students than are reflected in official crime statistics." (Rape is recognized to be the most underreported of all crimes, and date rape is among the least reported, least believed, and most difficult to prosecute, second only to spouse rape.)

Most victims of date rape initially blame themselves for what happened, and almost none report it to campus authorities. And most academic institutions prefer to keep it that way, judging from the lack of surveys on date rape—all of which makes one wonder if they don't actually blame the victim, too.

As long as such attacks continue to be a "hidden" campus phenomenon, unreported and unacknowledged by many college administrators, law enforcement personnel, and students, the problem will persist. Of course, the term has become much better known in the three years since *Ms.* reported on the prevalence of such experiences. It has been the subject of talk shows such as *The Phil Donahue Show* and TV dramas (*Cagney & Lacey*), but for most people it remains a contradiction in terms. "Everybody has a stake in denying that it's happening so often," says Martha Burt. "For women, it's self-protective . . . if only bad girls get raped, then I'm personally safe. For men, it's the denial that 'nice' people like them do it."

Statistics alone will not solve the problem of date rape, but they could help bring it out into the open. Which is why *Ms.* undertook the first nationwide survey on college campuses. The *Ms.* Magazine Campus Project on Sexual Assault, directed by Mary P. Koss at Kent State and funded by the National Center for the Prevention and Control of Rape, reached more than seven thousand students at a nationally representative sample of thirty-five schools to find out how often, under what circumstances, and with what aftereffects a wide range of sexual assaults, including date rape, took place.

RESULTS OF THE *MS.* STUDY

One-quarter of women in college today have been the victims of rape or attempted rape, and almost 90 percent of them knew their assailants. Preliminary results of the three-year study show the following:

- Fifty-two percent of all the women surveyed have experienced some form of sexual victimization.
- One in every eight women were the victims of rape, according to the prevailing legal definition.
- One in every twelve men admitted to having fulfilled the prevailing definition of rape or attempted rape, yet virtually none of those men identified themselves as rapists.
- Of the women who were raped, almost three-quarters did not identify their experience as rape.
- Forty-seven percent of the rapes were by first or casual dates, or by romantic acquaintances.
- Three-quarters of the women raped were between ages fifteen and twenty-one; the average age at the time of the rape was eighteen.
- More than 80 percent of the rapes occurred off campus, with more than 50 percent on the man's turf: home, car, or other.
- More than one-third of the women raped did not discuss their experience with anyone; more than 90 percent did not tell the police.

MS. HELPED TO REDIRECT the public's understanding and recognition of rape, debunking the presumption that it is perpetrated only by strangers. Over the decades, as the discourse has become more proactive and nuanced, so too have policy reforms and interventions—which now commonly address issues like consent, explicitly outlaw surreptitious drugging and drink spiking, and have even begun to consider the act of "stealthing" (removal of a condom during intercourse). While solid statistics are difficult to cull—so often these crimes go vastly underreported—by all accounts campus sexual violence remains pervasive.

Finding Celie's Voice

BY **ALICE WALKER** • DECEMBER 1985

THE SPRING OF 1984, as I was completing the daily scrutiny of each hollyhock bud in my garden, my neighbor on the next ridge, a lesbian sculptor and potter of great talent, arrived on my doorstep. She had just finished the evening milking of her goats, she said, when she received a call from a feminist bookstore in San Francisco, some 140 miles away. A television news van was apparently parked in front of their door, and the newspersons inside had informed the bookstore owners that *The Color Purple* was up for banning—because a local mother had objected to its use in the Oakland public schools—and since they sold the book, what did they think of this?

Their response was to put the newscaster on hold, call my neighbor, and ask her to tramp up the hills and down the ravines, through the trees and underbrush and sticker-briar, and cross the creek to ask me what they should say.

I learned that a certain Mrs. Green had objected to having her daughter, Donna, read *The Color Purple.* In her opinion the book was too sexually explicit, presented a stereotyped view, and degraded Black people by its "exposure" of their folk language.

Eventually, a committee was formed to study the merits of *The Color Purple* to determine whether it was degrading to Black people, repugnant to whites, and generally bad for growing minds. The committee, comprising all colors and both (or more) sexes, representative of the people as only a Bay Area committee can be, exonerated the book while at the same time treating Mrs. Green and her objections with patience, understanding, tact, and even gentleness—for which I was glad.

For I feel I know what Mrs. Green was objecting to . . . the first five pages of the book. The same five pages *my* mother objected to because she found the language so offensive. They are the pages that describe the brutal sexual violence done to a nearly illiterate Black woman-child who then proceeds to write down what has happened to her in her own language, from her own point of view. She does not find rape thrilling; she thinks the rapist looks like a frog with a snake between his legs. How could this not be upsetting? Shocking? How could anyone want to hear this? She spoke of "pussy," "titties," the man's "thang." I remember actually trying to censor this passage in Celie's voice even as I wrote it. Even I found it almost impossible to let her say what had happened to her as *she* perceived it, without euphemizing it a little. And why? Because once you strip away the lie that

Akosua Busia as Nettie and Desreta Jackson as a young Celie in *The Color Purple.*

rape is pleasant, that rapists have anything at all attractive about them, that children are not permanently damaged by sexual pain, that violence done to them is washed away by fear, silence, and time, you are left with the positive horror of the lives of thousands of children (and who knows how many adults)—lives we are even beginning to hear about now in *People, Newsweek,* and *Time*—who have been sexually abused and who have never been permitted their own language to tell about it.

Celie's stepfather, the rapist, warns her not to tell anybody but God about having been raped. But Celie's community had already made sure she would not feel free even to use the words she knew. In her backward, turn-of-the-century community the words "penis" and "vagina" did not exist. Indeed, so off-limits was any thought of the penis that the closest anyone got to it in language was to call it "the man's thing." As for "vagina"—well, this is how my grandmother taught her girls to bathe: "Wash down as far as possible, then wash up as far as possible, then wash possible."

Of course if I had written of Celie's rape from the point of view of the rapist or that of the voyeur, very few people—other than feminists—would have been offended. We have been brainwashed to identify with the person who receives pleasure, no matter how perverted; we are used to viewing rape from the rapist's point of view. I could have written that Celie enjoyed her abuse and done it in such pretty, distancing language that many readers would have accepted it as normal. But to do this would have been to betray Celie; not only her experience of rape, but the integrity of her life;

her life itself. For it is language more than anything else that reveals and validates one's existence, and if the language we actually speak is denied us, then it is inevitable that the form we are permitted to assume historically will be one of caricature, reflecting someone else's literary or social fantasy.

This is one reason I use the word "mammy" in the book as a word used by turn-of-the-century Black people instead of "mother," though already in a somewhat pejorative way. It is my hunch that "mammy"—which in America conjures up only an immensely fat and Black wide-eyed slave of thin Vivien Leigh– or Bette Davis–like white people—is in fact an African word. For certain it was a word used by early twentieth-century African Americans until it was expropriated and popularized by whites and used to designate a kind of contented, white-folks-comforting Black woman of enormous girth of whom Black people felt ashamed. I feel immensely

grateful that what little understanding I have of the probable transformation of this word comes from having had a grandfather who, while I was growing up, still used it. This is what he called his mother and this is what he called his children's mother—and as a child watching the "mammies" in films like *Gone with the Wind,* I wondered why. I knew his mother had been largely Cherokee Indian and was remembered mainly for her meanness and long hair. His wife, my mother's mother, was an obviously oppressed, long-suffering Black, Black woman who gave birth to twelve children and who, from pictures and memories that I have of her, apparently never smiled.

There is no reason to try to bring "mammy" back. Its intention in racist books and films was to undermine the integrity of the mother of the Black race, and in the minds of many, many people this was accomplished. This is the reason many Black people cannot even say the word aloud without cringing. It will be a great and amusing day in our nation's future when a film—perhaps many films—will be made about the old plantation South and the story will unfold from a real "mammy's" point of view. Then we will see why the real woman was locked inside the stereotype. It will be like watching a prison break.

But as of now "mammy" is a used, abused, disposed-of word, and the person to whom it applies has met the same fate. This was emphasized for me when a colleague was telling me about the horrors of the 1984 Republican National Convention, one of which was the presence of Black entertainers who sang.

Who were these entertainers? I asked. "The Mammies and the Pappies," she replied. She then elaborated on the personalities Reagan's staff had chosen to represent Black people at the convention. Her harshest words were reserved for the mammy figure whom she imagined consoling Ronald Reagan with johnnycake and clabbered milk in the "classic" mammy tradition. "Now don't you worry none, honey," this modern mammy would say, her sequined gown now replacing her apron of old, "them bombs you settin' up in Europe ain't botherin' nobody. And them shiftless shines you cuttin' off of welfare ought to find them some good white folks to work for like I done."

And yet we can learn from what has happened to "mammy" too. That it is not by suppressing our own language that we counter other people's racist stereotypes of us, but by having the conviction that if we present the words in the context that is or was natural to them we do not perpetuate those stereotypes but rather expose them. And more important, we help the ancestors in ourselves and others continue to exist. If we kill off the *sound* of our ancestors, the major portion of us, all that is past, is history, is human being, is lost, and we become historically and spiritually thin, a mere shadow of who we were on the earth.

For Celie's speech pattern in *The Color Purple,* Celie's words reveal not only an intelligence that transforms illiterate speech into something that is, at times, very beautiful—as well as effective in conveying her sense of her world—her speech also reveals what has been done to her by a racist and sexist system, and her intelligent blossoming as a human being despite her oppression demonstrates why her oppressors persist even today in trying to keep her down. For if and when Celie rises to her rightful, earned place in society across the planet, the world will be a different place, I can tell you.

How can you justify enslaving such a persona as Celie? Segregating or sexually abusing such a person? Her language—all that we have left of her—reveals her as irreducibly human. And the answer is, you cannot.

She has not accepted an alien description of who she is, neither has she accepted an alien tongue completely to tell us about it. Her being is affirmed by the language in which she is revealed, and like everything about her it is characteristic, hard-won, and authentic.

The system closed the door on people who sounded like Celie long before I was born. All of us who can *hear* her today open the shut doors in ourselves and in our society, wide.

And when Celie comes through those doors, buffalo soldiers on one side, Shug and Natty Dread and a clutch of dreadlocked Rastas perhaps on the other, and only when Celie comes through those doors, when Celie comes in from the cold of repression, self-hatred, and denial, and only when Celie comes in from the cold—do I come in. And many of you as well. And when all of us and all of the old ones are hugged up inside this enormous warm room of a world we must build very quickly, really, or die of a too-shallow mutual self-respect, you will see with me—through the happy spirits of our grandchildren—such joy as the planet has never seen.

And I can personally deliver the message that the old spirits are more alive today than anyone thought.

When I was a little girl, there was a song that was very popular on the gospel station of the radio. It was called "Will the Circle Be Unbroken?" It is about how death breaks the circle of loved ones on earth, but how, in heaven, "in the sky, Lord, in the sky," this will not be the case. In heaven neither father nor mother will die. Nor little sister, brother, lover or husband or wife, either. Heaven, according to the song, is different from here.

It is a mournful song that was written specifically, I think, about the loss of the songwriter's mother, and it used to make me sad and fearful of losing my own. Over the years I have worried about losing not only my mother and other members of my family, but poets, singers, philosophers, prophets, political activists as well. And many of these we have all lost, sometimes to sickness, accident, or disease, sometimes to assassination. But I have found that where there is spiritual union with other people, the love one feels for them keeps the circle unbroken and the bond between us and them strong, whether they are dead or alive. Perhaps that is one of the manifestations of heaven on earth.

After I had finished *The Color Purple* and it was winning prizes and being attacked, I had several extraordinary dream-visits from people I knew before they died and from people who died before I was born, but whose names and sometimes partial histories I knew. This seemed logical and right. But then, at my most troubled, I started to dream of people I'd never heard of and never knew anything about, except perhaps in a general way. These people sometimes brought advice, always excellent and upbeat, sometimes just a hug. Once a dark, heavyset woman who worked in the fields and had somehow lost the two middle fingers of her right hand took hold of my hand lovingly, called me "daughter," and commented supportively on my work. She was only one of the long line of ancestors who came to visit and take my hand that night, all apparently slaves, field workers, and domestics, who seemed to care about and want to reassure me. I remembered her distinctly next morning because I could still feel her plump hand with its missing fingers gently but firmly holding my own.

Since I am not white and not a man and not really Western and not a psychiatrist, I get to keep these dreams for what they mean to me, and I can tell you that I wake up smiling, or crying happily, as the case may be. It seems very simple: because they know I love them and understand their language, the old ones speak to me. It feels too good to be true!

I wrote this poem the morning after my dream, which I feel was not so much my dream as ours, and which I feel would sustain me forever, though Mrs. Green were joined by millions and my book banned from the planet itself.

The old ones	"Daughter, it's the best you've ever done."
visit me in dreams to thank me for *The Color Purple;*	I can't tell you how many rough old hands
They tell me	I've shook.

Since this dream I have come to believe that only if I am banned from the presence of the ancestors will I know true grief.

Divorce: Who Gets the Blame in "No Fault"?

BY **MARIANNE TAKAS** • FEBRUARY 1986

MOTHERHOOD," says Lillian Kozak, chair of NOW New York State Domestic Relations Law Task Force, "puts a woman behind the eight ball. Child raising can be a wonderful thing, but in our society it has no monetary value and accumulates no economic rights. If at any time the wage-earning father decides to leave, the mother and children can be financially devastated."

The facts support Kozak's claim. There are now more than eight million women raising children under twenty-one whose fathers are not living in the household, the U.S. Bureau of the Census reports. Fully one-third of them live below the poverty level. Nearly two-thirds of families entitled to child support collect no child support at all. And among the "lucky few" who do get some support, the average amount received is about $115 per child per month. According to Wayne Dixon, author of *The Child Support Enforcement Program: Unequal Protection Under the Law,* white families average about $12 per child per month and Black families about $7.

Alimony, once an important means of avoiding postdivorce poverty (particularly for older women or the mothers of young children), is now all but unknown. Less than 5 percent of all divorced, non-remarried women are entitled to receive alimony in a given year, and fewer still actually collect.

All women, married or unmarried, employed within and/or outside the home, are at risk. With the corporate world still largely insensitive to the needs of workers with family responsibilities, even professional couples face hard choices if they want to have children. Commonly, one parent—nearly always the woman—finds that she must interrupt or scale down her career in order to meet the family's needs at home. Coupled with the prevailing wage discrimination against women, the result is a serious disparity in earning power. The family becomes dependent upon the support of the male wage earner and ripe for economic disaster if that support is withdrawn.

Enter Lenore Weitzman, bearer of the bad news. Weitzman, associate professor of sociology at Stanford University, was the major researcher on a ten-year study of the effects of California's widely hailed—and widely imitated—no-fault divorce law. In her shocking and important new book, *The Divorce Revolution: The Unexpected Social and Economic Consequences for Women and Children in America*, Weitzman documents and explains how new divorce policies in California have resulted in severe financial losses to women and children. Her major finding: the effect of the average divorce decree is to decrease the

> "The old fault requirements provided only a crude bargaining tool that helped some women to escape the effects of the underlying problem: the failure of both law and society to recognize and reward the essential services offered by most women in the home."

standard of living of the woman and any minor children in her household by 73 percent, while actually *increasing* that of the man by 42 percent.

"The framers of the no-fault divorce laws," explains Weitzman, "were totally preoccupied with the negative aspects of the traditional adversarial system. In the past, to get a divorce, people were required to prove fault—that a spouse had done something improper like adultery or physical cruelty. That could bring out the worst in people in terms of anger and recriminations, and the legislators hoped that no-fault laws would reduce acrimony and restore dignity to the parties.

"What they didn't consider, however, was that requiring proof of fault had long provided the one protection for economically dependent homemakers and women raising children. If a woman hadn't given her husband grounds for divorce—hadn't committed adultery or other forbidden behavior—she had some leverage. She could agree to ask for the divorce herself on the grounds of the husband's behavior, but only if he first provided adequate support for her and the children."

Those who criticize the growing inequities under no-fault divorce laws do not, however, generally advocate a return to fault requirements. At best, explains NOW's Lillian Kozak, the old fault requirements provided only a crude bargaining tool that helped some women to escape the effects of the underlying problem: the failure of both law and society to recognize and reward the essential services offered by most women in the home.

"What we really need," says Kozak, "are laws and policies that recognize the family as a cooperative unit. If the facts show that a man within a family has been free to pursue his career fully while the woman has taken on most of the child-care responsibility—whether she's also held an outside job or not—his greater earning power is a family asset.

"That means that not only property but also in the years after the divorce income should continue to be shared. Otherwise, it's like dividing up a business partnership by giving half the capital and inventory to each partner but letting one of them keep the entire income-producing business."

"Women file for divorce in most cases because they are 'pissed-off,'" writes Ken Pangborn, president of Men International Inc., in the February 1985 issue of *Legal Beagle: A Family Law Reform Newsletter.* "Greed is a powerful motive. . . . The feminist agenda, when examined closely, is *not* a cry for a fair share of the pie. . . . It is an angry demand for the pie and the kitchen it was cooked in, along with everything else."

The solution, according to Pangborn? Since women cannot be trusted, men should strike back—by aggressively seeking sole custody of their children.

It would be comforting to believe that such extremes are limited to a few extremists, and indeed there *are* numerous calm, fair-minded male voices in the storm. Yet a glance at the steady stream of divorce advocacy books for men, written by male lawyers and published by prestigious houses, is indeed deeply disturbing.

The Lion's Share: A Combat Manual for the Divorcing Male, by J. Alan Ornstein, for example, is dedicated in part to divorcing women, the "Bitches of Buchenwald [with their] female chauvinistic greed." Leonard Kerpelman, author of *Divorce: A Guide for Men,* advised men to use "primitive democratic means" to reach their goals, explaining, "If [judges] see one person hollering and the other submitting, they'll rule for the one hollering." That same angry, competitive mentality pervades two books by Maurice Franks: *How to Avoid Alimony* and the more recent *Winning Custody.*

Perhaps the most chilling of all is *How to Win Custody,* by Louis Kiefer. Kiefer, a lawyer who won sole custody of his own children, offers helpful advice on using accusations of lesbianism as a bargaining technique, and on how to kidnap a child from the custodial mother.

"In recent years, when women began to get 'uppity'—began seeking economic independence and reproductive rights," says the psychologist Phyllis Chesler, author of *Mothers on Trial: The Battle for Children and Custody,* "the deepest patriarchal response was to go for the kids. Because when you go for the children, that keeps women in marriages that are bad, keeps them at home afraid to pursue careers. They're afraid to 'break the rules' that have traditionally defined good mothers. In fact, however, they're at risk even if they *don't* break the rules."

In a legal climate in which male custody victories appear not to require actual prior involvement in child raising, the potential for abuse is rife. While some men may in fact be involved in child raising during marriage, the law does not require or even encourage them to do so. Worse yet, children can be used as pawns for bargaining or expressing anger. Thus, in Weitzman's study, less than one man in ten actually sought physical custody of the children, but fully one-third used custody threats to gain leverage in financial bargaining.

According to Nancy Polikoff, staff attorney of the Women's Legal Defense Fund, the recent advance in male custody rights at first seemed reasonable even to feminist advocates. "In the early 1970s," explains Polikoff, "we saw a trend away from assuming that the mother was always the caretaker of the children and should therefore be their custodian. That seemed fine. We assumed that courts would then make a gender-neutral inquiry into who had actually been caring for the children, and whoever it was, the mother or the father, would be more likely to get custody.

"Well, it hasn't turned out that way. Instead of replacing an assumption that the mother was caring for the children with a gender-neutral inquiry, we've seen the work of the child raiser gradually devalued or ignored. Today the use of other factors to determine custody is flourishing. Courts look at financial status, the nicer home, even the new spouse the man is statistically more likely to have. Then, too, money generally buys the ability to litigate more effectively. In the end, the relationship between mother and child, the work that she's done raising

A memo to the staff of *The New York Times*—with a personal note from legendary editor Abe Rosenthal to the *Ms.* team offering "thanks for many ideas and inspiration"—on the day the newspaper finally mandated the use of "Ms." in all its reporting and communication. "Until now, 'Ms.' had not been used because of the belief that it had not passed sufficiently into the language to be accepted as common usage. The *Times* believes now that 'Ms.' has become a part of the language, and is changing its policy," he wrote, justifying the long delay.

the children, and the importance of continuity of care to the children is all but forgotten."

As the need for reform becomes ever more clear, women's activism on divorce equity is increasing. Just as we struggle for the freedom to choose or not choose men as partners, to marry or not to marry, and to have or not have children, we must also struggle to make those choices meaningful and safe. By insisting that our partings with men be free from oppression and coercion, we open the door to equality between women and men *within* relationships.

Kathy's Day in Court

BY **ANGELA BONAVOGLIA** • APRIL 1988

> **"Fifteen minutes later, Judge Nice returned and read his decision: he would not grant Kathy's request for an abortion; she was not mature enough; it was not in her best interest."**

ON WEDNESDAY, September 23, 1987, at 7:30 a.m., a pregnant seventeen-year-old we will call "Kathy"*—her court-designated name—left her home in a working-class neighborhood of Birmingham, Alabama, and drove alone to the Jefferson County Family Courthouse. Kathy wanted an abortion. But in Alabama, as in twenty other states in the nation, a law exists that forbids a minor (anyone under the age of eighteen) to give her own consent for an abortion. Alabama's minors must ask one parent for permission, and if they can't do that, they must get a judge's approval before they can have an abortion.

Kathy is a friendly young woman with a big hearty laugh. Her face is round with residues of baby fat and framed in a mane of blond hair. People tend to describe her as "sensible," which she is, but her sense of competence comes from having had to take care of herself much too early in life. Six years ago her mother remarried, to a man who is an alcoholic. For the last year and a half Kathy has lived mainly on her own, since she doesn't get along with her stepfather. Kathy always wears a delicate antique ring that belonged to her grandmother, and a man's watch, which she says she more or less pilfered from her stepfather, although "I don't wish to claim him as that," she insists.

---

* Some of the details of Kathy's life have been changed to protect her anonymity.

Normally, on Wednesday, Kathy would be driving to her $4.75-an-hour job as a salesgirl at a clothing store, a job she loves: "All the people coming through here, all the noise, the music on the sound system. I feel kind of funny if I'm in a quiet place." She works full time, with two weekdays off. Kathy has been working since school ended in May. She finished the twelfth grade, but didn't graduate because she failed several subjects. By her own admission, she was not "in the upper class of students, the ones that took the notes and knew everything that was going on." She had also been sick much of her senior year. "I had real bad headaches . . . all the time." Her mother took her to three doctors who believed they were caused by stress, but were unable to help her.

It's difficult for Kathy to talk about Tom, her nineteen-year-old boyfriend, a factory worker by day and drummer by night. Her answers are tense, whispered, monosyllabic. Yes, she loved him. Yes, they had been in a relationship for five months when she found out she was pregnant. At the time she went to court, he didn't know she was pregnant or that she wanted an abortion. "I knew a girl and she had an abortion," said Kathy. "Her boyfriend didn't like the idea of it too much and they broke up. . . . I'm kind of insecure and I didn't want that to happen."

Waiting for her at the courthouse that September day was the abortion provider Kathy had contacted when she realized she was pregnant. Diane Derzis, the director of Summit Medical Center, is a tough, chain-smoking rail of a woman with dark blond hair and long red fingernails. Besides running the center, she had been taking a full load of law school courses for the past three years. Every January, on the anniversary of *Roe v. Wade,* the Supreme Court decision that legitimated abortion, Derzis gives her roomfuls of patients—Black, white, teenagers and women in their forties, childless and mothers of many—a red rose and a note that tells them they are part of a critical, historical movement to protect a woman's right to choose.

Alabama's new consent law for minors' abortions incenses Derzis; she fought against it for a full seven years. When the state legislature finally passed it in June 1987, to be put into effect on September 23, Derzis decided that if she was going to have to live with the law, she would challenge it—immediately. The statute requires that if a minor cannot or does not want to ask one parent for consent to have an abortion, she must seek a judge's determination of whether she is, according to the law, "mature and well-informed enough to make the abortion decision," or if she is found to be immature, whether the "abortion would be in [her] best interest." The law gives no guidance as to how a judge should make these decisions. Diane Derzis wanted to find a teenager willing to go to court and take her chances with the ambiguous law. If a judge turned this test case down, she would help the girl appeal, going as far as necessary in the court system to show how punitive the statute is.

When Kathy, sounding calm and mature, called Summit Medical Center in mid-September to arrange an abortion, just before the law went into effect, Derzis asked to meet with her. She was struck by Kathy's composure: "She's a thirty-five-year-old, really." Derzis asked Kathy if she would wait five days and become the first girl in Jefferson County required to seek a judge's permission for an abortion because she could not go to her family for consent. (As it turned out, Kathy was the first minor in all of Alabama to have an abortion hearing.) In return, Derzis would arrange for Kathy's abortion to be performed for free; it would have cost Kathy $260 otherwise, since she could not put it on her mother's health plan without her mother finding out. Until September 22, Kathy could have had an abortion without parental or judicial involvement. Once she agreed to go to court, the decision of whether or not she would bear a child was up to the discretion of the judge.

"The money was a little bit of why I did it," said Kathy, "but I could have paid." More to the point for Kathy was that "Diane told me it would be a big help to the people who came after me. Everyone thought I was the perfect person to try this out: seventeen, living on my own. And, I thought, with all I've been through, I'm still here. I *know* I can handle this."

Following the instructions set forth in the Alabama law, Derzis had submitted Kathy's request for a judicial hearing to the Jefferson County Family Court. By law, the court had to provide Kathy with free legal representation for her hearing. Her papers were brought by a court officer to a Legal Aid lawyer, J. Wynell "Wendy" Brooks Crew, on September 21. That gave Crew two days to prepare for Kathy's hearing, which was scheduled for the day the law went into effect. Crew believed herself to be Kathy's lawyer even though Charles Nice, the judge who would be hearing the case, had not signed papers formally appointing her. According to Crew and the officer who gave her the papers, in most cases a formal appointment is not necessary for work to begin on a case, especially when there is a rush, as there would be with Kathy's abortion request. The officer had understood Judge Nice to say that minors' abortion requests should be handled by Legal Aid. Crew went to work on the case, researching the law and talking with Kathy by telephone several times during the two days before her court appearance. According to Kathy, it had been hard to talk to a stranger about her pregnancy and decision to abort, "but not as hard, because it was Wendy," who made her feel very comfortable.

But on the day after Crew believed herself to have been appointed as

Kathy's attorney, Judge Nice's bailiff approached her and a private attorney, Marcus Jones. According to Crew, the bailiff told Jones *he* had been appointed to represent the minor, and she was to represent the fetus. Wendy Crew said no. She pointed out that she had already talked to Kathy. She also noted that appointing a lawyer for the fetus would be unconstitutional, since, under *Roe v. Wade,* the fetus cannot be considered a person and does not have the right to representation. The bailiff, Crew recalls, told them to work it out themselves. A thirty-year-old dynamo who had left private corporate law three years earlier to join the staff of Legal Aid, Crew has earned a reputation as a fierce defender of children's rights. Once, when she represented a minor charged with murdering her violent stepfather, Crew was beaten up in court by the stepfather's family in a scene the local press referred to as "a 10-minute brawl." She had survived that and was not about to let herself get thrown off Kathy's case. She knew that without signed papers from Judge Nice, her position was precarious, but she felt the court officer had been following established procedure, and she told Jones she wanted to continue as Kathy's lawyer.

On the morning of the twenty-third she met with Kathy and Diane Derzis in the courthouse. Remembers Kathy, "I was just petrified. Me and Diane went upstairs and met with Wendy in this big conference room with a big humongous table." While they were sitting there, Crew was called out of the room. The same officer who had given her the papers told her she was off the case. He showed her the appointment papers from Judge Nice on which she saw that something had been whited out in the section naming Kathy's counsel—she presumed it was "Legal Aid"—and Marcus Jones's name written in.

Crew and Jones went into the judge's office. Nice, sixty-eight, a slightly built, benevolent-looking man, had in his office pamphlets from Lifeline, an adoption agency run by the virulently antichoice Sav-A-Life Christian ministry. Hanging on his wall was a photo of some of Lifeline's adoptive parents at their last reunion. Crew told him she wanted to stay on the case. She asked to be appointed Kathy's guardian or to be co-counsel. Judge Nice dismissed both requests and dismissed Crew.

Now Marcus Jones went into the conference room to meet Kathy. "I was mad," said Kathy. "I felt like I could pull through this with Wendy. Then they bring some man in fifteen minutes before the trial. Men don't really know about this. How is some man gonna stand up there and fight for me when he doesn't even know what's going on? I thought to myself, 'I'm gonna lose.'"

At approximately 9:45 a.m., Kathy and Diane Derzis walked down the hall from the conference room to Judge Nice's courtroom. Papers covered the window on the door, to guarantee the requisite confidentiality of the

Kathy's Day In Court

Because she didn't want to tell her parents, Kathy, like thousands of teens across America, had to ask a judge for permission to have her abortion. Eventually, she was allowed her choice. What do parental consent laws accomplish?

By Angela Bonavoglia

Wendy Crew believed she would represent Kathy, but when she entered Judge Nice's chambers he said she was dismissed from the case. Earlier, the bailiff had tried to get her to represent the fetus. The new lawyer had 15 minutes to discuss the case with Kathy.

ON WEDNESDAY, SEPTEMBER 23, 1987, AT 7:30 A.M., A PREGnant 17-year-old we will call "Kathy"*—her court-designated name—left her home in a working-class neighborhood of Birmingham, Alabama, and drove alone to the Jefferson County Family Courthouse. Kathy wanted an abortion. But in Alabama, as in 20 other states in the nation, a law exists that forbids a minor (anyone under the age of 18) to give her own consent for an abortion. Alabama's minors must ask one parent for permission, and if they can't do that, they must get a judge's approval before they can have an abortion.

Kathy is a friendly young woman with a big hearty laugh. Her face is round with residues of baby fat, and framed in a mane of blond hair. People tend to describe her as "sensible," which she is, but her sense of competence comes from having had to take care of herself much too early in life. Six years ago her mother remarried, to a man who is an alcoholic. For the last year and a half Kathy has lived mainly on her own, since she doesn't get along with her stepfather. Kathy always wears a delicate antique ring that belonged to her grandmother, and a man's watch, which she says she more or less pilfered from her stepfather, although "I don't wish to claim him as that," she insists.

Normally, on a Wednesday, Kathy would be driving to her $4.75-an-hour job as a salesgirl at a clothing store, a job she loves. "All the people coming through there, all the noise, the music on the sound system. I feel kind of funny if I'm in a quiet place." She works full-time, with two weekdays off. Kathy has been working since school ended in May. She finished the twelfth grade, but didn't graduate because she failed several subjects. By her own admission, she was not "in the upper class of students, the ones that took the notes and knew everything that was going on." She had also been sick much of her senior

*Some of the details of Kathy's life have been changed to protect her anonymity.

year. "I had real bad headaches ... all the time." Her mother took her to three doctors who believed they were caused by stress, but were unable to help her.

It's difficult for Kathy to talk about Tom, her 19-year-old boyfriend, a factory worker by day and drummer by night. Her answers are tense, whispered, monosyllabic. Yes, she loved him. Yes, they had been in a relationship for five months when she found out she was pregnant. At the time she went to court, he didn't know she was pregnant or that she wanted an abortion. "I knew a girl and she had an abortion," said Kathy. "Her boyfriend didn't like the idea of it too much and they broke up. . . I'm kind of insecure and I didn't want that to happen."

Waiting for her at the courthouse that September day was the abortion provider Kathy had contacted when she realized she was pregnant. Diane Derzis, the director of Summit Medical Center, is a tough, chain-smoking rail of a woman with dark blond hair and long red fingernails. Besides running the center, she has been taking a full load of law school courses for the past three years. Every January, on the anniversary of *Roe v. Wade*, the 1973 Supreme Court decision that legitimated abortion, Derzis gives her roomfuls of patients—black, white, teenagers and women in their forties, childless and mothers of many—a red rose and a note that tells them they are part of a critical, historical movement to protect a woman's right to choose.

Alabama's new consent law for minors' abortions incenses Derzis; she fought against it for a full seven years. When the state legislature finally passed it in June of 1987, to be put into effect on September 23, Derzis decided that if she was going to have to live with the law, she would challenge it—immediately. The statute requires that if a minor cannot or does not want to ask one parent for consent to have an abortion, she must seek a judge's determination of whether she is, according to the law, "mature and well-informed enough to make the abortion decision," or, if she is found to be immature, whether the "abortion would be in [her] best interest." The law gives no guidance as to how a judge should make these decisions. Diane Derzis

ILLUSTRATIONS BY MICHAEL NG

wanted to find a teenager willing to go to court and take her chances with the ambiguous law. If a judge turned this test case down, she would help the girl to appeal, going as far as necessary in the court system to show how punitive the statute is.

When Kathy, sounding calm and mature, called Summit Medical Center in mid-September to arrange an abortion, just before the law went into effect, Derzis asked to meet with her. She was struck by Kathy's composure: "She's a 35-year-old, really." Derzis asked Kathy if she would wait five days and become the first girl in Jefferson County required to seek a judge's permission for an abortion because she could not go to her family for consent. (As it turned out, Kathy was the first minor in all of Alabama to have an abortion hearing.) In return, Derzis would arrange for Kathy's abortion to be performed for free; it would have cost Kathy $260 otherwise, since she could not put it on her mother's health plan without her mother finding out. Until September 22, Kathy could have had an abortion without parental or judicial involvement. Once she agreed to go to court, the decision of whether or not she would bear a child was up to the discretion of a judge.

"The money was a little bit of why I did it," said Kathy, "but I could have paid." More to the point for Kathy was that "Diane told me it would be a big help to the people who came after me. Everyone thought I was the perfect person to try this out: seventeen, living on my own. And, I thought, with all I've been through, I'm still here, I *know* I can handle this."

Following the instructions set forth in the Alabama law, Derzis had submitted Kathy's request for a judicial hearing to the Jefferson County Family Court. By law, the court had to provide Kathy with free legal representation for her hearing. Her papers were brought by a court officer to a Legal Aid lawyer, J. Wynell (Wendy) Brooks Crew, on September 21. That gave Crew two days to prepare for Kathy's hearing, which was scheduled for the day the law went into effect. Crew believed herself to be Kathy's lawyer even though Charles Nice, the judge who would be hearing the case, had not signed papers formally appointing her. According to Crew and the officer who gave her the papers, in most cases a formal appointment is not necessary for work to begin on a case, especially when there is a rush, as there would be with Kathy's abortion request. The officer had understood Judge Nice to say that minors' abortion requests should be handled by Legal Aid. Crew went to work on the case, researching the law and talking with Kathy by telephone several times during the two days before her court appearance. According to Kathy, it had been hard to talk to a stranger about her pregnancy and decision to abort, "but not as hard, because it was Wendy," who made her feel very comfortable.

But on the day after Crew believed herself to have been appointed as Kathy's attorney, Judge Nice's bailiff approached her and a private attorney, Marcus Jones. According to Crew, the bailiff told Jones he had been appointed to represent the

hearing. Kathy walked to the large, wooden witness stand at the front of the courtroom and sat down. "I was having heart failure," she said. She wanted Derzis to stay, but only court personnel were allowed in the room. That left Kathy in a room with four men—Nice, Jones, the bailiff, and the court officer—she had never met before that morning. There was also a young, female court reporter.

Jones began his questioning. To establish her maturity, Jones asked about her school. She told him that since she had not graduated, she planned to take the high school equivalency test. She also testified that she had been working full time and part time for the last two years and contributed to her own support.

Marcus Jones asked about her family. Kathy testified that her alcoholic stepfather abused her mother and herself. According to Kathy, he beat her so badly one night she left and moved in with friends. "I told the judge my mother wanted me to come back home and I finally did, but then neither of us could stand it anymore," so both Kathy and her mother moved out. Her mother is back with the stepfather now. Kathy testified that for the last year and a half she has been living mostly by herself. She didn't want to tell her mother about the pregnancy because her mother told her stepfather everything and if he found out about this he might get mad and end by beating her mother.

Kathy testified that she considered adoption as well as abortion and remembers being surprised when Judge Nice continued to question her about this: "He asked whether I had thought about giving it to some adoption agency. He mentioned about three adoption groups and kept asking, 'Have you thought about this?' 'Yes, sir,' I said about two times. Then he asked Marcus if he wanted to ask me more questions about adoption, but Marcus told the judge I had already answered the question." Kathy had to say whether the pregnancy was the result of incest—a word that had to be explained to her before she could respond—or rape.

After forty-five minutes of testimony, Judge Nice left the courtroom to make his decision. Kathy stepped down from the witness stand and sat on a bench, talking nervously with the court reporter. Fifteen minutes later, Judge Nice returned and read his decision: he would not grant Kathy's request for an abortion; she was not mature enough; it was not in her best interest. The judge told Kathy she should talk to her mother about this decision.

Kathy was stunned. "I was about in tears. How can he say this about me? He didn't feel I was mature enough to make this decision myself? I could feel my eyes start pooling up, and I was going, 'Don't cry, don't cry.'"

"Everyone here at the clinic thinks I'm such a hard bitch," said Diane Derzis, "but I came back the day of that hearing and cried to think of what Kathy went through."

But they persevered, filing an appeal of Judge Nice's decision.

Fourteen days after the hearing, the Alabama Court of Civil Appeals overturned the judge's opinion, rendering a scathing decision:

> The trial judge in this case abused his discretion by denying the minor's request. . . . More importantly, we can neither discern from the trial court's judgment nor from the record any ground upon which the trial court's conclusion could rest. We can safely say, having considered the record, that, should this minor not meet the criteria for "maturity" under the statute, it is difficult to imagine one who would.

On Friday, October 9, Kathy arrived at Summit Medical Center for her abortion. Summit is housed in a neat redbrick building; its interior, decorated in bold prints and bright colors, strains for cheerfulness. Diane Derzis was there to greet and shepherd her through the procedures, but Kathy felt totally alone that day. "It was the most horrible experience of my life. I had to fill out a bunch more papers . . . do a little counseling thing. The counselor was talking to us about birth control and told us exactly what they were going to do. I couldn't really tell what she said 'cause I didn't pay attention, 'cause I didn't want to know."

Judge Nice continues to feel he made the proper judgment in Kathy's case. Asked in an interview four months later how he determined that Kathy was not mature, he told *Ms.,* "I based it on her looks . . . just something that comes across when you talk to her . . . her credibility."

Nice also told *Ms.* that he did not try to appoint Wendy Crew to represent the fetus in this case. However, he said he strongly believes the fetus should have an attorney. "After all, the fetus has a part in it . . . whether the fetus is going to exist or not." He said that in minors' consent cases he would consider not only what is in the minor's best interest but what is in the fetus's best interest as well. Asked if it would be hard to approve an abortion under these conditions, he replied, "Might be."

In all states, whether the law is parental consent or notification, the statutes have been developed and pushed through the legislatures by antichoice groups. Americans United for Life provides, along with its model statutes, line-by-line recommendations on how to write a bill that will withstand legal assault.

The consent and notification laws often contradict other state laws about minors' rights. For instance, they often exist side by side in many states with laws authorizing minors to approve their own medical care. According to a 1986 ACLU booklet on parental notice laws, forty states allow minors to consent to diagnosis and treatment of venereal disease; twenty-seven states allow them to consent to prenatal care, including cesarean section surgery; and nine states have developed "mature minor" laws allowing children under eighteen to consent to all forms of medical treatment. The State of Alabama has all of these statutes.

The solution to the real problem is clear to experts like Nicki Nichols Gamble, executive director of the Planned Parenthood League of Massachusetts. "If you as a parent want to play a supportive role in your children's

---

"KATHY," the Alabama teen in Bonavoglia's article, challenged state-sanctioned obstacles—parental consent or a judicial bypass—to get an abortion in 1987. Alabama would continue to have among the most restrictive abortion laws in the country and the number of clinics would dwindle.

Diane Derzis went on to own the Jackson Women's Health Organization, the named plaintiff in the lawsuit challenging Mississippi's 2018 law banning abortion after fifteen weeks of pregnancy, the case at the center of the Supreme Court's decision to overturn *Roe v. Wade*.

Today, both Alabama and Mississippi are among the ten states that ban abortion from the moment of fertilization with exceptions for the life of the woman. In Alabama, exceptions are also made if the woman is suffering from a condition that risks "substantial and irreversible impairment" of a "major bodily function"; in Mississippi, the ban includes an exception for rape.

lives, you need to convey from a very early age that you want to help them, even when you and they may disagree. . . . You need to talk to them about sexuality. You need to talk to them about contraception. You need to talk with them about the fact that contraception doesn't always work."

Kathy could never talk about sex with her mother or any adult in her family. Her abortion was the first medical treatment she had ever received without her mother's involvement. "All through the whole thing, I was wishing I could tell my mother," Kathy said. "Just to have her there with me would have made me feel better, or just knowing that I could tell her." Kathy still hasn't told her mother about the abortion and doubts that she ever will.

Chromosome Count

BY **ALISON CARLSON** • OCTOBER 1988

I AM AN ATHLETE, and I am a woman. At least I think I'm a woman. But if I were among that dazzlingly gifted number of female athletes preparing to compete in Seoul, my gender, like theirs, would be considered suspect. So much so that before any athlete is allowed to compete in women's events at the Games or in most other major international competitions, she must first submit to a "gender certification" test of her chromosomes. As a tennis pro who has competed on the regional level, I have never had to subject myself to this "Orwellian" inspection, nor contemplate the traumatic possibility of being told I am not female. But this is precisely what has happened to other women athletes, even though gender is far too complex to be evaluated by a laboratory test.

Since 1968, the International Olympic Committee (IOC) has been screening the chromosomes of all women competitors, "to insure femininity in the competitors" and "establish equality among ath-

> **"Critics are labeling the entire theory and practice of sex testing discriminatory . . . because athletes are disqualified on the basis of a postulated advantage that may not be an advantage after all."**

letes." Passing the test, which is called the "buccal smear," has nothing to do with the way a woman looks, her birth records, or her sense of self. Getting "certified feminine" depends on the results of the microscopic analysis of cells, scraped from inside the athlete's cheek to determine the pattern of her sex chromosomes. Normally, the female pattern is XX, and the male is XY. But that is not always the case. And when an abnormality appears, the athlete is subjected to a battery of gynecological and clinical exams to decide whether she is "feminine" enough to compete. So far, it is estimated that a dozen women have been disqualified from Olympic competition.

Those numbers don't begin to tell the chilling story of what's happening to young girls who are being pretested today at lower levels of competition, or of the inaccuracies in the test itself and the flawed assumptions about the very nature of sexuality, or the narrow definitions of femininity that its use is based upon. Neither do they reflect the havoc it wreaks in the lives of those who do not pass, or the stress the test imposes on female athletes on the eve of their competition. As the Olympic high jump champion Debbie Brill, who was first "certified feminine" in 1972, says, "It is scary having to report to a 'sex control' station. You go through all these what-ifs. You know you are a girl, but what if the test doesn't show that?"

Which is what happened to Ewa Klobukowska. The Polish sprinter was the first woman to be disqualified by the test when it was used on a trial basis at the European Track and Field Championships in 1967. Klobukowska might have had some internal male organs due to a birth defect, which is not unusual. Estimates of the incidence of sex chromosomal defects range from one in one thousand to one in four thousand births. At one end of the spectrum are people who look female, while at the other extreme are those who can have some ambiguity in their sex organs and secondary sex characteristics and are almost always treated medically and surgically to produce as concordant a sexual identity as possible.

What the officials told the twenty-one-year-old Klobukowska was that her test revealed an irregularity. Upon further examination, they said she showed "male-like characteristics." Even though she was neither hyper-muscular nor particularly more successful than her peers, their conclusion was that she had been competing "unwittingly as a man." Klobukowska was quoted as saying, "I know what I am and how I feel. . . . It's a dirty and stupid thing to do to me." After her disqualification, she went through severe and long-lasting depressions; it was rumored that she even submitted to surgery to try to correct her internal abnormalities and regain her eligibility. Although Klobukowska was an Olympic gold medalist and world record holder in the hundred-meter dash, her name was removed from the books, and all public recognition of her awards taken away. Today, she works for a Polish computer firm in Czechoslovakia and has broken off all contact with the sports world.

So why are female athletes being subjected to this? Because of rumors about men masquerading as women, and of women "who were not really women" competing at the Games. Although these allegations were not unfounded, they were greatly exaggerated and reflected a fundamental ignorance of the biological conditions of women like Klobukowska who were singled out.

At the 1966 European Track and Field Championships in Budapest, women were required to undress for what the press called a "nude parade" in front of a panel of gynecologists. All 234 competitors were inspected, and all of them, including Klobukowska, passed.

By 1968, the visual check was not enough. A year after Klobukowska's very public disqualification, the IOC decided to adopt the newly discovered buccal smear test, which it considered a simpler, more objective, and more dignified method of distinguishing the sexes. The IOC Medical Commission further justified its use by stating, "It would be unfair in a women's competition to allow chromosomally abnormal athletes with male-like characteristics."

From the first, concerned medical specialists have protested using the buccal smear in this context. The American College of Physicians and the American College of Obstetricians and Gynecologists recently passed resolutions calling for the test to be banned. Not surprisingly, critics are labeling the entire theory and practice of sex testing discriminatory, not just because men are not tested, but because athletes are disqualified on the basis of a postulated advantage that may not be an advantage after all. But at the very heart of the debate is the far more disturbing and complex question of whether testing should be done in the first place.

Although all normal women and men produce both male and female hormones—it is their relative proportion that is important in sexual development—there are also genetically normal women with medical conditions causing an overabundance of the male hormone testosterone. One of these, congenital adrenal hyperplasia, accounts for many if not most innately hypermuscular women. Then there are women who have testosterone-producing tumors on their ovaries, which can induce "male-like" characteristics. Even some hermaphrodites, who are born with both male and female internal organs, have the female XX pattern. And there are men who have the XX chromosome pattern, although this is extremely rare. All of these people would pass through the chromosome screen undetected, would never be subjected to further examination, and would not be banned.

The psychologist John Money, co-author of *Sexual Signatures: On Being a Man or a Woman,* emphasizes this: "The difference between male and female is not black and white; it is a biological continuum. I don't know of any statistical studies anywhere that could tell you what isn't overlap between men and women on anatomical scales. . . . Really, the range of difference within the same sex can be as great as that between men and women. Any dividing line is a matter of context."

Inevitably, drawing that line is a subjective decision. Just how much "male-likeness" is too much? When does it start to mean an unfair advantage?

Dr. Myron Genel, a pediatric endocrinologist, deems it absurd that the IOC is trying to guarantee such things as "physical equality" and "fair competition"—concepts that he says can't even be defined consistently in the first place. "If some women get disqualified for being extra strong, then why not also disqualify those with unusual height or more oxygen capacity?"

Or for that matter why disqualify only some women who have so-called genetic advantages? Genel cites the case of Flo Hyman, who suffered from Marfan's syndrome, a genetic disorder that causes extra height. At six feet five, she was one of the best volleyball players in the world. If anything, height is the anatomical parameter that correlates best with athletic success. Following the IOC's standards, should she have been disqualified?

If authorities begin selecting out designated bits of anatomy, John Money wonders, "what of the Masai with their huge long legs, or the Mexican Indian tribals with their extraordinary oxygenation capacity? Who gets excluded?" He contends that "sports are not democratic; they're elitist. The tallest play basketball; the shortest are jockeys. The ultimate would be to break the Olympics into biological classes and run them like the Westminster Dog Show."

The IOC's response to the debate? "If there is a better way, we would welcome suggestions," says the IOC Medical Commission chairman Prince Alexandre de Mérode. After twenty years, the IOC has finally agreed to set up a "working group" to address the problem. Chairman Mérode promises that by Seoul the medical commission will have decided "how and when the IOC will look into this issue."

The Finnish geneticist Albert de la Chapelle, although a member of that group, is somewhat skeptical, saying, "For so long I have asked the IOC to reassess their policy, and every four years they tell me, 'Let us just get through these next Games, and then we will look into it.' I know the IOC means no harm, but their policy is misguided."

Whatever is decided, the people the IOC claims it is trying to protect should be included in the discussion. To date, there has been no indication that women athletes have ever been asked.

Y DOESN'T ALWAYS MARK THE SPOT

The first time the U.S. swimmer Kirsten Wengler went for a sex test the results went awry. In 1985 she was scheduled to compete in an international student swim meet in Japan. At a coed team meeting, every girl but Kirsten was handed a certificate of femininity, or "fem card" as it is called. In front of the other athletes she was told by the team manager that she needed to go back to the lab.

Wengler, who was twenty-one at the time, said the "guys kidded me. But I knew I was a girl." At first she simply assumed it was a mistake. But when they retested her, the doctors confirmed the results showing the presence of a Y chromosome and said that she might not be able to have children. After some debate, she was finally allowed to compete, because the Japanese were not prepared to do the clinical and gynecological exams that are supposed to follow when the smear detects an abnormal pattern.

The full impact of the test results "really hit me on the plane home from Austin," said Wengler. "I was crying and really freaked out. I thought I would never be able to have children and that something was wrong with me."

Fortunately, Wengler's father is a physician and her mother teaches at a medical school. They quickly arranged for more sophisticated tests at great personal expense. It took four months to get the results, and during that time Wengler was worried and depressed. "I don't know what I would have done if I hadn't been a twenty-one-year-old biology major with doctors for parents," she said.

Wengler eventually learned that what the buccal smear had shown as a Y chromosome was in fact the presence on one of her autosomal or nonsex chromosomes of a protein that is similar to one in a Y. Although she now has her "fem card" and continues to compete in major events, Kirsten Wengler worries about other women who encounter similar results. "What about a poor girl from some backward country? She would probably go home, never find out about the mistake, and feel inadequate for the rest of her life."

BY 2004, the International Olympic Committee had begun allowing transgender athletes to participate, but none had done so openly until the Tokyo 2020 Games when the Canadian women's soccer team had a transgender member, a transgender woman competed in weight lifting for New Zealand, and the U.S. BMX freestyle team had a transgender cyclist. Several other transgender athletes—from track stars to volleyball players—vied to make the Olympic roster in 2020. It seemed a sure sign of progress.

Meanwhile across the United States, 2021 marked a record legislative session for the number of regressive, discriminatory bills introduced, with legislatures in thirty-seven states seeking to bar participation of transgender girls and women on youth, high school, and even college sports teams.

CHAPTER 3

1990s

THE DECADE STARTED under the leadership of Robin Morgan as editor in chief, Helen Zia as managing editor (soon to be executive editor), and Ruth Bower as publisher. Morgan brought global vision and perspective to the issues reported and stories told in the pages of *Ms.,* creating an international advisory board and pledging to ensure that coverage would be done "*by* women writers *from* those countries." And the decision was made to eliminate all paid advertising—a revolutionary call. When the "new" *Ms.* launched, sixty thousand copies were printed and, like the first time, sold out in days. Circulation quickly climbed to 200,000 with subscribers in 117 countries in addition to newsstand and bookstore sales.

Meeting of the Liberty Media for Women board, with then editor in chief Marcia Ann Gillespie (*third from right*) among the team at the table.

In 1993, Marcia Ann Gillespie, who had been a former contributing and executive editor at *Ms.,* took the reins as editor in chief. Gillespie further integrated coverage by and about women of color, lesbians, and young women. And she led a redesign of *Ms.*—partly to address rising supply costs as well as to modernize the format. By 1997, *Ms.* contended with yet another new owner, when Lang sold it to MacDonald Communications Corporation, kicking off another bout of financial uncertainty.

And so, in 1998, *Ms.* began charting a path to liberation: the creation of Liberty Media for Women as owner of the magazine. Envisioned and spearheaded by Gillespie together with Gloria Steinem, it was fueled with financial investments by influential women business leaders and philanthropists. Finally, by the turn of the twenty-first century, *Ms.* was once again the only national magazine for women owned and controlled by women—and able to chart its own destiny.

Ms. **Lives!**

BY **ROBIN MORGAN** • JULY/AUGUST 1990

COSMIC LAUGHTER . . .
They said it couldn't happen. They said no periodical should even try to get along without advertising. They said readers wouldn't want a major feminist magazine of substance, audacity, quality. They said this is a "postfeminist" era, that younger women were burned out. They said *Ms.* was dead.

> **"Welcome to liberated territory—where we defiantly proclaim the beginning of the post-patriarchal era."**

Well, welcome to liberated territory— where we defiantly proclaim the beginning of the post-patriarchal era. The "megabook" you hold in your hands at this moment is a piece of future history.

Your energy made it happen. You said you are age seventeen and age seventy; that you *do* want a challenging, intelligent publication; that you are willing to pay extra for one whose health and size won't be threatened by the absence or presence of ads. You said you cared very much about editorial freedom.

THE POWERFUL JUXTAPOSITION of Robin Morgan's introduction and Gloria Steinem's exhaustive "Sex, Lies, and Advertising" (*opposite*) from 1990 makes crystal clear why *Ms.* has best served its mission—and its readers—as an independent ad-free haven. During the course of a decade, *Ms.* changed hands among four commercial publishers—each offering distinct lessons for *Ms.* editors and a chance for *Ms.* readers to sound off on their preferences—and in 1998 a consortium of feminists launched Liberty Media for Women to create an independent home for *Ms.* But by 2001, turmoil in the magazine industry and insufficient capital reserves prompted Steinem to approach the Feminist Majority Foundation about acquiring Liberty Media for Women. And that is where *Ms.* proudly remains today.

All the tumult of the 1990s set *Ms.* up well for the modern era: the emergence of the internet, the ongoing changing dynamics of the magazine industry, and the continued rise of social media. Today, *Ms.* continues to publish quarterly in print, as well as to draw vast intergenerational audiences to its website, podcasts, and social accounts. Its time-honored traditions—in-depth investigative reporting and feminist political analysis by, with, and for influential leaders in the field—have never been more needed, and bring a new generation of writers and readers together to forge the feminism of the future.

So here we are, still crazy after all these years. Here we are with a hundred pages (including covers), a beautiful new design, *editorially free,* with *no advertising.* Here we are, stubborn as hell, committed to helping you feel validated, informed, furious, joyous, argumentative, and hopeful. Because distance is shrinking and the women's movement is growing, this *Ms.* will be international and unashamedly *feminist.* (A 1986 *Newsweek* poll showed that 56 percent of U.S. women under age forty-five identify as feminists; a 1989 *Time* poll showed a growing 82 percent say feminism improves their lives. It would be pretty foolish to jettison the word now.)

Sex, Lies, and Advertising

BY **GLORIA STEINEM** • JULY/AUGUST 1990

WHEN *MS.* BEGAN, we didn't consider *not* taking ads. The most important reason was keeping the price of a feminist magazine low enough for most women to afford. But the second and almost equal reason was providing a forum where women and advertisers could talk to each other and improve advertising itself. After all, it was (and still is) as potent a source of information in this country as news or TV and movie dramas.

We decided to proceed in two stages. First, we would convince makers of "people products" used by both men and women but advertised mostly to men—cars, credit cards, insurance, sound equipment, financial services, and the like—that their ads should be placed in a women's magazine. Since they were accustomed to the division between editorial and advertising in news and general interest magazines, this would allow our editorial content to be free and diverse. Second, we would add the best ads

> "That doesn't matter, he says. He knows his customers, and they would *like* to be kept women. That's why he will never advertise in *Ms.*"

for whatever traditional "women's products" (clothes, shampoo, fragrance, food, and so on) that surveys showed *Ms.* readers used. But we would ask them to come in *without* the usual quid pro quo of "complementary copy."

We knew the second step might be harder. Food advertisers have always demanded that women's magazines publish recipes and articles on entertaining (preferably ones that name their products) in return for their ads; clothing advertisers expect to be surrounded by fashion spreads (especially ones that credit their designers); and shampoo, fragrance, and beauty products in general usually insist on positive editorial coverage of beauty subjects, plus photo credits besides. That's why women's magazines look the way they do. But if we could break this link between ads and editorial content, then we wanted good ads for "women's products," too.

By playing their part in this unprecedented mix of *all* the things our readers need and use, advertisers also would be rewarded: ads for products like cars and mutual funds would find a new growth market; the best ads for women's products would no longer be lost in oceans of ads for the same category; and both would have access to a laboratory of smart and caring readers whose response would help create effective ads for other media as well.

I thought then that our main problem would be the imagery in ads themselves. Carmakers were still draping blondes in evening gowns over the hoods like ornaments. Authority figures were almost always male, even in ads for products that only women used. Sadistic, he-man campaigns even won industry praise. Even in medical journals, tranquilizer ads showed depressed housewives standing beside piles of dirty dishes and promised to get them back to work.

Obviously, *Ms.* would have to avoid such ads and seek out the best ones, but this didn't seem impossible. *The New Yorker* had been selecting ads for aesthetic reasons for years, a practice that only seemed to make advertisers more eager to be in its pages. *Ebony* and *Essence* were asking for ads with positive Black images, and though their struggle was hard, they weren't being called unreasonable.

Clearly, what *Ms.* needed was a very special publisher and ad sales staff. I could think of only one woman with experience on the business side of magazines—Patricia Carbine, who had recently become a vice president of *McCall's* as well as its editor in chief—and the reason I knew her name was a good omen. She had been managing editor at *Look* (really *the* editor, but its owner refused to put a female name at the top of his masthead) when I was writing a column there. After I did an early interview with Cesar Chavez, then just emerging as a leader of migrant labor, and the publisher turned it down because he was worried about ads from Sunkist, Pat was the one who intervened. As I learned later, she had told the publisher she would resign if the interview wasn't published. Mainly because *Look* couldn't afford to lose Pat, it *was* published (and the ads from Sunkist never arrived).

Though I barely knew this woman, she had done two things I always remembered: put her job on the line in a way that editors often talk about but rarely do, and been so loyal to her colleagues that she never told me or anyone outside *Look* that she had done so.

Fortunately, Pat did agree to take a huge cut in salary to become publisher of *Ms.* She became responsible for training and inspiring generations of young women who joined the *Ms.* ad sales force, many of whom went on

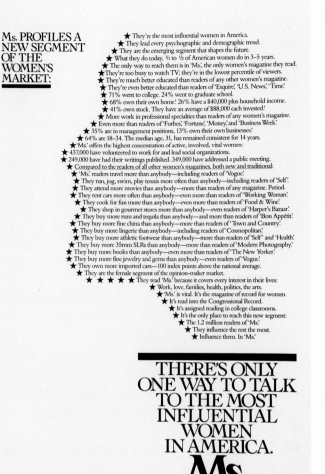

"There's only one way to talk to the most influential women in America": soliciting advertisers for *Ms.* in *The New York Times*, *Adweek*, and *Newsweek*.

to become "firsts" at the top of publishing. When *Ms.* first started, however, there were so few women with experience selling space that Pat and I made the rounds of ad agencies ourselves. Later, the fact that *Ms.* was asking companies to do business in a different way meant our saleswomen had to make many times the usual number of calls—to convince first agencies and then client companies—and to present endless amounts of research. I was often asked to do a final ad presentation, or see some higher decision maker, or speak to women employees so executives could see the interest of women they worked with. That's why I spent more time persuading advertisers than editing or writing for *Ms.* and why I ended up with an unsentimental education in the seamy underside of publishing that few writers see (and even fewer magazines can publish).

Let me take you with us through some experiences, just as they happened:

Cheered on by early support from Volkswagen and one or two other car companies, we scrape together time and money to put on a major reception in Detroit. We know U.S. carmakers firmly believe that women choose the upholstery, not the car, but we are armed with statistics and reader mail to prove the contrary: a car is an important purchase for women, one that symbolizes mobility and freedom.

But almost nobody comes. We are left with many pounds of shrimp on the table, and quite a lot of egg on our face. Thus begin ten years of knocking on hostile doors, presenting endless documentation, and hiring a full-time saleswoman in Detroit—all necessary before *Ms.* gets any real results.

This long saga has a semi-happy ending: foreign and, later, domestic carmakers eventually provided *Ms.* with enough advertising to make cars one of our top sources of ad revenue.

But long after figures showed a third, even half, of many car models being bought by women, U.S. makers continued to be uncomfortable addressing women. Unlike foreign carmakers, Detroit never quite learned the secret of creating intelligent ads that exclude no one, and then placing them in women's magazines to overcome past exclusion. (*Ms.* readers were so grateful for a routine Honda ad featuring rack-and-pinion steering, for instance, that they sent fan mail.)

In the *Ms. Gazette,* we do a brief report on a congressional hearing into chemicals used in hair dyes that are absorbed through the skin and may be carcinogenic. Newspapers report this too, but Clairol, a Bristol Myers subsidiary that makes dozens of products—a few of which have just begun to advertise in *Ms.*—is outraged. Not at newspapers or newsmagazines, just at us.

We offer to publish a letter from Clairol telling its side of the story. In an excess of solicitousness, we even put this letter in the news section, not in "Letters to the Editors," where it belongs. Nonetheless—and in spite of surveys that show *Ms.* readers are active women who use more of almost everything Clairol makes than do the readers of any other women's magazine—*Ms.* gets almost none of these ads for the rest of its natural life.

Meanwhile, Clairol changes its hair coloring formula, apparently in response to the hearings we reported.

Our saleswomen set out early to attract ads for consumer electronics: sound equipment, calculators, computers, VCRs, and the like.

We know that our readers are determined to be included in the technological revolution. We know from reader surveys that *Ms.* readers are buying this stuff in numbers as high as those of magazines like *Playboy,* or "men 18 to 34," the prime targets of the consumer electronics industry. Moreover, unlike traditional women's products that our readers buy but don't need to read articles about, these are subjects they want covered in our pages. There actually is a supportive editorial atmosphere.

"But women don't understand technology," say executives at the end of ad presentations. "Maybe not," we respond, "but neither do men—and we all buy it."

"If women *do* buy it," say the decision makers, "they're asking their husbands and boyfriends what to buy first." We produce letters from *Ms.* readers saying how turned off they are when salesmen say things like "Let me know when your husband can come in."

After several years of this, we get a few ads for compact sound systems. Some of them come from JVC, whose vice president, Harry Elias, is trying to convince his Japanese bosses that there is something called a "women's market." At his invitation, I find myself speaking at huge trade shows in Chicago and Las Vegas, trying to persuade JVC dealers that showrooms don't have to be locker rooms where women are made to feel unwelcome. But as it turns out, the shows themselves are part of the problem. In Las Vegas, the only women around the technology displays are seminude models serving champagne. In Chicago, the big attraction is Marilyn Chambers, who followed Linda Lovelace of *Deep Throat* fame as Chuck Traynor's captive and/or employee. VCRs are being demonstrated with her porn videos.

In the end, we get ads for a car stereo now and then, but no VCRs; some IBM personal computers, but no Apple or Japanese ones. In the electronics world, women and technology seem mutually exclusive. It remains a decade behind even Detroit.

Because we get letters from little girls who love toy trains, and who ask our help in changing ads and box-top photos that feature little boys only, we try to get toy-train ads from Lionel. It turns out that Lionel executives *have* been concerned about little girls. They made a pink train and were surprised when it didn't sell.

Lionel bows to consumer pressure with a photograph of a boy and a girl—but only on some of their boxes. They fear that if trains are associated with girls, they will be devalued in the minds of boys. Needless to say, *Ms.* gets no train ads, and little girls remain a mostly unexplored market. By 1986, Lionel is put up for sale.

But for different reasons, we haven't had much luck with other kinds of toys either. In spite of many articles on child rearing; an annual listing of nonsexist, multiracial toys by Letty Cottin Pogrebin; "Stories for Free Children," a regular feature also edited by Letty; and other prizewinning features for or about children, we get virtually no toy ads. Generations of *Ms.* saleswomen explain to toy manufacturers that a larger proportion of *Ms.* readers have preschool children than do the readers of other women's magazines, but this industry can't believe feminists have or care about children.

When *Ms.* begins, the staff decides not to accept ads for feminine hygiene sprays or cigarettes: they are damaging and carry no appropriate health warnings. Though we don't think we should tell our readers what to do, we do think we should provide facts so they can decide for themselves. Since the antismoking lobby has been pressing for health warnings on cigarette ads, we decide to take them only as they comply.

Philip Morris is among the first to do so. One of its brands, Virginia Slims, is also sponsoring women's tennis and the first national polls of women's opinions. On the other hand, the Virginia Slims theme, "You've come a long way, baby," has more than a "baby" problem. It makes smoking a symbol of progress for women.

We explain to Philip Morris that this slogan won't do well in our pages, but they are convinced its success with some women means it will work with all women. Finally, we agree to publish an ad for a Virginia Slims calendar as a test. The letters from readers are critical—and smart. For instance: Would you show a Black man picking cotton, the same man in a Cardin suit, and symbolize the antislavery and civil rights movements by smoking? Of course not. But instead of honoring the test results, the Philip Morris people seem angry to be proven wrong. They take away ads for *all* their many brands.

Gradually, we also realize our naïveté in thinking we *could* decide against taking cigarette ads. They became a disproportionate support of magazines the moment they were banned on television, and few magazines could compete and survive without them; certainly not *Ms.*, which lacks so many other categories. By the time statistics in the 1980s show that women's rate of lung cancer is approaching men's, the necessity of taking cigarette ads has become a kind of prison.

General Mills, Pillsbury, Carnation, Del Monte, Dole, Kraft, Stouffer's, Hormel, Nabisco: you name the food giant, we try it. But no matter how desirable the *Ms.* readership, our lack of recipes is lethal.

We explain to them that placing food ads *only* next to recipes associates food with work. For many women, it is a negative that works *against* the ads. Why not place food ads in diverse media without recipes (thus reaching more men, who are now a third of the shoppers in supermarkets anyway), and leave the recipes to specialty magazines like *Gourmet* (a third of whose readers are also men)?

These arguments elicit interest, but except for an occasional ad for a convenience food, instant coffee, diet drinks, yogurt, or such extras as avocados and almonds, this mainstay of the publishing industry stays closed to us. Period.

We hear in 1980 that women in the Soviet Union have been producing feminist samizdat (underground, self-published books) and circulating them throughout the country. As punishment, four of the leaders have been exiled. Though we are operating on our usual shoestring, we solicit individual contributions to send Robin Morgan to interview these women in Vienna.

The result is an exclusive cover story that includes the first news of a populist peace movement against the Soviet occupation of Afghanistan, a prediction of glasnost to come, and a grassroots, intimate view of Soviet women's lives.

From the popular press to women's studies courses, the response is great. The story wins a Front Page Award.

Nonetheless, this journalistic coup undoes years of efforts to get an ad schedule from Revlon. Why? Because the Soviet women on our cover *are not wearing makeup.*

Four years of research and presentations go into convincing airlines that women now make travel choices and business trips. United, the first airline to advertise in *Ms.,* is so impressed with the response from our readers that one of its executives appears in a film for our ad presentations. As usual, good ads get great results.

But we have problems unrelated to such results. For instance, because American Airlines flight attendants include among their labor demands the stipulation that they can choose to have their last names preceded by "Ms." on their name tags—in a long-delayed revolt against the standard "I am your pilot, Captain Rothgart, and this is your flight attendant, Cindy Sue"—American Airlines officials seem to hold the magazine responsible. We get no ads.

Women's access to insurance and credit is vital, but with the exception of Equitable and a few other ad pioneers, such financial services address men. For almost a decade after the Equal Credit Opportunity Act passes in 1974, we try to convince American Express that women are a growth market—but nothing works.

Finally, a former professor of Russian named Jerry Welsh becomes head of marketing. He assumes that women should be cardholders and persuades his colleagues to feature women in a campaign. Thanks to this 1980s series, the growth rate for female cardholders surpasses that for men.

For this article, I asked Welsh if he would explain why American Express waited so long. "Sure," he said, "they were afraid of having a 'pink' card."

Women of color read *Ms.* in disproportionate numbers. This is a source of pride to *Ms.* staffers, who are also more racially representative than the editors of other women's magazines. But this reality is obscured by ads filled with enough white women to make a reader snow-blind.

Pat Carbine remembers mostly "astonishment" when she requested African American, Hispanic, Asian, and other diverse images. Marcia Ann Gillespie, a *Ms.* editor who was previously the editor in chief of *Essence,* witnesses ad bias a second time: having tried for *Essence* to get white advertisers to use Black images, she sees similar problems getting integrated ads for an integrated magazine. Indeed, the ad world often creates Black and Hispanic ads only for Black and Hispanic media. In an exact parallel of the fear that marketing a product to women will endanger its appeal to men, the response is usually "But your [white] readers won't identify." In fact, those we are able to get—for instance, a Max Factor ad made for *Essence*—are praised by white readers, too.

By the end of 1986, production and mailing costs have risen astronomically, ad income is flat, and competition for ads is stiffer than ever. The sixty-forty preponderance of edit over ads that we promised to readers becomes fifty-fifty; children's stories, most poetry, and some fiction are casualties of less space; in order to get variety into limited pages, the length (and sometimes the depth) of articles suffers; and, though we do refuse most of the ads that would look like a parody in our pages, we get so worn down that some slip through. Still, readers perform miracles. Though we haven't been able to afford a subscription mailing in two years, they maintain our guaranteed circulation of 450,000.

Nonetheless, media reports on *Ms.* often insist that our unprofitability must be due to reader disinterest.

My healthy response is anger. My not-so-healthy response is constant worry. Also an obsession with finding one more rescue. There is hardly a night when I don't wake up with sweaty palms and pounding heart, scared that we won't be able to pay the printer or the post office; scared most of all that closing our doors will hurt the women's movement.

Out of chutzpah and desperation, I arrange a lunch with Leonard Lauder, president of Estée Lauder. With the exception of Clinique, none of Lauder's hundreds of products has been advertised in *Ms.* A year's schedule of ads for just three or four of them could save us.

Over a lunch that costs more than we can pay for some articles, I explain the need for his leadership. I also lay out the record of *Ms.:* literary and journalistic prizes won, new issues introduced into the mainstream, new writers discovered, and more impact on society than any other magazine; more articles that became books, stories that became movies, ideas that became television series, and newly advertised products that became profitable; and, most important for him, a place for his ads to reach women who aren't reachable through any other women's magazine. Indeed, if there is one constant characteristic of the ever-changing *Ms.* readership, it is their impact as leaders. Whether it's waiting until later to have first babies or pioneering PABA as sun protection in cosmetics, *whatever* they are doing today, a third to half of American women will be doing three to five years from now. It's never failed.

But, he says, *Ms.* readers are not *our* women. They're not interested in things like fragrance and blush. If they were, *Ms.* would write articles about them.

On the contrary, I explain, surveys show they are more likely to buy such things than the readers of, say, *Cosmopolitan* or *Vogue.* They're good customers because they're out in the world enough to need several sets of everything: home, work, purse, travel, gym, and so on. They just don't need to read articles about these things. Would he ask a men's magazine to publish monthly columns on how to shave before he advertised Aramis products (his line for men)?

He concedes that beauty features are often concocted more for advertisers than readers. But *Ms.* isn't appropriate for his ads anyway, he explains. Why? Because Estée Lauder is selling "a kept-woman mentality."

I can't quite believe this. Sixty percent of the users of his products are salaried and generally resemble *Ms.* readers. Besides, his company has the appeal of having been started by a creative and hardworking woman, his mother, Estée Lauder.

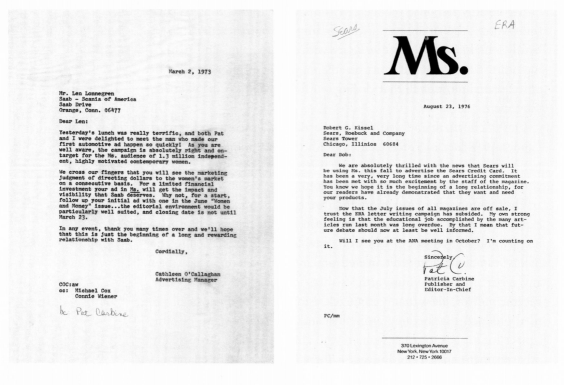

Early letters from the publishing staff regarding advertising in *Ms.*—thanking "the man who made our first automobile ad happen so quickly" (*left*) and sharing the staff's excitement over an advertisement for the Sears Credit Card while trying to appease the company (*right*), which was aggrieved over an ERA letter-writing campaign.

That doesn't matter, he says. He knows his customers, and they would *like* to be kept women. That's why he will never advertise in *Ms*.

In November 1987, by vote of the Ms. Foundation for Education and Communication (*Ms.*'s owner and publisher, the media subsidiary of the Ms. Foundation for Women), *Ms.* was sold to a company whose officers, the Australian feminists Sandra Yates and Anne Summers, raised the investment money in their country that *Ms.* couldn't find in its own. They also started *Sassy* for teenage women.

In their two-year tenure, circulation was raised to 550,000 by investment in circulation mailings, and to the dismay of some readers editorial features on clothes and new products made a more traditional bid for ads. Nonetheless, ad pages fell below previous levels. In addition, *Sassy*, whose fresh voice and sexual frankness were an unprecedented success with young readers, was targeted by two mothers from Indiana who began, as one of them put it, "calling every Christian organization I could think of." In response to this controversy, several crucial advertisers pulled out.

Advertisers' control over the editorial content of women's magazines had, by that time, become so institutionalized that it was written into "insertion orders" or dictated to ad salespeople as official policy. Procter & Gamble, one of this country's most powerful and diversified advertisers, stands out in the memory of Anne Summers and Sandra Yates: its products were not to be placed in *any* issue that included *any* material on gun control, abortion, the occult, cults, or the disparagement of religion. Caution was also demanded in any issue covering sex or drugs, even for educational purposes.

Since Anne and Sandra had not met their budget's projections for ad revenue, their investors forced a sale. In October 1989, *Ms.* and *Sassy* were bought by Dale Lang, owner of *Working Mother* and *Working Woman,* and one of the few independent publishing companies left among the conglomerates. In response to a request from the original *Ms.* staff—as well as to reader letters urging that *Ms.* continue, plus his own belief that *Ms.* would benefit his other magazines by blazing a trail—he agreed to try an ad-free, reader-supported *Ms.* and to give us complete editorial control.

It's almost three years away from life between the grindstones of advertising pressures and readers' needs. I'm just beginning to realize how edges got smoothed down—in spite of all our resistance.

I remember feeling put-upon when I changed "Porsche" to "car" in a piece about Nazi imagery in German pornography by Andrea Dworkin—feeling sure Andrea would understand that Volkswagen, the distributor of Porsche and one of our few supportive advertisers, asked only to be far away from Nazi subjects. It's taken me all this time to realize that Andrea was the one with a right to feel put-upon.

Even as I write this, I get a call from a writer for *Elle* who is doing a whole article on where women part their hair. Why, she wants to know, do I part mine in the middle?

It's all so familiar. A writer trying to make something of a nothing assignment; an editor laboring to think of new ways to attract ads; readers assuming that other women must want this ridiculous stuff; more women suffering for lack of information, insight, creativity, and laughter that could be on these same pages.

·   ·   ·

She

BY **ADRIENNE RICH** • JULY/AUGUST 1990

goes through what must be gone through:
that catalogue she is pitching out
mildew spores velvet between the tiles
soft hairs, nests, webs
in corners, edges of basins, in the teeth
of her very comb. All that rots and rusts
in a night, a century.
Balances memory, training, sits in her chair
comb in hand, breathing the smell of her own hair
and thinks: *I have been the weir*
where disintegration stopped.
Lifts her brush once like a thrown thing
lays it down at her side like a stockpiled weapon,
crushes out the light. Elsewhere
dust chokes the filters, dead leaves rasp in the grate.
Clogged, the fine nets bulge
but she is not there.

"Femicide": Speaking the Unspeakable

BY **JANE CAPUTI** AND
DIANA E. H. RUSSELL • SEPTEMBER/OCTOBER 1990

THE CANADIAN NOVELIST Margaret Atwood once asked a male friend why men feel threatened by women. He replied, "They are afraid women will laugh at them." She then asked a group of women why they feel threatened by men. They answered, "We're afraid of being killed."

However disproportionate, these fears are profoundly linked, as was demonstrated on December 6, 1989, at the University of Montreal. That day, the twenty-five-year-old combat-video aficionado Marc Lépine suited up for war and rushed the school of engineering. In one classroom, he

separated the women from the men, ordered the men out, and, shouting, "You're all fucking feminists," opened fire on the women. During a
half-hour rampage, he killed fourteen young women,
wounded nine other women and four men, then
turned the gun on himself. A three-page suicide note
blamed all his failures on women, whom he felt had
scorned him. Also found was a list of fifteen prominent
Canadian women.

> *"Whether individual
> hate killers are demented
> is beside the point."*

Unable to complete an application to the school of engineering, Lépine
felt humiliated by women he defined as "feminists" because they had
entered traditional male territory. His response to the erosion of white
male exclusivity was a lethal one. It was also an eminently political one.

In the massacre's aftermath, media reports regularly denied the political nature of the crimes, citing such comments as the Canadian novelist
Mordecai Richler's: "It was the act of an absolutely demented man [which
does not] lend itself to any explanation." This despite Lépine's clear explanation of his actions. *Whether individual hate killers are demented is beside
the point.* In a racist and sexist society, psychotics as well as the so-called
normal frequently act out the ubiquitous racist and misogynist attitudes
they repeatedly see legitimized.

Lépine's murders were hate crimes targeting victims by gender, not race,
religion, ethnicity, or sexual orientation. When racist murders—lynchings
and pogroms—occur, no one wonders whether individual perpetrators are
crazy or have had bad personal experiences with African Americans and
Jews. Most people understand that lynchings and pogroms are motivated
by political objectives: preserving white and gentile supremacy. Similarly,
the aim of violence against women—conscious or not—is to preserve male
supremacy.

Early feminist analysis of rape exposed the myths that it is a crime of
frustrated attraction, victim provocation, or uncontrollable biological
urges, perpetrated only by an aberrant fringe. Rather, rape is a direct expression of sexual politics, an assertion of masculinist norms, and a form of
terrorism that preserves the gender status quo.

Like rape, the murders of women by husbands, lovers, fathers, acquaintances, and strangers are not the products of some inexplicable deviance.
Murder is simply the most extreme form of sexist terrorism. A new word
is needed to reflect this political understanding. We think "femicide" best
describes the murders of women by men motivated by hatred, contempt,
pleasure, or a sense of ownership of women. Femicide includes mutilation
murder, rape murder, battery that escalates into murder; historical immolation of witches in Europe; historical and contemporary immolation of
brides and widows in India; and "honor crimes" in some Latin and Middle

Eastern countries, where women believed to have lost their virginity sometimes are killed by male relatives.

The misogyny motivating violence against women also distorts press coverage of such crimes. Rape, femicide, and battery are variously ignored or sensationalized in the media, depending on the victim's race, class, and "attractiveness." Police, media, and public response to crimes against women of color, poor women, lesbian women, women working as prostitutes, and drug users is particularly abysmal—usually apathy laced with pejorative stereotyping and victim blaming. Moreover, public interest is disproportionately focused on cases involving nonwhite assailants and white middle-class victims, such as the uproar over the 1989 Boston murder of Carol Stuart, a pregnant white woman who, her husband falsely claimed, was shot by a Black robber. (She had been murdered by her affluent white husband.)

Femicide is the ultimate end of a continuum of terror that includes rape, torture, mutilation, sexual slavery (particularly in prostitution), incestuous and extrafamilial child sexual abuse, physical and emotional battery, sexual harassment, genital mutilations (clitoridectomies, infibulations), unnecessary gynecological operations (gratuitous hysterectomies), forced heterosexuality, forced sterilization, forced motherhood (criminalizing contraception and abortion), psychosurgery, abusive medical experimentation (for example, some efforts to create new reproductive technologies), denial of protein to women in some cultures, cosmetic surgery, and other mutilations in the name of beautification. Whenever these forms of terrorism result in death, they become femicides.

Federal statistics do not reveal the scope of violence against women. Surveys by independent researchers show rates of female victimization that should shatter us all. For example, in Diana Russell's random sample survey of 930 San Francisco women, 44 percent reported being victimized by rape or attempted rape, 38 percent by child sexual abuse, 16 percent by incestuous abuse, 14 percent by wife rape, and 21 percent by marital violence.

As with rape and child sexual abuse, femicide is most likely to be perpetrated by a male family member, friend, or acquaintance. Ironically, the patriarchy's ideal domestic arrangement (heterosexual coupling) is the most potentially femicidal situation. Husbands (including common-law) account for 33 percent of all women murdered between 1976 and 1987 in the United States.

Violent crimes against women have escalated in recent decades. Some believe this increase is due to women reporting them more. But Russell's research on (largely unreported) rape, for example, establishes a dramatic escalation during the last fifty years.

We see this escalation of violence against females as part of a male backlash against feminism. This doesn't mean it's the *fault* of feminism: patriarchal culture terrorizes women whether we fight back or not. Still, when male supremacy is challenged, that terror is intensified.

A sense of entitlement is a major cause of sexist terrorism. Many males believe they have a right to get what they want from females. Consider the hatred exhibited in response to a trivial challenge to male dominance: female students at the University of Iowa complained about the loud stereos of male students on the floor above. A response in graffiti titled "The Top 10 Things to Do to the Bitches Below" was found in the men's bathroom and then published in the university newspaper, including exhortations to beat the women "into a bloody pulp with a sledgehammer and laugh" and instructions on "how to mutilate female genitalia with an electric trimmer, pliers, and a 'red-hot soldering iron.'" Similarly, the suggestion was made in the University of Toronto engineering students' newspaper that women "cut off their breasts if they were sick of sexual harassment."

To see where these students get such gruesome ideas, we need only look to pornography and mass-media "gorenography." An FBI study of thirty-six sex serial killers found that pornography was ranked highest of many sexual interests by an astonishing 81 percent. Such notorious killers as Edmund Kemper (the "Coed Killer"), Ted Bundy, David Berkowitz (the "Son of Sam"), and Kenneth Bianchi and Angelo Buono (the "Hillside Stranglers") were all heavy pornography consumers. Bundy maintained that pornography "had an impact on me that was just so central to the development of the behavior that I engaged in." His assessment is consistent with testimony from many other sex offenders, as well as research on the effects of pornography.

Femicidal atrocity is everywhere normalized, explained as "joking," and rendered into standard fantasy fare, from comic books through Nobel Prize–winning literature, box-office smashes through snuff films. Meanwhile, the FBI terms sex killings "recreational murder."

Just as many people denied the reality of the Nazi Holocaust, most people refuse to recognize the gynocidal period in which women are living—and dying—today. If all femicides were recognized as such and accurately counted, if the massive incidence of nonlethal sexual assaults against women and girls was taken into account, if incest and battery were recognized as torture (frequently prolonged over years), if the patriarchal home were seen as the inescapable prison it so frequently becomes, if pornography and gorenography were recognized as hate literature, then this culture might have to acknowledge that we live in the midst of a reign of sexist terror comparable in magnitude, intensity, and intent to the persecution, torture, and annihilation of women as witches from the fourteenth to the seventeenth century in Europe.

It is unspeakably painful for most women to think about men's violence against us, as individuals and collectively, because the violence we encounter, as well as the disbelief and contempt with which we are met when we do speak out, is often so traumatic and life threatening that many of us engage in denial or repression of our experiences.

The recollection and acknowledgment of history/experience that has been so profoundly repressed is what Toni Morrison in her masterpiece *Beloved* calls "rememory." In an interview, Morrison noted that there is virtually no remembrance—no lore, songs, or dances—of the African people who died in the Middle Passage: "I suspect . . . it was not possible to survive on certain levels and dwell on it. . . . There is a necessity for remembering the horror, but . . . in a manner in which the memory is not destructive." Morrison's concept of rememory is crucial as well for all women grappling with the torment of living in a femicidal world. We too must be able to face horror in ways that do not destroy but save us.

Progressive people rightly favor an international boycott of South Africa so long as apartheid reigns; why do they/we so rarely consider the potential efficacy of boycotting violent and abusive men and *their* culture? In 1590, Iroquois women gathered in Seneca to demand the cessation of war among the nations. We must now demand an end to the global patriarchal war on women. The femicidal culture is one in which the male is worshipped. This worship is obtained through tyranny, subtle and overt, over our bruised minds, our battered and dead bodies, our co-optation into supporting even batterers, rapists, and killers.

DIANA RUSSELL, who popularized the term "femicide," died on July 28, 2020, at the age of eighty-one. According to her obituary, Dr. Russell first used the word "femicide" publicly in 1976 at the International Tribunal on Crimes Against Women in Brussels, attended by two thousand women from forty countries. Her early definition—the killing of females by males because they are female—evolved over time to cover a range of calculated acts of violence, including setting a wife on fire for having too small a dowry, death as a result of genital mutilation, and the murder of prostitutes, as well as indirect forms of killing, such as deaths that result from barring women from using contraception or obtaining an abortion.

A Day in the Life:
Dispatches from Nome, Alaska, to Virginia Beach

BY **RITA HENLEY JENSEN** • SEPTEMBER/OCTOBER 1990

WHAT HAPPENED in Montreal on December 6, 1989, may forever stand out in our minds as the ultimate assault against women. Yet it's the monotonous quality of the violence—the threats, slaps, kicks, slugs, knifings, rapes, and murders—that is the backdrop of our daily lives. For most women, December 6, 1989, was another day of the routine yet terrifying acts of daily and nightly violence against women and female children. It just never seems to stop.

In an effort to gain a sense of the everyday brutality we live with—and the struggle of those who spend their lives helping the victims and survivors of misogynist violence—*Ms.* contacted battered women's shelters, rape crisis centers, and law enforcement officials across the country. We asked them what happened in their hometown on December 6, 1989. Here is some of what we found.

> **"Aguirre spends much of the hour-long conversation trying to assure the teenager that the rape is not her fault. The center never hears from her again."**

At 12:32 a.m., the 911 operator for the county surrounding Eugene, Oregon, receives a call reporting a violent fight between a man and a woman, which can be heard by the caller who lives across the street and two houses down. A police car is sent to investigate. The outcome of the incident is unknown.

Throughout that night and early morning hours, police in Gary, Indiana, search for Ray Williams, a suspect in the murders of Linda Bownes, forty-two, and her twenty-two-year-old twin daughters, Gena and Lesa Mabon. Lesa's three-month-old daughter survived the attack and was found in the house, crying.

At 5:15 a.m. a rape crisis hotline in Houston, Texas, is called by a local hospital. A fourteen-year-old girl has been raped by her twenty-year-old cousin during the early morning hours. The cousin had been left in charge of the teenager while her mother was out of town on a business trip. He woke her during the night and asked her to play cards. He told her one of the rules was that if she lost, she would have to drink beer. He also forced her to smoke marijuana. She fell asleep again, to be awakened once more by her cousin, who was on top of her, raping her. When he fell asleep, the teenager called her mother; her mother contacted a friend who took her to the emergency room.

At 7:35 a.m. in Cheyenne, Wyoming, a mother of three calls Safe House Sexual Assault Services. Her husband has beaten her again, blackened her eye again. She and her three children, including the six-year-old daughter who is being treated for cancer, are sheltered for two days until an order of protection goes into effect.

At 8:00 a.m., prospective jurors are questioned in circuit court room 4 in Virginia Beach, Virginia, in the opening stages of Randolph A. Rau's murder trial. He stands accused of hiring a contract killer to slay both his mother and his sister, Amber Rau. His sister, forty-nine, survived; his seventy-four-year-old mother did not. His wealthy mother was in the process of changing her will.

In Spokane, William Stevens II pleads not guilty at 9:30 a.m. to charges of possession of stolen automobiles. Stevens was a prime suspect in the Green River serial killings and disappearances of up to forty-nine women in the Seattle area between July 1982 and March 1984. But the week before, police had announced that Stevens was no longer a suspect, and Major Bob Evans, head of the King County Police Task Force, continued investigations into the fifty or so remaining suspects on a list that once contained fifteen hundred names.

Many of the forty-one dead women and eight of the missing women had links to prostitution. In a newspaper report on the crime, Evans said, "We just passed the 100th anniversary of Jack the Ripper. Murder goes hand in hand with this profession. It always has."

At 10:00 a.m. in California's northern Sacramento valley, Hope Aguirre, staff member for Rape Intervention of Northern California, a rape crisis center, is at work in her office in an old, Victorian-style house jammed with three desks, a file cabinet with a cat sleeping on top of it, and a coffeepot in the corner. A fourteen-year-old calls. She has been raped earlier that morning by an adult friend of the family. She is crying. Aguirre knows she can offer little comfort to her caller. If the caller reveals her name, Aguirre

IN MEMORY OF THE WOMEN WHO HAVE BEEN KILLED

Later in the decade, *Ms.*'s September/October 1994 cover listed the names, ages, and locations of some of the thousands of U.S. women and girls who had been murdered by former or current male partners between 1990 and the issue's publication.

is a "mandated reporter" under state law and must report the incident to the police. She knows, too, that the caller is probably correct when she says she cannot confide in her parents because her father will beat both her and her attacker. Aguirre spends much of the hour-long conversation trying to assure the teenager that the rape is not her fault. The center never hears from her again.

In Chicago, at around 11:15 a.m., Dr. Lee Robin, thirty-one, is committed to a hundred years in a mental institution for hacking his wife to death and drowning their two-month-old daughter. Robin had tried to commit suicide the week before the double murder and had warned his therapist that he might harm himself or his family. Informed of her husband's fears, Annette Robin decided to stay with her husband of four years.

Ninety miles below the Arctic Circle, the winter skies darken at midday; it is near dusk at the Bering Sea Women's Group in Nome, Alaska, when two calls come in. At 11:20 a.m., a fifty-five-year-old female member of the Siberian Yupik Eskimos calls. Her husband has beaten her. Her eyes are black; her lips are swollen. She lives in one of the fifteen Eskimo villages spread out over the 126,000-square-mile area in which the center's network of volunteers reside. The caller agrees to come to the shelter in Nome via the free-of-charge air taxi where she can receive counseling and assistance in obtaining an injunction against further violence.

At around 12:05 p.m., a twenty-one-year-old living in Nome calls the center. An Eskimo from a tiny island with a hundred inhabitants, she says she was raped the previous weekend by a sixty-year-old white male acquaintance. She has hidden herself in her apartment since then and has not eaten or slept. Volunteers go to her apartment, feed her, accompany her to the hospital and the police station, and bring her back to stay at the converted shingle house used as a shelter and counseling center.

In Honolulu, a middle-aged woman walks up the sidewalk to the Shelter for Abused Spouses and Children at about 1:30 p.m. In one direction, she sees lush green mountains; in the other, the ocean. In front of her, she sees safety.

She has been married to her abuser for the past three and a half years. One month after the wedding, he beat her so badly that he broke her leg. In the course of their marriage, he had broken her nose two times, subjected her to multiple concussions and other head injuries, and fractured her ribs.

The most recent incident began the night before. She was next door visiting friends when he arrived home. After she returned, he was outraged and began to batter her. He hit her in the face and broke her jaw in several places. The woman called the shelter at 7:00 a.m. from the local hospital.

As she enters the shelter, the workers notice her jaw is wired shut in several places.

At 2:00 p.m., midway through finals week, Susan Barnes, president of

Associated Students of the University of California, Irvine, finds a notice in her mailbox that a student has been raped at knifepoint the previous weekend in a poorly lit campus parking lot. She and others spend the day preparing a bulletin that will warn students of the danger. She also begins to protest the length of time it took the school administration to notify other students of the rape. The several-day delay means that by the time she and others post the special edition of "Crime and Safety Notesheet" across campus on Thursday, most of the students will have already left the campus for their midyear break.

In Jackson, Mississippi, a fourteen-year-old eighth grader calls at 3:20 p.m. She is seeking counseling from a local hotline after she and a friend were raped in separate incidents by a classmate.

At 3:30 p.m., a Juneau, Wisconsin, county judge rules that there is sufficient evidence for Chad Goetsch to stand trial on charges that he murdered his mother with a hunting arrow. The ruling comes after his father, the Wisconsin state representative Robert Goetsch, testified in tears that he was awakened by a thump and a scream in his bedroom. He saw his wife bleeding from an arrow wound and his son standing over her aiming a bow and arrow at him.

At 5:05 p.m., the Queens, New York, district attorney John Santucci announces the indictment of five Taiwanese gang members for raping and robbing a woman who they claimed owed $50,000 to a mutual friend. Of the five, four are teenagers. The 168-count indictment charges that the five, members of a gang called Taiwanese Brothers, played Russian roulette with their victim, holding a loaded gun to her head while they assaulted her. She knew her attackers from a bar where she worked as a hostess.

As evening falls in Montreal, there is a report that local gun shops are being swamped by requests for the same semiautomatic assault rifle used by Marc Lépine during the massacre at the university and that some weapon stores are sold out.

At 7:17 p.m., the 911 operator in Eugene, Oregon, receives a call. "My husband is trying to kill me," the caller says. "There are lots of guns at this location." No further details are available.

At 9:30 p.m. in a small, rural Wisconsin town, eight women are in a meeting at the local center for domestic violence and sexual assault. An impromptu support group, they are sharing their stories as they hug pillows and stuffed animals strewn throughout the room.

One woman is staying at the shelter with her twelve-year-old daughter. Her alcoholic husband abuses her, and she has been at the shelter for four days. A second woman, aged thirty, is married to a man who uses drugs and abuses her. She fled rather than reveal what she knows about his drug abuse to authorities, and had been living in her car in subzero weather for at least two weeks before she arrived at the center.

A third woman is a single twenty-year-old who is trying to escape her father's total control of her life.

Just as their meeting ends and they begin to leave, a stranger in her fifties rings the security bell and asks to come in.

She feels trapped, she says, because her husband beats her, won't permit her to write a check or drive the family car without permission. Can they help her? she asks.

Around 10:00 p.m., ten women and eight children are crowded into the Duluth Women's Coalition shelter. They watch as the gifts they brought are being opened. A nighthawk—a staffer who takes emergency calls during the night shift—is nine months pregnant, and the shelter residents have organized a baby shower for her. Although many are on public assistance, they have saved enough to buy a receiving blanket and sleepers for the forthcoming infant.

IN MEMORIAM:

Geneviève Bergeron, 21

Hélène Colgan, 23

Nathalie Croteau, 23

Barbara Daigneault, 22

Anne-Marie Edward, 21

Maud Haviernick, 29

Barbara Maria Klucznik, 31

Maryse Leclair, 23

Maryse Leganière, 25

Anne-Marie Lemay, 22

Sonia Pelletier, 28

Michèle Richard, 21

Annie St. Arneault, 23

Annie Turcotte, 21

•   •   •

Women **Rap Back**

BY **MICHELE WALLACE** • NOVEMBER/DECEMBER 1990

L IKE MANY BLACK FEMINISTS, I look on sexism in rap as a necessary evil. In a society plagued by poverty and illiteracy, where young Black men are as likely to be in prison as in college, rap is a welcome articulation of the economic and social frustrations of Black youth.

It offers the release of creative expression and historical continuity; it draws on precedents as diverse as jazz, reggae, calypso, Afro-Cuban, African, and heavy metal, and its lyrics include rudimentary forms of political, economic, and social analyses.

> "For a Black feminist to chastise misogyny in rap publicly would be viewed as divisive and counterproductive. The charge is hardly new."

But though there are exceptions, like raps advocating world peace (the W.I.S.E. Guyz's "Time for Peace") and opposing drug use (Ice-T's "I'm Your Pusher"), rap lyrics can be brutal, raw, and, where women are the subject, glaringly sexist.

Though styles vary—from that of the X-rated Ice-T to the sybaritic Kwamé to the hyperpolitics of Public Enemy—what seems universal is how little male rappers respect sexual intimacy and how little regard they have for the humanity of the Black woman.

At present there is only a small platform for Black women to address the problems of sexism in rap and in their community. For a Black feminist to chastise misogyny in rap publicly would be viewed as divisive and counterproductive. The charge is hardly new. Such a reaction greeted Ntozake Shange's play *For Colored Girls Who Have Considered Suicide, When the Rainbow Is Enuf,* my own essays in *Black Macho and the Myth of the Superwoman,* and Alice Walker's novel *The Color Purple,* all of which were perceived as being critical of Black men.

Rap is rooted not only in the blaxploitation films of the 1960s but also in an equally sexist tradition of Black comedy. In the use of four-letter words and explicit sexual references, both Richard Pryor and Eddie Murphy, who themselves drew upon the earlier examples of Redd Foxx, Pigmeat Markham, and Moms Mabley, are conscious reference points for 2 Live Crew. Black comedy, in turn, draws on an oral tradition in which Black men trade "toasts," stories in which dangerous badmen and trickster figures like Stackolee and Dolomite sexually exploit women and promote violence among men.

Rap remains almost completely dominated by Black males and this mindset. Although women have been involved in rap since at least the mid-1980s, record companies have only recently begun to promote them. And as women rappers like Salt-N-Pepa, Monie Love, MC Lyte, L.A. Star, and Queen Latifah slowly gain visibility, rap's sexism may emerge as a subject for scrutiny. Indeed, the answer may lie with women, expressing in lyrics and videos the tensions between the sexes in the Black community.

Today's women rappers range from a high ground that refuses to challenge male rap on its own level (Queen Latifah) to those who subscribe to the same sexual high jinks as male rappers (Oaktown 3.5.7). MC Hammer launched Oaktown 3.5.7, made up of his former backup dancers. These female rappers manifest the worst-case scenario: their skimpy, skintight leopard costumes in the video of "We Like It" suggest an exotic animalistic sexuality. Clearly, their bodies are more important than rapping. And in a field in which writing one's own rap is crucial, their lyrics are written by their former boss, MC Hammer.

Most women rappers constitute the middle ground: they talk of romance, narcissism, and parties. On the other hand, Salt-N-Pepa on "Shake Your Thang" uses the structure of the 1969 Isley Brothers song "It's Your Thing" to insert a protofeminist rap response: "Don't try and tell me how to party. It's my dance and it's my body." MC Lyte, in a dialogue with Positive K on "I'm Not Havin' It," comes down hard on the notion that women can't say no and criticizes the shallowness of male rap.

Queen Latifah introduces her video "Ladies First," performed with the English rapper Monie Love, with photographs of Black political heroines like Winnie Mandela, Sojourner Truth, Harriet Tubman, and Angela Davis. With a sound that resembles scat as much as rap, Queen Latifah chants "Stereotypes they got to go" against a backdrop of newsreel footage of the apartheid struggle in South Africa. The politically sophisticated Queen Latifah seems worlds apart from the adolescent, buffoonish sex orientation of most rap. In general, women rappers seem so much more grown up.

Can they inspire a more beneficent attitude toward sex in rap?

What won't subvert rap's sexism is the actions of men; what will is women speaking in their own voice.

MS. WEIGHED IN just as a host of rappers began to forge a new vision for female empowerment in the industry: artists like Salt-N-Pepa, Queen Latifah, and MC Lyte, who topped the charts in the 1980s. In the decades that have followed, a growing cadre of rappers have further shaped and elevated the genre with feminism, including stars like Lauryn Hill, who went on to break records for Grammy wins; Missy Elliott, who became the best-selling female rapper of all time; and Cardi B, the first female rapper to achieve multiple diamond records.

· · ·

The Search for Signs of Intelligent Life in the Twenty-First Century

BY **JANE WAGNER** • NOVEMBER/DECEMBER 1990

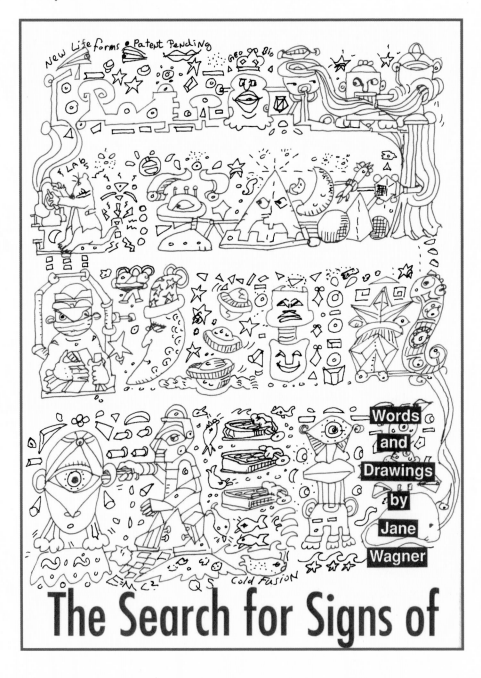

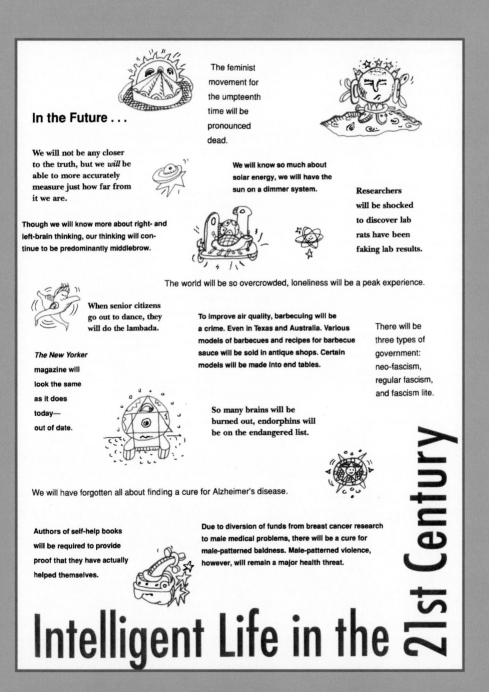

In the Future . . .

The feminist movement for the umpteenth time will be pronounced dead.

We will not be any closer to the truth, but we *will* be able to more accurately measure just how far from it we are.

We will know so much about solar energy, we will have the sun on a dimmer system.

Researchers will be shocked to discover lab rats have been faking lab results.

Though we will know more about right- and left-brain thinking, our thinking will continue to be predominantly middlebrow.

The world will be so overcrowded, loneliness will be a peak experience.

When senior citizens go out to dance, they will do the lambada.

To improve air quality, barbecuing will be a crime. Even in Texas and Australia. Various models of barbecues and recipes for barbecue sauce will be sold in antique shops. Certain models will be made into end tables.

There will be three types of government: neo-fascism, regular fascism, and fascism lite.

The New Yorker magazine will look the same as it does today— out of date.

So many brains will be burned out, endorphins will be on the endangered list.

We will have forgotten all about finding a cure for Alzheimer's disease.

Authors of self-help books will be required to provide proof that they have actually helped themselves.

Due to diversion of funds from breast cancer research to male medical problems, there will be a cure for male-patterned baldness. Male-patterned violence, however, will remain a major health threat.

Intelligent Life in the 21st Century

In the Future . . .

New Marketing Ventures:

Concept lens: breakthrough product to put over your eyes to get new perceptions and ideas.

Press-on nails will still be popular, but the big thing will be *press-on teeth*. They will come in different sizes, shapes, and colors. Traditional white will be popular for day wear. For festive occasions anything goes.

There will be a new magazine called *Others*. However, with most people it will not catch on.

To protect themselves from those pesticides that will be still allowed, apples will mutate to form a cantaloupe-like exterior. From then on they will be marketed as a trendy new fruit: appleloupes.

Flesh-colored Band-Aids will come in many colors.

There will be no major advance in the design of sardine cans.

New Slanguage:

Squeakonomics: when our economy is so bad we can barely squeak by.

Junk bonds: new usage meaning the junk bonds formed when two Boesky-like businessmen form a relationship.

Global glaucoma: condition referring to people who can't see the world as a whole.

Delusions of candor: when you are fooled into thinking someone is telling the truth.

Newrotics: cutting-edge group of people who will find new ways to be just as neurotic as we've always been.

Morewellian: word coined to describe conditions even more Orwellian than George Orwell himself could have ever imagined.

Facial prejudice: discrimination against the unpresentable appearance of older people who refuse plastic surgery.

New Ideas Whose Time Will Come:

Boot camp think tank: where people will go to be trained to think before being admitted to think tanks.

Rethink tanks: where people from think tanks can be sent to rethink things.

Letters

Last fall I sent a subscription to *Ms.* for the women residents of the prison in Muncy, Pennsylvania, in care of their educational director. I thought you might be interested in the attached copy of a letter I received; maybe it might encourage others to send subscriptions.

MARY B. SADDLEMIRE
Bowling Green, Ohio
May/June 1991 issue

This week on a cold and lonely Friday night I had the pleasure of receiving two issues of *Ms.* forwarded to us here at the State Correctional Institute at Muncy as a gift. I was deeply touched by the understanding and pure kindness inherent in this type of gesture, and I extend our sincere thanks.

I am employed here at the prison in the garment shop as a bookkeeper, and I thought that it might be a great idea to share the magazine with the other thirty-five women I work with. We have an interesting mix of young, old, Black, white, and Hispanic women in our shop, and the magazine holds things of interest for all.

I never expected to cry when I put myself to bed on Friday night, yet the very first piece I read was written by a Catholic feminist about a church that has repeatedly asked for her blind faith while turning a deaf ear to her humble voice for equity. I send you gratitude from the many different women who live here at Muncy.

JUDITH WAGNER
Muncy, Pa.
May/June 1991 issue

I am writing in response to your survey on violence. My husband battered me for the ten years of our marriage. When he first began, I tried to fight back, but that only increased the intensity of the beatings. I learned to endure the violence passively, the beatings never stopped.

Five years ago I shot and killed my husband in a misguided attempt to save my life. I am now incarcerated at the California Institution for Women, serving a sentence of fifteen years to life for committing the heinous crime of self-preservation. Society's message seems clear: men may batter, abuse, or even kill women and such behavior will be tolerated, but the woman who dares strike back and challenge the status quo will be dealt with harshly.

BRENDA ARIS
Frontera, Calif.
July/August 1991 issue

Three Generations of Native American Women's Birth Experience

BY **JOY HARJO** • JULY/AUGUST 1991

IT WAS STILL DARK when I awakened in the stuffed back room of my mother-in-law's small rented house with what felt like hard cramps. At seventeen years of age, I had read everything I could from the Tahlequah Public Library about pregnancy and giving birth. But nothing prepared me for what was coming. I awakened my child's father and then ironed him a shirt before we walked the four blocks to the Indian hospital because we had no car and no money for a taxi. He had been working with another Cherokee artist silk-screening signs for specials at the supermarket and making $5 a day, and had to leave me alone at the hospital because he had to go to work. We didn't awaken his mother. She had to get up soon enough to fix breakfast for her daughter and granddaughter before leaving for her job at the nursing home. I knew my life was balanced at the edge of great, precarious change, and I felt alone and cheated. Where was the circle of women to acknowledge and honor this birth?

> "I knew my life was balanced at the edge of great, precarious change, and I felt alone and cheated."

It was still dark as we walked through the cold morning, under oaks that symbolized the stubbornness and endurance of the Cherokee people who had made Tahlequah their capital in the new lands. I looked for handholds in the misty gray sky, for a voice announcing this impending miracle. I wanted to change everything; I wanted to go back to a place before childhood, before our own tribe's removal to Oklahoma. What kind of life was I bringing this child into? I was a poor, mixed-blood woman heavy with child who would suffer the struggle of poverty, the legacy of loss. For the second time in my life, I felt the sharp tug of my own birth cord, still connected to my mother. I believe it never pulls away, until death, and even then, it becomes a streak in the sky symbolizing that most important warrior road. In my teens I had fought my mother's weaknesses with all my might, and here I was at seventeen, becoming like my mother, who was in Tulsa, cooking breakfasts and preparing for the lunch shift at a factory cafeteria as I walked to the hospital to give birth. I should be with her; instead, I was far from her house, in the house of a mother-in-law who later would try to use witchcraft to destroy me.

After my son's father left me, I was prepped for birth. This meant my pubic area was shaved completely and then I endured the humiliation of an enema, all at the hands of strangers. I was left alone in a room painted government green. An overwhelming antiseptic smell emphasized the sterility of the hospital, a hospital built because of the U.S. government's treaty and responsibility to provide health care to Indian people.

I intellectually understood the stages of labor, the place of transition, of birth, but it was difficult to bear the actuality of it, and to bear it alone. Yet in some ways I wasn't alone, for history surrounded me. It is with the birth of children that history is given form and voice. Birth is one of the most sacred acts we take part in and witness in our lives. But sacredness seemed to be far from my lonely labor room in the Indian hospital. I heard a woman screaming in the next room with her pain, and I wanted to comfort her. The nurse used her as a bad example to the rest of us who were struggling to keep our suffering silent.

The doctor was a military man who had signed on to this watch not for love of healing or out of awe at the miracle of birth but to fulfill a contract for medical school payments. I was another statistic to him; he touched me as if he were moving equipment from one place to another. During my last visit I was given the option of being sterilized. He explained to me that the moment of birth was the best time to do it. I was handed the form but chose not to sign it, and am amazed now that I didn't think too much of it at the time. Later I would learn that many Indian women who weren't fluent in English signed, thinking it was a form giving consent for the doctor to deliver their babies. Others were sterilized without even the formality of signing. My light skin had probably saved me from such a fate. It wouldn't be the first time in my life.

When my son was finally born, I had been deadened with a needle in my spine. He was shown to me—the incredible miracle nothing prepared me for—then taken from me in the name of medical progress. I fell asleep with the weight of chemicals and awoke yearning for the child I had suffered for, had anticipated in the months proceeding from his unexpected genesis when I was still sixteen and a student at Indian school. I was not allowed to sit up or walk because of the possibility of paralysis (one of the drug's side effects), and when I finally got to hold him, the nurse stood guard as if I would hurt him. I felt enmeshed in a system in which the wisdom that had carried my people from generation to generation was ignored. In that place I felt ashamed I was an Indian woman. But I was also proud of what my body had accomplished despite the rape by the bureaucracy's machinery,

Joy Harjo in 2019

and I got us out of there as soon as possible. My son would flourish on beans and fried bread, and on the dreams and stories we fed him.

My daughter was born four years later, while I was an art student at the University of New Mexico. Since my son's birth I had waitressed, cleaned hospital rooms, filled cars with gas (while wearing a miniskirt), worked as a nursing assistant, and led dance classes at a health spa. I knew I didn't want to cook and waitress all my life, as my mother had done. I had watched the varicose veins grow branches on her legs, and as they grew, her zest for dancing and sports dissolved into utter tiredness. She had been born with a caul over her face, the sign of a gifted visionary.

My earliest memories are of my mother writing songs on an ancient Underwood typewriter after she had washed and waxed the kitchen floor on her hands and knees. She, too, had wanted something different for her life. She had left an impoverished existence at age seventeen, bound for the big city of Tulsa. She was shamed in a time in which to be even part Indian was to be an outcast in the great U.S. system. Half her relatives were Cherokee full-bloods from near Jay, Oklahoma, who for the most part had nothing to do with white people. The other half were musically inclined "white trash" addicted to country-western music and Holy Roller fervor. She thought she could disappear in the city; no one would know her family, where she came from. She had dreams of singing and had once been offered a job singing on the radio but turned it down because she was shy. Later one of her songs would be stolen before she could copyright it and would make someone else rich. She would quit writing songs. She and my father would divorce, and she would be forced to work for money to feed and clothe four children, all born within two years of each other.

As a child growing up in Oklahoma, I liked to be told the story of my birth. I would beg for it while my mother cleaned and ironed. "You almost killed me," she would say. "We almost died." That I could kill my mother filled me with remorse and shame. And I imagined the push-pull of my life, which is a legacy I deal with even now when I am twice as old as my mother was at my birth. I loved to hear the story of my warrior fight for my breath. The way it was told, it had been my decision to live. When I got older, I realized we were both nearly casualties of the system, the same system flourishing in the Indian hospital where later my son, Phil, would be born.

My parents felt lucky to have insurance, to be able to have their children in the hospital. My father came from a fairly prominent Muscogee Creek family. *His* mother was a full-blood who in the early 1920s got her degree in art. She was a painter. She gave birth to him in a private hospital in Oklahoma City; at least that's what I think he told me before he died at age fifty-three. It was something of which they were proud.

This experience was much different from my mother's own birth. She and five of her six brothers were born at home, with no medical assistance. The only time a doctor was called was when someone was dying. When she was born, her mother named her Wynema, a Cherokee name my mother says means "beautiful woman," and Jewell, for a can of shortening stored in the room where she was born.

I wanted something different for my life, for my son, and for my daughter, who later was born in a university hospital in Albuquerque. It was a bright summer morning when she was ready to begin her journey. I still had no car, but I had enough money saved for a taxi for a ride to the hospital. She was born "naturally," without drugs. I could look out the hospital window while I was in labor at the bluest sky in the world. I had support. Her father was present in the delivery room—though after her birth he disappeared on a drinking binge. I understood his despair, but did not agree with the painful means to describe it. A few days later, Rainy Dawn was presented to the sun at her father's pueblo and given a name so that she will always be recognized as part of the people, as a child of the sun.

That's not to say that my experience in the hospital reached perfection. The clang of metal against metal in the delivery room had the effect of a tuning fork reverberating fear in my pelvis. After giving birth, I held my daughter, but they took her from me for "processing." I refused to lie down to be wheeled to my room after giving birth; I wanted to walk out of there to find my daughter. We reached a compromise and I rode in a wheelchair. When we reached the room, I stood up and walked to the nursery and demanded my daughter. I knew she needed me. That began my war with the nursery staff, who deemed me unknowledgeable because I was Indian and poor. Once again, I felt the brush fire of shame, but I'd learned to put it out much more quickly, and I demanded early release so I could take care of my baby without the judgment of strangers.

I wanted something different for Rainy, and as she grew up, I worked hard to prove that I could make "something" of my life. I obtained two degrees as a single mother. I wrote poetry and screenplays, became a professor, and tried to live a life that would be a positive influence for both of my children. My work in this life has to do with reclaiming the memory stolen from our peoples when we were dispossessed from our lands east of the Mississippi; it has to do with restoring us. I am proud of our history, a history so powerful that it both destroyed my father and guarded him. It's a history that claims my mother as she lives not far from the place her mother was born, names her as she cooks in the cafeteria of a small college in Oklahoma.

When my daughter told me she was pregnant, I wasn't surprised. I had known it before she did, or at least before she would admit it to me. I felt despair, as if nothing had changed or ever would. She had run away from Indian school with her boyfriend, and they had been living in the streets of Gallup, a border town notorious for the suicides and deaths of Indian peoples. I brought her and her boyfriend with me because it was the only way I could bring her home. At age sixteen, she was fighting me just as I had so fiercely fought my mother. She was making the same mistakes. I felt as if everything I had accomplished had been in vain. Yet I felt strangely empowered, too, at this repetition of history, this continuance, by a new possibility of life and love, and I steadfastly stood by my daughter.

I had a university job, so I had insurance that covered my daughter. She saw an obstetrician in town who was reputed to be one of the best. She had the choice of a birthing room. She had the finest care. Despite this, I once again battled with a system in which physicians are taught the art of

---

JOY HARJO—renowned musician, writer, and storyteller of the Muscogee (Creek) Nation—is the twenty-third poet laureate of the United States, the first Native American to serve in the role, and only the second poet to be appointed for three terms.

The lyrical account she wrote for *Ms.*—the generational joys and traumas of birth in her own family—foretells much of what is now recognized as a state of crisis for reproductive justice and maternal health and mortality in the United States, especially for indigenous women and women of color. Today, women in the United States are more likely to die from pregnancy-related causes than anywhere else in the developed world, with rates of death for Native women more than double those for women who are white. Globally, indigenous women also continue to experience significantly worse maternal health outcomes than majority populations.

healing by dissecting cadavers. My daughter went into labor a month early. We both knew intuitively the baby was ready, but how to explain that to a system in which numbers and statistics provide the base of understanding? My daughter would have her labor interrupted; her blood pressure would rise because of the drug given to her to stop the labor. She would be given an unneeded amniocentesis and would have her labor induced—after having it artificially stopped! I was warned that if I took her out of the hospital so her labor could occur naturally, my insurance would cover nothing.

My daughter's induced labor was unnatural and difficult, monitored by machines, not by touch. I was shocked. I felt as if I'd come full circle, as if I were watching my mother's labor and the struggle of my own birth. But I was there in the hospital room with her, as neither my mother had been for me, nor her mother for her. My daughter and I went through the labor and birth together.

And when Krista Rae was born, she was born to her family. Her father was there for her, as were both her grandmothers and my friend who had flown in to be with us. Her paternal great-grandparents and aunts and uncles had also arrived from the Navajo reservation to honor her. Something *had* changed.

Four days later, I took my granddaughter to the Saguaro forest before dawn and gave her the name I had dreamed for her just before her birth. Her name looks like clouds of mist settling around a sacred mountain as it begins to speak. A female ancestor approaches on a horse. We are all together.

Letters

I am an eleven-year-old and I have a subscription to your magazine. When I was completing your "Race and Women" survey I noticed that question #67b, "How old are you?" did not include young people of my age. In the future, it would be appreciated if you would change the question and start considering my generation as young feminists also! Other than that, I think your magazine is excellent.

KATIE GORDON
Northfield, Minn.
November/December 1991 issue

I thought no one heard me! All those tired phrases, like "women and minorities," "women and people of color," reinforce the idea that white is the standard of womanhood and everyone else is "other."

I almost cried from relief and joy when I saw that *Ms.* did hear me. Your May/June 1991 issue included several examples of progressive language, such as "Black people . . . and all women" and "with women and with men of color." I am proud to support a feminist magazine that not only talks the talk but walks the walk!

NICOLE HALL
Torrance, Calif.
September/October 1991 issue

I Am Not **One of the**

BY **CHERYL MARIE WADE** • NOVEMBER/DECEMBER 1991

I am not one of the physically challenged—

I'm a sock in the eye with gnarled fist
I'm a French kiss with cleft tongue
I'm orthopedic shoes sewn on a last of your fears

I am not one of the differently abled—

I'm an epitaph for a million imperfect babies left untreated
I'm an ikon carved from bones in a mass grave at Tiergarten, Germany
I'm withered legs hidden with a blanket

I am not one of the able disabled—

I'm a black panther with green eyes and scars like a picket fence
I'm pink lace panties teasing a stub of milk white thigh
I'm the Evil Eye

I'm the first cell divided
I'm mud that talks
I'm Eve   I'm Kali
I'm The Mountain That Never Moves
I've been forever   I'll be here forever
I'm the Gimp
I'm the Cripple
I'm the Crazy Lady

I'm The Woman With Juice

•   •   •

OPPOSITE Renowned artist Barbara Kruger designed the cover for the January/February 1992 issue of *Ms.* using her signature style: photo-based images overlaid with blocks of provocative text boxed in red. It captured women's anger and outrage following the Anita Hill/Clarence Thomas hearings in 1991. This cover is now featured on the website of the Museum of Modern Art in New York City.

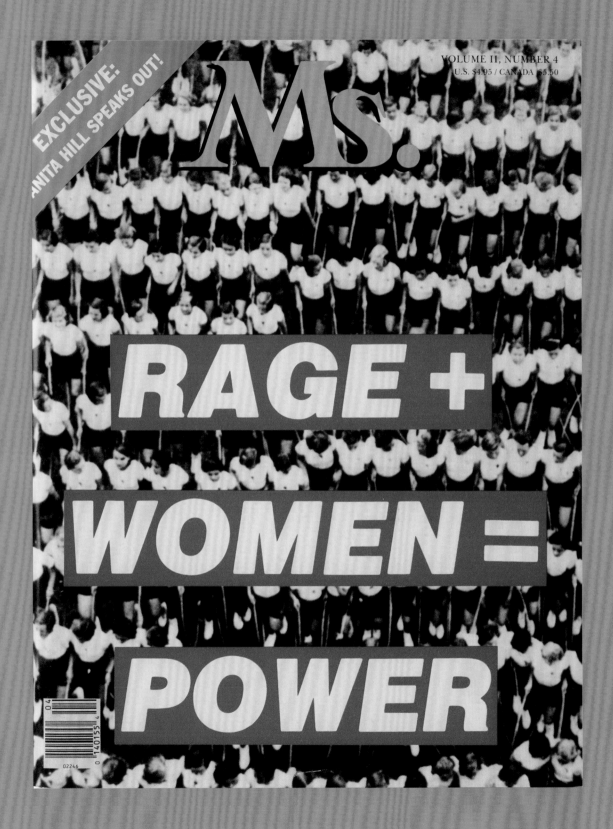

VOLUME II, NUMBER 4
U.S. $4.95 / CANADA $5.50

Ms.

EXCLUSIVE: ANITA HILL SPEAKS OUT!

RAGE +
WOMEN =
POWER

04

0 140155 4

02246

And the Language Is Race

BY **ELEANOR HOLMES NORTON** • JANUARY/FEBRUARY 1992

I SELDOM VISIT my colleagues on the Senate side, although the Senate is a short walk from the House and you can use the Capitol's long hallways or its byzantine underground tunnels to get there. But on October 8, 1991, seven of us who are congresswomen took a walk to the Senate. Most of the twenty Democratic congresswomen also would have walked, but some remained on the House floor, where the Republican men were raising parliamentary points against the one-minute speeches we were trying to make in support of Professor Anita Hill. The Republican men argued that House precedent barred discussion of proceedings in "the other body." They could raise their points of order if they liked, but nothing could keep us from reaching "the other body" in the most direct way. So we walked.

We were in step with U.S. women and men, who jammed the Senate and the House phones like nothing in memory, to stop the clock. It was incredible, but it was happening. The Senate was going to vote in the face of a serious charge that could have two colossal consequences. If checked, it could disqualify Clarence Thomas for a seat on the Supreme Court. If not checked, it could strain the court itself. An unresolved charge of sexual harassment would have followed Thomas to the court, spreading the stain on an institution that must be spotless.

> "Anita Hill was everybody's daughter, every community's model student, every sister. At the same time, she was an enigma in the African American community."

The best evidence of Hill's credibility was the desperation of Thomas's supporters to push the vote without looking into her charges. Her press conference revealed a woman of awesome credibility, not to mention brains, dignity, attractiveness of person, and a personality so compelling that the official Thomas advocates never dared to attack her personally.

If Anita Hill was so credible, why did the public disbelieve her? Why did her revelations seem to drive Thomas's support up, capping her charges with irony? Or was it so ironic, after all?

If these allegations, made by a remarkably believable person with nothing to gain, had come out in the ordinary course of the hearings, they almost surely would have ended the nomination. Instead, the outcome was controlled by the law of unintended consequences—the leak caused an effect that was the reverse of what apparently was desired. The last-minute leak of lewd sex-based allegations during a hard-fought nomination gave the taint of unfairness to everything that followed. All of this was a major factor in saving Thomas. He should be grateful for small favors.

The leak that almost buried the nomination was universally seen as offensive, on that point uniting Thomas proponents and opponents alike. Disastrously, the leak also put the Judiciary Committee Democrats on the defensive, because their prior opposition to Thomas appeared to confer a motive. Moreover, Hill burst like a meteor with testimony much worse in the sexual crudeness it attributed to Thomas than anticipated. The testimony, said to betray the inner sex life of a man on his way to the court, deeply embarrassed the public.

After all, the American people are not fools. During any normal hearing process, those who saw Hill (most did not; Thomas got to testify during evening hours) could figure out who had a motive to lie. Instead, the public was asked to respond with instant reflection to sexual crudeness so marginal most had never heard of the expression used. Worse, a response against Thomas might seem to *condone* the leak through which the boorish pornographic conversation was revealed. In the minds of many Americans, Hill's charges, and the sexual images they portrayed, were not so much overcome as they were suppressed.

The leak sealed the matter for many African Americans, who were always the key to success or failure of the nomination. Race had been responsible for the nomination and only race could undo it. Thus, it is a mistake to read the outcome of the hearings as a comment on feminism; it is a comment on the continuing potency of race to push all else aside. Not surprisingly, with a nomination of a Black man to the Supreme Court at stake, race trumped sex.

Thomas understood very well that his nomination was anchored to race and that to save himself he must cling to that anchor. Faced with a Black woman who was too honest to use race and too believable to be denied, Thomas reached below the belt. That Anita Hill was also Black did not count for much; she declined to use her race (or her gender, for that matter) to enhance her charges, while Thomas made race his central, indeed his only, defense.

Though he had spent his entire career criticizing Blacks for ascribing their condition to race, Thomas reached for a racial rock and angrily hurled it at the monolith that composed the Senate Judiciary Committee. To many Blacks, the committee looked like nothing so much as an all-white jury. Thomas took no chance that this symbolism would be missed. Declining subtle racial allusions, he brought race front and center with brazenly undiluted charges of racism—"high-tech lynching" and the rest—sending the message, especially to Blacks, that the leak and the public hearing had come *because* he was Black. Thomas's charges lit a racial flame, the functional equivalent of screaming "Fire!" in a crowded theater.

Until Anita Hill's revelations, Thomas had been protected by his race and by skillful administration handling of the Pin Point, Georgia, roots story to cover up his record. That chilling record began to come alive in documentation from witness after witness during the hearings: Thomas's career-long hostility to civil rights laws and to much of the current interpretation of the Bill of Rights. Slowly the man's own animus had begun to seep through the gauze that had seemed to seal off his government record and writings. In a *New York Times* poll three days after the first of Hill's revelations was published, only 36 percent of Blacks said Thomas should be confirmed, down from 61 percent in September—when all that most Blacks had known about Thomas was that he, too, was Black.

By the end, most African Americans did not support Thomas, and the nomination barely survived—by a vote of 52 to 48, the closest since 1888. But southern senators who were the decisive swing votes did not get a clear enough message to oppose Thomas from southern Blacks. Why not?

In addition to the racial confusion deliberately sown by Thomas, two motivations account for the Black response.

First, the leak had a particularly deep effect. Victimized historically by racism and unfair tactics, some Blacks found the leak especially suspect. More important, it reinforced the notion of racial dirty tricks. "They" (whoever was "behind" Anita Hill) came after the Black guy just as he was about to cross the finish line. Historically conditioned to identify with Black victims, some Blacks felt the leak reinforced Thomas's charge that "they" were out to get him because he was an "uppity Black."

Second, given a history impossible to ignore, many saw Thomas entirely through black-tinted glasses. Many Blacks believed he was all they could expect or get from a conservative president who had vetoed one civil rights bill and was loudly promising to block yet another. For African Americans, the Supreme Court has been both the first and the last line of defense. In the lifetime of most, the court had recognized rights the other branches of government had denied and had saved rights that Americans historically could not be trusted to ensure. Given this history, not having a Black man on the Supreme Court was unthinkable. Never mind that the court seemed bent on marching backward. All the more reason for the appearance—and the hope—of racial fairness.

What was seldom stated and what many Blacks did not consider is that an all-white Supreme Court probably could not long be left that way. Racism is still a salient part of this country's life, and the court's central role in its unraveling is too recent to be put aside. (Today, of course, the court poses the opposite danger, as it retracts civil rights laws, most recently requiring Congress to reenact the basic job discrimination statute, Title VII of the 1964 Civil Rights Act.) An all-white court would lack the appearance of elementary fairness. If not this president, then surely the next one would have chosen an African American.

But race, and the race of the only nominee Blacks could imagine from *this* president, blocked notions that there would be a better day. What if another Black was not nominated for forty years? Even some Blacks who distrusted Thomas and others who opposed him on his record saw a bird in the hand. The far more ominous and obvious possibility receded: that Thomas could *block* for a very long time the appointment of a Black in the tradition of the Black legal experience. That of course is what happened. Blacks who supported Thomas focused on the Black nominee, hoping he would allow if not his racial identity, at least his racial memories, to overcome his expressed ideology.

Nothing can disturb the shining character of Anita Hill. In this period when high moral values are preached more than practiced, Anita Hill prevailed. She emerged with enhanced stature while Thomas was diminished. Most of us know from personal experience whereof she speaks, but few of us have the courage to attempt what she did. We are in her debt.

The African American community has been left with an old dilemma. We saw it first when the Fifteenth Amendment enfranchised Black men but not Black women and led Sojourner Truth to oppose it. It is race that has defined the Black experience in this country. Everything else has been considered secondary.

Hill unintentionally brought forward the race-sex tension that is unavoidable when ethnicity is the mark of oppression. Color, country, culture, and language define an entire group; sex only half of it. This is a country where racism has been the longest-standing national neurosis. Is it any wonder that it sometimes has been difficult for the Black community to come to grips with its internal complexity? Some believe that even a concession to gender could threaten the solidarity necessary to resist and defeat racism. Nevertheless, after some initial confusion in the 1970s, many Black women embraced feminism and women's rights. This proved far less difficult than had been imagined, in part because the two identities seldom competed on the same stage at the same time. This time the two emerged together when the prospect was all-white justice. It was not a fair fight.

> **ELEANOR HOLMES NORTON,** the crusading civil rights attorney and feminist leader, is now in her fifteenth term as the delegate to Congress from the District of Columbia; among her lifetime of barrier-breaking accomplishments, she was the first woman to chair the U.S. Equal Employment Opportunity Commission.

Nevertheless, the majority of African Americans got past the race-sex confusion inherent in this conflict. Just before the confirmation vote, Thomas's support in the Black community had risen, but only by four points, to 40 percent, and then only because it seemed to be a take-it-or-leave-it proposition. Blacks did not squarely veto Thomas, but whites carried Thomas over.

Anita Hill was everybody's daughter, every community's model student, every sister. At the same time, she was an enigma in the African American community, still struggling with racism, still searching for its rightful place in its own country, still sorting out race and sex and class. Anita was ahead of a time she has helped define—a time to be Black and a woman.

Letters

Ms. is too good not to share with those who are most in need of broader perspectives—the policy makers in both the public and the private sectors. I'd like to suggest that *Ms.* initiate an adopt-a-policy-maker campaign wherein gift subscriptions can be purchased for the policy maker(s) of your choice. To start the campaign off, I am enclosing a check. Please start a gift subscription in my name for each of the U.S. Supreme Court justices. When the one-year subscriptions are up, send me the renewal notice(s).

Even if the policy makers themselves don't read a word, perhaps a staff member or friend or relative will. Dandelions have been fairly successful for some time without worrying much about the seeds that don't find fertile soil.

> WES CHRISTENSEN
> San Jose, Calif.
> January/February 1992 issue

Sexual harassment was never a major issue as long as it only threatened the careers of millions of women. It only became a major issue when it threatened the career of one man [Clarence Thomas]. Click!

> SUSAN PEPPERDINE
> Fairway, Kans.
> January/February 1992 issue

Even though Clarence Thomas has been sworn in as the newest member of the U.S. Supreme Court, speaking as a dedicated feminist, I know that the women's movement has still made history. Thinking with regard to sexual attitudes will never be the same. The greatest clarion call of feminist activism should now be to fight for those issues that Thomas and his Senate supporters continued to show the greatest disregard toward. Namely, women's rights.

> LINDA MAURO
> Passaic County, N.J., NOW
> January/February 1992 issue

Recently, my local NOW chapter sent a flyer announcing a rally for reproductive freedom; I haven't been to a rally in nineteen years. My seventeen-year-old son saw the flyer and left a note attached to it: "Mom, I want to go—let's do it!" So we drove one and a half hours to the rally; he questioned me on how I became involved; it was a wonderful experience! He said, "Next time I'm going to get some of my friends and we'll take a van full."

I'm hoping my fifteen-year-old will also become involved. I had to share this; someone has to know what success really is.

> MARGARET HIGUERA
> Bloomfield Hills, Mich.
> January/February 1992 issue

The Politics of Housework

BY **PATRICIA MAINARDI** • MAY/JUNE 1992

T SEEMS PERFECTLY REASONABLE. We both had careers, both had to work a couple days a week to earn enough to live on, so why shouldn't we share the housework? So I suggested it to my mate and he agreed—most men are too hip to turn you down flat. "You're right," he said. "It's only fair."

Then an interesting thing happened. I can only explain it by stating that we women have probably been brainwashed more than even we can imagine. Probably too many years of seeing TV women in ecstasy over their shiny waxed floors or breaking down over dirty shirt collars. Men have no such conditioning. They recognize the essential fact of housework from the very beginning: it stinks. The longer my husband contemplated these chores, the more repulsed he became, and so proceeded to change from the normally considerate Dr. Jekyll into the crafty Mr. Hyde who would stop at nothing to avoid the horrors of housework. As he felt himself backed into a corner laden with dirty dishes, brooms, mops, and reeking garbage, his teeth grew longer and pointier, his fingernails haggled, and his eyes grew wild.

> "Men have no such conditioning. They recognize the essential fact of housework from the very beginning: it stinks."

So ensued a dialogue that's been going on for several years. Here are some of the high points:

- "I don't mind sharing the housework, but I don't do it very well. We should do the things we are best at." *Meaning:* Unfortunately, I'm no good at things like washing dishes or cooking. *Also meaning:* I don't like the dull stupid boring jobs, so you should do them.
- "I don't mind sharing the work, but you'll have to show me how to do it." *Meaning:* I ask a lot of questions and you'll have to show me everything every time I do it because I don't remember so good. Also don't try to sit down and read while I'm doing my jobs because I'm going to annoy the hell out of you until it's easier to do them yourself.
- "We have different standards, and why should I have to work to your standards? That's unfair." *Meaning:* I can provoke innumerable scenes over the housework issue. Eventually, doing all the housework yourself will be less painful to you than trying to get me to do half.

- "I've got nothing against sharing the housework, but you can't make me do it on your schedule." *Meaning:* Passive resistance. I'll do it when I damned well please, if at all. If my job is doing the dishes, it's easier to do them once a week. If taking out the laundry, once a month. If washing the floors, once a year. If you don't like it, do it yourself oftener, and then I don't do it all.
- "I hate it more than you. You don't mind it so much." *Meaning:* Housework is the worst crap I've ever done. It's degrading and humiliating for someone of my intelligence to do it. But for someone of your intelligence . . .
- "Housework is too trivial to even talk about." *Meaning:* Housework is beneath my status.
- "Women's liberation isn't a political movement." *Meaning:* The revolution is coming too close to home. *Also meaning:* I am only interested in how I am oppressed, not how I oppress others. Therefore, war, the draft, and the university are political. Women's liberation is not . . .

Participatory democracy begins at home. If you are planning to implement your politics, there are certain things to remember:

1. He is feeling it more than you. He's losing some leisure and you're gaining some. The measure of your oppression is his resistance.

2. If human endeavors are like a pyramid with men's highest achievements at the top, then keeping oneself alive is at the bottom. Men have always had servants (us) to take care of this bottom stratum of life while they have confined their efforts to the rarefied upper regions.

3. It is a traumatizing experience for someone who has always thought of himself as being against the exploitation of one human being by another to realize that in his daily life he has been accepting and implementing (and benefiting from) this exploitation: that the oldest form of oppression is perpetuated by half of the population on the other half.

4. Keep checking up on who's actually doing the jobs. These things have a way of backsliding so that a year later the woman is again doing everything. Use time sheets if necessary. He will accuse you of being petty. Alternate the bad jobs.

5. Beware of the double whammy. He won't do the little things he always did because you're now a "Liberated Woman," right? Of course he won't do anything else either . . . I was just finishing this when my husband came in and asked what I was doing. Writing a paper on housework. Housework? Oh my God, how trivial can you get.

Twenty Years of Feminist Bookstores

BY **CAROL SEAJAY** • JULY/AUGUST 1992

THERE WAS A TIME when a committed feminist could store everything in print about the women's liberation movement in a few file folders on her desk. Now there are more than a hundred women's bookstores scattered across the United States and Canada. The larger stores stock fifteen thousand to eighteen thousand titles, and most have more books than any one woman could read over the course of her lifetime.

The women's liberation movement became a print movement out of necessity. In the late 1960s, little of what we needed to know was available in any written form. When we did get coverage in mainstream publications, our ideas were distorted and trivialized, and it became increasingly clear that if we wanted feminist ideas in print, we would have to do it ourselves.

Freedom of the press, we learned by the early 1970s, belonged to those who owned printing presses. When male printers refused to print our articles about self-help vaginal exams, the real lives of women in prostitution, or lesbian self-esteem, we established our own

> **"The demand for books that tell the truth about women's lives, contrary to the impression given by mainstream media, continues to grow rather than decline."**

printing presses so that no man could ever again tell women what we could read. To further that autonomy, we established our own typesetting shops, binderies, wholesale distributors, and bookstores to put the literature into women's hands. It was a wonderfully exhilarating time.

The development of the women-in-print movement was a part of that drive for women's independence, and its growth has been phenomenal. Articles like "The Myth of the Vaginal Orgasm," "The Woman-Identified Woman," and "Why I Want a Wife," as well as women's liberation magazines and newspapers, were passed from hand to hand. Newspapers and pamphlets with no visible means of distribution traveled thousands of miles in the backpacks and cars of women who took the new publications everywhere they went.

Activists set up tables filled with the new feminist literature at conferences and demonstrations, at women's liberation meetings, and later in women's centers. These tables offered pamphlets, newspapers and magazines, and the first books published by the first feminist publishers (staple-bound copies of *Child of Myself; Edward the Dyke, and Other Poems; Notes from the First Year; Notes from the Second Year; Our Bodies, Ourselves; Sleeping Beauty: A Lesbian Fairy Tale; Songs to a Handsome Woman;* and *Woman to Woman*). They were the first generation of women's bookstores. Some contemporary stores, such as Lioness Books in Sacramento, trace their beginnings back to when these literature tables moved to permanent quarters in women's centers. Other early bookstores started on front and back porches, or in an extra room in a women's living collective.

Even when women deliberately opened bookstores *in* storefronts, it was difficult to tell the difference between a women's bookstore and a women's center. There were always places to sit; the coffeepot was always on; there were usually more plants and bulletin boards than books. Toys, "kids' corners," and even playrooms welcomed children. The women who worked in the bookstore provided information and meeting space. They were as likely to be found answering questions or aiding a battered woman as they were to be selling books.

Women from all walks of life and experiences found community and resources as well as books and ideas. Some women walked around the block many times before they found the courage to enter. Once they made it through the doorway, they took what they found and changed their lives— left abusive relationships, found new self-images, came out, found sisterhood and a community. Many went on to become activists whose work has changed all of our lives.

There was one important difference between women's centers and women's bookstores, however: selling the books paid the rent. During the years when women's centers lost funding or were "deprioritized," the financially independent bookstores stood firm.

Many of the stores in the early 1970s were the result of a burst of energy in a circle of women who worked together on other projects. If someone had the idea to start a bookstore, two or five or twenty women would join together and start one. Most of these stores were collectively run in styles as diverse as the communities that started them. Many if not most of those who felt strongly enough to get involved, raise funds, build bookcases, and do volunteer shifts week after week were lesbians. For all the women, their weekly shifts were an important part of their social and community networks. Some of these stores lasted only a few months. Others, including Everywomans Books, Fan the Flames, Mother Kali's, Sisterhood Bookstore, and the Vancouver Women's Bookstore, are still serving women's need for information today.

In those wonderfully anarchistic days, little attention was given to details of ownership, structure, long-term goals, or financial planning. Creating equality-based, nonhierarchical organizations where each woman would be respected for her unique gifts was deemed to be far more important than setting up procedures to deal with such unlikely eventualities as conflict, collective members who failed to keep commitments, or (unthinkable lack of faith in women!) embezzlement. Traditional business practices (the domain of the patriarchy) were automatically suspect. Most stores survived—and thrived—on constant fundraising, volunteer labor, and donated supplies (often "liberated" from patriarchal institutions). Collective members often wrote personal checks to pay for books or magazines they wanted to see stocked. "Long-term financial planning" often meant raising money—or saving it out of sales—to pay the rent.

The earliest bookstores closed for various reasons: the constant turnover among volunteers, the loss of skills when staff turnover occurred more rapidly than skills could be passed on. Some collectives developed structures to deal with disagreements, but others were closed by unresolved and unresolvable conflicts. Lack of access to enough capital to allow a bookstore to prosper has probably killed more bookstores than any other single problem.

Despite these obstacles, the survival rates for feminist stores are surprisingly high. Of the sixty women's liberation bookstores in the United States and Canada in 1978, nineteen are still open fourteen years later. More than half of the seventy-three feminist bookstores that were listed in the September 1983 issue of *Ms.* are still serving their communities nine years later. These are excellent survival rates for any small businesses—never mind undercapitalized, politically based bookstores.

Better yet, more feminist bookstores open each year than close, and the total number increases each year. The demand for books that tell the truth about women's lives, contrary to the impression given by mainstream media, continues to grow rather than decline. Even a recession of current proportions has not stopped that climb. Sales in feminist bookstores increased from $4 million to $30 million between 1981 and 1991.

But staying open should not be the only measure of success for feminist bookstores: during the months and years the now-defunct stores *were* open, these hotbeds provided women with access to books, magazines, pamphlets, *ideas* that weren't available anywhere else, and they changed women's lives. They helped to build our information and communication networks. Simply by existing, these stores taught women to feel entitled to books that reflected their experiences.

Financially speaking, *none* of the first generation of bookstores or publishers should have survived: there simply weren't enough books for feminist bookstores to sell to stay afloat, nor enough bookstores to sell enough books to make feminist publishing financially viable. But women keep opening feminist bookstores and publishing companies just the same, and kept them open as long as possible, until time came when there *were* enough outlets to make feminist publishing viable and enough books to support feminist bookstores.

By the 1980s, new bookstores were less likely to be run by collectives: more stores were opened by triads, partners or lovers, and sole proprietors who, in addition to providing a community with literature, wanted to create a satisfying livelihood for themselves. Volunteer labor was increasingly in short supply, and more and more of the stores were staffed by paid workers. There were many more books and fewer coffeepots (booksellers having learned how many books can be damaged with a single spilled cup of coffee) and ever more nonsexist, antiracist children's books, reflecting the baby booms in both the lesbian and the heterosexual communities. Overstuffed couches gave way to the additional bookcases needed to display all the new books. Sidelines such as cards, calendars, music, and women-oriented jewelry continued to provide images not available elsewhere as well as to supplement bookstore incomes. Potted ferns were no longer essential, but virtually every feminist bookstore now had large sections of books by and about women of color, out of passion for validating the diversity of women's lives and experiences. International sections grew as more feminist works became available in translation. Stores that were thriving had broad-based stock, reflecting the wide range of class, age, race, sexuality, politics, and priorities of the women who use the stores. Women's bookstores are still the first place women turn to find community resources of all kinds.

Bookselling in the 1990s is a complex (though eminently learnable) skill. Lacking experience and capital, many women have built thriving community centers/bookstores through vision, idealism, and commitment. There's nothing like telling a feminist that she can't do something to guarantee that she will.

·   ·   ·

Persephone **Abducted**

BY **RITA DOVE** • JULY/AUGUST 1992

She cried out for Mama who did not
hear. She left with a wild eye thrown back,
she left with curses, rage
that withered her features to a hag's.
No one can tell a mother how to act:
there are no laws when laws are broken, no names
to call upon. Some say there's nourishment for pain,
and call it Philosophy.
That's for the birds, vulture and hawk, the large ones who praise
the miracle of flight because
they use it so diligently.
She left us singing in the field, oblivious
to all but the ache of our own bent backs.

"**We Are Who You Are**"

BY **BONNIE SHERR KLEIN** • NOVEMBER/DECEMBER 1992

WHAT HAPPENS when a successful feminist filmmaker (*Not a Love Story: A Film About Pornography*) who is also a wife and mother is struck down in her prime by a catastrophic brain-stem stroke and becomes disabled?

It all began in 1987. I am forty-six years old and enjoying an athletic and sexy vacation with my husband, Michael. On a hot day, we bicycle ten miles to the town tennis courts. I feel weak and nauseated, and play badly. We think it must be food poisoning.

> "*Every* issue is a women's issue; relationships, dependence, and autonomy are as much a part of feminism as day care and violence. I have undersold feminism."

Within several hours, I am staggering and slurring my speech. I have double vision. Michael, a family physician, recognizes the signs of central nervous system damage. At midnight, he speeds me home to Montreal, to the emergency room of the hospital where he works.

Diagnostic tests are inconclusive. We are shocked and scared, but I begin to stabilize. Within a few days, I am released from the intensive care unit and take a few steps with a walker. After two weeks, we celebrate our twentieth anniversary in the hospital with our children. I feel blessed and happy to be alive.

The next day I become totally paralyzed. Semiconscious, I am "locked in" and unable to speak. A respirator breathes for me. A magnetic resonance imaging test reveals that a congenital malformation at the base of my brain stem has bled, resulting in several strokes. It is like a time bomb waiting to explode again. Local specialists declare it inoperable because of its inaccessible location. Close family and friends come to say goodbye.

Michael refuses to accept this fatal verdict. He locates a surgeon who is prepared to remove the malformation.

I am jet-ambulanced on a respirator to London, Ontario. By my bed, the surgeon posts a newspaper clipping: a picture of me with Kate Millett from my documentary *Not a Love Story*. I overhear a staff remark, "She used to be a filmmaker." I remain in intensive care for several months. Michael stays with me, acting as husband, family doctor, nurse, and advocate. He will not resume work for several months.

As I come back to life but cannot move, speak, or breathe, I have frequent panic attacks. Only Michael can talk me down. He breathes with me until I fall asleep. The literal meaning of "conspire" is "to breathe together." We are in a conspiracy for my life. This becomes the metaphor of our partnership. This *is* a love story.

RECOVERY

Back in Montreal, I spend more months in the hospital and then in a rehabilitation institute. Like a helpless baby, I learn how to swallow, speak, sit upright, use the toilet, stand.

Several months after the stroke, as soon as I can use a pencil, the occupational therapist helps me to copy circles and squares like a schoolgirl. My first communication is an illegible letter to our daughter, Naomi—then seventeen—in which I share my fear about how slow recovery may be, an admission I make to no one else. Once I can write, I begin my journal, which becomes a tool for my survival. I use it to process the strange and troubling events happening in my body, to record thoughts I cannot trust my damaged mind to remember, to remind myself how far I have come.

THE LONG HAUL: REHABILITATION

After seven months in the hospital, I am at home over the next two and a half years, in the long process of rehabilitation. I have conventional physical, occupational, and speech therapy. As I gradually improve, I remember my old feminist wisdom that I know my body better than anyone else. I take control. I experiment with so-called alternative approaches like acupuncture. Michael and I dance and play, in whatever motivating ways we can invent to push my physical limits. And I learn to rest. In my pre-stroke life, this was never easy for me, juggling the three *F*s: family, film-making, and feminism. Now I have no choice. My body's messages are nonnegotiable.

The anguish is profound when I let it emerge, and it comes out at the slightest invitation.

The stroke hit me in the middle of editing a film. The producer and the editor bring the film to the hospital and my home so we can work on it together. *Mile Zero* is the story of four teenagers—one of whom is my son, Seth—who are organizing against nuclear arms. The premiere, sixteen months after my stroke, is the most triumphant moment in my rehabilitation. I have reclaimed the important piece of myself that was a filmmaker.

Yet I still do not accept myself as disabled; disability is "a stage I am just passing through." For the premiere, I reject a fully accessible educational institution and choose a glamorous cinema with inaccessible bathrooms, even though I am in a wheelchair.

I am coming up against multiple barriers, personal and social. I cannot return to my former life, and I do not know what my life will be now. Even feminism has betrayed me. It seems too narrow a lens for the new realities of my life. I also feel an unresolved conflict between feminism and my increased dependence on—and appreciation for—Michael.

About two and a half years post-stroke, I have an experience that begins to clarify my thinking about feminism. We spend the winter in Beersheba, Israel, where Michael is working to help me escape Montreal's ice and snow. A woman from the local chapter of the Israel Women's Network phones: As a visiting feminist, would I speak on a "women's issue" of my choosing at their next meeting? Again, my first reaction is negative: "I am no longer engaged with women's issues; I have been so self-obsessed with my stroke that's all I could possibly talk about." Her response is quick: "That's exactly what we want to hear about, but were too shy to ask!"

I have forgotten how wonderful it is to share intimately with a group of women! I read bits from my journal, and my story prompts theirs. One woman says, "My relationship with my husband is fine as long as I'm healthy, capable, and available sexually, but I don't know what would happen if I were incapacitated." She hadn't read the United Nations statistic that disabled women are twice as likely to get divorced or separated as disabled men. We realize that we rarely talk about illness, disability, and dying, though we all confront these realities.

Every issue is a women's issue; relationships, dependence, and autonomy are as much a part of feminism as day care and violence. I have undersold feminism. I slowly recognize that the way I am living my stroke has everything to do with myself as a feminist—as well as with implications for feminism itself.

"COMING OUT" DISABLED

I feel comfortable and stimulated in this group of Israeli women; they are middle-class, middle-aged, married Jewish women like me. But no one else there is disabled. I am "other." I desperately need company.

I had first learned of DAWN (the DisAbled Women's Network of Canada) years earlier when it approached Studio D to make our screenings more accessible. We appreciated being sensitized, favored wheelchair-accessible venues, and enjoyed the aesthetics of sign language interpretation with our movies. But sometimes DAWN's demands seemed "excessive"; our meager resources were already exhausted by items on our agenda that seemed to affect *most* women. But in retrospect, I know that as a not-yet-disabled woman I was afraid of disability.

As soon as I return to Canada, I dig DAWN's phone number out of a feminist newsletter. I realize that its agenda is identical to mine (and feminism's): dependence and autonomy; image and self-esteem; powerlessness, isolation, violence, and vulnerability; equality and access; sexuality. Three years after my stroke, I go to my first DAWN meeting at the local YWCA.

I feel apologetic, illegitimate, because I was not born disabled and am not as severely disabled as many other people. I feel guilty about my privileges of class, profession (including my disability pension), and family. I am a newcomer to the disability movement: I have not paid my dues. (Doesn't this litany sound "just like a woman"?)

Our talk keeps moving between the personal and the political, because disability—like gender, race, age, and sexuality—is a social as well as a biological construct. The DAWN members, typical of disabled women, are mostly unemployed, poor, and living alone. It is like the early days of consciousness-raising in the women's movement: sharing painful (and funny) experiences, "clicks!" of recognition; swapping tips for coping with social service bureaucracies and choosing the least uncomfortable tampons for prolonged sitting. It is exhilarating to cry and laugh with other women again.

Here, I am not the other, because everyone is other. It is the sisterhood of disability. The stroke has connected me with women who were not part of my world before—working-class women with little education, women with intellectual and psychiatric disabilities, women with physical "abnormalities" from whom I would have averted my eyes in polite embarrassment. All women like me.

I discover it is easier for me to be a disabled feminist than a disabled person. Feminism means loving myself as I am. After three long years, I am finally ready to accept myself as permanently, irrevocably disabled: acceptance is not an event but an ongoing process. I learn more about the disability rights movement. I meet other women with disabilities who become my buddies, sisters, teachers, and "rolling" models. I learn, not surprisingly, that women are leaders in the disability movement.

WHERE AM I NOW?

In retrospect, the "clicks!" in my consciousness about disability paralleled my coming to feminist consciousness two decades earlier. For a long time, I denied I was disabled, and kept my distance from the "cripples" in the hospital gym because I was an exception to the rule. Later, I was sure I could "overcome" it; I would be supercrip (superwoman); I would support the rights of other people with disabilities, but *I* was not oppressed. As time passed, I experienced with great pain the ways in which other people's attitudes and societal barriers disempowered me. At first, I internalized the oppression and lost all self-esteem. Then, as I reconnected with feminism and discovered my commonality with other women (and men) with disabilities, I began to see more clearly. With solidarity came strength.

Between writing this piece and correcting the galleys, I have taken a giant step in my journey. I went to Independence 92 in Vancouver, an international conference on disability—more than two thousand of us from more than a hundred countries! For one week, I had the heady feeling that we were taking over the world. Even better—we were making it, creating a world in which difference is not the problem but part of the solution.

It is a feat for this disabled filmmaker's eyes: a gridlock of wheelchairs on a freight elevator, a shoulder chain of the blind leading the blind, signing and singing, nursing babies in wheelchairs—images we have not seen because we disabled are invisible, even to each other; images so rare and precious they have not yet been co-opted or trivialized.

Somehow, I think I will be making films again.

·   ·   ·

Today Could Be the Day

BY **AUDRE LORDE** • MARCH/APRIL 1993

> **AUDRE LORDE** died on November 17, 1992, after a fourteen-year battle against cancer. To the end, she remained more than the sum of her parts—in her words, "a Black, lesbian, feminist, warrior poet, fighting the good fight in spite of it all." This poem—one of the last she wrote—appeared in her posthumous collection *The Marvelous Arithmetics of Distance*. Her presence has been sorely missed, her legacy greatly cherished.

I can't just sit here
staring death in her face
blinking and asking for a new name
by which to greet her

I am not afraid to say
unembellished
I am dying
but I do not want to do it
looking the other way.

Today is not the day.
It could be
but it is not.
Today is today
in the early moving morning
my sun shining down upon
the farmhouse in my belly
lighting the wellswept alleys
of the town growing in my liver
intricate vessels swelling with the
   heat

of one goddess or another
Mother Mawu's gift
or her mischievous daughter
Afrekete   my beloved

feel the sun of my days surround
   you
joining our pathways   our labor
we have water to carry
honey to harvest
bright seed to plant for the next
   fair
sweet oil to exchange as we linger
over each other's long ashy legs
the evening light
a crest on your cheekbones.

By this rising
a piece of our labor is half-done
a taste of loving
doing a bit of work
and having some fun
riding my wheels so close to the
   line
my eyelashes blaze.
. . .

This could be the day.
I could slip anchor and wander
to the end of the jetty
uncoiling   into the waters
vessel of sun   moonglade

ride the freshets to sundown
and when I am gone

another stranger will find you
coiled on the warm sand
beached treasure   and love you
for the different stories
your seas tell
and the half-finished blossoms

growing out of my season
will trail behind
with a comforting hum.

But today
is not
the day.
Today.

—April 22, 1992

What, Menopause Again?
A Guide to Cultural Combat

BY **MARGARET MORGANROTH GULLETTE** •

JULY/AUGUST 1993

NINETEEN NINETY-TWO was the year of the horrific menopause anecdote and the full-scale launch of the menoboom, inundating women with "information" that detailed all the loss, misery, humiliation, and despair supposedly in store for us. Women's magazine articles, talk-show discussions, advice books, and menopause diaries have led (since men overhear everything) to prime-time innuendo about midlife women's troubles, and thus around back again into private life.

> **"It's the end of menstruation. That is the only absolute. It is not, and I repeat *not*, a disease or a disorder."**

Why *now*? Here's the stock answer: "Sexual enlightenment has gone so far that it's time to tackle the last taboo subject." This view presents current menopause discourse as a triumph of feminism, like taking sexual harassment public, shaming *MacNeil/Lehrer* into finding more women experts in economics and international politics, or writing the names of date rapists on the bathroom walls of college campuses. Silence implies taboo, feminism breaks silences; ergo, women need to "speak menopause." But how can it be a taboo subject when the word appears everywhere you look? When women are signing the articles? When women can be told by a woman writer that other women are talking about "it" at dinner parties? Far from being taboo, it's in real danger of becoming obligatory.

Menopause discourse flourishes at a moment when women are seen to be getting powerful, independent, and increasingly self-assured. What woman, sniffing the stale sweat of male alarm, can't anticipate the backlash? Older women get hit with ageism in the form of widespread public discussion about menopause, male science that assumes we've all got a deficiency disease, and male commerce that sells us the supposed remedies. If women internalize the messages, we are weakened.

Let me say in a sentence what menopause means as a biological universal. It's the end of menstruation. That is the only absolute. It is not, and I repeat *not,* a disease or a disorder. Everything else they tell us about menopause is not universal.

In fact, for many women so much else is going on that the incident doesn't loom large in their whole life story. Postmenstrual women are unlikely to spend much time in the beauty parlor, their women's group, their kitchens, or conference rooms talking about it. (Two of my closest friends passed through this allegedly major marker without mentioning it.) And we should be wary of judging our mothers' silence about menopause. My mother never told me anything about hers until I asked, and then she said there wasn't anything to remember. Then I recalled her telling me occasionally at the time that she was having a flush (although I hadn't observed it). But she doesn't remember having them, nor can either of us recall how old she was. Her memory is excellent, by the way, and her health too.

Despite the enormous cultural pressures to reveal all about menopause, magnify it, and make it an event, might real power consist in refusing to join the public discussion? Yes and no. Our main goal should be to take control of the flood of "news" about menopause to ensure that its place in our whole life story is proportional. Is it possible that most of the silence about menopause reflects one real truth, that biologically and even psychologically speaking on the whole nothing of major significance occurs? Obviously, we need to make the true meaning of our silence clear. That "nothing happened" or "it was nothing that you couldn't handle" has become a bigger part of our woman-to-woman conversations, as well as more public discussions.

And when we speak, we should eschew unframed anecdotes—"my most humiliating experience"—and carefully decide what questions we will and will not answer. We are being encouraged to tell all in the name of "frankness," but a selection of our worst anecdotes is being plucked like plums and reheated by mainstream commentators to prove their point, that "menopause is hush-hush because it's too awful to talk about; it dominates your life." Their menopause does. Ours need not.

The culture has managed to make women fearful that midlife marks the fall into aging, and menopause means you wake up overnight an alarmingly diminished person. The fear of the sudden loss of self begins long before a woman nears the likely age of her menopause. As a result, menopause is on its way to becoming a psychosomatic disease for women who haven't had it yet, who are being made hyperconscious of the ailments of old-old age and of "female" causes of death. The last half of adulthood is collapsed into itself, mercilessly shortened. This is a form of cultural terrorism.

No other age group gets told a future-health-risk story like this. Nor is there an equivalent discourse that makes men of forty as anxious about their aging. Although they can suffer from impotence, for which there seems to be no female equivalent, the media are not (yet) touting their need for hormones. By making women's problems so medical, so visible, so traumatic, and so tied up with aging, the culture not only treats women as if they alone aged—bad as that would be in itself—it treats longevity, because it's female, as if it were solely a disaster. And it presents the problems of old-old age as the model for life after menopause. As a result, women have been made to feel anxious and defensive and taught to buy the products that are sold to relieve anxiety.

Ageism internalized is a stressor, a depressant—in itself a psychosomatic illness. Feeling demoralized when you look in the mirror, assuming that no one will take a sexual interest in you henceforth, and believing that your future ended yesterday are all symptoms of ageism, not aging. Women and men both need to acknowledge that midlife crisis is a disease created in European cultures. Learning this should make us angry, and learning its effects should make us resistant. We know we'll all age by the rule of nature. Should we let ourselves be aged by the tyranny of our culture too?

Letters

As a cradle Catholic, raised in Catholic schools, I was outraged at the statement by Cardinal Franjo Kuharić, quoted in your coverage on rape victims in Bosnia and Herzegovina ("Will the World Remember? Can the Women Forget?," March/April 1993), that "for those who have become pregnant, we will try to awaken their maternal instincts and encourage them to give birth to the child." Let me put it in common parlance: Fuck the cardinal. Let the cardinal "awaken" his own maternal instincts. Perhaps he would like to bear children such as these.

KATHRYN ELIZABETH KIRBY
Glen Ellyn, Ill.
July/August 1993 issue

Raising Sons

BY **MARY GORDON** • NOVEMBER/DECEMBER 1993

WE WERE ONE of a minority of couples—one in ten, is it? one in a hundred?—who were hoping for a girl. The delivery room nurses, knowing my passionate wish, let out a joyous shout when they saw that the baby was a daughter. It took her twenty-two hours to be born, a difficult birth; she wanted to come into the world chin up, and she's kept it that way for thirteen years. Anna looked at us, and at the world, with a gimlet eye; as soon as she could focus, she understood her job description: separating the sheep from the goats.

She so delighted us that three years later we decided to try again. This time I was older and decided on an amniocentesis. We opted to know the gender of the fetus before it was born; we thought it was absurd that the lab technician should know more about our child-to-be than we did. The six weeks waiting for the results of an amnio are among the longest days in anyone's life, and when the doctor called, saying he had good news, I was elated. "Everything's fine," he said. "It's perfectly healthy. And it's a boy!"

"Oh my God," I said. "What am I supposed to do with one of them?"

"They're very cute," the doctor said.

"Yes, but I don't know what to do with them."

He told me I'd figure it out.

I'd lived an unusually female-centered life. I am an only child, and my father died when I was seven. My mother and I then moved in with my grandmother and my aunt. I went to an all-girls high school and a women's college. I wasn't a tomboy, and I wasn't someone who had a lot of male friends. The important relationships in my life were with women friends and male lovers; for most of my life it was in that order. Now I was (and still am) married when I learned the news that I was to have a son, so I was going to be bringing one of them up alongside one of them. You would think I needn't have been so alarmed. But I was.

It's one thing to be angry at a grown-up male, even unjustly sometimes, for acting according to type, or representing the values of a gender with a history of oppressing, but what about a kid? What about one who lived inside your body for nine months, who is sustained by the milk in your breasts? This is the kind of thing I was afraid of: Would I take my generalized anger against male privilege out on this little child who was dependent upon me for his survival, physical to be sure, but mental as well?

And what would I do with him? I didn't like sports; I wasn't interested in soldiers, or cowboys, or cops, or cars. What would we talk about? If I

OPPOSITE Cartoon by Alison Bechdel (*Dykes to Watch Out For; Fun Home*), which ran on the back cover of the July/August 1993 issue.

brought him up to be interested in what I was interested in—so we could have a good time hanging out—would I be depriving him of his rightful place in the world of men, a world he had no choice but to inhabit?

In retrospect, I realize that I was thinking about what men did all day in ways that were grotesquely stereotyped. I didn't imagine that my daughter and I were going to spend the day talking about cooking or hairdos; why did I think my son would come into the world equipped with a football helmet and a six-pack?

I had a lot to learn. Of course, the body is a great teacher. If my mind told me, occasionally, that the creature inside me was the "other," my heart leaped with joy every time I felt him move inside me. The slow grinding of his head against my belly, the undulant curve of his midnight swim, wiped out the very hint of separateness. Then he was born: an easy birth, three hours. And he was David. He wasn't *him*.

From the beginning, he was less fierce than his sister; he always seemed to have more of those qualities Carol Gilligan says girls have than his sister did. He was much more interested in pleasing, in cooperating; she was interested in what was right. She could block out the world to achieve mastery of a task. I once saw her literally step over a weeping classmate in nursery school in order to get to the shelf where the books were kept. He could be distracted from his pursuits by the presence of other people, particularly if he felt they weren't happy.

From the moment he noticed other people, he's had a tendency—anguishing for a mother to observe—to suffer when other people are suffering, to intuit their suffering, to turn himself into a pretzel—telling jokes, giving them toys—in order to make them happier. When he was in kindergarten, there was a child in his class who'd been born addicted, who'd had a difficult life, moving, often several times a month, from one welfare hotel to another. Each morning, he began his day sitting on David's lap, and David rocked him for a few minutes until he was ready to join the other children at their play. He always went out of his way to include difficult or isolated children. Anna, however, has never had any tolerance for bad behavior, no inclination for charity playdates. David's guilt (which he, but not Anna, took in with his mother's milk) often leads him to invite people he doesn't like and then feel trapped by their presence. Anna knows her limits and states them clearly. When she was a kindergartner, we went (God help us all) to Disney World. There, the characters walk around, and children get their autographs. Mickey, Donald, and Goofy were mobbed. But no one was around Chip and Dale. I said to my daughter, "Why don't you ask Chip and Dale for their autographs. They must feel sad that no one's asking them."

"I didn't tell that guy to be Chip," she said. "It's his choice and his problem." My daughter could hear the unexpurgated Grimm stories, delighting Bruno Bettelheim's heart, and not turn a hair at the most bloodthirsty myths (Beowulf was a favorite with her), but we quickly learned that David was very troubled by cruelty or violence in stories or on the screen. *Raiders of the Lost Ark* did him in at age eight. A friend of mine had invited him over to watch it, and David came back, pale and distraught. "He invited me to see another Indiana Jones movie tomorrow," David said. "Tell him you won't let me go. Tell him you think it's too violent." When my friend walked in the house the next day, David said, "She won't let me see it. I just begged her to let me see it, but she said she thinks it's too upsetting." He knew what he didn't like, but he felt it unmanly to admit that he was frightened by something. So he came up with a public strategy, one that he could be confident would be a hit: bend the truth and blame Mom. Whereas Anna is Joe Friday's ideal respondent—just the facts, ma'am— David's not above a little creative storytelling to grease the world's wheels, to make people happier, to spare their feelings, to make himself well liked.

You often hear mothers of boys and girls say that their boys are more fragile than their girls, and in the case of my family it seems to hold. But thinking of your son as fragile can lead a feminist to the pitfall that my daughter insists is my chief one: overprotecting the son. Because many of us tend to characterize the world of men as predatory, aggressive, ruthlessly competitive, we fear for our sons more than mothers who see the world of men as more benign. We may worry that, growing up in homes that stress feminist virtues, they have been underprepared for the cold, tough world that is still run on the whole by men who haven't been very susceptible to the feminist message.

I never expect to be loved again with the uncomplicated sweetness with which David loved me when he was small. I always felt that Anna and I were shoulder to shoulder in the world, but I knew she saw me clearly, warts and all. For David, I was the most beautiful, the most charming, the best cook, the most brilliant writer in the history of the world. He would look through catalogs and tell me which clothes he was going to buy for me when he grew up. I basked in this adoration—who wouldn't?— and worried what I'd do when it stopped. This year, I got a clue that the romance was ending. "You know," he said, "my friend Tommy's mother is very beautiful. I think she's a lot younger than you." He asked me if I knew how much gray there was in my hair and if I'd ever considered dyeing it. A few months ago he said, "My friend Johnny said he thinks you have a big butt, and I couldn't tell him he was wrong."

This is the year he discovered basketball. Ten months ago, I coaxed him to join a team because a friend of mine was coaxing her son as well. Suddenly he discovered he was very good at it. He practiced obsessively. He spent his money on basketball cards, hats, and posters. He watched games on TV that were broadcast from cities I'd never even heard of. What was worse, he asked me to watch with him. My husband couldn't be pulled in, but I couldn't say no to my son. Also, I had to admit that it was something of a relief to me to see him involved in a traditionally male activity that wasn't horribly aggressive, that seemed as if it was fun, that might be able to teach him the good side of competitiveness and those things that women are said to lack because we didn't play team sports.

There I was, watching basketball. The very person who'd always made fun of people who talked sports and accused women interested in sports of trying to please their fathers. As a teenager, I'd invented something called "sport-speak," a skill I tried to pass on to younger women. "Sport-speak" was based on the theory that any woman could learn three sentences and convince any man that she knew a lot about sports by inserting them, in well-chosen places, into his monologue. You could do fine by saying, "Well, at this point in the season, it's hard to tell"; "Of course, it all depends on what happens in the clutch"; and "Sometimes they start slow and pick up speed, and sometimes they just run out of gas."

The trouble came when he wanted me to actually play basketball with him. I told him I wasn't very good. He said he'd coach me. After a few minutes, he turned to me in near despair. "Mom," he said, "are you going to hold that ball like a baby, or are you going to hold it like a ball? Because if you're going to hold it like a baby, I'm going to grab it out of your hands." I told him I'd try to hold it like a ball. It wasn't good enough. "Mom," he said, "you're just not aggressive enough. You have to really want to get that ball away from me." I told him that our relationship had been based on my not being aggressive with him, and rather than wanting to take things away from him, I always wanted him to have things. "Mom," he said, "don't think of me as your son. Think of me as your opponent."

For a few months, everything was basketball. He didn't want to go to museums with me anymore. Going to museums had been one of our favorite things to do; talented at drawing and painting himself, he was excellent at describing how he thought paintings had been constructed. But one day on our way to the Metropolitan Museum of Art, he asked if we couldn't just go for an ice cream instead. "I think I'm not into art anymore," he said. I took a deep breath and asked if he wanted hot fudge. A few months later, he said, "Why don't you take me to the museum anymore? You know art's one of my favorite things." We went to the museum and spent twenty minutes in front of a Hopper lighthouse, talking about the shadings of the sky. He's still obsessed with basketball. But there are other things, things that came to him partly as a result of knowing me. But maybe he needed to know he could get away from me, that he could move in a world I wasn't in charge of, that he could share a world with me, but on his terms.

Our boys have to contend with boys who are surrounded by people who give them enough rope to hang all of us and then excuse their behavior with a shrug, remarking that "boys will be boys." But what boys will be what boys? And what men will these boys become? As feminist mothers of sons, we have a stake in the world of men. We can't afford wholesale male bashing, nor can we afford to see the male as the permanently unreconstructable gender. Nor can we pretend that things are all right as they are. We have hints that our sons are different from us, but it may be impossible to tease out what is DNA and what is environment. The task of setting limits while allowing a child to be her- or himself is the central one for all parents, but a feminist mothering a son may find the limit/freedom tightrope a particularly vexing one to walk. We must love them as they are, often without knowing what it is that made them that way.

Hate **Radio**

BY **PATRICIA J. WILLIAMS** • MARCH/APRIL 1994

THREE YEARS AGO, I stood at my sink, washing the dishes and listening to the radio. I was tuned to rock and roll so I could avoid thinking about the big news from the day before: George Bush had just nominated Clarence Thomas to replace Thurgood Marshall on the Supreme Court. I was squeezing a dot of lemon Joy into each of the wineglasses when I realized that two smoothly radio-cultured voices, a man's and a woman's, had replaced the music.

"I think it's a stroke of genius on the president's part," said the female voice.

"Yeah," said the male voice. "Then those Blacks, those African Americans, those Negroes—hey, 'Negro' is a good enough word for Thurgood Marshall—whatever, they can't make up their minds [what] they want to be called. I'm gonna call then Blafricans. Black Africans. Yeah, I like it. Blafricans. Then they can get all upset because now the president appointed a Blafrican."

"Yeah, well, that's the way those liberals think. It's just crazy."

> **"If racism, homophobia, jingoism, and woman hating have been features of natural life in pretty much all of modern history, it rather begs the question to spend a lot of time wondering if right-wing radio is a symptom or a cause."**

"And then after they turn down his nomination, the president can say he tried to please 'em, and then he can appoint someone with intelligence."

Back then, this conversation seemed so horrendously unusual, so singularly hateful, that I picked up a pencil and wrote it down. I was certain that a firestorm of protest was going to engulf the station and purge those foul radio mouths with the good clean soap of social outrage.

I am so naive. When I finally turned on the radio and rolled my dial to where everyone else had been tuned while I was busy watching *Cosby* reruns, it took me a while to understand that there's a firestorm all right, but not of protest. In the two and a half years since Thomas has assumed his post on the Supreme Court, the underlying assumptions of the conversation I heard as uniquely outrageous have become commonplace, popularly expressed, and louder in volume. I hear the style of that snide polemicism everywhere, among acquaintances, on the street, on television in toned-down versions. It is a crude demagoguery that makes me heartsick. I feel more and more surrounded by that point of view, the assumptions of being without intelligence, the coded epithets, the "Blafrican"-like stand-ins for "nigger," the mocking angry glee, the endless tirades filled with nonspecific, nonempirically based slurs against "these people" or "those minorities" or "feminazis" or "liberals" or "scumbags" or "pansies" or "jerks" or "sleazeballs" or "loonies" or "animals" or "foreigners."

What does it mean that a manic, adolescent Howard Stern is so popular among radio listeners, that Rush Limbaugh's wittily smooth sadism has gone the way of prime-time television, and that both vie for the number one slot on all the best-selling books lists? What to make of the stories told by our modern radio evangelists and their tragic unloved chorus of callers? Is it really just a collapsing economy that spawns this drama of grown people sitting around scaring themselves to death with fantasies of Black feminist Mexican able-bodied gay soldiers earning $100,000 a year on welfare who are so criminally depraved that Hillary Clinton or the Antichrist-of-the-moment had no choice but to invite them onto government payroll so they can run the country?

As I listened to a range of such programs, what struck me as the most unifying theme was not merely the specific intolerance on such hot topics as race and gender but a much more general contempt for the world, a verbal stoning of anything different. It is like some unusually violent game of Simon Says, this mockery and shouting down of callers, this roar of incantations, the insistence on agreement.

The audience for this genre of radio flagellation is mostly young, white, and male. Two-thirds of Rush Limbaugh's audience is male. According to *Time* magazine, 75 percent of Howard Stern's listeners are white men. Most of the callers have spent their lives walling themselves off from any real experience with Blacks, feminists, lesbians, or gays. In this regard, it is probably true, as the former secretary of education William Bennett says, that Rush Limbaugh "tells his audience that what you believe inside, you can talk about in the marketplace." Unfortunately, what's "inside" is then mistaken for what's outside, treated as empirical and political reality. The *National Review* extols Limbaugh's conservative leadership as no less than that of Ronald Reagan, and the Republican Party provides Limbaugh with books to discuss, stories, angles, and public support. "People were afraid of censure by gay activists, feminists, environmentalists—now they are not because Rush takes them on," says Bennett.

U.S. history has been marked by cycles in which brands of this or that hatred come into fashion and go out, are unleashed and then restrained. If racism, homophobia, jingoism, and woman hating have been features of natural life in pretty much all of modern history, it rather begs the question to spend a lot of time wondering if right-wing radio is a symptom or a cause. For at least four hundred years, prevailing attitudes in the West have considered African Americans less intelligent. Recent statistics show that 53 percent of people in the United States agree that Blacks and Latinos are less intelligent than whites, and a majority believe that Blacks are lazy, violent, welfare dependent, and unpatriotic.

I think that what has made life more or less tolerable for out-groups has been those moments in history when those "inside" feelings were relatively restrained. In fact, if I could believe that right-wing radio were only about idiosyncratic, singular, rough-hewn individuals thinking those inside thoughts, I'd be much more inclined to agree with the Columbia University media expert Everette Dennis, who says that Stern's and Limbaugh's popularity represents the "triumph of the individual" or with *Time* magazine's bottom line, that "the fact that either is seriously considered a threat . . . is more worrisome than Stern or Limbaugh will ever be." If what I was hearing had even a tad more to do with real oppressions, with real white *and* Black levels of joblessness and homelessness, or with the real problems of real white men, then I wouldn't have bothered to slog my way through hours of Howard Stern's miserable obsessions.

Yet at the heart of my anxiety is the worry that Stern, Limbaugh, Bob Grant, and their ilk represent the very antithesis of individualism's triumph.

As the *National Review* said of Limbaugh's ascent, "It was a feat not only of the loudest voice but also of a keen political brain to round up, as Rush did, the media herd and drive them into the conservative corral." When asked about his political aspirations, Bob Grant gloated to *The Washington Post,* "I think I would make rather a good dictator."

The polemics of right-wing radio are putting nothing less than hate onto the airwaves and into the marketplace, electing it to office, teaching it in schools, and exalting it as freedom. What worries me is the increasing-to-constant commerce of retribution, control, and lashing out, fed not by fact but by fantasy. What worries me is the reemergence, more powerfully than at any time since the institution of Jim Crow, of a socio-centered self that excludes the likes of, well, me, for example, from the civic circle and that would rob me of my worth and claim and identity as a citizen. As *The Economist* rightly observes, "Mr. Limbaugh takes a mass market—white, mainly male, middle-class, ordinary America—and talks to it as an endangered minority."

I worry about this identity whose external reference is a set of beliefs, ethics, and practices that excludes, restricts, and acts in the world on me, or mine, as the perceived if not real enemy. I am acutely aware of losing *my* mythic individualism to the surface shapes of my mythic group fearsomeness as Black, as female, as left wing. "I" merge not fluidly but irretrievably into a category of "them." I become a suspect self, a moving target of loathsome properties, not merely different but dangerous. And that worries me a lot.

What happens in my life with all this translated license, this permission to be uncivil? What happens to the social space that was supposedly at the sweet mountaintop of the civil rights movement's trail? Can I get a seat on the bus without having to be reminded that I *should* be standing? Did the civil rights movement guarantee us nothing more than to use public accommodations while surrounded by raving lunatic bigots? "They didn't beat this idiot [Rodney King] enough," says Howard Stern.

How real is the driving perception behind all the Sturm und Drang of this genre of radio harangue—the perception that white men are an oppressed minority with no power and no opportunity in the land that they made great? While it is true that power and opportunity are shrinking for all but the very wealthy in this country (and would that Limbaugh would take on that issue), the fact remains that white men are still this country's privileged citizens and market actors.

Given deep patterns of social segregation and general ignorance of history, particularly racial history, media remain the principal source of most Americans' knowledge of each other. Media can provoke violence or induce passivity.

The outright denial of the material crisis at every level of U.S. society, most urgently in Black inner-city neighborhoods, but facing all of us, is a kind of political circus, dissembling as it feeds the frustrations of the moment. We as a nation can no longer afford to deal with such a crisis by *imagining* an excess of bodies, of babies, of job stealers, of welfare mothers, of overreaching immigrants, of too-powerful (Jewish, in whispers) liberal Hollywood, of lesbians and gays, of gang members ("gangsters" remain white and, no matter what the atrocity, less vilified than "gang members," who are Black), Arab terrorists, and uppity women. The reality of our social poverty far exceeds these scapegoats. This right-wing backlash resembles, in form if not substance, phenomena like anti-Semitism in Poland: there aren't but a handful of Jews left in that whole country, but the giant balloon of heated anti-Semitism flourishes apace, Jews blamed for the world's evils.

The overwhelming response to right-wing excesses in the United States has been to seek an odd sort of comfort in the fact that the First Amendment is working so well that you can't suppress this sort of thing. Look what's happened in eastern Europe. Granted. So, let's not talk about censorship or the First Amendment for the next ten minutes. But in western Europe, where fascism is rising at an appalling rate, suppression is hardly the problem. In eastern and western Europe, as well as the United States, we must begin to think just a little bit about the fiercely coalescing power of media to spark mistrust, to fan it into forest fires of fear and revenge. We must begin to think about the levels of national and social complacence in the face of such resolute ignorance. We must ask ourselves what the expected result is, not of censorship or suppression, but of so much encouragement, so much support, so much investment in the fashionability of hate. What future is it that we are designing with the devotion of such tremendous resources to the disgraceful propaganda of bigotry?

IF THERE'S ANY SINGULAR CONSTANT on America's path to political polarization, it has been the outsized influence of right-wing talk radio. Tens of millions of listeners tune in daily to nationally syndicated programming that—by design—fuels the flames of hate. Racism, white nationalism, xenophobia, misogyny, homophobia, transphobia—all are staples of scripts that peddle misinformation and conspiracy theories. Radio hosts have used their platforms to incite acts of violence, including the January 6 insurrection.

Rush Limbaugh drove the rise of the medium, dating back to the late 1980s. His show reached more than fifteen million listeners each week. Even as the internet yields competing platforms that amplify right-wing voices—from podcasts to YouTube videos to a growing array of social media sites, mainstream and fringe—hate radio continues to retain its vast power.

Letters

Cynthia Enloe's story, "The Globetrotting Sneaker" (March/April 1995), should raise concerns among your readers and your editorial staff about reporting practices, as well as accuracy. Enloe chose to present dated misinformation, failed to supply appropriate context for quotes taken from other sources, and neglected to tell the story of our ongoing efforts to guarantee safe working conditions and provide fair wages to our subcontractors' employees.

Had Enloe done her homework, she would have learned that the accounting firm Ernst & Young audits workplace standards in our subcontractors' factories in Indonesia. Its audits provide objective documentation that contradicts much of what has been reported: the average wage paid is well in excess of the minimum wage; subsidies for transportation, housing, food, and health care are paid in addition to the wage base—not deducted from wages as Enloe implies.

Manufacturing jobs that Nike supports in the Asia Pacific region are among the best paying in those economies. The income of an Indonesian entry-level factory worker is five times that of a farmer.

KEITH G. PETERS
Media Relations Director
Nike Inc.
Beaverton, Ore.
September/October 1995 issue

CYNTHIA ENLOE REPLIES: As *Ms.* readers will appreciate perhaps more than Nike's media relations director, what was more important in "The Globetrotting Sneaker" was to give voice to Korean and Indonesian women working for multinational companies. These women clearly are less than fully persuaded that Nike and the other sneaker companies are simply to be thanked for providing them with a daily wage that barely takes them over the poverty line.

And let's be clear about this—it is Nike that fails to supply the appropriate context for its claims. Not only have Nike subcontractors just recently stopped deducting "subsidies" from their workers' pay, but most tried to get away with paying less than the minimum wage, according to Jeff Ballinger, the former head of the Asian-American Free Labor Institute's Indonesia office.

Peters also fails to tell readers that a worker's wages and subsidies combined rarely amount to more than $2.60 a day, says Ballinger. (Only food, transportation, and work-related accidents are subsidized; regular health care is not.) Not what you'd call "well in excess" of the minimum daily wage of $2.10.

Guest Room

SAYING THE WORD

BY **V (FORMERLY EVE ENSLER)** • MAY/JUNE 1997

VAGINA"—there, I've said it. "Vagina"—said it again. I've been saying it over and over again for the last three years. I've been saying it in theaters, at colleges, in living rooms, in cafés, at dinner parties, and on radio programs all over the country. I would be saying it on TV if someone would let me. I say it 128 times every evening I perform my show, *The Vagina Monologues* (an evening based on interviews with hundreds of women of all ages and races about their vaginas). I say it in my sleep. I say it because I'm not supposed to say it. I say it because it's an invisible word that stirs up anxiety, awkwardness, contempt, and disgust.

I say it because I believe that what we don't say, we don't see, acknowledge, or remember. What we don't say becomes a secret, and secrets often create shame and fear and myths. I say it because I want to eventually feel comfortable saying it, and not ashamed and guilty.

I say "vagina" because I want people to respond, and they have. Wherever *The Vagina Monologues* has traveled, they have tried to censor the word: in ads in major newspapers, on tickets sold in department stores, on banners that hang in front of theaters, on box-office phone machines where the voice says only *"Monologues"* or *"V. Monologues."*

V (formerly Eve Ensler) rehearsing at the American Conservatory Theater in San Francisco in 2004.

"Why is this?" I ask. "'Vagina' is not a pornographic word; it is actually a medical word, a description of a body part—like 'elbow,' 'hand,' or 'rib.'" "It may not be pornographic," people say, "but it's dirty—what if our little daughters were to hear it? What would we tell them?" "Maybe you could tell them that they have a vagina," I say, "if they don't already know it. Maybe you could celebrate that." "But we don't call their vaginas 'vaginas,'" they say. "What do you call them?" I ask.

"Pooki," "poochie," "poopee," "peepee," "poopelu"—the list goes on.

I say "vagina" because I have read the statistics, and bad things are happening to women's vaginas everywhere: more than 350,000 women are raped every year in the United States, and it is estimated that 100 million women are genitally mutilated worldwide. I say "vagina" because I want these bad things to stop. I know they will not stop until we acknowledge that they are going on, and the only way that happens is by creating the safety for women to talk without fear of punishment or retribution.

It's scary saying the word. "Vagina." At first, it feels as if you were crashing through an invisible wall. "Vagina."

Then you begin to say the word more and more. You say it with a kind of passion, a kind of necessity, because you sense if you stop saying it, the fear will overcome you again and will fall back into an embarrassed whisper. So, you say it everywhere you can, bring it up in every conversation. You're excited about your vagina; you want to study it and explore it and introduce yourself to it, and find out how to listen to it and give it pleasure, and keep it healthy and wise and strong. You learn how to satisfy yourself and teach your lover how to satisfy you.

And as more women say the word, it becomes less of a big deal to say it; it becomes part of our language, part of our lives. Our vaginas become respected. Sacred. They become part of our bodies, connected to our minds, fueling our spirits. Shame leaves and violation stops because vaginas are visible and connected to powerful, wise, vagina-talking women.

We have a huge journey in front of us. This is the beginning. Here's the place to think about our vaginas, to learn about other women's vaginas, to hear stories, to answer questions and to ask them. Here's the place to release the myths, shame, and fear. Here's the place to celebrate. Here's the place to practice saying the word, because we know that the word is what propels us and sets us free. "Vagina."

THE VAGINA MONOLOGUES first ran off-Broadway in New York City in 1996 and then followed with a national tour, television version, and myriad adaptations and celebrity renditions. One year after this essay ran in *Ms.*, in 1998, the show morphed into V-Day, the global activist movement connecting art and advocacy to call for an end to violence against women and girls. Feminists across the country and around the world staged thousands of events—performances, benefits, protests—on campuses and in communities, and have continued to do so over the decades. In 2006, *The New York Times* called out *The Vagina Monologues* as "probably the most important piece of political theater of the last decade."

Letters

So I'm poring through the twenty-fifth anniversary issue of *Ms.* on some airplane going somewhere in the amorphous blur that amounts to my life and I'm finding it endlessly enlightening and stimulating as always, when, whaddaya know, I come across a little picture of little me. I was flattered to be included in the issue's "21 Feminists for the 21st Century" thingybob. I think y'all are runnin' the most bold and babe-olishious magazine around, after all.

Problem is, I couldn't help but be a little weirded out by the paragraph next to my head that summed up my me-ness and my relationship to the feminist continuum. It largely detailed my financial successes and sales statistics. My achievements were represented by the fact that I "make more money per album sold than Hootie & the Blowfish" and that my catalog sales exceed three-fourths of a million. It was specified that I don't just have my own record company but my own "profitable" record company. And the ironic conclusion is a quote from me insisting "it's not about the money." Why then, I ask myself, must "the money" be the focus of so much of the media that surround me? Why can't I escape it, even in the hallowed pages of *Ms.*?

I'm just a folksinger, not an entrepreneur. My hope is that my music and poetry will be enjoyable and/or meaningful to someone, somewhere, not that I maximize my profit margins.

I have so much respect for *Ms.* If I couldn't pick it up at newsstands, my brain probably would've atrophied by now on some transatlantic flight and I would be lying limp and twitchy in a bed of constant travel, staring blankly into the abyss of the gossip magazines. *Ms.* is a structure of media wherein women are able to define themselves, and articulate for themselves those definitions.

We've gone beyond the limited perceptions of sexism, and so we should move beyond the language and perspective of the corporate patriarchy.

We have the facility to judge each other by entirely different criteria from those imposed upon us by the superstructure of society. We have a view that reaches beyond profit margins into poetry, and a vocabulary to articulate the difference.

Thanks for including me, *Ms.*, really. But promise me one thing: if I drop dead tomorrow, tell me my gravestone won't read,
    ani d.—CEO.
    Please let it read:
    Songwriter
    Musicmaker
    Storyteller
    Freak.

ANI DIFRANCO
Buffalo, N.Y.
January/February 1998 issue

Women **in Prison**

BY **NINA SIEGAL** • SEPTEMBER/OCTOBER 1998

HAMEDAH A. HASAN began her journey to federal prison when she was just twenty-two years old. Trying to escape an abusive boyfriend, in 1989 she moved briefly from her home in Portland, Oregon, to Omaha, where she stayed with two cousins. It was there that federal investigators linked her to her cousin's drug-trafficking exploits. That connection later landed her a life sentence.

Hasan sits at the warden's conference table at the Federal Correctional Institution in Dublin, California, just southeast of San Francisco, dressed in her khaki, brown, and green prison uniform. Outside, the winter morning fog lifts over a group of brown ranch-style prison units and the large fields of the Tri-Valley area beyond. Groups of women dressed in greens and browns cluster in aimless congregations.

From the warden's office, the place seems almost tranquil, except for the ubiquitous barbed-wire fences topped with loops of thick razor wire, the guards positioned at every door, and the loud crack of locks being opened and shut. And then there are the invisible reminders that this is, in fact, no summer camp. In early March, the Federal Bureau of Prisons settled a suit with three former Dublin inmates who claimed they were prostituted and sexually and physically assaulted by guards while being held in the men's detention facility adjacent to the building where we sit.

Less shocking but more persistent is the problem of overcrowding. Ask any inmate at Dublin about the housing, and she'll tell you, "It's like living in a bathroom with two other people." The prison, which first opened in the 1970s, was designed so that each eight-by-eleven-foot cell would house two people, but today most women, including Hasan, share the tiny quarters with two other inmates.

The overcrowding is the result of an alarming new trend: for the past decade, women have been entering prison at a much faster rate than men.

The reason for the accelerated rate of female incarceration can largely be summed up in three words: "mandatory drug sentencing." In 1986, Congress passed—and in 1987 the U.S. Sentencing Commission adopted—a new set of minimum penalties for commerce in illicit drugs. Ostensibly designed to stem the tide of drug trafficking by going after "kingpins," the measure set up strict new rules for sentencing drug offenders. For example, anyone convicted of possessing fifty grams of crack would automatically receive ten years behind bars.

Most research into these drug sentencing laws, however, has concluded that instead of being used to crack down on "kingpins," they are more likely to be applied to small-time drug offenders—often women. Since the federal legislation was adopted, the number of women serving time for federal drug convictions has increased more than tenfold.

Margaret Owens, director of the National Center for Women in Prison, based in Washington, D.C., believes there's no question about who has borne the brunt of mandatory minimums. "It's women who have been caught in the cross fire of this policy," she says.

The new laws have had a visible impact on the types of female inmates now filling up the system, says Ida McCray Robinson. Currently the director of Families with a Future, a San Francisco–based family support organization for incarcerated women, Robinson spent ten years in Dublin. When she first entered prison in the 1980s, the inmates were predominantly white-collar criminals, and their faces were mostly white too. "I never saw so many women of color until after the beginning of the mandatory minimums," she says. "What happened was a change in the colors of the faces of the women there."

AN AVERAGE CRIMINAL

Hamedah Hasan has the "face" of the average woman in prison today. She's thirty years old, African American, and a single mother of three, and she comes from a low-income community. A warm, articulate, and devoutly religious Muslim woman with large almond-shaped eyes and an engaging smile, Hasan is certainly not what most people would think of when they imagine a lifer in federal prison.

But when one looks at the statistics, she turns out to be a "typical" female prisoner. Forty-six percent of all women in state prisons are Black, and 50 percent are between the ages of twenty-five and thirty-four. Seventy-eight percent of all women in prison are mothers. Forty-five percent have never been married. Like 92 percent of women in federal prison, Hasan is in for a nonviolent crime, and like 62 percent she's in on her first offense.

Hasan's story is like that of many women in prison today. Already the mother of two daughters at age twenty-two, she was living on welfare in federally subsidized housing in a depressed section of Portland. Having returned from Omaha, she was completing Steps to Success, a Portland program to move people from welfare to work, while volunteering at the Black United Fund of Oregon, a nonprofit grant maker.

But then she was indicted on a drug conspiracy charge. She was charged, along with nine other individuals, with distribution of 12.6 kilograms of crack cocaine over a two-year period in Omaha. To this day, Hasan contends that she was not involved in drug dealing, and when she returned to Omaha to face trial, that's what she told prosecutors.

They offered her a deal—ten years in exchange for information about the drug ring—but she turned it down. She simply didn't know anything, she says, and she refused to play games to get a lighter sentence. "She was insistent that there would be no plea because she was innocent," says Susan Koenig, Hasan's court-appointed private attorney.

This was Hasan's first arrest, and she didn't think prosecutors had any evidence to prove her guilty. What they did have was testimony from a woman who said she had witnessed a man giving Hasan one kilo of cocaine, as well as evidence that Hasan had wired some $72,000 to family members. Hasan contends that these transfers were made for business and personal reasons that had nothing to do with drugs.

In Omaha federal court, Hasan's case was lumped together with those of other defendants, and they were charged as "co-conspirators." After a trial of just six days, Hasan returned to court to hear the verdict, still certain of acquittal. "I was thinking it would be put to rest, and I would go home that day," she says. "Then they started off, 'Guilty on this charge. Guilty on this,' and they never stopped. I was guilty all the way through."

Six months later, the U.S. district judge Richard G. Kopf read Hasan's sentence as per federal sentencing requirements: two life sentences, two forty-year sentences, two twenty-year sentences, plus a five-year sentence and a four-year sentence to run concurrently, and five years of supervised release. Upon completing this litany, the judge said he did not think Hasan should spend the rest of her life in prison. He called mandatory sentencing "a tragic error" and added, "Had I the discretion, I would have imposed a sentence of between ten and fifteen years."

EQUALITY WITH A VENGEANCE

Women still make up only a small fraction—6.4 percent—of the total U.S. prison population. Because men compose the overwhelming majority of inmates, the nation's prisons, by and large, are designed to deal with men. Men in prison are more likely than women to be serving time for violent crime and are much more likely to be violent repeat offenders. Women's crimes are more often drug and property offenses.

The pattern of illegal activity is different for men and women because crime is "distinctively gendered," says Beth E. Richie, associate professor of criminal justice and women's studies at the University of Illinois at Chicago and author of *Compelled to Crime,* a book focusing on African American battered women and their paths to crime. "Drug offenses and other nonviolent crimes that women commit are often linked to persistent poverty and biased law enforcement practices in low-income communities of color," she says.

The feminist activist and scholar Angela Davis agrees. She argues that many crimes committed by women are "directly related to their economic status," because poor women are driven into "underground economies" of drugs and prostitution or theft in order to support their families. The majority of drug crimes committed by women, she says, are also linked to addiction.

Thea R. DuBow, a founding member and vice chair of the National Network for Women in Prison, and a former prisoner, says women's crime tends to be linked to abuse in their past. According to a 1994 report by the Bureau of Justice Statistics (BJS), 34 percent of women behind bars reported having been physically abused before they went to prison. Violent crimes committed by women, says DuBow, are also more likely to be defensive or retaliatory.

Mental illness is also a key factor in women's crime. According to a study published in the *Archives of General Psychiatry* of the American Medical Association in June 1996, more than half of women in prisons nationwide suffer from some form of psychiatric disorder. "If you've had some form of victimization, you're likely to have mental health problems," explains B. Kathleen Jordan, the sociologist who conducted the study. "That is often the root cause whereby women come into the system. They have some sort of troubled background and then they have a psychiatric disorder—an impulse control problem or a drug and alcohol problem—that gets them into trouble. If you're rich, you're more likely to be able to afford mental health care, but if you're poor, you're more likely to end up in a psychiatric institution or in prison."

Prisons are not constructed to take women's differences into account. Brenda V. Smith, senior counsel with the National Women's Law Center, says that women don't get the same kinds of services as men in prison— "services like drug treatment programs, medical services. Gynecological care is considered to be 'specialty care,' but, of course, it's not, if you're a woman."

"Women experience gender bias at every level of the criminal justice system," says Margaret Owens. "The bottom line is that the U.S. correctional system was not created with women in mind. And it is very clear that the male model is failing women and girls."

HEALTH-CARE HORRORS

Within days of learning the jury's verdict, Hasan learned more devastating news: she was pregnant. She wanted to get an abortion, but she couldn't.

For the past several years, Congress, through its annual appropriations bills, has banned the use of federal funds for abortions in prison. The Bureau of Prisons is allowed to pay for inmates' abortions only in cases of rape or if giving birth would endanger the life of the woman. Federal prisons are required to transport prisoners to clinics to get abortions if the women can pay for them themselves, but in Hasan's case that never happened.

But if the system forces women to carry their pregnancies to term, it does not ensure that they have healthy babies. Hasan says that her prenatal care was far from professional and that a jail doctor misdiagnosed spotting, telling her she had had a miscarriage.

MOTHERS BEHIND BARS

Hasan was lucky. She received some prenatal care while in prison, and although she lost forty pounds during her pregnancy instead of gaining the typical twenty-five to thirty-five pounds, she was able to carry her baby to term. In January 1994, at a hospital near the prison, she gave birth to a seven-pound baby girl. The next day, the newborn was taken away. "I didn't even spend twenty-four hours with my daughter," she says.

Some correctional systems offer community-based residential treatment in lieu of incarceration for offenders who have recently given birth, known primarily as mother-infant care programs. This option allows a mother to bond with her newborn while learning parenting skills. Studies have shown that these programs help mothers to overcome addiction, reform, and keep their families together.

But there are far too few slots available. The federal Family Unity Demonstration Project Act, passed in 1994, authorized states to seek federal funding to create new mother-infant care programs, but Congress never appropriated the funds.

When mothers can't enter such programs, it causes great disruption to families, since the moms are usually the primary—and often the only—caregivers. Only 20 percent of children end up living with their fathers when their mothers go to jail, says Denise Johnston, director of the Center for the Children of Incarcerated Parents at Pacific Oaks College in Pasadena, California. Most of the children—60 percent—are sent to live with their grandmothers. Ten to 15 percent end up in foster care, and the rest move in with other relatives.

The long-term effects prove devastating. Children of incarcerated parents are at least three times as likely as other children to end up in prison themselves, according to Johnston. And the link to adult incarceration is easy to make: almost half of women in state prisons today report that someone in their family was, at one time, in jail or prison, according to the BJS.

Now thirty years old, Hasan says she's learned the lessons prison has to teach her. She doesn't believe that anyone would call her a threat to society anymore, and she wants the chance to go home and care for her kids. But she's still got a lifetime to serve behind bars.

WHAT TO DO?

More than 100,000 children nationwide now have a mother behind bars. That fact alone, say advocates, is a good reason for the nation to take a hard look at sentencing alternatives. "The first concern we have is that women, wherever possible, not be separated from their children," says Margaret Owens. "It's totally unacceptable for nonviolent felons to be sent away to a facility and to not be treated in the community."

Next, advocates contend, we need to start reconsidering the mandatory sentences that are placing women in prison at such a rapid rate. Many are strongly questioning whether the punishments are remotely appropriate for the offenses and pointing out the negligible effects of mandatory minimums on the drug trade in the United States.

The Supreme Court considered several challenges to mandatory sentencing guidelines in 1989 and 1991, did not find constitutional reasons to overturn the measures, and subsequently washed its hands of the debate. In 1994, Congress passed a crime bill that included a provision that allowed judges to ignore mandatory minimums in a narrow range of cases in which the defendant was a nonviolent first-time drug offender. But since then, there have been few attempts to change mandatory sentencing laws on the federal level.

EVERY YEAR, *Ms.* sends its magazines to more than five thousand federal, state, and county prisoners and to hundreds of domestic violence shelters around the country. When *Ms.* launched this program in 2004, women and girls were becoming the fastest-growing incarcerated population in the United States.

Knowledge is power. *Ms.* wants women in prison to know they are seen and valued. And because domestic violence shelters can be almost as isolating as prisons—often lacking reading material, as many prisons do—shelters are included in this program too.

Here's what one incarcerated reader wrote: "It was hard to feel heard, to feel like my personhood mattered to anyone. *Ms.* . . . was a spark of dignity. Prison itself is founded on unknowing and isolation, and I am not content to consent to its dehumanization."

Meanwhile, the prison-industrial complex continues to expand. Before 1990, there were fifty-three women's prisons in the United States. Since then, at least fifteen new women's prisons have been built, and many more are planned. Without ongoing attention to the ways in which the laws, the courts, and the prisons themselves perpetuate gender biases, our mothers, sisters, and daughters will continue to feed that system.

Hasan's friend Danielle Metz, also thirty, a mother of two who is serving a life sentence at Dublin on a drug conspiracy conviction, summed it up best: "Now the prisons they're building are for our kids. I don't want to see my daughter come down this road."

Letters

I would like to respond to Gloria Steinem's article "Yes Means Yes, No Means No" [May/June 1998]. I was thankful to hear a refreshing angle on the Clinton harassment issue. With all the media coverage screaming to lynch Clinton, I found it hard to stand my ground. Although I notice a tendency among feminists to let Clinton off the hook because he's the most pro-woman president to date (considering presidential history, this isn't saying much), the article said to me, "Think for yourself," which is the foundation of what feminism is all about.

In all honesty, I couldn't care less about what any political figure does with another consenting adult. But amid those who said, "You're a feminist, you should be appalled by Clinton's behaviors," I questioned why I wasn't more dismayed with old Bill. Steinem's article helped me see that those who are shouting "Down with Clinton!" are predominately the right-wingers, seeking only to serve their own agenda.

The issue isn't about Clinton's abuse of power. It's about the difference between sexual harassment and sex scandals. Neither is acceptable for the commander in chief, but there is a critical difference.

Thank you, *Ms.*, for helping me find my voice on this issue.

DEBORAH WINSLOW
Fort Collins, Colo.
September/October 1998 issue

So Who Gets the Kids? Divorce in the Age of Equal Parenting

BY **SUSAN J. DOUGLAS** • JUNE/JULY 1999

T'S 3:47 A.M. Hour of the Wolf. That deep pocket in the night when anxieties and self-doubts gnaw at already ragged psyches. I get up and go to my daughter's room. I got home from work too late to put her to bed. I brush the hair off her face and kiss her warm, sweet-smelling forehead. And I wonder if Robert Young is doing the same, only with a much more desperate sense of urgency and impending loss. And is his ex-wife, Alice Hector, also up in the night staring into her daughters' empty rooms, her stomach in a knot?

I am up because I hate this story. It's too upsetting. But that pales beside Young's and Hector's battle: for both of them, their daily relationship to their daughters, ages ten and thirteen, is on the line. In a highly publicized case, Alice Hector, once a partner in a prominent Miami law firm and now head of her own, lost custody of her two daughters in June 1998 because a panel of three male judges ruled that her work schedule was too demanding for her to remain their primary caretaker. They overturned a trial judge's decision to keep the girls with their mother, and awarded custody to Young, the girls' father, who until two years ago was a stay-at-home dad and who now has a job with flexible work hours. Hector appealed the ruling in December and, as of this writing, awaits a decision.

Young had done things like start a Brownie troop for their younger daughter when none existed, organize a soccer team for the elder daughter when that didn't exist either, and then coach the team as well. He also volunteered at school. Hector couldn't do these kinds of things. But she did get up at the crack of dawn so she'd have time with the girls in the morning, she devoted her weekends to them, and she claimed in court that in the middle of the night, when either one of them was sick, they came to her. Young and his attorneys have been very careful not to label Hector a bad mother;

> **"In a custody battle, if Dad knows the name of the kids' dentist and went to one PTA meeting, he's the Albert Schweitzer of parenting; if Mom gets up at 5:00 a.m. to do the laundry and read files from work so she can have more time with her kids, she's still suspect."**

on the contrary, they have praised her efforts to juggle her work as a litigator with the demands of motherhood. Young's point is simple: we're both devoted parents, we both love our kids, but I'm home much more than she is and have much more time to take care of the kids, so they should live with me.

Florida does not favor joint custody, as many other states do. Florida law assumes that moving back and forth between parents' homes is bad for kids. Instead, the law promotes "shared parental responsibility," meaning that both parents are supposed to remain active in the children's lives, but the kids maintain a primary residence with only one of the parents. This is, in part, where the battle started. Both sides say they agreed to share the house while they worked out the divorce settlement—an arrangement

that kept the parents in daily touch with the kids but might have exacerbated their intense competition over who deserves custody. Deep resentments and intransigent stereotypes snarl through the case. Hector claims she never wanted Young to be a stay-at-home dad, but instead encouraged him to try to find work. She increasingly resented having the burden of supporting the family entirely on her shoulders and clearly felt it was unfair for her to have to put in sixty-hour weeks while her husband did no work outside the home.

It is very difficult for most women, however liberated, to overcome our culture's easy equation of bringing home the bacon and true manhood. Difficult for the courts, too: during the initial hearing, when Hector won custody, the judge said to Young, "Maybe I'm missing something. Why don't you get a job?" Young found himself dismissed elsewhere as well for staying home with the kids. He recalled a partner in his wife's law firm greeting him with "It's nice to meet you, Mr. Alice."

In a comment feminists should find poignant, he told a reporter, "I was only perceived as Alice's husband." Hector, of course, has been stereotyped, too, as a selfish, uncaring mother who brought legal briefs with her to a child's recital. "There is this idea that I wanted this life and this was the life I chose," Hector said in an interview. "The opposite is true. I'm not saying I don't enjoy my work—I do—but it is not my first choice."

Which one of them should I be rooting for? Why is this a contest, a war? Does being a feminist mean that I automatically root for her, no matter what? If my husband and I ever found ourselves in divorce court, would I, too, face losing custody of my daughter because there have been nights, like this one, when I wasn't home for dinner and didn't tuck her in? Or could he be suddenly ripped out of the daily routine of her life—even though he takes her back and forth to school almost every day, helps her with her homework, and wouldn't be able to stand not seeing her for days on end—simply because I'm the mother? According to David Chambers, a professor of law at the University of Michigan, in most custody cases the courts prefer to place a child with the parent who is the primary caretaker, and in the overwhelming majority of cases this is the mother. The primary caretaker presumption was designed, in part, to thwart the potential threat by fathers to sue for custody so their ex-wives would give in on other aspects of a divorce settlement, like money. But what if you're both the primary caretakers?

I guess that one of the reasons I hate this story is that this case, more than many other custody battles that have received media attention, does, in fact, require us to confront our contradictory stances about what we want and expect from fathers now that we're thirty years into the women's movement. Three decades ago, we argued that our treatment before the law should be gender-blind because when it wasn't, we lost. We've also been insisting, with some limited success, that fathers become more involved in child rearing. Those of us who work outside the home are tired of the utter unfairness of the second shift, when both parents come home from work but Dad gets to read the paper while Mom makes dinner, helps with geometry homework, fends off telemarketers, and does ten loads of laundry.

And many of our husbands have responded.

So if some men have become equal, or even more than equal, partners in child rearing, as we'd hoped, then shouldn't those men have the same rights that women would in court? But if we grant this, are we opening the floodgates to thousands of frivolous and even unjust custody challenges by fathers who work but won't face the same prejudices in court about their commitment to their children as a working mother automatically does? In a custody battle, if Dad knows the name of the kids' dentist and went to one PTA meeting, he's the Albert Schweitzer of parenting; if Mom gets up at 5:00 a.m. to do the laundry and read files from work so she can have more time with her kids, she's still suspect if she isn't standing in the doorway at 3:30 p.m. offering baked goods to the kids as they come home from school. A 1989 report commissioned by the Michigan Supreme Court found that stereotypes bias judges against working mothers: they granted custody to fathers showing the most minimal interest in parenting, and they viewed mothers who placed emphasis on their careers to be less fit as parents than fathers who did exactly the same thing.

Many feminists, women lawyers, and women's organizations have expressed outrage over the ruling against Hector. After all, this case has not occurred in a vacuum: it comes on the heels of quite a few well-publicized and outrageous cases in which mothers lost custody of their children simply because they worked outside the home or worked "too many hours." Some studies claim that when custody disputes end up in court, fathers win more than 60 percent of the time, and women lose custody for behavior that is utterly acceptable for men, such as having ambitious career goals. The list is long and infuriating. In 1994, Sharon Prost, deputy chief counsel of the Senate Judiciary Committee, lost custody of her two sons because a female judge determined that she devoted too much time to her job. It didn't matter that Prost got up at 5:30 a.m. to fix breakfast and drive her older son to school or that she brought her younger son with her to the Senate day-care center every day, usually had lunch with him, and often left for home before 6:00 p.m. It didn't matter that a court-appointed psychologist affirmed that Prost's children were primarily attached to their mother. Nor did it matter that her ex-husband, Kenneth Greene, insisted that the couple retain an au pair, even when he was unemployed and at home for over a year, or that when he was employed, he put in extremely long workdays himself.

Meanwhile, shortly after Hector lost custody of her daughters, *Sports Illustrated* reported that Pamela McGee, who plays for the WNBA's Los Angeles Sparks, lost custody of her four-year-old daughter while the court investigated whether McGee's work prevented her from being a good mother. In his motion for temporary sole custody, McGee's ex-husband, the Reverend Kevin E. Stafford, asserted that a career and motherhood are mutually exclusive. McGee's "level of achievement," he argued, "impairs her ability to parent her daughter." At issue, according to *Sports Illustrated,* was whether McGee's travel schedule—she's on the road about four weeks a year—took her away from her daughter too much. The court was not investigating whether Stafford's travel schedule—he's on the road seven to eight weeks a year—made him an unfit father.

In 1982, a father who had refused to acknowledge paternity, wouldn't pay child support, and didn't visit his son until he was fifteen months old sued for custody after the mother tried to get child support. He won, because the mother had worked two jobs to support her son, while his new wife didn't have a job and could be home with the child. This mother has had to watch her child be raised by another woman. When sexist judges with outdated and inaccurate biases against day care apply the "best interests of the child" standard, working mothers can easily lose. And child-care providers, whether housekeepers, babysitters, or day-care centers, are routinely dismissed as inferior, second-rate caretakers.

So it's no surprise that we feminists have our hackles up. We see a vengeful backlash against mothers who work outside the home in which we detect a barely disguised glee in meting out the most painful punishment there can be: separating us from our children. There seems to be a real bloodlust—not just in the courts, but in much of the culture—to take working women down a peg, especially if they are more successful than their ex-husbands. At its core, this trend of taking children away from their working mothers is about punishing women for having what is perceived to be too much power. This has occurred within the broader backlash against feminism that continues unabated, where we see an assault on women's reproductive rights, punitive policies toward poor mothers, ridicule of women's studies programs, trivialization of date rape, and calls by a bevy of antifeminist women for us to get back into the kitchen.

Yet too many feminists, in our outrage over this punitive trend, have been dismissive of Young. He has had to pay for every sexist judge's decision, every mother wronged in court. His feminist attorney, Barbara Green, who saw this as a case about gender equality, has been stung by reactions from other women attorneys who treat her like a traitor. We should admit to the other truth that we know: many fathers are deeply connected to their children and then, after a divorce, are relegated to every-other-weekend cameo appearances. I think we've let this case be too easy for us, and we've used Hector and Young as caricatures onto whom we can project a host of fears, rages, and anxieties about work and the family.

The case also dramatizes how very far we still have to go as a culture to devise family-friendly work environments. For most professional people, being overworked means you're important and productive. It also means you have less time for your family. While women rightly want the same opportunities as men, feminists once had a dream that we could humanize the workplace; many of us didn't want to have to become just like workaholic, absentee men. Cases like Hector-Young allow us to focus on particular individuals—the classic way the news media cover major trends—instead of on the deep systemic problems of overwork.

It is impossible for me not to feel torn by this case. If one is committed to gender equity, and to granting custody to the primary caretaker, Robert Young should retain custody. In my head, I am with him. But in my heart, I am with Hector. Because I know that if I ever found myself in a courtroom, it wouldn't matter that I know the names of all my daughter's dolls, or that I lie in bed with her at night to talk about friendship, or decimals, or God, or that I know which kinds of socks she loves and which ones she absolutely refuses to wear. It would only matter that I work longer hours than my husband, and so, as a working mother, I am a bad mother. Until the courts banish this stereotype, it is going to be impossible for many feminists, however deeply committed they are to gender equity, to support the sorts of role reversals we once celebrated in our dreams.

Studying Womanhood

BY **NOELLE HOWEY** • OCTOBER/NOVEMBER 1999

WHILE I AM in my room playing, Dad is down in the basement, a place where all dads like to be. It's cold and made of concrete; there's a sawhorse, a tool kit, and an extra fridge filled with Budweiser. He says he is working on a project. I assume that means shellacking an end table. It doesn't.

My father has tucked himself away in the windowless back room of the basement. He takes out a portable makeup mirror from behind the solvents, a cache of old dresses from under the camping equipment. He leans toward the mirror, trying on a new pair of eyelashes. He slicks on Ruby Red Max Factor and puckers. When he hears a creak on the steps, he starts frantically unscrewing his jar of Pond's Cold Cream. It's just the cat.

> **"Liberating the notion of father from that of man hasn't been easy. But my father is alive because she is female, and she has made herself into one hell of a woman."**

Exhaling, he slips into a green hausfrau number. He imagines himself done up in an apron, merrily folding the laundry for the whole clan. In the dim light of the basement, he can barely see his stubble or Adam's apple. He runs his hands over the padded bra, trying to ignore the stray chest hairs. "This is ridiculous," he mutters. He needs another drink. Stoically, he wipes all trace of the cosmetics from his face. He goes upstairs and barks at me to get away from the TV because it's time for the PGA championship. When my mother comes home, he tells her he spent the afternoon finishing the end table.

My father is a transgendered lesbian, a biological male who thought of his Y chromosome as a cruel cosmic joke and wanted, above all things, to become a female. Over the course of my teenage years, he metamorphosed into a woman through exhaustive estrogen therapy, electrolysis on every last facial hair follicle, and sex reassignment surgery. But, for both of us, the process of becoming a woman was more complicated than mere physical transformation. We spent years unconsciously trying on and discarding several different, and equally limiting, images of Woman before we were able to create versions that fit.

I got a jump start on the whole woman thing, being born a girl in the summer of 1972. From the time I could walk, I embodied the sugar-and-spice nursery-rhyme image of girldom. And I charmed the hell out of everyone—except, unfortunately, my father.

He was raised in the testosterone-poisoned atmosphere of the 1950s and spent much of his adolescence being mocked in public bathrooms because boys sensed his effeminacy. He learned that the only way to survive was to emulate the bullies, to swagger and scoff like a varsity letterman. It worked, superficially. He married my mother at twenty-four, right on schedule, and then glad-handed his way up the old-boy corporate ladder. By the time I was born, my father had acquired all the requisite guy accessories: a convertible, a clunky gold watch, a *Sports Illustrated* swimsuit calendar, and a major chip on his shoulder.

As far as I could tell, my father was cold, brusque—and normal. Most of the kids I knew loathed and feared their rarely there, always-angry fathers. But I didn't want to settle for that; I craved his approval and longed for a connection. So, when he came home, downed a few screwdrivers, and slowly eased into his drunkenness, I would climb up on his lap to cajole a hug or an Eskimo kiss. If he was feeling affectionate, he might pat me abruptly on the head. Usually, he would squirm and complain that I was blocking the screen. My mother always apologized for him. "He loves you but doesn't know how to express it," she would say. "Some men can be like that."

These days, my father says she loves me with every phone call, in every handwritten birthday card. She can do that openly now that she has been untethered from her male body and, so she says, the cold distance she felt she needed to keep from breaking down and admitting who she was. I sympathize with the anguish she felt sitting there in that recliner, so paralyzed by self-loathing and terror that she could not embrace her own young daughter. But it will take me the rest of my life to truly understand why my father couldn't find a way to express love for me while she lived in a male body.

I was in ninth grade when my mom dropped the news. In a halting, whispery voice, she said that Dad liked to wear girls' clothes and needed to move out in order to understand exactly what that was all about. I was predictably shocked. So, Dad is like Tootsie? Or Boy George? It seemed impossible that my dad could be anything but a tough guy. But oddly, I felt an enormous flood of relief rush over me. So that's why he's such a jerk, I thought, almost giddy with the revelation. He's a freak. It's not me. I am not the problem.

Later that week, my father took me out to lunch, still wearing his guy clothes. I scrutinized him for any noticeable signs of femininity and found only that his nails were kind of long for a man—way longer than mine were. Over cheeseburgers and nacho fries, he told me he wasn't just a transvestite but a transsexual, which meant he believed he should have been born a woman. He said he felt trapped in the wrong gender his whole life,

BY NOELLE HOWEY

studying womanhood

and that's why he had so many problems communicating with me and my mom. He still loved us, but he couldn't live in a man's body anymore. I nodded. I didn't have any questions—yet.

Like many children of divorce, I saw my dad at lunch every weekend. He was still somewhat closeted, so he looked like a man. But each Saturday he would appear just a little more girlish. Maybe he would be wearing pedal pushers, or open-toed sandals. Sometimes his long fingernails were polished. Often, now, he would sit with his legs crossed instead of wide apart, or gently dab the corners of his lips with a napkin instead of rubbing vigorously. His voice started to get a little squeakier and giggly, as though he had been sucking on a helium balloon. Watching my father week after week was like watching a film progress one frame at a time. And each subtle change sent a visceral shock through my body.

To my relief, no one else really seemed to notice. No waiters called him "ma'am," no clerks gave him bemused glances. Dad still drove his sports car and made the same six-figure income. I coped by telling myself that this little "transgender thing" was an odd diversion, a personality quirk with no real impact on our day-to-day lives. I focused my energies on being a perfect student and burgeoning political activist. And by my junior year of high school, on sex.

Sex provided a powerful distraction from thoughts of my father. The first crack in my purposefully indifferent teen exterior came when I saw my father fully dressed as a woman. She loped up the driveway sporting nautical wear from the Gap, with a mop of brown curls and pink lipstick. She looked like a quintessential PTA mom—no *Some Like It Hot* drag queen here. My God, I thought, she is really doing this.

Except for her suspiciously thick wrists, there was not a single sign that she was genetically a middle-aged man. I knew she had been having electrolysis treatments, and I had witnessed the purple bruises from the eye tuck and chin lift that briefly mottled her face. I also realized she had been taking major hormones. But I had no idea how smoothly she could morph into a passable—even attractive—female. It scared me beyond belief. My stomach clenched when I saw her hairless arms, the small bumps on her chest. What hit me hardest, though, was spotting a thin Timex watch where her gold Rolex had been. My dad always wore that thick gold watch. Now it was gone, packed away in a box as though he were dead. I didn't say a word. I hugged her tensely and ran upstairs to do homework.

I wonder now if my family could have used a mourning period. But instead, we believed our own rhetoric—that he was the same, only different, and that our family was still intact and loving, only divorced and a little confused. We did not acknowledge that the change my father was making was more than cosmetic, and that even if it was ultimately for the better, it still entailed a profound loss.

I saw my dad's new home on my first spring break from college. The two-story in a neighboring suburb was unquestionably Martha Stewart. Three of the rooms were painted mauve, rose-shaped guest soaps lay in a cup in the bathroom, and everything was spick-and-span, as though she had just discovered housework. And in a way, she had, since the extent to which she had ever participated in housecleaning until then was to lift up her legs while my mother vacuumed between the recliner and the ottoman.

Beaming, she had told me that she had taken up flower arranging in place of bowling—her guy obsession. Indeed, small vases of dried pink flowers sat on every tabletop on the first floor. One sat next to a plate of freshly baked chocolate chip cookies.

A recently declared women's studies minor who proudly eschewed makeup and cut my hair butchy short, I was irritated by my father's apparently simplistic notion of what it meant to be a woman. I couldn't believe she would go through physical pain and risk the enmity of everyone she had ever known in order to act the role of domestic goddess. I thought femininity was oppressive and not a remotely valid point on the spectrum of women's choices.

On the third day I was home, my father prepared yet another string of meticulous menus: mesclun salad and wild mushroom lasagna. The fancy food sent me careening over the edge. Halfway through dinner I exploded. "This isn't what being a woman is all about, Dad," I informed her. "Look at me. I'm a real woman. I go on marches for choice and sign petitions and fight against sexual harassment. You're playing house. You're reinforcing every single stereotype of what a woman is supposed to be, circa, like, 1956." My father sniffled—as she often did those days—and insisted she didn't think a woman was all about housework and that I should give her a little more credit, thank you very much. She said she was trying out some things that she hadn't been allowed to do as a man. "Isn't feminism about being able to choose the lifestyle that works for you?" she demanded. "Well, yeah," I scoffed, "but *this* isn't what we mean by choice."

My father and I did not stay angry at each other; rather, our seemingly endless series of debates over whether or not transgenderism was inher-

ently sexist drew us closer. And over time, I began to understand that my dad's desire to be a woman transcended all these arguments. Observing my father—once embittered and half drunk much of the time—bask in an almost Zen-like contentment even as her friends and family and work clients were drifting away made me realize the profundity of her longing. I began to trust that what she was doing was essential to her happiness, and probably even her survival.

When I was twenty-two, I accompanied my dad to Belgium for her sex reassignment surgery. It was an act of contrition and a sign that I accepted her decision to be the fullest woman she could be. She was white-knuckled with fright the night before the surgery. She paced around the hotel room suddenly paranoid that her penis had become too small from the hormones and would not invert into a sufficiently deep vaginal canal. I felt for her but was also aware that such talk would—and did—make me sick; I threw up most of my dinners during our week in Brussels. Still, I didn't realize that surgery would reopen my own wounds about losing my father as a man.

Lying there in the hospital awaiting surgery, with Magic Marker indicating where the incisions would be made in her groin, my dad looked like a train wreck of genders: bald and breastless (she had removed her padded bra), but immaculately manicured. During the next several hours, as the doctor cut off her testicles and converted her penile tissue into a clitoris and vagina, I sobbed into her bed pillow until my throat hurt and my stomach tied in knots. I was in mourning. For perhaps the first time, I realized that my old dad was gone for good.

In the aftermath of the surgery, I fell into a deep clinical depression.

Finally, I was grieving the death of a man I barely knew and didn't like but still loved. Moreover, I was lamenting the permanent loss of white-bread normalcy. The surgery made everything final: he was a woman, my parents weren't ever going to reunite, and no one would ever look at us as a standard middle-American family again.

In the years since my father's surgery, I have had to reinvent the mythology of family. Liberating the notion of father from that of man hasn't been easy. But my father is alive because she is female, and she has made herself into one hell of a woman. As she has grown into her womanhood, she has stopped the frenetic housecleaning and flower arranging. These days she cooks only pasta, and two years ago she joined a women's bowling league. I still struggle now and then with the selfishness she exhibited during my childhood. I can get furious with her over the smallest disagreement. But for the most part, we spend less of our time arguing over whether she's a woman and more commiserating on how difficult it is to be one in this often-oppressive world. She scolds me when I worry about having a bubble butt, and I console her when she gets dissed by a lesbian who can't deal with her male past. I still ache over the disassociation she felt with her own body and life. But now her struggle is ours together, and in the pact we have made, I found a father I never had.

Letters

I, too, had been shouting at the television, correcting the reporters on their usage of "our children" when describing who committed these violent acts. "Boys," I yelled. "It's young white boys." And then Gloria Steinem's article ("Supremacy Crimes," August/September 1999) stated eloquently what I intuitively knew, that the expectation of supremacy, when unfulfilled, can easily produce violence.

A couple of years ago, I read the results of a poll that asked young males what made them feel most like men. The top three answers were financially supporting the family,

producing children, and protecting the family. Instantly it struck me that women no longer require the efforts of men exclusively for any one of these conditions to occur. The result? Increasingly frustrated men. Translated, they can't be men because women won't let them.

Yes, I am concerned about the daily violence in men's lives. But as the article suggests, men's frustrations are exploding in all directions, making women, racial minorities, and gays (and potentially more lesbians, I'm afraid) targets of the unspoken promise not kept.

PAT HAMILTON
Sharpsburg, Md.
December 1999/January 2000 issue

CHAPTER 4

2000s

AS THE MILLENNIUM KICKED OFF, so too did the next chapter of *Ms.*

Again, in the throes of financial constraints, Gloria Steinem and Marcia Ann Gillespie, with the support of *Ms.* staff, approached the Feminist Majority Foundation (FMF) to assume the role of nonprofit publisher of *Ms.* Other options had been considered—women's colleges, university women's centers, national foundations—but the FMF stood apart. A major national and global advocacy and research organization, with myriad campaigns and connections involving a worldwide network of activists, the FMF was celebrated as "a movement in itself" in the Spring 2002 issue announcing the deal. The synergy and alignment were undeniable and exciting—from FMF's long-standing work against gender apartheid in Afghanistan, to its efforts to counter antiabortion violence and bring medication abortion into the United States.

FMF's president, Eleanor Smeal, and executive director, Katherine Spillar, set about rebuilding the systems and structures, forging modern models

for production and distribution at a time when print media were struggling to survive. They determined how best to maximize shared resources, moving the editorial operations of *Ms.* to Los Angeles while keeping the publishing function at the FMF's metro Washington, D.C., headquarters.

The magazine entered the digital era: launching a website and online platforms that

ABOVE Feminist Majority Foundation president Eleanor Smeal (*left*), who would soon become *Ms.*'s publisher, with chair of the board Peg Yorkin at the *Ms.* Women of the Year awards in New York City in 2001.

LEFT Then editor in chief Marcia Ann Gillespie, former publisher Pat Carbine, and then publisher Fayne Erickson at the *Ms.* Women of the Year awards in New York City in 2001.

Yoko Ono, reading the *Ms.* article about her life and work, at the *Ms.* Women of the Year awards in New York City in 2001; she was among the honorees that year.

Speaker Nancy Pelosi, executive editor Katherine Spillar, publisher Eleanor Smeal, and actor Amy Brenneman in Washington, D.C., in 2009 at a *Ms.* event celebrating the inauguration of President Obama.

would expand and engage its robust feminist community. A full digital library and curriculum for women's and gender studies programs created out of *Ms.*'s impressive trove of content—Ms. Classroom—reached thousands of college students each year on campuses in the United States and around the globe. *Ms.* also developed a series of writers' workshops to train and feature feminist scholars, as well as a cohort of student and teen contributors.

Who Wants
to Marry a Feminist?

BY **LISA JERVIS** • JUNE/JULY 2000

THE WINTER I GOT ENGAGED, a college friend was using some of my essays as course material for a Rhetoric 101 class she was teaching at a large midwestern university. She couldn't wait to alert her students to my impending marriage. "They all think you're a lesbian," she told me. "One of them even asked if you hate men." I was blown over by the cliché of it all—how had we come to the end of the twentieth century with such ridiculous, outmoded notions even partially intact? But I was, at least, pleased that my friend was able to use my story to banish the stereotype once and (I hoped) for all in the minds of thirty corn-fed first-years. "To a man?" they reportedly gasped when told the news.

I'd been married less than a year when a customer at the bookstore where my husband works approached the counter to buy a copy of the feminist magazine I edit. "You know," a staffer told her while ringing up the purchase, "the woman who does this magazine is married to a guy who works here." The customer, supposedly a longtime reader, was outraged at the news—I believe the phrase "betrayal of feminism" was uttered—and vowed never to buy the magazine again.

These two incidents may be extreme, but they are nonetheless indicative. Although we are far from rare, young married feminists are still, for some, something of a novelty—like a dressed-up dog. We can cause a surprised "Oh, would you look at that" or a disappointed "Take that damned hat off the dog, it's just not right."

Let's take the disappointment first. Marriage's bad reputation among feminists is certainly not without reason. We all know the institution's tarnished history: women as property passed from father to husband; monogamy as the simplest way to assure paternity and thus produce "legitimate" children; a husband's legal entitlement to his wife's domestic and sexual services. With marriage rates declining and social sanctions against cohabitation falling away, why would a feminist choose to take part in such a retro, potentially oppressive, bigotedly exclusive institution?

Well, there are a lot of reasons, actually. Foremost are the emotional ones: love, companionship, the pure joy that meeting your match brings with it. But, because I'm wary of the kind of muddled romanticizing that has ill-served women in their heterosexual dealings for most of recorded history, I have plenty of other reasons. To reject marriage simply because of its history is to give in to that history; to argue against marriage by saying that a wife's identity is necessarily subsumed by her husband's is to do nothing more than second the notion.

And wasn't it feminists who fought so hard to procure the basic rights that used to be obliterated by marriage? Because of the women's rights movement, we can maintain our own bank accounts, we can make our own health-care choices; we can refuse sex with our husbands and prosecute them if they don't comply. In the feminist imagination, "wife" can still conjure up images of cookie-baking, cookie-cutter Donna Reeds whose own desires have been forced to take a back seat to their stultifying helpmate duties. But it's neither 1750 nor 1950, and Donna Reed was a mythical figure even in her own time. Marriage, now, is potentially what we make it.

Which brings me to the "surprise" portion of our program. And as long as wives are assumed—by anyone—to be obedient little women with no lives of their own, those of us who give the lie to this straw bride need to make ourselves as conspicuous as possible.

I want to take the good from marriage and leave the rest. I know it's not for everyone, but the "for as long as we both shall live" love and support thang really works for me. Sure, I didn't need the wedding to get that love and support, but neither does the fact of marriage automatically consign me and my man to traditional man-and-wife roles. Like so many relationships, married and un-, ours is a complex weave of support, independence, and sex. We achieve this privately—from the mundanities of you-have-to-cook-tonight-because-I-have-this-deadline-tomorrow to sleepy late-night discussions on more profound matters, like the meaning of life or how many steps it takes to link Kevin Bacon to John Gielgud by way of at least one vampire movie. But also publicly—with our name change, for example (explaining to folks like the Social Security Administration and whoever hands out passports that, yes, we both needed new papers, because we each had added the other's name, was, and I mean this quite seriously, a thrill). And it's this public nature of marriage that appeals. It's what allows me to take a stab at all this I've been yammering about.

I won't pretend I meet with success all the time. Disrupting other people's expectations is hard, and sometimes it's neither possible nor desirable to wear the workings of one's relationship on one's sleeve. An appropriate cocktail party introduction is not "This is my husband, Christopher, who knows how to truss a turkey, which I don't, and who, by the way, doesn't mind at all that I make more money than him. Oh, and did I mention that the last time our toilet got scrubbed, it wasn't by me?"

By and large I do believe that we're culturally ready to accept changes in the way marriages are viewed. Increasing rates of cohabitation and the growing visibility of long-term same-sex partnerships are changing popular notions of relationships.

It's true that the most important parts, the actual warp and weft of Christopher and my relationship, could be achieved without a legal marriage (and I could have kept my third wave street cred). In the end, though, the decision to marry or not to marry is—no matter how political the personal—an emotional one. I wanted to link my life to Christopher's, and, yes, I admit to taking advantage of the universally understood straight-shot-to-relationship-legitimacy that marriage offers. But it is a testament to the feminists who came before me, who offered up all those arguments about marriage's oppressive roots and worked tirelessly to ensure that my husband owns neither my body nor my paycheck, that I can indulge my emotion without fear of being caught in those roots. Instead, I can carry on their struggle and help forge a new vision of what marriage is.

Making the Cut

BY **MARTHA COVENTRY**   •   OCTOBER/NOVEMBER 2000

ON NEW YEAR'S EVE, I sit with an acquaintance and talk. We are nearing the end of a long, pleasant evening. My friend, also a writer, leans toward me into the little circle of privacy we've created. "So, you mean what happens to African girls?" she asks, after I tell her what I am working on. "No," I say. "I mean what happens to children in the United States." And as I explain the details of the story, she earnestly watches my face, then sits back, stunned. "I am astonished," she says, and I have to agree with her. It is an astonishing story.

> **"He lists what he calls eight stages of progressive disease triggered by masturbation."**

The tale begins in England. It is 1858, and the Victorian era is in full swing. A respected gynecologist named Isaac Baker Brown, who later served as president of the Medical Society of London, has an interesting theory about women: excitement of the nervous system, and the pubic nerve, which runs into the clitoris, is particularly powerful. When aggravated by habitual stimulation, this nerve puts undue stress on the health of women. He lists what he calls eight stages of progressive disease triggered by masturbation: first comes hysteria, followed by spinal irritation, hysterical epilepsy, cataleptic fits, epileptic fits, idiocy, mania, and finally death.

The cure Brown offered was complete excision of the clitoris with scissors, packing the wound with lint, administering opium via the rectum, and strictly observing the patient. Within a month, the wound usually healed, and according to Brown intractable women became happy housewives, rebellious teenage girls settled back into the bosom of their families, and married women formerly averse to sexual duties became pregnant.

Eventually, Brown fell out of favor with a medical establishment that would have preferred more discretion about women's genitals. But before his fall from grace, Brown influenced U.S. doctors who were discussing his procedure in medical journals by 1866. It was used off and on for decades to stop masturbation, nymphomania, and hysteria. In 1894, a surgeon reported in *The New Orleans Medical and Surgical Journal* that he had excised the clitoris of a two-and-a-half-year-old child to stop her from masturbating and slipping into insanity. He noted that after the operation she had "grown stouter, more playful, and [had] ceased masturbating entirely." As late as 1937, Emmett Holt's *Diseases of Infancy and Childhood,* a respected medical school text, stated that the author was "not averse to circumcision in girls or cauterization of the clitoris." Toward the middle of the 1950s, just as U.S. medicine seemed to be awakening to the brutality and ineffectiveness of clitoridectomies as a means to control behavior, it found another use for the procedure. This time the rationale was that the operation could be used to make a child whose clitoris appeared bigger than other girls' look "normal," thus helping the child, and everyone around her, to feel more comfortable.

In 1966, a full century after Brown's clitoridectomies were first discussed in this country, this recommendation appeared in the journal *Surgery:* "Some persons have been reluctant to advocate excision of even the most grotesquely enlarged clitoris . . . half-way measures are much less satisfactory than complete clitoridectomy." Given this attitude, in 1966, was any girl in the United States whose clitoris protruded noticeably beyond her labia at risk of getting it amputated? Yes. Would a girl in the year 2000 still be at risk of losing at least part of her clitoris? Yes.

By eight weeks of gestation, all external fetal genitals have the potential to develop into what we think of as female or male genitals. The genitals will become female if testosterone, or a hormone that mimics testosterone, does not interfere. If it does, then the clitoris extends to make a penis and the inner labia wrap around the underside of the penis and fuse to form the penile urethra. The outer labia come together to create the scrotum. The process for the internal sexual organs is similar. All fetuses start out with precursors of female and male sex organs. By the third fetal month, if the rudimentary male ducts have not been triggered to mature into testes and vas deferens, they will disappear. The female ducts will then grow and develop into ovaries and a uterus.

But this intricate and elegant development of external and internal sexual organs is a journey prone to detours caused by all sorts of influences, like maternal hormones, drugs, genetic disposition, environmental hazards, and chance. Sometimes clitorises look more like penises. Sometimes the outer labia on a girl baby fuse into a scrotal-looking sac so her genitals may appear almost indistinguishable from a typical newborn baby boy's. Some-times a boy's scrotum is empty, his testes undescended, and his penis tiny. Some vaginas end before they reach the uterus.

These variations occur more frequently than most of us assume. According to Anne Fausto-Sterling, professor of biology and women's studies at Brown University and author of *Sexing the Body: Gender Politics and the Construction of Sexuality*, in almost 2 percent of live births, or approximately eighty thousand births a year, there is some genital abnormality. Approximately two thousand children a year have genital surgery in the United States. Experts say the vast majority are girls who lose parts of their clitorises, and less commonly, little boys whose penises are pared down to approximate a clitoris in an attempt to give them what doctors believe will be a better life.

These children are called "intersexed" by the medical world, no matter what their chromosomal makeup. Surgeons perform cosmetic genital surgeries on these children so that they and their parents and caregivers will have an unwavering notion of them as one sex or the other.

All over this country there are people whose clitorises have been removed, either totally or partially. They range from your great-aunt's roommate in the nursing home to your neighbor's two-year-old child. They include hundreds of women from every generation. Some were born clearly female; some were born clearly male but were reassigned as female and then had their genitals altered; and some were babies whose sex was not easy to define.

Approximately five times a day in the United States, surgeons change the size and shape of a child's healthy clitoris. Few of those children are capable of expressing what they want. Some, if given the choice later in life, might choose clitoroplasty. But judging from the responses of women who had the surgery done with or without their agreement—or at an age when they were too young to know what they were agreeing to—many would have preferred to stay the way they were.

The U.S. public had no idea these surgeries were going on, and most doctors considered them a necessary treatment for a rare group of people. Medical schools spend only a few hours on the subject of intersexuality, with surgery hardly mentioned at all. Intersexed children with "abnormal" genitals are depicted in medical books naked with a black band across their eyes in photographs, lending an aura of freakishness to them. They historically have been given the label "hermaphrodite," and further categorized as "true hermaphrodites" (people who have some ovarian and some testicular tissue) or "pseudohermaphrodites" (boys with testes and some feminine characteristics or girls with ovaries and some masculine characteristics). These names also serve to marginalize children, hiding the fact that this is a far larger group than anyone realizes. Even the doctors who care for these patients as children know little or nothing about them as they grow into their adult lives.

Activists and health-care providers are calling for a new protocol: raise the children with atypical genitals in a gender most appropriate to their bodies, provide counseling for them and their families, and allow decisions about genital plastic surgery to be made by the person whose genitals will be changed, at an age when they, not their anxious parents or well-meaning doctors, can give informed and educated consent. As William Reiner, a pediatric urologist turned child psychiatrist at Johns Hopkins puts it, "If you've got a fourteen-year-old girl who comes in and says, 'I absolutely cannot tolerate this. It makes me think I'm a boy. I'm a girl, and I want my clitoris made smaller,' then after appropriate counseling, if she's still serious, we have to listen to her. She's a human being. She's not an adult, but so what? In other words, you can leave these clitorises alone for a long time and let the kids decide what they want to do."

A big clitoris on a girl or woman in the sixteenth century, when discovered by a witch-hunter, was seen as a "devil's teat." It alone was enough to condemn her to death. We are more civilized today. We're beyond witch-hunting, and we're appalled by countries that routinely clitoridectomize their daughters. But we still treat a bigger than average clitoris on a child as fair game for surgery. If her parents or doctors want it made smaller, it will be made smaller. She can do nothing to stop it. But the world is changing. People with atypical genitals are no longer solely relegated to "interesting case" status and tucked away in medical books. Their stories, in their own voices, can be read in books, in magazines, or on the web. These stories bring a new and crucial perspective to an old and damaging view of difference.

People are talking to each other at last, and change is in the air. The story of clitoridectomy in the United States—a procedure whose name, technique, and intention change with the society it serves—began with Isaac Baker Brown, but it might just end with us.

MY OWN STORY

I did not choose clitoridectomy as a subject; it chose me. In 1958, when I was six years old, my mother took me to the doctor. "Seen for evaluation re: enlargement of clitoris; parents have been concerned about genital anomaly since child was small. Exam: neg. except definite enlargement of clitoris," read the report. My clitoris, I now know, had become enlarged because my mother was given progesterone to prevent miscarriage when she was pregnant with me. Three days after our visit, a surgeon performed a clitorectomy, cutting off my clitoris at the surface along the hood and most of the inner labia.

After five days in the hospital, I returned to first grade as if nothing had happened. But my pleasant childhood was shadowed by a nagging question: What was that operation I had? The only time I made an effort to find out, my loving but practical surgeon-father recommended, "Don't be so self-examining." So, I worried about why my parents took me to the hospital when I wasn't sick and why I felt so ashamed about whatever the doctors did to me there. And I was afraid I was some kind of boy-like creature. I didn't know girls had anything between their legs you could cut off. I was certain no one, anywhere, looked or felt as I did.

My marriage fell apart when I was in my forties, and with that ending came the desire to lay to rest the fears about myself. I got my medical records, asked every question I could think of, and, with the help of a kind gynecologist, made a clay depiction of my presurgery vulva. Perhaps most important, I stumbled upon the Intersex Society of North America. Soon I found people who had stories like mine, people who spoke a familiar language of childhood loss and bewilderment.

Since 1996, I have written and spoken about clitoral surgery in the United States. Recently, my eighteen-year-old daughter asked, "Mom, aren't you getting tired of clitorises?" I laughed and said, "Yeah, pretty much," and smiled at the easy way that word rolled off her tongue. How wonderful that "clitoris" is a household word in my family of two daughters. How thankful I am that my children will not carry on the concerns and fears of their mother.

The Dykes Next Door

BY **JUDITH LEVINE** • OCTOBER/NOVEMBER 2001

MO CAN'T SLEEP. She's worried that her girlfriend is cheating on her. To keep her mind off her troubles, she dips into *GirlFrenzy* magazine, only to learn that its editors have rated Monsanto—maker of genetically modified foods, pesticides, and other evil products—the second-best "lesbian place to work" in the United States. Removing her wire-rimmed glasses and lying back in bed, our endearingly neurotic, perennially politically exasperated heroine throws her arm across her forehead and cries (inside a thought bubble), "Did I have to live to see the principles of lesbian-feminism betrayed so utterly?" Once again, one of the characters in

> **"It's hard to say what— besides the defining fact that she has sex with a woman—qualifies the life of Alison Bechdel as 'lesbian,' authentic or otherwise."**

Alison Bechdel's *Dykes to Watch Out For* has put her finger squarely on the Dykegeist. Since 1983, this little comic-strip community has been griping, groping, and gossiping its way through the cultural and political events of our time, from the butch-femme debates to the second coming of Bush; from El Salvador to civil unions; from Reaganomics to postmodernism. In biweekly installments of ten to twelve panels each, and nine collections

AS LESBIAN CULTURE MOVES INTO THE "MAINSTREAM," WHAT WILL BECOME OF ALISON BECHDEL'S "ALTERNATIVE" COMIC

ALISON (LEFT) AND MO

published by the little lesbian-feminist press Firebrand Books, Bechdel has created what some aficionados consider the preeminent cartoon record of modern lesbian-feminist history—and one of the preeminent oeuvres in the comic genre, period. Yet, in keeping with the modesty of both the form and the artist herself, Bechdel says she strives in each strip to produce a "small moment" in which "hardly anything happens. Just like real life."

The DYKES Next Door

BY
JUDITH LEVINE

Mo can't sleep. She's worried that her girlfriend is cheating on her. To keep her mind off her troubles, she dips into *GirlFrenzy* magazine, only to learn that its editors have rated Monsanto—maker of genetically modified foods, pesticides, and other evil products—the second-best "lesbian place to work" in the U.S. Removing her wire-rimmed glasses and lying back in bed, our endearingly neurotic, perennially politically exasperated heroine throws her arm across her forehead and cries (inside a

Lately, however, a lot has been happening in real lesbian life. Lesbians and gays have been on the cover of every newsweekly and are in the scripts of every sitcom. Bechdel's home state, Vermont, has legally recognized same-sex civil unions. Even Attorney General John Ashcroft was compelled to promise he wouldn't blackball homosexual nominations for the judiciary. But assimilation—for most, the goal of gay liberation—also has its downside. The far-reaching, left feminist vision that used to give dykes their multiculti cohesiveness is being edged out by the likes of the Log Cabin Republicans (in 2000, about 25 percent of homosexuals voted for the GOP, compared with only 9 percent of Black people, for example). Moderate and conservative homosexuals are demanding inclusion in the military, the kiddie-paramilitary (Boy Scouts), and what feminists have long argued is one of history's most oppressive institutions, marriage. The very identity that glued the gay and lesbian movement together is being domesticated and deconstructed out of business. And still, homophobia is far from vanquished; the ghastly image of Matthew Shepard crucified on a fence post certifies that. It seems the only act in which lesbian and gay identities have undisputed purchase is, literally, the purchase. The last Gay Pride March looked more like a shopping mall than a protest. Wails Mo, "Another liberation movement up Madison Avenue without a paddle!"

Perched on a straight-backed chair in her roomy home studio in Burlington, Bechdel gathers one long leg up to her chest as she discusses the crossroads at which she and her characters find themselves. Unlike Mo's strict anti-mainstream stance, the artist admits to being somewhat ambivalent about assimilation. After all, many of the changes in the last decade or so have made life easier for lesbians and gays, even though they might have made the community less cohesive. Vermont's civil unions bill, Bechdel says, encapsulates this contradiction. "Something irrevocable has been lost. That feels tragic. But [the law] took me by surprise: I felt a sense of relief. A weight was lifted that I didn't know was there." She looks toward the snowy woods outside her studio windows. "I didn't think I cared about being legitimate," she continues, "but now that someone was saying I was legitimate, it was intoxicating. You want these things, but you don't want them."

Viewing herself as something between a journalist, a historian, and a soap-opera writer, Bechdel describes her challenge this way: "to have [my characters] segue into more contemporary life, but without losing their personalities and their relationships." She grounds *Dykes,* especially the persona of Mo, in the history and values that she and her oldest fans still believe in. At the same time, says her longtime editor and publisher, Nancy K. Bereano, "she has to stay au courant for the current generation."

It's a precarious act, straddling epochs.

Bechdel faces the challenge of finding new sources of motivation and inspiration. Before, she tells me, she worked from inside a "huge, fascinating, burgeoning subculture, reflecting back to lesbians what their real lives were like." Now that those reflections can be found elsewhere, however incompletely, her passion comes from another place. "My attitude is, why can't I write a very detailed, authentic representation of what my life as a lesbian is like and have people read it?"

The catch is, it's hard to say what—besides the defining fact that she has sex with a woman—qualifies the life of Alison Bechdel as "lesbian," authentic or otherwise. Indeed, the former outsider artist shows signs of becoming virtually normal herself. She owns a nice house and forty wooded acres with her longtime partner. Her commentary on modern lesbian mores is as much a product of intelligence gathering on college speaking tours as it is a record of her own personal experience. Just like her characters, Bechdel feels her identity turning with the century. And her life is no longer as purely party line as Mo might endorse. These changes may have as much to do with Bechdel's own impending middle age as with that of the movement in which she came of age. "I feel like I'm growing up at the same rate as the community," she says. "In that way, my strip is a reflection of myself."

The strip is syndicated in almost seventy publications, an increasing number of which are alternative, but non-gay-specific, weeklies. Her books sell steadily—more than 100,000 copies to date—making her the best-selling author on Firebrand's list. Bechdel knows from her correspondence that many of her fans are not queer or even female.

In the end, Alison Bechdel's future may be decided less by lesbian legitimacy than by audiences' appreciation of good literature, which evokes the universal by creating a specific world. After all, you don't have to be a nineteenth-century Russian aristocrat to get caught up in *Anna Karenina.* If we're all lucky, Bechdel will move into new realms and also, with *Dykes,* guide newcomers into an evolving subculture that probably won't disappear soon. Maybe she'll even do her part in the recruitment effort. A lesbian friend who teaches English as a second language recently told me that a Taiwanese student, who "may be gay," has gotten hooked on *Dykes.* Said my friend, "She asks me questions like 'What does "flannel" mean as an adjective?'"

· · ·

ALISON BECHDEL, in addition to syndicating *Dykes to Watch Out For* until 2008, created wildly successful graphic novel family memoirs, including *Fun Home: A Family Tragicomic*—named one of *Time* magazine's ten best books of 2006 and later adapted into a Broadway musical that swept the 2015 Tony Awards. Among her iconic imprints on American culture, Bechdel appeared in a cameo on *The Simpsons,* won a prestigious MacArthur "genius" award, and, of course, is the source and namesake of the "Bechdel Test" (*next page*). Bechdel credits her friend Liz Wallace for the idea, which has lived on in force since it first debuted in her comic strip in 1985.

A NEW RATING SYSTEM FOR MOVIES: "D"

IN AN EARLY STRIP, one of the Dykes lays out her requirements for a good film. It should (a) have at least two women, who (b) talk to each other, about (c) something other than a man. We put some recent Oscar winners to this test.

GLADIATOR, 2000
SUMMARY: After his family is murdered on orders from the evil prince Commodus, the brooding Roman general Maximus is sold into slavery.

> At least two female characters? Yes.
> Do they have a conversation? No.
> About something other than a man? N/A.

COMMENTS: Maximus's wife is martyred before she can utter a word.

AMERICAN BEAUTY, 1999
SUMMARY: A frustrated suburbanite, Lester, has a tumultuous midlife crisis that sucks in his wife, Carolyn; his daughter, Jane; and her friend, Angela.

> At least two female characters? Yes.
> Do they have a conversation? Yes.
> About something other than a man? Yes.

COMMENTS: Jane's discussions with Angela mostly concern men, but Jane and her mom have non-male-related fights: "You ungrateful little brat! When I was your age, I lived in a duplex!"

SHAKESPEARE IN LOVE, 1998
SUMMARY: The upper-class aspiring actor Viola, engaged to a noxious scion of wealth, meets the scruffy bohemian playwright Will Shakespeare. Passion ensues.

> At least two female characters? Yes.
> Do they have a conversation? Yes.
> About something other than a man? Yes.

COMMENTS: Viola enthusiastically discusses the theater with both her handmaiden and the unexpectedly sassy Queen Elizabeth.

TITANIC, 1997
SUMMARY: The upper-class aspiring free spirit Rose, engaged to a noxious scion of wealth, meets the scruffy bohemian artist Jack. Passion ensues.

> At least two female characters? Yes.
> Do they have a conversation? Yes.
> About something other than a man? Barely.

COMMENTS: Rose's mom, aware that her once-rich family is penniless, forbids Rose to end her engagement. But she's talking about money, not men: "Do you want to see me working as a seamstress?"

—Lisa Gidley

Sneak Attack: **The Militarization of U.S. Culture**

BY **CYNTHIA ENLOE** • DECEMBER 2001/JANUARY 2002

THINGS START to become militarized when their legitimacy depends on their associations with military goals. When something becomes militarized, it appears to rise in value.

But it is really a process of loss. Even though something seems to gain value by adopting an association with military goals, it actually surrenders control and gives up the chain to its own worthiness.

Militarization is a sneaky sort of transformative process. Sometimes it is only in the pursuit of *de*militarization that we become aware of just how far down the road of complete militarization we've gone. Representative Barbara Lee (D-Calif.) pulled back the curtain in the aftermath of the September 11 attacks when she cast the lone vote against giving George W. Bush carte blanche to wage war. The loneliness of her vote suggested how far the militarization of Congress—and its voters back home—has advanced. In fact, since September 11, publicly criticizing militarization has been widely viewed as an act of disloyalty.

> **"Sometimes it is only in the pursuit of *de*militarization that we become aware of just how far down the road of complete militarization we've gone."**

Whole cultures can be militarized. It is a militarized U.S. culture that has made it easier for Bush to wage war without most Americans finding it dangerous to democracy. Our cultural militarization makes waging war seem like a comforting reconfirmation of our collective security, identity, and pride.

Other sectors of U.S. culture have also been militarized:

- **EDUCATION.** School board members accept Junior ROTC programs for their teenagers, and social studies teachers play it safe by avoiding discussion of past sexual misconduct by U.S. soldiers overseas. Many university scientists pursue lucrative Defense Department weapons research contracts.
- **SOLDIERS' GIRLFRIENDS AND WIVES.** They've been persuaded that they are "good citizens" if they keep silent about problems in their relationships with male soldiers for the sake of their fighting effectiveness.
- **BEAUTY.** This year, the Miss America pageant organizers selected

judges with military credentials, including a former secretary of the navy and an air force captain.
- **CARS.** The Hummer ranks among the more bovine vehicles to clog U.S. highways, yet civilians think they will be feared and admired if they drive them.

Then there is the conundrum of the flag. People who reject militarization may don a flag pin unaware that doing so may convince those with a militarized view of the U.S. flag that their bias is universally shared, thus deepening the militarization of culture.

The events post–September 11 have also shown that many Americans today may be militarizing non-U.S. women's lives. It was only after Bush declared "war on terrorists and those countries that harbor them" that the violations of Afghan women's human rights took center stage. Here's the test of whether Afghan women are being militarized: if their well-being is worthy of our concern only because their lack of well-being justifies the U.S. bombing of Afghanistan, then we are militarizing Afghan women—as well as our own compassion. We are thereby complicit in the notion that something has worth only if it allows militaries to achieve their missions.

It's important to remember that militarization has its rewards, such as newfound popular support for measures formerly contested. For example, will many Americans now be persuaded that drilling for oil in the Alaskan wilderness is acceptable because it will be framed in terms of "national security"? Will most U.S. citizens now accept government raids on the Social Security trust fund in the name of paying for the war on terrorism?

Women's rights in the United States and Afghanistan are in danger if they become mere by-products of some other cause. Militarization, in all its seductiveness and subtlety, deserves to be bedecked with flags wherever it thrives—fluorescent flags of warning.

· · ·

OPPOSITE *Ms.* celebrates its thirtieth anniversary with a collector's issue and gets a new publisher, the Feminist Majority Foundation, which has remained in that role ever since.

AFGHAN WOMEN · A FEMINIST FAMILY TREE

Ms.

VOLUME XII NUMBER 2 · SPRING 2002 · U.S. $5.95 CANADA $6.95

the best of

30 years

Reporting Rebelling & Truth-telling

Plus Updates:
Moving into the Future

A Cruel Edge:
The Painful Truth About Today's Pornography—and What Men Can Do About It

BY **ROBERT JENSEN, PHD** • SPRING 2004

AFTER AN INTENSE THREE HOURS, the workshop on pornography is winding down. The forty women present all work at a center that serves battered women and rape survivors. These are the women on the front lines, the ones who answer the twenty-four-hour hotlines and deal directly with the victims. These women have heard and seen it all, and there is no way to one-up them with stories about male violence. But after three hours discussing the commercial heterosexual pornography industry, many of these women are drained. Sadness hangs over the room.

One woman has held back throughout the workshop, her arms wrapped tightly around herself. Now, finally, she speaks. "This hurts," she says. "It just hurts so much."

Everyone is quiet as the words sink in. Slowly the conversation restarts, but her words hang in the air.

It hurts.

It hurts to know that no matter who you are, you can be reduced to a thing to be penetrated, and that men will buy movies about that, and that in many of those movies your humiliation will be the central theme. It hurts to know that so much of the pornography men buy fuses sexual desire with cruelty.

Even women who cope daily with those injured by male violence struggle with this knowledge. It's one thing to deal with overt acts; it's another to face the thoughts and fantasies that fuel so many men's sexual lives.

People routinely assume that pornography is such a difficult and divisive issue because it's about sex. I think that's wrong. This culture struggles unsuccessfully with pornography because it is also about men's cruelty to women, and about the pleasure that men sometimes take in that cruelty. And that is much more difficult for everyone to face.

There are different pornographic genres, but my studies of pornographic videos over the past seven years have focused on the stories told in mainstream heterosexual pornography. By that I mean the videos and DVDs that are widely available in the United States, marketed as sexually explicit (what is commonly called "hard-core"), rented and purchased primarily by men, and depict sex primarily between men and women. The sexual activity is not simulated: what happens on the screen happened in the world.

To obtain mainstream pornographic videos for study, I visited stores that sold "adult products" (the industry's preferred term) and asked clerks and managers to help me select the most commonly rented and purchased tapes. I wanted to avoid the accusation that feminists analyzing pornography pick out only the worst examples, the most violent material, to critique.

> **"Men who consume these images are everywhere: men who can't get a date and men who have all the dates they want."**

While many may find what is described here to be disturbing, these are not aberrations. These tapes are broadly representative of the 11,303 new hard-core titles that were released in 2002, according to *Adult Video News,* the industry's trade magazine. They are standard fare from a pornography industry with an estimated $10 billion in annual sales. They are what brothers and fathers and uncles are watching, what boyfriends and husbands and, in many cases, male children are watching.

The 2003 film *Sopornos 4* was produced by VCA Pictures, one of the "high-end" companies that create films for the "couples market." These films, sometimes called "features," typically attempt some plot and character development. The industry claims these films appeal to women as well as men.

The plot of *Sopornos* is a takeoff on the popular HBO series about New Jersey mobsters. In the last of six sex scenes, the mob boss's wife has sex with two of his men. Moving through the standard porn progression—oral sex and then vaginal sex—one of the men prepares to penetrate her anally. She tells him, "That fucking cock is so fucking huge. . . . Spread [my] fucking ass. . . . Spread it open." He penetrates her. Then, she says, in a slightly lower tone, "Don't go any deeper." She seems to be in pain. At the end of the scene, she requests the men's semen ("Two cocks jacking off in my face. I want it") and opens her mouth. The men ejaculate onto her at the same time.

Two in the Seat #3, a 2003 "gonzo" release (meaning, there is no attempt to create characters or story lines) from Red Light District, contains six scenes in which two men have sex with one woman, culminating in a double penetration (the woman is penetrated vaginally and anally at the same time). In one scene, twenty-year-old Claire, her hair in pigtails, says she has been in the industry for three months. Asked by the off-camera interviewer what will happen in the scene, she replies, "I'm here to get pounded." The two men then enter the scene and begin a steady stream of insults, calling her "a dirty, nasty girl," "a little fucking cunt," "a little slut." After oral and vaginal sex, she asks one, "Please put your cock in my ass." During double penetration on the floor, her vocalizations sound pained. She's braced against the couch, moving very little. The men spank her, and her buttock is visibly red. One man asks, "Are you crying?"

Claire: "No, I'm enjoying it."

Man: "Damn, I thought you were crying. It was turning me on when I thought you were crying."

Claire: "Would you like me to?"

Man: "Yeah, give me a fucking tear. Oh, there's a fucking tear."

Finally, there's *Gag Factor 10,* a 2002 release from JM Productions also in the "gonzo" category. One of the ten sex scenes involves a woman and man having a picnic in the park. While she sits on the blanket, he stands and thrusts his penis into her mouth. Two other men who walk by join in. One man grabs her hair and pulls her head into his penis in what his friend calls "the jackhammer."

At this point the woman is grimacing and seems in pain. She then lies on the ground, and the men approach her from behind. "Eat that whole fucking dick. . . . You little whore, you like getting hurt," one says. After they all ejaculate into her mouth, the semen flows out onto her body. She reaches quickly for the wineglass, takes a large drink, looks up at her boyfriend, and says, "God, I love you, baby." Her smile fades to a pained look of shame and despair.

I can't know exactly what the women in these films were feeling, physically or emotionally. But here is what Belladonna, one of the women who appeared in *Two in the Seat #3,* told a television interviewer about the sex scenes: "You have to really prepare physically and mentally for it. I mean, I go through a process from the night before. I stop eating at 5 p.m. I do, you know, like two enemas, and then the next morning I don't eat anything. It's so draining on your body."

Even if the pain shown in the above scenes is acted and not real, why don't directors edit *out* pained expressions? I see only two possible answers: either they view such pain as being of no consequence to the viewers' interest—and hence to the goal of maximizing film sales—or they believe viewers enjoy seeing the women's pain. So why, then, do some men find the infliction of pain on women during sex either not an obstacle to their ability to achieve sexual pleasure or a factor that can *enhance* their pleasure?

I believe it's all about the edge.

There are only so many ways that human beings can, in mechanical terms, have sex. There are a limited number of body parts and openings, a limited number of ways to create the friction that produces the stimulation and sensations. That's why stories about sexuality generally tap into something beyond the mechanical. When most nonpornographic films deal with sex, they draw, at least in part, on the emotions most commonly connected with sex: love and affection. But pornography doesn't have that option, since my research has shown that men typically consume it to *avoid* love and affection and go straight to sexual release.

And that means pornography, without emotional variation, will become repetitive and uninteresting, even to men watching primarily to facilitate masturbation. So pornography needs an edge.

When the legal restrictions on pornography gradually loosened in the 1970s and 1980s, anal sex captured that edge, because it was seen as something most women don't want. Then, as anal sex became routine in pornography, the gonzo genre started routinely adding double penetrations and gag-inducing oral sex—again, acts the men believe women generally do not want. These days, pornography has become so normalized and so mainstream in our culture that the edge keeps receding. As Jerome Tanner put it during a pornography directors' roundtable discussion featured in *Adult Video News,* "People just want it harder, harder, and harder, because . . . what are you gonna do next?"

It's not surprising that the new edge more and more involved overt cruelty—an easy choice given that the dynamic of male domination and female submission is already in place in patriarchy. All people are capable of being cruel, of course. But contemporary mainstream heterosexual pornography forces the question: Why has cruelty become so sexualized for some men?

Feminist research long ago established that rape involves the sexualization of power, the equation in men's imaginations of sexual pleasure with domination and control. The common phrase "rape is about power, not sex" misleads, though; rape is about the fusion of sex and domination, about the eroticization of control. And in this culture, rape is normal. That is, in a culture where the dominant definition of sex is the taking of pleasure from women by men, rape is an expression of the sexual norms of the culture, not a violation of those norms. Sex is a sphere in which men are trained to see themselves as naturally dominant and women as naturally passive. Rape is both nominally illegal and completely normal.

By extension, there should be nothing surprising about the fact that some pornography includes explicit images of women in pain. But my question is, wouldn't a healthy society want to deal with that? Why aren't more people, men or women, concerned?

Right-wing opponents of pornography offer a moralistic critique that cannot help us find solutions, because typically those folks endorse male dominance (albeit not these particular manifestations of it). Conversely, some feminists want us to believe that the growing acceptance of pornography is a benign sign of expanding sexual equality and freedom. Meanwhile, feminist critics of pornography have been marginalized in political and intellectual arenas. And all the while, the pornographers are trudging off to the bank with bags of money.

I think this helps explain why even the toughest women at rape crisis centers find the reality of pornography so difficult to cope with. No matter how hard it may be to face rape, at least our society still brands it a crime. Pornography, however, is not only widely accepted but sold to us as liberation.

I don't pretend to speak for women; my focus is on men. And I believe that the task for men of conscience is to define ourselves and our sexuality outside the domination/submission dynamic. It is not easy: like everyone, we are products of our culture and have to struggle against it. But as a man, I at least have considerable control over the conditions in which I live and the situations in which I function. Women sometimes do not have that control. They're at far more risk of sexual violence, and they have to deal with men who disproportionately hold positions of power over them. Mainstream pornography tips that power balance even further.

For example, when a female student has a meeting about a research project with a male college professor who the night before was watching *Gag Factor 10,* who will she be to him? Or when a woman walks into a bank to apply for a loan from a male loan officer who the night before was watching *Two in the Seat #3,* what will he be thinking? And when a woman goes in front of a male judge who the night before was watching *Sopornos 4,* will she be judged fairly?

But some will argue, how can you assume that just because men watch such things they will act in a callous and cruel manner, sexually or otherwise? It is true that the connection between mass-media exposure and human behavior is complex, and social scientists argue both sides. But taken together, the laboratory evidence, the research on men who abuse, and the voluminous testimony of women clearly indicate that in some cases pornography influences men's sexual behavior. Pornography may not *cause* abuse, but it can be implicated as an accessory to the crime.

If we could pretend that these images are consumed by some small subset of deviant men, then we could identify and isolate those aberrant men, maybe repair them. But men who consume these images are everywhere: men who can't get a date and men who have all the dates they want. Men who live alone and men who are married. Men who grew up in liberal homes where pornography was never a big deal and men who grew up in strict religious homes where no talk of sex was allowed. Rich men and poor men, men of all colors and creeds.

When I critique pornography, I am often told to lighten up. Sex is just sex, people say, and I should stop trying to politicize pornography. But pornography offers men a politics of sex and gender, and the politics is patriarchal and reactionary. In pornography, women are not really people; they are three holes and two hands. Women in pornography have no hopes, no dreams, and no value apart from the friction those holes and hands can produce on a man's penis.

As with any political issue, successful strategies of resistance, I would suggest, must be collective and public rather than solely personal and private. Pornographers know that to be true, which is why they try to cut off the discussion. When we critique pornography, we typically are accused of being people who hate freedom, sexually dysfunctional prudes who are scared of sex, or both.

Pornographers also want to derail any talk of sexual ethics. They, of course, have a sexual ethic: anything—and they mean anything—goes, and consenting adults should be free to choose. I agree that choice is crucial. But in a society in which power is not equally distributed, "anything goes" translates into "anything goes for men, while some women and children will suffer for it."

There are many controversial issues in the pornography debate, but there should be nothing controversial about this: to critique pornography is not repressive. We should be free to talk about our desire for an egalitarian intimacy and for sexuality that rejects pain and humiliation. That is not prudishness or censorship. It is an attempt to claim the best parts of our common humanity: love, caring, empathy. To do that is not to limit anyone. It is to say, simply, that women count as much as men.

·   ·   ·

One Secret Thing

BY **SHARON OLDS** • SPRING 2004

One secret thing happened
at the end of my mother's life, when I was
alone with her. I knew it should happen—
I knew someone was there, in there,
something less unlike my mother than
anything else on earth. And the jar
was there on the table—the space around it
round, and pulled back from it, like the awestruck
handmade air around the crèche,
and her open mouth, not shut for two
days, was parched. I have always feared her.
It was evening, no one was there. The lid
eased off. I watched my finger draw through
the jelly, its egg-sex essence, the four
corners of the room were not creatures, if I did not
do this, what was I—I rubbed the cowlick of
petrolatum on the skin around where the
final measures of what was almost not
breath swayed, and her throat made a guttural
stream-bed sound, like pebbly relief. But each
lip was stuck by dried chap to its row
of teeth, stuck fast. And then I worked
for my motherhood, my humanhood, I
slid my forefinger slowly back and
forth along the scab-line and underlying
canines and incisors, upper lip and then
lower lip, until, like a basted
seam, softly ripped, what had been
joined was asunder, I ran the salve inside the folds, along the gums,
common mercy. The secret was
how deeply I did not want to touch
inside her, and how much the act
was an act of escape, my last chance
to free myself.

· · ·

What's So Funny?

BY **GINA BARRECA** • SUMMER 2004

WOMEN ARE FUNNY. We are certainly funnier than men. Which is why you always hear laughter coming from the women's room—we're having a riot in there.

You rarely hear laughter coming from the men's room. And the fact that they don't have separate stalls is only *part* of the reason.

Put three women together for more than three minutes and—whether or not they have ever met before—they will have exchanged vital details of their inner lives and started to laugh.

Guys aren't like this. Their conversations consist of asking each other questions that can be answered numerically. Men can play poker together for twenty-two years and know precisely two things about their comrades: their first names and what kinds of cars they drive. Humorous interaction between men instantly becomes a joke-off.

> **"Put three women together for more than three minutes and—whether or not they have ever met before—they will have exchanged vital details of their inner lives and started to laugh."**

Women don't joke-off that way.

You'll notice, in fact, that we rarely tell jokes; instead, we tell stories.

We move from gritty details of intimate life to the generalities of politics and culture within a single sentence. We use humor to name things in our lives the world wants to keep mysterious. The comic Pam Stone has a great story about this: "I had a girlfriend who told me she was in the hospital for female problems. I said, 'Get real! What does that mean?' She says, 'You know, *female* problems.' I said, 'What? You can't parallel park? You can't get credit?'"

Using humor to bridge gaps in conversation and in our lives was illustrated for me most poignantly as I waited in line at the local all-night Stop & Shop. It was nearly midnight and the place looked like a cross between a hospital and an airport in an eastern bloc country: huge, clean, and empty.

I stood behind a woman whom I'd never met but who was, from all appearances, my match. She was around my age. In my cart were milk, juice, cereal, peaches, and kitty litter. Basics. In contrast, hers had filet mignon, baking potatoes, sour cream, parsley—the works. As she started placing these on the belt at the register, I leaned over and said with half a laugh, "Excuse me, but can I go home with you? This looks like one great meal."

Looking me straight in the eye as she counted out some tangerines, she said without missing a beat, "It's for tomorrow night's dinner. If *we don't decide to move in together* tomorrow night, it's over."

Now, I'd never met her before, but of course I knew exactly what she meant and could supply, in the shorthand of all female existence everywhere, all the necessary information.

"How long has it been?" I asked.

"Five years," she replied, arching an eyebrow for effect as I nodded. "I'm forty-four years old," she continued. "If I'm going to learn to live with another adult, it had better be *now*."

Meanwhile, the woman working the register started ringing up the steak and said, "Honey, sounds like a bad deal to me. You've been on your own and you've liked it because otherwise you would have hooked up with somebody. Trust me. This way you can have a relationship without all the attendant garbage of cohabitation. You have any coupons?" She said this as she expertly scanned the produce under the magic green eye that records the price. She knew what everything cost, including, it seemed, the relationship under discussion. By now we were all double bagging the groceries and talking at the same time. We were laughing, but the laughter was underscored—yet in no way undermined—by the gravity of the story.

Even though there is no follow-up memo, even though we do not know each other's names, we know this is real work, the telling of our tales; the turning of anxiety into humor is the equivalent of spinning straw into gold. We take it seriously.

Our humor is both public and private. We exchange information for the purpose of helping one another—wherever we happen to be. Consider this story about Tallulah Bankhead: In a public restroom during an intermission, Tallulah discovered that there was no toilet paper. "I beg your pardon, but do you have any toilet tissue in your cubicle?" she asked her neighbor. Receiving a negative reply, Tallulah tried again: "Do you have any Kleenex perhaps?" Again, the reply was negative. "Not even some cotton wool? A piece of wrapping paper?" A long pause followed the third negative, after which could be heard the sound of a purse opening. A resigned drawl finally came through the partition: "Darling, do you have two fives for a ten?"

Humor works by bending or breaking the rules; it always has. But at this moment in our culture, we are uncertain which rules apply. This is one reason why the relationship of women to humor is at an important point of what can be best called "conflagration," of destruction and, literally, re-creation. It does not come down to whether women telling small-dick jokes or men telling beating-up-women jokes is politically correct; it comes down to whether we laugh at them because of rage and fear, using our humor foremost as a way to bludgeon or gag the opponent. The "gags" directed at women in masculinist humor have for too long served exactly that purpose: to shut women up.

The writer Kate Clinton has come up with a compact word for feminist humorists—"fumerists"—because it captures the idea of being funny and wanting to burn the house down all at once. Feminist humor, according to Clinton, "is about making light in this land of reversals, where we are told as we are laughing, tears streaming down our faces, that we have no sense of humor." She goes on to say that "men have used humor against women for so long—we know implicitly whose butt is the butt of their jokes—that we do not trust humor. Masculine humor is deflective. It allows denial of responsibility, the oh-I-was-just-kidding disclaimer. It is escapist, something to gloss over and get through the hard times, without ever having to do any of the hard work of change. Masculine humor is essentially not about change."

The difference, in fact, between men's humor and women's humor seems to be the difference between revolt and revolution. Masculine humor has of course included digs at the conventions of the world, poked fun at the institutions and establishments, but without the truly anarchic edge that characterizes feminine humor. Women's humor calls into question the largest issues, questions the way the world is put together.

Women's humor has a particular interest in challenging the most formidable structures because they keep women from positions of power.

Why has the feminine tradition of humor, ubiquitous as it is, remained essentially hidden from the mainstream? In part it is due to the Tupperware mentality that sought to preserve humor by keeping it away from the potentially hazardous male gaze. If men didn't find funny what we found funny, then they would think we were foolish. If they thought our joking was foolish, we might learn to like it less ourselves. It wasn't worth the risk. One of the other answers is a paradox: when women joke—as we all know women do, and do well—we are exploring a particularly feminine tradition of humor. The laughter in the kitchen, dorm room, and locker room is evidence of women's ability to joke and appreciate joking in an all-female group. We are exploring, in our laughter, female territory. The idea that women have our own humor, that a feminine tradition of humor could exist apart from the traditional masculine version, is not considered a viable possibility, and so women who initiate humor are seen as acting like men.

Studies by sociologists and psychologists go far in proving what we've all suspected as amateurs, namely "that society may hold different expectations regarding boys' and girls' humor." These social norms, argues the psychologist Paul McGhee, dictate that "males should be the initiators of humor, while females should be responders." McGhee outlines the ways in which early childhood experiences form the expectations we have concerning how men and women use humor. Theorizing that "humor in interpersonal interaction serves as a means of gaining or maintaining dominance or control over the situation," McGhee argues that "because of the power associated with the successful use of [humor] . . . the initiation of humor has become associated with other traditionally masculine characteristics, such as aggressiveness, dominance, and assertiveness."

If these studies are right, and the "witty person in a natural group is among the most powerful members of the group," then it is not in society's interest to allow girls to learn to use humor unless it is willing to accept that by doing so, girls will be learning to use power. Many stand-up performers have learned to command authority in other settings before facing an audience. Joy Behar, whose insights into relationships are profound, brings the authority she once used in an inner-city classroom to the stage. Having taught in a school where "they sent kids who would otherwise be behind bars" to her classroom, Behar translates her self-assurance to other areas of life. There is no hesitation in her remarks, no self-effacement. Behar's comedy proceeds from her personal authority and power. This is, once again, the equation that makes women's humor so subversive—the equation between women using humor and women using power.

Our humor, finally, is really about it being okay to answer back. When Lizz Winstead replies to the question "Why aren't you married?" with the retort "I think, therefore I'm single," we want to applaud. In response to Pat Buchanan's speech at the 1992 Republican National Convention, in which women's reproductive rights were considered the handmaidens of witchcraft, Molly Ivins suggested that we could not condemn Buchanan's speech because, after all, "it probably sounded better in the original German."

Women's humor is not for the fainthearted or the easily shocked. But then again, neither is waking up in the morning. Nobody said life would be easy. By seeing the ironies and absurdities of the world around us, we can lighten up and be less weighed down; humor permits perspective, and perspective is essential for change.

There is something clarifying, redemptive, and vital about using humor. So, make some trouble and laugh out loud. And always have two fives for a ten.

·   ·   ·

How Everything Adores Being Alive

BY **MARY OLIVER** • SUMMER 2004

What
　if you were
　　a beetle,
　　　and a soft wind

and a certain allowance of time
　had summoned you
　　out of your wrappings,
　　　and there you were,

so many legs
　hardening,
　　maybe even
　　　more than one pair of eyes

and the whole world
　in front of you?
　　And what if you had wings
　　　and flew

into the garden,
　then fell
　　into the up-tipped
　　　face

of a white flower,
　and what if you had
　　a sort of mouth,
　　　a lip

to place close
　to the skin
　　of honey
　　　that kept offering itself—

what would you think then
　of the world
　　as, night and day,
　　　you were kept there—

oh happy prisoner—
　sighing, humming,
　　roaming
　　　that deep cup?

Between a Woman and Her Doctor

BY **MARTHA MENDOZA** • SUMMER 2004

I COULD SEE my baby's amazing and perfect spine, a precise, pebbled curl of vertebrae. His little round skull. The curve of his nose. I could even see his small leg floating slowly through my uterus.

My doctor came in a moment later, slid the ultrasound sensor around my growing, round belly, and put her hand on my shoulder. "It's not alive," she said.

She turned her back to me and started taking notes. I looked at the wall, breathing deeply, trying not to cry.

I can make it through this, I thought. I can handle this.

I didn't know I was about to become a pariah.

I was nineteen weeks pregnant, strong, fit, and happy, imagining our fourth child, the newest member of our family. He would have dark hair and bright eyes. He'd be intelligent and strong—really strong, judging by his early kicks.

And now this. Not alive?

I didn't realize that pressures well beyond my uterus, beyond the too-bright, too-loud, too-small ultrasound room extending all the way to the boardrooms of hospitals, administrative sessions at medical schools, and committee hearings in Congress, were going to deepen and expand my sorrow and pain.

> **"I'd been through labor and delivery three times before, with great joy as well as pain, and the notion of going through that profound experience only to deliver a dead fetus . . . was horrifying."**

On November 5, 2003, President Bush signed what he called a "partial birth abortion ban," prohibiting doctors from committing an "overt act" designed to kill a partially delivered fetus. The law, which faces vigorous challenges, is the most significant change to the nation's abortion laws since the U.S. Supreme Court ruled abortion legal in *Roe v. Wade* in 1973. One of the unintended consequences of this new law is that it puts people in my position, with a fetus already dead, in a technical limbo.

Legally, a doctor can still surgically take a dead body out of a pregnant woman. But in reality, the years of angry debate that led to the law's passage, restrictive state laws, and the violence targeting physicians have reduced the number of hospitals and doctors willing to do dilations and evacuations (D&Es) and dilations and extractions (intact D&Es), which involve removing a larger fetus, sometimes in pieces, from the womb.

At the same time, fewer medical schools are training doctors to do these procedures. After all, why spend time training for a surgery that's likely to be made illegal?

At this point, 74 percent of obstetrics and gynecology residency programs do *not* train all residents in abortion procedures, according to reproductive health researchers at the National Abortion Federation. Those that do usually teach only the first trimester abortion procedures such as dilation and curettage—D&C, the fifteen-minute uterine scraping. Less than 7 percent of obstetricians are trained to do D&Es, the procedure used on fetuses from about thirteen to nineteen weeks. Almost all the doctors doing them are over fifty years old.

"Finding a doctor who will do a D&E is getting very tough," says Ron Fitzsimmons, executive director of the National Coalition of Abortion Providers.

My doctor turned around and faced me. She told me that because dilation and evacuation is rarely offered in my community, I could opt instead to chemically induce labor over several days and then deliver the little body at my local maternity ward.

"It's up to you," she said.

I'd been through labor and delivery three times before, with great joy as well as pain, and the notion of going through that profound experience only to deliver a dead fetus (whose skin was already starting to slough off, whose skull might be collapsing) was horrifying.

I also did some research, spoke with friends who were obstetricians and gynecologists, and quickly learned this: study after study shows D&Es are *safer* than labor and delivery. Women who had D&Es were far less likely to have bleeding requiring transfusion, infection requiring intravenous antibiotics, organ injuries requiring additional surgery, or cervical laceration requiring repair and hospital readmission. A review of three hundred second-trimester abortions published in 2002 in the *American Journal of Obstetrics & Gynecology* found 29 percent of women who went through labor and delivery had complications, compared with just 4 percent of those who had D&Es.

The American Medical Association said D&Es, compared with labor and delivery, "may minimize trauma to the woman's uterus, cervix and other vital organs."

There was this fact, too: the intact D&E surgery makes less use of "grasping instruments," which could damage the body of the fetus. If the body were intact, doctors might be able to more easily figure out why my baby died in the womb.

I'm a healthy person. I run, swim, and bike. I'm thirty-seven years old and optimistic. Good things happen to me. I didn't want to rule out having more kids, but I did want to know what went wrong before I tried again.

We told our doctor we had chosen a dilation and evacuation.

"I can't do these myself," said my doctor. "I trained at a Catholic hospital."

My doctor recommended a specialist in a neighboring county, but when I called for an appointment, they said they couldn't see me for almost a week.

I could feel my baby's dead body inside mine. This baby had thrilled me with kicks and flutters, those first soft tickles of life bringing a smile to my face and my hand to my rounding belly. Now this baby floated, limp and heavy, from one side to the other, as I rolled in my bed. And within a day, I started to bleed. My body, with or without a doctor's help, was starting to expel the fetus. Technically, I was threatening a spontaneous abortion, the least safe of the available options.

I did what any pregnant patient would do. I called my doctor. And she advised me to wait.

I lay in my bed, not sleeping day or night, trying not to lose this little baby's body that my own womb was working to expel. Wait, I told myself. Just hold on. Let a doctor take this out. I was scared. Was it going to fall out of my body when I rose, in the middle of the night, to check on my toddler? Would it come apart on its own and double me over, knock me to the floor, as I stood at the stove scrambling eggs for my boys?

On my fourth morning, with the bleeding and cramping increasing, I couldn't wait anymore. I called my doctor and was told that since I wasn't hemorrhaging, I should not come in. Her partner, on call, pedantically explained that women can safely lose a lot of blood, even during a routine period.

I began calling labor and delivery units at the top five medical centers in my area. I told them I had been nineteen weeks along. The baby is dead. I'm bleeding, I said. I'm scheduled for D&E in a few days. If I come in right now, what could you do for me? I asked.

Don't come in, they told me again and again. "Go to your emergency room if you are hemorrhaging to avoid bleeding to death. No one here can do a D&E today, and unless you're really in active labor you're safer to wait."

More than sixty-six thousand women each year in the United States undergo an abortion at some point between thirteen and twenty weeks, according to the Centers for Disease Control and Prevention (CDC). The CDC doesn't specify the physical circumstances of the women or their fetuses. Other CDC data shows that four thousand women miscarry in their second trimester. Again, the data doesn't clarify whether those four thousand women have to go through surgery.

Here's what is clear: most of those women face increasingly limited access to care. One survey showed that half of the women who got abortions after fifteen weeks of gestation said they were delayed because of problems in affording, finding, or getting to abortion services. No surprise there: abortion is not readily available in 86 percent of the counties in the United States.

Although there are some new early diagnostic tests available, the most common prenatal screening for neural tube defects or Down syndrome is done around the sixteenth week of pregnancy. When problems are found—sometimes life-threatening problems—pregnant women face the same limited options that I did.

At last, I found one university teaching hospital that, at least over the telephone, was willing to take me.

"We do have one doctor who can do a D&E," they said. "Come in to our emergency room if you want."

But when I arrived at the university's emergency room, the source of tension was clear. After examining me and confirming I was bleeding but not hemorrhaging, the attending obstetrician, obviously pregnant herself, defensively explained that only one of their dozens of obstetricians and gynecologists still does D&Es, and he was simply not available. Not today. Not tomorrow. Not the next day. No, I couldn't have his name. She walked away from me and called my doctor.

"You can't just dump these patients on us," she shouted into the phone, her high-pitched voice floating through the heavy curtains surrounding my bed. "You should be dealing with this yourself."

Shivering on the narrow white exam table, I wondered what I had done wrong. Then I pulled back on my loose maternity pants and stumbled into the sunny parking lot, blinking back tears in the dazzling spring day, trying to understand the directions they sent me out with: Find a hotel within a few blocks of a hospital. Rest, monitor the bleeding. Don't go home—the forty-five-minute drive might be too far.

The next few days were a blur of lumpy motel beds, telephone calls to doctors, cramps. The pre-examination for my D&E finally arrived. First, the hospital required me to sign a legal form consenting to terminate the pregnancy. Then they explained I could, at no cost, have the remains incinerated by the hospital pathology department as medical waste, or for a fee have them taken to a funeral home for burial or cremation.

They inserted sticks of seaweed into my cervix and told me to go home for the night. A few hours later—when the contractions were regular, strong, and frequent—I knew we needed to go to the hospital.

"The patient appeared to be in active labor," say my charts, "and I explained this to the patient and offered her pain medication for vaginal delivery."

According to the charts, I was "adamant" in demanding a D&E. I remember that I definitely wanted the surgical procedure that was the safest option. One hour later, just as an anesthesiologist was slipping me into unconsciousness, I had the D&E and a little body, my little boy, slipped out. Around his neck, three times very tight, was the umbilical cord, source of his life, cause of his death.

This past spring, as the wildflowers started blooming around the simple cross we built for this baby, the Justice Department began trying to enforce the Bush administration's ban, and federal courts in three different cities heard arguments regarding the new law. Doctors explained that D&Es are the safest procedure in many cases, and that the law is particularly cruel to mothers like me whose babies were already dead. In hopes of bolstering their case, prosecutors sent federal subpoenas to various medical centers, asking for records of D&Es. There's an attorney somewhere, someday, who may poke through the files of my loss.

I didn't watch the trial, because I had another appointment to keep— another ultrasound. Lying on the crisp white paper, watching the monitor, I saw new life, the incredible spine, tiny fingers waving slowly across my uterus, a perfect thigh. Best of all, there it was, a strong four-chamber heart, beating steady and solid. A soft quiver, baby rolling, rippled across my belly.

"Everything looks wonderful," said my doctor. "This baby is doing great."

The Dialectic of Fat

BY **CATHERINE ORENSTEIN** • SUMMER 2005

FAT—OUR PREOCCUPATION WITH LOSING IT, its meaning for our identity, its effect on our desirability, work prospects, and social status—has become a trademark American obsession. As our waistlines expand (two-thirds of Americans are now overweight, according to government statistics; a third of us are officially obese), the press coverage and cultural reflections on our obesity crisis seem to be expanding endlessly as well. There's something for everyone, from the aggressively wistful makeover shows to Neil LaBute's recent and darkly cynical off-Broadway play *Fat Pig*, which charts a man's inability to publicly embrace the plus-size woman he loves.

It's no coincidence that these fat commentaries revolve around female bodies: even though women are statistically less likely than men to be over-weight (but somewhat more likely to be obese), feminists have long pointed out how the twin fantasies of beauty and thinness torment us.

The late Andrea Dworkin saw the battle of the sexes as waged on the female body in an unbroken history of oppression extending from ancient foot binding to modern-day waxing, tweezing, and dieting. Naomi Wolf, in *The Beauty Myth,* exposed the staggering amount of time, effort, and money that women are compelled to spend on their outward appearance in order to be socially acceptable, employable, and manageable. And Susie Orbach, in her 1978 clas-sic, *Fat Is a Feminist Issue,* saw story lines playing out upon women's flesh. She presented food as language and fat as a metaphor—a filter between us and the world, telling a story about our rela-tionship with our mothers, men, and ourselves. She urged women to stop dieting and instead seek to understand the reasons why they were fat in the first place. Fat, she wrote, has hidden agen-das and can express many things: the desire for protection, to remain unseen, or to rebel against imprisoning social ideals.

> "The late Andrea Dworkin saw the battle of the sexes as waged on the female body in an unbroken history of oppression extending from ancient foot binding to modern-day waxing, tweezing, and dieting."

But whatever wisdom we might have absorbed about the tyranny of the health and beauty industry and its relentless glorification of thinness seems to have had a limited, and ambiguous, impact. Today, eating disorders affect five to ten million Americans, most of them women. *Time* reports that 80 percent of children have been on a diet by the time they reach the fourth grade. According to one survey, 40 percent of women would trade three to five years of their lives to achieve their goal body weight. Mean-while, the ideal body has become even more narrowly defined, even as it is presented as increasingly accessible to all.

Part of the torment of fat, and fatism, is how it grows. Dominant Ameri-can (read privileged and white) body ideals have spread along with our pathologies. Despite the conventional wisdom about African American and Latino cultures' appreciation for more voluptuous female body types, eating disorders are on the rise for both those groups.

We are also exporting our body issues to faraway places, with disturb-ing success. Studies funded by Harvard Medical School tracked the eating habits of girls on the island of Fiji, where television was first introduced in 1995. Between 1995 and 1998, the islanders watched *Melrose Place* and *Bev-erly Hills 90210,* and 11 percent of the girls surveyed developed bulimia—a disease previously unknown to them. Television, it seems, can carry disease.

That is not to say those affected were unwilling victims. "The girls were articulate and explicit about why they were making themselves throw up," says the Harvard medical anthropologist Anne Becker, who led the study. "They felt that if they had a Jennifer Aniston body, they would look more modern and more Western, and they would have a better chance of getting a job." Their dream job? "Stewardess."

"Not only is fat still a feminist issue," Susie Orbach comments, "now it's a global feminist issue."

In an introduction to the 1990 reedition of her book, Orbach wrote enthusiastically about the progress that women had achieved since she had penned *Fat Is a Feminist Issue* twelve years earlier. But today Orbach—a psychotherapist and co-founder of the Women's Therapy Center Institute in New York City—is less optimistic. She says she underestimated the extent to which young women are "assaulted by visual culture—by mono-imagery." She also worries about the "normalization of disordered eating: that is, compulsive eating and dieting that is no longer considered abnormal."

Several forthcoming books, and substantial anecdotal evidence, echo Orbach's worries as we see the emergence of "pro-ana" websites created to support anorexics not in gaining weight but in more effectively *starving* themselves. (Visitors can click on "thinspiration" photos or seek tips on eating fewer than four hundred calories a day.)

Fortunately, as an intriguing new anthology points out, the stories fat tells about us aren't written in stone. In *Fat: The Anthropology of an Obsession,* thirteen anthropologists and an activist tell a few lesser-known plots.

In Niger, Rebecca Popenoe writes, desert Arabs idolize fat bodies, girls are force-fed, and women don extra clothing before stepping on the scale; stretch marks are beloved. In the world of fat pornography, Don Kulick observes, astonishingly obese women are eroticized as goddesses: instead of having sex, they have food. And in hip-hop culture, Joan Gross reminds us, girth is a sign of power. The term "phat" seeped into that culture through music, and its original meaning—a full, rich sound—expanded to an expression of general praise.

Indeed, it's hip-hop that provides the pseudo-reality show *Fat Actress* with one of its more memorable scenes: at the end of one episode, as credits roll, Kirstie Alley does a lap dance for the singer Kid Rock, accompanied by the Sir Mix-a-Lot song "Baby Got Back." "I'm tired of magazines / Sayin' flat butts are the thing," go the lyrics. "I like big butts!" After the deluge of tabloid photos and headlines that shouted Alley's weight as if it were a national threat, it's hard not to like a woman who dances to that. At the same time, it's worth noting that the lyrics—like the tabloids—are fixated on her fat.

Ms. Conversation: Lesley Gore and Kathleen Hanna

FALL 2005

THE MOST SUCCESSFUL female solo recording artist of the 1960s ("It's My Party," "You Don't Own Me") talks with the punk-rock star (from the bands Bikini Kill and Le Tigre) about feminism, the record industry, sexual abuse, karaoke, music, joy, and more.

KATHLEEN HANNA: *Lesley, I'm a real fan. First time I heard your voice, I went and bought everything of yours—trying to imitate you but find my own style. I wish I had a "feminist reason" for the connection I feel, but . . .*

LESLEY GORE: Well, a musical reason's okay, too!

HANNA: *The great thing about your new record* [Ever Since] *is that it's not a caricature of yourself. I'm sure some fans will always want "It's My Party." But in these new songs, I hear a grown woman's voice. It's not you ten or twenty years ago, yet I got the same chills. Even with a signature song like "You Don't Own Me," on this CD it's different from any version I've ever heard.*

GORE: A whole new arrangement, that's why. Same with "Out Here on My Own" [the hit from the film *Fame*], which I wrote and I've sung but never actually recorded until now. You know, this is my first album since 1976. I had to rethink those lyrics.

HANNA: *It doesn't sound like you thought about it at all.*

GORE: To have a song sound effortless takes an enormous amount of work! I've worked with some wonderful producers, Quincy Jones not being the least, back when I was only sixteen. In this case, we wanted the record to sound organic: four pieces, maybe some backgrounds—but no horns, strings, synthesizers. Just my voice—and great material.

HANNA: *Funny, I wrote "organic" in my notes! You accomplished that. And it's mixed perfectly—the production quality is really amazing, even more so for an indie. The sound is rich, super mellow—smoky—the music complements your voice without distracting from it. Your voice is lying on top of . . .*

GORE: Exactly.

HANNA: *I tuck my vocals. You're not tucking, you're lying right there on top. But it sure doesn't sound like karaoke. [Gore laughs.] You know what I mean: reverb here, vocals here. [Hanna laughs.] Hey, wait a minute! I used to be a karaoke host!*

GORE: You're kidding!

HANNA: *I had to reinvent myself, too. After being in one band, Bikini Kill, for nine years, then being caught in the Riot Grrrls phenomenon while the press anointed me Riot Grrrl Queen, I quit to start a rebelliously different project: more hard-core punk rock. I was tired of singing in a limited way and wanted to have more dynamics. It took me ten years to realize that if you sing full out for the whole song, it's not going anywhere.*

> **"How are we supposed to be artists in a world where you have to be a nineteen-year-old supermodel in order to get a record contract?"**
> —Kathleen Hanna

GORE: Also, if you don't pace yourself for a seventy-minute show, you're a mess.

HANNA: *Yes! I was destroying my voice. I want longevity, like you. So I needed to find new ways to sing and not become one-dimensional. Now I finally don't have to be the opposite of who I was; I can take from all aspects of my life. So how do you use everything, yet keep pushing the envelope? You've been at the top, but you're at your peak form now. That's important to me as a younger artist, in an industry where careers aren't being built anymore, artists aren't given time to develop and—*

GORE: And women have never been the favored gender in the recording business.

HANNA: [Laughing.] *Yeah! Where's the female Elvis Costello?*

GORE: Hel-LO!

HANNA: *Guys get support for their new projects. Costello is allowed to do a Burt Bacharach [collaboration]—*

GORE: Anything he wants. Which is fine. But what about women? The industry is even more one hit oriented than it used to be, and as—or more—male focused than ever. Unlike the film industry, there's almost never been a woman at the top of the music industry. Well, maybe Florence Greenberg in the 1960s, with Scepter Records.

HANNA: *We met with a woman who headed Elektra; she'd signed [the rap artist] Missy Elliott. Then we read she was about to get fired. So we didn't sign there.*

GORE: That's one reason I chose to go indie. In fact, with technology changing everything anyway, the "big boy" labels are becoming irrelevant.

HANNA: *I definitely think indies are the future of women in music. The weird thing is, after being indie all my life, my band, Le Tigre, went with a major label—Universal—for our latest record,* This Island. *Actually, we have our own label, Le Tigre Records, and we're keeping our already-independent releases. Of course, you've been on major labels, and now you just went—*

GORE: Indie! In fact, you've gone to the major I came from. [Laughter.]

HANNA: *So, what do you find the difference is?*

GORE: Freedom! Early on, basically I was working for the label. Quincy was great, but did I have much to say? No. Though I also didn't know much then. Why did *you* go with a non-indie after so long?

HANNA: *I was nineteen when I started, booking my own tours, driving the van. Screw you, industry, we won't play your crappy Britney Spears game, we're gonna do it ourselves! Empowering! After fifteen years, I realized that as a woman I've been trained to be a damn volunteer—and here I am selling records out of my car trunk, writing a check with one foot, on the phone with the other arm, reenacting all the women in my family being social workers. I thought, Maybe I could write better songs myself if I wasn't on the phone all the time! So, it's my feminist statement to say, finally, I want help! But even so, it's in our contract that we do what we want,* then *hand them the record.*

GORE: Good.

HANNA: *I do worry. How are we supposed to be artists in a world where you have to be a nineteen-year-old supermodel in order to get a record contract?*

GORE: Preferably with no voice, no rhythm.

HANNA: *We've worked with great people at Universal, but I was nervous. Our label-mate JoJo is fourteen and was the biggest thing since sliced bread the day we signed. I can't compete with JoJo, you know? Still, given how bad things are with the U.S. government, I thought, I'm not seeing a lot of feminist faces in the mainstream. So, it was like a science experiment: Can a feminist band make it right now?*

GORE: You've been touring, right?

HANNA: *We're just finishing eight months across Europe, and we're about to go out again for two more months, opening for Beck.*

GORE: I don't know how anyone survives such tours. Thank God my parents never let me go on one of those Dick Clark caravans. They work those kids unbelievably. Sometimes Clark flew me in for certain shows, but I never did the long hauls. Well, if I was working Vegas, maybe a four- or five-week stint.

HANNA: *Tell me, have you ever had a really bad experience, when your confidence gets wrecked?*

GORE: Are you kidding? Like once, I don't even remember the name of the record exec, but I was just told, "He passed on it." Period.

HANNA: *I've had indie labels pass on things I've done. Once, I had an awful experience. I was coming to consciousness as a feminist, working with sexual-abuse survivors, and I was pissed off, all the while mastering this really heavy record with this guy—who then asked me to go fetch coffee for him! I kept going into the parking lot, crying, then thinking of all the artists who've lumbered on. So, I dived back in, ordering him, "Turn up the bass."* [Gore laughs.] *How did you not totally freak out at only age sixteen?*

GORE: When you walked into the studio, it was all men. The only time you'd see another woman is when background singers came in—and that felt great. There was never even a woman assistant engineer. It was just the way it was.

HANNA: *How did you find feminism?*

GORE: When I first recorded "You Don't Own Me," I didn't think of it as a feminist song. Then seeing young women respond so completely . . . !

HANNA: *It's still modern in a lot of ways. The Slits have songs called "Love und Romance" and "Typical Girls" on the same theme.*

GORE: A former manager of mine once said, "No one took Lesley seriously because of 'It's My Party.'" You'd think "You Don't Own Me" would've changed that, but . . . So I was conscious while making this album that I intended to be taken seriously.

HANNA: *It is a serious record. But also, well, joyful. Songs like "Someday" and "Better Angels"—wow!*

GORE: The odd thing is if you'd hung out at the piano with me when I was seventeen, these would have been the types of songs we'd have been playing. I grew up listening to Ella Fitzgerald, Sarah Vaughan, Dinah Washington.

HANNA: *I also wanted to ask you about fans.*

GORE: Well, after "It's My Party" became a hit, the fans started—letters, calls, people sleeping on the lawn—a bizarre time. See, I was brought up fairly sheltered. I didn't know about lots of things until I started getting letters from young women who were being abused at home, who had alcoholic parents, battering boyfriends. It helped politicize me very quickly.

HANNA: *For me, it was "I'm a feminist!" so this song is about rape, or about fighting back. I wrote a lot about female conditioning. I was a white middle-class kid in college, too. But I'd survived abuse, which is part of what drew me into writing about it. And the response from women! It was—*

GORE: *Tremendous.* Women feel they can communicate with you, that you can kind of help. And I guess by doing what we do, we are helping. I like to think that.

· · ·

Letters

FOLLOWING *MS.*'s RELAUNCH of its 1972 "We Have Had Abortions" campaign, readers responded.

I just answered a call from *Ms.* to confirm that yes, I do want my name printed in the "We Had Abortions" area of the Fall issue. I have such mixed feelings about the entire thing. Sadness that it still needs to be said, and that a woman's right to autonomy over her body is still threatened. Fear of what could happen to me [for] making such a public admission. Relief that there is something I can do to stand up for my beliefs. And, finally, pride mixed with amusement that I was asked to do this in my ninth month of pregnancy.

With the deluge of stories about more and more clinics being closed and laws against driving a minor woman over state lines for an abortion, I had been feeling such a rage of hopelessness over the entire issue. I marched on Washington at the March for Women's Lives, I donated money to the cause, and I've escorted women through protest lines, but it all seems so futile. Despite the fact that I resent the need to make public a deeply private decision, I am happy to be able to contribute to what I hope to be the innumerable voices who declare that we have chosen to exercise control over our own bodies.

SHAWNA LISK-SPRESTER
Redwood City, Calif.
Fall 2006 issue

In 1969, when I was twenty, in college, unmarried, and living at home, I became pregnant. This was during the pre–*Roe v. Wade* days when there weren't many options available to unwed mothers. I could go to Sweden or Mexico. I opted for Mexico. . . .

I was given instructions that sounded more like an undercover operation than an abortion. I had to fly a specific airline, stay in a specific hotel, call a specific phone number for the clinic from a phone booth down the street from the hotel, and take two taxis to get to the clinic to assure I wasn't being followed.

I was terrified to do it and terrified not to go through with it. Traveling by myself and following the instructions to the letter, I found myself at a very clean clinic staffed with compassionate doctors and nurses. I woke in the post-op room with another girl in the bed beside me whose mother was with her. When she saw that I was alone, she came over to comfort me and stayed with me until I was able to leave. This all happened on the weekend that man first walked on the moon and my first niece was born. It's been thirty-seven years, and each year we celebrate my niece's birthday I think about the abortion I underwent when she was being born. I'm thankful that I was able to do it.

VICKI LANZING
Via email
Winter 2007 issue

A Brave Sisterhood

BY **BAY FANG** • WINTER 2006

O N ELECTION MORNING, the Jefaya mosque in eastern Kabul is packed with women of all ages, many in blue burqas, squeezed together in disorderly lines. While other polling sites across the Afghan capital remain quiet, with a lower turnout than expected, this one bustles with activity.

Women of the Shiite minority, historically one of the most mistreated groups in Afghanistan, have come out in force to make sure their voices are heard. But many, being illiterate, are having trouble navigating the seven-page ballot.

Halima, seventy-five, who like many Afghans goes by only one name, has a confused look on her wrinkled face. She has been sitting in the corner for at least half an hour, scanning the packed ballot like a newspaper. "I know it's very important to vote," she says, "so from eight a.m. I've been sitting here, looking for my candidate."

Afghanistan's historic parliamentary election on September 18 was the last step on the path to democracy dictated by the Bonn Agreement, which set out a process of democratization for the country after the fall of the Taliban in 2001. It was a significant step as well for women's participation in the country's political process, both as voters and as candidates. Of the 5,700 candidates running for 249 seats in the House of the People, or Wolesi Jirga—the lower house of parliament—and 420 seats on provincial councils, 575 were women. But the relatively low number of female candidates was deceiving, since the 2004 constitution had already determined that at least 25 percent of the seats in the House of the People would be filled with women.

> **"The week before the election . . . a gang of men with covered faces and AK-47s appeared and tried to make her group go with them. When the petite woman refused, they shot her in the leg."**

It's a remarkable boost in achievement for the female population of the country, considering that Afghanistan's problems are still magnified for women. Eighty percent of the country's women are illiterate. A woman dies every twenty-seven minutes in childbirth. Under an ineffectual judicial system, men illegally sell their daughters to prospective husbands, while women who are raped fear prosecution for adultery. Teenage girls and young women still set themselves on fire to escape forced marriages or violence.

Election workers in Kabul tally votes at a polling station.

A Brave Sisterhood

Women overcame years of gender apartheid—and even bullets—to run for office and vote in Afghanistan's recent elections.

BY BAY FANG
PHOTOGRAPHS BY ANDREA CAMUTO

ON ELECTION MORNING, THE JEFAYA mosque in eastern Kabul is packed with women of all ages, many in blue burqas, squeezed together in disorderly lines. While other polling sites across the Afghan capital remain quiet, with a lower turnout than expected, this one bustles with activity.

Women of the Shiite minority, historically one of the most mistreated groups in Afghanistan, have come out in force to make sure their voices are heard. But many, being illiterate, are having trouble navigating the seven-page ballot.

Halima, 75, who like many Afghans only goes by one name, has a confused look on her wrinkled face. She has been sitting in the corner for at least half an hour, scanning the packed ballot like a newspaper. "I know it's very important to vote," she says, "so from 8 a.m. I've been sitting here, looking for my candidate."

Many believe that women's political gains have been achieved faster than the society is ready for. But that couldn't stop women from running for office or voting.

On the day before the elections, an American organization hosts a gathering of women in the aging InterContinental Hotel in Kabul, high on a hill overlooking the city. For security reasons, its location had to be kept secret until the last minute, and bags are carefully inspected at the door. Inside, women candidates mingle with veteran women's rights workers from Afghanistan and beyond.

"Women work in offices now, and in government," says Laila Ahmadzai, program coordinator for the NGO Women for Afghan Women, who spent thirteen years in Pakistan as a refugee, returning to Kabul three years ago after the Taliban was driven from power. "When people moved to Pakistan, we saw different cultures and brought changes to our own lifestyles. Now women have more rights in their homes."

Hosai Andar is familiar with these changes. A forty-one-year-old with a ready smile, she has been running as a candidate in her home province of Ghazni, southwest of Kabul. She receives visitors in her small apartment, which doubles as campaign headquarters, but shoos the men out so she can speak freely. Under the Taliban regime, she ran an underground school for girls here. In four years, she says, five hundred girls attended, taking classes in math, physics, chemistry, English, and the Quran. When Taliban officials became suspicious, she told them she had a tailoring shop and taught girls handicrafts. She called the program Tailoring and Embroidery for Girls.

Andar had problems campaigning in Ghazni, a city that is largely under the control of Abdul Rasul Sayyaf, the feared leader of one of the main mujahideen groups that fought against the Soviets. "I don't trust my own mother," says Andar. "Everyone is from a political party. I tell them I'm running for one of the three seats set aside for women, but they know my campaign is very wide [in the constituency she hopes to serve]. People are tired of Sayyaf—they want democrats, educated people."

Many women ran on the platform of having "clean hands"—unstained by affiliation with armed factions and the violence or religious extremism of the country's past. But without strong political or financial backing, the new women parliamentarians could find themselves sidelined among the commanders and clerics who were expected to win the majority of seats in the House of the People.

The best hope is that the new female parliamentarians will have a moderating influence on their colleagues. "Afghan women can provide an important counterbalance to the political and religious extremism that threatens to undermine democracy in Afghanistan," said a February 2005 study done by the Women Waging Peace Policy Commission (now the Initiative for Inclusive Security Policy Commission), a Harvard University–launched group that explores conflicts around the globe.

But running for office in Afghanistan called for bravery far beyond that required of, say, an American woman running for the U.S. Congress. The candidate Malalai Joya, twenty-seven, a women's rights activist campaigning in the western Farah province, gained fame at the 2003 Afghan constitutional assembly by saying that the jihadi commanders who fought the civil war in the 1990s—many of whom were sitting there—were criminals and should face punishment from national and international courts. Death threats ensued, and Joya had to travel incognito for security reasons.

Hawa Nuristani faces similar pressure this time around. She lies back in bed with a grimace, crutches propped up next to her. The former television news presenter is running for a seat in her home province of Nuristan, an impoverished region bordering China, despite having heard that a mullah in Nuristan had issued a fatwa, or edict, that anyone voting for a woman was an infidel. Her sisters had begged her to restrict her travels to Kabul and its environs, especially since, unlike many of the male candidates, she had no money to hire cars or gunmen and did much of her campaigning on foot. But the week before the election, as she was walking to a remote village, a gang of men with covered faces and AK-47s appeared and tried to make her group go with them. When the petite woman refused, they shot her in the leg.

"The fact that I am a candidate to parliament in itself is positive work," Nuristani says. "We shouldn't have the expectation that everything will change overnight. Tradition is still ruling; it's a religious society."

Nuristani wanted to run in Nuristan rather than Kabul, where she now lives, because she thought the people of Nuristan—especially the women— needed more help to bring about change. However, she says in doing so they must be careful not to move too fast. "If you want to go to the roof, you have to go step by step," she says. "In Nuristan, women's faces are totally covered. You can't tell them, suddenly, 'Lower your scarf.' That would create a bad reaction."

Most of the candidates have faced a steep political learning curve. Nasrine Gross, an Afghan American women's rights activist, ran a training seminar for women candidates in the run-up to the election, introducing them to such concepts as fundraising and public speaking. Her training guide includes sections titled "Dealing with Men's One-Upmanship" and lessons on how to make people remember you. About two hundred candidates, from the ages of eighteen to seventy-three, attended. Once elected, Gross says, the women will need extensive coaching on basics such as how laws are made and how to link up with other women to form voting blocs.

She tells the story of one thirty-one-year-old candidate with six children from Ghor province who was engaged at the age of ten and married at twelve. With only a sixth-grade education, she wanted to run on a platform of education for women. "Women have a very local, native understanding of the problems in their areas," says Gross. "It's important that they gain a voice."

Massouda Jalal, the minister for women's affairs, agrees. She was a candidate for president in October 2004, campaigning in a rickety yellow taxicab with her husband/manager while other candidates drove around in large SUVs with an entourage of staffers. Like the women running for parliament this year, she ran as an independent with little financial backing.

"I am trying to give them training, resource centers, and a chance to meet other female parliamentarians," says Jalal. "I expect them to develop a sisterhood, and stand for women's rights." She has a ten-year plan, she says, by the end of which time there should be no need for a ministry of women's affairs.

But many think Jalal and others are too optimistic. A month after the election, Ali Mohaqiq Nasab, editor of the magazine *Haqoq-e-Zan* (Women's Rights), was sentenced to two years in jail for blasphemy, because of articles he wrote that questioned the severity of Islamic punishments for crimes such as adultery. Jalal said that this was due to parts of the Afghan government still needing reform, and she made an oblique reference to those Islamic clerics called the "ulema," who continue to dominate Afghan courts.

"We need legal and judicial reform," Jalal declared. "There are a lot of unprofessionals and uncertified people working in the judicial area."

Back at the Jefaya mosque, Halima finally finishes voting. She puts her ballot in the box, lowers her burqa, and walks out into the blinding sun to find her husband and children. "I don't usually get to come out and participate," she says. "Today is a great day."

POSTSCRIPT: After accusations of election fraud delayed official results, it was announced that seventy-three women won election to parliament. Malalai Joya won an unreserved seat, garnering the second-largest number of votes in Farah. Hawa Nuristani won. Hosai Andar lost. Several candidates were wounded and eight killed during their campaigns. Warlords, clerics, and candidates linked to warlords won the majority of seats in the House of the People, including Abdul Rasul Sayyaf, who won seats for himself and his supporters. Warlords and allies also constituted a substantial majority of those elected to provincial councils, which elect thirty-four of the delegates to the House of Elders.

Since the Taliban stormed back into power in August 2021, two decades of gains for women's rights in Afghanistan hang in the balance. Under Taliban control once again, Afghan women and girls stand to suffer the ongoing loss of basic freedoms and safety.

Ms.'s real-time reporting has long featured the voices of women on the ground—including in this latest era of crisis. As Sahar Azimi, news anchor and international multimedia broadcaster for Voice of America, explained to *Ms.*, women and girls in Afghanistan didn't fight "to be outspoken, only to suddenly sacrifice all that they have learned." She proclaimed, "Once you teach a bird to fly, you cannot imprison them. Our women are not meant to be caged, and we must support them in finding freedom from the Taliban's chains once again."

Letters

After reading *Ms.* magazine's Spring 2007 article "Changing His Name" by Bailey Porter, the state senator Vicki Walker wanted to clarify Oregon's marriage statutes to bring them into the twenty-first century. [So] Senator Walker set about drafting an amendment to an already existing marriage certificate bill moving from the Oregon House to the Senate.

The amendment adds a "legal name upon marriage" line for both the bride and the groom on the Oregon application, license, and record of marriage. The amendment specifies that the surname may be changed to either the bride's or the groom's surname or to a hyphenated combination of the surnames of both spouses. (If same-sex domestic partnerships become law in Oregon, these amendments will also apply to the statutes that govern domestic partnerships.)

The Oregon Senate and House approved the bill, and it is expected to be signed by Governor Ted Kulongoski. Thank you for inspiring Senator Walker to make this great stride for equality in Oregon.

ALLISON DE LA TORRE, legislative assistant to State Senator Vicki Walker
Salem, Ore.
Summer 2007 issue

Before his election, Barack Obama assured *Ms.* publisher Eleanor Smeal that he too was a feminist. Following his inauguration, *Ms.* captured the excitement of Obama's new administration and the president's pledge to address issues of long concern to feminists. Near the end of his presidency, at a White House summit on women, he famously declared, "I may be a little grayer than I was eight years ago, but this is what a feminist looks like."

Too Poor to Parent?

BY **GAYLYNN BURROUGHS** • SPRING 2008

WHEN A RECURRING PLUMBING PROBLEM in an upstairs unit caused raw sewage to seep into her New York City apartment, twenty-two-year-old Lisa (not her real name) called social services for help. She had repeatedly asked her landlord to fix the problem, but he had been unresponsive. Now the smell was unbearable, and Lisa feared for the health and safety of her two young children.

When the caseworker arrived, she observed that the apartment had no lights and that food was spoiling in the refrigerator. Lisa explained that she did not have the money to pay her electric bill that month, but would have the money in a few weeks. She asked whether the caseworker could help get them into a family shelter. The caseworker promised she would help—but left Lisa in the apartment and took the children, who were then placed in foster care.

> **"When state child-welfare workers come to remove children from Black mothers' homes, they rarely cite poverty as the factor putting a child at risk."**

Months later, the apartment is cleaned up. Lisa still does not have her children.

Monique (also a pseudonym), too, lost her children to foster care despite all her efforts to keep her family united. The impoverished Georgia mother of three had been left by her boyfriend after discovering that their infant son needed heart surgery. Undeterred, she sent her older children to live with family out of state, while she moved to a shelter close to the hospital. When the baby recovered, she moved to New York and was reunited with her other kids.

Unemployed and without financial resources, Monique hoped to live with family, but when they couldn't take her in, she looked for a shelter again. This time, though, she got caught up in endless red tape from the emergency housing *and* medical systems—the latter of which kept her waiting months for an appointment with a cardiologist and medication for her child.

Finally, settled in an apartment lent by a friend, Monique began a job search, leaving the baby at home with a sitter, and that's when the *real* nightmare began. One day police found the baby alone and took him into protective custody. The next day, child-welfare officials charged Monique with inadequate guardianship *and* medical neglect (because the child hadn't seen a cardiologist or gotten his medication), and put all three children in foster care. Monique can now visit them only once a week, supervised, for just two hours.

It is probably fair to say that most women with children worry about their ability as mothers. Are they spending enough time with them? Are they disciplining them correctly? Are they feeding them properly? When should they take them to the doctor, and when is something not that serious? But one thing most women in the United States do not worry about is the possibility of the state removing children from their care. For a sizable subset of women, though—especially poor Black mothers like Lisa and Monique—that possibility is very real.

Black children are the most overrepresented demographic in foster care nationwide. According to the U.S. Government Accountability Office, Black children make up 34 percent of the foster-care population, but only 15 percent of the general child population. In 2004, Black children were more than twice as likely to enter foster care as white children. Even among other minority groups, Black mothers are more likely to lose their children to the state than Hispanic or Asian American parents—groups that are slightly underrepresented in foster care.

The reason for this disparity? Study after study reviewed by the Northwestern University law professor Dorothy Roberts in her 2002 book, *Shattered Bonds: The Color of Child Welfare,* shows that poverty is the leading cause of children landing in foster care. According to one researcher, poor families are up to twenty-two times more likely to be involved in the child-welfare system than wealthier families. And nationwide, Black people are four times more likely than other groups to live in poverty.

But when state child-welfare workers come to remove children from Black mothers' homes, they rarely cite poverty as the factor putting a child at risk. Instead, these mothers are told that they neglected their children by failing to provide adequate food, clothing, shelter, education, or medical care. The failure is always personal, and these mothers and children are almost always made to suffer individually for the consequences of one of the United States' most pressing social problems.

Federal spending for foster care skyrocketed in the 1980s, but funding for antipoverty services to prevent foster-care placement—or speed reunification with birth parents—stagnated. As explained by the child-welfare expert Martin Guggenheim, a professor at New York University School of Law, "Between 1981 and 1983, federal foster-care spending grew by more than 400 percent in real terms, while preventive and reunification spending grew by only 14 percent, and all other funds available for social services to the poor declined."

As a result of the failure to fund programs servicing poor families—helping them secure housing, jobs, health care, subsidized day care, mental health services, and drug treatment programs—the number of poor children in foster care began to soar. In 1986, the foster-care population numbered around 280,000 children. Just five years later, that number had jumped by 53 percent to 429,000. The latest data available shows an estimated 514,000 children in foster care.

Troubled not only by the number of children in foster care but by their longer stays in the system, Congress passed the Adoption and Safe Families Act (ASFA) in 1997. Its purpose is to achieve a permanent family environment more quickly for children in foster care, but the legislation accomplishes that goal by placing time limits on family reunification—thus encouraging adoption instead of the return of children to their parents.

Supporters of ASFA claim that the legislation is child-friendly because it measures time from the perspective of a child's development and strives to place children in safe homes away from "bad parents" who are unlikely to stop putting their children in harm's way. Certainly there are situations in which temporarily placing a child in foster care, or even terminating parental rights, is the only responsible outcome. However, as Guggenheim points out, "ASFA makes no distinction between parents whose children were removed because of parental abuse and parents whose only crime is being too poor to raise their children in a clean and safe environment without additional benefits the government refuses to supply."

While ASFA was making it more difficult for some parents to win back their children, changes in federal antipoverty policies were making it more difficult for families struggling to keep their children. President Clinton's welfare reform in the mid-1990s eliminated federal cash assistance for single mothers and their children in favor of block grants to states, so individual states now have wide discretion to set benefit levels, establish work requirements for welfare assistance, and create time limits for public assistance. For some women, the effect of welfare reform was a low-paying job or unemployment, coupled with the loss of a government safety net. Still poor, many of these women continued to lose their children because of the predictable consequences of poverty: lack of health care, inadequate housing, and simply the inability to meet basic needs.

Yet public perception of parents accused of neglecting their children remains extremely negative, regardless of the actual allegations. Child-welfare workers in New York City, citing emergency conditions, routinely remove poor children from their homes without notifying the parents, without securing a court order, and without informing parents of their legal rights. Sometimes they even remove children from school, day care, or a friend's home without giving parental notice. It's not uncommon in court on Monday morning to meet frantic parents whose children were removed on Friday night and who have still not learned where their children were taken.

The legal system often provides no haven for these parents. Based on even the flimsiest allegations, they are essentially presumed guilty and pressured to participate in various cookie-cutter services that often do not directly address the concerns that brought them to court. For example, after her children went into foster care, Lisa was asked to attend parenting classes, undergo a mental health evaluation, seek therapy, and submit to random drug testing before her children could be returned. But child-welfare authorities did not assist her in repairing her home or finding a new apartment, nor have they gone after her landlord for allowing deplorable conditions. Lisa's poverty has led government authorities to pathologize her; she's automatically considered sick, careless, or otherwise unfit if she attempts to parent while poor.

And what about children who are physically or sexually abused by their parents? A myth of child welfare is that foster care is full of such children, but in fact the majority of children who encounter the child-welfare system have *not* been abused. At least 60 percent of child-welfare cases in this country involve solely allegations of neglect. Lacking private resources, poor women may also come to the attention of government authorities more often than other mothers do, because they must often rely on public services such as shelters, public hospitals, and state welfare offices. That gives government workers more opportunities to judge, and report on, parental fitness. So poor mothers must cope not only with the daily frustrations of parenting but also with the crushing gaze of the state.

Until this country comes to terms with its culpability in allowing widespread poverty to exist, poor Black mothers will continue to lose their children to the state. And we will continue to label these women "bad mothers" to assuage our own guilt.

Forty Years of
Women's Studies

BY **BEVERLY GUY-SHEFTALL** • SPRING 2009

WOMEN'S STUDIES, as a distinct entity within U.S. higher education, made its debut in 1970 with the establishment of the first program at San Diego State University. Forty years later, there are more than nine hundred programs in the United States, boasting well over ten thousand courses and an enrollment larger than that of any other interdisciplinary field. And women's studies has gone international in a big way: students can find programs and research centers everywhere from Argentina to India to Egypt to Japan to Uganda—more than forty countries in all, from nearly every region of the globe.

During the 1970s, the pioneers of women's studies focused on establishing the field as a separate discipline with autonomous programs. In the 1980s, the focus expanded to include "mainstreaming" women's studies throughout the established curriculum, incorporating feminist scholarship within many academic disciplines. In that way, women's studies wouldn't remain in an academic ghetto, but could begin to transform and gender balance every aspect of the curriculum.

Also in the 1980s, women of color began to critique both women's studies and gender-focused curriculum projects for their relative lack of attention to questions of race, ethnicity, class, and cultural differences.

Responding to such critiques, a new field of study emerged—Black women's studies, which now provides a framework for moving women of color from the margins of women's studies to its center. The 1982 book *All the Women Are White, All the Blacks Are Men, but Some of Us Are Brave* (edited by Gloria Hull, Patricia Bell Scott, and Barbara Smith) helped catalyze this transformation of women's studies, providing

> **"Because of its potential for societal transformation, women's studies should be supported more than ever during this paradoxical period of assault or backlash."**

a theoretical rationale for incorporating "minority women's studies" and "intersectional" analyses into all teaching and research on women.

In these forty years since its inception, women's studies has revamped and revitalized major disciplines in the academy. It has challenged curricular and pedagogical practice. It has disrupted the male-centered canon. It has altered or blurred the boundaries between disciplines. It has introduced the social construction of gender and its intersections with race, class, ethnicity, and sexuality as a major focus of inquiry. And it has experienced phenomenal and unanticipated growth, becoming institutionalized on college and university campuses, spurring the hiring of feminist faculty, adding graduate courses of groundbreaking content, generating a large body of educational resources, and providing the impetus for the establishment of feminist research centers. It has stimulated the development of *other* academic fields as well: gay and lesbian studies, cultural studies, gender studies, men's studies, peace studies, and more.

Even more compelling, perhaps, are the profound changes that have occurred over the past forty years as a result of the feminist activism, teaching, and research stimulated by women's studies. There is heightened consciousness and advocacy around rape, incest, battering, sexual harassment, sex trafficking, the feminization of poverty, and health disparities related to race, gender, and class. In addition, there is more intense dialogue about government-subsidized child care, health-care reform, sex equity in education, and spousal leave. It is unfortunately still the case that empowerment strategies for women do not necessarily address the particular experiences and needs of women of color or poor women, but this just gives women's studies scholars and activists a challenge for the future.

Because of its potential for societal transformation, women's studies should be supported more than ever during this paradoxical period of assault or backlash, on the one hand, and increased demand from students plus the growing imperatives of diversity and inclusion, on the other. A well-organized right-wing movement, inside and outside higher education, still employs outmoded but persistent racist, sexist, and homophobic schemes to try to reverse progressive reforms.

This is the greatest challenge for our field: to transcend the boundaries of race, ethnicity, class, sexuality, age, geography, and language in the interest of a feminism that is expansive and responsive. After forty years, we know that women's studies is more than up to it.

Intersections

BY **BONNIE THORNTON DILL** • SPRING 2009

AS A BLACK SCHOLAR writing about women's issues in the late 1970s, I joined others in arguing that women's studies needed to incorporate a more complex approach to understanding women's lives. My colleagues and I contended that the gender analyses of that period were too often derived from the experiences of white middle-class women and ignored the oft-untold stories of women of color and those without economic privilege. We wanted feminist theory to incorporate the notion of difference, beginning with race, ethnicity, class, and culture.

Today, one of the *first* things students learn in women's studies classes is how to look at women's lives through these multiple lenses. The concept of intersectionality has been a key factor in this transition. Intersectionality has brought the distinctive knowledge and perspectives of previously ignored groups of women into general discussion and awareness and has shown how the experience of gender differs by race, class, and other dimensions of inequality.

For example, one impact of gender in schools is that girls are more likely than boys to be steered away from math and science. Class differences then compound the effects of gender, because low-income girls interested in math and science are likely to attend schools with poorly equipped labs and fewer certified teachers—thus their training may make it harder for them to compete successfully at higher levels. Race adds another layer of differentiation because white and middle-class teachers—who are the majority of educators—are likely to have higher expectations of white girls than of Black girls. As research has shown, they give white girls tasks that develop their academic abilities while giving Black girls tasks that focus on their social maturity and caretaking competencies.

> "We wanted feminist theory to incorporate the notion of difference, beginning with race, ethnicity, class, and culture."

Women's studies students tend to grasp the concept of intersectionality most readily in relationship to personal identity. They understand immediately that their sense of self is multifaceted, that they have been shaped by a number of different (and sometimes conflicting) social factors, and that their behaviors cannot be understood in a one-dimensional manner.

Yet intersectionality is also an important way of understanding the organization of society—the distribution of power within it and the relationship of power and privilege to individual experience. At the societal level, intersectional analysis seeks to reveal the ways systems of power are used to develop and maintain privileges for some groups and deprivations for others. As an example, well-financed and well-equipped public services—schools, health and recreational facilities, libraries—are more likely to be located in communities with high concentrations of middle- and upper-income white people.

Finally, intersectionality is a tool for social justice. Its focus is to transform knowledge by fully incorporating the ideas, experiences, and critical perspectives of previously excluded groups. That knowledge can then be used to advocate for policies and practices that will eliminate inequality.

·   ·   ·

Letters

Thank you for your touching article regarding the life of Dr. George Tiller ["A Man Who Trusted Women," Summer 2009] and the families he helped save. Antichoice conservatives often speak of the "freedom" we soldiers fight for, but in truth people like Dr. Tiller are the true fighters of freedom for women everywhere. George Tiller woke up each day risking his life so that women could have the freedom to choose. For him, the fighting never stopped, and even when the workday was over, the threats of losing his life for something he believed in followed him. He never took off the uniform, he was never off duty, and he rarely got recognized for the dangerous yet noble line of work he chose. I am in awe of Dr. Tiller and his work, for I cannot ever imagine myself doing the dangerous yet highly necessary work he did. To Dr. Tiller and abortion providers everywhere: thank you. In fighting for women's right to choose, you enhanced the lives of my mother, sisters, friends, classmates, and fellow soldiers, and as a result you also enhanced mine.

SGT. MARC LOI
Baghdad, Iraq
Fall 2009 issue

A MAN WHO TRUSTED WOMEN

DR. GEORGE TILLER LEAVES A LEGACY OF COURAGE, TENACITY AND AN ABIDING DEDICATION TO WOMEN'S RIGHTS

BY MICHELE KORT

DR. GEORGE TILLER PLANNED TO BE A DERMATOLOGIST. He could have led a comfortable, secure life with his wife, Jeanne, their four children and, ultimately, their 10 grandchildren. Instead, Tiller decided to enlist in what shouldn't be—but is—one of the most perilous jobs in the United States: women's reproductive health care.

In addition to a family practice, Tiller decided to treat women who chose to have abortions. It was a specialty that did not become legal nationally until 1973 with the U.S. Supreme Court's decision in *Roe v. Wade*. Nonetheless, some brave physicians performed abortions on the sly before then, risking their licenses and livelihoods because they recognized how strong women's needs were for their services.

George Tiller's father, Jack, was one of them. A family practice physician himself, Jack died in a 1970 plane crash that also took the lives of his wife, daughter and son-in-law—a tragedy that led George to leave dermatology, return to his hometown of Wichita, Kan., and take over for his father. That was when the younger Tiller learned, to his great surprise, that his father had been performing abortions, inspired to do so in the mid-1940s after a woman he had refused to help lost her life from a botched abortion. Would the new Dr. Tiller, some patients asked, be willing to help?

He eventually said yes, taking on a lifelong mission that by then had become legal. Tiller called it "making the world a better place...one woman at a time."

Over the decades, given a highly organized movement of escalating vehemence and, ultimately, violence against abortion providers—it proved a dangerous undertaking. Only a doctor steadfast about a woman's right to choose would dare take it on.

"SOME PEOPLE WANT TO WALK ACROSS THE bridge, others want to follow," says Susan Hill, speaking of pioneering abortion providers like herself and George Tiller. "Some people are on the front lines."

Hill, who had been a hospital social worker, helped open an abortion clinic just two weeks after *Roe v. Wade* was decided, and has subsequently operated as many as 11 at a time in various underserved communities. Like Tiller, she came to know not just the gratitude of her patients, but the horror of anti-abortion terrorism. At first, however, there were just nuns protesting at her clinic, sent by their church. "Peaceful," says Hill.

As early as 1976, though, peaceful protests turned violent. "The rhetoric escalated, the protests outside clinics escalated, we started to get threatened," says Hill. Anti-abortion extremists turned to arson, bombings, severe vandalism. "We used to say, 'Gee, where are the nuns?'" says Hill.

Tiller, too, hadn't expected terrorism—like having his clinic bombed in 1986. Some 1,100 were arrested for blockading Tiller's clinic during the "Summer of Mercy" demonstrations organized by Operation Rescue in 1991, and even on the most ordinary day five to 10 protestors showed up. Besides being bombed, the clinic was also repeatedly vandalized—the last time this past May.

"While I was developing this practice between 1973 and 1985 I thought I was just Joe Blow family physician, raising my kids, stamping out disease and taking family vacations," he told the Feminist Majority Foundation's National Young Women's Leadership Conference in March 2008. "[But] it has been impressed on me that there are a lot of people in the United States who don't like what we do."

He used a similar dark humor in telling conferees, "The phrase 'a shot in the arm'...has had an entirely different meaning to me." Anti-abortion extremist Rachelle "Shelley" Shannon shot Tiller in both arms in 1993 during an assassination attempt as he tried to leave his clinic. The attack didn't stop him: He just hired a Brink's armored car for a time to take him to and from work, and gradually built his clinic into a fortress. "Hell no, we won't go" became his motto.

Tiller had become particularly known by anti-abortion forces—and demonized with such epithets as "Tiller the Killer"—because he was a dedicated advocate and political activist for women's right to choose. In 2002, the anti-abortion group Operation Rescue and its leader, Troy Newman, moved to Wichita from Southern California with the express purpose of closing down Tiller's clinic. In subsequent years, Newman employed aggressive and highly unsettling harassment of Tiller, his family and clinic workers.

Tiller also became well-known for providing what the anti-abortion movement turned into a hot-button rallying point: *late* abortions, performed at the end of the second or third trimester. Most providers don't perform these, both because they're highly specialized and for fear of running afoul of ever-more-stringent state and federal laws regulating what techniques can be employed.

Blinded by inflammatory rhetoric, the country lost sight of what late abortions *really* are: rare procedures needed by women carrying fetuses that have died or carry severe abnormalities, or for women facing irreparable physical or mental harm should they continue their pregnancies. Here's how Tiller explained one significant reason for late abortions:

"Chromosomal abnormalities make up about 24 percent of our [late abortion] patients, and sometimes the heart, the lung, the intestines, all of this is outside of the body [of the fetus]. Most places in the United States say that even if you have this kind of a problem you may not have a termination of pregnancy. ...What this says is that...women are not smart enough, they are not tough enough and they do not love enough to make these family decisions about their children and their families."

IN HER 28TH WEEK OF A VERY WANTED PREGNANCY IN 2000, Miriam Kleiman, a government employee in Washington, D.C., and her husband, Jason, learned that their male fetus had a severe brain malformation. He would probably die shortly after birth.

The couple immediately went for second, third and fourth opinions. The news stayed the same.

"This is not a fair life for a baby," they decided. "Even with every medical intervention, the baby's going to die. It's not if,

TILLER BELIEVED IN "MAKING THE WORLD A BETTER PLACE ...ONE WOMAN AT A TIME."

Domestic Workers
Take It to the Streets

BY **PREMILLA NADASEN** • FALL 2009

FOR MORE THAN TWO YEARS, Irene, a Colombian woman in her mid-sixties, slept in the sewage-filled basement of a house in the New York City area. Upstairs, she worked an average of seventy-two hours a week—cleaning, cooking, and caring for a disabled boy. Her wages: less than $2 an hour.

When Irene (not her real name) was suddenly fired without notice or severance, she was distraught, despite the privations she'd endured. "[My boss] offered no explanation. I asked her for permission to stay in the house that night. . . . I could not even sleep thinking about where I would go next."

Her story would have remained unknown, her former employers unchallenged, had she not come upon Domestic Workers United (DWU), a New York City organization fighting for the

> "Major U.S. unions have long favored manufacturing over service-sector workers . . . job categories where white men tend to dominate."

rights of an estimated 200,000 housekeepers, nannies, and caregivers for the elderly. DWU demanded back pay and a public apology from Irene's employers and launched a boycott of the Italian restaurant they owned. It also led a public "shaming" outside the house where Irene had given so much for so little compensation: "Tell Dem Slavery Done," read the signs held by protesters, appropriating Old South vernacular for today's version of servitude.

Last February, after a four-year battle, Irene won a court settlement for an undisclosed amount. Once again, DWU had shown itself to be at the vanguard of a growing, innovative global movement to organize private household workers. It's not an easy task. Such workers are among the most challenging to find and talk to, let alone unionize. They labor in individual homes rather than larger workplaces, frequently change employers, speak a polyglot of languages, and are often undocumented, making them wary of outsiders.

They're without an umbrella of labor protection as well. When the Fair Labor Standards Act (FLSA) and National Labor Relations Act were passed in the 1930s as part of the landmark New Deal legislation, domestic and agricultural workers were purposefully excluded—because southern congressmen insisted on control over "their" African American labor force. New Deal supporters acquiesced. In fact, in 1938 President Roosevelt responded to FLSA opponents, who claimed the bill would require employers to "pay your Negro girl 11 dollars a week," with the assurance that "no law ever suggested intended a minimum wages and hours bill to apply to domestic help." Domestic workers thus were not guaranteed the rights to minimum wage, overtime pay, and collective bargaining that were afforded other U.S. workers.

Nor were they championed by the twentieth-century labor movement. The American Federation of Labor and the Congress of Industrial Organizations (now the AFL-CIO), in the first half of the twentieth century, tolerated segregation and discrimination among their member unions, as well as the exclusion of women, African Americans, and other people of color. Equally important, major U.S. unions have long favored manufacturing over service-sector workers, full-timers over part-timers, skilled over unskilled workers, and steady over intermittent workers—job categories where white men tend to dominate.

Nonetheless, domestic workers do have a long history of organizing. They formed associations in the 1930s and again in the 1960s and 1970s. The most recent campaigns have come at a propitious moment: the mainstream labor movement is in crisis, battling declining membership and facing mounting challenges as a result of free trade and mobile capital.

DWU organizers are modeling alternative strategies. Instead of going into workplaces and getting employees to sign union cards, DWU organizers converge on New York playgrounds to meet other domestic workers and pass out buttons, brochures, and flyers, then sit down to chat with them. DWU directly assists workers like Irene by publicizing their cases and pushing for judicial remedies. The group has won more than $450,000 in back wages for domestic workers through the twenty-plus lawsuits it has brought against exploitative employers.

DWU uses another novel strategy: it takes pay and benefit negotiations straight to state and local legislatures, bypassing employers altogether. The group has gotten legislation passed in Nassau County (on Long Island) and New York City requiring employment agencies to inform domestic workers of their rights and employers of their responsibilities.

Now DWU is pushing for a precedent-setting New York State Domestic Workers' Bill of Rights that will guarantee household employees such basic rights as overtime pay, paid sick leave and holidays, and cost-of-living raises.

"The Domestic Workers' Bill of Rights is a model for innovative labor laws to protect vulnerable and informal sector workers," says Ai-jen Poo, the lead organizer of DWU. And the bill's impact could reverberate well beyond the boundaries of New York state. As the assembly member Keith Wright, sponsor of the bill, explains, "We are hoping that this legislation will become a model for similar laws throughout the country."

Because domestic workers still lack the basic protections accorded other workers, they are often stiffed on pay and benefits. African American women domestic workers organizing in the 1970s gained a few basic rights, such as minimum wage, but the sheer number of work sites, the power imbalance between employers and employees, and the fact that domestic workers still cannot legally form a union make enforcement difficult. Nine out of ten workers don't receive health insurance from their employers, and just over one-quarter earn below the poverty line. Two-thirds of the domestic workers surveyed don't receive overtime. DWU's proposed bill of rights would upend those statistics.

The work of DWU and similar organizations gives workers a voice and hope that the patterns of exploitation may be addressed. As Irene said at a public testimonial, "I, Irene, ask with all my heart to those who make the laws—the governor, Congress, and everyone here today—to do your part so that domestic workers are heard. We are fighting for a just cause."

HISTORICALLY AND STILL TODAY the vast majority of America's 2.5 million domestic employees—nannies, home health aides, housecleaners—are women; more than half of the domestic workforce is women of color. The global pandemic shined a light on the crucial importance of essential labor that's too often invisible in the public eye. A movement continues to mobilize across the United States—winning campaigns to ensure fair wages, legal protection, and respect and recognition for the vital role of those who make all work possible. To date, ten states and the cities of Philadelphia and Seattle have passed domestic workers' bills of rights.

CHAPTER 5

2010s

MS. BEGAN THE DECADE doubling down on investigative reporting, winning awards for its work to uncover the network of extremists linked to the assassination of Dr. George Tiller, documenting the criminal prosecution of young girls who had been trafficked for sex, and the cover-up of rapes in the military. The magazine's campaign—Rape Is Rape—helped secure changes in the FBI's more than eighty-year-old definition of rape to finally include *all* forms of rape.

Ms. celebrated its fortieth anniversary with a major two-day symposium at Stanford University and events at the National Press Club in Washington, D.C., and the Paley Center for Media in New York City. And in 2017, *Ms.* got a street named after it in New York City, near its birthplace at the former offices of *New York* magazine.

But the decade was disrupted by deep political upheaval. The United States went from reelecting its first Black president . . . to the Democratic Party running a feminist woman candidate for president . . . to the devastating outcome of the 2016 election. The Trump administration's all-out war on women meant that *Ms.*'s coverage and presence took on new and crucial import: the entire movement was front and center like never before, from the Women's March to #MeToo to Black Lives Matter.

Then president Barack Obama awards Gloria Steinem the Presidential Medal of Freedom in a ceremony at the White House in 2013. In her speech at a *Ms.* event at the National Press Club celebrating the honor, Steinem said, "It would be crazy if I didn't understand that this was a medal for the entire women's movement." She proclaimed, "Our revolution has just begun."

Not a Lone Wolf

BY **AMANDA ROBB** • SPRING 2010

AS SOON as Scott Roeder was named the sole suspect in the point-blank shooting death of the Wichita, Kansas, abortion provider Dr. George Tiller in the vestibule of the Reformation Lutheran Church Tiller attended, a predictable story began to be told. Following the lead of a recent Department of Homeland Security report characterizing right-wing terrorists as lone wolves, the *Los Angeles Times,* CNN, ABC, NBC, and Fox News all ran stories calling Roeder a "lone wolf" gunman.

It is the oldest, possibly most dangerous abortion story out there.

But for loners, these guys have a lot of friends. A lot of the same ones, in fact. Over the past six months, I have interviewed Scott Roeder more than a dozen times, met several times with his supporters at the Sedgwick County Courthouse in Wichita where he was tried and convicted, and permissibly recorded numerous three-way telephone conversations Roeder had me place to his friends. Using information gleaned from these sources, along with public records, I was able to piece together the close, long-term, and ongoing relationship between Roeder and other antiabortion extremists who advocate murder and violent attacks on abortion providers.

> **"The how-to manual for would-be terrorists provides instructions on vandalizing clinics, including arson, super-gluing locks, constructing bombs, and 'disarming the persons perpetrating the [abortions] by removing their hands.'"**

Now meet Roeder's antiabortion associates, beginning with Roeder himself.

Scott Roeder, fifty-two, was born in Denver. His family moved to Topeka, Kansas, when he was a toddler. He worked for the Kansas City electric company, and at age twenty-eight he married and had a son. For about five years family life was stable, but then in the early 1990s Roeder suddenly could not cope—with anything.

While under financial stress in 1992, Roeder happened upon the right-wing televangelist Pat Robertson's *700 Club* on television. He claims he fell to his knees and became a born-again Christian. According to his own recollections and those of his ex-wife, he immediately fixated on what he considered two earthly evils: taxes and abortion.

In very short order, he affiliated himself with Christian antigovernment groups such as the Freemen militia and eventually became involved with antiabortion groups such as Operation Rescue and the Army of God, the latter of which openly sanctions the use of violence to stop abortion.

Roeder told me that his first act as an antiabortion activist was to protest outside a Kansas City women's clinic. Among the protesters he came to know were Anthony Leake, a proponent of the "justifiable homicide" of abortion doctors, and Eugene Frye, the owner of a Kansas City construction company who, together with another antiabortion activist, had been arrested in 1990 for attempting to reinsert the feeding tube of a Missouri woman in a persistent vegetative state. Frye had also been arrested for blockading abortion clinics during the 1991 Summer of Mercy in Wichita, which was organized by Operation Rescue.

Through Frye, Roeder says, he soon met Rachelle "Shelley" Shannon. She, like Frye, had attended the Summer of Mercy protests; over the next two years she would commit eight arson or acid attacks on abortion clinics in the Pacific Northwest. Then, most horrifically, on August 19, 1993, she would try to murder Dr. George Tiller, succeeding only in shooting and wounding him in both his arms.

Roeder says Frye took him to visit Shannon where she was incarcerated in Topeka. Roeder was instantly smitten with the intense, unrepentant shooter. Frye had made a match.

Roeder began visiting Shannon without Frye. Over the years, while she served her thirty-year sentence for the clinic attacks and the attempted murder, Roeder would see her some twenty-five times. As his marriage began disintegrating, he even considered asking the raven-haired Shannon about beginning a romance. But, he told me, he did not because of the obvious obstacles involved in dating an incarcerated woman.

Still, Roeder and Shannon stayed close, and he began contemplating killing Dr. Tiller himself. Maybe it would be a car crash; maybe he'd shoot him sniper-style from a rooftop near Tiller's clinic. Or maybe he would just cut off Dr. Tiller's hands with a sword. Roeder testified to all of these at his trial.

While protesting at a Kansas City abortion clinic, Roeder also met Regina Dinwiddie, who had been arrested along with Frye during Operation Rescue's Summer of Mercy.

Dinwiddie, an admitted member of the violence-promoting Army of God, was also arrested at Operation Rescue's 1988 Siege of Atlanta. Authorities housed the antiabortion activists in a separate unit, which became a terrorist seedbed. Also arrested and incarcerated along with Dinwiddie were Shannon, Jayne Bray, and James Kopp. Bray is the wife of Michael Bray, the so-called lifetime chaplain of the Army of God, who was, at that time, incarcerated elsewhere for a series of clinic bomb attacks. Kopp went on to murder the New York abortion provider Dr. Barnett Slepian in a sniper attack in 1998 at Slepian's home, and is the lead suspect in the shooting and wounding of four abortion providers at their homes in upstate New York and Canada between 1994 and 1997.

It is widely believed some of those jailed in Atlanta in 1988 were involved in the creation of "The Army of God Manual," in which they receive "special thanks" under monikers such as "Shaggy West" (Shelley Shannon), "Atomic Dog" (James Kopp), "Kansas City Big Guys," the "Mad Gluer," and "Pensacola Cop Hugger." The how-to manual for would-be terrorists provides instructions on vandalizing clinics, including arson, supergluing locks, constructing bombs, and "disarming the persons perpetrating the [abortions] by removing their hands." The manual was discovered buried in Shannon's backyard during a search by law enforcement following her attempted murder of Dr. Tiller in 1993.

Back in 1994, Dinwiddie had enjoyed special fame in antiabortion circles because Paul Hill had stayed at her house two weeks before he shot and killed Dr. John Britton and his volunteer escort James Barrett outside an abortion clinic in Pensacola, Florida. Shortly after that double murder, Scott Roeder enters our story again: he is invited to Dinwiddie's along with Frye to meet a special guest, Michael Bray.

Bray is a linchpin among the extremists; his influence over those who commit abortion-related violence is hard to overstate. Author of *A Time to Kill*—a theological justification for violence—Bray is a convicted clinic bomber (he served from 1985 to 1989 for his crimes). He helped draft and was the first to sign the "Defensive Action" statement endorsing the murder of abortion providers that Hill began circulating in the months before he killed Britton and Barrett. Shannon says she was moved to violence by reading Bray's writings; according to her diary, when an early arson attempt failed to produce much damage, she wrote to him in despair, and Bray reassured her, "Little strokes fell mighty oaks." James Kopp first met Bray in 1983 at an extremist religious retreat in Switzerland and, according to law enforcement sources, stopped at Bray's home in 1998 as he was fleeing the country after murdering Dr. Slepian.

Bray has obviously privately supported violence as a means to stop abortion since the mid-1980s, but by 1991 he and his wife, Jayne, were open enough to discuss his views with a reporter from *The Washington Post*:

> "Is there a legitimate use of force on behalf of the unborn?" Bray asks rhetorically. "I say yes, it is justified to destroy the [abortion] facilities. And yes, it is justified to . . . what kind of word should I use here?"
>
> "Well, they use 'terminate a pregnancy,'" Jayne Bray says.
>
> "Yeah, terminate an abortionist," he says.

When Scott Roeder arrived at Regina Dinwiddie's house with Eugene Frye in 1994 or 1995 to meet Michael Bray, he was nearly giddy, by his own recollection to me:

SCOTT ROEDER: I think it was right after Paul Hill . . . I got to meet [Bray] and I heard that he'd been on *60 Minutes*. . . . I just kept asking Mike [Bray] questions because I was so fascinated with him, you know. . . . As a matter of fact, Gene [Frye] had to tell me to quit asking him questions.

AMANDA ROBB: [But] did you guys discuss justifiable homicide? If it was justifiable to shoot a doctor?

ROEDER: Oh yeah, yeah. We definitely discussed that, and like I say, Michael [Bray], he's been outspoken, and he's always said, as long as I've known him, he's always said it's been justified to do that.

Another admitted Army of God member whom Roeder has become close to is Jennifer McCoy. In 1996, she was arrested and pleaded guilty to conspiring to burn down abortion clinics in Norfolk and Newport News, Virginia. During her two and a half years in prison, she was in contact with Bray, who honored her in absentia at the White Rose Banquet in Washington, D.C.—an annual event organized by Bray to recognize those jailed for their (mostly violent) antiabortion activities and attended by many in the extremist network (including McCoy in 1996).

After her release, McCoy began protesting regularly with Operation Rescue in Wichita shortly after its president, Troy Newman, moved the headquarters there in 2002 for the sole purpose of tormenting Dr. Tiller into shuttering his clinic.

As Roeder's conversations with me have indicated, McCoy has been among his most regular visitors since he was arraigned for Dr. Tiller's murder, although according to Roeder they did not know each other before May 2009. But McCoy is close to people Roeder is connected to, people Roeder could try to implicate as co-conspirators and/or accessories, such as Bray or Newman, the latter of whom extremely angered Roeder by denying their acquaintance.

Perhaps this is why McCoy has been more than a supporter; she has been a flatterer and even a fabulist. At one point, according to Roeder, McCoy told him that a seventeen-year-old woman in Wichita was scheduled to have an abortion but after Dr. Tiller's murder changed her mind and had the baby. Roeder believed that young woman would testify in court on behalf of his defense that the murder was justified to save lives. But there is no evidence that any woman who was planning to abort her pregnancy before Dr. Tiller was killed changed her mind afterward.

Roeder first stalked Tiller at his Wichita church, Reformation Lutheran, in 2002, the year Operation Rescue moved there. Operation Rescue had already begun demonstrating at the church, and on the group's website Newman had announced plans to gather at Tiller's clinic, church, and home.

Also that year, Roeder says he went to lunch with Newman and asked him about using violence to stop abortion.

ROBB: What did you say to him?

ROEDER: Oh, something like if an abortionist—I don't even know if it was specifically Tiller—was shot, would it be justified? . . . And [Newman] said, "If it were, it wouldn't upset me."

According to Roeder's trial testimony, he became an active and regular participant in Operation Rescue events. He told me he has donation receipts, event T-shirts, and a signed copy of Newman's 2001 book, *Their Blood Cries Out,* to prove it. During an Operation Rescue event at Dr. Tiller's clinic in 2007, Roeder posted on the Operation Rescue website: "Bleass [*sic*] everyone for attending and praying in May to bring justice to Tiller and the closing of his death camp. Sometime soon, would it be feasible to bring as many people as possible to attend Tillers [*sic*] church (inside not just outside)."

Moreover, when Roeder was apprehended for Dr. Tiller's murder, news cameras photographed a piece of paper on the dashboard of Roeder's car. It contained the phone number of Cheryl Sullenger, Operation Rescue's senior policy adviser, who served two years in prison for conspiring to bomb abortion clinics in the late 1980s. Roeder also told me that Sullenger was present at the lunch with Newman where they discussed "justifiable" homicide, and that Newman had given Roeder the autographed copy of his book just three months before Roeder killed Tiller when Roeder visited Operation Rescue headquarters. Sullenger was there as well, Roeder said.

Yet Newman has denied any formal link between Roeder and Operation Rescue. He said to me, "I have no recollection of ever meeting Scott Roeder." Immediately after Roeder killed Dr. Tiller, Newman issued a statement saying, "We deplore the criminal actions with which Mr. Roeder is accused. . . . Operation Rescue has diligently and successfully worked for years through peaceful, legal means [to stop abortion]." In his writings, though—his book, *Their Blood Cries Out,* is still for sale on the Operation Rescue website—he talks about the bloodguilt of those who condone abortion. The biblical atonement for bloodguilt is death.

Scott Roeder, Eugene Frye, Shelley Shannon, Regina Dinwiddie, and Michael Bray all know one another.

Jennifer McCoy and Anthony Leake know all of them, too, except perhaps Shelley Shannon.

Troy Newman knows McCoy, Frye, and possibly others.

Dinwiddie and Bray have signed "Defensive Action" (justifiable homicide) statements, stating in part, "We, the undersigned, declare the justice of taking all godly action necessary to defend innocent human life including the use of force." Leake has said publicly he supports the use of deadly force against abortion providers.

McCoy, Shannon, Dinwiddie, and Bray are admitted members of the Army of God.

"We're like circles that overlap," McCoy told me in an anteroom in the Sedgwick County Courthouse near where Scott Roeder was being sentenced on April 1, 2010. "We all don't know each other—we may not agree on a lot of things, like religion, say—but we're all completely committed to one purpose: stopping abortion."

"Uh-huh," Dinwiddie concurred, looking up from the character statement she was getting ready to give on Roeder's behalf. "That's right."

Across from the women was Frye, along with David Leach—who calls himself the secretary-general of the Army of God and is another justifiable homicide advocate. They were working on their statements on behalf of Roeder's character, too.

They let me sit with them because I said I was Scott's acquaintance, and also because I'm the niece of Dr. Barnett Slepian, the abortion provider murdered by James Kopp in upstate New York. I was especially close to Bart because he lived with my family for nearly a decade after my own father died when I was four years old. During Roeder's trial, and again at his sentencing, I explained my presence to his supporters the same way I had explained my interest in him when I had first written to him six months earlier: I really need to understand how someone could be moved to murder to stop abortion.

I feel that I now understand. Circles that overlap.

One circle encompasses the Army of God, including Bray, Shannon, Leach, Dinwiddie, McCoy, and Kopp, the man who killed my uncle.

A second circle includes the justifiable homicide advocates Bray, Shannon, Leach, Dinwiddie, Leake, and the murderer Paul Hill, who was executed in 2003 by the State of Florida.

And a third circle holds Operation Rescue, Troy Newman, McCoy, and Cheryl Sullenger.

Scott Roeder overlaps with all of them.

Police, prosecutors, and the military define a cell as a circle of individuals—usually three to ten people—who are joined in common unlawful

The opening spread from 2010 shows (*top to bottom*) Dr. George Tiller's killer, Scott Roeder; the Army of God's Michael Bray; and Dr. Barnett Slepian's killer, James Kopp.

purpose. *A Military Guide to Terrorism in the Twenty-First Century,* a U.S. Army training manual, describes a cell as the "foundation" of most terrorist organizations. Most often, and most effectively, these cells are networked, "depend[ing] and even thriving on loose affiliation with groups or individuals from a variety of locations."

In international terrorism cases, in organized crime cases, even in drug-trafficking cases, conspiracy charges can be filed when two or more people enter into an agreement to commit an unlawful act. In fact, of the 159 people convicted of international terrorism by the United States since 9/11, more than 70 percent were sentenced for conspiracy (or for "harboring" terrorists). Once a person becomes a member of the conspiracy, she or he is held legally responsible for the acts of other members done in furtherance of the conspiracy, even if she or he is not present or aware that the acts are being committed.

The government does not have to prove that conspirators have entered into any formal agreement. Because they are trying to hide what they are doing, criminal conspirators rarely do such things as draw up contracts. Nor does the government have to show that the members of the conspiracy state between themselves what their object or purpose or methods are. Because they are clandestine, criminal conspirators rarely discuss their plans in a straightforward way. The government only has to prove beyond a reasonable doubt that the members of a conspiracy, in some implied way, came to mutually understand they would attempt to accomplish a common and unlawful plan.

Given the broad latitude in proving conspiracy, you'd think the same legal theory could have been used in prosecuting slayings of abortion doctors. Yet to date, only the individual murderers of abortion providers have been charged and prosecuted. No charges have been brought against any individuals for conspiracy to commit those murders.

Shortly after Roeder's trial—when I met Michael Bray and he told me he had met Scott Roeder only *after* he killed Dr. Tiller—Roeder stopped communicating with me. But during one of our last phone calls, I was able to ask Roeder a critical question:

ROBB: Wait, just tell me how it works . . . when the use of force comes up in conversation, it has to come up sometimes.

ROEDER: I've always said [it] over the years, and I would see what level of comfort they were willing to talk about it. . . . Michael Bray, he would talk about it forever. He went on *60 Minutes* for Pete's sake. Other people, they might say, "Well, you know, I just don't think it's right." Then I'd explain to them why, and if they're still not comfortable with it, I would drop it. I wouldn't keep pushing it. Regina [Dinwiddie] obviously agrees with the use of force, and Gene Frye, I believe, does.

Roeder, his associates, and "The Army of God Manual" could not be more plain. The manual ends, "'Whosoever sheds man's blood, by man shall his blood be shed' [Genesis 9:6] . . . we are forced to take up arms against you."

Taking up arms. Shedding man's blood. Bloodguilt. Circles that overlap. In other words, wolves run in packs.

Letters

My jaw about dropped when I saw articles about Wichita, Kansas, and Dr. George Tiller ["Standing Up to Terror," Summer 2013]. I wish I never would have needed to cross his path, but I am so grateful for Dr. Tiller and the work that he did. I was six and a half months pregnant with my second daughter, happily married, and in good health. We went for a routine ultrasound [only] to have our world crash—[I was told that] if I carried to term, my child would not survive the birth. We were referred to Dr. Tiller's office.

I literally thought I was going to die of grief and guilt. My body failed to protect my child; I still feel her loss daily. Dr. Tiller and his staff were absolutely amazing. I don't know if I would have made it physically or mentally without their help.

TARA
Shakopee, Minn.
Winter/Spring 2014 issue

Jailing Girls for Men's Crimes

BY **CARRIE N. BAKER** • SUMMER 2010

B.W. WAS THIRTEEN YEARS OLD when she offered to perform oral sex for $20 on an undercover officer in Texas. The officer arrested her and booked her as an adult. Despite evidence that B.W. had a history of sexual and physical abuse, was living with a thirty-two-year-old "boyfriend," and under Texas law was considered incapable of consenting to sex because she was under fourteen, the county DA charged her with prostitution and obtained a conviction.

Is a thirteen-year-old girl selling sex on the streets a criminal? This question is now being asked around the nation, generating vigorous debate and concrete action. In April, New York became the first state to enact a policy *against* prosecuting girls under age eighteen for prostitution, with its groundbreaking Safe Harbor for Exploited Children Act. The act also provides support and services to sexually exploited youth under sixteen.

Similarly, Connecticut, Illinois, and Washington recently passed laws that decriminalize prostituted children. The activists behind these laws all argue the same thing: that prostituted girls are victims of sex trafficking.

At this point, "sex trafficking" tends to conjure images of girls in Southeast Asian brothels or women from former Soviet bloc states. Rarely do we think of U.S. girls as trafficked. Only this year, for the first time, did the U.S. State Department include this country in its annual *Trafficking in Persons Report.*

> **"We care about abused girls abroad but not at home, we prosecute underage girls but not the adult men buying and pimping them, and we charge some young girls with prostitution while protecting others with statutory rape laws."**

"As a nation, we've graded and rated other countries on how they address trafficking within their borders and yet have effectively ignored the sale of our own children within our own borders," said Rachel Lloyd of the New York–based anti-trafficking organization Girls Educational and Mentoring Services (GEMS), in recent testimony before Congress. "Katya from the Ukraine will be seen as a real victim, and provided with services and support, but Keisha from the Bronx will be seen as a 'willing participant,' someone who is out there because she 'likes it' and who is criminalized and thrown in detention or jail."

The idea that the commercial sexual exploitation of girls is sex trafficking has, in fact, been established in U.S. federal law since the Trafficking

Victims Protection Act went on the books in 2000, defining sex trafficking to include the commercial sexual exploitation of youth under eighteen, whether by consent or not. At the federal level, this policy has been enforced: the FBI's Innocence Lost National Initiative has removed more than a thousand children from prostitution and convicted more than 570 pimps since 2003. However, the federal directive has been slow to take hold on the state and local levels: police officers across the country still arrest sexually exploited girls and treat them as criminals. And studies show there are plenty of girls out there to arrest.

The National Center for Missing and Exploited Children estimates that 100,000 U.S. children each year are victims of commercial sexual exploitation within our borders. The Justice Department's Child Exploitation and Obscenity Section estimates that nearly 300,000 U.S. youth are currently at *risk* of becoming victims of commercial sexual exploitation because they are runaways, throwaways, homeless, or in other circumstances that make them particularly vulnerable to exploitation. In fact, according to 2009 figures from the Department of Justice, a third of sex-trafficking allegations in the United States involved minors, mostly girls. The median age of entry into prostitution in the United States is shockingly young: twelve to fourteen years old for girls.

Despite these statistics, activists in this country have had to fight hard to get people to recognize and care about the situation. New York's Safe Harbor Act is revolutionary in stating that sexually exploited girls under eighteen are to be considered sex-trafficking victims, not criminals. Yet the State of Georgia recently rejected a similar safe-harbor law that would have exempted minor girls from prosecution for prostitution.

And who opposed it? The Georgia Christian Coalition, the Georgia Baptist Convention, and other conservative organizations staged protests and letter-writing campaigns, claiming the law would legalize child prostitution. They argued that arresting girls was the best way to get them off the streets and out of the hands of pimps. Wrote Sue Ella Deadwyler, a conservative Christian activist, in her newsletter, *Georgia Insight,* "Some boys and girls know the law, defy the law and decide to choose prostitution as a way to make money." So Georgia continues to criminalize prostituted girls—even though, under Georgia's statutory rape law, a girl under sixteen is not considered capable of consenting to sex.

The decision to prosecute these girls rather than provide a safe harbor only makes them more vulnerable and more numerous. A 2010 study shows that five hundred girls aged seventeen and under are sold for sex each month in Georgia, with seventy-two hundred men paying for sex with adolescent females (whether they know their age or not). Meanwhile, as in Texas, the considerably older pimps and buyers almost always avoid arrest.

Nonetheless, activists in Atlanta are continuing their fight to change the situation. Arresting sexually exploited girls for prostitution is an egregious form of blaming the victim. Society's treatment of these girls is rife with double standards: we care about abused girls abroad but not at home, we prosecute underage girls but not the adult men buying and pimping them, and we charge some young girls with prostitution while protecting others with statutory rape laws.

Lloyd attributes the lack of concern for the girls being prostituted to the fact that "the young people who are impacted by this in this country . . . are young people who live in poverty, they are young people who are in the child-welfare system or the juvenile justice system, and they are just not highly valued by society on many levels." The buyers, however, are "regular men" from all parts of society: our legislatures, law enforcement, media, and the justice system, as well as teachers and clergy—"folks in power" who don't want change.

Rather than blaming the victims, advocates around the country are calling on governments to stop arresting these girls and instead provide them with the social services they need, reserving criminal prosecution for the perpetrators—the pimps and johns. "In the last year or two," says the attorney Karen Harpold of the Houston-based Children at Risk, "there has been so much more awareness about human trafficking and these problems. I think it's changing, and I think there's definitely that critical mass of people who are working on it to make real changes."

"In ten years," adds Rachel Lloyd of GEMS, "we will look back and consider it ludicrous that we ever prosecuted children for prostitution."

·　·　·

Calling All Grand Mothers

BY **ALICE WALKER** • FALL 2010

We have to live
differently

or we
will die
in the same

old ways.

Therefore
I call on all Grand Mothers
everywhere
on the planet
to rise
and take your place
in the leadership
of the world

Come out
of the kitchen
out of the
fields
out of the
beauty parlors
out of the
television

Step forward
& assume
the role
for which
you were
created:
To lead humanity
to health, happiness
& sanity.

I call on
all the
Grand Mothers
of Earth
& every person
who possesses
the Grand Mother
spirit
of respect for
life
&
protection of
the young
to rise
& lead.

The life of
our species
depends
on it.

& I call on all men
of Earth
to gracefully
and
gratefully

stand aside
& let them
(let us)
do so.

An Acequia Runs Through It

BY **PATRICIA MARINA TRUJILLO** • WINTER 2010

FOR ACEQUIAS, the communal water-sharing systems of New Mexico, winter is a time of rest and renewal.

The deep purple, snowcapped mountains jutting across the horizon are harbingers of the health and vitality of the next crop's growing season. Each snowstorm gives added reassurance that there will be a strong springtime flow of water downstream. Having grown up in northern New Mexico, I was taught a reverence for snow, because in the long, dry months of the spring and summer growing seasons, it transforms into water, which is often scarce and must always be shared.

My grandmother was a *parciante*—an irrigator and member of her local acequia association in the tiny town of El Guache, on the west bank of the Rio Grande. Growing up on the acequia, I remember afternoons spent with my family working her fields for a harvest of corn, chilies, beans, carrots, radishes, *calabacitas,* and *alberjones.* While the adults farmed, my siblings and I often jumped into the water, walking the path of the acequia underneath bridges and fence lines to the connected water shared with our neighbors. Splashing and playing, we'd explore the vivid ecology of the acequia by catching jumping spiders, toads, and, on rare and lucky occasions, a water snake.

> "Just as drought and climate change are being shown to have an inordinate impact on women, it's pertinent to note the new roles women are taking locally to conserve water resources— including acequias."

When the weeding was complete, our parents would yell for us to get out of the water, and then we'd all fight to pull open the *compuerta* (head gate) to release the acequia's water onto the field. Ruled only by gravity, the water followed its natural instincts, descending slowly from the *compuerta* through the careful architecture that encouraged its movement along rows of plants as it had for at least six generations before.

At a time when water has become a contested resource globally—with droughts, climate change, and corporate profiteers putting tremendous stress on this vital resource—the acequia system provides a traditional model to reflect upon. Acequias are founded on the principle that water should be cared for and shared with anyone who needs it. Water, in this context, is always a community resource and right, never a commodity. The acequia running through the land connected us not only to food production; it was a shared resource that ran through the lives of our family and neighbors and continues to run through our collective histories. Acequias are central to understanding who we are as a community, inspiring our sense of belonging.

And just as drought and climate change are being shown to have an inordinate impact on women, it's pertinent to note the new roles women are taking locally to conserve water resources—including acequias. For nearly four hundred years, the practice of governing, managing, and maintaining acequias has been a male-dominated endeavor. But now that is changing; women are emerging as the new generation of acequia leadership, especially at the state level. These women leaders seek to bring new understanding to the long history of acequias—maintaining the old tradition of sharing natural resources while starting new traditions that address issues facing agricultural communities today.

In New Mexican communities, women traditionally were seed savers, food preservers, gardeners, and irrigators, as well as food preparers, and these roles are all part of acequia culture. Lucille Trujillo, fifty-eight, remembers when she and her mother were left to tend to their ranch after migrant work lured her father away from home in the 1950s. When the men were gone, she recalls, "the women had to take over."

"The acequia is a community," says Paula Garcia, executive director of the New Mexico Acequia Association (NMAA), and that point is ignored if the focus is on acequias as "the domain of men as the head of household, the water-right owner, the person who goes to dig the acequia." Bringing women out of the shadow of men's acequia culture recovers women's historical roles; we begin to understand that women have *always* been part of the acequia.

But the erasure of women in acequia history was not only due to the actions of individual men; according to Garcia, the modernization of agriculture displaced some of the traditional women's roles in the acequias. For instance, women were driven from their role as seed keepers by the commercialization of seed stock and the production of genetically modified seeds—a pattern that has been repeated worldwide as corporate agriculture encroaches on local farming.

Like other states in the Southwest, New Mexico is facing unprecedented growth and demand for water. In the 1980s and 1990s, cities began buying water rights from agricultural users to support industrial and housing growth in major population centers like Albuquerque. Those developments threatened the water base of northern New Mexico's traditional agricultural communities, and the NMAA went on the defensive.

Garcia, Lucille Trujillo, and Janice Varela helped coordinate some of the

The opening spread shows (*clockwise from left*) LeAnn Pino, who participated in the New Mexico Acequia Association's youth program Sembrando Semillas (Sowing Seedings); an acequia winding through the New Mexico landscape in winter; another youth-program participant on her father's tractor in Urraca, New Mexico.

most successful campaigns for acequia and water rights in New Mexico history, including the 2003 legislative fight for basic acequia rights. Last April, Governor Richardson signed another water-rights bill supported by the NMAA, which "puts water used by an acequia, community ditch, irrigation district, conservancy district or political subdivision of the state beyond the reach of condemnation."

Under protection of the new laws, the NMAA continues to fight attacks by developers and businesses that seek to separate water rights and profit from them. NMAA is also busy educating acequia members on their legal rights, preparing them for leadership roles, and training a new generation of heritage farmers. Since 2003, the focus of NMAA has broadened to include many of the acequia-related practices that women traditionally maintained. Each spring now brings not only the cleaning of the acequias but a seed exchange coordinated with like-minded agricultural groups, such as the New Mexico Food and Seed Sovereignty Alliance, the Traditional Native American Farmers Association, Honor Our Pueblo Existence, and Tewa Women United. In 2007, women from these groups crafted the declaration "*Las Mujeres Hablan:* Women, Seeds, and Agriculture," calling for recognition of the contributions of women to New Mexico agriculture. Last year, the NMAA also introduced two new voting bodies to the statewide *congreso:* the young adult's caucus and the women's caucus.

Members of the NMAA women's caucus, Las Comadres de las Acequias, are hard at work in the fields. They honor the shared cultural knowledge of Hispano and Native American communities, driven by a sense of having a common homeland and not wanting to be displaced by either overdevelopment or the ravages of climate change.

This concept of traditional resilience is at the heart of acequia work, highlighting the community's relationship to natural resources, which predates the current environmental movement by hundreds of years. It is also the force behind the NMAA's work in coalition with other groups to support local farming and the recovery and saving of heritage seeds, and to protest the production of genetically modified seeds. And it could well be a model for other groups hoping to preserve and protect their local environments, traditions, and healthy food production.

Pilar Trujillo proposes that the strength of acequias is how they connect contemporary activism to long, geographically specific traditions of sustainability. New Mexicans can trace their traditions back hundreds of years, she says, but most people in modern cities must come up with new traditions altogether. Acequias are not going to be found everywhere, and they may not even be a viable method for water sharing in all places, but the important part is identifying land-based practices unique and sustainable for each region.

Paula Garcia envisions a larger mission for NMAA: "Everyone is looking for that sense of community, . . . and we've taken that on."

"Yeah, we're very resilient," chimes in Quita Ortiz, one of the young women whose work involves reinforcing women's place in acequia culture. "There was such a lack of balance living in a society that is ruled by patriarchy; we've finally realized that is not the best way to carry everything out," she goes on. "We need balance, and we are trying to bring that back with women."

Sitting around a table, as many women have before us, our conversation comes to an end with a renewed sense of purpose and belonging—and an acequia runs through it.

What Would bell hooks Say?

BY **JENNIFER WILLIAMS** • SPRING 2011

I N 1981, *Ain't I a Woman: Black Women and Feminism* introduced us to bell hooks, a writer who would become one of the twentieth century's foremost critical voices on feminism, race, class, culture, and sexual politics. Since then, the famously lowercased hooks has published more than thirty books, ranging from feminist film criticism and studies of Black masculinity to essays on teaching and community to works of memoir and poetry.

Her definition of feminism, in *Feminism Is for Everybody: Passionate Politics,* as a "movement to end sexism, sexist exploitation, and oppression" equipped feminists with an accessible response for students and naysayers who felt alienated from the f-word. Agree or disagree with every analysis, we came to rely on hooks's sharp perceptions of the myriad ways that "white supremacist capitalist patriarchy" shapes representations of women, people of color, and sexual minorities in American culture.

> **"I really believe that love as a political transformative force in our society can change the world. It's been love that motivates people to the most deep and profound change."**
>
> **—bell hooks**

In the past few years, especially in light of the social changes that have taken place in America's so-called post-racial and post-feminist culture, we've missed that voice we'd come to depend on to "tell it like it is." So I was thrilled at the opportunity to catch up with bell hooks in her home state of Kentucky, where she is a distinguished professor in residence at Berea College, which launched the bell hooks Institute for Critical Thinking, Contemplation, and Dreaming last year.

I talked to her about how to *live* feminism and not just *think* it.

MS.: *Feminists were used to hearing from you and we've missed you. We even celebrated bell hooks week on the* Ms. *blog last fall. Some of our readers felt you had disappeared—did you?*

BELL HOOKS: Not at all. I left New York in part because my parents were aging. I also grew up in Kentucky and wanted to give back to the kind of people who had given a lot to me, so I went to teach at Berea College, which is a needs-based college. None of our students pay tuition. I wanted them to see what Kentucky can bring. You can be cosmopolitan *and* be a country girl from Kentucky.

MS.: *How did the return home influence the direction of your work?*

HOOKS: I wrote a book called *Belonging: A Culture of Place,* which came out about a year ago, about organic farming, Black people and sustainability, and ecofeminism. Those are big issues in Appalachia. I feel like what's happening with people in Appalachia is what's going to happen with everybody in the United States—food shortages, lots of people growing their own food.

I also just finished a big essay on Simone de Beauvoir and her influence on my thinking.

MS.: *In what ways did you feel her influence?*

HOOKS: I came upon Simone de Beauvoir as a late teen and thought, This is it. This woman is an intellectual. I want to be an intellectual. She is going to be the person that I follow. My dad had always said if you're too educated, you're not going to have partnerships, and her long-term love relationship with Sartre inspired me and so many other young women in the late '60s/early '70s. Of course we found out that the romance wasn't all that we thought it was. It was very conventional in some ways, but still she was a great inspiration to me.

MS.: *And you serve that role for a lot of us, myself included.*

HOOKS: Hallelujah!

MS.: *With my generation of feminists—I'm thirty-nine—do you think there's been a failure to carry the torch?*

HOOKS: I wouldn't say there's a failure. It's much harder for young women today to practice feminism because so much is expected of you all. And you really see, if you watch television, that you're expected to be slim and beautiful, smart and the equals of men, but to subordinate yourselves to men whenever that's appropriate for getting ahead. So many mixed messages leave a lot of young women feeling depressed—not in feminist practice, but not subjugated either. More like *lost.* It's our responsibility as feminist thinkers and advocates to share more of how to live in the world.

Gloria Steinem and I had a conversation recently at Berea with around twenty women from the college and community. People want to know how to *live* in this world as feminists, not just how to *think* feminism. When I walk out my door and some redneck white old man calls me "doll baby," how do I deal with that? *I* deal with it by recognizing in the scheme of what people are enduring in the world, if all I have to address in that moment is a man calling me "doll baby," I don't have to freak out about that because I'm an advocate of feminist politics.

And women who are heterosexual want to know how to have partnerships with men. I meet a lot more young men who advocate feminism than ever before, but they're often not the men that young women desire.

MS.: *So clearly there need to be more conversations taking place across generations as well as across genders.*

HOOKS: I agree. One of the negatives of the whole idea of the "first wave, second wave, third wave" is that it divided people off from one another, rather than recognizing that if we're talking about feminism as a political movement to end domination, to end sexism and sexist oppression, then we're not talking about categories. We're just talking about politics. How do we advocate feminist politics in such a way that it permeates every aspect of our lives, of our government, of religion? One of the worst things to happen to feminism is that people perceive it as a lifestyle that some people choose and not a politics.

MS.: *I noticed that you've appeared on Twitter. Is social media a useful tool to reach across generations?*

HOOKS: I've been a person who doesn't use the internet or have a cell phone, and it's because of young feminists, men and women, because of their demand for my work, that I've come more into technology. All media can be used to educate for critical consciousness. A lot of people don't realize that before his death Martin Luther King Jr. was already warning us about the danger of being too enamored of new technologies and not using them for social justice.

MS.: *I also noticed that you've been tweeting about love.*

HOOKS: I'm still obsessed with love! I really believe that love as a political transformative force in our society can change the world. It's been love that motivates people to the most deep and profound change. . . . So many bell hooks readers [were] upset that I was writing about love; it was like "bell's gone soft," and I kept thinking, They don't get it. It's not about going soft at all; it's about knowing what can save our planet. Which is people connecting, communicating, showing loving-kindness.

MS.: *A* woman *who talks about love is still suspect.*

HOOKS: Oh, definitely. I always tease people that if Cornel West had started talking about how we need to go back to love, people would say, "Oh gosh, he's just a genius. That's brilliant." But when I talk about love, people say, "Oh, she's gone soft; it's trivial." And that's really sad because to speak of love as a force against domination is just such a powerful call.

MS.: *There are so many hot-button issues I'd like to get your thoughts on. So let's do a kind of "what would bell hooks say?" talkback. To start, what do you think about the revolutions in Africa and the Middle East, and women's roles in those uprisings?*

HOOKS: It is vital that so many of these movements have been called forth and women are active in them, because a resurgence of patriarchal domination is part of why the resistance on the part of women in many cultures has gotten greater. Women are being wrongly blamed for a lot of social ills.

MS.: *Okay, how do you feel about gay marriage?*

HOOKS: I think *marriage* in general is not a healthy institution in our society. If people want civil rights, then that's what I feel we should be fighting for. Couples, people who are each other's kin or primary intimacies, a friend who takes care of a friend for thirty years in the same household—all should have basic civil rights. To bring that whole movement for social justice under the rubric of "gay marriage" seems to me just to reinforce patriarchal notions of who is worthy of care and support. It also lets down the gay people who don't want to be married.

The movement for gay marriage has had a strong push among very class-privileged people, because they are the people with trusts and with property and with health care. If you're gay, Black, poor, and you don't have any access to insurance, the question of whether your partner can be included on your insurance is just not relevant to the health needs of your life. What would be more relevant is national health care!

MS.: *While we're on health and medical issues, what do you think about the recent attack on women's reproductive rights?*

HOOKS: On one hand, we're being told that feminism failed, but if it failed, why do people want to go back and take away some basic successes of the movement? I think it's because having choice empowers women who have unwanted pregnancies. There's no way we can surrender the struggle to maintain reproductive rights because it's so tied to the future of what females of all ages can do. I think we forget about the level of bondage many women felt prior to birth control, prior to so many reproductive freedoms, of just feeling like your body was an agent of your destruction.

MS.: *Where is feminism today?*

HOOKS: Overall, the theory and practice of feminism can transform your life in so many positive ways, starting with calling forth healthy self-esteem and self-love. Feminism offers young women and men incredible tools that can allow them to live well in an unwell society. Many of us over-fifty women who've found our lives so enhanced and our capacity to love, to think, to act, so fueled by feminist thinking and practice stand by and watch young people think this is a worthless movement. And it's sad because it's been part of the energizing catalyst for us to have incredible lives.

Gloria Steinem and I were on the cover of *Ms.* magazine some years ago with Urvashi Vaid and Naomi Wolf, and we look back on that and think about where our lives are now, that we've all just grown more powerful, stronger, and even richer. I just want young *Ms.* readers to know that power and that joy, the joy in struggle.

BELL HOOKS—feminist author, poet, thinker, teacher, scholar—died on December 15, 2021, at the age of sixty-nine. Throughout her career, she wrote and spoke prolifically and profoundly of the crucial intersections of race, gender, class, and sexuality. And called upon generations of readers to commit to the act of loving—and embrace the life-changing power of love.

On the day of her death, *Ms.* shared a powerful statement issued by Karsonya Wise Whitehead, president of the National Women's Studies Association, excerpted here:

> On December 15, we lost a giant. A genius. A fire. A brilliant incandescent spirit. For those of us who knew her or knew her work, we lost our radical intellectual spirit guide who helped us to find our way. I am not okay. Black women are not okay. None of us—feminists, scholars, activists, truth seekers, survivors—who sat at the feet of her work are okay. Not today. Not at this moment and not for a minute.
>
> bell hooks never gave up. She never gave in. She was more than we could have asked for and gave us more than we could have ever imagined.

Letters

Thank you for writing about the whole "forcible rape" issue ["Rape Is Rape," by Stephanie Hallett, Spring 2011]. Forcible rape as opposed to what? Welcomed rape? If it was welcomed, it would just be plain, regular sex.

Just like Joe Biden said loud and clear, "Look, guys, no matter what a girl does, no matter how she's dressed, no matter how much she's had to drink, it's never, never, never, never okay to touch her without her consent. This doesn't make you a man. It makes you a coward."

CHELSEA GAST
Boone, N.C.
Summer 2011 issue

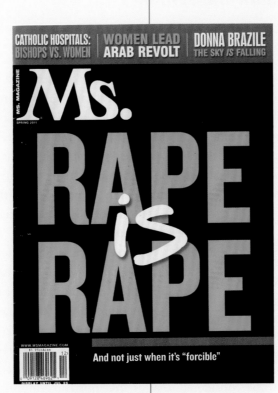

CATHOLIC HOSPITALS: BISHOPS VS. WOMEN | WOMEN LEAD ARAB REVOLT | DONNA BRAZILE THE SKY *IS* FALLING

MS. MAGAZINE

SPRING 2011

Ms.

RAPE *is* RAPE

WWW.MSMAGAZINE.COM

And not just when it's "forcible"

It was in the magazine rack of the university's women's center exactly when I needed it—when giving up seemed wise. Another audience had responded with disbelief to my revelation that coerced sex is rape. I felt like I was back in that metal chair at the police station, trying to explain to the detective why the bruises on my body weren't "evidence of passionate lovemaking." At such times, when it's clear that those in power just don't get it, the fight against rape seems endless. In 2011, lawmakers reminded us that they didn't get it when they quietly tried to affirm the FBI's distinction of real rape as "forcible." Yet also in 2011, *Ms.* reminded us that anti-rape work has not been in vain. Survivors aren't alone anymore; those who abuse power—in the back of a car or from behind a government desk—will be called out.

ANDREA HARRIS
Beavercreek, Ohio
Winter 2012 issue

Ms. launched its Rape Is Rape campaign to change the way we talk about, and the way federal law enforcement must define and tally, the crime of rape. The FBI's definition of "rape" in 2011—"the carnal knowledge of a female forcibly and against her will"—excluded nonconsensual oral and anal sex; attacks with fingers, fists, and other objects; assaults when the victim is unconscious or otherwise unable to consent; and all male victims.

If the Clothes Fit

BY **MINH-HA T. PHAM** • FALL 2011

"[MY] PASSION for fashion can sometimes seem a shameful secret life," wrote the Princeton University English professor Elaine Showalter in 1997.

And indeed, after these words appeared in *Vogue,* more shame was heaped on her. Surely she must have "better things to do," said one colleague. Graduate students accused her of flaunting her privileged standing ("None of us can even entertain the idea of buying clothes as expensive as the Prada ones you talk about"). Showalter admittedly described having some champagne tastes, but she convincingly made the point that feminists shouldn't feel bound to solely the "ovarian earth-mother look"; they should consider fashion "free speech."

> **"Fashion, like so many other things associated primarily with women, may be dismissed as trivial, but it shapes how we're read by others."**

The experience of Showalter, one of the founders of feminist literary criticism, is just one small illustration of how fashion makes some contemporary feminists uncomfortable. Part of the reason is a well-placed mistrust of an industry that, at its worst, polices our bodies and empties our wallets—an industry that can tell women we have to wear crippling six-inch stilettos to be considered sexy or that our three-month-old blouse is "so last week." Better, some might conclude, to resist it altogether and avoid the trappings of a "fashion victim" or "shopaholic."

Easier said than done.

Fashion, like so many other things associated primarily with women, may be dismissed as trivial, but it shapes how we're read by others, especially on the levels of gender, class, and race. In turn, how we're read determines how we are treated, especially in the workforce—whether we are hired, promoted, and respected and how well we are paid. That most ordinary and intimate of acts, getting dressed, has very real political and economic consequences.

If feminists ignore fashion, we are ceding our power to influence it. Fortunately, history has shown that feminists can, instead, harness fashion and use it for our own political purposes.

In 1993, Carol Moseley-Braun, the first African American woman elected to the U.S. Senate, unintentionally changed fashion history by wearing a pantsuit on the Senate floor, thus forcing an end to a decades-long ban on women sporting pants there. "I didn't know what I had done until some [women Senate employees] started thanking me," she said later.

The fact that even the most politically and culturally commanding women must walk a razor's edge between looking powerful and still appearing "appropriately feminine" underscores the visual theorist John Berger's concise description of mainstream society: "Men act and women appear." In other words, men are judged by their deeds; women, by their looks.

In U.S. politics, Hillary Clinton has experienced the damned-if-you-do, damned-if-you-don't double bind for strong women. If she wears a power pantsuit, it's a "desexualized uniform," but if she shows a hint of cleavage—as she famously did in 2007—it can ignite a media firestorm that eclipses her political platform.

The significance of women's dress and grooming habits is supported by research on workplace psychology. One often-cited study by Denise Mack and David Rainey found that women's grooming held more weight with potential employers than did their qualifications for the job.

A laid-back look may be acceptable for certain modern entrepreneurial men (think Facebook's Mark Zuckerberg and his hooded sweatshirts), but the message women still receive is that without careful maintenance of their appearance they risk personal and professional failure. The Chicago Bar Association's April 2010 professionalization event for law students advised men to simply wear a tailored suit with a necktie and polish their shoes. Women, on the other hand, were given an extensive list of fashion don'ts that even included wearing too-nice jewelry that might inflame the jealousy of female employers. A blogger who attended the event wryly dubbed it "How to Dress Like a Lawyer as Told by Some Women Haters, Old Men, and Random Law Students."

While all women's fashion choices are more carefully policed than men's, women of color endure heightened scrutiny. Racist stereotypes that cast some women of color as "out of control" (the angry Black woman, the hypersexual Latina) and others as easily controllable (the traditional Asian woman, the sexually available Indian woman) serve women poorly in the workplace. Professional women of color thus consciously and unconsciously fashion themselves in ways that diminish their racial difference. One Asian woman interviewed by the sociologist Rose Weitz for the academic journal *Gender & Society* admitted that she permed her hair for work "because she felt that she looked 'too Asian' with her naturally straight hair." A Black woman interviewed by Charisse Jones and Kumea Shorter-Gooden for their book, *Shifting: The Double Lives of Black Women in America,* explains that "she never goes into an interview or a new job experience without first straightening her hair. . . . 'I don't want to be prejudged.'"

For working-class women of color, fashion policing can be more explicit, especially when they're required to wear a uniform. While some uniforms are used simply to identify store employees who provide customer service, those worn by women in traditionally gendered and racialized occupations are typically designed to make them inconspicuous. As Mimi Nguyen has written of hotel maids in *Threadbared* (a blog on the politics of fashion and beauty, which I co-author), their uniform "deindividuates," making them invisible so they can "work unobtrusively around the perceptual periphery of the guest." Janitorial uniforms for men have a similar function, but the hospitality industry does reserve several positions for men (for example, doormen and butlers) in which the uniforms locate them at the center rather than the margins of bourgeois society.

Fashion's cultural appropriation is nothing new. Sally Roesch Wagner uncovered an early moment of appropriation in her book *Sisters in Spirit,* recounting the little-known history of the bloomer: the long baggy pants that narrowed at the ankles, usually associated with dress reformers in the mid-nineteenth century. While prevailing fashion histories credit the white New Yorker Elizabeth Smith (second cousin to Elizabeth Cady Stanton) with inventing the billowy pants and Amelia Bloomer with popularizing them, Wagner finds that Smith was influenced by Native Haudenosaunee women.

Smith "was among the first to shed the twenty pounds of clothing that fashion dictated should hang from any fashionable woman's waist, usually dangerously deformed from corseting," wrote Wagner. "The reform costume Elizabeth Smith adopted . . . promised the health and comfort of the loose-fitting tunic and leggings worn by Native American friends." That the contributions of Native women go largely unmentioned in accounts of this iconic garment is a reminder of the racial exclusions that prevail in fashion history.

If fashion has been used to introduce new ways of expressing womanhood, it has also been a tether that keeps women's social, economic, and political opportunities permanently attached to their appearances. At a time when makeover reality TV shows suggest that self-reinvention is not only desirable but almost required, and the ubiquity of social media encourages everyone to develop a "personal brand," the pressure on women to be fashionable has never been more pervasive. One-click shopping and personalized makeover sites are supposed to make it so easy to maintain your appearance that there's no excuse not to.

Today, fashion blogs that celebrate an array of non-normatively raced, gendered, sexed, and sized bodies have emerged to challenge the dominant messages of gender, beauty, and style. And bloggers are using their clout to speak out against offensive fashion and beauty products.

A blog-initiated campaign in 2010 persuaded the cosmetics company MAC and the Rodarte design team to abandon their collection of nail polish and lipstick with names such as "Ghost Town," "Factory," and "Juarez" (referencing the Mexican border town notorious for the serial murders of women working in local factories). As MAC's president, John Demsey, posted on the company's Facebook page, "We have heard the response of concerned global citizens loud and clear and are doing our very best to right our wrong." Similar online campaigns have also been waged against designers and magazines that employ blackfacing and yellowfacing, as well as against retailers like Abercrombie & Fitch and American Apparel that perpetuate racist, sexist, and sizeist beauty ideals. In the age of interactive social media, consumers have at least one ear of the fashion establishment; we should continue to speak up.

Showalter ended her *Vogue* article with this musing: "If Erma Bombeck learned all she needed to know in the dressing rooms at Loehmann's, I got at least some of my feminist education at Au Printemps [the Parisian department store]. . . . Looking at clothes, feeling the pace, picking up idioms in the aisles, watching other women invent themselves, is a kind of sisterhood."

Her point is that fashion opens up social and creative spaces for women. Throwing fashion out the window because of its oppressive tendencies wastes the political potential of one of the rare women-centered cultural realms. And to ignore fashion is to dismiss the notion that self-care and personal pleasure can be feminist acts, since women are historically socialized to care only for others. Wearing fashion does not have to mean that we allow it to wear us down.

Letters

Could we please have pockets, strong ones? May we please wear comfortable shoes that look nice? Could durable, classic styles please endure for more than one season? And might we large women look tailored, powerful, and womanly, instead of like baskets of fruit or Hawaiian Punch?

ROGI RIVERSTONE
www.rogiriverstone.com
Winter 2012 issue

Most. Effective. Speaker. Ever.

BY **LINDA BURSTYN** • WINTER 2011

FEW PEOPLE have been as unjustly maligned as former House Speaker Nancy Pelosi.

Republicans spent an estimated $75 million during last November's election campaigns, the vast majority to attack Pelosi and make her a national target for voter unrest. Even the outmatched Republican challenger in her congressional district raised $2 million and put out a video comparing her to the Wicked Witch of the West, which echoed the sorts of ridicule aired on Fox News and elsewhere when Pelosi became Speaker in 2007. The barrage of negativity pulled Pelosi's poll ratings so low that *The New York Times* has called her one of the nation's least popular politicians.

> **"Could it be that Pelosi's remarkable success in both these areas contributed to her being targeted in such an unprecedented way by the Republican Party?"**

Adding to the insults, *Time* and *Newsweek* didn't think Pelosi newsworthy enough to feature on their covers when she became the first woman Speaker (nor since); *Ms.* was the only national magazine to recognize her immediately on its cover. Yet both major newsweeklies featured incoming Republican Speaker John Boehner on their covers even before he officially took over his new position.

All of which is pretty frustrating, especially considering that—according to many historians and political scientists—Nancy Pelosi was probably the most successful House Speaker in U.S. history.

"No one before her has been able to move the activist agenda she's been able to move," says the congressional history expert Ron Peters, Regents Professor of Political Science at the University of Oklahoma and co-author with Cindy Simon Rosenthal of *Speaker Nancy Pelosi and the New American Politics*. "She went for years without losing a vote. That's extraordinary."

Even Norman Ornstein, resident scholar at the conservative American Enterprise Institute, agrees: "We're looking at an extraordinary set of accomplishments over a brief period of time. She ranks with the most consequential Speakers, certainly in the last seventy-five years. The range and dramatic quality of the legislation achieved in an extremely difficult and contentious Congress is incredible."

Pelosi herself knows just why the Republicans tried to demonize her. "They tried to shoot me down because I got the job done," the new House minority leader told me. "Because I was effective fighting Wall Street, big

MOMS, JOBS AND BIAS
BRAVE WOMEN SPEAK OUT
206 FEMINIST ARTISTS

Ms.

WINTER 2007

NANCY PELOSI
TAKES CHARGE

Exclusive
BARBARA EHRENREICH:
Dancing in the Streets

The Beauty of Salma Hayek's Ugly Betty

THIS IS WHAT A SPEAKER LOOKS LIKE

WWW.MSMAGAZINE.COM
U.S. $5.95 CANADA $6.95
DISPLAY UNTIL APRIL 8

HAITI'S WOMEN
RISE FROM THE RUBBLE

CONSUMER WATCHDOG
ELIZABETH WARREN

NANCY PELOSI
BEST. SPEAKER. EVER.

Ms.

WINTER 2011

The Woman TIME & NEWSWEEK Won't Put on Their Covers

Ms.

SPRING 2019

MS. SPEAKS WITH THE SPEAKER

NANCY PELOSI
EMERGES VICTORIOUS

SAUDI WOMEN FLEE GENDER APARTHEID

TOXIC MASCULINITY GETS TRUMPED UP

THE YOUNG WOMEN OF SUNRISE

WWW.MSMAGAZINE.COM
$6.95US/CAN

Ms. was the first and only national magazine to feature Speaker of the House Nancy Pelosi on the cover when she became Speaker the first time. During her tenure as House leader in the Obama, Trump, and now Biden administrations, her iconic look—power suits and a power stride, her bold gestures and expressions—led the rest of the world to follow *Ms.*'s lead as she became popular fodder for feminist memes. *Ms.* later put Speaker Pelosi on the cover, memorializing one of her many iconic moments—in this case, when she emerged victorious from a White House confrontation with President Donald Trump.

oil, and the insurance industry. Because I have been the best fundraiser for the Democrats. Because of the issues that are important to me in protecting working families."

Many scholars and experts feel that there are two critical ways to judge the effectiveness of modern Speakers: their success rate in passing legislation and their ability to create majority party status. Could it be that Pelosi's remarkable success in both these areas contributed to her being targeted in such an unprecedented way by the Republican Party? Judge for yourself.

In terms of passing legislation, Pelosi faced a House so divided along party lines that she couldn't count on garnering even a single Republican vote. That meant that every piece of legislation required Democrats to demonstrate a discipline and unity they have not been famous for. A daunting prospect, but something Pelosi was able to achieve with enormous success.

"If you look at what was passed through the House to produce significant public policy, the record is unmatched since the Great Society legislation [of the 1960s]," says the University of Oklahoma political science professor Cindy Simon Rosenthal. "And much of it is because of her."

Consider the historic legislation passed over the last four years: health-care reform, additional health-care coverage for eleven million children (SCHIP), the financial-reform act, the Lilly Ledbetter Fair Pay Act, student aid, ethics reform, raising the minimum wage, the $787 billion stimulus package, Don't Ask, Don't Tell's repeal, and the list goes on. And those are just the bills that were made into law: that list doesn't include more than three hundred pieces of legislation passed by the House that did not make it through the Senate.

"There have been very effective Speakers of the House before, and there have been periods that were important in terms of passing important legislation, but no Speaker of the House has ever done more to pass historic legislation than Nancy Pelosi," says Harold Meyerson, the *Washington Post* columnist and editor of *The American Prospect*. "In the passage of the New Deal and Great Society legislation, the Speakers were not key players. In contrast, Pelosi mattered hugely on the stimulus, on financial reform, and above all on health care."

When it comes to supporting women's issues in the House, Pelosi has always been a committed ally, says the Feminist Majority Foundation president (and *Ms.* publisher) Eleanor Smeal. "She is a feminist and she is for women's rights unequivocally. She made sure the health-care bill ended blatant discrimination on the basis of sex; she made sure it covers maternity benefits and eliminates charging more for women's health insurance. As the Speaker herself says, 'No longer is being a woman considered a preexisting condition.'"

Speaking up for women is something Pelosi does without question. "I have a responsibility to open doors and opportunities to women both in politics and in government," she says. "Everything from rocking the baby to serving in the military to heading corporations—removing barriers to women participating is a responsibility we all have. It's not only good for women; it's good for America."

While Pelosi was intent on passing historic legislation, she faced an uphill battle in selling some of her own party members on votes. Explains Ornstein, "In the mid-1960s [under Speaker] John McCormack . . . it wasn't a piece of cake to get the civil rights bill and Medicare [passed], but the numbers were so overwhelming and the opportunity for Republicans to step up made it a much easier process for him. For Pelosi every vote that was of consequence meant she'd have to find a majority among the Democrats alone. And that included a large number of people whose natural inclinations were not to join with progressive legislation, along with a group of liberal purists who didn't want to compromise, so it made it a real challenge."

"Every single person in the caucus—Pelosi knows what they care about, what they're angry about, their families, whatever it takes to get the job done," says Representative Rosa DeLauro (D-Conn.).

"She hustles votes like nobody else can," says Representative Lois Capps (D-Calif.). "It's retail politics. It's hand-to-hand combat out there."

The result: The 111th Congress is now considered to have been the most productive since the 89th Congress during Lyndon B. Johnson's term, and through most of it Speaker Pelosi didn't lose a single vote.

As for putting the Democrats in the House majority in 2007, Pelosi went around the country recruiting candidates who could win in tough districts. And she raised money for them—more than anyone ever has. The totals are more than $231 million since 2002, and $64.8 million in this past election cycle alone.

But should she be held responsible for the loss of Democratic seats in 2010? Most would concede that not as many seats would have been lost if more had been done to stimulate jobs in the United States—something Pelosi tried to do, despite resistance from the Senate and the White House.

"The Democrats in the House were passing stimulus bills that were being quashed in the Senate at a time in which both the Obama administration and the Senate thought they'd done enough to fix the economy," says Meyerson. "But Pelosi's people concluded not enough had been done and the recession wasn't going to get better. The House passed a second stimulus package back in December of 2009. They were never able to get anywhere with it in the Senate."

Now Pelosi, reelected as the leader of House Democrats but in the minority, must face in the 112th Congress a Republican Party united toward what the Senate majority leader Mitch McConnell said is his party's goal: "for President Obama to be a one-term president."

Among other tasks in this heated partisan environment, Pelosi will be trying to protect the hard-won health-care bill from the heavy artillery the Republicans have promised to launch upon it. She remains undaunted.

"I didn't come here to keep a job; I came here to do a job, and that's what I'm very, very proud of," she told me. "When you get in the public arena, it's treacherous. But you can't run from a fight if you haven't achieved your purpose yet, and I still haven't achieved my purpose."

Stopping the Republicans' drive to repeal health care and to take down the president is one fight Nancy Pelosi is willing and determined to take on. Knowing her success rate—even with the deck stacked against her—we're betting on her to win.

Court-Martialing the Military

BY **MOLLY M. GINTY** • SPRING/SUMMER 2012

MYLA HAIDER was pinned down by a fellow soldier and raped at 2:00 a.m., then held captive in his barracks room until after dawn. But the crime she endured was never punished, and that injustice resulted in anxiety and depression from which she still suffers to this day.

When she was attacked in 2002, Haider was interning for a branch of the U.S. Army that investigates sexual assaults. She did not initially report the crime, because her attacker was an established law enforcement agent and she was afraid she would not be believed. It was only two years later, when she learned the perpetrator was being investigated as a serial sex offender, that she agreed to testify against him. But he was never prosecuted.

> "In many cases, military rape can result in not only broken bones or shattered psyches but charges that the survivor is herself 'guilty.'"

"I pursued every possible avenue, including a congressional inquiry, and found there is no recourse for victims," says Haider. So in 2010, she joined the first of three lawsuits spearheaded by the Washington, D.C., attorney Susan Burke.

From 2001 to 2011, an estimated 200,000 U.S. soldiers were sexually assaulted by their comrades in arms. Thirty-seven of them, plus Haider, have now stepped forward to sue the military for its handling—or, rather, mishandling—of their attacks and attackers.

The first suit filed by the firebrand Burke, who previously took on the military contractor Blackwater and Abu Ghraib torture cases, included twenty-eight plaintiffs. In many cases, military rape can result in not only broken bones or shattered psyches but charges that the survivor is herself "guilty."

That first case, in which two former secretaries of defense were sued for violating the plaintiffs' constitutional rights and "openly subjecting them to retaliation," is currently on appeal—after a district court judge ruled that rape is an "occupational hazard" in the military.

But that didn't stop Burke, the daughter of an army colonel herself. In the second case she filed, on March 6, 2012, eight plaintiffs charged the current and former heads of the Department of Defense (DOD), U.S. Navy, and Marine Corps for failing to obey rules designed to thwart rape and for exhibiting "high tolerance" for the crime but "zero tolerance" for those who report it.

Those plaintiffs include Ariana Klay, a marine officer and Iraq War vet who was raped by a senior Marine Corps commanding officer and his civilian friend while stationed at Marine Barracks Washington, D.C. It was a prestigious assignment, but she had been sexually harassed from the outset of her service there, routinely called a slut and whore—insults that the military determined she had "welcomed" because she wore shorts while jogging and makeup on the job. The harassment was so abhorrent that she formally requested a transfer to Afghanistan several times, preferring to go back to an actual war zone. Instead, she was forced to stay in D.C. and was brutally assaulted.

Another plaintiff, Elle Helmer, also a marine lieutenant, was required by her commanding officer to go on a pub crawl and was later knocked unconscious and raped by him. She was subsequently accused of "conduct unbecoming an officer." Such victim blaming is "a double betrayal," says Burke.

The third military rape case filed by Burke, on April 20, charges the heads of the DOD, U.S. Army, U.S. Navy, U.S. Naval Academy, and U.S. Military Academy at West Point with the same wrongdoings listed in the second case—but this time on behalf of two female cadets, Karley Marquet (West Point) and Anne Kendzior (Naval Academy). Marquet alleged that she was raped by an upperclassman in her freshman year, then forced to do punitive "walking hours" with him as a penalty for reporting him. Kendzior alleges being raped by two different cadets, but discouraged from reporting the assaults by the academy counselor she finally sought out to deal with the trauma. Marquet ended up resigning from West Point, and Kendzior was forced out of the Naval Academy, which used her mental health records to deny her commissioned officer status.

AFTER YEARS OF ADVOCACY AND LEADERSHIP, in 2021 Senator Kirsten Gillibrand (D-N.Y.) and Representative Jackie Speier (D-Calif.) won a major advance in the fight for federal legislation to address sexual assault in the military. The bipartisan Military Justice Improvement and Increasing Prevention Act—with a remarkable sixty-six co-sponsors and seventy supporters in the Senate—would require independent prosecutions of higher-ups and bolster prevention measures, education, and training across units. Senator Joni Ernst (R-Iowa) spoke powerfully about it: "As a former combat commander and a survivor of sexual assault, I understand the traumatic experiences too many of our service members have faced. Sexual assault has no place in our military—or anywhere else—and it's far past time we take more steps toward preventing and reducing these heart-wrenching crimes."

By the close of 2021, the House passed a disappointingly watered-down version of the Senate bill, a frustrating setback in the pursuit of justice for those who serve and protection for victims of sexual assault. The fight continues.

Congress has been holding hearings for years about the problem of rape in the military, and the DOD has attempted to improve the protocol for training, reporting, and prosecution. But victims too rarely find justice, while perpetrators commit assaults with impunity. If the military brass realize they can be successfully sued for damages, though, says Burke, "they would be forced to take responsibility, prosecute rapes, and at long last clean up their act."

Various loopholes allow many military rape cases to escape prosecution. Rather than face potentially vicious reprisals, a quarter of survivors choose to make confidential "restricted reports" that entitle them to follow-up care but do not trigger an official investigation. And rather than face a court of law after these reports, accused sex offenders are allowed to simply step down (called "resign in lieu of courts-martial").

Another problem arises from the military's insistence on chain of command. The military hands responsibility for deciding whether to investigate rape complaints to the most junior officer in an accused service member's command.

What's more, the same employee rights offered to civilians are not granted to military workers. "Service members cannot sue the military or its personnel for negligence or discrimination," says Rachel Natelson, legal director of the Service Women's Action Network, a national advocacy group that also provides direct aid for women veterans and those still on duty. "If [the military] legal system fails them, they are essentially stuck."

Burke hopes to get around this by suing on constitutional grounds—the claim that the military has violated her clients' legal rights, including due process, equal protection under the Fifth Amendment, and First Amendment free-speech rights to report sexual assault without retaliation.

In April, following Burke's legal filings and the premiere of a hard-hitting documentary on military rape called *The Invisible War,* Secretary of Defense Leon Panetta promised to put higher-ranking officers in charge of adjudicating rape cases. He also pledged to give rape-response coordinators better training, to provide counseling to survivors' families, and to create Special Victims Units to better investigate rapes. But Burke wasn't impressed.

"Secretary Panetta's plans fall far short of effective reform," she says. "After decades of DOD inaction on the military rape issue, the time for unenforceable promises must end."

Myla Haider says she sees "progress." But she would still like to add other reforms to the DOD's list: emergency medical leave and reassignment for assaulted soldiers, the immediate arrest of perpetrators, and an end to the practice of restricting rapists to barracks, where they can still prey on their comrades.

"The DOD must demonstrate true zero tolerance of rape," says Haider. "But at least it's finally taking some steps toward justice."

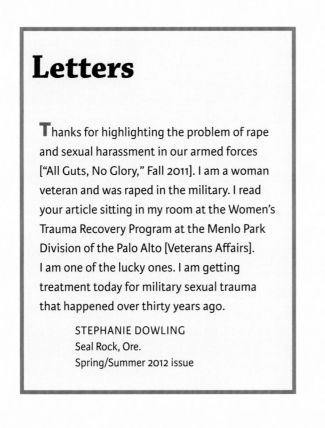

Letters

Thanks for highlighting the problem of rape and sexual harassment in our armed forces ["All Guts, No Glory," Fall 2011]. I am a woman veteran and was raped in the military. I read your article sitting in my room at the Women's Trauma Recovery Program at the Menlo Park Division of the Palo Alto [Veterans Affairs]. I am one of the lucky ones. I am getting treatment today for military sexual trauma that happened over thirty years ago.

STEPHANIE DOWLING
Seal Rock, Ore.
Spring/Summer 2012 issue

For the Price of a Pad

BY **LINDA VILLAROSA** • SPRING/SUMMER 2012

EVERY WOMAN remembers her first period.

Although the timing can be a surprise and cause some embarrassment, for most American girls and women menstruation is, at most, an inconvenience. We grab a pad or a tampon and continue on our way to class or the office.

But in impoverished and developing nations, menstruation can signal the beginning of the end of a girl's formal education. Surprising statistics show that vast numbers of girls all over the world drop out of school because they can't afford sanitary protection. This translates into dreams deferred, all for the price of a menstrual pad.

The connection between menstruation and girls' dropout rates has largely been overlooked, yet global equality in education is a United Nations Millennium Development Goal—one that was missed in 2005 and that observers doubt will be achieved by 2015. In southern Asia, just seventy-six girls are enrolled in formal education for every one hundred boys; the rate drops to 67 percent in sub-Saharan Africa.

> **"In impoverished and developing nations, menstruation can signal the beginning of the end of a girl's formal education."**

In India, inadequate menstrual protection forces adolescent girls to miss five days of school each month. According to a report by Nielsen, "Sanitary Protection: Every Woman's Health Right," only 12 percent of India's 355 million menstruating women use sanitary napkins. Africa is another trouble spot: the nonprofit Girl Child Network Worldwide reports that at least three-fifths of the 1.5 million menstruating girls in Kenyan primary and secondary schools (872,000) miss four to five days of school per month because they don't have money to purchase sanitary pads and underwear.

"Chronic absenteeism is a major problem among girls who can't afford sanitary pads," says Lorna Macleod, founder and executive director of Huru International, an organization that is working on the issue. "It's as if once a month they feel like prisoners in their own lives."

The staggering numbers of girls missing or leaving school cause a ripple effect of illiteracy and poverty that impacts communities and entire countries. And on individual girls and their families, an incomplete education has profound negative consequences, both physical and psychological.

For women and girls who don't have pads, necessity has long been the mother of invention. They've made do with tattered pieces of cloth, torn-up old mattresses, and even ashes. In addition to being ineffective at stopping leakage, these makeshift products are unsanitary and can cause infection and disease.

Many schools don't have a latrine or water source, so girls have no privacy to manage their periods. Without clean pads or a hygienic place to change, they stay home. As a result, menstruating girls fall behind with their schoolwork. According to Macleod, "These gaps in their education [are] almost impossible to overcome."

But there are some rays of hope: in areas of the world where education inequality is greatest, activists and entrepreneurs are finding innovative ways to make a difference.

In India, Arunachalam Muruganantham, a.k.a. the Tampon King, is out to start a cultural revolution to empower women one pad at a time.

Muruganantham, founder of Jayaashree Industries, has come up with a machine that makes low-cost sanitary napkins.

The pad problem came to his attention in 1998 when he noticed his wife, Shanthi, walk past while hiding something. "I asked her what she had in her hands and she replied, 'It's none of your business.' I looked anyway and saw it was a rag, and was shocked when I realized she was using this unsanitary bit of cloth for her period."

When he suggested that she just buy sanitary napkins in the market, she told him that it was either buy milk or buy pads. "I had no idea this problem existed," says Muruganantham.

So he set out to create a low-cost, homemade napkin. He unsuccessfully tried to get his wife and sisters to test it, then approached female medical students to wear them and fill out feedback sheets, but no woman wanted to talk to a man about such a personal subject. He eventually wore the pads himself and rigged an udder of goat blood to create a more realistic experience, thus becoming the "first man to have a period and wear a pad."

After much analysis he finally came up with the formula for his pad. It took another four years to build a machine to shape, compress, and then sanitize wood fibers and other materials. For about $2,500, a fraction of the cost of those used by big-name manufacturers, the machine is capable of producing about 120 pads per hour at a cost of 1.5 rupees (around 3 cents) per napkin.

Muruganantham's machines are now up and running in more than five hundred locations across India, serving more than 250,000 women. (He's also getting inquiries from other areas, including Nigeria, Ethiopia, Kenya, Uganda, and Nepal.) Each machine can produce more than a thousand napkins a day, which retail for about twenty-five cents for a package of eight but are often sold or bartered for individually. "Many women in India have never used a pad and would not be comfortable going to a store to buy it," explains Muruganantham, "much less having to ask the salesman how to attach it to their underwear."

To overcome the social hurdles, Muruganantham's pads are distributed through a female social entrepreneurial model. Saleswomen go house to house, and women can buy a single pad for a few rupees—or trade, say, an onion or a potato for the pad. Self-help groups of low-income women now have sales and distribution jobs that earn them much more than ordinary labor. Some intrepid businesswomen have even hired their own saleswomen to sell the napkins at homes, offices, and colleges.

INNOVATIONS IN MENSTRUATION have gone mainstream—including on the big screen. Arunachalam Muruganantham was listed among *Time* magazine's 100 Most Influential People in 2014, and his work and life have since inspired numerous films and documentaries—even a Bollywood blockbuster, *Pad Man,* released in 2018 and starring Akshay Kumar.

After learning about Muruganantham's work, a group of high school students in California—part of the Feminist Majority Foundation's Girls Learn International network—formed the Pad Project to raise funds and purchase a pad-making machine for a village outside New Delhi, India. They documented the process and produced a short film, *Period. End of Sentence,* which won an Academy Award in 2019; it inspired a 2021 book of the same name written by the best-selling author of *The Red Tent,* Anita Diamant. The Pad Project continues to expand its reach and increase access to menstrual supplies and education to communities around the world.

Letters

Forty, wow! You look great! Really you do. Don't give me that look—it's okay to care about your looks if you're a feminist. A lot of other magazines have very bloated advertising and a rather eerie glossy finish. But not you. Yes, you've freshened yourself up over the years, but that's what keeps you modern and relevant.

Do you remember the first time you came to my house? Me neither. But I remember you being there in those early years. My housewife mother must have heard about you at her consciousness-raising group and invited you home. I'm guessing you got passed around a bit. Household expenditures were tightly monitored (it was the 1970s, after all, [and] things were tough all over). Come to think of it, it took some chutzpah to start a magazine . . . on the cusp of the recession, didn't it? But you never did shy from a challenge. They laughed at you. Who did you think you were? A serious magazine for women? A business run by women?

It must have been hard at times, all that bullying. They even made fun of your name. You know, that name is now a standard fixture in the English language, appearing on all official documents and forms. You were the first to talk about abortion openly, instigating untold honest conversations in homes across the country. You shined the spotlight on domestic violence, helping to place the shame where it belongs—on the perpetrators. You gave voice to issues that often had no visible

champion. You helped us to understand our bodies and minds and how they can work.

I've no doubt you played some part in my mother returning to school and becoming the writer she always longed to be. You probably had a hand in the household responsibilities being distributed to all family members (yeah, that was just great, thanks!). I can see your handiwork now in my own outlook on life. I struggle, like I know you do, with the backlash to some of our progress. There are times I thought we'd be further ahead by now. We still have work to do, don't we, *Ms.*? Maybe forty really is the new thirty!

Happy Birthday, *Ms.*, and thank you. Now get back to work.

BRENDA TOBIAS
Via email
Fall 2012 issue

Four (Same-Sex) Weddings and a Funeral

BY **SUSAN GOLDBERG** • WINTER 2012

MY GIRLFRIEND PROPOSED—if you could call it a proposal—over the phone, long-distance, on a Sunday afternoon in October 2003. Cordless in hand, I was rooting through my fridge for something to eat when she said, "So, what do you think about getting married?"

I paused, the cold air from the refrigerator blowing in my face.

The previous summer, the Canadian province of Ontario had, finally, granted same-sex partners the right to wed, and all of a sudden "gay marriage" was the topic of every conversation, garnering its own special section of the editorial pages each day and forcing Canadian queers to consider the question: Will you or won't you now that you can?

> "Seven years and two children later, it's still difficult for me to talk about my wedding. When I tell the story I get weepy."

Not us, I had thought about me and Rachel. After all, we were good feminists. We both had master's degrees in women's studies, for God's sake. We had been well schooled in marriage's economic, not romantic, origins—in the idea that modern marriage is rooted in archaic notions of women as chattel. Not for us the need for state sanction, that piece of paper from city hall. Not for us the capitulation to tradition.

And then she asked. And all of a sudden it was us. When I asked her why, Rachel simply said, "It felt like a good approximation of where our relationship was at the time."

She had a point. Eight and a half years in and counting, there we were. We'd just spent the previous year rescuing the relationship from near ashes, sitting across from a skilled therapist as we learned to talk to each other all over again, to wipe clear that pane of murky glass that seemed to grow up between us and distorted our images of each other. She'd finished her doctorate, had gotten a tenure-track job teaching at a northern Ontario university. I'd built up my freelance career. We were looking at houses up north; I planned to move from the apartment we had shared in Toronto to be with her in the fall. And we had booked the first flight for our sperm donor to fly in from Vancouver so we could begin the process of trying to have a baby.

"Um," I said to Rachel, "okay."

And that was that. We were getting hitched.

We didn't tell anyone for a few weeks. At first Rachel didn't want to tell anyone, ever. She wanted to elope, have a secret ceremony at city hall, and never mention it again. I think she was scared. If we said it out loud, if we told anyone, it would be real.

But we were also scared of my family's influence. I come from a family big on big Jewish weddings—weddings of the white-dress variety, with dozens of attendants. Weddings that cost tens, if not hundreds, of thousands of dollars. Weddings with DJs and klezmer bands, with first dances, with disposable cameras on the tables, with open bars and mashed-potato bars and (I swear) kosher hot dog carts wheeled in at midnight. Weddings preceded by a year's worth of Friday-night dinners in honor of the engaged couple. Did I mention my aunt owns a bridal store? We had lots of reasons to be afraid.

Slowly, though, we both warmed to the idea of a public ceremony—on our own terms. We began to plan our ideal wedding: outside in the summer, maybe on one of Lake Ontario's islands. Fancy outfits. A big party with family and close friends. A string quartet. We'd find a way to afford it.

And then we told my parents. More precisely, on a Sunday evening in November, we invited ourselves over for dinner at their suburban Toronto home and told them about our baby plans.

"And there's one more thing," I said.

"There's more?" my mother said, weakly. My father just grinned as he sat next to her on the family room couch, where she spent most of her time these days.

"There's more," I confirmed. "We're getting married."

What I thought was an afterthought became the main event.

"You're getting *married*? When?" asked my mother. "Where? How?"

We began to outline our vision: summer, outside, family and close friends.

"Well," she interrupted, "you'll have to do it here. At our house."

Rachel and I looked at each other. I was about to explain why we couldn't possibly hold the wedding at my parents' house when Rachel said, "That would be lovely."

"What were you *thinking*?" I asked her in the car on the way home.

"Well," she said, "it's just that it's your *mom*."

My mom. Who had reached out in dozens of small ways to my girlfriend over the years. Who had helped pave the way toward my father's slow but eventually steadfast acceptance of both my relationship and my sexuality. Whose chicken soup Rachel—at the time a vegetarian—ate without hesitation. My mother, battling breast cancer, lying there on the couch.

And that was the end of our first wedding and the beginning of the second. By the next morning, my mother had notified all our relatives. I came home that evening to half a dozen messages of mazel tov from scattered cousins, aunts, and uncles, all promising to be there for our "big day." By Tuesday morning, my mother was in full swing, brainstorming caterers and flower arrangements, guest lists and officiants.

"Um," I said, "I'm not sure we can afford all this."

She paused. "Oh, Susan," she said, "we'd like to pay for it." It was a vast gesture of acceptance that I should have anticipated and didn't, and the fact that I didn't suggests that I was more caught up in doubts about the legitimacy of my own marriage than were my parents. For them, this wasn't a "gay wedding." It was their daughter's wedding, and, damn it, they were going to do it up right.

So we set the date, June 13. We met with the caterer. We negotiated the guest list, capping the number of my parents' friends to, in my mother's opinion, an impossibly small amount that continually edged upward. We found a rabbi—possibly the only one in the city who would agree to perform both an interfaith (Rachel is a very lapsed Catholic) and a same-sex wedding. A secular humanist Jew, the rabbi insisted only that the ceremony contain no reference to God and no sexism. We could live with that.

We booked the string quartet, asked my sister-in-law to do the flowers. I applied for our marriage license. The forms hadn't yet been updated to reflect the new legislation, and so my name was entered under the heading "groom." I wondered which of the two men in line ahead of me at the registrar's office would be a bride. After much convincing on the part of family and friends, we even registered, spending a couple of giddy hours debating china patterns and testing the fine blades of luxurious German knives.

In the meantime, we bought a house up north. We flew our donor in for a second try, and then I flew to Vancouver for the third—which "took." I was pregnant. My parents were over the moon. So was the rabbi.

Then my mother's chemo failed.

Through all the planning, we had tried to ignore the question that hovered, unspoken, in the backs of our minds: Would she make it to June 13? Back in October, we had been optimistic. Yes, my mom was weak, but for the past three years each successive round of chemotherapy, each new drug, had held the disease at bay. Over the past twenty years, she had survived, against astonishing odds, two previous bouts with cancer, one ovarian, one breast.

We thought she was invincible. We were counting on her track record of almost miraculous resilience. Why would this occurrence—breast cancer, now metastasized—be any different?

And yet it was. By April, she was vomiting up most of what she ate and had started spending nights as well as days on the couch, because the walk up the stairs was too hard. She found it increasingly difficult to breathe.

We all saw a third wedding coming, but we hesitated. Finally, my mother said out loud the words no one else had been able to say. She'd spent the night at the hospital in respiratory distress; the doctors had drained two liters of fluid from around her right lung, the one that didn't have a catheter in it already. We had an appointment with the palliative care doctor the next morning.

"Susan," she said, "I don't think I'm going to make it to June 13."

"We'll change the date," I said. "We'll do it sooner." She nodded. My father just looked into his lap as he sat next to her on the couch. I didn't cry until I phoned the rabbi to reschedule.

We settled on Mother's Day, May 9, three weeks away. It was the closest we could fathom pulling everything together. It would be a truncated affair, just family and a few close friends at my parents' house. No quartet. Our families changed their flights. We flew up north, signed the lawyers' papers on the house, flew home, found rings and outfits at a local shopping mall, met with our midwife. We printed our ketubah (no God, no sexism) off the internet; no time to commission anything custom. I had a pre-wedding pedicure and then burst into tears when the polish smudged.

"All I want is for my toenails to look nice," I wailed in the car on the way home. Rachel looked at me sideways. "Is it really your toes you're upset about?"

Meanwhile, my mother deteriorated rapidly. She had moved from the couch to a hospital bed we'd set up in the family room, but she could no longer get comfortable. Even small efforts, such as going to the washroom, became overwhelming. My father spent hours trying to persuade her to eat something, anything, but she wasn't hungry, so her body wasted, wisps of chemo-thin hair framing her gaunt face. She had coughing fits that left her exhausted. Some combination of drugs and disease left her unfocused and anxious, confused or annoyed.

"I know I'm not making sense," she told me.

"It's okay," I said. "You don't have to make sense."

The night before the ceremony, we ordered in Thai for the immediate family members who had congregated. My mom napped in the family room while we ate quietly in the kitchen, unsure how to work her decline into the celebration, how to acknowledge such sorrow in the midst of what was supposed to be joy.

"I'm not sure I can go through with this," I told Rachel at the door as she left to meet her mother at our downtown apartment. I was going to sleep at my parents' home, on night duty.

The next morning, the tips of my mother's fingers had turned dusky and I wasn't able to rouse her. But her chest rose and fell, and so I called up denial, found the now-much-too-big clothes she wanted to wear and laid them out, to help her into later. She died while I left the room to eat breakfast, while my father was at his computer, printing out his toast to the brides.

"Excuse me?" said the home-care worker. "Miss? I think that your mother is not breathing."

I closed her eyes, rested my forehead against hers for a moment. We held the funeral the following day. My cousins, already assembled for the wedding, were pallbearers. The wedding caterer fed the hundreds of people who showed up at the house following the burial.

Rachel and I exchanged rings privately, then sat shivah.

The fourth wedding was on June 13, in my parents' backyard—a much smaller affair than we'd originally planned, just family and a few close friends. We served hors d'oeuvres and lunch. In the photos of the ceremony, we all look so sad under the chuppah. My father and brother are holding back tears, my sister-in-law wears dark glasses, and Rachel and I clutch each other's hands while staring into each other's eyes, biting our lips. At three months pregnant (with, as it turned out, a boy, who would be named for his Bubbe), I am barely showing.

When the time came to break the glass at the wedding—because, according to Jewish tradition, in each simcha we are always reminded of our sorrows—we couldn't do it. We tried, but maybe there had been too much sorrow already. Our high heels simply pushed the glass deeper into the soft ground, where it stayed resolutely whole, unbroken, unbreakable.

Seven years and two children later, it's still difficult for me to talk about my wedding. When I tell the story, I get weepy. When I hear other people, queer or straight, talk about their own nuptials, I get jealous.

On the outside I nod and smile, but on the inside I am consumed with longing for what could have been: the party, funny toasts, the quartet, the champagne, the joy. I fantasize about my mother standing up with us, reveling in family and food and friends.

And then I remind myself that there is no such thing as a perfect wedding, despite what the marketers would have us think. And I remind myself that my wedding(s), as vastly imperfect as they were, brought together family and friends from around the world. That, because of my queer, shotgun wedding, my mother's siblings and nieces and nephews, as well as Rachel's mother, got a chance to see and talk to her and say goodbye. I think about the day of her death and how we were already gathered at my parents' house, and how we cried and talked and ultimately laughed about my mom. Her big talent had been bringing people together, and she had managed to do it one more time. All because her daughter was getting married. To another woman.

And that's the thing about weddings. Done right, they bring together more than two people. They knit families and friends together, make us collectively stronger. And that's why, for me at least, the issue of gay marriage resonates: the human rights it protects and enshrines extend beyond the two brides or two grooms to their parents, their siblings, their communities.

Has getting married changed anything for me and for Rachel? Hard to say. Our wedding was just one of half a dozen major life events that took place within a six-month span: my mom's death, obviously, but also the move to a new city, the transition from urban student renters to suburban professional homeowners, the baby. The combined stress of all of these (compounded by severe sleep deprivation) nearly drove us apart within the first year of our first son's life; by the time our second son arrived, we'd mostly recovered.

On the ring finger of my left hand, under the gold wedding band that I picked out so hastily, I wear my mother's diamond engagement ring. My sons like it when it catches the light and throws rainbows onto the walls. I twist the ring and tell my mother about her grandchildren, about how six-year-old Rowan reads and reads, about how his little brother, Isaac, finally consented to his first "big boy" haircut, about our kitchen renovations, what we're having for dinner. Both kids are fascinated by death at the moment; Rowan in particular asks us to tell him the story of my mother's last day—in intimate detail—at regular intervals.

"And then what happened?" he asks. "And then what did you do?"

I explain about burial, about bodies returning to the earth, but my stubborn romantic streak whispers: *She's right here, inside us.* He likes that I wear my mother's ring—"To remember her. Because she died. Right, Mom?"

And Rowan likes, he tells us, that we are married. "Why?" we ask him. "Why do you like it?"

"I don't know," he says. "It's just good."

. . .

Beyoncé's Fierce Feminism

BY **JANELL HOBSON** • SPRING 2013

THE SINGER/ACTOR/POPULAR-CULTURE ICON known simply by her first name—Beyoncé—does not hesitate to embrace the feminist label. She has especially shined a light on women's power: the power to perform in a male-dominated music industry; the power to acquire fame and fortune; the power to delight in one's beauty and sexuality; the power to cross over into mainstream media while championing a "girl power" anthem. Yet when women like Beyoncé proudly proclaim feminism, they tend to invite more debates than affirmation.

There was no denying the sheer audacity of Beyoncé's performance at this year's Super Bowl in early February as she strode confidently on a stage that highlighted her silhouetted figure. The spectacle invoked goddess power, represented by Oshun—an African orisha (spirit or deity) known for her self-love, generosity, and wealth—and Durga, the Hindu warrior goddess whose multiple hands emerged via digital screen as an extension of Beyoncé's essence. Beyoncé also summoned the collective power of women—representing diverse racial and ethnic backgrounds—by having an all-woman ten-piece backing band (the Sugar Mamas), women backup singers, and 120 women dancers. There was even a moment when the fans in the mosh pit seemed to be all women.

> **"Despite this performance of feminism for a mass audience, Beyoncé's critics still question her brand of female empowerment."**

And while Beyoncé and troops captivated hundreds of millions of Super Bowl spectators and TV viewers with their overtly sexual moves, the lead guitarist and music director Bibi McGill was given a spotlight moment to appropriate rock-star masculinity with her pyrotechnic guitar playing. In thirteen minutes, Beyoncé exploded all the symbols associated with the Super Bowl: football, male virility, and violence. Even the omnipresent objectification of women in Super Bowl ads momentarily lost its power.

"Lights out!!! Any questions??" tweeted Beyoncé's marital and music partner, Shawn "Jay-Z" Carter, when the New Orleans Superdome had a power failure after his wife's halftime show.

If this is what Beyoncé had in mind when she prophetically sang "Run the World (Girls)," I say, "Bring it on!"

But despite this performance of feminism for a mass audience, Beyoncé's critics still question her brand of female empowerment. There were those who wanted her to wear more clothes onstage, or not be so sexy in her dance moves.

And others who came to her defense.

In an article for *The Telegraph* in the U.K., Emma Gannon wrote, "If we accept that Lena Dunham [of the much-debated HBO series *Girls*] likes to take her clothes off and celebrate her body (with the majority of the media giving her a firm thumbs up), then how come Beyoncé is branded 'not a feminist' for doing the same?"

The talented and successful entertainer has been performing in show business since the age of fifteen, but we need not dismiss Beyoncé's brand of feminism as mere marketing. Feminism is political consciousness, not a product, and as Brittney Cooper, the women's and gender studies professor and author, notes, "Beyoncé has certainly evolved in her thinking about feminism—where before it was about her women friends, now she's critiquing patriarchy."

Here Cooper refers to Beyoncé's interview earlier this year with Amy Wallace in *GQ*, in which the pop star declared, "I truly believe that women should be financially independent from their men. And let's face it, money gives men the power to run the show. It gives men the power to define value. They define what's sexy. And men define what's feminine. It's ridiculous."

Beyoncé has been advocating for women's financial independence since her early Destiny's Child years, singing about unreliable lovers careless with their money in "Bills, Bills, Bills," or later, during her solo career, admonishing her ex to "not touch her stuff" as he exits "to the left / to the left" in "Irreplaceable." Especially telling is her financial bravado in a song like "Suga Mama" ("Puttin' you on my taxes already . . . I promise I won't let no bills get behind"). In a culture that focuses too much on consumerism, we may rightly feel uncomfortable with this emphasis on materialism, but Beyoncé's recognition of the economic inequalities between men and women certainly fuels her rhetoric and performance of what our society defines as "power."

Without a doubt, Beyoncé holds both financial and cultural power, and it will be intriguing to watch how they unfold. The blogger Danielle Belton would like to see the pop star more informed about women's realities: "There needs to be more substance behind the girl-power mantle she's been carrying."

For Aishah Shahidah Simmons, Beyoncé is already practicing feminism—even if it's confined to the music industry. "As far as I'm concerned we need all hands on deck [in ushering feminist social movements]."

Despite Beyoncé's contradictions—finding it "ridiculous" that men still define what's sexy while she maintains her body and image through conventional portrayals of sexiness and white beauty standards, or preaching "girl power" while calling us "bitches" in the next breath—her albums and soundtracks provide more than enough catchy beats and hooks to empower and encourage solidarity. If a battered woman can feel empowered to leave her abuser while booming "I'm a survivor / I'm not gon' give up" in her get-away car, or if a woman running for public office can make "Run the World (Girls)" her campaign slogan, need we expect more from our pop stars?

"Beyoncé just needs to wear a T-shirt that says, 'This is what a feminist looks like,'" Simmons suggests slyly. "Maybe she'll wear it on her Mrs. Carter world tour."

I can see it now. *Lights on! Any questions?*

Marriage **Is Marriage**

BY **SARAH BOONIN** • SUMMER 2013

L IKE MANY OTHER LAW PROFESSORS I KNOW, I eagerly awaited the U.S. Supreme Court's decision in *United States v. Windsor,* anticipating that the court would strike down at least a portion of the Defense of Marriage Act (DOMA). Within minutes of downloading the opinion on the morning of June 26, I found myself no longer a law professor analyzing the text but simply a wife and mother mesmerized by the court's words.

I immediately called my wife and began reading aloud to her from the opinion: "DOMA's principal effect is to identify a subset of state-sanctioned marriages and make them unequal," it read. A 5–4 majority would no longer accept that inequality. As I read further, my wife fought through tears to say, "This changes everything for us."

> **"The court's opinion signified a revolution of hearts and minds. By declaring federal same-sex marriage discrimination unconstitutional, our highest court affirmed the dignity and equality of our families."**

DOMA had been passed in 1996, defining marriage—once the province of state law—as being, for federal purposes, between one man and one woman. That meant that as states such as Massachusetts and Iowa began to recognize same-sex marriages like mine—we were married in Massachusetts in 2007—we became subject to all the protections and obligations of marriage at the *state* level but none at the *federal* level. DOMA's impact, invisible to most people, was profound in my world. DOMA made more than a thousand federal laws referencing marriage inapplicable to us.

Now, with the majority of justices in the *Windsor* opinion finding this federal definition of marriage to be a violation of equal protection, same-sex families will enjoy a whole new world of federal benefits. Here's what this means to my family:

I am married to a woman who is a federal employee, and we have a two-year-old daughter. Before *Windsor,* I had been precluded from joining my wife's health insurance plan, because the federal government viewed our relationship no differently than the way it views your relationship with a neighbor down the block. I could have opted to carry my wife and daughter on my employer's health plan (I work at a private university), but the federal government would have taxed me on the value of *my* employer's contribution as if it were overtime pay. Now I can finally join my wife's health insurance plan. Beyond economic savings, I have the added assurance that I could maintain my health insurance should I leave my job by choice or illness.

Each April, my wife and I have had to prepare a contradictory and onerous set of four tax returns. We filed joint state returns in Massachusetts, as state law demands of married couples. We filed two separate federal returns, as federal law requires of "unmarried" individuals. But in order to prepare our joint state return, we had to create a *fake* joint federal return—which we submitted to Massachusetts but were precluded from filing federally. In perhaps the greatest indignity of all, my wife and I had to choose which one of us would claim our daughter as a dependent.

Sarah Boonin (*left*) and her wife at their wedding.

Now, post-DOMA, we'll be like every other married couple in Massachusetts: we will file joint state and federal returns that declare our dual support of our child. There are a host of other federal spousal benefits for which I am now eligible. For example, I'll have a right to collect my wife's pension should she predecease me. I can participate in my wife's life insurance, long-term care insurance, dental and vision insurance, and flexible spending account. Should my wife become ill, I can now take leave under the Family and Medical Leave Act to care for her.

While these changes have real and immediate meaning in my life, the impact of *Windsor* on other same-sex families will be even more dramatic. The same-sex spouses of service members will now be entitled to housing, health, and survivor's benefits. Gay and lesbian U.S. citizens who marry immigrants can now live with them legally in the United States. Older same-sex married couples can collect Social Security benefits based on their spouse's earnings. Seriously ill spouses of same-sex partners can access health care through their spouse's insurance plans.

Beyond the tangible, the court's opinion signified a revolution of hearts and minds. By declaring federal same-sex marriage discrimination unconstitutional, our highest court affirmed the dignity and equality of our families.

Still, *Windsor* did not dismantle all the barriers to full marriage equality. Again, I'll use my family as an example.

In May, my wife, daughter, and I took a family vacation to Florida—a state that prohibits same-sex marriages. In preparation, we brought snacks and books for the plane; bathing suits, sandals, and SPF 50+ sunblock for the beach—and copies of our wills, health-care proxies, durable powers of attorney, marriage certificate, and the adoption papers for our daughter (my wife gave birth to her, but we had to jointly adopt her to ensure I would be treated as her legal parent when traveling). The *Windsor* opinion stopped short of requiring that Florida, or the other thirty-six states that don't permit same-sex marriage, recognize our marriage. While federal recognition of my Massachusetts marriage may add a layer of legitimacy to my family when we travel outside "marriage-equality states," we remain legal "strangers" in most states throughout the country.

The Supreme Court also expressly limited federal recognition of same-sex marriages to those sanctioned under state law (in thirteen states and Washington, D.C.). Because the court allowed states to continue to choose discrimination over marriage equality, it left a foothold for those who claim our love is less deserving than theirs.

These legal contradictions that persist in the wake of *Windsor* are untenable—legally, politically, and socially. However, legal advocates and supporters of marriage equality, emboldened by the court's recognition of the equality of same-sex marriages, will now pick up where the court left off. Further litigation is inevitable and imminent (it has already begun in Pennsylvania). Somewhere in the United States, a legally married same-sex couple will move from a marriage-equality state to a discriminatory state, and the state benefits and federal recognition they had come to rely on will crumble. That couple, supported by many of the brilliant legal strategists who brought us the *Windsor* case, will sue. Eventually, by the very principles articulated in *Windsor,* they will win.

.   .   .

The Feminist Factor

BY **ELEANOR SMEAL** • WINTER 2013

I'VE BEEN THINKING about the gender gap since the early 1970s, when I was doing graduate work on women's political attitudes. And in 1980, I proved its existence while analyzing job-approval polling, segmented by gender, for President Ronald Reagan, who opposed the Equal Rights Amendment (ERA). Women approved of him less than men—a statistic borne out in the election, in which there was an eight-point gap between women's votes for Reagan and men's. A team of us at NOW (the National Organization for Women), who were campaigning hard for the ERA, named it the gender gap, and we even had a ditty that we chanted toward politicians we opposed: "The gender gap will get you if you don't watch out!"

> "While there were many reasons for President Obama's decisive victory, the feminist factor may be one of the most significant."

The gap—the measurable difference between the voting behavior and political attitudes of women and men—has grown considerably since then. It was decisive in November, both in the presidential race and in maintaining a Democratic majority in the U.S. Senate.

To begin with, women (53 percent of all voters) cast some eight million more votes for the president than men did. And 55 percent of those women chose Obama, compared with just 45 percent of men—for a 10 percent gender gap. If only men had voted, Mitt Romney would have won the presidency, 52 percent to 45 percent.

The gender gap and women's votes were also decisive in some key Senate races in which the Democratic candidate won, including Elizabeth Warren's in Massachusetts (a 12 percent gender gap) and Chris Murphy's in Connecticut (11 percent). If only men had voted in each of these races, the Republican candidate would have won.

But now it's time to add another metric beyond the gender gap to our postelection analysis: the "feminist factor." While there were many reasons for President Obama's decisive victory, the feminist factor may be one of the most significant.

We dubbed it that after analyzing an in-depth poll *Ms.* commissioned with the Communications Consortium Media Center and the Feminist Majority Foundation. Conducted November 4–6, 2012, by Lake Research Partners, it found that 55 percent of women voters and even 30 percent of men voters consider themselves feminist.

Publisher Eleanor Smeal and co-founder Gloria Steinem, celebrating the fortieth anniversary of *Ms.* in 2013 at the National Press Club in Washington, D.C.

These results are generally nine points higher than they were in 2008, when the same question was posed to voters, and this upward trend is likely to continue given the strong identification with feminism by younger women and women of color.

Speaking of younger women, a solid majority of them (58 percent) identify as feminists—as did 54 percent of older women, nearly three-quarters (72 percent) of Democratic women, and a respectable 38 percent of Republican women. The feminist factor cuts across race and ethnic lines, with a majority of Latina, African American, and white women voters considering themselves feminists.

Most important, voters' views on feminism correlated with their choice of candidates. Among feminist women, some two-thirds (64 percent) voted for Obama, as did 54 percent of feminist-identified men. Looking at voters who identified as pro-choice, 61 percent cast their ballot for Obama.

Although feminists feel that the election was a victory for us in the "war on women"—the term now commonly used by feminists and the media to describe initiatives in state legislatures and Congress that severely restrict women's rights in such areas as reproduction, violence, and pay equity—we can't savor it for long. The 2012 election wins have prevented some of the worst attacks on women's rights from succeeding, but we won just a battle: the opposition to women's rights, especially at the state level, is certainly not going away. We have much to do if we are to realize the pro-choice, pro–women's rights agenda upon which President Obama and other candidates ran—an agenda that will move women and the nation forward.

· · ·

Fiction

SAVING MOTHER **FROM HERSELF**

BY **MARGE PIERCY** • WINTER 2013

MY DAUGHTER, SUZIE, and my brother, Adam, really got after me about what they called my hoarding. I live alone. My husband died when he was just fifty-eight of one of those heart attacks that hit without warning. He was playing golf—something he enjoyed but was never much good at—with another dentist and two podiatrists on the Wednesday when he just keeled over on the fifth hole trying to bang his way out of a sand trap. At first they thought he was kidding them. I was only fifty then.

I continued working, of course. I was a paralegal for thirty years in a small law office that did mostly real estate, wills and probate, and small-business stuff. I was really as much a secretary as a paralegal, if I'm honest. But it wasn't all that taxing. I liked the two men I worked for and it paid decently, a middling middle-class wage, you might say. Four years ago, I retired. Actually they retired and closed the office, and at fifty-nine I wasn't about to get hired to do anything better than greeting folks at Walmart or bagging at the supermarket.

I had the insurance from Walt. I'd banked it. I had his Social Security, which was better than mine would have been. I was okay. The mortgage on our house we paid off decades ago. It was the same house I raised Suzie and my son, Brady, in. Brady's out in Arizona, so I only see him maybe every couple of years when he sends me tickets to fly out there. The last time was for my granddaughter Olivia's wedding. A very nice affair that must have set him back I can't imagine how much. Olivia's pregnant now, he tells me. I'll be a great-grandmother before I can take that in. Amazing. Makes me feel ninety.

Suzie tried to get me to move into an apartment, but why? I'm used to this house. I know my neighbors and they know me. We don't hang out together, but we keep an eye on each other's property and have a friendly chat over the fence now and then. I have a nice little garden out back and a two-car garage. This house has three bedrooms so I have plenty of room for my things. That's what Suzie and Adam object to, as if there's something wrong with liking bargains and pretty things and useful things other people throw away. If you ask me, people discard too many items nowadays. I feel sorry when I see a perfectly good lamp or glassware or a rug that's still usable or even a flowerpot sitting in a dumpster or out on the street waiting for the pickup to be taken to the landfill and left to rot. So I bring them home. I know I'll get some use out of them by and by. And books and magazines. Perfectly fine to read. And VCR tapes. At garage sales I can always find something interesting. When you live alone, you appreciate entertainment. I always have the TV on even when I'm reading. It's company. I like to keep up with the news and a few of my favorite programs, but mostly I appreciate hearing another human voice.

So I collected. Who cares except my busybody daughter and then she enlisted my older brother, who always used to try to boss me around before I married. He and his wife, Liz. She gives me a pain in the you-know-where. She seems to feel superior that she never worked. So she stayed home and raised two children. Big deal. I worked and raised two children and they turned out just fine. She always has her hair done and her nails too. As if at our age anybody gives a damn, excuse my language, what her nails look like and if they're pink or red or purple. I'm too busy to fuss about my nails. Long red talons would never survive one of my scouting trips, collecting the wonderful stuff people discard. Besides, until Suzie butted in, Liz and Adam had no idea about my hobby. We always met in a restaurant (they

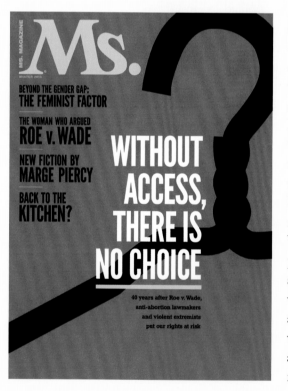

paid). Liz had no desire to come by my house, and I have even less of a desire to visit them. I'd come once and everything was so tidy and white and black I kept being afraid I'd spill coffee on that huge white couch as big as a boat. Adam and I never did have much in common. So what I filled up the dining room with my finds and the spare bedrooms and the hall that leads to them and half the living room. Who am I about to dine with, anyhow? What do I need spare bedrooms for? In the living room I store my reading material and VCR tapes and some extra VCRs people threw away. You can't buy a simple VCR any longer, and I keep about a dozen spares for when they go on the fritz. I'm always watching for them because I have a library of almost a thousand perfectly good tapes I can watch whenever I choose. My daughter calls it a mess, but I have them all cataloged. Just ask me. I can pull out any show I want, great old movies, some I saw and loved, others I never got a chance to see. Going to the movies used to be cheap, but now it's too rich for my purse. Why would I need to go to the movies anyhow with people nowadays being so rude and talking all through the movie and yakking on their cell phones? I have enough movies so I can see one whenever I choose.

Now, isn't that luxury? Every tape is cataloged. I have an old file cabinet I found behind the office building on Eighth Street, and in it every single book and magazine and VCR tape is listed, so I can pull out what I want. It may look a junkyard to Suzie, but it just plain isn't—or rather wasn't.

It isn't like Suzie is over here much. She likes to call me every couple of weeks and complain. I only hear from Brady when he has something to boast about or wants to fly me down there for some event where a grandmother is welcome as some kind of certification of family. So he has his life, Suzie has hers, and, by the way, I also have mine.

I was just going along living my life happy as could be, collecting and sorting and cataloging, collecting and storing all the useful things I might need later. I'm not Bill Gates (you didn't think I'd know who he was, but I saw a documentary on him, one of my tapes), so why should I ever have to buy what I can get free? Chairs, tables, lamps, cabinets, nice ornamental stuff like this stuffed owl I found—where else would I ever get a fine creature like Roscoe? Some people collect art or even stupid things like license plates or baseball cards, and nobody calls the feds on them. What's wrong with collecting useful things, I ask you? I feel bad for them, thrown on the rubbish heap when there's still lots of life in them. So I save them.

Then there's my daughter yelling at me that I have a sickness.

"What are you talking about? I always get my flu shots at the senior center. I hardly ever get a cold."

"You're a hoarder. I saw it all on TV," she said. "We have to get you help." Clutching my hand, super dramatic. "We care for you, Mama, so we're going to make things right."

"What do I need help for? I'm doing fine. I'm happy. That's more than I can say for you." I meant it. Suzie is always complaining on the phone to me about her husband Ron's bad habits—he won't stop smoking, he leaves his underwear on the bedroom floor and his socks on the couch. As if I want to know about Ron's underwear, give me a break.

She went on and on but I tuned her out. If I hadn't learned to do that decades ago, I wouldn't be such a good-natured person, believe me.

But two weeks later Suzie showed up at the door with a woman—blond, in her forties, and wearing a navy suit. This simpering bitch was a therapist and she plumped her skinny behind down on my couch, which is sideways between the walls of books and zines stacked, neatly I might say, on one wall and my entertainment section on the other wall, my 1,247 tapes. I only have about ten inches' clearance between the couch and the entertainment section, but I can squeeze through, so what is the problem?

This therapist woman goes on about how hoarding is a disease but it can be treated. Then my daughter chimes in that if I don't let them come into my house and take away all my wonderful things, she will call elder services and have me moved into a home. For this I raised her from a squalling baby and put her through community college and paid for her wedding?

They had me over a barrel, so finally after three of these sessions with the woman who pretended to be on my side but never was, I agreed. She insisted on a tour of my house, making notes on her gizmo, talking into it. She checked the basement where I do laundry, the attic where I store stuff I don't need yet, and the garage with my car in it. It turned out that same TV program that my daughter had been watching that got me into trouble was going to come to my house and film everything. They were going to clean up my house and make everything neat and orderly, the way surely I wanted it, and it wouldn't cost me a penny. They'd clear things out with my approval, of course (smirk)—with that threat hanging over my head the whole time. I was sweating by then with anxiety.

"When will all this be happening?"

She consulted her electronic gizmo. "We can schedule you for two weeks from today. The film crew will come in the day before. Then we'll have two days to clear all this junk out and clean and make your house like new again. I know it will be hard for you to adjust, but in the end your house will be livable again."

Livable? What have I been doing here, dying? That gave me some time. I started moving my best stuff to the garage. At least I could protect that. I jammed the garage door opener so they couldn't get inside and moved my car to the driveway.

The film crew came. They moved a lot of my stuff around to make it look messy. They pushed some of the stuff from the hall into my bedroom so I could barely reach my bed that night. I could not sleep, facing the ordeal. Aside from when Walt died and when Brady had appendicitis and we just got him into the hospital in time, those two days were just about the worst of my life. They top my first delivery, when I was in labor for twenty hours, the time I broke my ankle tripping on my neighbor's dog and was in a cast for a month, and the time Walt had food poisoning from some stupid mayonnaise chicken salad at a picnic. Needless to say, I didn't make that. Adele Fortunata did. Never forgave her.

They arrived early, the therapist, a cleaning crew, and muscle, along with four huge semis labeled "WE GOT JUNK." Junk they called my stuff. I never picked up anything that wasn't useful. They were going to strip me bare. I had a stomachache. I couldn't eat breakfast and the coffee bored a hole in my belly.

When she saw how upset I was, the therapist took my hand as if I were a baby she was leading out of danger. "You need all these objects because you never properly processed your husband's death. It was so sudden and unexpected, you couldn't cope with the grief. You must let it out. You must experience your loss so you can let go of all these substitutes for him."

The therapist sat down with me as they carried all my precious things out to the front lawn. The neighbors were gaping. I'd never live this down. I was supposed to pick through everything and save a few things. Whatever I picked, they said I was saving too much. The therapist kept talking about processing grief. She insisted that I had never properly "processed" Walt's premature death and that hoarding, as she called it, was caused by that. Bunch of hooey. Process? Like can or freeze it? Walt didn't go collecting with me, but he liked the way I was frugal and found things instead of spending our hard-earned cash on a chair or a vase or some good reading matter. They couldn't understand how much pleasure I took in saving money and protecting good things that would otherwise end up in the dump. Finally I agreed with everything. Suzie cried and hugged me and I pretended to cry with her. I really did manage to shed a few tears when I saw them carrying out the VCRs and the Oriental rug I'd found rolled up and set out for the trash collector. I had planned to put it down in my bedroom when I had time.

I'd saved four VCRs in the garage, anyhow. "Now, what would you ever need six VCRs for? They don't even make them any longer. Don't you see how much room they take for no use?"

"How many suits do you have?"

She looked blank and stared at me. "I don't know. . . . Maybe six?"

"Why not just one? And how many lipsticks?"

She ignored that. Then I saw my stuffed owl Roscoe going out into the trash. I made a grab for him.

"Now, why on earth would you want a dusty mangy old stuffed owl?"

I lied. "It belonged to my late husband."

"It's a poor substitute for him, isn't it? Can't you remember him without something probably full of dust and insect eggs?"

I loved Roscoe, his yellow eyes looking at me from the mantel. I made another grab for him but Suzie held me down in the chair. The therapist said, "If it bothers you so much, we can send it to the resale shop."

The crew along with Suzie was dividing all my property into things to be dumped and items to go to a resale shop. I found out which one. I could have tried to find out where what they were trashing was going to end up, but I am not a garbage picker and those places stink. I counted my losses but I bore with them; I had no choice. My lovely oak bookcase, my gilt elephant with a howdah on top, Walt's golf clubs, a round mirror with only a little damage to the left edge, three platters in the shape of fish, the tin of buttons, straight chairs that just needed a bit of work. I imagined running away to Florida or Mexico or Puerto Rico when they were done, to escape scrutiny, but I love my house and I know my way around here, so I sat in the lawn chair and picked through my treasures and watched them disappear. I wished for a hurricane or a blizzard, but the sky stayed blue and the day stayed mild for early November. I imagined a great wind carrying them all off and me returning to my own home, my private home, and putting everything back where I keep it. But they kept stealing my things and carting them off and I had to sit there and smile for the cameras and listen to that simpering therapist's bull dung. Inside I was boiling, but I'm not stupid, no matter what they think. They had the upper hand—for now.

Finally they had "restored" my home to what it had never looked like in all the years I'd lived there, raised my ungrateful children, been married and happy with Walt, made a life for myself that satisfied me. The therapist set up an appointment with me for some other meddler. I promised to go. I could sit through more bull dung if that would get them all off my back.

Adam and Liz had decamped before the last truck roared off with my things inside.

They had a fundraiser to attend for some private school. Adam is in real estate. I don't know what he does and I don't particularly care, so long as he lets me alone. Finally Suzie, who had hung around to the bitter end—bitter for me—left, telling me how wonderful the house looked. At last they were all gone, relatives, therapist, musclemen, cleanup crew, and trucks. I sat in my boring living room with only the TV for company, a single bookcase of books they'd agreed to leave me, one VCR, and ten tapes. The dining room was set up for company who would never arrive. At least they cleaned everything. It does tend to get dusty, but I don't have allergies, so what do I care. I was exhausted and furious. How would you like a bunch of strangers to invade your house, take three-quarters of your possessions away, tell you what you're supposed to think and feel—all of which was being filmed for anybody in the country to gape at. I felt humiliated. I felt violated. And they had kept saying how nice it was now and expecting me to thank them. The next morning I brought my few saved treasures from the garage into the house. It still felt bare and lonely. My house and I were bereft, robbed, pillaged!

Monday I went to the bank and withdrew $500 in cash. Then I rented a U-Haul and headed for the resale shop. I figured after three days, they'd have my stuff out. I recognized twenty-three pieces of mine, so I bought them back. I told the lady I was furnishing a condo. When I unloaded the stuff into my house and set everything up, it was still barren, but at least I had a few things to look at and use like that easy chair. The maroon upholstery was worn but it was comfy. Some of the glassware and dishes I'd collected, good pieces. My extra china closet that I could begin to fill. That nice table with the inlaid chessboard. A few cracks didn't spoil it. The stuffed owl, put back on the mantel. Welcome home, Roscoe. Two salad bowls. I like wood. Two end tables. I can always use end tables. Another bookcase. It was a humble beginning but better than they'd left it. I didn't feel quite so strongly I was rattling around alone in the house.

I had the locks changed so Suzie couldn't come barging in. I found some thick drapes in a different resale shop so she couldn't see in any longer from the porch. I've learned to protect myself. They won't catch me again. I went to the therapist, a man this time but just as opinionated and misguided as that lady. I parroted what they expected me to say. I'm not stupid. He said he was very pleased with my progress and my cure.

Every weekend I search for yard and garage sales and slowly I am collecting things that make my life worthwhile, treasures others have abandoned that I can enjoy. My home is beginning to feel like mine again, comfy and full of objects I have rescued. The month before last, I was on TV and lay low for a while. The show was just as humiliating as the experience itself. They made my home look disgusting. I found an auburn wig in a consignment shop I put on to go hunting now. If people stare at it, I say I had chemo and they shut up. I know people will forget that show shortly (there was a man on half the show who collected so many toys and dolls he couldn't get to his bathroom; I've never had trouble getting to mine. I love to take baths). People nowadays discard memories as fast as they discard perfectly good objects. But here I am ready to save what shouldn't be thrown on the trash heap, like this old woman and many another. I'm gradually getting my life back, the way I like it. I'm settling back into my home.

SAVING MOTHER FROM HERSELF

A longtime favorite of feminists, multigenre author and social activist Marge Piercy is back with new fiction, which *Ms.* is thrilled to be the first to publish. In this short story, poignancy and empowerment mix as a woman resists her family's efforts to clean up what they consider her messy life.

BY MARGE PIERCY

MY DAUGHTER, SUZIE, AND MY BROTHER, ADAM, really got after me about what they called my hoarding. I live alone. My husband died when he was just 58 of one of those heart attacks that hit without warning. He was playing golf—something he enjoyed but was never much good at—with another dentist and two podiatrists on the Wednesday when he just keeled over on the fifth hole trying to bang his way out of a sand trap. At first they thought he was kidding them. I was only 50 then.

I continued working, of course. I was a paralegal for 30 years in a small law office that did mostly real estate, wills and probate, and small-business stuff. I was really as much a secretary as a paralegal, if I'm honest. But it wasn't all that taxing. I liked the two men I worked for and it paid decently, a middling middle class wage, you might say. Four years ago, I retired. Actually they retired and closed the office, and at 59, I wasn't about to get hired to do anything better than greeting folks at Walmart or bagging at the supermarket.

I had the insurance from Walt. I'd banked it. I had his social security, which was better than mine would have been. I was okay. The mortgage on our house we paid off decades ago. It was the same house I raised Suzie and my son Brady in. Brady's out in Arizona, so I only see him maybe every couple of years when he sends me tickets to fly out there. The last time was for my granddaughter Olivia's wedding. A very nice affair that must have set him back I can't imagine how much. Olivia's pregnant now, he tells me. I'll be a great-grandmother before I can take that in. Amazing. Makes me feel 90.

Suzie tried to get me to move into an apartment, but why? I'm used to this house. I know my neighbors and they know me. We don't hang out together, but we keep an eye on each other's property and have a friendly chat over the fence now and then. I have a nice little garden out back and a two-car garage. This house has three bedrooms so I have plenty of room for my things. That's what Suzie and Adam object to, as if there's something wrong with liking bargains and pretty things and useful things other people throw away. If you ask me, people discard too many items nowadays. I feel sorry when I see a perfectly good lamp or glassware or a rug that's still usable or even a flower pot sitting in a dumpster or out on the street waiting for the pickup to be taken to the landfill and left to rot. So I bring them home. I know I'll get some use out of them by and by. And books and magazines. Perfectly fine to read. And VCR tapes. At garage sales I can always find something interesting. When you live alone, you appreciate entertainment. I always have the TV on even when I'm reading. It's company. I like to keep up with the news and

JUNK?

Letters

As winter came to a cold close in the forty-ninth state, some residents of Fairbanks, Alaska, turned up the heat on a local legislator who wanted *Ms.* magazine off the shelves of the local co-op market.

The conservative Fairbanks assemblyman Lance Roberts, one of twenty-three hundred members of the natural foods market/deli, posted on his website that he had noticed "an extremely liberal magazine promoting killing babies" on sale at the co-op. (That would be the Summer 2013 issue of *Ms.*, featuring the Texas state senator Wendy Davis, who bravely filibustered against draconian antiabortion legislation.) He described another *Ms.* cover (Fall 2013), which pictured Rosie the Riveter as a fast-food worker, as "promoting ways to destroy the economy and kill jobs"—presumably because fast-food workers are radical enough to demand a living wage.

Keeping his promise, Roberts withdrew his co-op membership. Not that anyone minded. Here's how the co-op's general manager, Mary Christensen, responded:

Lance—

I am sorry that you see it this way. Co-op Market doesn't take a political position by the content of the literature it offers. [Ms.] magazine exists to tell stories about all kinds of issues that affect women and children; teaching them, loving them, and raising them to be kind and love life . . . is that political? You made this a political issue. My mother always told me that the things you put energy into grow. You made interest in Ms. *magazine grow by*

putting your energy there. We at Co-op Market welcome everyone. We offer an opportunity for people on all sides of the political spectrum to find common ground in healthy food and community. We ordered another magazine, the National Review, *that I hope offers a balance in perspectives. It was started by William F. Buckley, one of the foremost conservative thinkers of our time. As always, you are welcome at Co-op Market, and we respect that you choose not to be a member-owner.*

We really appreciated Christensen's letter to Roberts. We also thought Avril Wiers Ester's letter to the editor of the Fairbanks paper *Daily News-Miner* was right on point:

The uproar over the Co-op Market stocking Ms. *is ridiculous. Just because Barnes & Noble stocks* High Times *does not mean that [the bookstore] advocates the legalization of marijuana, and just because my dentist has copies of* Shooting Illustrated *doesn't mean he's trying to shove his ideals down my throat. Consumers have the choice of whether they choose to purchase a good. By admitting that pro-choice people do exist in the world, I could buy my organic groceries and get a dose of much-needed feminism, which is (shhh—don't tell the Right) my freedom. . . .*

Sounds to me like we need more people who read Ms. *and stand up for women's rights in Alaska. Women are 48 percent of the population of Alaska.*

And thank you, Fairbanks feminists!

THE EDITORS
Summer 2014 issue

Aftermath of Isla Vista

BY **DONNA DECKER** • FALL 2014

I T WAS IN 1968 that the poet Muriel Rukeyser asked, "What would happen if one woman told the truth about her life? The world would split open."

In 2014, the world did split open, and female truth gushed forth, after one beleaguered man too many committed another "supremacy crime." The outcome: the world can now spell *m-i-s-o-g-y-n-y.*

The catalyst: on May 23, 2014, twenty-two-year-old Elliot Rodger murdered six people in Isla Vista, California. After stabbing to death his two roommates and their visitor, all young men, the heavily armed shooter knocked on the door of Alpha Phi sorority at UC Santa Barbara and, when there was no response, shot and killed two Tri Delta sorority members who happened to be outside. He then drove off and fatally fired at a young man at an eatery before killing himself.

A day earlier, Rodger had laid out his "Day of Retribution" plans in a YouTube video. "I'll give you exactly what you deserve. All of you," he said calmly. "All you girls who rejected me and looked down upon me and, you know, treated me like scum while you gave yourselves to other men."

He had also written a 137-page manifesto in which he described his personal "war on women" to "punish all females for the crime of depriving me of sex." After his murderous rampage, people discovered he had put up other disturbing You-

> **"After each horrifying crime, only a few commentators made the connection between the violence and toxic masculinity, or hypermasculinity, nor was there a deeper questioning of cultural forces behind such actions."**

Tube videos as well and had posted on internet boards that attracted "men's rights activists," "pickup artists" (PUA, who purport to teach men how to manipulatively seduce women, believing that they're *entitled* to women's sexual attention, even in the face of clear rejection), or "incels" (involuntary celibates). He seemed to particularly align himself with PUAHate, which criticizes PUA as a scam. In November, Rodger posted to an online message board, "One day incels will realize their true strength and numbers, and will overthrow this oppressive feminist system. . . . Start envisioning a world where WOMEN FEAR YOU."

A mass murder fueled by misogyny and a toxic version of masculinity isn't a new story. Most famously, in the 1989 Montreal Massacre, Marc

Lépine killed fourteen women at an engineering school, at one point announcing, "You're women, you're going to be engineers. You're all a bunch of feminists. I hate feminists." And in the 2009 Collier Township shooting, George Sodini—who, like Rodger, had chronicled his rejections by women (on a blog)—killed three women at their aerobics class in a Pittsburgh suburb.

But after each horrifying crime, only a few commentators made the connection between the violence and toxic masculinity, or hypermasculinity, nor was there a deeper questioning of cultural forces behind such actions.

One of those forces is men's rights groups, which, in a backlash to feminism, see men as the oppressed sex and promote a stereotypical macho ideology that forces men into a narrow cultural script. Harris O'Malley, who blogs under the name of Dr. NerdLove, says the worst of men's rights activists promote such cultish and toxic thinking by "berating and insulting women and talking about how women 'manipulate' men and how women are men's 'natural enemy.' They're obsessed with being 'alpha,' with being 'real men,' not 'manginas.' They're all about asserting manhood by force, 'showing' women and punishing them. Manhood by violence. Manhood by force. Manhood by sex. This is the world that Rodger was drowning himself in."

The cost of such narrow thinking is hefty to women *and* men. And not just women are appalled by it. The White Ribbon Campaign, launched in Ontario in 1991 in response to the Montreal Massacre, is the "world's largest movement of men and boys working to end violence against women and girls, promote gender equity, healthy relationships and a new vision of masculinity." The educational campaign, which conducts trainings in gender equality among other activities, has spread to more than sixty countries, asking men to wear white ribbons as a symbolic "pledge to never commit, condone or remain silent about violence against women and girls."

The motivation for the tragedy in Isla Vista can't be reduced to one tidy explanation. But the fact that Rodger had revealed his hate-filled motivations online before he began his killing spree set a national and international dialogue into overdrive, with both social and mainstream media racing to keep up.

A new Twitter hashtag was born—#YesAllWomen—which turned the #NotAllMen meme and hashtag upside down. The idea behind #NotAll Men was this: all too often, when a woman complains about patriarchy or misogyny, someone, usually a defensive man, will respond with the riposte "not all men" or "I'm a good guy" or "The killer was just a crazy dude. This is an extreme, isolated thing. Why are we even having this discussion?" Such comments, deliberately or not, derail discussion of male violence against women.

Once launched, it took off: #YesAllWomen tweets peaked at 61,500 on May 25 and reached more than a million worldwide, as far away as Pakistan, Indonesia, and Qatar. Women claimed #YesAllWomen as a space in which to share stories of their own rapes, sexual assaults, and everyday misogynist vexations. Famous personalities weighed in with the rest of us.

Mainstream media could not look away from this social media blitz, with all major outlets reporting or opining on it. But, inevitably, the backlash came. In a particularly smug and lethal column that appeared two weeks after Isla Vista and its attendant feminist outrage, *The Washington Post*'s George Will attacked "the supposed campus epidemic of rape, a.k.a. 'sexual assault'" (quotes his), determining that "the 20 percent assault rate is preposterous. . . . [V]ictimhood," he purported, is "a coveted status that confers privileges."

Posthaste, the activist Wagatwe Wanjuki kick-started #SurvivorPrivilege, a hashtag movement that documented the "perks" of this so-called coveted status. "Where's my survivor privilege?" tweeted Wanjuki on June 9. "Was expelled & have $10,000s of private student loans used to attend school that didn't care I was raped."

Is it enough, this textual flurry of fury?

At the Ms. Wonder Awards in November 2014 at the National Press Club in Washington, D.C.: (*above*) executive editor Katherine Spillar; and (*left*) award-winning fast-food strikers from Chicago, New York City, Pittsburgh, Philadelphia, and North Carolina, with Feminist Majority Foundation board member Dolores Huerta.

In the 2012 Barnard Center for Research on Women report *#FemFuture: Online Revolution,* the authors Courtney Martin and Vanessa Valenti assert that online feminism is "'consciousness raising for the 21st century' . . . [and] young women across the country—and all over the world, in fact—are discovering new ways to leverage the Internet to make fundamental progress in the unfinished revolution of feminism."

The #RapeIsRape campaign (promoted by *Ms.* and the Feminist Majority Foundation) helped spur the FBI to finally change its outdated definition of rape. The #FBrape campaign pressured Facebook to remove content that promotes gender-based violence. Facebook, Twitter, and petition campaigns helped expose Susan G. Komen's decision to remove funding from Planned Parenthood. Hashtags such as #StopRush and #FlushRush helped persuade corporate sponsors to drop their ads from Rush Limbaugh's show after he slut-shamed the Georgetown law student Sandra Fluke. And the recent virtual action against a column in the *Chicago Sun-Times* about the transgender actor/activist Laverne Cox led the newspaper to pull the column and apologize.

Clearly, the attention paid to the link between hypermasculinity and violence against women has taken root as well. Yet Gish Jen, author of *Mona in the Promised Land,* warns, "This incident [Isla Vista] has helped regalvanize women in an important way. We have certainly made progress over the years, but what with such a long way to go, it's no time for complacency."

No indeed, feminism has never enjoyed complacency.

A CATALOG OF THE MASS SHOOTINGS that have occurred since Donna Decker's article was published—and names of those who've been gunned down in schools, houses of worship, movie theaters, shopping malls, salons—would fill pages of this book. It has become an all-too-common exercise in America to examine, after the fact, the violent, antisocial ideologies—racism, xenophobia, white supremacy—fueling deadly rampages. But the common strain—and stain—of misogyny undergirds it all. A 2019 investigation by *Mother Jones* reveals a stark, predictable pattern of toxic masculinity and domestic violence—not just among men who use guns to harm and kill intimate partners, but also among men who commit public mass shootings.

Since the Isla Vista massacre, a new vernacular has taken hold—that of "incels," shorthand for involuntary celibate men. A recent report by the National Threat Assessment Center (a division of the U.S. Secret Service) called attention to the rise in the threat of violence against women by self-identified incels and emphasized the importance of identifying early warning signs in men who are a potential danger.

The Women of Black Lives Matter

BY **BRITTNEY COOPER** • WINTER 2015

O N LABOR DAY WEEKEND 2014, I sat in the basement of St. John's United Church of Christ in St. Louis, organizing with a group of young women who helped mount the local response to police killing the unarmed Ferguson, Missouri, teenager Michael Brown. Comprising many women—both queer and straight, national and local—our group co-facilitated a "learn-in" about what a gender-progressive racial-justice framework might entail.

The way in which the Black Lives Matter (BLM) national organizing network—the group with whom I had traveled by bus more than twenty hours from New York—conceptualizes this new movement is starkly different from both the civil rights and the Black Power eras of the 1960s and 1970s. Recently, I had a chance to chat again with some of the women I met during our Ferguson rides, and with others who have joined the work along the way.

Patrisse Cullors, one of the BLM co-founders, told me, "We are not just talking about a Black cis [one whose gender identity matches his or her gender assignment at birth] man who is a preacher." Alluding to the predominance of Christian male leaders in the 1960s, Cullors made clear that the new framework must reject this charismatic male model. Also established in the heat of a long summer that saw police kill other unarmed Black men and boys, including Eric Garner in Staten Island, twelve-year-old Tamir Rice in Cleveland, and John Crawford III in Beavercreek, Ohio (shot in Walmart while holding one of the store's BB guns), is that the politics of this moment must prove vigilant, expansive, and visionary enough to withstand a protracted struggle.

> **"I'm inspired by the fervor of young people I've worked with who have resolved that white supremacy 'has got to go.'"**

That struggle has been intensified by the failure to indict Darren Wilson, the police officer who shot Michael Brown, and Daniel Pantaleo, the officer who held Eric Garner in a choke hold as Garner cried out repeatedly, "I can't breathe."

These killings have galvanized consciousness-raising, particularly among young people. They have staged marches, rallies, and die-ins at local malls, blocked traffic, and inspired well-known athletes to wear "I can't breathe" T-shirts and put their hands up in a "don't shoot" position.

The Women of #BLACK LIVES MATTER

A new civil rights movement has emerged from the tragic killings of young African Americans—and women are at the activist forefront

BY BRITTNEY COOPER

ON LABOR DAY WEEKEND 2014, I SAT IN THE basement of St. John's United Church of Christ in St. Louis, organizing with a group of young women who helped mount the local response to police killing unarmed Ferguson, Missouri, teenager Michael Brown. Composed of many women—both quiet and straight, national and local—our group co-facilitated a "learn-in" about what a gender-progressive racial-justice framework might entail.

The way in which the Black Lives Matter (BLM) national organizing network—the group with whom I had traveled by bus more than 20 hours from New York—conceptualizes this new movement is starkly different from both the civil rights and Black Power eras of the 1960s and 1970s. Recently, I had a chance to chat again with some of the women I met during our Ferguson rides, and with others who have joined the work along the way.

Patrisse Cullors, one of the BLM cofounders, told me, "We are not just talking about a Black cis [one whose gender identity matches his or her gender

In Oakland, California, Chinyere Tutashinda speaks at a "Millions March" protest against the police killing of unarmed Black men.

assignment at birth] man who is a preacher." Alluding to the predominance of Christian male leaders in the 1960s, Cullors made clear that the new framework must reject this charismatic male model. Also, established in the heat of a long summer that saw police kill other unarmed Black men and boys, including Eric Garner in Staten Island, 12-year-old Tamir Rice in Cleveland and John Crawford III in Beavercreek, Ohio (shot in Walmart while holding one of the store's BB guns), is that the politics of this moment must prove vigilant, expansive and visionary enough to withstand a protracted struggle.

That struggle has been intensified by the failure to indict Darren Wilson, the police officer who shot Michael Brown, and Daniel Pantaleo, the officer who held Eric Garner in a chokehold as Garner cried out repeatedly, "I can't breathe."

These killings have galvanized consciousness-raising, particularly among young people. They have staged marches, rallies and die-ins at local malls, blocked traffic, and inspired well-known athletes to wear "I can't breathe" T-shirts and put their hands up in a "don't shoot" position.

Yet these many months of collective fervor since August 2014 have so far netted zero victories in terms of indictments. So protesters and organizers now ask, "What next?" Jamila Lyiscott, a faith and social-justice organizer with Cyphers for Justice and Urban Word in New York, shared with me that a 17-year-old man with whom she works texted her excitedly (but naively), "I want us to sit down and dismantle white supremacy."

Like Lyiscott, I'm inspired by the fervor of young people I've worked with who have resolved that white supremacy "has got to go." I wonder how to hold on to the truth that change takes time—yet not kill the momentum with the impotent rhetoric of gradualism. And I'm inspired by young women like Johnetta "Netta" Elzie, one of the organizers from St. Louis, who told me, "I'm fighting for future kids that I don't even have and I'm fighting for myself because I'm only 25." She's been on the ground since the day Michael Brown was killed, enduring harrowing days of rubber bullets and tear gas. Now a field organizer with Amnesty International, Elzie also continues her local activism through a daily ThisIsTheMovement newsletter, which she organizes and distributes with her friend DeRay McKesson.

Cullors, who along with Alicia Garza and Opal Tometi created the #BlackLivesMatter hashtag and organized the Black Lives Matter campaign after the 2012 killing of unarmed young Floridian Trayvon Martin by a self-appointed vigilante, told me, "Movement and change take a significant amount of time. We are in a state of emergency, [but] things take decades, centuries to change. To unearth those systems—racism, patriarchy, transphobia—takes consistency and perseverance."

This commitment to an intersectional framework—involving class, sexuality, gender identity and more, in addition to race—makes this movement different than 20th-century civil rights efforts. BLM intentionally elevates both cis and trans women of color in its leadership and activism. Lourdes Ashley Hunter, cofounder of the Trans Women of Color Collective, reinforces the view that racial justice cannot focus only on Black men. "The same system that is killing Black men is killing Black trans women. One of the many ways is by denying access to housing, jobs, education, food," Hunter says. Adds Cullors, "We need a national campaign that has to resonate locally, a new poor people's campaign that targets gentrification, law enforcement violence and collective labor, [and involves] Black trans organizations and Black women's organizations."

Cullors laid out a two-part framework for a Year of Resistance and Resilience, with the first phase—currently underway—involving government resolutions declaring the need to value Black life. The second phase will push various bills that, for example, require the Department of Justice to "grade" police departments on how they police communities of color. Departments that fail would be subject to defunding, in hopes that the monies would be rerouted to public schools and other social services.

Other issues on the table include anti-gentrification and food justice. Cullors and Hunter are particularly outraged about the structural violence faced by trans and cis Black women with restricted access to safe housing, healthy food and good jobs.

Communal racial trauma is another thing the movement will address. Elzie says her focus will be on "helping people build communities out of tragedy." Hunter adds, "There needs to be healing for everyone. White people, too. They are wrapped up in a system they were born into." Cullors spoke of the need to move beyond the buzzword of "self-care" and to think about "collective care."

"There is no manual for the movement," Elzie points out. Moving forward will involve a fair share of trial and error. But wherever these women lead, we should follow. Something tells me they are in the sure pursuit of freedom. ■

BRITTNEY COOPER is assistant professor of women's and gender studies and Africana studies at Rutgers University and cofounder of Crunk Feminist Collective. Her book, tentatively titled Race Women: Gender and the Making of a Black Public Intellectual Tradition, *is forthcoming.*

> **This commitment to an intersectional framework—involving class, sexuality, gender identity and more, in addition to race—makes this movement different than 20th-century civil rights efforts.**

Yet these many months of collective fervor since August 2014 have so far netted zero victories in terms of indictments. So protesters and organizers now ask, "What next?" Jamila Lyiscott, a faith and social justice organizer with Cyphers for Justice and Urban Word in New York, shared with me that a seventeen-year-old man with whom she works texted her excitedly (but naively), "I want us to sit down and dismantle white supremacy."

Like Lyiscott, I'm inspired by the fervor of young people I've worked with who have resolved that white supremacy "has got to go." I wonder how to hold on to the truth that change takes time yet not kill the momentum with the impotent rhetoric of gradualism. And I'm inspired by young women like Johnetta "Netta" Elzie, one of the organizers from St. Louis, who told me, "I'm fighting for future kids that I don't even have and I'm fighting for myself because I'm only twenty-five." She's been on the ground since the day Michael Brown was killed, enduring harrowing days of rubber bullets and tear gas. Now a field organizer with Amnesty International, Elzie also continues her local activism through a daily *This Is the Movement* newsletter, which she organizes and distributes with her friend DeRay Mckesson.

Cullors, who along with Alicia Garza and Opal Tometi created the #BlackLivesMatter hashtag and organized the Black Lives Matter campaign after the 2012 killing of the unarmed young Floridian Trayvon Martin by a self-appointed vigilante, told me, "Movement and change take a significant amount of time. We are in a state of emergency, [but] things take decades, centuries to change. To unearth those systems—racism, patriarchy, transphobia—takes consistency and perseverance."

This commitment to an intersectional framework—involving class, sexuality, gender identity, and more, in addition to race—makes this movement different from twentieth-century civil rights efforts. BLM intentionally elevates both cis and trans women of color in its leadership and activism. Lourdes Ashley Hunter, co-founder of the Trans Women of Color Collective, reinforces the view that racial justice cannot focus only on Black men. "The same system that is killing Black men is killing Black trans women. One of the many ways is by denying access to housing, jobs, education, food," Hunter says. Adds Cullors, "We need a national campaign that has to resonate locally, a new poor people's campaign that targets gentrification, law enforcement violence, and collective labor, [and involves] Black trans organizations and Black women's organizations."

Cullors laid out a two-part framework for a Year of Resistance and Resilience, with the first phase—currently under way—involving government resolutions declaring the need to value Black life. The second phase will push various bills that, for example, require the Department of Justice to "grade" police departments on how they police communities of color. Departments that fail would be subject to defunding, in hopes that the money would be rerouted to public schools and other social services.

Other issues on the table include anti-gentrification and food justice. Cullors and Hunter are particularly outraged about the structural violence faced by trans and cis Black women with restricted access to safe housing, healthy food, and good jobs.

Communal racial trauma is another issue the movement will address. Elzie says her focus will be on "helping people build communities out of tragedy." Hunter adds, "There needs to be healing for everyone. White people, too. They are wrapped up in a system they were born into." Cullors spoke of the need to move beyond the buzzword of "self-care" and to think about "collective care."

"There is no manual for the movement," Elzie points out. Moving forward will involve a fair share of trial and error. But wherever these women lead, we should follow. Something tells me they are in the sure pursuit of freedom.

Ms.'s Fall 2016 issue was slated to have this photo on the cover with the words "This Is What a President Looks Like." With a print deadline one week after the 2016 election, the *Ms.* editors made the choice to still run the photo on the inside front cover, but with Hillary Clinton's concession speech—a proud, hopeful message for all of us.

contents | FALL 16
VOLUME XXVI • NUMBER 3

"TO ALL THE WOMEN, AND ESPECIALLY THE YOUNG WOMEN, WHO PUT THEIR FAITH IN THIS CAMPAIGN AND IN ME, I WANT YOU TO KNOW THAT NOTHING HAS MADE ME PROUDER THAN TO BE YOUR CHAMPION. I KNOW WE HAVE STILL NOT SHATTERED THAT HIGHEST AND HARDEST GLASS CEILING, BUT SOMEDAY SOMEONE WILL, AND HOPEFULLY SOONER THAN WE MIGHT THINK RIGHT NOW."
—HILLARY RODHAM CLINTON

We marched, an estimated 5.6 million of us in at least 999 marches worldwide, throughout the United States and in ninety-two countries on all seven continents, even in Antarctica. Never before in the history of the world had so many people in so many places taken to the streets on a single day for a single purpose.

—from "Feet on the Ground. Not Backing Down!,"
Spring 2017

FEET ON THE GROUND. NOT BACKING DOWN!

ON TRUMP'S FIRST DAY IN OFFICE, WOMEN DELIVERED A HUGE MESSAGE—TOO MASSIVE TO IGNORE

THERE WAS A MOMENT DURING THE NEW YORK MARCH WHEN THE BELLS OF A FIFTH AVENUE CHURCH RANG OUT WOODY GUTHRIE'S "THIS LAND IS YOUR LAND" AND WE OLDER MARCHERS SPONTANEOUSLY SANG ALONG, FEEDING THE LYRICS TO SOME OF THE YOUNGER MARCHERS BESIDE US. HUNDREDS OF WOMEN ON FIFTH AVENUE SINGING THEIR MESSAGE TOGETHER.
—ELLEN STERN WITCHELL, MARCHING IN NEW YORK CITY

I watched a little girl on Constitution Avenue talking to a female member of the D.C. National Guard. The conversation ended in a hug. That moment said it all for me. We're all in this together.
—KATHERINE LARSEN, MARCHING IN WASHINGTON, D.C.

As an Afro-Caribbean woman, I marched because we women are all connected. I marched for my mother, aunts, sisters, grandmothers and elders who made a way out of no-way through immigration and migration.
—SYLVIA LEWIS, MARCHING IN NEW YORK CITY

I marched with a bunch of dykes, and hearing women nearby exclaiming, "I've found my people!" as we stomped and chanted "The dykes are here" was my favorite thing about that amazing, womyn-powered day.
—KATIE WATKINS, MARCHING IN WASHINGTON, D.C.

[1] Sister March occupies 42nd Street in New York City. NYC's was the third largest—with an estimated 500,000 protesters. [2] We're looking at you, Mr. Trump. Also seen: "Men of quality do not fear equality." [3] The march of the penguins: Penguins for Peace join in from their expedition ship off the coast of the Antarctic Peninsula.

www.msmagazine.com

Ms. SPRING 2017 | 11

I MARCHED FOR MY UNDOCUMENTED MOTHER; FOR MY AUNTS WHO DO NOT SPEAK ENGLISH; FOR MY DARK AND BEAUTIFUL COUSINS; FOR THE UNDOCUMENTED, UNAFRAID AND UNAPOLOGETIC LATINX WOMYN; FOR THE FUTURE AND RIGHTS OF MY DAUGHTERS; FOR ALL THE WOMYN FORGOTTEN ON ELECTION DAY.
—JULIA RAMIREZ, MARCHING IN WASHINGTON, D.C.

[1] Girl power in Las Vegas. Also seen: "I vote in 8 years." [2] Carrie Fisher inspires D.C. protester. [3] Young women work together to carry a banner—solidarity in action. [4] Inspired by Shepard Fairey's iconic Barack Obama "Hope" poster, the Amplifier Foundation commissioned a new series from three artists responding to Trump's inauguration; it features Muslim Americans, African Americans, Native Americans, Latinas and lesbian women. [5] Demonstrators gather around the reflecting pool in Hermann Square, within view of Houston City Hall. [6] The birthplace of the women's suffrage movement saw 10,000 marchers.

Special Women's March issue: *Ms.* was the only publication to cover the marches in such detail, including a tally of every march location worldwide.

On the edge of one of the most conservative states in the United States, almost 3,000 people gathered in downtown Fargo to show their support for women—and refugees, peace, the LGBTQ+ community and Black Lives Matter.
—BAILEY HOVLAND, MARCHING IN FARGO, NORTH DAKOTA

WE MARCHED WITH WOMEN, CHILDREN AND MEN OF ALL RACES, RELIGIONS, GENDER IDENTITIES AND NATIONALITIES. THE ORGANIZERS EXPECTED 600 WHO WOULD MARCH ON THE SIDEWALKS. WHEN 11,000 SHOWED UP, THEY GAVE US THE STREETS!

—DEB BALLAM, MARCHING IN ANN ARBOR, MICHIGAN

[1] The 5-degree weather doesn't stop Alaskan marchers. [2] Girl protester Niko at Los Angeles march already gets intersectionality. [3] Northern Virginians march. [4] High school students Colette Raptosh (left) and Nora Harren organized the Boise march, which brought 5,000 demonstrators to the steps of the Idaho statehouse. [5] Also seen: "Did I survive a dictator to be: deported for being a foreigner, registered for being a Muslim, grabbed for being a woman in America?" [6] Los Angeles feminists [7] The scene at Boise's capitol

1 GUSTAVUS, AK

2

3 WINCHESTER, VA

DIVERS STRENGTH GUSTAVUS AK

BLACK LIVES MATTER
WOMEN LIVES MATTER
DISABLED LIVES MATTER
LGBT LIVES MATTER

4

5 NASTY WOMAN NASTY WOMAN

6 WE WILL FIND A WAY LOVE TRUMPS HATE

7 BOISE, ID

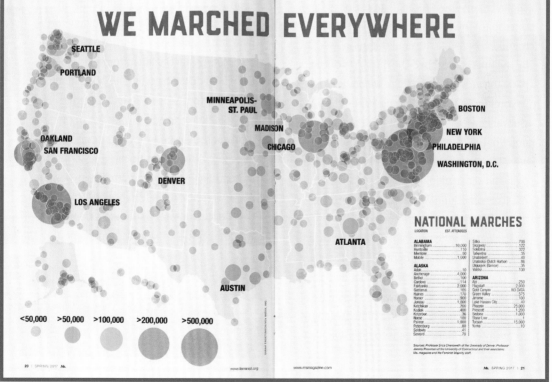

WE MARCHED EVERYWHERE

SEATTLE
PORTLAND
MINNEAPOLIS-ST. PAUL
BOSTON
MADISON
NEW YORK
OAKLAND
SAN FRANCISCO
CHICAGO
PHILADELPHIA
WASHINGTON, D.C.
DENVER
LOS ANGELES
ATLANTA
AUSTIN

<50,000   >50,000   >100,000   >200,000   >500,000

NATIONAL MARCHES

LOCATION	EST. ATTENDEES
ALABAMA	
Birmingham	10,000
Huntsville	110
Mentone	50
Mobile	1,000
ALASKA	
Adak	10
Anchorage	4,000
Bethel	100
Cordova	114
Fairbanks	2,000
Gustavus	105
Haines	170
Homer	900
Juneau	1,000
Ketchikan	200
Kodiak	400
Kotzebue	36
Nome	100
Palmer	1,000
Petersburg	80
Seldovia	41
Seward	70

LOCATION	EST. ATTENDEES
Sitka	700
Skagway	122
Soldotna	322
Talkeetna	35
Unalakleet	40
Unalaska (Dutch Harbor)	86
Utqiaġvik (Barrow)	35
Valdez	130
ARIZONA	
Ajo	250
Flagstaff	2,000
Gold Canyon	NO DATA
Green Valley	575
Jerome	100
Lake Havasu City	40
Phoenix	25,000
Prescott	1,200
Sedona	1,000
Show Low	1
Tucson	15,000
Yuma	10

Sources: Professor Erica Chenoweth of the University of Denver; Professor Jeremy Pressman of the University of Connecticut and their associates; Ms. magazine and the Feminist Majority staff.

Letters

When I saw the notice for the Women's March, I didn't care if it turned out to be just a sad little group of shell-shocked women like myself. I just wanted my teenage daughter Rosie to see how people are supposed to respond to injustice of this magnitude. You don't sit silent. So with a need to do *something,* we made a sign and bundled up in warm clothes and walked to the bus stop that morning. When the bus arrived, it had room for just two more to stand in the aisle.

My daughter smiled up at me. We weren't alone.

As the bus drove down Lincoln Street getting closer to the capitol, we began to see all the bus stops filling with people. Streets began to jam up with cars. Three blocks from the capitol the driver announced we'd have to unload because she couldn't get closer. By the time we reached the outskirts of the park, the crowd was so thick we couldn't see beyond those surrounding us. When the wave we were part of inched its way to the starting point of the march more than an hour later, we joined the surge chanting our anger and pain and sense of injustice. It was cathartic. It felt like something was coming back to life.

My friend sent Rosie a copy of *Ms.* magazine with the coverage of the march, a neatly bound keepsake of photos, interviews, and commentary to remember that day. She brought it to school to show her classmates and teachers, and it opened a dialogue about what this presidency means to girls, what can be done to survive it, and what good could come out of it.

"You know," I told my Rosie, "it will be better for you." But I could tell from her attitude that she already knew. She saw the biggest crowd of people she's ever seen in one place, saw the coverage of people coming out into the streets in cities around the country and the world, the biggest mobilization of protest in our history. She knows we made it happen and understands from firsthand experience the force we can be, we women.

SUSAN BURNS
Denver, Co.
Summer 2017 issue

I am writing about a special project some women and I have in mind for educating the Wyoming state legislators about women's rights. To name a few problems that have spurred this project: Wyoming came in fifty-first in the wage pay gap (below forty-nine states and D.C.). Abortion is almost completely inaccessible. Domestic violence isn't prosecuted harshly. Our state minimum wage ties for the lowest with Georgia's ($5.15).

I would like to subscribe each of our sixty representatives and thirty state senators to *Ms.* magazine. Wyoming has a supermajority of Republicans and a supermajority of men. My impression is that Wyoming legislators think that women's issues are a nonissue, that they don't know that 50 percent of their constituents are women.

ISABEL RUCKER
Pinedale, Wyo.
Summer 2017 issue

Peace Strength Wisdom Wonder

BY **AVIVA DOVE-VIEBAHN** • FALL 2017

MOMENTS BEFORE DIANA LEAVES her lush island home, Themyscira, in the director Patty Jenkins's summer blockbuster *Wonder Woman,* the Amazon princess receives what may be all-too-familiar advice for many women. "Be careful in the world of men, Diana," Queen Hippolyta (Connie Nielsen) counsels her superhuman daughter. "They do not deserve you."

Young and naive of the world outside her all-woman paradise, Diana (Gal Gadot) is not deterred. And she does not need to be. Half goddess, astonishingly strong and in possession of unmatched courage, she dives headlong into World War I with her sword, shield, and lasso of truth. The cruelty and horrors Diana witnesses galvanize her further: she will not sit by idly while innocents suffer. Saving the world is not just her duty; as she assures her mother, she is "willing to fight for those who cannot fight for themselves." Indeed, Diana's compassion and fearlessness are some of her greatest strengths, grounds for her status as a distinctive and welcome new style of superhero.

Then again, Wonder Woman is not new. She has an enduring, if mottled, seventy-six-year legacy as a comic book hero, feminist icon, television idol, action figure, animated character, and, now, more than $800 million box-office draw. *Ms.* magazine aligned itself with the Amazonian fighter for peace and justice from its inception, featuring the red, white, and blue bedecked heroine on the cover of its first full issue. Five times, to date, Wonder Woman has graced this magazine's cover, linking her inexorably with women's empowerment and feminism writ large.

Like feminism, Wonder Woman is not without her controversies or detractors. Created in 1941 by the psychologist William Moulton Marston (who used the pen name Charles Moulton), *Wonder Woman* marked the first entry of a significant female superhero onto the comic book scene. Comics were an influential entertainment market, especially for children and teenagers, and the Amazon hero's appearance just as America officially entered World War II meant she could serve as constructive propaganda, espousing American values and urging women and men to do their part in the war effort.

In this original version of Diana's story—and there have been variations since—the goddess Athena herself implores the queen of the Amazons to allow her daughter to accompany Steve Trevor, a pilot Diana rescues from the shore of her island after his plane crashes during pursuit by a Nazi fighter. "American liberty and freedom must be preserved!" Athena maintains. "You must send with him your strongest and wisest Amazon—the finest of your wonder women!—for America, the last citadel of democracy, and of equal rights for women, needs your help!"

America of the 1940s was certainly no haven of equal rights for women, but Marston fervently believed in the necessity of "femininity" to help counter the "blood curdling masculinity" of other popular superheroes, who always relied on violence and force to save the day. Reflecting on his decision to create Wonder Woman a few years after the character proved her popularity, Marston explains how "not even girls want to be girls so long as our feminine archetype lacks force, strength, power." It's disappointing, but perhaps not surprising, that Marston still championed "feminine tenderness and allure" for his superheroine, in addition to her more practical powers: superstrength, altruism, and love.

> "Diana's compassion and fearlessness are some of her greatest strengths, grounds for her status as a distinctive and welcome new style of superhero."

While we may find Marston's staunchly antiwar attitude and belief that the greater empowerment of women would achieve a more peaceful and happy society laudable, his insistence upon Wonder Woman's tender femininity is not as appealing. Nor is his seeming obsession with depicting his hero in frequent situations of sexualized vulnerability (sometimes even bound by her own magic lasso!) or his conceit that Diana's main reason for leaving her island home is her instantaneous love for Steve, the first man she's ever met. Thankfully, the 2017 film emphasizes Diana's love for humanity, peace, and justice as her primary motivations for venturing from Themyscira's shores. Although Steve does become a romantic interest eventually, he is not Diana's primary focus. During one heated exchange, she even tells him pointedly, "What I do is not up to you."

The distinction between love and romance—and, in a related sense, the degree to which the character caters to men—has been a sticking point of Wonder Woman's feminist credentials since the beginning. In the cover article of the first issue of *Ms.* magazine (July 1972), the co-founding editor Joanne Edgar discusses how her childhood love of the comic faced disenchantment when romance featured more heavily in later narratives. Edgar saw early Wonder Woman as a character who "captured the Amazonian spirit of strength and self-sufficiency, but added the peacefulness and revulsion toward killing that have culturally distinguished women from men."

There was no question that Wonder Woman was worth rehabilitating, via the cover of *Ms.* and in the comic itself, which saw a shift in story lines due at least in part to the interventions of Gloria Steinem and other advocates of women's rights. Edgar recalls how *Ms.* editors wanted an iconic, feminist symbol for their first issue, not a real woman who would then bear the brunt of everyone's heightened expectations. The comic book hero fit the bill nicely: she was antiwar, believed in sisterhood, and fought for those less fortunate. Of 2017's *Wonder Woman,* Edgar told the *Pacific Standard,* "The spirit is absolutely right up there with what we had in mind." The film "just reaches into this place where you believe that things can work. That the belief in justice and the belief in love, and using power to achieve that, is possible."

For better or worse and real or not, Wonder Woman has not escaped the burden of representation faced by other "firsts" or "onlys" at her level. As a character, she is often expected to speak for and to all women, an impossible task. In her long history, Wonder Woman has served as a lightning rod on issues around race, class, sexuality, and gender. She's been accused of being a corporatized symbol of white liberal feminism; she's faced dueling allegations of inspiring girls to pursue lesbianism versus too often falling victim to heterosexual romance plotlines for someone from an all-female island; she's withstood arguments over whether her minimal outfit catered to the male gaze or merely emphasized her freedom from patriarchal fashion constraints; and, despite her antiwar bona fides and her preference for defensive fighting over gratuitous bloodshed (at least in the early comics, the television show, and the new film), she's been criticized as overly violent.

Many of the criticisms lobbed at Wonder Woman in her various incarnations have validity, but it's a testament to her symbolic significance that she's endured nonetheless. Epitomizing women's potential, the possibilities of feminism, and the hopes of humanity, Wonder Woman "has still managed to reach icon status, which isn't accidental," writes Angelica Jade Bastién in *Vulture.* "It's indicative of the hunger for female-oriented stories, especially coming-of-age tales, that go against the usual depictions of female strength."

The lead in the top-grossing film at the box office this summer, Wonder Woman stands tall as a symbol for women and for feminism whether we're convinced of her credentials or not. As the film emphasizes frequently, believing in yourself is the first step toward changing the world. During Diana's initial training, the Amazon general Antiope (Robin Wright) tells her young charge, "You are stronger than you believe. You have greater powers than you know." Later, Diana proves herself a formidable opponent and an atypical hero. In one of the film's most tremendous scenes, Diana ignores Steve's warning that no-man's-land can't be crossed. "We can't save everyone in this war," Steve admonishes. "This is not what we came here to do." In response, Diana sheds her cloak to reveal her full armor and climbs out of the trench to face the German soldiers on the other side head-on, responding, "No, but it's what I'm going to do."

The word "mankind" is used frequently and deliberately throughout the film, setting the island of the Amazons apart from our world, perhaps not literally a "world of men," but certainly one suffering under patriarchal and otherwise oppressive impulses to dominate and destroy. Briefly disillusioned by humanity's capacity for destruction, Diana eventually realizes that the complexity of humanity isn't its downfall but its strength. At the end of the film, a powerful enemy reminds her of Hippolyta's warning. "You were right, Diana, they don't deserve our help," he says. "They have always been and always will be weak, cruel, selfish, and capable of the greatest horrors." No, Diana ultimately counters, "you're wrong about them. They're everything you say, but so much more. . . . It's not about deserve. It's about what you believe. And I believe in love."

When Hippolyta uses the word "deserve," it carries a meaning far more expansive than when we mere mortals articulate the same sentiment. For Hippolyta, the terrible, cruel world of men has done nothing to earn the protection of a hero as powerful and empathetic as her only child. When women angrily insist or furtively whisper these words to each other, we often mean that the indifference, disrespect, abuse, or exploitation has become too much to bear.

On its cover, the July 1972 issue of *Ms*. declares "Wonder Woman for President." It's a blow looking back on this inspiring slogan forty-five years later, so soon on the heels of being robbed of our first real chance at a woman president. But what if equality is about not what we deserve but what we believe—and what we, like Wonder Woman, are willing to fight for?

Needlework

BY **ROBIN MORGAN** • SUMMER 2018

A sewing basket of sorts: swatches, patches,
bits and scraps, Post-it jottings, scribbles
in the margin of a grocery list—an overheard
remark that warrants remembering. Or images:
the incurled claw of a frozen finch
corpse in the garden. Sometimes just a word.
Or a newspaper clipping, brittle, yellowed.

This one, for instance, on the nameless sister
of the Pharaoh Khufu, he who built the Great
Pyramid. She disobeyed him, about what we don't
know. As punishment, he exiled her from royal burial
plans and sentenced her to a brothel. So she charged
each customer a stone for her favors, and this way
built her pyramid of a thousand vengeful stones.

Or these two remnants, scribbled notes from early
America: Deborah Franklin, common-law wife of Ben
for forty-four years. She raised his child by another woman,
ran his printing press, wrote and edited his almanac, and
while he was in London trying to negotiate
a truce—yet finding time to do his own experiments—
back in the colonies, she died alone.

Deborah never met Sarah, wife of evangelical
theocrat Patrick Henry. She brought him as dowry
a Virginia plantation, small, with six enslaved persons.
He imprisoned her in the cellar for the rest of her life—
an alternative to the asylum, he claimed, since she suffered
from melancholia. Meanwhile, confident he'd done
God's will, he boasted, "Give me liberty or give me death."

Lives of such women, unlived, wait patiently to be
embroidered as they deserve. But if you rummage down
among the rags, you find the selvage of anger hemmed
long ago by those mourned only now by this stranger
to Khufu's sister, Deborah, Sarah, so many selves—
including the self who stitched together, before she died,
the old woman who survived to write this poem.

·   ·   ·

In late 2017, *Ms.* got
its own street in New
York City. East Thirty-
Second at Third Avenue
is co-named Ms.
Magazine Way. The
location commemorates
Ms.'s birth: when the
preview issue appeared
as an insert in *New York*
magazine, the latter's
offices were located on
East Thirty-Second Street.

Letters

In 1972, I taught my first women's studies course at Ramstein Air Base in Germany for the University of Maryland University College. The brand-new *Ms.* magazine was for sale in the Stars and Stripes bookstore, and everyone in the class, including me of course, gobbled it up. Since that time, I have always been a *Ms.* subscriber. In 2015, I moved to the Carol Woods continuing care retirement community. Last year, our Women's Rights Study Group continued with the Ms. Classroom project, with about twenty women participating, many over ninety years old. Congratulations on your work educating us all!

MAGGIE MCFADDEN
Chapel Hill, N.C.
Fall 2017 issue

My daughter cracked up at the *Ms.* cover title "Women Who Know Their Place (the U.S. House)"! Today, I'm not despairing on the sluggish pace of change. I'm choosing to stay inspired—read the individual accounts of those incredible women via @MsMagazine.

MARION GROH MARQUARDT
@thecroissants
Spring 2019 issue

Thank you for your steadfast coverage of the issue of menstrual equity and for sharing an excerpt of Anna Dahlqvist's excellent book, *It's Only Blood* [Summer 2018]. The stories that she highlights—of the burden of stigma, of the crisis of lack of education or access to products—are essential for fueling the kinds of policy change we're now seeing in the United States and around the globe.

From new laws to provide menstrual access for those who are incarcerated, to those that reconfigure tax codes to make products more affordable, this agenda occupies a unique place in American politics: it has rare bipartisan buy-in and popular support.

At its core, menstrual equity is about making the case that our laws must account for menstruation—and that this is a critical component to advancing gender and economic parity.

Periods, as we're seeing, are a potent rallying force. Those of us who experience them are half the population. When we leverage our collective voice, we draw power to reframe the experience.

JENNIFER WEISS-WOLF
Author, *Periods Gone Public: Taking a Stand for Menstrual Equity*
New York
Fall 2018 issue

What a lovely article, "Alias Jane" [by Cindy Wolfe Boynton, Fall 2018].

Anyone who knows me will not be too surprised to learn that I had an abortion—I worked at the National Abortion Rights Action League (NARAL) for nine years and I was its president from 1975 to 1981.

I self-induced an abortion when I was in college. This was in 1964. I was like the hundreds of thousands of women at that time who did not know where to turn if they had an unplanned pregnancy.

I wish we would no longer use the phrase "pro-choice," but instead say we support safe and legal abortion. We should not add to the stigma by avoiding the use of the word "abortion."

KAREN MULHAUSER
Washington, D.C.
Winter 2019 issue

The Crime Was Pregnancy

BY **AMBER KHAN** • SUMMER 2019

R EGINA MCKNIGHT GREW UP and lived with her mother in a lovely, historic town near Myrtle Beach, South Carolina. But when her mother was killed by a hit-and-run driver, McKnight found herself homeless and depressed. She turned to cocaine. In 1999, a pregnant twenty-two-year-old McKnight went into labor and was transported to Conway Medical Center, where she gave birth to a stillborn baby, for whom she had already chosen the name Mercedes. McKnight was heartbroken. She asked to hold Mercedes. She asked for photographs. She asked for footprints to be taken. She asked to take home the hospital bracelet the nurses had placed on the baby.

> **"The antiabortion movement has been working to create a framework that recognizes fertilized eggs, embryos, and fetuses as separate 'persons' under the law to be protected, even from the women who carry them."**

But McKnight was not given much time to grieve. Within months she was arrested and charged and later convicted and ordered to serve twelve years on a twenty-year prison sentence.

What were McKnight's crimes? She was Black. She had been pregnant. She was poor. She had experienced a stillbirth. She tested positive for cocaine. In a South Carolina courtroom, after a jury deliberated for only fifteen minutes, McKnight was convicted of homicide by child abuse. She was the first person in South Carolina to be convicted under such a criminal theory for experiencing a stillbirth. Greg Hembree from the prosecutor's office said that he wanted pregnant women with a substance use disorder to know that there would be consequences for their actions.

Thirty-five years ago in this publication, the feminist attorney Janet Gallagher asked, "What lies in store for pregnant women in the future?" Writing eleven years after *Roe v. Wade,* Gallagher was concerned about the growing "fetal rights" movement and all the ways it could be used to violate the rights of women. *Roe* recognized the constitutionally protected right to have an abortion, but also acknowledged the state's "interest in potential life" in later stages of a pregnancy.

With the increasingly conservative majority on the U.S. Supreme Court, there is understandable anxiety surrounding the future of *Roe.* However, what is at stake today is more than the right to abortion; it is the ability of half of our population to be free from state surveillance and punishment, to make our own medical decisions, to have access to health care, to have our government protect and not violate our human rights.

The antiabortion movement has been working to create a framework that recognizes fertilized eggs, embryos, and fetuses as separate "persons" under the law to be protected, even from the women who carry them. This framework has been utilized to prosecute; civilly commit to hospitals, treatment programs, and mental institutions; and force medical procedures upon hundreds of pregnant women in the United States.

In the late 1980s, when stories of pregnant women being prosecuted for drug use emerged, Dorothy Roberts, a legal scholar of race and gender, wrote, "I immediately suspected that most of the defendants were Black women." Roberts was right; the cases were overwhelmingly brought against people of color. With the expansion of the war on drugs came the exaggerated and race-based fears surrounding crack cocaine use and pregnancy.

Dr. Hallam Hurt, education director of the neonatal follow-up program at the Children's Hospital of Philadelphia, began a study in the late 1980s to understand the impacts on children from prenatal exposure to cocaine. Hurt found "no differences between the exposed and the nonexposed" children studied, but she did find that poverty negatively impacted both sets of children. However, the myth of the "crack baby" endured. "It was easier to focus on drug use than to fix poverty," Hurt explains. It also played right into the drug scare tactics and law enforcement policies of the time, providing another justification for the prosecution of people of color, especially poor people: the need to protect the "unborn" from their own mothers.

Lynn Paltrow, executive director of National Advocates for Pregnant Women (full disclosure: I also work for NAPW), explains, "Because of the enormous mythology and stigma created by the war on drugs, many people were inclined to think that those women—African American mothers whose motherhood has been degraded since slavery, and where there is drug use involved—are terrible women who deserve to be punished." Over the past three decades, unjust drug policies have caused the female prison population to skyrocket. "Women are the fastest-growing correctional population nationwide," says a joint report by Human Rights Watch and the American Civil Liberties Union. A disproportionate number are Black and brown mothers. The scientific community might have rejected the crack baby myth, but the demonization of Black motherhood continues, and so does the criminalization of pregnant women.

Since 1997, South Carolina's criminal legal system has recognized a viable fetus as a "child" under the law. In other words, for more than twenty years prosecutors have been empowered to go after pregnant women for anything they believe could harm an "unborn child," leading to scores of women being arrested, prosecuted, and incarcerated. Paltrow, who worked on McKnight's case and many others like it, believes that what underlies these cases is "the effort to expand state control over women, to use the intersection of the war on drugs and the war on abortion to create laws that actually provide state authority for creating a second-class status for pregnant women."

McKnight served eight years in prison before she succeeded in having the South Carolina Supreme Court overturn her conviction. The court reasoned that the trial counsel failed to call experts who would have testified about studies "showing that cocaine is no more harmful to a fetus than nicotine use, poor nutrition, lack of prenatal care or other conditions commonly associated with the urban poor." In fact, experts determined that an infection and inflammation in the umbilical cord were the cause of fetal death, and they ruled out cocaine as the cause of the complication.

But McKnight's ordeal didn't end there. The court didn't strike down the dangerous notion that a woman could be criminally prosecuted for the outcome of her pregnancy. Nor did it rail against what appeared to be a prosecution inspired by racial stereotypes and resulting from the state's failure to provide necessary services. The court instead ordered a new trial, and McKnight took a plea to get out of prison. She didn't want to stand trial for homicide again. She wanted the nightmare to end.

Once the legal system accepts that a pregnant woman who has used a controlled substance can be prosecuted for harming her fetus, it eases the way to prosecute others like Purvi Patel in Indiana for terminating her own pregnancy or Anne Bynum in Arkansas for experiencing a stillbirth. Currently at least thirty-eight states and the federal government recognize fetuses as separate victims of a crime, and seven states have laws on their books permitting the prosecution of women for terminating their own pregnancies.

Tennessee passed a fetal assault law in 2014, the first of its kind nationwide, that specifically targeted pregnant women for prosecution. The law faced widespread opposition and was criticized for its potential to deter women from seeking necessary health care out of fear of arrest. Though it remained in effect for only two years, the law was used to prosecute more than 120 women.

Judicial decisions in Alabama have permitted the prosecutions of more than six hundred pregnant women under the charge of "chemical endangerment" of a child. The law was intended to prosecute people for bringing children to dangerous environments like meth labs, not people for being pregnant and using a controlled substance. In 2013, the Alabama Supreme Court heard appeals on these cases and decided women could be prosecuted under this felony charge simply for being pregnant: the word "child" was redefined to include a fetus.

Today, more and more states are attempting to amend their own constitutions to afford full protections to fetuses—more protections, in fact, than those afforded to women. In 2018, Alabama successfully passed an amendment that enshrines fetuses' "right to life." Currently, a similar proposal is pending in South Carolina, McKnight's home state.

But her case—along with the cases of hundreds of other women—have taught us that rights cannot be granted to fetuses without also stripping them from pregnant women.

To promote healthy pregnancy outcomes, we must respect the rights of those who become pregnant, including their right not to be. Founders of the reproductive justice movement teach us that "all oppressions impact our reproductive lives," and so we must use an intersectional lens to work together toward a solution. We must improve access to necessary health care, including abortion and treatment for substance use disorders. We must address the causes of homelessness instead of criminalizing the poor. We must confront the role of racism in the systems of mass incarceration and child welfare, which, like federal agents at the U.S.-Mexico border, cause trauma and separate families. We must address the staggeringly high maternal health and morbidity rates in the United States, especially those of Black women.

Protecting the lives of pregnant women, children, and families should be the government's priority, but sending McKnight and others like her to prison, banning abortion, and criminalizing pregnant women—that's no way to do it.

NOT SURPRISINGLY, with abortion rights under attack, the United States has seen an escalation of criminalization of pregnancy outcomes—a burden that falls heaviest on Black women and women of color and those who are lower income.

The prosecution and conviction in 2021 of Brittney Poolaw is a chilling example. The mere allegation that the Oklahoma teen's drug use contributed to miscarriage led to her arrest for first-degree manslaughter; she was jailed for a year and a half before trial, unable to afford $20,000 bail, and then sentenced to four years in prison. Experts weighing in on the case highlight that the cause of miscarriage is unknown and that the rate of stillbirths for Native American women like Poolaw is almost 50 percent higher than that of white women.

Among those sounding the alarm, the National Association of Criminal Defense Lawyers warns that the reversal of *Roe v. Wade* is likely to "open the floodgates to massive overcriminalization" of pregnancy.

A Social Movement
That Happens to Play Soccer

BY **DAVE ZIRIN** • FALL 2019

T HE 2019 U.S. women's national soccer team will be remembered throughout the annals of history as a social movement that happened to play soccer. Its impact will be measured not in World Cups won but in laws and lives changed. This is a team that has joyously embraced the mantle. The players have shown themselves to be more than willing to not only work their way to a World Cup triumph but also continually raise the issues of equal pay and equal rights in a fearless and appealing manner that's just devastating to defenders of the status quo.

What these political buccaneers of the pitch have done is take a struggle that women have painstakingly agitated around for decades—the seemingly simple concept of equal pay for equal work—and turned it from a moribund talking point into a cause célèbre.

> "They will not be co-opted. They will not be used for photo ops. . . . They are not calling for peace. They are calling for justice."

Their protest for equal pay stems from their own lived experiences: a set of circumstances deeply entrenched in the structural sexism that defines soccer's governing body, the Fédération Internationale de Football Association (FIFA). The numbers are a slap in the face, especially in the wake of the team's titanic triumph in France. For the 2018 (men's) World Cup, FIFA gave out $400 million in prize money. This year, the total purse for the Women's World Cup was $30 million. That's a thirteen-to-one pay disparity.

The know-nothing naysayers, like President Donald Trump, argue that this is because "you've got to look at the numbers." In the United States, that simply is not true. It's a talking point as dead as the nineteenth-century idea that women should not be allowed to play sports at all.

Here in these United States, the women have the number one selling jersey ever sold on Nike.com in a single season and the larger following. And according to *The Wall Street Journal*, since winning the 2015 World Cup, they've been generating more revenue than the men. An estimated one billion people watched the Women's World Cup, making the tournament like a steadily ringing cash register: a license to print money. Despite that, U.S. women earn, according to the lawsuit they filed against the U.S. Soccer Federation, about thirty-eight cents on the dollar compared with what the men make. This is why, as the women basked in triumph following their finals 2–0 victory over the Netherlands, it wasn't a chant of "U.S.A." that rang out in the Stade de Lyon but "equal pay." It is why, when they took their victory parade at the Canyon of Heroes in New York City, thousands of people arrived with homemade signs with slogans calling for gender and economic justice, like "Equal Pay for Equal Play" and "FIFA: Explain Yourself!"

These grassroots demands for equal pay have people looking well beyond the world of sports, connecting the clarion call to workplaces across the country. It's generally reported that U.S. women earn eighty cents to a man's dollar, but this understates the true magnitude of the gap. The "income" gap is a better measure because it takes into account not only wages but also benefits including life and health insurance, pension contributions, bonuses, stock options, and other forms of remuneration that accrue disproportionately to men. Using this more inclusive measure means the disparity between women's and men's earnings is significantly larger.

This soccer team of outspoken women has burst the complacency that settled around this issue and put it on the front burner of the collective consciousness. It inspired Senator Elizabeth Warren (D-Mass.) to tweet, "The @USWNT is #1 in the world & contributes higher revenues for @USSoccer than the men's team, but they're still paid a fraction of what the men earn. Women deserve equal pay for equal (or better!) work in offices, factories, AND on the soccer field."

The attorney Jeffrey Kessler, who is representing the team in its lawsuit against the U.S. Soccer Federation, commented to PolitiFact that Warren's statement is "entirely accurate." He added, "The women earn more revenues than the men, are world champions and make substantially less. It is legally and morally wrong." The team is moving beyond the mere call for equal pay and looking for legislative remedies. As the World Cup Golden Boot and Golden Ball winner Megan Rapinoe put it, "Everyone is kind of asking what's next and what we want to come of all of this. It's to stop having the conversation about equal pay and are we worth it." She added to Rachel Maddow, "If you're not down with equal pay at this point . . . you're so far out of reality and the conversation that we can't even go there. I think it's time to go to the next phase."

That next phase has included an invitation to the women's team signed by all twenty-five women members of the U.S. Senate—Democratic and Republican alike—for a meeting to discuss the issue. The team has also received tweeted invites from Speaker Nancy Pelosi (D-Calif.) and Representative Alexandria Ocasio-Cortez (D-N.Y.) to celebrate the team's victory and take a tour of the House of Representatives. These accepted political invitations exist alongside the invitation the women conspicuously rejected from Trump's White House. As Rapinoe put it on *Anderson Cooper 360°*, "I would not go, and every teammate that I've talked to explicitly about it would not go. I don't think anyone on the team has any interest in lending the platform that we've worked so hard to build, and the things that we fight for, and the way that we live our life—I don't think that we want that to be co-opted or corrupted by this administration."

They will not be co-opted. They will not be used for photo ops. They will not be positioned as some symbol of national unity during these deeply divided times. They are not calling for peace. They are calling for justice.

Those who—like the scolds on Fox News—are shocked by their brash impatience are not understanding the ways that the passage of time has marked this team. The players are done with waiting. Commentators have referred to them as the children of Title IX. In one sense that's true. In another, it doesn't do justice to this moment. It is certainly true that without the landmark 1972 law, women's sports, and in particular women's soccer, would be a sclerotic dead zone, smothered by the sexism and absence of access that defined women's athletics for most of the twentieth century. According to the Women's Sports Foundation, two out of five high school girls were playing sports by the end of 2016. Before Title IX, that number was one in twenty-seven.

But the law was signed almost fifty years ago. Members of this 2019 team are not the "daughters" of Title IX. That was a generation ago. The daughters of Title IX were the famed 1999 World Cup soccer victors led by Mia Hamm and Brandi Chastain.

These 2019 women—led by Rapinoe, Alex Morgan, and Tobin Heath—are the grandchildren of Title IX, and they are done waiting. They are not content with mere access to their sport, not content to be the subject of puff pieces about how far they have come. They want to know where they are going. They don't want a feel-good narrative about how much progress has been made since 1972. They would rather drive a discussion that asks greater structural questions about institutionalized sexism and pay inequity.

What makes this team—and Rapinoe in particular—so dynamic is that equal pay is hardly the only issue on which it speaks out. This is a squad of women who live the politics of intersectionality, connecting their fight against sexism with the promotion of LGBTQ rights and the struggle against racism. They proudly embrace their LGBTQ teammates, including the coach Jill Ellis, in a way that feels unforced and normalized. Rapinoe was the first female athlete to take a knee in support of the former NFL star Colin Kaepernick. She said to *Time* magazine about her support for the quarterback blackballed over his anthem protests against police violence, "I am in solidarity with Colin Kaepernick in trying to continue a conversation. It's no secret that we still have very tense race relations in this country.

I don't think everybody is as free as everybody else. Until people with the most privilege—and I would consider myself in that group—put our own skin in the game, then things aren't really going to change."

It is no surprise that one of Rapinoe's heroes is the great poet and activist Audre Lorde. Rapinoe even once wore a jersey with Lorde's name on her back as tribute. It was Lorde who famously once said, "I began to ask each time: 'What's the worst that could happen to me if I tell this truth?' . . . Our speaking out will irritate some people, get us called bitchy or hypersensitive and disrupt some dinner parties. And then our speaking out will permit other women to speak, until laws are changed and lives are saved and the world is altered forever."

The world—despite the shock of some conservative commentators—certainly has been altered, and this team has only just begun.

Letters

We know that we stand on the shoulders of women who have come before us and blazed the trail so that we can declare our yea votes for the Equal Rights Amendment in Virginia, in that chamber where Madison and Jefferson did not imagine twenty-eight women delegates were going to have a seat at the table.

It is amazing to see the progress we made [getting within one vote of ratification in Virginia]. More progress is yet to happen as we take the ERA across the finish line—and we will.

We've had the conversations; we've toured through the Commonwealth of Virginia to get people educated and excited about the Equal Rights Amendment. Now we'll accept no more lip service from our colleagues, no more empty promises, no more "I respect you by shaking your hand." Respect will be shown when we gain equality in the Constitution. We're telling our colleagues, "If you stand with women, you will vote for women. And if we can't change your minds, then we're gonna change your seats in the 2019 election."

Democracy is not a spectator sport. We all have skin in the game. And as we can now see, our lives depend on these elections, our children's lives depend on these elections, so we cannot sit on the sidelines, we cannot be on the bench. We all must do what is necessary to get the ERA passed. The women delegates of Virginia can't do it alone; we need your support. Help us become the thirty-eighth state that passes the Equal Rights Amendment.

STATE DELS. HALA AYALA AND
JENNIFER CARROLL FOY
Richmond, Va.
Summer 2019 issue

CHAPTER 6

2020s

TODAY, *MS.* CONTINUES TO PUBLISH a quarterly print issue that is sold on newsstands and in bookstores and is also distributed via membership subscriptions, at feminist events and conferences, and through the *Ms.* Prison and Domestic Violence Shelter donation program.

Ms. maintains its award-winning, action-packed website, MsMagazine .com, where a dedicated digital team posts upwards of 150 articles every month. *Ms.* creates specialty online platforms too—like a new "Women and Democracy" multimedia series and a 2022 tribute site to commemorate the two hundredth anniversary of the birth of Harriet Tubman with interactive stories, timelines, art, and poetry. And of course, with the rise of social media, *Ms.* continues to engage millions from Twitter to TikTok.

In 2020, *Ms.* launched its first two podcasts, *On the Issues with Michele Goodwin* and *Fifteen Minutes of Feminism*. As the host and executive producer Michele Goodwin explains, "*Ms.* podcasts appeal to those who believe, as we do, that women's voices matter, that equality for all persons cannot be delayed, and that rebuilding America and being unbought, and unbossed, and reclaiming our time are important." The launch of *Ms.*'s latest brainchild—*Ms.* Studios—brings even further depth and opportunities for audience interaction, including new podcasts and video programming.

And so, the *Ms.* legacy continues in force. *Ms.* looks ahead to the next fifty years with resolve and gratitude—for those whose vision is reflected in these pages, and for the generations of feminist readers, contributors, and leaders who have been a part of the *Ms.* story.

Ms. commemorated Virginia's ratification of the Equal Rights Amendment—the thirty-eighth and final state needed—with this cover.

We Want In

BY **CARRIE N. BAKER** • SPRING 2020

O N THE AFTERNOON OF JANUARY 15, hundreds of women packed the gallery of the Virginia House as delegates voted on whether to ratify the Equal Rights Amendment and make Virginia the thirty-eighth and final state needed to enshrine the ERA in the U.S. Constitution.

When House Speaker Eileen Filler-Corn (D)—the first female and first Jewish Speaker in Virginia—announced a 59–41 vote in favor of ratification, the women in the gallery erupted in cheers, waving their arms and hugging each other. "Today is a major victory for women and girls throughout the country," declared Delegate Hala Ayala (D), who co-sponsored the ERA ratification bill along with the chief sponsor, Delegate Jennifer Carroll Foy (D), both women of color elected for the first time in 2017.

> **"We know that equality for women will always elude us when it isn't etched into the Constitution."**

For decades, Republican leadership had blocked the ratification bill from a floor vote in the Virginia House. But in 2017, Democrats flipped fifteen seats, decreasing the Republicans' sixty-six-to-thirty-four majority to a razor-thin fifty-one-to-forty-nine margin. Then, in 2019, Democrats—backed by tremendous get-out-the-vote efforts by feminist groups—flipped the legislature, gaining control of both the house and the senate.

As a result, women stepped into key leadership positions. Filler-Corn became the first woman Speaker in the four-hundred-year history of the Virginia House. Louise Lucas became the first woman and first African American president pro tempore of the senate. Charniele Herring became the first African American and the first woman to be house majority leader. The leadership made quick work of passing the ERA.

The Trump administration and conservative state attorneys general are now trying to block recognition of the amendment, despite polling showing massive public support for the ERA. The vast majority of respondents—men and women, Republicans, Democrats, and independents—want the ERA, and most think the ERA is already a part of the Constitution. Nearly two-thirds believe that the ERA would have a positive impact for women.

But hostile attorneys general from Alabama, Mississippi, and South Dakota have sued to prevent the archivist of the United States, David Ferriero, from certifying that the conditions for ratification have been met. Donald Trump's attorney general, William Barr, backed them up with a thirty-eight-page opinion arguing that the timeline for ratification expired in 1979.

"The Trump administration has concocted a scheme to try to nullify the will of millions of Americans," the Virginia attorney general, Mark Herring, declared. Herring's filed a civil suit along with the attorneys general from Nevada and Illinois—the thirty-sixth and thirty-seventh states, respectively, to ratify the ERA—arguing that the timeline is invalid and that the executive branch (including Barr) has no role in the ratification of an amendment. Their suit demanded that the archivist certify the amendment. Meanwhile, the U.S. House of Representatives has approved a bipartisan resolution to remove the timeline. Yet despite some bipartisan support for the ERA in the Senate, Majority Leader Mitch McConnell (R-Ky.) is now blocking a vote on the resolution.

"The leadership needs to change," says the Feminist Majority Foundation president (and *Ms.* publisher), Eleanor Smeal, who for part of the 1970s and 1980s was president of the National Organization for Women, which led the ERA fight. Smeal told *Ms.* that McConnell's refusal to allow a vote on the resolution echoes earlier fights for the ERA.

A LONG HISTORY OF OBSTRUCTION, DELAY, AND TRICKERY

Back in the early 1970s, when there were only fifteen women in Congress—two in the Senate and thirteen in the House—powerful male leaders of key House and Senate committees blocked votes on the Equal Rights Amendment.

The most powerful opposition, says Smeal, were business interests, especially the insurance industry, which opposed equality because sex discrimination is highly profitable. "'Women's equality' is not just words," Smeal says. "It means real things, especially in the area of money. It means you have to stop discriminating against women in employment and in annuities, life insurance, and health insurance. It involves billions and billions of dollars.

"It was one hell of a fight," Smeal continues. "We marched, we picketed, we demonstrated. We had sit-ins. People were arrested. Some women went on hunger strikes. Every nonviolent protest that could be done was done. NOW had a silent vigil on the steps of the Senate, around the clock."

Women's protests finally got the ERA out of committee in 1971, but with a seven-year ratification timeline in the preamble to the amendment. So the women's movement fought tooth and nail to quickly win state ratifications.

Hawaii ratified within hours of Congress approving the ERA in 1972, and other states soon followed. In many states, however, business interests and elected state legislators—overwhelmingly men—blocked the ERA from a vote. By the end of the seven-year timeline, the amendment fell three states short of ratification. Feminists battled in Congress to pass an extension of the timeline, which they did until 1982, but no additional states voted to ratify the ERA—until 2017.

After Trump became president, the fight for the ERA became more urgent. The massive rollback of women's rights and Trump's appointment of the archconservatives Neil Gorsuch and Brett Kavanaugh to the U.S. Supreme Court made it clearer than ever that women need explicit protection for their equal rights in the U.S. Constitution.

Feminists turned with laser focus to a three-state strategy—seeking three more states to ratify the amendment and then a congressional joint resolution to remove the timeline.

But as feminists sought three more state ratifications, mostly male conservative leaders in state legislatures once again refused to allow the ERA out of committee. So feminists focused on electing more women to office and flipping legislatures from red to blue.

In Nevada, with the election of a record number of women and people of color in 2016, Democrats took control of the legislature. Under the leadership of the state senator Pat Spearman, the new Democratic majority ratified the ERA in 2017. In the spring of 2018, Illinois ratified the ERA after a strong pro-ERA movement succeeded in pressuring the Democratic Speaker to finally allow a vote on the amendment.

Weeks after Virginia's ratification this year, the state attorneys general Herring, Kwame Raoul of Illinois, and Aaron Ford of Nevada filed suit to ensure that the Equal Rights Amendment would be added to the Constitution. These three AGs argue that under Article 5, which sets out the process to amend the Constitution, a proposed constitutional amendment automatically becomes part of the U.S. Constitution as soon as it is ratified by the legislatures of three-fourths of the states.

Opponents argue that four states—Idaho, Kentucky, Nebraska, and Tennessee—have voted to rescind their ratification of the ERA. And South Dakota stated its ratification would simply lapse after 1979. But historical precedent suggests that states cannot do so. After the Civil War, two states rescinded their ratification of the Fourteenth Amendment, but Congress refused to recognize these rescissions. "States that rescinded their ratification were counted toward the three-quarters of states necessary for ratification of the Fourteenth Amendment," notes the constitutional law scholar Erwin Chemerinsky. "That indicates that states that have rescinded can still be counted."

The former dean of Stanford Law School Kathleen Sullivan agrees: "Article 5 speaks to ratification but not rescission."

Dear *Ms.* Community Member,
While we were at work on this issue, our world changed suddenly, terribly. As we go to print, we're still reeling from the tragedy—the increasing number of cases of COVID-19, the increasing number of deaths, the increasing anxiety and feelings of helplessness. By the time you read this, the numbers of sick and dying will only be greater and the losses more tragic.

These are difficult times for us all. And yet, we continue.

Here at *Ms.*, we'll keep providing up-to-the-minute reporting—both in the magazine and online at **msmagazine.com**. We'll salute our heroes and mourn those who are lost. *Ms.* will remain focused on aspects of the crisis not often reported on by mainstream media: how this virus disproportionately impacts women, many of whom are on the front lines of this public health crisis. The vast majority of nurses, home health care workers and those who look after the elderly in nursing homes are women. So are the overwhelming majority of teachers, school counselors and school cafeteria workers, domestic workers and child care providers.

When we shelter in place, what happens to women experiencing domestic violence, homelessness or mental illness? For women who can't afford not to work, what happens when family members become ill or children's schools close?

This crisis has become a national teaching moment, exposing some of the most glaring inequities in our country. We're outraged that 69 percent of low-income workers making $10.80 or less per hour—who are mostly women and disproportionately women and men of color—do not have even

Continued on Page 1

Ms.'s Spring 2020 issue went to press days after the pandemic sent the world into lockdown. Already, *Ms.* predicted that the crisis would become "a national teaching moment, exposing some of the most glaring inequities in our country."

"Ultimately, the Constitution and Supreme Court precedent leave to Congress the question of when an amendment is properly ratified," Chemerinsky adds. "If Congress by joint resolution says the ERA is part of the Constitution, then it is."

Feminists are now focusing their efforts on the U.S. Congress. The huge electoral victories for women and Democrats in the U.S. House of Representatives in 2018 paved the way for advancing the ERA in Congress. Women were elected to a record 23 percent of House seats, and Democrats gained forty-one seats.

This year, Representative Jackie Speier (D-Calif.) introduced a joint resolution to remove the arbitrary timeline for the ERA. "This is very simple," Speier said during the House floor debate. "Women want to be equal, and we want it in the Constitution. . . . Women of America are done being second-class citizens. We are done being paid less for our work. Done being violated with impunity. Done being discriminated against for our pregnancies. Done being discriminated against simply because we are women."

Under the leadership of Speaker Nancy Pelosi (D-Calif.), the House voted on February 13 to pass the joint resolution with a bipartisan 232–183 vote (5 Republicans voted with Democrats in favor of the legislation).

"With this resolution, we take a giant step toward equality for women, progress for families, and a stronger America—because we know when women succeed, America succeeds," Pelosi said at a press conference ahead of the vote.

"Our message here today is quite simple," added Speier, holding up a pocket-sized copy of the U.S. Constitution. "We want in."

Senators Ben Cardin (D-Md.) and Lisa Murkowski (R-Alaska) introduced a similar resolution in the Senate. In response to the Justice Department's opinion letter, they released a joint statement arguing that Congress certainly has the authority under Article 5 of the Constitution to set and change deadlines for the ratification of constitutional amendments and has done so on numerous occasions. "There is no reason to put a time limit on achieving equality under the law," they wrote.

Because Senator McConnell has indicated he would block the resolution—he says he's "personally not a supporter" of the ERA—Democrats must flip the Senate in the November election in order to secure passage of the resolution.

WHERE WE GO FROM HERE

"We know that equality for women will always elude us when it isn't etched into the Constitution," Congresswoman Carolyn Maloney (D-N.Y.) says.

We are in the final homestretch of the long-fought battle for the ERA, but the fate of the amendment rides on the fall elections. "The ERA resolution is being blocked by McConnell and by the leadership of the Republican Party," Smeal notes. "That's why we have to flip the Senate. It isn't individual Republicans. I believe if the ERA were put on the Senate floor, we would pass it. The problem is the leadership, and whomever they are beholden to. We must flip the Senate to have leadership that will remove the timeline.

"I think that women's rights will be on the ballot in some key states this November. It will be the reason people will say, 'I've had it with these Republicans. I want equality for women.'"

As Smeal says, "It was never a matter of *if*, only *when* the ERA would be ratified. Women have fought long and hard for equal rights under the law and waited too long for full equality. It's time—long overdue—for the thirty-eight states that have ratified the ERA to be recognized and for the ERA to be enshrined in the U.S. Constitution. The days of women working twice as hard for half as much must end."

Beijing + 25

BY **ELLEN CHESLER** • FALL 2020

TWENTY-FIVE YEARS AGO, the United Nations hosted the largest gathering of women (and more than a few good men) in its fifty-year history. Some seventeen thousand participants—among them official government delegates, representatives of accredited nongovernmental organizations, international civil servants, and members of the press—registered for the Fourth World Conference on Women in Beijing. Another thirty thousand global activists, including eight thousand from the United States, met in Huairou, a district some forty miles away, to mount an impassioned parallel forum.

Women came together united by common bonds of disadvantage in a world of male privilege, but also divided by significant distinctions of race, class, religion, culture, and geography. I, for one, will never forget the thrill of being part of that joyous, colorful assemblage.

> "Ideas matter. They drive progress, inspire concrete change, and lift the human spirit. They are among the UN's most precious legacies, nowhere perhaps more significantly than in advancing women's rights."

The then U.S. First Lady, Hillary Rodham Clinton, confidently attired in a stylish pink jacket and skirt, brought the crowd to its feet with her rousing opening speech. She argued the issue of women's rights as a moral imperative, characterizing everyday forms of oppression and violence against women, long protected by local custom, as behaviors demanding universal legal remedy. And she also made her case on instrumental grounds, framing equality and opportunity for women as necessary conditions to advance prosperity and security among nations. Adapting a central tenet of the global women's movement—actually first heard a few years earlier among grassroots women's groups in the Philippines—Clinton memorably said, "Women's rights are human rights, once and for all," a paradigm she helped transform into a global mantra.

Benazir Bhutto, then serving as prime minister of Pakistan, echoed the sentiment. Quoting from the Quran, she characterized respect for women's rights as principles inherent to Islamic scripture and lived experience. She dismissed contrary interpretations from fundamentalists as "social taboos spun by the traditions of a patriarchal society." Later the victim of an assassination, she might well have sacrificed her life for these views.

Days of intense deliberations followed. A new generation of profession-

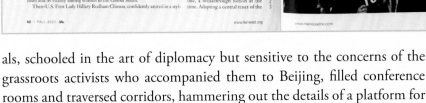

BEIJING+25

Adopted in 1995, the U.N.'s Beijing Declaration and Platform for Action shaped aspirations for women's equality in the 21st century—and no amount of resistance or repression since has been able to reverse its momentum

BY ELLEN CHESLER

TWENTY-FIVE YEARS AGO, THE UNITED NATIONS HOSTED THE largest gathering of women (and more than a few good men) in its 50-year history. Some 17,000 participants—among them, official government delegates, representatives of accredited nongovernmental organizations, international civil servants and members of the press—registered for the Fourth World Conference on Women in Beijing. Another 30,000 global activists, including 8,000 from the U.S., met in Huairou, a district some 40 miles away, to mount an impassioned parallel forum.

Women came together united by common bonds of disadvantage in a world of male privilege, but also divided by significant distinctions of race, class, religion, culture and geography. I, for one, will never forget the thrill of being part of that joyous, colorful assemblage. Women in vibrant African batik, stunning Indian saris, elegant caftans and handwoven textiles stood side by side with those of us in the drab, structured, European-style suits so popular back then. The clothes were indicative of a larger reality—the universality of feminism and its vitality among women in the Global South.

Then-U.S. First Lady Hillary Rodham Clinton, confidently attired in a stylish pink jacket and skirt, brought the crowd to its feet with her rousing opening speech. She argued the issue of women's rights as a moral imperative, characterizing everyday forms of oppression and violence against women, long protected by local custom, as behaviors demanding universal legal remedy. And she also made her case on instrumental grounds, framing equality and opportunity for women as necessary conditions to advance prosperity and security among nations; she framed it not as a "soft" foreign policy issue but as an essential one, a breakthrough notion at the time. Adapting a central tenet of the global women's movement—actually first heard a few years earlier among grassroots women's groups in the Philippines—Clinton memorably said, "Women's rights are human rights, once and for all," a paradigm she helped transform into a global mantra.

Benazir Bhutto, then serving as prime minister of Pakistan, echoed the sentiment. Quoting from the Quran, she characterized respect for women's rights as principles inherent to Islamic scripture and lived experience. She dismissed contrary interpretations from fundamentalists as "social taboos spun by the traditions of a patriarchal society." Later the victim of an assassination, she may well have sacrificed her life for these views.

Days of intense deliberations followed these provocative plenary speeches. A new generation of professionals, schooled in the art of diplomacy but sensitive to the concerns of the grassroots activists who accompanied them to Beijing, filled conference rooms and traversed corridors, hammering out the details of a Platform for Action that would shape aspirations for the 21st century.

With determination and savvy, they managed to achieve consensus among the 189 U.N. member countries on an unusually optimistic blueprint for change. Some critics dismiss Beijing, along with prior U.N. assemblies addressing women's rights, as lacking focus and practical strategies for implementation. I would argue that these conferences, the outcome documents they produced and the civil society mobilization they inspired have raised awareness, changed norms, altered behaviors, fostered activism, expanded legal protections and improved conditions around the world in countless ways. However slow progress may be—however intense the backlash every step of the way—no amount of resistance or repression has been able to reverse this momentum.

So where do we stand today?

There have been widely acknowledged gains in several of the critical areas Beijing prioritized:

• Norms have certainly changed, but the actual legal status of women in most countries has also improved. State obligation to protect women in the home and workplace was a relatively new concept in 1995. Sexual harassment as an enforceable provision of state criminal and civil law did not exist in the U.S. until

Left, in 1995, some 30,000 global women's rights activists convened a parallel forum just outside Beijing; below, a protest in Seoul, South Korea—the global #MeToo movement has put pressure on private businesses to improve treatment of women workers.

> Today, a majority of countries have criminalized violence against women at home and at work, and many have also trained police and social welfare professionals and funded shelters.

the 1980s, for example. And we took no legislative action to marshal federal resources to address violence against women until 1994. Today, a majority of countries have criminalized violence against women at home and at work, and many have also trained police and social welfare professionals and funded shelters. The International Labour Organization has adopted legal protections for transnational domestic workers and for women working in factories that are engaged in global trade. Compliance remains a challenge, of course, but is becoming a greater priority, as many countries condition new trade agreements upon enforcement of these provisions, and as private businesses come under increased pressure from an emboldened, global #MeToo movement, ever vigilant today as the COVID-19 pandemic poses new obstacles.

• The gender gap in education between boys and girls has closed at the primary school level, with an estimated 39 million more girls in school. Families still living in extreme poverty, or in the many countries disrupted by conflict today, remain hardest to reach. And significant economic gains for women may be achievable only once they reach parity in secondary schools, colleges and universities, but even there, trends are moving in the right direction.

• Women's health and well-being have improved. Maternal deaths have been drastically reduced, as public health professionals recognize the value of saving the lives of women and babies by investing in measures that increase access to obstetrical interventions in breech births and

---

als, schooled in the art of diplomacy but sensitive to the concerns of the grassroots activists who accompanied them to Beijing, filled conference rooms and traversed corridors, hammering out the details of a platform for action that would shape aspirations for the twenty-first century.

With determination and savvy, they managed to achieve consensus among the 189 UN member countries on an unusually optimistic blueprint for change. Some critics dismiss Beijing, along with prior UN assemblies addressing women's rights, as lacking focus and practical strategies for implementation. I would argue that these conferences, the outcome documents they produced, and the civil society mobilization they inspired have raised awareness, changed norms, altered behaviors, fostered activism, expanded legal protections, and improved conditions around the world in countless ways. However slow progress may be—however intense the backlash every step of the way—no amount of resistance or repression has been able to reverse this momentum.

So where do we stand today?

There have been widely acknowledged gains in several of the critical areas Beijing prioritized:

- Norms have certainly changed, but the actual legal status of women in most countries has also improved. State obligation to protect women in the home and workplace was a relatively new concept in 1995. Today, a majority of countries have criminalized violence against women at home and at work, and many have also trained police and social welfare professionals and funded shelters. The International Labour Organization has adopted legal protections for transnational domestic workers and for women working in factories that are engaged in global trade. Compliance remains a challenge, of course, but is becoming a greater priority, as many countries condition new trade agreements upon enforcement of these provisions and as private businesses come under increased pressure from an emboldened, global #MeToo movement.

- The gender gap in education between boys and girls has closed at the primary school level, with an estimated thirty-nine million more girls in school. Families still living in extreme poverty, or in the many countries disrupted by conflict today, remain hardest to reach.

- Women's health and well-being have improved. Maternal deaths have been drastically reduced. Expanded access to modern methods of contraception has empowered women to plan and space pregnancies, which also makes them safer. Breaking long-established taboos against providing sex education and birth control to unmarried women and to adolescents has significantly improved health outcomes as well. Sadly, bold pledges to fund family planning have never been fully met, and unmet need for reliable services still extends to millions of women. In thrall to social conservatives, the Trump administration has instead reduced U.S. aid for development assistance generally, including family planning.

- Women's political representation has increased, if haltingly. The global average for representation of women in national legislatures reached a record 24.9 percent at the start of 2020, up from negligible numbers a generation ago. Southern countries, including Rwanda, Cuba, Bolivia, Mexico, and the United Arab Emirates, have joined pioneers like Sweden, Finland, and France in surpassing or reaching near gender parity in their parliaments. In 2018, the United States, although still slightly below the global average in Inter-Parliamentary Union rankings, saw more than a hundred women join Congress. Only twenty-one countries currently have women as national executives.

In the workplace, women have seen few gains. Women's formal labor force participation has stagnated at a global rate of about 48 percent, and numerous countries that were once doing much better have witnessed declines in recent years, including the United States.

"Last Word," a new series on the final page of each issue, honors (*clockwise from top left*), the late Supreme Court justice and trailblazer Ruth Bader Ginsburg, 2020; poet Amanda Gorman, who was a source of energy and optimism at President Joe Biden's inauguration, 2021; the legendary Black feminist scholar bell hooks, 2021; and Supreme Court justice Sonia Sotomayor, who issued a scathing dissent to her colleagues' decision to allow a six-week ban on abortion to go into effect in Texas in September 2021.

MS. MAGAZINE

Ms.

WINTER 2021

THIS IS WHAT DEMOCRACY LOOKS LIKE

WWW.MSMAGAZINE.COM
$6.95US/CAN

11>

0 74820 46962 0

DISPLAY UNTIL APR 26

ERA YES

BLACK LIVES MATTER

A recent analysis by Rachel Vogelstein of the Council on Foreign Relations cites three sets of barriers to economic progress for women. The first is legal. More than a hundred countries still restrict women from many high-paying occupations like construction or mining. Seventy-five countries, many with large rural populations, still deny women the right to own property, even though they perform most of the agricultural work. And women entrepreneurs have a harder time accessing credit and sustaining small retail businesses, although innovation in banking by cell phone could help close gaps in this sector.

The second barrier, however, is structural. Women are vastly overrepresented in jobs outside the formal, taxable economic sector, as well as in low-wage factory jobs that provide them with fewer benefits and protections. And this segregation is unlikely to change without substantial gains in secondary schooling and higher education. At the same time, state and local government workplaces that disproportionately employ women as office workers and in health care have declined dramatically in the past three decades as a result, I believe, of neoliberal, macroeconomic policies that starved the public sectors of many developing countries in the misguided notion that only unfettered capitalism would foster economic growth. Instead, we have seen stagnant wages and vastly widening inequalities.

And finally, much of the problem is cultural. In most countries, women remain constrained by the obligation to balance paid work with 75 percent of the burden of unpaid housework, child care, and elder care. A recent study shows that more than a third of men in China and Korea (and nearly that many women) still wish that women could stay at home all the time. In many Middle Eastern countries, even as the number of women earning college degrees has exceeded men, prevailing mores have kept married women out of the workforce, just as they often did until the 1970s in the United States, where this is again becoming a problem. Although both parents work in nearly two-thirds of married-couple families with kids, more women are leaving the labor market so they can manage family responsibilities during the COVID-19 pandemic. The United States does not even rank in the top ten countries of the world as measured by the Council on Foreign Relations' Women's Workplace Equality Index.

Recent research demonstrates conclusively that women's work drives economic growth. Studies from once blinkered institutions like the World Bank, the World Economic Forum, and the McKinsey Global Institute estimate that bringing women to parity with men in workforce participation and earnings would translate into trillions of dollars and expand

OPPOSITE *Ms.* celebrates the historic election of Kamala Harris as vice president in 2021 and President Joe Biden's appointment of a gender-balanced presidential cabinet for the first time in U.S. history.

global gross domestic product by more than 25 percent. Concrete evidence from India, Japan, and many other countries long unfriendly to women shows that gender-sensitive taxation, expansion of social welfare, and infrastructure investment make a real difference. With the issue now gaining mainstream attention from international financial institutions and national treasuries as well as the private sector, the arguments first sounded by feminist activists in UN forums are finally gaining greater traction.

Data to support policy innovation is abundant. What is harder to marshal is political will. Crises unforeseen when bold verbal commitments to women's equality were made in the 1990s have sapped energy and diminished resources. Conflicts in the Middle East and elsewhere have spawned large refugee populations. Pandemics like HIV-AIDS and COVID-19 have wrought further havoc. Extreme weather resulting from a warming climate has caused costly environmental damage and increased displacement.

An unsettled world has unleashed political reaction and the rise of authoritarian regimes unfriendly to women in many countries, most dramatically, perhaps, here at home in the United States. International alliances have been severed, funding for foreign aid has been eroded, and essential programs have been cut. But worse, one could argue, is the fundamental intellectual challenge the Trump administration has posed to the human rights and development architecture that U.S. leadership has nurtured at the United Nations for many years.

In a jaw-dropping report issued in July, Secretary of State Mike Pompeo challenged the expansive definition of rights across civil, political, social, and economic sectors that was inscribed in the Universal Declaration of Human Rights in 1948. And he argued against the fundamental principle that these rights are indivisible. In a flagrant threat to women and gender nonconforming individuals, he insisted that rights claims have become excessive and must be contained, and he defended the administration's earlier decision to leave the UN Human Rights Council on these and other grounds.

Ideas matter. They drive progress, inspire concrete change, and lift the human spirit. They are among the UN's most precious legacies, nowhere perhaps more significantly than in advancing women's rights.

Seventy-five years ago, in the dark shadow of World War II, the United Nations was born out of the improbable idea that sovereign nations might come together to shape a new world order secured morally and legally by human rights instruments and safeguarded by an impressive and unprecedented array of new development and humanitarian institutions.

At the time of its founding, just thirty of the fifty-one original member states guaranteed women the right to vote. Diplomacy was still essentially a man's game. Only four women gathered among the 160 public delegates to the UN's first meeting in San Francisco in 1945. But with support from a robust community of civil society activists, they inscribed women's rights into the charter of the organization and affirmed in its preamble "faith in fundamental human rights, in the dignity of the human person, in the equal rights of men and women and of nations large and small."

The journey since has been long and often grueling, but as the UN celebrates its seventy-fifth anniversary this year and marks twenty-five years since Beijing, gender equality occupies an ever more secure position at the center of its agenda. This stunning accomplishment results from the dogged determination and agency of women from every country in the world. Our job as Americans in this critical moment is to go out and vote to defend it!

Do We Care?

BY **RAKEEN MABUD** AND
LENORE PALLADINO   •   SPRING 2021

THE COVID-19 PANDEMIC "is the most discriminatory crisis we [women and girls] have ever experienced," Phumzile Mlambo-Ngcuka, executive director of UN Women, said at the opening of the sixty-fifth session of the Commission on the Status of Women in mid-March.

Her statement rings just as true in the United States as elsewhere in the world. Since the start of the pandemic a little more than a year ago, American women have lost a net total of 5.4 million jobs—1 million more than men—and by the end of February nearly 3 million women had left the workforce entirely, many of them to care for their families. As the pandemic subsides, we must address this deep economic upheaval, which is resulting in an estimated $64.5 billion per year in lost wages for mothers alone. As a central component of our response, we must confront the total collapse of America's patchwork care infrastructure.

> **"Addressing our caregiving crisis is a moral and economic imperative."**

The Biden-Harris administration and the 117th Congress have an opportunity to center care work as *essential* work through major public investments that could establish universal access to high-quality care. Investing in care cannot be an afterthought in our recovery response.

Federal investment in child care, residential health care, and home health care can create high-quality employment opportunities for millions of workers, lifting the disproportionately women-of-color workforce out of poverty while enabling unpaid family caregivers to join the paid workforce. And as care workers spend wages on goods and services, new jobs will also be created in major employment sectors like retail and food service.

Our current caregiving crisis is the inevitable outcome of an outdated ideology that has resulted in insufficient investments in our care infrastructure and in our people. This has put the essential yet deeply undervalued task of caring for our young, elderly, sick, and disabled family and community members onto individuals—when this can, and must, be a shared priority for all of us and, therefore, a responsibility of our government.

It's time for the nation to act on a fundamental truth: our economy and society are stronger when all people can live lives of stability and dignity.

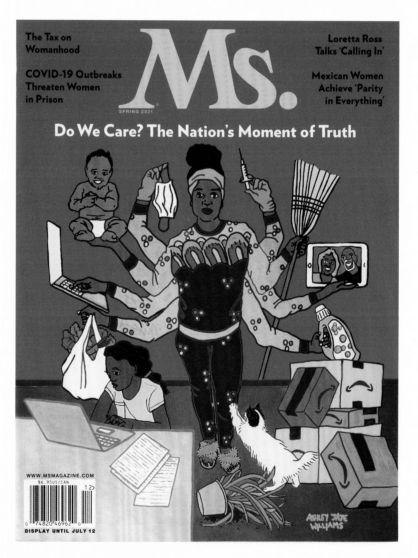

A modern reboot of *Ms.*'s inaugural cover, inspired by the many moments of truth for gender equity and the care economy that the global pandemic forced to the surface.

A BREAKING POINT FOR WOMEN

The COVID-19 pandemic has made it more evident than ever that women, especially Black women and Latinas, are trapped in an economy that is set up to extract their labor without paying them their due—all while also relying on them to solve the caregiving needs of their families on their own.

Millions of women, particularly low-income women, were pushed from the labor force by business closures and cutbacks, or they were driven to leave jobs or reduce their work hours when child-care centers and schools closed or, lacking paid leave, when they or their family members became sick.

A year on, women's labor force participation is down two percentage points, with nearly 275,000 women leaving the labor force in January 2021 alone; the crisis is far worse for Black and Asian women, as well as Latinas, all of whose employment levels remain far below those of white women.

A recent survey from the National Employment Law Project, Color of Change, the Worker Institute at Cornell, and Time's Up Foundation suggests that the sudden need to provide care is playing a major role in keeping women out of the paid labor force: more than half of Latinas surveyed and 44 percent of Black women said that unpaid caregiving responsibilities would negatively affect the amount of paid work they would be able to take on going forward. And there's no end in sight: nearly half of all child-care centers could close permanently as a result of the pandemic, and the flight from nursing homes has left many women caring for older relatives.

A PIVOTAL MOMENT

During the presidential campaign, Joe Biden and Kamala Harris committed to establishing a robust care infrastructure as a key economic plank of their "Build Back Better" platform. As the economic crisis continues, extensive government spending is necessary to provide immediate relief and to ensure long-term recovery for those most impacted.

Addressing our caregiving crisis is a moral and economic imperative.

The care sector is the backbone of the U.S. economy. Care jobs are job-supporting jobs, and when care workers earn family-supporting compensation, their own spending activity will create new jobs in other sectors as well. Our research for Time's Up Foundation finds that one crucial way to provide relief and set the foundation for a more inclusive economy going forward is to invest in our caregiving infrastructure.

Our findings likely understate the true benefits of investing in care. Our calculations cannot take into account the unknown droves of women who have been forced out of the labor market because of unmet child- and elder-care needs over the course of the pandemic (and even before).

And our model is limited to analyzing the impacts of job creation at *current* wages for care workers, though *family-supporting* wages would enable higher economic activity. Investing in a robust care infrastructure would not only create new jobs but also allow many others to come back, spurring the country's economic engine.

To be effective, investments for the care sector must support high-quality jobs and accessible, affordable care for all. Care labor is undervalued and unappreciated precisely because we undervalue the women of color who provide it. We must ensure that women are not simply returning to the insecure, underpaid jobs they occupied before the pandemic but that we are reshaping what those jobs look like.

An inclusive approach that centers the well-being and success of Black women in response to this crisis—what Janelle Jones (the Labor Department's chief economist), Kendra Bozarth, and Grace Western call "Black Women Best"—is a necessary pathway to begin to build equity now and to undo the exclusion inherent in U.S. policies, systems, and institutions.

The public gets it: investments in care are incredibly popular. A poll commissioned by Time's Up Foundation, Caring Across Generations, and Paid Leave for All Action found that more than 90 percent of voters are in favor of a comprehensive plan to provide services and support for people who are responsible for family and child care. Less than a third of voters thought that these needs could be met through individual actions. Polling by Data for Progress demonstrates overwhelming support for large-scale public spending to meet the COVID-19 crisis.

This moment of crisis calls for deep and extensive public investments in the people and communities who have supported our economy for generations. When we choose not to spend our public funds on a public problem we are making an active choice about whom we value in our economy—and whom we don't. Choosing to invest in care would serve as an important signal that as a society we cannot and will not take women for granted any longer. In this moment of relief and recovery, if we settle for benching half the population because of a care crisis, there is no way we will enjoy a sustainable, inclusive economy going forward.

We have a once-in-a-generation opportunity to enact transformative change and to rethink our economy at large and also how we value and treat women's labor. Let's not let it pass us by.

· · ·

Parity in Everything

BY **JENNIFER M. PISCOPO** • SPRING 2021

I N 2018, women won half the seats in Mexico's federal Congress. They then championed a groundbreaking constitutional reform: gender parity for all candidates for elected office and for top posts in the executive and judicial branches. Called "parity in everything," the reform sailed to victory in June 2019. Not a single member of Congress voted against it.

This easy success seems astounding, but "parity in everything" capped a decades-long process of increasing Mexican women's access to political power. By 2019, political parties already respected fifty-fifty rules when nominating candidates for the federal Congress, state legislatures, and municipal governments, including mayors. The last holdouts among elected positions were the coveted governor positions.

Other newly implemented rules further level the electoral playing field for women, and not just in the governors' races. Those convicted of violence against women cannot stand for elected office. And of the campaign resources that political parties distribute to candidates, 40 percent of the money and 40 percent of the advertising time must go to women.

While U.S. feminists were focused on breaking the 25 percent barrier for women in the House of Representatives, Mexico became the world's leader on gender parity. Mexican women spent decades chipping away at men's political dominance, turning incremental gains into deeper changes. Working across ideological divides, women in Mexico's political parties forged partnerships with activists and election authorities, and together they held party leaders accountable for fulfilling democracy's promise of political equality.

> **"Women from the Right made common cause with women from the Left. Issues like abortion could divide them, but political equality would unite them."**

FORCING PARTIES TO CHANGE

The idea of gender quotas for women candidates goes back nearly fifty years, to the United Nations' First World Conference on Women, coincidentally held in Mexico City in 1975. At the time, the UN recommendations merely emphasized the importance of women's political inclusion, but women activists and elected officials knew party leaders would need requirements, not pretty words. So in Latin America and elsewhere, women began pushing party leaders to set targets for nominating women.

In 1991, Argentina became the first country in Latin America and the world to adopt a 30 percent gender quota law for women political candidates. Mexico followed, with a 1996 law recommending that parties nominate 30 percent women for the federal Congress and a 2002 law requiring them to do so. Key to this shift was Mexico's democratization.

Electoral reform gave women legislators—who made up about 12 percent of Congress throughout the 1990s—an opportunity. They could introduce gender quotas as amendments to election laws, tying targets for women candidates to the parties' broader efforts to kick out the old-timers and the dinosaurs. They connected women's inclusion to improving democracy. As the academic and political leader Rosa Icela Ojeda Rivera noted at the time, representative models that excluded half the population lacked democratic legitimacy.

On this point of fairness, women from the Right made common cause with women from the Left. Issues like abortion could divide them, but political equality would unite them. As one woman senator explained, "Each woman thinks, fundamentally, that if there is more space for women in politics, then there is more space for me."

FROM GENDER QUOTAS TO GENDER PARITY

All legislation requires bargaining. Women won the mandatory gender quota in 2002 because they agreed to loopholes. Most famously, parties who chose their candidates using internal primaries (rather than direct selection by the party leadership) would not need to fill the 30 percent quota.

Loopholes notwithstanding, the quota did succeed in electing more women to Congress. In the 2003 elections, women went from 16.8 percent of the lower house to 24.9 percent. And they became even more determined to work for their inclusion.

In 2008, women legislators took advantage of yet another electoral reform, adding an amendment that raised the gender quota to 40 percent. Party leaders agreed, so long as they could keep their work-arounds. They claimed to select candidates using primaries, and election authorities took them at their word. They nominated more women, but in districts where the party expected to lose.

And then party leaders went too far. Women made few gains in the 2009 elections, increasing their presence in the lower house to just 27.6 percent. Even worse, sixteen women winners—from parties of the Left and the Right—forfeited, allowing men to claim their seats. Women legislators cried foul and fraud. Journalists called the sham candidacies "cheating" and "an undignified trick." Prominent women leaders came together to form a network of politicians, journalists, academics, activists, and policy makers known as Mujeres en Plural (Women as Multiple). Together, they brought a class-action lawsuit before Mexico's federal electoral court, which has final say over election law.

The court, led by the then chief magistrate María del Carmen Alanís, sidestepped the partisan arguments and went back to basics: Mexico's Constitution promised women and men equal rights. Alanís explained, "Gender equality is a constitutional principle equal to other constitutional principles." In other words, gender equality cannot play second fiddle to other constitutional principles, like political parties' freedom to choose candidates. The court wrote that each party must nominate men and women in "equality of conditions" and that the quota needed to be filled "without exception."

This landmark ruling tied the gender quota to fulfilling Mexico's constitutional promise of gender equality. Parties lost their loopholes. Soon after, a 2014 Constitution reform replaced the 40 percent gender quota with gender parity for the federal Congress and the state legislatures. Further, the 2015 electoral reform added that parties could not send women candidates exclusively to losing districts.

These changes triggered gains in the municipalities. As states updated their own constitutions and laws to require gender parity for state legislative races, some used imprecise language, implying that gender parity also applied to municipal elections. Mujeres en Plural had prepared for this possibility and reacted quickly, petitioning state election courts to resolve the ambiguity in women's favor. By early 2015, the federal electoral court weighed in, announcing gender parity for municipal races across Mexico beginning in 2018.

TACKLING POLITICAL VIOLENCE
AGAINST WOMEN

Gender parity alone cannot bring about political equality, of course. Women across the globe face unequal treatment and even violence on the campaign trail and in office, including abuse and harassment on social media and threats and assaults targeting them, their family members, and their staff. Attackers pursue women not because of their political views but because they dare enter, participate in, and claim power within a man's world.

Mexico proves no exception.

But Mexican women are, once again, not enduring misogyny in silence. With about half the seats in Mexico's lower house and senate, women exercise considerable influence over legislation. After passing "parity in everything" in June 2019, they passed a law to prevent and sanction political violence against women in April 2020.

This reform adds "political violence against women for reasons of gender" as an offense to Mexico's law penalizing violence against women. Political violence against women includes abuse, harassment, and assault in person and online and, more generally, placing obstacles to women's political campaigns such that "they cannot participate in conditions of equality."

With preparation for the 2021 elections already under way, women lawmakers worked to translate this mandate into reality. Congresswoman Martha Tagle and her colleagues asked election authorities to implement the "3-of-3 rule": that any man or woman previously sentenced by the courts for the failure to pay child support, for committing domestic violence, or for committing sexual violence would be ineligible to stand for office. The National Electoral Institute agreed, and the political parties conceded to not challenge this measure before the election court.

"The intention is that all people who seek to hold public office are people with no history of violence, because decisions that affect the lives of women are in their hands," Tagle explains.

She specifically referenced her party's gubernatorial candidate in Guerrero, Félix Salgado Macedonio, whom five women have denounced for sexual assault. Because Salgado has been accused but not convicted, the 3-of-3 rule leaves his candidacy intact—for now. "But this has to end," Tagle says. "We can no longer have public servants willing to cover up violence against women, but [rather] those who commit to stopping it."

MEXICAN WOMEN RULE

Mexico is the first country in the world to implement gender parity so thoroughly and effectively. The journey has not been easy. From running sham candidates to keeping the most prestigious races the preserve of men, political parties have resisted women's inclusion at every turn. But women fought back, making common cause across ideological divides and finding strength in their shared resolve. They went to war with the dinosaurs, and they won.

.   .   .

Call In for Equality

BY **CARRIE N. BAKER** • SPRING 2021

THERE'S TOO MUCH INFIGHTING in the feminist movement," the feminist activist Loretta Ross recently told *Ms.* "We're too vulnerable. Our weaknesses become our opponents' opportunities." Ross is raising an alarm about the corrosive practice of "calling out" in social justice movements and proposes an alternative— "calling in"—which she describes as a "feminist practice of intersectionality."

Calling out is publicly criticizing others in a way that humiliates them. Calling out can be a useful tactic for holding human rights violators accountable, Ross says, particularly for less powerful people trying to stop harm by more powerful people or entities. But calling out is often counterproductive when it takes the form of public shaming within social movement spaces, Ross notes, particularly when it results in banishing others because they are not "woke" enough.

> " 'Being so quick to take offense is not a statement of how woke you are. It's a statement of how much you need to grow.' "

"Calling out is about power," Ross says. "It's a way of gaining power in social interactions. In a group, if you can call somebody else out, then you all of a sudden control the group and you can set the agenda. It cuts off conversation. You can no longer have a give-and-take. You no longer can compromise. You no longer can work together. All of a sudden somebody's been banished. And they can't talk anymore. And then others are afraid to speak up for fear of being targeted themselves."

Ross says that calling out is toxic to the women's movement because it creates a discouraging atmosphere that drives people away from feminist activism. She argues that it replicates the carceral system of punishment by isolating people rather than unifying them, increases harm rather than healing, makes accountability difficult, and creates a culture of cynicism and hopelessness.

"First of all," Ross says, "we need to stop having this trigger fuse that when somebody says something that you don't perfectly agree with that you just set a firecracker off in the middle of their lives and blow them up. Stop and say, 'Wait a minute, we're all on the same team. Even if we've got different roles to play and different pathways, we're all on the same team.' . . . Being so quick to take offense is not a statement of how woke you are. It's a statement of how much you need to grow."

She gives the example of the calling out that happened around the women's marches. "All that calling out around the pink pussy march of 2017 is totally emblematic," she says. Callouts at the time focused on condemning the pink pussy hats as exclusionary of transgender women and women of color. Others berated white women who were new to the movement rather than focusing their energy on the real danger of the Trump administration.

Ross is also critical of people who insist on safe spaces and use significant time in movement meetings for somatic exercises and processing their feelings.

"We need to stop seeing feminism as our personal therapy spaces," she says. "The purpose of feminism is to end the oppression of women. Full stop. Not to create safe spaces where your feelings won't get hurt. . . . We've got to stop seeing the world through a victim-trauma lens. Because what that does is make you not only conflict averse but presumes that everything that you see is harming you. . . . Calling in is a brave-space practice, not a safe-space practice."

Ross defines calling in as initiating difficult dialogues with those you disagree with while respecting their human rights and differences. Ross began her work on calling in back in 2015, when she organized a daylong conference at Smith College. The overwhelmingly positive response from students led her to continue holding workshops on the topic. In February 2020, she held a second conference on calling in, again at Smith College, with Mia Mingus, Katherine Cross, and Asam Ahmad—all thought leaders on the practice.

When COVID-19 hit, Ross began teaching an online course, Calling In the Calling Out Culture. The first time she ran the class, four hundred people enrolled. The second time, seven hundred people signed up. Ross is now speaking out to mainstream media about calling in, including *The New York Times,* National Public Radio, and MSNBC's *Morning Joe,* and she has a forthcoming book on the topic.

"Calling in is a learnable art," Ross says. "To walk around life with short fuses is not a way to be a human rights feminist. We need to create a culture of forgiveness. You've got to find out your own trip wires and be in charge of them so you're not ruled by your emotions. Then you've got to practice self-forgiveness and forgiveness of others."

Ross adds that there's also "calling on": "a middle step between calling in and calling out." The author and activist Sonya Renee Taylor advocates for "calling on" people to be better human beings by shifting their perspectives. Whereas calling in requires the investment of labor in someone else's growth, "calling on" places responsibility for the growth on the other person by centering the person's behavior that needs to change.

"Calling out is an invitation to a fight. Calling in is an investment in another person's growth. I believe in calling on—calling on people to be better," Ross says. "Sometimes people will say a microaggression to you, and you don't have the time to invest in their growth, and you don't want to call in, so you can just respond, 'You know, I'm calling on you to rethink what you just said,' and walk away. 'I'm calling on you to be a better human being.'"

PROFESSOR LORETTA J. ROSS teaches at Smith College, where her course White Supremacy, Human Rights, and Calling In the Calling Out Culture has been widely covered and acclaimed. Through it, she advances her belief that private engagement is more compassionate—and ultimately more effective—than public outrage. Among the ways she's practiced "calling in" over the course of her own life: as executive director of the D.C. Rape Crisis Center in 1979, she used her own story of being sexually assaulted to teach Black feminist theory to men incarcerated for rape; later she taught antiracism to women whose families had ties to the Ku Klux Klan. Ross is among the Black activists who coined the phrase and frame of "reproductive justice" (which is the title of another of the courses she teaches at Smith).

The End of *Roe v. Wade*?

ON THE ISSUES, HOSTED BY MICHELE GOODWIN •
EPISODE 44, SEPTEMBER 15, 2021

MICHELE GOODWIN: On today's show, we're talking about reproductive health rights and justice.

I'm joined by Professor Dorothy Roberts, author of the award-winning *Killing the Black Body,* as well as the forthcoming page-turner *Torn Apart: How the Child Welfare System Destroys Black Families—and How Abolition Can Build a Safer World.*

In the past week, news cycles have turned to Texas and the Supreme Court and *Roe v. Wade,* and now they're beginning to see that the Texas law S.B. 8 has remnants of racism in it, that's embedded in it, in the language of it, but these are issues that are not new. You have long spoken about these issues at the intersection of race and sex and women of color's bodies and Black women's bodies. So, what began your work in this lane?

DOROTHY ROBERTS: Well, my very first entrée into the topic of reproductive freedom, at least as a scholar and an activist, was contesting the prosecutions of Black women for drug use during pregnancy in the late 1980s, early 1990s. I became a law professor in part because of those prosecutions and other ways in which pregnant women were being constrained and controlled.

> "It was just so obvious to me that this was not about protecting Black children. That's not how U.S. policy has been ever."
>
> —Dorothy Roberts

I started teaching in 1988, which was right when the so-called crack epidemic was going through Black communities, but more important, the U.S. government and state governments were attacking Black communities for crack use as if it were an especially horrendous form of drug use, and prosecutors were beginning to prosecute Black women in particular.

This was a time when the false image of the crack baby was being promoted. The idea that Black women's drug use somehow had stronger, more horrific effects on their babies than other kinds of drug use, that played on all sorts of stereotypes about Black women being irresponsible reproducers, and the criminalization of Black women and their children because the crack baby was supposed to turn into a criminal.

GOODWIN: This was what was being written about in newspapers.

ROBERTS: That's right. There was this idea that for some reason crack cocaine in particular deprived women of maternal instinct, and that Black children who were exposed to crack cocaine in utero were deprived of any kind of social consciousness. They were supposed to all become criminals at an early age and be predestined to welfare dependency and incapable of learning.

Of course, now we know that was all shoddy science and just made-up hyperbole. It was a total myth we know was false, but when I started reading about the prosecutions, I immediately thought of them as turning a public health crisis into a crime, and a way of punishing Black women for having babies. It was just so obvious to me that this was not about protecting Black children. That's not how U.S. policy has been ever.

GOODWIN: It's actually hard to find U.S. policy that was steeped in protecting Black children, Black women, Black men, right?

ROBERTS: Right. So the facts show that white women use drugs during pregnancy at the same rates, but yet, Black women were being reported by doctors for drug use to social services and prosecutors. One study in Pinellas County, Florida, found that Black women were being reported at ten times the rate as white women who used drugs during pregnancy. So, this was clearly targeted at Black people, and there's just no plausible way you could say that these prosecutors were more interested in protecting Black babies than white babies.

Also, it's not protecting a fetus to lock the fetus's mother up in a dingy jail cell without prenatal care. . . . It was clearly devaluing Black women for having children, and at the time there wasn't that much being written about prosecuting pregnancy, criminalizing pregnancy.

There was a mainstream reproductive rights movement that was advocating for abortion rights, but that movement tended to see these issues as separate, and I really saw them as the same issue. It's about controlling women's bodies . . . and the way in which racism has always intersected with misogyny and sexism in order to control, in particular, the bodies of women of color.

GOODWIN: You opened the door to this conversation about Texas and S.B. 8. How are you responding to what's taking place in Texas right now?

ROBERTS: I think it's just an atrocious attack on women's autonomy, women's freedom, women's health, women's lives. We know that without access to safe, legal abortion, women, especially impoverished women, low-income women, and women of color, are going to be forced into dangerous, life-threatening situations. The idea that the state can ban a health decision shows a lack of valuing of women's lives and freedom. It's really horrific.

In order to get around the idea that what they're actually doing is punishing women and deterring them from getting health care

and risking their lives, instead of having any kind of penalty on the person who's seeking an abortion, the penalties are on doctors who perform abortions.

How is the state going to go about imposing these penalties? Well, it's deputized ordinary, private citizens to sue anyone they suspect has performed an abortion or aided and abetted the performance of an abortion. So it's done two things. It's deputized citizens to hunt down women and deputized ordinary citizens to spy on and report on and interfere in the health and freedom of their fellow citizens. That's like a police state.

GOODWIN: For you, did it trigger any sense of "we've seen this before"?

ROBERTS: I'll tell you, it triggered two things. One is the Fugitive Slave Law deputizing U.S. citizens to track down escaped enslaved people and help in their capture. It sounds like that. The other thing it reminded me of relates to the work I've been doing on the child-welfare system . . . , which I call "family policing," in which citizens are deputized to report people for child abuse and neglect.

You might think, Oh, that sounds good to have people report on other people who are harming their children, but what actually happens is that people report on people out of revenge. They report on ex-boyfriends. They report on their girlfriend and claim that she is maltreating the children.

Whenever you have this kind of deputizing of people to investigate, spy on, and report on others, it's impossible to separate that from the kinds of stereotypes about Black women in particular that circulate in our society and the way in which many Americans have been willing to put Black women in harmful situations in order to achieve some other broader policy goal.

GOODWIN: Right. As Loretta Ross mentioned to me, Black women being used as roadkill in the fight for white women to have restricted reproductive rights. What's interesting is that there have been some who have said, "Oh, we shouldn't compare this to slavery." Because white women weren't enslaved. And what they're forgetting is that there are Black women in Texas.

ROBERTS: And affected more, both because Black women are less likely to have the means to go to another state or find a doctor who will perform the abortion, somehow secretly. That's always happened throughout history, even when abortion was banned. Black women are less likely to have the means to do it. And that means the money. It means the ability to leave work and go on a trip to seek out an abortion, maybe you have to wait, . . . and also, Black women have a higher rate of abortions. So, they're more likely to be affected by a law that severely restricts, really virtually bans, abortions in the state.

Also, another way in which abortion and pregnancy—wanted pregnancy—are connected is the high rate of maternal mortality for Black women, which is, I've seen, two, three, four times the rate of white women. We should remember that maternal mortality means death from pregnancy-related causes, which covers the gamut of reasons why a woman may die from a pregnancy.

GOODWIN: The claim that what they're doing is protecting Black women, their safety and health, by enacting laws that would restrict Black women's rights to abortion. What do you make of Justice Clarence Thomas along that line of thinking, and also the state efforts that claim that abortion harms Black women?

ROBERTS: Well, they're just bogus arguments. They're historically flawed. Thomas's argument that abortion was a tool of eugenics is just historically wrong. Eugenicists preferred sterilization, and there's been a long history of sterilization abuse of Black women, as well as impoverished women and women who were seen to have disabilities.

GOODWIN: I usually ask at the end of our show, what's the silver lining? It's hard to kind of ferret out a silver lining here, although maybe one comes to us from history: What did Black women do centuries ago to try to address these issues? What do you see as pathways forward?

ROBERTS: The reproductive justice movement, which really came into its own in the 1990s. The term was coined in the 1990s, and it now has blossomed into a really strong movement that understands the connections among these issues and has been spearheaded by Black women and other women of color. I think it's a really exciting movement.

Also, the prison abolition movement, the idea of abolishing the prison-industrial complex from the 1980s. People around the world learned about it last summer with the global protests against police violence. I write about it in *Torn Apart,* and one of the reasons I decided to write a new book about the child-welfare system was because of an emerging movement to end this punitive, really horrible way of addressing children's needs that ends up harming children.

So, I really have great hope that as these movements understand the connections we've been talking about and come together in a common mission to end these punitive ways of addressing human needs and addressing violence, that instead we have an approach that is caring, that treats all people as equal human beings. That dismantles these hierarchies of gender and race and class and ability, and that builds a world that takes care of people. I think Black women's history of taking care of families and communities in loving, emancipatory ways is a wonderful road map for us. We just need to pay more attention to it and learn from those examples.

·   ·   ·

A Case for the
Equal Rights Amendment

BY **VICTORIA F. NOURSE** • FALL 2021

WHEN SHE WAS a college freshman in 1994, Christy Brzonkala says she was gang-raped by two students on the Virginia Tech campus in Blacksburg, Virginia, thirty minutes after she met them.

Months after the alleged rape, she says one of her assailants announced in the dorm's dining room that he "like[d] to get girls drunk and fuck the shit out of them." This same man also admitted at the school hearing that he had sex with Brzonkala (he claimed it was consensual, though she'd said no twice), but ultimately the school didn't discipline him. The other alleged assailant was never prosecuted at all.

Distraught, Brzonkala attempted suicide and then dropped out of school. In 1995, Virginia Tech allowed the man who'd been prosecuted (both were athletes on the football team) to return to class.

After a Richmond grand jury refused to indict her alleged assailants, Brzonkala turned to a law newly passed in 1994 called the Violence Against Women Act (VAWA). That law allowed survivors a civil rights remedy to sue their assailants for gender-based violence in civil court—to achieve some measure of legal accountability when officials disbelieved the allegations or took no action.

Brzonkala's alleged assailants argued that the new law was unconstitutional, that Congress had no power to pass it. Almost every court to hear their constitutional claim rejected it until the case reached the Supreme Court, where, in 2000, women's right to equal protection from violence died in the case *United States v. Morrison*. (Antonio Morrison was one of Brzonkala's alleged rapists.)

There are many reasons to fight for an Equal Rights Amendment to the Constitution. But Brzonkala's case offers a particularly poignant one. As the late justice Antonin Scalia once explained, "Certainly the Constitution does not require discrimination on the basis of sex. The only issue is whether it prohibits it. It doesn't. Nobody ever thought that that's what it meant.

"Nobody ever voted for that," the famously conservative justice said, adding, "If the current society wants to outlaw discrimination by sex, hey we have things called legislatures, and they enact things called laws."

But here's the rub: that might work if Congress had the constitutional power to enact laws against gender violence. The *Morrison* decision holds that the Constitution bars Congress from passing such a law. That could all change with the adoption of the Equal Rights Amendment.

THE SUPREME COURT V. VAWA

The Violence Against Women Act, passed twenty-seven years ago, did many things, but its sponsor, the then senator Joe Biden (whom I worked for at the time), believed that the civil rights remedy was the heart of it.

To see how big a deal that was, consider Harvey Weinstein, who was sentenced to twenty-three years in prison for rape and sexual assault and was alleged to have assaulted dozens of women over decades. No federal law allows his victims to sue him for gender-based violence.

Title VII of the Civil Rights Act, which prohibits sex discrimination in employment, though well known, is quite limited. It gives some people a right to sue for sexual harassment—but only in some situations. If you are not an employee, you have no right under the law. (Many of Weinstein's victims, for example, were looking for jobs; they did not have them.) And even when the survivors are employees, the law does not cover sexual assault that occurs outside the workplace (a much larger problem) and allows lawsuits only against employers with more than fifteen workers.

> "'Certainly the Constitution does not require discrimination on the basis of sex. The only issue is whether it prohibits it. It doesn't. Nobody ever thought that that's what it meant.'"

There was, and still is, a very big gap in the law of gender-based violence. VAWA's civil rights remedy aimed to close it.

But the Supreme Court ruled in *Morrison* that Congress had no power to protect women from violence because crime is a matter for the states. It did not appear to matter to the justices that state criminal prosecutions for sexual assault were rare, then and now. The *Morrison* decision announced grand principles of federalism (deference to the states), but its history carried the stench of racism and judicial power politics. Its author, Chief Justice William Rehnquist, had spearheaded a lobbying effort against VAWA's civil rights remedy trying to prevent it from passing.

Per ethics rules, judges are not supposed to lobby at all, and certainly not on laws that they themselves will rule on. But the chief justice took a very public stand against the legislation, claiming it would flood the federal courts with "a whole host of millions of domestic relations disputes" and "be invoked as a bargaining tool within the context of divorce negotiations"—implying that women would lie about violence in divorce proceedings. After his very public lobbying efforts, Rehnquist held the remedy unconstitutional, writing an opinion that equated sexual violence with what high-powered, white-collar lawyers viewed as relatively trivial legal matters of family law—marriage and divorce—and thus beneath the attention of federal authorities.

The *Morrison* decision largely avoided talking about gender equality—the very reason Congress had passed the civil rights remedy. The Senate Judiciary Committee, which proposed the law, noted that criminal prosecutions for gender violence were rare and that there was pervasive gender bias in state law and in the criminal and civil justice systems. Congress needed to intervene because the states had failed to protect women. The problem was structural: the system was set up to make it difficult for anyone, prosecutors or survivors, to hold assailants to account.

None of these well-known facts mattered enough to the Supreme Court majority who decided *Morrison*.

ERA NOW

Most gains in women's rights have come not from the Supreme Court via the Constitution but from Congress via legislation. Laws like Title VII and Title IX were held constitutional based on the fiction that they were primarily about commerce or federal educational funding, not fundamental gender equality, and thus apply only at work or school. Outside those contexts, women's rights too often stop.

Since *Morrison* was decided, the Supreme Court has only become more conservative. Now six justices, including former president Donald Trump's three appointments to the court, believe in "originalism": the theory that the meaning of the Constitution was fixed more than two hundred years ago in 1787, when women were legally regarded as the property of their husbands and fathers.

If strictly applied, originalism would eradicate women's progress and allow this court to overturn all the decisions applying the Fourteenth Amendment to women because no one thought women were included in the Fourteenth Amendment at the time it was ratified. Forget about abortion. Under the originalism doctrine, states could pass laws that expressly discriminate based on sex, barring women from jobs and denying equal pay.

The ERA would block that move by placing the words "sex" and "equality" in the U.S. Constitution. Even originalists bow to the actual text of the Constitution. Perhaps more important, the ERA would spark Congress to enact new laws on gender violence, including redrafting the VAWA civil rights remedy, and chart a path to overturn *Morrison*.

It is long past time to add the ERA to the Constitution—to address this matter and right a constitutional wrong.

Women's Rights Are Not "Western Values"

BY **SIMA SAMAR** • FALL 2021

I N THE WAKE of the fall of the Afghan government to the Taliban, many in the international community and media have said that efforts in Afghanistan to secure women's rights and human rights were doomed to fail because of the traditions and culture in my country. This is absolutely the wrong lesson to take away from our experience in Afghanistan.

> **"The lesson that we need to take from what has happened in Afghanistan is that peace and security are not possible without respect for women's rights and human rights."**

Human rights and women's rights are not "Western values." They do not belong to the West. They are universal values. As laid out in the Universal Declaration of Human Rights in 1948, human rights are universal for everyone, everywhere, regardless of nationality, race, gender, religion, locale, or political system.

Over the past twenty years, despite the continued fighting in the country, the people of Afghanistan made remarkable achievements on human rights, including reforming the law according to the principles of human rights and equality. Women were represented in the parliament, the judiciary, ministries, the army, the police, the media, business, and sports. A generation of young women were able to attend school and have the freedom to work. A generation of young women and men were educated about human rights and women's rights, and these are lessons they will not forget—even in the current situation. These achievements on human rights and women's rights cannot be denied by anyone.

The lesson that we need to take from what has happened in Afghanistan is that peace and security are not possible without respect for women's rights and human rights. My country was plunged into forty-two years of conflict beginning in 1979, when the Soviets invaded Afghanistan. And throughout the decades, women's rights have been violated.

During the Soviet invasion, the civil war that followed, and then the Taliban regime, women and girls were denied their most basic human rights in the name of religion and Afghan tradition. "Tradition" was used as an unwritten code to control women's bodies and abilities. And families put more restrictions on female members in the name of protection, further reducing their space in society.

We must end the fighting in Afghanistan, but women's rights and human rights cannot be sacrificed in the process.

The international obligations of the Afghan government, particularly the international human rights instruments and agreements to which Afghanistan is a party, should be respected by the new government. These include equality between people from different ethnic religious groups and differ-

DR. SIMA SAMAR, a medical doctor and fierce advocate for girls and women, was the highest-ranked woman official in Afghanistan. Appointed to key panels by the secretary-general of the United Nations, she also held leadership roles as special envoy of the president of Afghanistan and state minister for human rights and international affairs. In addition, she served as chair of the Afghanistan Independent Human Rights Commission, as minister of women's affairs (one of only two women in the transition government at that time), and as UN special rapporteur on human rights in Sudan. A long-standing partner of the Feminist Majority Foundation, she has been featured by *Ms.* for her groundbreaking work over two decades to expose the dire conditions for Afghan women and girls, to champion social, economic, and human rights policy interventions, and to create educational opportunities.

ent genders. We, as Muslims, believe that all human beings are born with equal dignity. Promotion and protection of human rights is a shared and moral responsibility for us all.

Sustainable peace will not be possible without the full and meaningful participation of women, who are half of the population. As history has shown, without peace in Afghanistan, the problem will reach other countries. Unfortunately, recent events in Afghanistan show that history repeats itself. We should learn from our mistakes.

Abortion Is Essential to Democracy

BY **KATHERINE SPILLAR** AND
JENNIFER WEISS-WOLF • WINTER 2022

AFTER S.B. 8 WENT INTO EFFECT in Texas on September 1, and following the Supreme Court's egregious 5–4 ruling allowing its enforcement, a cohort of staff from across the Brennan Center for Justice came together to show solidarity, express outrage, and articulate a response. That conversation morphed into an electrifying brainstorm with *Ms.,* the result of which is captured in the array of essays on a dedicated *Ms.* microsite (msmagazine.com/abortion-is-essential-to-democracy).

The Brennan Center for Justice, a law and policy institute affiliated with NYU Law School, is a central and invaluable leader in the fight for democracy and justice in America. Every day, it works to protect voting rights, ensure free and fair elections, champion a diverse judiciary, and advocate for equal justice.

> **"The fight for abortion rights, the fight for equality and the fight for representative democracy are all in service of the same goal: justice for all."**

After oral arguments in *Dobbs v. Jackson Women's Health Organization* on December 1, it is all too clear that myriad democratic dysfunctions have led us to this dire moment. By formally joining our voices, we hope to demonstrate that the fight for abortion rights, the fight for equality, and the fight for representative democracy are all in service of the same goal: justice for all.

THE GOVERNMENT HAS A LONG HISTORY OF CONTROLLING WOMEN— ONE THAT NEVER ENDED

BY **ELIZABETH HIRA**

"WOMEN CAN 'CONTROL THEIR REPRODUCTIVE LIVES' without access to abortion; they can do so by refraining from sexual intercourse."

This stunning statement was written in a "friend of the court" brief submitted to the Supreme Court in July by Texas Right to Life and signed by Jonathan Mitchell, one of the architects of Texas law S.B. 8. And it makes crystal clear that outlawing abortion isn't the only end game. Control over women is.

The ability to control one's body is intrinsic to controlling one's life. This is true along the entire reproductive continuum, from sex to abortion to delivery. In her 1993 Supreme Court confirmation hearing, Ruth Bader Ginsburg explained to the Senate Judiciary Committee, "The decision whether or not to bear a child is central to a woman's life, to her well-being and dignity. It is a decision she must make for herself. When government controls that decision for her, she is being treated as less than a fully adult human responsible for her own choices."

In short, she is being treated differently—and less—than a man.

Twenty-five years later, the then senator Kamala Harris made the point more plain during Brett Kavanaugh's confirmation hearing, asking, "Can you think of any laws that give government the power to make decisions about the male body?" Judge Kavanaugh replied, "I'm not aware—I'm not—thinking of any right now, Senator."

Throughout modern history, government control over women's bodies—and, by extension, women—has been a prevalent theme, built into our very systems. Rape was initially deemed a property crime against the victim's father. And as property themselves, married women could not own property under the common-law principle of coverture. U.S. laws long forbade women to fully participate in society. For instance, only beginning in 1973 could women serve on a jury in all fifty states, and until 1974 women lacking their husband's permission could be refused credit cards.

Of course, we've since achieved advances—legislative, jurisprudential, societal—that make these examples seem archaic. Yet the work to secure true equality under the law has never been completed. We may have it better than our foremothers, but the current state of the law is not enough. Texas law S.B. 8—and the public statements made by its architects—show just how much worse it could get.

And that is because abortion is not (just) a health issue. Whether we are

The reproduced magazine spread reads:

ABORTION IS ESSENTIAL TO DEMOCRACY

Despite the fact that a majority of Americans support *Roe v. Wade*, the Supreme Court appears poised to overturn or dramatically weaken the landmark decision. In this excerpt from *Ms.'* collaboration with the Brennan Center for Justice, the organization's experts explain how we got here—and offer some ways forward.

After SB 8 went into effect in Texas on Sept. 1, and following the Supreme Court's egregious 5-4 ruling allowing its enforcement, a cohort of staff from across the Brennan Center for Justice came together to show solidarity, express outrage and articulate a response. That conversation morphed into an electrifying brainstorm with *Ms.*, the result of which is captured in the array of essays on a dedicated *Ms.* microsite (see sidebar) and excerpted here.

The Brennan Center for Justice, a law and policy institute affiliated with NYU Law, is a central and invaluable leader in the fight for democracy and justice in America. Every day, it works to protect voting rights, ensure free and fair elections, champion a diverse judiciary and advocate for equal justice.

After oral arguments in *Dobbs v. Jackson Women's Health Organization* on Dec. 1, it is all too clear that myriad democratic dysfunctions have led us to this dire moment. By formally joining our voices, we hope to demonstrate that the fight for abortion rights, the fight for equality and the fight for representative democracy are all in service of the same goal: justice for all.

—KATHERINE SPILLAR AND JENNIFER WEISS-WOLF

The Government Has a Long History of Controlling Women—One That Never Ended
BY ELIZABETH HIRA

"WOMEN CAN 'CONTROL THEIR REPRODUCTIVE LIVES' WITHOUT ACCESS to abortion; they can do so by refraining from sexual intercourse."

This stunning statement was written in a "friend of the court" brief submitted to the Supreme Court in July by Texas Right to Life and signed by Jonathan Mitchell, one of the architects of Texas law SB 8. And it makes crystal clear that outlawing abortion isn't the only end game. Control over women is.

The ability to control one's body is intrinsic to controlling one's life. This is true along the entire reproductive continuum, from sex to abortion to delivery. In her 1993 Supreme Court confirmation hearing, Ruth Bader Ginsburg explained to the Senate Judiciary Committee: "The decision whether or not to bear a child is central to a woman's life, to her well-being and dignity. It is a decision she must make for herself. When government controls that decision for her, she is being treated as less than a fully adult human responsible for her own choices."

In short, she is being treated differently—and less than—a man.

Twenty-five years later, then-Sen. Kamala Harris made the point more plain during Brett Kavanaugh's confirmation hearing, asking, "Can you think of any laws that give government the power to make decisions about the male body?" Judge Kavanaugh replied, "I'm not aware—I'm not—thinking of any right now, senator."

Throughout modern history, government control over women's bodies—and by extension, women—has been a prevalent theme, built into our very systems. Rape was initially deemed a property crime against the victim's father. And as property themselves, married women could not own property under the common law principle of coverture. U.S. laws long forbade women from full societal participation. For instance, only beginning in 1973 could women serve on a jury in all 50 states; and until 1974, women lacking their husband's permission could be refused credit cards.

Of course, we've since achieved advances—legislative, jurisprudential, societal—that make these examples seem archaic. Yet the work to secure true equality under the law has never been completed. We may have it better than our foremothers, but the current state of the law is not enough. Texas law SB 8—and the public statements made by its architects—shows just how much worse it could get.

And that is because abortion is not (just) a health issue. Whether we are willing to let women and people capable of becoming pregnant control their

It appears likely that the Supreme Court will, at the very least, uphold Mississippi's abortion law, which bans the procedure after 15 weeks.

20 | WINTER 2022 *Ms.*   www.feminist.org   www.msmagazine.com   *Ms.* WINTER 2022 | 21

---

willing to let women and people capable of becoming pregnant control their own bodies, for health or any other reason, is an equity issue—a question of who deserves bodily autonomy and freedom to reach their full potential.

TEXAS'S ABORTION BANS AND VOTER SUPPRESSION LAWS LET CITIZENS DO "DIRTY WORK" OF OPPOSING CONSTITUTION

BY **IZABELA TRINGALI** AND **JULIA KIRSCHENBAUM**

SINCE THE JIM CROW ERA, states have flouted the Constitution by enlisting private citizens and organizations to do the "dirty work" of enforcing laws that violate fundamental rights. Texas has been a notable offender.

In 1927, for example, when no longer permitted to exclude Black Americans from political primaries, it enacted a law delegating the power to establish qualifications for electoral participation to political parties; in Fort Bend County, political organizations were permitted to run private, pre-

Ms. partnered with the Brennan Center for Justice at New York University School of Law on a special section of the Winter 2022 issue, "Abortion Is Essential to Democracy," which links key issues of civic participation and engagement to the fight for abortion rights.

primary elections to cut Black voters out of the candidate selection process. The Supreme Court determined that these systems were unconstitutional more than fifty years ago.

Texas lawmakers have resurrected this tactic once again—not only in the context of voting rights, but to shut down abortion access, too. Texas's S.B. 8 went into effect on the same day that S.B. 1, an omnibus voter suppression package, was passed by both chambers of the state legislature. The parallels between these laws extend well beyond their synchronized timelines.

Each law hands over an aspect of what would traditionally be the state's enforcement power to civilians, encouraging and empowering a type of citizen vigilante. S.B. 8 does this by creating a bounty system in which "any person, other than an officer or employee of a state or local governmental entity in this state," may be awarded a minimum of $10,000 for successfully suing an abortion provider or anyone who "aids and abets" someone getting an abortion after six weeks of pregnancy.

S.B. 1, meanwhile, expands the authority of partisan poll watchers by giving them "free movement," while also imposing criminal penalties on election workers who try to regulate poll watcher conduct. For example, even if an election worker receives several complaints that a watcher is harassing and intimidating voters, S.B. 1 prohibits removal of the watcher from the polling place unless the worker witnesses a violation of election law or the watcher has breached the state's penal code.

Both laws penalize the provision of assistance to those exercising a constitutional right. By allowing private citizens to sue anyone they suspect of providing or helping a person access abortion care, S.B. 8 creates liability for abortion providers and myriad others, whether they be neighbors, family, rideshare drivers, or members of the clergy. And S.B. 1 makes it more difficult for voters—especially those who have disabilities, less formal education, or limited English proficiency—to receive assistance.

Another similarity between the laws is the purposeful imposition of restrictions that make exercising the right in question more time-consuming and inconvenient and therefore more expensive and out of reach. S.B. 8 has pushed the majority of people seeking an abortion to find care outside Texas, adding long-distance travel to the list of direct costs, as well as a cascade of collateral costs like child care, time away from work, and lost wages—all expenses that are felt most acutely by low-income and Black and brown Americans.

Similarly, S.B. 1's ban on twenty-four-hour early voting and drive-through voting prohibits some of the most accessible options for low-wage workers and others who have limited flexibility.

S.B. 1 and S.B. 8 are linked not only in their tactics but also in a larger antidemocratic power play. Both laws aim to undermine basic rights and privatize certain enforcement powers in an attempt to entrench conservative political ideology in the public sphere. The result is not "liberty" or "small government": it is the deliberate outsourcing of the state's power in order to disenfranchise and marginalize.

THE POWER OF STATE COURTS IN SECURING ACCESS: "IT'S TIME TO GIVE THEM CENTER STAGE"

BY **ALICIA BANNON**

THE SUPREME COURT'S early September ruling on Texas law S.B. 8 was a chilling moment, but also a wake-up call. Progressives are giving new attention to reforming the Supreme Court, but it would be a mistake to stop there. We also need to pay greater attention to state courts and state constitutions as a promising, underappreciated, and frequently threatened venue for protecting abortion rights.

Why focus on state courts? A key feature of our federal system is that state courts get to interpret laws under their own state's constitution. Therefore, it's state supreme courts, not the Supreme Court, that get to be the final word in interpreting the meaning of state constitutional provisions, and they can interpret their constitutions to go further than the federal Constitution in establishing and protecting rights. In other words, when it comes to protecting civil and human rights, the U.S. Constitution functions as a floor, not a ceiling. With state constitutions, you can build a skyscraper.

This isn't news to reproductive rights litigators, who have increasingly looked to state courts as promising venues. Consider Kansas and Iowa, where in the past three years state supreme courts have issued rulings protecting abortion rights, all under their state constitutions. Yet the broader progressive movement has paid surprisingly little attention to state courts—not who sits on them or how to defend them when their rulings prompt political attacks.

And there's been little attention given to the stark lack of diversity on state supreme courts across the country, where women hold only 39 percent of seats. Meanwhile, people of color are completely absent from high-court benches in twenty-two states.

Equally troubling is what's happened in many states when courts have issued rulings that are out of step with entrenched political interests. In 2019, for example, Alaska's governor used his line-item veto authority to strip $335,000 from the judiciary's budget after the Alaska Supreme Court issued a ruling requiring state funding of certain abortion services. It's part of a broader trend where rulings on issues such as abortion rights, voting rights, education equity, and death penalty abolition have all put targets on state courts in recent years—including impeachment campaigns, efforts to strip away courts' power, and moves to give politicians more control over judicial selection.

State courts in many of the places most likely to attack reproductive rights may not have judges ready to defend them. But with federal rights increasingly at risk, it makes sense to use every available tool and to invest in building fair courts that can be on the vanguard of protecting reproductive rights.

The decades since *Roe v. Wade* make clear that courts can't be the only path to achieving reproductive justice but also that we won't have reproductive justice without them. State courts have usually been afterthoughts in these strategies. It's time to give them center stage.

Ms. Harriet Tubman at Two Hundred

BY **JANELL HOBSON** • SPRING 2022

TWO HUNDRED YEARS AGO, a child was born into chattel slavery. She grew up to become a liberator. Abolitionist. Diviner. Healer. Nurse. Naturalist. Freedom fighter. Military raid leader. Spy. Scout. Suffragist. Daughter. Sister. Wife. Mother. Aunt. Friend. National icon. This is the legacy of Harriet Tubman, born Araminta Ross around 1822, nicknamed "Minty" in her youth and heralded as "Moses" in her extraordinary adult years of emancipatory action.

The Harriet Tubman Bicentennial Project launched in February 2022 on *Ms.*'s online platform (msmagazine.com/tubman200), culminating on March 10—the anniversary of Tubman's death in 1913. The project sought to honor one of America's greatest feminist heroes by teaching about her vibrant, complex, and complicated life.

Few know Tubman beyond her status as an Underground Railroad conductor who self-liberated from slavery in 1849 before freeing others during the 1850s. Fewer still know the conditions of enslavement that she sought to flee. Or that she continued liberating others during the U.S. Civil War, when she worked as a nurse, cook, spy, and scout. Or that she devoted her later years to establish the Home for the Aged.

In the interest of public education, the Tubman 200 Project features a timeline chronicling Tubman's life; an interactive calculator configuring the amount Tubman is owed for her enslaved labor; conversations with experts, artists, and Tubman's living descendants; and a series of essays from scholars in diverse fields. The biographer Kate Clifford Larson encourages us to discern the distortions and myths from the facts and truth of the historical record. The historians Deirdre Cooper Owens and Edda L. Fields-Black reveal the lesser-known stories of Tubman, respectively including the impact of her disability on her life and her military-raid leadership on the Combahee River during the Civil War. Tubman's history is given much more depth that extends her heroism across the length of her ninety-one years. To that end, the archaeologist Douglas V. Armstrong pieces together the life Tubman led in freedom in Auburn, New York, through fragments of artifacts uncovered at the site of the Harriet Tubman property, while the fashion historian Jonathan Michael Square uses the visual record to comment on Tubman's styling choices, which reveal both her femininity and her humanity.

Digital artist Nettrice Gaskins titled her illustration of Harriet Tubman *Beacon of Hope* because Tubman "dreamed for herself a future . . . she had to create something that [didn't] exist yet and something that [was] only in her mind," Gaskins told *Ms.*

Still others use provocative frameworks to reinterpret Tubman's actions. The ethnomusicologist Maya Cunningham views Tubman's musical gifts as subversive forms of liberation, while the cultural studies scholar Michelle D. Commander traces Tubman's visions, stemming (most likely) from her epileptic seizures, through the lens of Afrofuturism. Moreover, the astrophysicist Chanda Prescod-Weinstein proclaims Tubman to be "one of the greatest astronomers in American history" for following the North Star to freedom. Other pieces demonstrate how her iconic status is powerful enough to signal needed social change, whether in the art traditions that Michele Wallace analyzes when commenting on Tubman's representations in the art of Wallace's mother, Faith Ringgold, or in the antiracist and feminist education explored by the game design instructors Rebecca Rouse and Amy Corron, who centered Tubman as a heroic avatar in their own classroom. Keisha N. Blain questions the meaning of Tubman's image on the planned redesign of the $20 bill if economic justice for Black women as a group is not included in these future plans.

As the project tackles these social issues, it also seeks to inspire through original creative works, including the artist Nettrice Gaskins's digital portrait of Tubman and Alexis Pauline Gumbs's powerful poem "dark energy."

We salute a groundbreaking feminist and liberator who never lost sight of freedom. Harriet Tubman has stood the test of time through her incomparable example of bravery, fierceness, persistence, faith, self-assurance, compassion, and commitment to solidarity. May her memory serve as a guiding light, much like the North Star she followed, steering us all in the right direction at this critical juncture.

DARK ENERGY

for Harriet Tubman

BY **ALEXIS PAULINE GUMBS** • 2022

1822
the Astronomical Society
of London meets
to write down what they know of
    stars

in eastern shore Maryland
araminta screams
into an unmeasurable life

1835
sap dark root of love

opening out your skull
praise the girl who watched the
    comet and knew
praise the girl who tracked the
    north star and knew
praise the girl who studied herself
    and knew one thing:

sky is a map

1844
expand the universe

open the wet reflective road
blood bashed temporal lobe

let everything that is not love
escape your skull
like so much stardust

1849
and while they chart
the pricks of light
    use night
    love night
    be night
    free night
    write night

if colonialism is a starving hunter
    and slavery is a splintered pencil
        go
            become untraceable

1851
if all you breathe is freedom
they can't hear you
if all you take is freedom
they can't steal you

if all you feel is freedom
they can't find you
if all you give is freedom
they can't stop you
if all you love is freedom
they can't catch you

girl you look just like freedom
they can't see you

1863
sing to the river
wake the people
sing to the rice fields
wake the land
sing to the trees
the vines
the moss
sing to the river
the people come running
buildings burning in their wake
like stars

1865
walk away from the broken
   promise
walk away like you walked before
walk away from the muddled battle
walk on into your own front door

freedom is the people you choose
the air you breathe

1896
sometimes
the meeting room
is a night sky

you see infinite versions
of the universe
looking back at you
in each blinking face

1910
the comet comes back
around
the ground
has changed

1913
if you build it right
if you know the trees
if you make it sweet enough for
   your parents
and big enough for your
   community
and soon enough to live in it
   yourself
the old folks home can be a
   spaceship

1922
somebody thinks
they can fix the cosmos
get black history down in writing
fix your image keep you there
somewhere the first and last
   astronomer laughs

2022
and laughs

JUSTICE AND THE MEANING OF THE TUBMAN $20

BY **KEISHA N. BLAIN**

It is only fitting that Harriet Tubman should receive national recognition for her life of service and sacrifice. And the decision to replace the image of President Andrew Jackson with Tubman's on the $20 bill is a powerful, symbolic gesture.

The irony is that her life story brings into bold relief the economic struggles Black women face in American society and the creative ways they have managed to use limited material resources to help—and indeed liberate—others. Tubman's lived experiences reflect the broader challenges that Black women endured in American society—often celebrated, but hardly ever protected.

Despite the end of legal slavery in the United States in 1865, Black people remained in a precarious position as they worked to build a new life with few material resources and in the face of much violent resistance. A white supremacist and sexist society relegated Black women to the bottom of the socioeconomic ladder. Tubman was no exception. She gave so much to the nation, yet the nation offered so little in return. In the years following the Civil War, Tubman was believed to have struggled to maintain her monthly payments for the property she purchased in Auburn, New York. She also assumed financial responsibility for her parents, extended family, and several members of the community.

Though she made every effort to overcome it, the economic precarity that shaped Tubman's life under slavery remained fixed in place in the decades that followed. The headline of a *New York Age* article from June 8, 1911—"Harriet Tubman Ill and Penniless"—illustrated the difficult circumstances of Tubman's final years. The article appealed to the public for assistance to help meet the mounting bills associated with her care. The fact that Tubman would, at the end of her life, face such dire circumstances serves as a bitter reminder that celebratory acclaim offers little to meet tangible needs.

And while symbolically meaningful, Tubman's face on a $20 bill brings us no closer to liberation. This historic development will hold much greater meaning if we commit to addressing the tangible needs of Black women—including better access to quality health care, a fair wage, equal opportunity, and economic security. Let us work toward making this commitment a reality by the time Tubman appears on the redesigned $20.

· · ·

The Patriarchs' War on Women

BY **ZOE MARKS** AND **ERICA CHENOWETH** • SPRING 2022

U.S. FEMINISTS have been raising alarms about persistent assaults on gender equality. Across the country, GOP-led legislatures are rolling back reproductive rights, legislating against trans youth and their families, and censoring school curricula about racism, sexism, LGBTQ+ issues, and even what to expect at the gynecologist's office.

These developments in the United States reflect a troubling pattern: around the world, patriarchal authoritarianism is on the rise, and democracy is on the decline. The connection between sexism and authoritarianism is not coincidental or a mere character flaw of individual misogynists in chief.

Women's political power is essential to a properly functioning multiracial democracy, and fully free, empowered women are a threat to autocracy. Assaults on women's and LGBTQ+ rights—and attempts to put women "in their place"—constitute a backlash against feminist progress expanding women's full inclusion in public life.

> **"Women's political power is essential to a properly functioning multiracial democracy, and fully free, empowered women are a threat to autocracy."**

As women's participation becomes more prominent in domestic and international politics, our research sheds light on why political sexism and gender policing are also becoming more virulent—and what to do about it.

PATRIARCHAL AUTHORITARIANISM

Authoritarianism rejects political competition and promotes a strong central power that upholds the political and social status quo. Autocrats try to maintain control by attacking the rule of law, separation of powers, political expression, and fair elections.

But strongmen and their enablers also tend to usurp power in part by promoting a conservative and binary gender hierarchy. Patriarchy is, in the words of the political scientist Valerie Hudson and her colleagues, the "first political order." And it is closely related to authoritarianism. Authoritarian backsliding occurs when women are stripped of equal access, opportunity, and rights in the workplace, in the public sphere, and at home. By strengthening men's control over the women and girls in their lives, authoritarian leaders strike a patriarchal bargain, doling out private authority in exchange

for public loyalty to the strongman. Incidentally, many women buy into the bargain, too. Women from dominant groups and classes are often willing to promote conservative gender norms and policies that entrench the status quo. The policing of gender expression and relations becomes a powerful tool for promoting a hegemonic racial, religious, or ethnic national identity.

Thus, alongside assaults on democracy, patriarchal authoritarians also promote increased state control over women's bodies; the subordination of women in public office and the workforce; permissiveness toward sexual assault, harassment, or abuse; hypermasculine ideals; the criminalization of LGBTQ+ people; tolerance of violence toward women and girls; and an emphasis on the "traditional family," in which the role of women is primarily domestic. Put simply, the patriarchal authoritarian worldview is that men are "men," while women are wives and mothers. Everyone else is a threat to the system.

It's not hard to recognize patriarchal authoritarianism in U.S. political life today, but is it rhetoric or reality? Four key domains are under sustained legal and political attack by legislators seeking to set back gender equality: access to reproductive health care, workplace equality and economic inclusion, protection from sexual and gender-based violence, and LGBTQ+ rights.

Last year saw record-setting restrictions on abortion access, with nineteen states passing new laws and just six expanding access. Yet despite enthusiasm for forcing women into motherhood, Republicans continue to stonewall paid parental leave.

The United States remains the only country among the Organization for Economic Cooperation and Development's thirty-eight member states without mandated paid leave for new parents, even though more than 80 percent of Americans support such a policy, and only 60 percent of current workers are covered by the Family and Medical Leave Act's guaranteed *unpaid* leave. At the same time, workforce participation plummeted during the pandemic, with women's unemployment and nonparticipation nearly double that of men in 2020.

Not all countries experienced this "shecession," which reflects structural inequalities in the U.S. economy, gender segregation by job sector, and lack of access to affordable child care and health care. Democrats in Congress have attempted to address some of these issues in the "Build Back Better" bills. But components designed to support working women—such as child care and extending child tax credits—met opposition, primarily from Republicans, that effectively killed the bills.

Meanwhile, laws against gender-based violence have loosened in the United States, thanks, in part, to what the scholar Ruth Ben-Ghiat describes as the GOP's "culture of lawless masculinity." The reauthorization of the Violence Against Women Act, first championed by the then senator Joe Biden in 1994, was blocked for years by Republicans and a few Democrats who refused to close the "boyfriend loophole" that allows certain convicted abusers to keep firearms. When VAWA was finally approved by Congress in March, tacked onto a spending bill, it lacked the gun control provision.

Finally, anti-transgender legislation has become a go-to wedge issue for the Republican Party, which has introduced discriminatory bills at an exponential rate: 79 in 2020, 147 in 2021, and more than 280 already slated for 2022 legislative sessions. Many of these proposals aim to pit cisgender girls and women against transgender people, claiming to protect equity in sports and safety in bathrooms. But the crisis in fairness actually cuts in the other direction: marginalizing and harming gender minorities, not female athletes. In Florida, the "Don't Say Gay" law bans discussions of gender and sexuality in primary school classrooms and requires teachers to disclose their students' gender and sexuality questions to their parents. Anti-LGBTQ+ legislation uses the power of the government to police the gender binary, which underpins male dominance.

Patriarchal authoritarians rely on stable, narrow constructions of masculinity and femininity to assert control in homes, families, and private lives. The Republican Party is promoting an old yet predominant vision of family values by cynically pretending families are under threat from increased tolerance of LGBTQ+ people and rising antiracist agitation. In doing so, it's positioning itself as the party of "parents' rights"—a direct bid for white women's votes—while restricting rights of parents whose children are transgender or subject to racial discrimination in schools. These seemingly inconsistent policies have a common through line: they restrict discussions of racial and gender equality in public schools while inserting ever more state control over women's and LGBTQ+ families' rights. It is consonant with the GOP's unironic co-optation of "my body, my choice" as an anti-vaccine slogan by people who proudly restrict women's access to medical care.

AUTOCRACY TO DEMOCRACY . . . AND BACK AGAIN

Democracy and equal rights for women are rare in world history. Every country that is a democracy today was once an autocracy (or was part of one). When countries have transformed into durable democracies, it is because democratic movements mobilized to challenge the status quo and, over time, successfully pushed forward change.

In fact, it was women's activism—demanding the right to vote, to own property, to have constitutionally protected bodily autonomy, and to have civil and political rights for all people—that inaugurated the expansion of global democracy in the twentieth century. Our research finds that during the postwar period mass movements demanding independence and democracy were more successful at achieving their aims when women participated in larger numbers at the front lines. From the Philippines to Brazil, from Tunisia to Argentina, from Chile to Sudan, "people power" movements were more likely to usher in sustained democratization when at least 25 percent of their participants were women.

Yet in recent years, many democracies have slid back into authoritarianism, unable to stave off the rise of illiberal forces. For the sixteenth consecutive year, the world has been moving toward authoritarianism—what some have called a "democratic recession." Today, the Varieties of Democracy (V-Dem) project reports that only 30 percent of people in the world live in democracies.

Often dismissed as simply a feature of autocrats' personalities, misogynistic leadership appears to help bring authoritarianism to fragile democracies. Unsurprisingly, researchers have also discovered that women's rights and gender equality gains have stalled or, worse, are being reversed. For instance, India, Myanmar, and Venezuela have seen recent downgrades in levels of both democracy and women's equality.

Fully autocratic countries like Russia, Turkey, and China show us what consolidated patriarchal control looks like: women are considered subordinate to men in the home, in the workplace, and in public office. In Turkey, President Recep Tayyip Erdoğan has called women who choose to work rather than have children "half persons."

In these countries—and many others—reproductive rights are under threat or, in some cases, nonexistent. In China, women's reproduction was policed for decades under the "one child" policy. That has been relaxed to increase the country's population, but some Chinese feminists now worry that the government's call for Chinese women to produce three children might inspire future intrusive reproductive policies.

Calls for "traditional values" facilitate the subjugation of women and LGBTQ+ people. The Russian president, Vladimir Putin, justified his own authoritarian power grab in 2012 by invoking patriarchal and homophobic rhetoric. In his February 24 speech, in which he rationalized his armed forces' invasion of Ukraine, Putin invoked a defense of Russia's "traditional values" against the West's "false values" that "are directly leading to degradation and degeneration, because they are contrary to human nature"—a reference to the expansion of feminist and LGBTQ+ rights within the West.

TOWARD A FEMINIST DEMOCRACY

There is much we can do to protect and expand the hard-won rights that are already enshrined in policy and that, in turn, protect democracy. First, it is crucial to fully understand that assaults on women's and LGBTQ+ autonomy, well-being, and rights are assaults on constitutional democracy. A country in which more than half the population is subordinated politically, socially, economically, and culturally is not a democracy.

Corresponding assaults on democracy—including restrictions on ballot access, protest, and public expression, as well as the weakening of the rule of law—can unravel women's equality, particularly for marginalized and subjugated groups. The fate of women's rights is tied to the fate of democracy, and women's mobilization can help to secure both.

More than a hundred years ago, women worldwide mobilized for their inclusion in democracy. And they have since used their political power to demand fundamental rights in health care, employment, and domestic life. As a result, women have become key constituents with whom authoritarian leaders and parties have to contend—and often seek to control.

This finding is instructive: women and their allies mobilize when their rights are under assault, but they are even more powerful when they mobilize on broad-based issues. Women from all walks of life must continue to be vocal champions of inclusive democracy.

Feminist candidates, women elected officials, and feminist policies are fundamental to the health and well-being of democracy. Feminists must find their political homes and invest in them. Women, gender minorities, and feminists of all genders who are already engaged need to stay engaged. For those who have taken these hard-won rights for granted, the time has come to take a stand.

Letters

Who would have thought that today we need *Ms.* more than we ever needed it before?

As many of us were coming of age, *Ms.* magazine was born. During this time, women were fighting for civil rights and women's empowerment in every aspect of their lives, including women like myself. Women of color and African American women were challenged because we encountered so many barriers, including our race, to pursuing our dreams. It was good to find inspiration from Gloria Steinem and Black women like Barbara Jordan and Shirley Chisholm, who were part of this beautiful movement. Our sister Gloria and *Ms.* magazine stood up for us early. As *Ms.* grew, it captured all of our voices. We were galvanized for our cause. As we continued to fight, we had such hope—such a sense of brightness for the future—because we believed that if we collectively came together the nation and even the world were going to understand and accept the strength of women, the power of women, and the fact that women were also the builders of this nation.

Who would have believed that the fiftieth anniversary of *Ms.* magazine would find us in a fight for our bodies, our lives, and our dignity? But aren't we grateful to have had the personal stories, the news articles reflecting the movement, and the encouragement of our magazine for all of these years preparing us to never accept "NO" and to never go back!

CONGRESSWOMAN SHEILA JACKSON LEE,
chair of the House Judiciary Committee Subcommittee
on Crime, Terrorism, and Homeland Security; chief deputy whip;
founder and chair of the Congressional Children's Caucus,
Summer 2022 issue

Postscript

On June 24, 2022, the unthinkable happened: the U.S. Supreme Court, in *Dobbs v. Jackson Women's Health Organization,* struck down *Roe v. Wade,* taking away a fundamental constitutional right that women had fought for and won and lived with for almost fifty years, and sending shock waves across the country and the world.

As news of the Court's decision spread, women in clinic waiting rooms in states with trigger laws banning abortion were told their appointments were canceled. "We had a waiting room full of people," Dr. Sanithia Williams told *Ms.,* recalling the day the decision came down. "People were horrified and desperate. Some people offered to pay extra if we could just do the procedure—not fully understanding what was happening. We had to turn all those people away."

The tragic consequences for women and girls quickly emerged as the most extreme bans took effect. Pregnant as a result of rape, a ten-year-old girl in Ohio, where abortion is banned after six weeks with no exceptions for rape or incest, was forced to travel to Indiana for an abortion. Women with wanted pregnancies in emergency rooms actively miscarrying have been denied routine surgical procedures or medication for treatment. In states with the strictest bans and vaguely defined exceptions for severe health conditions or for the life of the woman, doctors and hospitals, fearing criminal liability, seek legal advice before intervening even in cases where a woman's condition is rapidly deteriorating.

With virtual unanimity, the medical community has spoken out, warning of ever more dire consequences as more women are denied abortion care and as the full range of reproductive health services, including access to birth control and prenatal care, is impacted with the closure of clinics. Maternal mortality and morbidity rates—already a crisis in Black, Native American, and rural communities—will increase.

Young women are especially angry and worried about the Supreme Court's decision overturning *Roe,* and say their lives already are significantly impacted. In the *Ms.* poll conducted across nine battleground states in September 2022, three months following the Court's decision, young women (eighteen to twenty-nine) said they are making plans about where they are willing to live and work based on whether abortion is protected or banned in states: 44 percent either have considered moving or already are making plans to move to a state where abortion is protected; 10 percent already have declined a job in a state where abortions are banned. Not only has the decision affected their plans, but young women and people close to them are taking actions in response to the Court's decision. They are obtaining long-acting birth control, the morning-after pill, and the abortion pill. And shockingly, 10 percent said they or their partner or someone close to them has already received sterilization services.

But this is not how this story will end.

The conservative majority on the Court and the extremist Republican state legislators and governors enacting bans and severe restrictions on abortion have no public mandate. At rallies and demonstrations in Washington, D.C., and in every state, red or blue, the Court's ruling was met immediately with outrage and with a deep determination to fight back.

Millions of women—some one in four of all U.S. women—have had abortions and know how important having access to safe abortion has been for their lives. Women are determined not to go back. And make no mistake, we will not cede this fight. The fight for abortion is at its core a fight for self-determination, dignity, and autonomy—for women's full equality.

This is not the first time the feminist movement has engaged in this battle, having organized and won hard-fought changes to abortion laws in a number of states in the 1960s and early 1970s, even *before* the Court's 1973 *Roe v. Wade* ruling. The movement is larger and more powerful today than it was in 1973, and the struggles, setbacks, and gains of the past forty-nine years have only strengthened and better positioned feminists to take on this fight.

Unlike forty-nine years ago, women possess tremendous political power. The gender gap—the measurable difference between women and men in public opinion polling and in voting—has grown significantly, and it's women's votes that can determine the outcome of local, state, and national contests, favoring candidates who support women's equality and the right to abortion.

Despite constant predictions by pundits and pollsters of the time that abortion was no longer top of mind for voters five months after the Supreme Court's ruling was handed down in June 2022, abortion ranked either first or second in key election contests according to the exit polls, delivering victories to Democrats in critical Senate and gubernatorial races and reducing the projected Republican "red wave" in the House of Representatives to a puddle. Democratic candidates outperformed all expectations—despite documented voter suppression and intimidation and having to run in gerrymandered districts—and defied historical trends for a midterm election, which typically spell doom for the party in control of the White House. Quite simply, voters—especially women and young voters—took seriously

Republican-announced plans to pass a national abortion ban were they to capture the Congress.

In the five states where abortion measures were on the ballot, abortion rights activists secured double-digit victories in California, Michigan, and Vermont, as voters chose to amend their state constitutions to include the right to reproductive freedom. And voters in the Republican-leaning states Kentucky and Montana decidedly rejected efforts to restrict abortion access, just as they did earlier in the election season in red-state Kansas, showing once again that the majority of Americans support abortion rights and reproductive freedom, regardless of political party.

We must continue to organize and channel women's collective rage that was triggered by the Court's reversal of *Roe* to restore abortion rights across the nation, ensuring all those who seek abortion care have access, including poor women, girls, and trans and nonbinary people. In addition to massive organizing efforts to pass state laws and constitutional amendments to ensure abortion rights, feminists are filing court cases challenging abortion restrictions as violations of state constitutions and providing support and funding to those who must travel from states where abortion is banned in order to access health care. And, despite efforts to suppress access to medication abortion (abortion pills), which a French health minister once described as the "moral property of women" and that can be delivered to your mailbox even in states that have banned abortion, women are undeterred, supported by courageous global networks of activists and providers. There is no way the movement can be stopped.

But we must do more. The legal reasoning used in the *Dobbs* case by the current majority to overturn *Roe* indicates they are willing to reverse other rights. Justice Clarence Thomas in his concurring opinion even specified which rights he wants the Court to revisit: the right to birth control and the right to same-sex marriage. The Court's majority opinion also threatens other rights won by women in the 1970s and 1980s, including the right to be free from sexual harassment, parental rights, control of marital property, and much more.

As the current rising authoritarianism around the world shows, the attacks on women's fundamental rights precede other attacks on democracy. Without women's rights and the ability to participate fully in civic life, there can be no real democracy. We must drive up the numbers of women in elective office at all levels of government. Too often in state after state where abortion bans have passed, it has been predominantly older white men debating the morality of abortion even as they vote to cut already underfunded social safety net programs that support children. Winning equal representation at the decision-making tables will require changes in the election systems and rules that are stacked against us.

And we must finally enshrine the Equal Rights Amendment in the U.S.

Constitution, securing a nationwide, permanent safety net for women's rights. The current conservative majority on the Supreme Court subscribes to the same originalist philosophy in interpreting the Constitution that led the late Supreme Court justice Antonin Scalia to assert that the Constitution does not prohibit sex discrimination and it was never intended to do so: "Nobody ever thought that that's what it meant. Nobody ever voted for that."

The Equal Rights Amendment, which will put the prohibition against sex discrimination in the Constitution, is needed more urgently now in the wake of *Dobbs*. Moreover, women are connecting the ERA and abortion, with nearly three-quarters (73 percent) in the *Ms.* poll saying it is important to support the ERA in light of abortion bans. Sixty percent of men agree. A state ERA on the 2022 ballot in Nevada passed overwhelmingly (58.6 percent in favor).

Women's passion and determination must be directed toward making real gains and will require sustained efforts. As we begin this battle in the long struggle for full equality—and for our very democracy—we at *Ms.* promise to be a trusted source for accurate, timely, and actionable information in print, online, on social media, through the acclaimed podcasts and programs of *Ms.* Studios, and by whatever new forms of communication yet to be developed. We will meet this historic challenge, and together we will illuminate a way forward—for all of us.

—the *Ms.* editors

Acknowledgments

Special thanks and appreciation go to my collaborator on this project, *Ms.* managing editor Camille Hahn, whose keen judgment and thoughtful insights were crucial in selecting and shaping the collection of articles you read in this book. Her steady "we can do this" assurances even as we were juggling each new issue of the magazine kept us moving forward.

Thanks to Jennifer Weiss-Wolf for her publishing expertise—and for contributing the insightful commentaries appearing throughout the book. To Aviva Dove-Viebahn, whose elegant writings shine in this volume's opening pages.

Grace Jidoun agreed to tackle the arduous task of locating fifty years of *Ms.* contributors and collecting their permissions. *Ms.* editorial assistant Meliss Arteaga performed countless thankless tasks—scanning, printing, transcribing, cataloging. Her hands have been on each issue in the archives and each page of this book. Thanks to CarolLee Kidd and her team at CLK Transcription for their services and their excitement for the project.

Our appreciation to Susan Grode and her amazing team of lawyers at Katten Muchin Rosenman LLP: Melanie Tomanov, Joshua Tate, David Halberstadter, Tami Kameda Sims, and Janie Freedman. Their expertise and guidance were crucial—without them, this book would never have happened.

Thanks to *Ms.* art director Brandi Phipps for many of the beautiful covers and layouts featured in this book—and for her research and coordination of many of the other images appearing in these pages. To Jenny Warburg for offering the collection of her photographs of *Ms.* events over the past twenty-four years.

Carrie Baker, JD, PhD, professor of the Study of Women and Gender at Smith College, delved into the archives of the first fifteen years of *Ms.* at the Sophia Smith Collection of Women's History at Smith. The artifacts in this book were her excellent finds.

Laura Mazer of Wendy Sherman Agency helped conceive this project and provided critical guidance at each step of the process for magazine editors who knew nothing about creating a book.

Our gratitude to editor extraordinaire Victoria Wilson and her team at Knopf. From our first meeting, she offered her faith in and enthusiasm for this project and, crucially, her understanding of the importance of *Ms.*—not only over the past fifty years but also at this most pivotal moment for women's rights in the United States and around the globe.

We salute Gloria Steinem and the visionary co-founders of *Ms.,* including the magazine's first publisher, Patricia Carbine, as well as the talented chief editors throughout the magazine's first thirty years: Suzanne Braun Levine, Robin Morgan, and Marcia Ann Gillespie.

And finally, thanks to the Feminist Majority Foundation's board members, who have worked to sustain *Ms.* in a time of tremendous challenges for the movement and for magazines—in particular Peg Yorkin, Eleanor Smeal, Dolores Huerta, Dee Martin, Bonnie Thornton Dill, Lorraine Sheinberg, Rita Haft, Irasema Coronado, Kimberly Adams, Mavis Nicholson Leno, and Carol Leif.

—Katherine Spillar

Contributors

ALAN ALDA has earned international recognition as an actor, writer, and director. Alda played Hawkeye Pierce on the classic television series *M*A*S*H* and wrote and directed many of the episodes. In addition to *The Aviator,* for which he was nominated for an Academy Award, Alda's films include *Crimes and Misdemeanors, Manhattan Murder Mystery, And the Band Played On,* and, recently, Steven Spielberg's *Bridge of Spies.* In 1975, Alda was a member of the National Commission on the Observance of International Women's Year.

CARRIE N. BAKER, JD, PhD, is the Sylvia Dlugasch Bauman Professor of American Studies and a professor in the Program for the Study of Women and Gender at Smith College. She is a contributing editor and regular writer at *Ms.* and co-chair of the Ms. Committee of Scholars.

GINA BARRECA, distinguished professor of English at the University of Connecticut, wrote the best-selling *They Used to Call Me Snow White . . . but I Drifted* and *Babes in Boyland: A Personal History of Co-education in the Ivy League,* as well as eight other books. Editor of *The Penguin Book of Women's Humor, The Signet Book of American Humor, Fast Funny Women, Fast Fierce Women,* and *Fast Fallen Women,* Barreca has helped establish the study of women's humor as a Thing.

ALISON BECHDEL is a cartoonist whose work includes the long-running comic strip *Dykes to Watch Out For,* as well as the graphic memoirs *Fun Home, Are You My Mother?,* and *The Secret to Superhuman Strength.* But she is best known in some quarters for being the originator of the "Bechdel Test."

KEISHA N. BLAIN, a 2022 New America Fellow, is an award-winning historian, writer, and professor. She is the author of several books, including *Until I Am Free: Fannie Lou Hamer's Enduring Message to America.*

The longtime *Ms.* writer and former contributing editor **ANGELA BONAVOGLIA** has written for such outlets as *The Nation, Chicago Tribune,*

Salon, the Women's Media Center, and *HuffPost.* Her books include *Good Catholic Girls: How Women Are Leading the Fight to Change the Church* and *The Choices We Made: 25 Women and Men Speak Out About Abortion,* with a foreword by Gloria Steinem.

SARAH BOONIN is a clinical professor of law at Suffolk University Law School, where she serves as the director of Clinical Programs and teaches in the areas of mental health and disability law, reproductive health and the law, and legal ethics. Boonin has written on these topics, as well as LGBTQ+ rights and clinical law teaching. She holds her BA magna cum laude from Duke University and her JD cum laude from Harvard Law School.

SUSAN BROWNMILLER is the author of *Against Our Will: Men, Women, and Rape; Waverly Place,* a novel; and *Shirley Chisholm,* a biography for children. She has written for *The New York Times, The Village Voice, Esquire, Vogue, Rolling Stone, The Nation,* and many other publications. Brownmiller lives in New York City.

GAYLYNN BURROUGHS, an attorney with a lifelong commitment to racial and gender justice, began her career at the Bronx Defenders, representing caregivers in child abuse and neglect cases and proceedings to terminate parental rights. She has since held key positions at the Feminist Majority Foundation, the Leadership Conference on Civil and Human Rights, and the National Women's Law Center.

LINDA BURSTYN is a political speechwriter, a strategist, a journalist, a writer/producer of TV drama—and always, a feminist. She's written hundreds of speeches for politicians and for celebrities giving political talks, has been a writer/producer for a dozen TV dramas, and was an Emmy Award–winning writer/producer for Ted Koppel's *Nightline.* She has written several articles for *Ms.*

JANE CAPUTI teaches at Florida Atlantic University. Her books are *The Age of Sex Crime; Gossips, Gorgons, and Crones; Goddesses and Monsters;* and *Call Your "Mutha": A Deliberately Dirty-Minded Manifesto for the Earth Mother in the Anthropocene.* She also has made two documentaries, *The Pornography of Everyday Life* and *Feed the Green: Feminist Voices for the Earth.*

For decades, **ALISON CARLSON** has turned cutting-edge knowledge in health, environment, investing, and athletics into results for public good. She co-launched the International Work Group on Sex/Gender Verification Policy in Sports, public radio's first hour-long sports program, and the University of California, San Francisco's Program on Reproductive Health and Environment. She's currently founder and chair of Forsythia Foundation. Alison graduated Phi Beta Kappa from Stanford in human biology.

ERICA CHENOWETH is the Frank Stanton Professor of the First Amendment at Harvard Kennedy School and a Susan S. and Kenneth L. Wallach Professor at the Radcliffe Institute for Advanced Study at Harvard University.

Trained as a historian, **ELLEN CHESLER,** PhD, has spent much of her professional career in government and philanthropy and brings both practical and intellectual perspectives to her writing on women. Currently a senior fellow at CUNY's Ralph Bunche Institute for International Studies, she is the author of more than a hundred essays and, most notably, of *Woman of Valor: Margaret Sanger and the Birth Control Movement in America.*

BRITTNEY COOPER is associate professor of women's, gender, and sexuality studies and Africana studies at Rutgers University. She is the author of the *New York Times* best seller *Eloquent Rage: A Black Feminist Discovers Her Superpower* and *Beyond Respectability: The Intellectual Thought of Race Women,* co-author of *Feminist AF: A Guide to Crushing Girlhood,* co-editor of *The Crunk Feminist Collection,* and co-founder of the Crunk Feminist Collective.

MARTHA COVENTRY lives and raised her family in the Midwest. She has had a long and happy career as a writer and editor and loves to ski, fly-fish, read, and cook. Her concerns for the world focus on hunger and homelessness, and she finds solace and joy in the Northwoods and in loving her family and friends.

Through her activism and scholarship over many decades, **ANGELA DAVIS** has been deeply involved in movements for social justice around the world. Her work as an educator—both at the university level and in the larger public sphere—has always emphasized the importance of building communities of struggle for economic, racial, and gender justice. She is the author of eleven books, including *Abolition. Feminism. Now.,* co-authored with Gina Dent, Erica Meiners, and Beth Richie, and a new edition of her *Autobiography.* Having helped to popularize the notion of a "prison-industrial complex," she now urges her audiences to think seriously about the future possibility of a world without carceral systems and to help forge a twenty-first-century abolitionist movement.

DONNA DECKER is the author of *Dancing in Red Shoes Will Kill You,* a novel about the 1989 murder of fourteen engineering students in their Montreal classrooms—all of them women. She is professor of English at Franklin Pierce University and a member of the Diversity, Equity, and Inclusion Council. Her article about the function of feminist revenge literature and films, "#DismantlingTools," appears in *South Central Review.*

BETTY DODSON (1929–2020), artist, author, and PhD sexologist, was one of the principal voices for women's sexual pleasure and health for more than four decades. Her first book, *Liberating Masturbation: A Meditation on Self Love,* became a feminist classic. *Sex for One* sold more than a million copies and is an international best-selling book. Most recently, she released *Sex by Design,* which details her experiences with America's sexual revolution, the women's movement, and her feminist sexual activism. In 2011, Dodson received the public service award from the Society for the Scientific Study of Sexuality and the Masters and Johnson Award presented by the Society for Sex Therapy and Research.

SUSAN J. DOUGLAS is the Catherine Neafie Kellogg Professor of Communication and Media at the University of Michigan. Her books include *In Our Prime: How Older Women Are Reinventing the Road Ahead; The Rise of Enlightened Sexism; The Mommy Myth;* and *Where the Girls Are: Growing Up Female with the Mass Media.*

RITA DOVE received the 1987 Pulitzer Prize for Poetry and served as U.S. poet laureate from 1993 to 1995. She is the only poet to have received both the National Humanities Medal and the National Medal of Arts. She teaches creative writing at the University of Virginia; her latest book, *Playlist for the Apocalypse,* was published in 2021.

AVIVA DOVE-VIEBAHN is an assistant professor of film and media studies at Arizona State University and a contributing editor to *Ms.* for its Scholars Writing Program. She has a PhD in visual and cultural studies and an MA in art history. Her scholarly research and public writing explore gender, race, and sexuality in television, film, and popular culture.

JOANNE EDGAR is a co-founder of *Ms.,* where she worked as an editor for seventeen years. She subsequently became communications director of the Edna McConnell Clark Foundation. Currently a consultant to nonprofits and foundations, she specializes in chronicling child-welfare reform efforts. She still loves the spirit of Wonder Woman.

SUSAN EDMISTON, a former editor at *Redbook* and *Glamour,* writes for *New York, The New York Times Magazine* and *Book Review, Esquire,* the

San Francisco Chronicle, and *Woman's Day.* The co-author of *The Cow in the Parking Lot: A Zen Approach to Overcoming Anger,* Edmiston lives in Berkeley, California.

BARBARA EHRENREICH is an investigative journalist, essayist, and activist and is the author of twenty-one books, including *Nickel and Dimed: On (Not) Getting By in America* and her memoir, *Living with a Wild God: A Nonbeliever's Search for the Truth About Everything.* With the Institute for Policy Studies, she launched the Economic Hardship Reporting Project in order to force this country's crisis of poverty and economic insecurity to the center of the national conversation. She was born in a mining town in Montana and now lives in Virginia.

NAWAL EL SAADAWI (1931–2021) was a world-renowned Egyptian writer, a novelist and physician, a fighter for the liberation of mind and women, and the founder of the Arab Women's Solidarity Association. She was dismissed from her work at the Egyptian Ministry of Health because of her revolutionary and enlightening writings; her struggle to prevent the circumcision of children, girls and boys; her motto to "unveil the mind"; and her promotion of solidarity among women. Her scientific and literary writings amount to eighty books, translated from Arabic into forty languages.

CYNTHIA ENLOE is research professor at Clark University. Among her fifteen books are *Bananas, Beaches, and Bases* and *The Big Push: Exposing and Challenging the Persistence of Patriarchy.* Her work appears in Turkish, French, Spanish, and Japanese. She was selected for the Gender Justice Legacy Wall at the International Criminal Court, The Hague.

BAY FANG is president of Radio Free Asia, where she oversees award-winning journalism bringing free press to closed societies in Asia. A former Beijing bureau chief for *U.S. News & World Report* who also covered the wars in Afghanistan and Iraq, she served in government as a deputy assistant secretary of state for press and public diplomacy. Fang earned her undergraduate degree at Harvard University and was a visiting fellow at Oxford University and a Fulbright scholar in Hong Kong. She trained as a French chef at Le Cordon Bleu in Paris and holds a brown belt in kung fu.

MARC FASTEAU, the founder of American Strategic Insurance Group, which was later sold to Progressive Insurance, is a former investment banker. He is an investor in and serves on the boards of an early-stage pharmaceutical manufacturing company and an advanced medical materials company. Early in his career he was staff director for a Rockefeller

Foundation commission on U.S. policy toward South Africa. He is now a vice chair of a think tank that lobbies for a trade and industrial policy that will revive U.S. manufacturing and our middle class. He is the author of *The Male Machine.*

ANNETTE FUENTES is a longtime journalist and the author of *Lockdown High: When the Schoolhouse Becomes a Jailhouse.*

MOLLY M. GINTY is a journalist, yoga instructor, and community-gardening activist based in New York City.

SUSAN GOLDBERG's work has appeared in, among other places, *The New York Times, Toronto Life, Catapult, Full Grown People, Lilith, Stealing Time,* and *The Manifest-Station,* as well as on the CBC and in several anthologies. She is co-editor of the anthology *And Baby Makes More: Known Donors, Queer Parents, and Our Unexpected Families.* She lives with her sons in Thunder Bay, Ontario, where she can't/won't stop collecting and refinishing midcentury modern furniture.

MICHELE GOODWIN is the executive producer of *Ms.* Studios, host of the popular podcast *On the Issues with Michele Goodwin* at *Ms.,* and author of the award-winning book *Policing the Womb: Invisible Women and the Criminalization of Motherhood.* She is also a chancellor's professor at the University of California, Irvine, and founding director of the Center for Biotechnology and Global Health Policy. Goodwin is an acclaimed bioethicist, constitutional law scholar, and prolific author. She directed the first ABA-accredited health law program in the nation and established the first law center focused on race and bioethics. Goodwin is a 2022 Margaret Brent Award honoree of the American Bar Association, an award named for the first woman lawyer in the United States.

MARY GORDON, Millicent C. McIntosh Professor in English and Writing, retired from Barnard College in 2020. She is the author of seven best-selling novels. She has also published two collections of stories, a book of essays, two memoirs, a biography of Joan of Arc, and *Reading Jesus: A Writer's Encounter with the Gospels.* Her latest books are *The Love of My Youth,* a novel, and *The Liar's Wife,* a collection of novellas. Gordon has received a Lila Acheson Wallace Reader's Digest Writer's Award and a Guggenheim Fellowship. She was elected to the American Academy of Arts and Letters in 2007.

LOIS GOULD (1931–2002) was an American novelist, journalist, and essayist. Her first novel, *Such Good Friends,* was adapted for the screen by Elaine

May and Otto Preminger. Gould published more than a dozen novels and nonfiction works. She was among the first contributors to *Ms.* and is a noted member of the so-called second wave of Western feminism.

ROBERTA BRANDES GRATZ was a reporter for the *New York Post* in 1972, when she wrote an award-winning series about rape and the inequities of the law. She has been observing and writing about cities—how they grow, fall apart, recover—for more than forty years, including authoring six books on urban change. Her last one, *It's a Helluva Town: Joan K. Davidson, the J. M. Kaplan Fund, and the Fight for a Better New York,* draws on her observations, understanding, and involvement in the critical issues of the city.

MARGARET MORGANROTH GULLETTE, the author of *Ending Ageism, or How Not to Shoot People,* is writing a new book, *American Eldercide.* She is a resident scholar at the Women's Studies Research Center at Brandeis University and a *Cognoscenti* contributor to WBUR in Boston.

ALEXIS PAULINE GUMBS, PhD, is a Black feminist love evangelist, an aspirational cousin to all life, and the author of the forthcoming *The Eternal Life of Audre Lorde.* She is a 2022 National Endowment for the Arts Fellow, and she was a 2020–21 National Humanities Center Fellow. Gumbs is the creative writing editor of *Feminist Studies,* the literary adviser for the Ntozake Shange Trust, and the co-creator of the Mobile Homecoming Trust, a living library amplifying generations of Black LGBTQ+ brilliance in Durham, North Carolina.

BEVERLY GUY-SHEFTALL is the founding director of the Women's Research and Resource Center (1981) and Anna Julia Cooper Professor of Women's Studies at Spelman College. She has published a number of texts within African American and women's studies that have been noted as seminal works by other scholars, including the first anthology on Black women's literature, *Sturdy Black Bridges: Visions of Black Women in Literature,* which she co-edited with Roseann P. Bell and Bettye J. Parker. She is the past president of the National Women's Studies Association and was recently elected to the American Academy of Arts and Sciences.

JOY HARJO, the twenty-third poet laureate of the United States, is a member of the Muscogee (Creek) Nation. She is the author of nine poetry collections, seven music albums, and two memoirs. Harjo is a chancellor of the Academy of American Poets and chair of the board of directors of the Native Arts & Cultures Foundation. She lives in Tulsa.

JANA HARRIS has taught creative writing at the University of Washington, the University of Wyoming, and the Writer's Workshop in Seattle. She is the editor and founder of *Switched-On Gutenberg.* Her most recent publications are *You Haven't Asked About My Wedding or What I Wore: Poems of Courtship on the American Frontier* and the memoir *Horses Never Lie About Love.*

DAVID HELLERSTEIN, MD, is a research psychiatrist at the New York State Psychiatric Institute and professor of clinical psychiatry at the Columbia University Irving Medical Center. His book *Heal Your Brain: How the New Neuropsychiatry Can Help You Go from Better to Well* was published by the Johns Hopkins University Press. A Distinguished Life Fellow of the American Psychiatric Association, he has served as president of the New York County District Branch of the American Psychiatric Association.

JANELL HOBSON is professor of women's, gender, and sexuality studies at the University at Albany, State University of New York, and the author of *When God Lost Her Tongue: Historical Consciousness and the Black Feminist Imagination, Venus in the Dark: Blackness and Beauty in Popular Culture,* and *Body as Evidence: Mediating Race, Globalizing Gender.* She is the 2021–22 Community Fellow at the University at Albany's Institute for History and Public Engagement in support of her role as the *Ms.* guest editor of the Harriet Tubman Bicentennial Project. She is a contributing writer for *Ms.* with a research focus on Black women's histories and representations in popular culture.

NOELLE HOWEY is a cultural strategist, social justice advocate, and writer. She is a principal in impact entertainment at the Raben Group, a progressive public policy firm, and author of the memoir *Dress Codes,* which was honored by the American Library Association and Lambda Literary Awards. She has written for *The New York Times, Glamour, Dame,* and *Real Simple,* among other publications.

RITA HENLEY JENSEN (1947–2017) started off in the 1960s as a plucky single mother from Ohio who survived domestic violence, put herself through college, and graduated from Columbia University with a master's in journalism. Taking on the male-dominated profession, she garnered awards for her daring investigative reporting. Later, she headed Women's eNews, a daily news service that served as a hub of inspiration for advocates for women worldwide. On the brink of launching her next nonprofit for Black maternal health advocacy, she succumbed to her third round of breast cancer in 2017.

ROBERT JENSEN is professor emeritus in the School of Journalism at the University of Texas at Austin and a founding board member of the Third Coast Activist Resource Center. He collaborates with New Perennials Publishing and the New Perennials Project at Middlebury College. Jensen is the associate producer and host of *Podcast from the Prairie,* with Wes Jackson.

LISA JERVIS is the founding editor and publisher of *Bitch: Feminist Response to Pop Culture.* After fifteen years as a writer, she shifted her attention to organizational operations, got a master's in information management and systems from UC Berkeley, and is now a principal at Information Ecology, a consultancy that supports movement builders and organizers in getting what they need from other information systems and technology.

AMBER KHAN is the director of the Health Justice Program at New York Lawyers for the Public Interest, where she leads NYLPI's work on healthcare advocacy with a focus on racial equity and immigrant justice. Before joining NYLPI, Amber advocated for the constitutional and human rights of pregnant and parenting people and worked with international nongovernmental organizations documenting human rights abuses and the treatment of refugees. Amber received her JD from George Washington University Law School, her master's degree in international human rights from Columbia University, and her BA from American University.

BONNIE SHERR KLEIN's essay " 'We Are Who You Are' " was one of the first personal narratives about disability. Its publication in *Ms.* led to a book contract to write her memoir, *Slow Dance: A Story of Stroke, Love, and Disability.* Eighteen years after her stroke, she made the film *Shameless: The ART of Disability* with five disability artists. More recently, she wrote *Beep Beep Bubbie,* a children's picture book, now awaiting a sequel.

JUDITH LEVINE is a journalist and author whose work investigates the intersections of the body and the body politic—sex, gender, race, dis/ability, bioeconomics, social movements, and the law. She is the author of five books, most recently *The Feminist and the Sex Offender: Confronting Sexual Harm, Ending State Violence,* with Erica R. Meiners.

The Black feminist, lesbian, poet, mother, and warrior **AUDRE LORDE** (1934–1992) was a native New Yorker and daughter of immigrants. Both her activism and her published work speak to the importance of struggle for liberation among oppressed peoples and of organizing in coalition across differences of race, gender, sexual orientation, class, age, and ability. An internationally recognized activist and artist, Lorde was the recipient of many honors and awards, including the Walt Whitman Citation of Merit, which conferred the mantle of poet laureate of New York for 1991–92. In designating her New York State's poet laureate, Governor Mario Cuomo observed, "Her imagination is charged by a sharp sense of racial injustice and cruelty, of sexual prejudice. . . . She cries out against it as the voice of indignant humanity. Audre Lorde is the voice of the eloquent outsider who speaks in a language that can reach and touch people everywhere."

HARRIET LYONS was a founding editor of *Ms.,* a journalist, and an art collector. In 1971, she wrote a cover story for *The Village Voice* about women's sexuality in art at a time when women were starting to challenge male definitions of art. A leading figure in the feminist movement, she supported artists through her writing, personal art collection, and activism, which included being a member, alongside Alice Neel, of the board of advisers to the New York Feminist Art Institute, which launched in 1979.

RAKEEN MABUD is the chief economist and managing director of policy and research at the Groundwork Collaborative. Mabud is an expert on economic inequality and the twenty-first-century workplace, with a particular focus on how structural factors such as racism and sexism perpetuate inequities. Mabud holds a PhD in government from Harvard University and received her BA in economics and political science from Wellesley College.

PATRICIA MAINARDI was part of the radical feminist group Redstockings in the 1970s, and in 1977, she became an associate of the Women's Institute for Freedom of the Press. A professor of eighteenth- and nineteenth-century European art at CUNY Graduate Center, Mainardi has also taught at Harvard University, Princeton University, and Williams College. She has received fellowships from the National Endowment for the Humanities, the American Council of Learned Societies, the Center for Advanced Study in the Visual Arts at the National Gallery of Art, and the Institute for Advanced Study.

ZOE MARKS is a lecturer in public policy at Harvard Kennedy School and a faculty affiliate at the Weatherhead Center for International Affairs and the Center for African Studies at Harvard University.

MARTHA MENDOZA is a two-time Pulitzer Prize winner and one-time finalist. Her reports have prompted congressional hearings and new legislation, Pentagon investigations, and White House responses and led to the freedom of more than two thousand enslaved fishermen. She's reported from dozens of countries, won a 2020 Emmy Award, and was a Stanford University Knight Fellow and a Princeton University Ferris Professor.

CASEY MILLER (1919–1997) was a feminist author and editor best known for promoting the use of nonsexist writing in the English language. Along with her writing partner, Kate Swift, Miller authored *The Handbook of Nonsexist Writing* and *Words and Women.*

An award-winning poet, novelist, journalist, activist, and best-selling author, **ROBIN MORGAN** has published more than twenty books of poetry, fiction, and nonfiction. Her 1970 anthology, *Sisterhood Is Powerful,* has been widely credited with helping to start the contemporary feminist movement and was cited by the New York Public Library as "one of the 100 most influential books of the 20th century." Recipient of the National Endowment for the Arts Prize (Poetry) among other honors, and former editor in chief of *Ms.,* she founded the Sisterhood Is Global Institute and co-founded (with Jane Fonda and Gloria Steinem) the Women's Media Center. She currently writes and hosts *WMC Live with Robin Morgan,* a syndicated weekly radio program, and serves as global editor of *Ms.*

PREMILLA NADASEN is professor of history at Barnard College. She is most interested in the activism and visions of liberation of poor and working-class women of color. She has been involved in social justice organizing for many decades and published extensively on the multiple meanings of feminism, alternative labor movements, and grassroots community organizing. She is the author of two award-winning books, *Welfare Warriors: The Welfare Rights Movement in the United States* and *Household Workers Unite: The Untold Story of African American Women Who Built a Movement,* and is currently writing a biography of the South African singer and anti-apartheid activist Miriam Makeba.

ELEANOR HOLMES NORTON, now in her fifteenth term as the congress-woman for the District of Columbia, is the chair of the House Subcommittee on Highways and Transit. She serves on two committees: the Committee on Oversight and Reform and the Committee on Transportation and Infrastructure. She is a former professor of law at Georgetown University, was chair of the EEOC from 1977 to 1981, and is the author of the federal guidelines on sexual harassment in the workplace.

VICTORIA F. NOURSE is one of the nation's leading scholars on statutory interpretation, Congress, and the separation of powers. She has had a distinguished career in government up and down Pennsylvania Avenue. In 2015–16, she served as chief counsel to the vice president of the United States. Prior to that she served as an appellate lawyer in the Justice Department and as special counsel to the Senate Judiciary Committee. The story of her role in the fight for the original Violence Against Women Act is told in Fred Strebeigh's book *Equal: Women Reshape American Law.* Nourse is currently the director of Georgetown Law's Center for Congressional Studies.

JOYCE CAROL OATES is the author of more than seventy books, including novels, short story collections, poetry volumes, plays, essays, and criticism, including the national best sellers *We Were the Mulvaneys* and *Blonde.* Among her many honors are the PEN/Malamud Award for Excellence in Short Fiction and the National Book Award. Oates is the Roger S. Berlind '52 Professor of the Humanities at Princeton University and has been a member of the American Academy of Arts and Letters since 1978.

SHARON OLDS is the author of twelve books of poetry, with her newest collection, *Balladz,* released in 2022. *Arias* was short-listed for the 2020 Griffin Poetry Prize, and *Stag's Leap* won both the Pulitzer Prize and England's T. S. Eliot Prize. Olds is the Erich Maria Remarque Professor of Creative Writing at New York University's Graduate Creative Writing Program. She lives in New York City.

The New York Times acknowledged **MARY OLIVER** (1935–2019) as "far and away, this country's best-selling poet." Born in a small town in Ohio, Oliver published her first book of poetry, *No Voyage, and Other Poems,* in 1963 at the age of twenty-eight. She lived for several years at the home of Edna St. Vincent Millay in upper New York state, companion to the poet's sister Norma Millay. It was there, in the late 1950s, that she met the photographer Molly Malone Cook. For more than forty years, Cook and Oliver made their home together, largely in Provincetown, Massachusetts, where they lived until Cook's death in 2005. Over the course of her long and illustrious career, Oliver received numerous awards, including the Pulitzer Prize for Poetry in 1984 for her fourth book, *American Primitive.*

JANE O'REILLY grew up in St. Louis and graduated in 1958 from Radcliffe College. She was a co-founder of *Ms.,* known for writing its first cover story, "Click! The Housewife's Moment of Truth." She was also a freelance writer and a regular contributor to *The New York Times, Time, Vogue,* and *New York* magazine. After the defeat of the Equal Rights Amendment in 1982, O'Reilly lived in Key West for several years with a group of treasure divers before moving to Vermont and teaching writing workshops. A distinguished political reporter, book reviewer, and travel writer, she now lives in East Boston, Massachusetts, where she is an amateur printmaker and fair housing activist. She will soon be releasing her newsletter, *The Diary of My Eighty-Sixth Year.*

CATHERINE ORENSTEIN is a folklorist, writer, and founder of the OpEd Project, a global thought leadership initiative founded to diversify public knowledge and change who writes history.

LENORE PALLADINO is assistant professor in the School of Public Policy and the Department of Economics and a research associate at the University of Massachusetts Amherst Political Economy Research Institute, as well as a fellow at the Roosevelt Institute. She holds a PhD from the New School in economics and a JD from Fordham Law School.

LINDA PASTAN's fourteenth book of poems, *Insomnia,* was published in October 2015 and won the Towson University Prize for Literature. She has twice been a finalist for the National Book Award, and in 2003, she won the Ruth Lilly Poetry Prize for lifetime achievement. Her most recent books are *A Dog Runs Through It* and *Almost an Elegy: New and Later Selected Poems.*

MINH-HA T. PHAM has published widely on the intersections of race, gender, class, fashion media, and capitalism. Her essays appear in academic journals as well as arts, culture, and politics magazines and media sites. She is the author of *Asians Wear Clothes on the Internet: Race, Gender, and the Work of Personal Style Blogging.*

MARGE PIERCY has written seventeen novels including the *New York Times* best seller *Gone to Soldiers,* the national best sellers *Braided Lives* and *The Longings of Women,* and the classic *Woman on the Edge of Time;* nineteen volumes of poetry including *The Hunger Moon: New and Selected Poems, 1980–2010;* and the critically acclaimed memoir *Sleeping with Cats.* Born in center-city Detroit, educated at the University of Michigan and Northwestern, and the recipient of four honorary doctorates, Piercy is active in antiwar, feminist, and environmental causes.

JENNIFER M. PISCOPO is associate professor of politics and director of the Center for Research and Scholarship at Occidental College in Los Angeles. Her research on gender, elections, and politics has appeared in more than twenty peer-reviewed journals and numerous books. She appears frequently in domestic and international media and consults regularly for UN Women on boosting women's political empowerment.

LETTY COTTIN POGREBIN, a founding editor of *Ms.,* is a writer and activist, the author of twelve books, and a consulting editor on Marlo Thomas's *Free to Be, You and Me.* Co-founder of the National Women's Political Caucus and the Ms. Foundation for Women, Pogrebin is also past president of the Authors Guild and board member of the Harvard Divinity School Women's Studies in Religion Program and the Brandeis University Women's and Gender Studies Program. Her honors include a Yale University Poynter Fellowship in Journalism, a Matrix Award for excellence in communication and the arts, and an Emmy Award for *Free to Be, You and Me.*

ADRIENNE RICH (1929–2012) was an American poet, writer, feminist thinker, and activist in progressive causes. In a career spanning seven decades, she wrote and published two dozen volumes of poetry and more than half a dozen of prose. Rich's poetry includes the collections *The Dream of a Common Language, A Wild Patience Has Taken Me This Far,* and *An Atlas of the Difficult World.* Her prose work includes the collections *On Lies, Secrets, and Silence* and *Blood, Bread, and Poetry;* an influential essay, "Compulsory Heterosexuality and Lesbian Existence"; and *Of Woman Born,* a scholarly examination of motherhood as a sociohistorical construct. She received the National Book Award for Poetry in 1974 for *Diving into the Wreck* and was a finalist an additional three times, in 1956, 1967, and 1991.

AMANDA ROBB is an award-winning investigative reporter whose work has appeared in *The New York Times, New York, The New Republic, The Guardian, Rolling Stone, GQ, Cosmopolitan,* and many other national and international publications. Before becoming a journalist, Robb worked as a soap-opera scriptwriter (ABC's *All My Children*) and political speechwriter (for the U.S. Senate majority/minority leader Harry Reid). Among the prizes Robb has won are a Mirror/Newhouse Award, a Deadline Award, a Maggie Award (twice), and a Writers Guild Award. Robb is also an Emmy nominee, a Headline Award finalist, and a National Magazine Award (Ellie) nominee.

REBECCA ROSENBLATT moved to New York City in the early 1970s from a coal-mining town in Pennsylvania. For months, she drove a taxicab in New York, one of the first of the very few women to do this. Her taxicab became the subject of her first formal writing, published in *New York* magazine. Her essay in *Ms.* was followed by an article on hunting for *womenSports* magazine, the first periodical for women's athletics. Rosenblatt later produced and wrote a documentary on women in policing for WNBC, NBC's New York City flagship. She married and moved to Long Island, learned to spearfish off Montauk Point, and hunted south of the Allagash Wilderness in Maine.

DIANA E. H. RUSSELL, PhD (1938–2020), was one of the foremost pioneers and experts on sexual violence and abuse of women and girls in the world. For forty years she was deeply engaged in research on these crimes and authored, co-authored, edited, and/or co-edited seventeen books and numerous articles, many of which have become authoritative sources on rape, incest, femicide, and the causal relationship between porn and sexual violence.

SIMA SAMAR, MD, is a physician and an outspoken advocate for women's and human rights in Afghanistan. She previously served as Afghanistan's deputy president and minister of women's affairs, and she was the chair of the Afghanistan Independent Human Rights Commission. She is a member of the UN secretary-general's high-level advisory boards on mediation and internal displacement.

CAROL SEAJAY co-founded the Old Wives' Tales bookstore in San Francisco and published and edited the *Feminist Bookstore News.*

MARIE SHEAR (1940–2017) defined herself as a writer and editor by trade, a satirist and musical-comedy lover by temperament, and a feminist by necessity (she was known for her definition of feminism as "the radical notion that women are people"). Her work has appeared in more than twenty professional and popular magazines.

NINA SIEGAL is a regular contributor to *The New York Times* from Amsterdam and the author of three novels and one nonfiction book, *The Diary Keepers.*

ELEANOR SMEAL is co-founder and president of the Feminist Majority Foundation, the publisher of *Ms.,* and the former president of the National Organization for Women (NOW). Smeal has led efforts for the economic, political, and social equality and empowerment of women worldwide for more than four decades. One of the architects of the modern drive for women's equality, Smeal is known as a political analyst, strategist, and grassroots organizer. Smeal was the first to identify the "gender gap"—the difference in the way women and men vote—and popularize its usage in election and polling analysis to enhance women's voting clout. As president of NOW, Smeal led the drive to ratify the Equal Rights Amendment, the largest nationwide grassroots and lobbying campaign in the history of the modern women's movement, and she continues to be a leading strategist in the current drive to ensure the ERA is added to the Constitution.

KATHERINE SPILLAR is the executive director of the Feminist Majority Foundation, and as one of its founders, she has been a driving force in executing the organization's diverse programs securing women's rights both domestically and globally. When the Feminist Majority Foundation acquired *Ms.* in December 2001, becoming the sole nonprofit publisher of the iconic magazine, Spillar oversaw relocation of *Ms.*'s editorial operations from New York City to Los Angeles and became the executive editor in 2005. Under her oversight, *Ms.* has increased its investigative reporting and in-depth analysis and today is the largest print and online feminist news site reaching readers from across the globe. She is an executive producer of *Ms.*'s highly acclaimed podcasts, *On the Issues with Michele Goodwin* and *Fifteen Minutes of Feminism.* Spillar graduated magna cum laude with a degree in urban studies from Texas Christian University, earned an MS in urban studies and economics from Trinity University, and received an honorary doctor of letters from Texas Christian University.

GLORIA STEINEM, a co-founder of *Ms.,* is an American feminist, journalist, and social and political activist who became nationally recognized as a leader and spokeswoman for the feminist movement in the late 1960s and early 1970s. In 1969, she published an article, "After Black Power, Women's Liberation," which brought her to national fame as a feminist leader. In 2005, Steinem, Jane Fonda, and Robin Morgan co-founded the Women's Media Center, an organization that works "to make women visible and powerful in the media."

CATHARINE R. STIMPSON regards her work with *Ms.*—writing, chairing the *Ms.* Advisory Board on Research, Scholarship, and Education—as among the happiest of her publishing experiences. She has taught at Barnard College, where she founded *Signs: Journal of Women in Culture and Society;* Rutgers University; and New York University. Her public service includes the presidency of the Modern Language Association and board roles for Scholars at Risk.

ELLEN SWEET held various executive positions in nonprofit communications for more than fifteen years, most recently as vice president for external affairs at Physicians for Reproductive Choice and Health. She was also communications director at the Center for Reproductive Rights, vice president of public affairs at the International Women's Health Coalition, and communications director at the Vera Institute of Justice. Prior to that, she worked for many years on staff and as a freelancer at national magazines including *Ms.,* where she served as senior editor and writer from 1980 to 1988. She is currently volunteering her time for Girls Write Now, a New York nonprofit that pairs aspiring high school writers with professional writers as mentors.

KATE SWIFT (1923–2011) was a feminist author and editor best known for promoting the use of nonsexist writing in the English language. Along with her writing partner, Casey Miller, Swift authored *The Handbook of Nonsexist Writing* and *Words and Women.*

MARIANNE TAKAS is the author of several books on child support, custody, adoption, fostering, and well-being. An attorney who represented children and parents, she has also worked for the ABA Center on Children and the Law, Voices for America's Children, and the National Foster Parent Association. She currently directs the nonprofits World Culture USA and the Birthday Books Project.

BONNIE THORNTON DILL is dean of the University of Maryland's College of Arts and Humanities and professor in the Harriet Tubman Department of Women, Gender, and Sexuality Studies. A pioneering scholar of intersectionality, she served as president of the National Women's Studies Association, vice president of the American Sociological Association, and chair of the Ms. Committee of Scholars and is currently on the board of the Feminist Majority Foundation.

JOHNNIE TILLMON (1926–1995) founded one of the first grassroots welfare mothers' organizations, ANC (Aid to Needy Children) Mothers Anonymous, in 1963. ANC Mothers later became a part of the National Welfare Rights Organization (NWRO). Tillmon quickly emerged as a leader and became a chair of the NWRO. Together with other welfare mothers, she struggled for adequate income, dignity, justice, and democratic participation.

PATRICIA MARINA TRUJILLO is a Chicana feminist scholar from Española, New Mexico. She writes about women's issues in northern New Mexico with an emphasis on representation of acequia and land-based cultures. She sits on the boards of Tewa Women United and NewMexicoWomen.org. Trujillo is currently the deputy secretary of the New Mexico Department of Higher Education.

V (FORMERLY EVE ENSLER) is a Tony and Obie Award–winning, *New York Times* best-selling playwright, author, and activist with plays and books published in more than forty-eight languages and performed in more than 140 countries. The founder of V-Day, the global grassroots movement to end violence against all women and girls (cisgender, transgender, those who hold fluid identities, and nonbinary people) and the planet, she is also the founder of One Billion Rising, the biggest mass action campaign to end violence against all women and girls in more than two hundred countries, and the co-founder of City of Joy, a revolutionary leadership center for Congolese women survivors of violence in Bukavu, D.R.C.

LINDSY VAN GELDER is a freelance writer based in San Diego. She has written for many mainstream newspapers and magazines, and her beats have included beauty, politics, personal computers, the Times Square porn industry, and gay European travel. But writing for *Ms.* remains a highlight; no other publication had readers who were so fiercely heart-and-brains engaged.

LINDA VILLAROSA is a journalist in residence and associate professor at the Craig Newmark Graduate School of Journalism at CUNY. A contributing writer at *The New York Times Magazine,* she is also the author of *Under the Skin: The Hidden Toll of Racism on American Lives and on the Health of Our Nation.*

CHERYL MARIE WADE (1948–2013) was ten when she was diagnosed with juvenile rheumatoid arthritis. She received bachelor's and master's degrees in psychology from the University of California, Berkeley. She co-founded the AXIS dance troupe. From 1985 to 1989, Wade performed with Wry Crips, which presented poetry and drama written by women with disabilities. Her solo career led her to perform in several videos. Wade also wrote poetry, plays, and articles about disability culture.

JANE WAGNER, one of America's most distinguished playwrights, has won numerous awards, including several Emmys for writing and producing and a Writers Guild Award for her work in television. Wagner has also won a New York Drama Critics' Circle Special Award and a New York Drama Desk Award for her Broadway success, *The Search for Signs of Intelligent Life in the Universe;* three Grammy nominations for comedy albums she wrote with Lily Tomlin, *Modern Scream, And That's the Truth,* and *On Stage;* and two Peabody Awards, the first for the CBS special *J.T.* and the second for the ABC special *Edith Ann's Christmas: Just Say Noël.*

ALICE WALKER was an editor at *Ms.* from 1974 to 1978. She is an internationally celebrated writer, poet, and activist whose books include seven novels, along with four short story collections, four children's books, and volumes of essays and poetry. She won the Pulitzer Prize for Fiction in 1983 and the National Book Award. Her work has been translated into more than two dozen languages, and her books have sold more than fifteen million copies.

MICHELE WALLACE was born in 1952 in Harlem. She is the author of *Black Macho and the Myth of the Superwoman, Invisibility Blues,* and *Dark Designs and Visual Culture.* Wallace is professor emerita of English at the City College of New York and CUNY Graduate Center. She has a PhD in cinema studies from the Tisch School of the Arts at NYU.

JENNIFER WEISS-WOLF is executive director of strategy and partnerships at *Ms.* She directs the Birnbaum Women's Leadership Center at NYU School of Law and is the author of the book *Periods Gone Public.*

JENNIFER WILLIAMS is an assistant professor of English at Howard University. Her research and teaching interests include twentieth- and twenty-first-century African American literature and women's, gender, and sexuality studies, particularly in relation to space, race, and class.

PATRICIA J. WILLIAMS, one of the most provocative intellectuals in American law and a pioneer of both the law and literature and the critical race theory movements in American legal theory, holds a joint appointment between Northeastern University's School of Law and its Department of Philosophy and Religion in the College of Social Sciences and Humanities. Williams has published widely in the areas of race, gender, literature, and law. Her books, including *The Alchemy of Race and Rights,* illustrate some of America's most complex societal problems and challenge our ideas about socio-legal constructs of race and gender.

DAVE ZIRIN writes about the politics of sports for *The Nation* and is its first sportswriter. He is the author of *The Kaepernick Effect: Taking a Knee, Changing the World* and the host of the *Edge of Sports* podcast and *The Collision: Sports and Politics,* with Etan Thomas, on WPFW in Washington, D.C.

Index

Page numbers of illustrations appear in italics.

ILLUSTRATION CREDITS

Page 4   Mary Ellen Mark
Page 5   Mary Ellen Mark
Page 61   Bettye Lane / Library of Congress
Page 99   Mary Ellen Mark
Page 104   Mary Ellen Mark
Page 123   Gerda Lerner Literary Trust
Page 154   Warner Bros.
Page 175   Jenny Warburg
Page 206   Shawn Miller / Library of Congress
Page 243   ZUMA Press, Inc. / Alamy Stock Photo
Page 265   Jenny Warburg
Page 266   Jenny Warburg
Page 325   Jenny Warburg
Page 376   Jenny Warburg
Page 387   Elliott O'Donovan
Page 402   Jenny Warburg

All other images are courtesy of *Ms.* magazine.

A NOTE ON THE TYPE

This book was set in Adobe Garamond. Designed for the Adobe Corporation by Robert Slimbach, the fonts are based on types first cut by Claude Garamond (c. 1480–1561). Garamond was a pupil of Geoffroy Tory and is believed to have followed the Venetian models, although he introduced a number of important differences, and it is to him that we owe the letter we now know as "old style." He gave to his letters a certain elegance and feeling of movement that won their creator an immediate reputation and the patronage of Francis I of France.

The display typefaces for this book were both designed by women. The headline typeface, Chaparral Pro, was designed by Carol Twombly in 1997. Karmina, the sans serif typeface, was designed by TypeTogether, a foundry formed by Veronica Burian and José Scaglione in 2007.

COMPOSED BY NORTH MARKET STREET GRAPHICS, LANCASTER, PENNSYLVANIA
PRINTED AND BOUND BY C & C OFFSET, CHINA
DESIGNED BY MAGGIE HINDERS